The
Religion
of Tomorrow

The
Religion
of Tomorrow

A Vision for the Future of the Great Traditions
—*More Inclusive, More Comprehensive, More Complete*

Ken Wilber

 Shambhala + Boulder + 2017

Shambhala Publications, Inc.
4720 Walnut Street
Boulder, Colorado 80301
www.shambhala.com

9 8 7 6 5 4 3 2 1

First Edition

Printed in the United States of America

♾ This edition is printed on acid-free paper that meets the American National Standards Institute Z39.48 Standard.
♻ This book was printed on 30% post-consumer recycled paper. For more information please visit www.shambhala.com.

Distributed in the United States by Penguin Random House LLC and in Canada by Random House of Canada Ltd

Designed by Greta D. Sibley

Library of Congress Cataloging-in-Publication Data
Names: Wilber, Ken, author.
Title: The religion of tomorrow: a vision for the future of the great traditions—more inclusive, more comprehensive, more complete / Ken Wilber.
Description: First Edition. | Boulder: Shambhala, 2017. | Includes bibliographical references and index.
Identifiers: LCCN 2016017248 | ISBN 9781611803006 (hardcover: alk. paper)
Subjects: LCSH: Religion—Philosophy. | Religion—History—21st century. | Buddhism.
Classification: LCC BL51 .W5863 2017 | DDC 200.1/12—dc23
LC record available at https://lccn.loc.gov/2016017248

Contents

The
Religion
of Tomorrow

Introduction

This is a book about what a possible religion of tomorrow might look like. It is meant to apply across the field of the Great Traditions; I believe that all of them will, in fact, most likely end up incorporating many of these elements into their own fundamental teachings at some point, simply because the forces driving toward such are so varied and far-reaching and, on balance, indeed make such a great deal of sense.

Nonetheless, in this particular presentation, I have chosen one religion—that of Buddhism—to use as a concrete instance, because specifics need to be given as actual examples of what is directly involved, and that requires a real religion to use as an example. I am not suggesting that Buddhism is somehow superior or more advanced and thus more open to this (in fact, as only one example, there are already a dozen books in print using exactly the same framework I will be introducing here to create a similarly "futuristic" Christianity). So there is no particular bias involved here; I believe any of the Great Traditions could be used as examples, and versions of many of them (including Christianity, Islam, Hinduism, and Judaism, as well as Buddhism) have already been presented following the same suggestions made in this book to show what would be involved in their own cases, with each of them indeed appearing to end up much more inclusive, complete, and comprehensive (not to mention fitting more easily with modern and postmodern developments, including those of basic science, without violating any of their main teachings).

So if you hail from a different faith—or if you are yourself "spiritual but not religious"—please work with me in the following pages and see how these suggestions could apply to your own spiritual path, formally or informally, and see if they don't help address many problems that your approach may be facing in today's world. Just see if the suggestions I'm about to offer don't make a certain basic sense to you in many, many ways.

But we start with Buddhism. It has been close to three thousand years since Gautama Buddha sat under the Bodhi tree and arose with his Enlightenment, which marked the First Great Turning of the Wheel of Dharma (ultimate Truth); some eighteen hundred years since Nagarjuna and his genius birthed the Emptiness realization and the Second Great Turning; and some sixteen hundred years since the half brothers Asanga and Vasubandhu made the Third (and final) Turning of the Wheel of Dharma with the refinement of the Yogachara view. And even looking at the wondrous developments of Tantra, especially as pioneered in the great Nalanda University in India from the eighth to the eleventh centuries CE, it has been close to a thousand years since something profoundly new has been added to Buddha Dharma.

The world's other Great Traditions find themselves in not much different circumstances, most of them being anywhere from one to three thousand years old. At the time that the major texts in all of these Great Traditions were first written, people really did think the earth was flat and was circled by the sun; slavery was taken to be the natural state of affairs, the way things were supposed to be (and this was challenged by none of the traditions); women were second-class citizens, if even that; atoms and molecules were unknown; DNA was unheard of; and evolution crossed nobody's mind.

And yet the world's great contemplative and meditative systems—East and West—looked into the minds, hearts, and souls of men and women and came up with staggeringly astonishing discoveries, many as timelessly true and profoundly significant today as they were two thousand years ago. After World War Two, Jean-Paul Sartre was touring Stalingrad, scene of an epic battle between the Russians and the Germans, where the Russians—finally, and barely—defeated the Germans, at the cost of millions dead. "They were amazing," Sartre mumbled under his breath. "The Russians?" his aide asked. "No, the Germans, that they got this far."

That's the only appropriate sentiment you can take toward these great adepts and ancient sages—that thousands of years ago, they got this far; they saw into the core of human beings and discovered, virtually each and every one of them, the ultimate Ground of Being, not only of humans but of the entire manifest universe. With no telescopes, microscopes, MRIs, or PET scans, they saw into the very essence of an ultimate reality that not only anchored all of manifestation but, when discovered, acted to radically free men and women from suffering itself, and introduce them to their own True Nature, known by many different names, but pointing to the same groundless Ground—Buddha-nature, Brahman, Godhead, Ayn Sof, Allah, Tao, Ati, Great Perfection, the One, Satchitananda, to name but a few.

Most of these traditions divided their teachings into two broad areas, often called "exoteric" and "esoteric." The exoteric was the "outer teaching," meant for the masses and the ordinary, and consisted of a series of tales, usually in mythic form, and it was taught that those who believed them would live everlastingly in a heaven with that tradition's ultimate Being or God or Goddess. But the esoteric teachings were the "inner teachings," the "secret teachings," usually kept from the public and open only to individuals of exceptional quality and character. These teachings weren't merely mythic stories and beliefs; they were psychotechnologies of consciousness transformation. By performing the specific practices and exercises, an individual could reach an actual awakening to his or her own True Nature, gaining a Great Liberation and ultimate Freedom from the terror-inducing limitations of ordinary life and a direct introduction to ultimate Reality itself. This Great Liberation was also known by various names—Enlightenment, Awakening, moksha, kensho, satori, metamorphosis, emancipation, salvation. In all cases, it was said to be the discovery of the timeless and eternal, spaceless and infinite, Unborn and Undying, Unlimited and Unfettered, the one and only One and Only, ultimate Reality itself. As Arthur Machen's fictional character Hampole so truthfully put it, of these esoteric practices:

Some have declared that it lies within our choice to gaze continually upon a world of equal or even greater wonder and beauty. It is said by these that the experiments of the alchemists of the Dark Ages . . . are, in fact, related, not to the transmutation of metals, but to the transmutation of the entire Universe. This method, or art, or science, or whatever we choose to call it (supposing it to exist, or to have ever existed), is simply concerned . . . to enable men [and women], if they will, to inhabit a world of joy and splendour. It is perhaps possible that there is such an experiment, and that there are some who have made it.[1]

This experiment does indeed exist, and there are in fact many who have made it—that's what the esoteric Paths of the Great Liberation are all about. Many of the original meditative schools that taught such practices are still flourishing to this day. Zen Buddhism, as one example, has been training individuals to discover their own Buddha-nature since the sixth century CE, when it was brought to China from India by Bodhidharma; Tibetan (Vajrayana) Buddhism, whose most famous follower is the Dalai Lama, was brought to Tibet in the eighth century by Padmasambhava and others, and is flourishing to this day; Vedantic Hinduism, one of the most sophisticated and philosophically astute of the Paths of the Great Liberation, is alive and well in India; and numerous contemplative schools exist in the West (from Jewish Kabbalah to Christian contemplation to Islamic Sufism) and are still passing on this "knowledge which is unto liberation." All in all, they represent one of the great and extraordinary treasures of human history.

But they are, the lot of them, becoming less and less influential in the modern and postmodern world. One reason is that the only "religion" the West is generally familiar with is the "exoteric," "outer," mythic-story type of religion, which retains much of the often childish qualities of the age that produced it, and becomes more and more embarrassing to modern men and women, silly even. Moses really did part the Red Sea? God really did rain locusts down on the Egyptians? Elijah really rose straight to heaven in his chariot while still alive? We're supposed to believe that stuff? It's not exactly an easy sell in today's world, given that the same essential worldview can be produced by any five-year-old child.

But another reason is that, in the one or two thousand years since these Great Traditions were first created—and whose fundamental forms have not substantially changed since that time—there has been an extraordinary number of new truths learned about human nature, about the mind, emotions, awareness, consciousness, and especially the growth and development of human traits and qualities, not to mention the explosion in knowledge related to brain chemistry and its functioning, things that the ancients simply had no way to know, and so did not include in their otherwise so-impressive meditative systems.

But what if that which we have since learned in the past thousand years, even the past fifty years, would actually affect how, for example, a person would directly experience Enlightenment or Awakening? What if we have discovered aspects of human awareness that most definitely determine how humans interpret any and all experiences that they have, and what if these interpretive frameworks, which will determine the different ways we directly experience Enlightenment, not only exist, but actually grow and develop through over a half-dozen well-documented stages during a human's overall life—and that they continue to develop during a human's adult years? Awakening or Enlightenment is traditionally taken as being the unity of the individual self with ultimate Reality—what the Sufis call "the Supreme Identity"—resulting in a Wholeness or Nonduality, which, including all of reality, conveys a sense of utter Freedom and total Fullness to the individual. But what if these interpretive frameworks actually govern how individuals see and experience "Wholeness," and thus directly determine how an individual experiences Enlightenment itself? That would change the nature of the Paths of the Great Liberation profoundly, with, in effect, a different "Liberation" being experienced at each of these different stages of growth and development. But the evidence is already in: those framework stages definitely exist—they have been found in over forty cultures (in every culture checked so far, in fact)—and they definitely alter how one experiences Enlightenment, or any other experience, for that matter. The very ground has shifted under the Great Traditions, and they don't even know it.

All of the Great Traditions are certainly in need of this information; and I am going to suggest that all of them need to incorporate the types of facts that I will be introducing in the following pages. Of course, I say this in all humility, and in the spirit of suggestions to be considered honestly, not commands to be taken unreservedly. But I am going to present a series of arguments—and significant evidence and research—to back up every suggestion I make. The idea is not for any of the Great Traditions to throw over their accepted truths, dharmas, or gospels, but simply to *add* some of the following facts to their overall teachings. None of what follows threatens the essential truths of any of the traditions—these facts are rather additions, simple supplements, that could be quite easily included in any major tradition. (In fact, I will provide several examples from every single major tradition where these facts are *already* being used and are already incorporated into their core teachings—all with extremely positive outcomes.)

This "Integral" approach (meaning "inclusive," as in including these new and major facts) is actually an approach that can be used in virtually any human discipline. Indeed, we already have seen the rise of things such as Integral Medicine, Integral Education, Integral Therapy, Integral Architecture, Integral Business and Economics and Leadership—all told, over sixty different disciplines have found this Integral approach enormously helpful and gratifying. And, as I said, virtually every major Great Tradition has some teachers who have included this Integral approach in their own teachings—including many "Integral Buddhists."

And I believe that if spirituality is going to start having a real impact on the modern and postmodern world, it will have to include a fair number of these modern and postmodern facts that I am about to summarize for you. Failing to include them just makes the spiritual approach look truly dated, outmoded, and archaic, and that is one of the major reasons that religion is continuously losing ground in the modern and postmodern world—only 11 percent of northern Europe, for example, is "churched." That is, only one out of ten people have anything to do with institutional religion; nine out of ten find it unbelievable and useless.

Not to mention the growing number of people who feel deeply spiritual but do not feel moved by any of the existing Great Traditions. There is a phrase for this that has become quite common: "I'm spiritual but not religious." Polls show that some 20 percent of Americans identify overall with that phrase. And some polls have shown that, in the younger generation—those between eighteen and twenty-nine—this percentage explodes to an astonishing 75 percent![2] In other words, three out of four young individuals have a deep spiritual yearning that no existing religion is addressing. And I believe—and there is already a significant amount of evidence supporting this claim—that a more truly "Integral" spirituality speaks compellingly to this demographic.

Although various teachers in all the Great Traditions have begun using this Integral approach, I chose Buddhism to use as an example, in this presentation, of what exactly would be involved. I did this for several reasons. As I pointed out earlier, this Integral approach has already been applied to many other Great Traditions (and this includes several Integral Buddhists), and I have written about many of these other traditions as well (the first book outlining this Integral approach for spirituality—namely, *Integral Spirituality*—was written as a non-denominational presentation designed and meant for any and all traditions).[3] But it seemed an appropriate time to specifically address Buddhism as one of the many examples. Although I have practiced virtually all of the world's great religions to varying degrees, I have spent an unbroken thirty years practicing Buddhism—fifteen years in Zen, then fifteen in Dzogchen and Mahamudra Tibetan Buddhism. But Buddhism also has a tradition—referred to as "the Three Turnings of the Wheel"—of tracing out its own evolutionary unfolding into wider and wider forms of belief and practice over the years, as if it understood that spiritual truths continue to grow and evolve, and that any spiritual system that wants to stay current and up-to-date needs to continue to expand its own teachings and include these new truths as they come into being. I therefore called a preliminary version of this present book *The Fourth Turning* (which is now out as an eBook available from Shambhala Publications); the title of that book itself implies a series of suggestions for Buddhism to actually take a Fourth Turning, in addition to its first Three Turnings, and incorporate some of the new facts I'll be presenting here. Whether Buddhism actually takes a "Fourth Turn" or not, of course, depends upon Buddhism itself. But as the years stretch on, and it increasingly becomes longer and longer than a thousand years since new truths have been added in a new turning, the more likely it becomes that Buddhism itself will be seen as increasingly obsolete, out of date, out of touch, outmoded. This would be a disaster—not only for any Great Tradition that doesn't take the leap—but especially for Buddhism, which contains perhaps the world's most sophisticated and stunning understanding of meditation of any tradition anywhere, anytime. But what these new modern and postmodern discoveries have found, for example, is that the stages of meditation themselves will actually be interpreted and experienced quite differently depending on the stage of development of the individual doing the meditating—and this has been happening all along; it's just that none of the Great Traditions were aware of it.

That particular discovery (which is only one of the half dozen or so major types of facts we'll be looking at)—the idea that all humans grow and develop through up to a dozen stages of interpretive frameworks that govern how they interpret and therefore experience their world—involves something much like the existence of grammar. Every person brought up in a particular language-speaking culture (German, English, Mexican, and so forth) will end up speaking that culture's language quite accurately—they will put subjects and objects together accurately, they will use adverbs and adjectives accurately, and in general they will end up following the rules of grammar of that language quite correctly. But if you ask any of them to write down the rules of grammar that they are following, virtually none of them can do it. In other words, they are all following the rather extensive rules of grammar perfectly, and yet they have no idea that they are doing so, let alone what those rules are!

These stages of interpretive frameworks are just like grammar— they are "hidden maps" that determine how we see, think, and generally experience the real territory around us. If it were possible for a six-month-old to have a real Enlightenment experience—just play along here—whatever it would be like, we could be pretty certain that it would be different from how an adult would experience it. And the main reason, of course, is that the infant hasn't yet really grown up. And it turns out that "growing up" means moving, growing, and developing through these stages of increasingly adequate interpretive frameworks—so much so, that I refer to the sequence of these stages as "Growing Up." In that regard, these stages are distinguished from, say, the stages of meditative development that lead to Enlightenment, or Awakening—stages that I refer to as "Waking Up." So, as we'll continue to see in clarifying detail, human beings have two major types of development available to them: Growing Up and Waking Up.

And here's the point. The states of awareness that constitute meditative states, or Enlightenment states, or Awakening states, or other types of "peak experience" states—these have been seen, known, and understood by humans for thousands and thousands of years, going back at least fifty thousand years to the first great shamans, who, in their vision quests, explored "altered states of consciousness" that were the forerunners to Enlightenment or Awakening experiences. These are direct, immediate, 1st-person experiences that are very clear and very obvious when you have them, and these are the foundations of Waking Up. But these "hidden maps," these hidden stages governing the overall processes of Growing Up, are *not* so obvious—just like the rules of actual grammar, they weren't discovered until just about one hundred years ago. All the Great Traditions had long, long since been fixed, and none of them had a chance to include these stages of Growing Up with their carefully researched stages of Waking Up.

Does that really matter? I mean, Waking Up is Waking Up—when you discover your True Nature, or ultimate Reality, or pure Nondual Suchness, or radical Godhead, who cares what your "relative self" is like; you've just discovered your one and only Real Self, or true Suchness. But that's exactly the point. In terms of the Buddhist notion of Enlightenment, which is the union of Emptiness (pure unqualifiable ultimate Reality) and all Form (the actual manifest world in its entirety), we could put it this way: Emptiness is not affected by whatever stage of Growing Up you might be at (although a certain minimum stage might be required—we don't really think, for example, that six-month-olds could really experience Emptiness, even though they are drenched in it), but how you experience Form is directly related to the stage of Growing Up that you are at. As you will amply see in the following pages, the very experience of Form changes from stage to stage of Growing Up. Emptiness, being beyond manifestation per se, doesn't grow or evolve—it has no moving parts—but remains rather the timeless Thusness, or Suchness, of what is; but the world of Form is exactly what does grow and evolve and change. Therefore, the *union* of Emptiness and Form will likewise change from stage to stage. In other words, the very core of the Enlightenment experience itself will differ considerably from stage to stage.

Not a single Great Tradition is even vaguely aware of this or has anything even close to these stages of Growing Up, for the simple reason that you can't see these "hidden maps" by looking within. Just as if you look within right now, you will find no hint as to the actual rules of grammar that you are faithfully and fully following every time you think, speak, or write, so too if you look within, you will not see any of these "hidden maps" that, research confirms time and again, you are as faithfully and fully following as any rules of grammar. And yet exist they do, and they are largely determining how each one of us thinks, feels, and behaves, and these ways of thinking, feeling, and behaving change stage by stage by stage. The stage we happen to be at will even determine the likelihood that we will be interested in meditation to begin with! (In the following pages, as we go through these stages, you will quite easily be able to spot which stage you are likely at, and what you can do about it. . . .)

The discovery of these stages of Growing Up is one of around five or six other, equally important, modern and postmodern discoveries that affect the Paths of Waking Up in far-reaching and profound ways. So the suggestion is simple: read over the following evidence, see if it makes sense to you, and if it does, then begin applying these facts to any discipline you're now involved with—including, as noted, medicine or nursing, business, leadership, therapy, education, politics, law, international relations, among numerous others—or, the specific topic at hand, to whatever spiritual system you happen to be practicing, including, of course, Buddhism. The teachers of the Great Traditions who have already done so uniformly report a greater, more effective, more enhanced system of practice when these new areas are added to their standard training, which itself remains essentially the same— again, these are simple additions, not subtractions, supplements to be added to the standard practice, not things to be taken away from it. See if, by applying this Integral approach, your own practice doesn't work better, faster, more effectively, and more efficiently.

And remember, these aren't specifically my ideas; I'm simply taking research that has already been done by hundreds of other people and suggesting ways that it can be applied across the board in various areas. This isn't something like "deconstruction," a mere theory invented by Jacques Derrida that you can believe in or not, as you wish; it's much more like "science," research performed by knowledge communities in dozens of areas, repeated and confirmed, representing discoveries that have been made by humanity in the past thousand years—or even the past hundred years, or even the past ten. I have no doubt whatsoever that if any of the Great Traditions were being created today, they would categorically and absolutely include this information in their fundamental teachings, dharma, gospel, or dogma. In the areas we will examine, from "Cleaning Up" to "Showing Up" to "Growing Up," these are facts that affect "Waking Up" in profound, far-reaching, and absolutely crucial ways, affecting and changing the very nature of the Paths of Waking Up in ways that, I honestly believe, can no longer be ignored in our modern and postmodern worlds. It is time to bring all of the Great Traditions up to speed in this world, or watch the demographic they influence continue to shrink to 11 percent or less of the population, as the world increasingly looks to systems more up-to-date for guidance on when, where, why, and how to live their lives.

And this is an urgent, utterly urgent, task, because virtually none—not one—of the world's modern and postmodern worldviews has anything resembling Waking Up. They know about Growing Up, and Cleaning Up, and Showing Up (the latter terms to be discussed below)—those are the only maps they use to make sense of the territory in which they find themselves—but of Waking Up, they know nothing, literally and absolutely nothing. This is a catastrophe of the first magnitude, a cultural disaster of unparalleled proportions.

The traditions uniformly divide truth into two categories: relative truth and ultimate Truth. Something like "Water consists of two hydrogen atoms and one oxygen atom" is a relative truth. But something like "Water itself is a manifestation of an ultimate Ground of Being" is an ultimate Truth. And ultimate Truth can't readily or easily be put into words, although it can be experienced, or directly and immediately realized—namely, by taking up the meditative stages leading to a Waking Up. What one wakes up to is exactly ultimate Truth.

Our culture is awash in relative truths, in every sort of area imaginable, but it is absolutely bereft of ultimate Truth. Moreover, it doesn't even suspect its existence; it is absent ultimate-Truth knowledge, and absent an awareness of its absence—a double lack. It's like frostbite: the affected area doesn't hurt, so the person thinks that things are just fine, whereas it doesn't hurt, not because things are fine, but because the person is numb and hence numb to the numbness itself. It's a double absence, and it is killing this culture, top to bottom.

We are not short of criticisms of Western culture; it's a hobby for any would-be philosopher or sociologist anywhere, a cottage industry. We have critiques of capitalism, consumerism, sexism, racism, patriarchy, greed-driven business, fossil fuel energy, multinational economics, environmental despoliation, global warming, militarism, worldwide poverty, the gap between rich and poor, human trafficking, epidemic drug use and marketing, worldwide hunger, global water shortages, worldwide disease epidemics, increasing food shortages—and on and on and on.

I find merit in virtually all of those critiques. But there is one critique that is, arguably, as important as, or more important than, any of them that is never, but never, even mentioned—a critique based on the fact that Western culture has lost track of its own sources of Waking Up. It has no ultimate Truth as a North Star to guide its overall actions, which means, ultimately, it has no idea where it is actually heading. So it generally throws its hands up, and awaits technological advances to address any really severe and persistent headaches—after all, we do have the hi-tech singularity headed this way, right? And it will soon enough solve all our problems, even some problems so difficult that we don't even know we have them yet, but beyond-brilliant computers will ferret out, pinpoint, and solve them, ushering in a transhuman heaven on earth, hallelujah!

It's not that I have major disagreements with any of those views, either. It's that they are all relative truths, relative realities, relative solutions. There is still no ultimate Truth, no Waking Up to an ultimate Reality, which, as the groundless Ground of Being, anchors and gives reality to any such relative endeavors in the first place. We are diving headfirst into the shallow end of the pool, and encouraging all of our fellow citizens to do the same as fast as they possibly can. It's mass suicide; that's what it is. And to make matters worse, we're proud of it! Proud that we are wallowing in relative truths and that we adamantly maintain that there is no ultimate Truth anywhere anyway.

But ultimate Truth is not something that can be rationally demonstrated or proven. As the Great Traditions would put it, humans have at least three modes of knowing: the eye of flesh, the eye of mind, and the eye of contemplation. The eye of flesh is what grounds conventional science—all conventional science rests its proofs in sensory experience (or extensions of the senses, such as telescopes, microscopes, CAT scans, and X-rays). The eye of mind gives us rationality, logic, and reason. Mathematics, for example, is a mental experience (nobody has ever seen the square root of negative one running around out there in the sensory world—it is a mental experience, pure and simple), and likewise logic, its rules and regulations, are mental experiences. And there are no sensory proofs for mental realities—there is no sensory proof for math or logic; can't be done. The "eye of mind" is a higher-level development than the eye of flesh, and the lower cannot prove the higher. Likewise with the "eye of contemplation"—a higher level yet, which cannot be proven either by the eye of flesh or the eye of mind (senses, reason, or logic). The eye of contemplation is the eye with which a human has authentic spiritual experiences, and just as sensory experiences are the foundation for the natural sciences, and mental experiences are the foundation for mathematics and logic, so spiritual experiences are the foundation for Waking Up realizations—for Enlightenment, Awakening, metamorphosis, gnosis, jnana. And scholars of the mystical, or esoteric, or inner teachings of the world's Great Traditions are fairly unanimous in saying that although the outer teachings of each tradition are considerably different, often even contradictory, the inner esoteric teachings, the teachings based not on beliefs but on direct spiritual experiences of Waking Up, show a remarkable similarity in what they say, which is why the mystics of virtually all the world's religions have great ease in understanding each other, even as their exoteric brethren argue themselves silly.

But this universal core of Waking Up and ultimate Truth is, as we noted, slowly but surely becoming less and less influential everywhere in the world, and this is for two basic reasons: First, they are too often confused with the outer, exoteric, childish, mythic narratives that constitute probably 90 percent of the world's religions as presently taught (and as humanity continues to mature, it increasingly finds these childish myths embarrassing and silly). Second, and this is what I am emphasizing, even the Waking Up schools have become out of touch, out of date, outmoded in certain ways, by simply failing to continue to add new and profoundly important truths to their own teachings. As I said, I have no doubt whatsoever that were these paths being created today, the Waking Up schools would absolutely include these truths as crucial components of their Waking Up teachings. Including these new truths and facts makes Waking Up work even better! Why on earth wouldn't they include them?

I mentioned that the "hidden maps" of Growing Up are so hard to spot that they weren't discovered until around one hundred years ago. Humans have been on this planet for hundreds of thousands of years, and only in the last one hundred years did they discover these maps, even though humans have been growing through them from the start! Another discovery, barely any older, is that of evolution itself. All of human history, and it was only around 150 years ago that evolution itself was discovered. Modern science now believes that evolution touches essentially everything in existence (even though it is lagging behind theoretically on exactly how to explain this). But the fact of evolution (if not the "how" of evolution) is now undeniable. There are even leading-edge thinkers who maintain that what humanity took to be immutable "laws of nature" are actually closer to "habits of nature," that these "laws" themselves evolved over the years.

But that makes one thing certain: spiritual and religious systems themselves have undergone, and continue to undergo, evolution. It's hard to read the Bible, for instance, and not notice the "growth" in God, from a childish, malicious, malevolent little monster—who in over six hundred passages early in the Bible recommends that his own people commit aggression and murder—to a being who recommends loving your enemies in all cases and always turning the other cheek. And what are the Buddhist "Three Turnings" but something close to an evolutionary unfolding of deeper and deeper truths and realizations? But one thing is for sure: whatever that evolution was, it didn't up and totally stop one or two thousand years ago; no, evolution continued to unfold, whether it was realized or not. You can even see evolution as driven by "Spirit-in-action," which I think is the only theory that can actually explain the mysteries of evolution satisfactorily; but in any event, spiritual realities have continued to unfold, to evolve, to follow what Alfred North Whitehead called that inexorable "creative advance into novelty."[4] And part of catching the traditions up with the modern and postmodern world is to simply follow their own evolutionary unfoldings as they continued over the ages (and they did continue, even if often in hidden and obscure sects and followings; but a trained eye can look at the history of virtually any religion and see, overall, movement through the stages of Growing Up—and these are parts of what need to be included in any new and updated Fourth Turning in any and every Great Tradition, if it is to find its way in the modern and postmodern worlds).

So that is the suggestion. Please take your time, and look over the following evidence, facts, and research, particularly as it applies to any spiritual system for Waking Up—I generally use Buddhism as an example, but my suggestions are meant to apply across the board—and see if some of it, at least, doesn't make some sort of sense. And remember, we're not taking anything away; this is not a painful subtraction of truths that you have become accustomed to; it is a simple addition, and in terms that can be completely accommodated to the already fundamental truths and doctrines of any tradition to which they are being added. These additions can be made in completely "kosher" forms to any tradition, as the many teachers in each tradition using an Integral approach have already demonstrated.

Above all, it is to preserve the ultimate Truth disclosed in the process of Waking Up that this effort is dedicated; this is such a precious, such a gorgeously glorious discovery of humankind, that the percentage of the population aware of its existence cannot be allowed to drop to 11 percent, then 5 percent, then 0 percent, as the only ultimate Truth ever uncovered by humankind is allowed to slip into the gutter and wash away into obscurity. A greater crime could hardly be imagined. But something, indeed, must be done, in terms of the packaging in which this ultimate Truth and Waking Up is presented— thousands-of-years-old packaging not only has no interest for today's humans, it isn't even keeping up with Spirit-in-action itself. Spirit-in-action has itself moved and evolved well beyond the forms in which it presented itself to humans thousands of years ago, and it has been moving forward ever since, driving new discoveries in science, art, morals, education, politics, economics, and, yes, even religion and spirituality. However, the latter two fields suffer from arrested development, as it was believed that the original forms of spiritual presentation were somehow cut in stone, never to be changed or improved on again, and not to believe in their original forms was the equivalent of heresy, blasphemy, and horrid disbelief. Thus, the effects of Spirit-in-action were listened to in virtually every other area of human activity—from science to morals to medicine to economics—except in religion and spirituality itself, perhaps history's greatest (and saddest) irony.

And remember, the discovery of this ultimate Reality is said to be not only the groundless Ground of all Being "out there" but also "in here"—it is the discovery of your own, truest, deepest Self and Suchness, the utterly most central and most real Reality of your own being, the discovery of which constitutes directly your own Awakening, your own Enlightenment, your own Metamorphosis:

> Some have declared that it lies within our choice to gaze continually upon a world of equal or even greater wonder and beauty. It is said by these that the experiments of the alchemists of the Dark Ages . . . are, in fact, related, not to the transmutation of metals, but to the transmutation of the entire Universe. This method, or art, or science, or whatever we choose to call it (supposing it to exist, or to have ever existed), is simply concerned . . . to enable men [and women], if they will, to inhabit a world of joy and splendour. It is perhaps possible that there is such an experiment, and that there are some who have made it.[5]

Well, there is such an experiment; and men and women for thousands of years have made it; and all have returned to tell a remarkably similar tale of what they saw and witnessed first hand, of the ultimate Reality to which they were introduced and that changed them deeply and forever. This is humanity's one and only discovery of something that, once experienced, individuals almost unanimously claim to be an ultimate Reality, an Absolute Truth, the most real and most certain experience that they have ever had. This is the precious jewel that we must not let perish. This is the treasure we must not let go uncovered. This is the Truth that we must not let die. Please join me in taking steps that hopefully will help prevent perhaps the greatest catastrophe in humankind's history, won't you?

Part One

A Fourth Turning
of the Dharma

1

What Is a Fourth Turning?

Buddhism is a unique spiritual system in many ways, while also sharing some fundamental similarities with the other Great Wisdom Traditions of humankind. But perhaps one its most unique features is its understanding, in some schools, that its own system is evolving or developing. This is generally expressed in the notion of the Three Great Turnings of Buddhism, the three major stages of unfolding that Buddhism has undergone, according to Buddhism itself. The First Turning of the Wheel is Early Buddhism, now generally believed to be represented by the Theravada school and thought to contain the historical Gautama Buddha's original teachings, which developed in the great Axial period around the sixth century BCE. The Second Turning of the Wheel, represented by the Madhyamaka school, was founded by the genius philosopher-sage Nagarjuna around the second century CE. The Third and final (to date) Great Turning of the Wheel, represented by the Yogachara school, originated in the second century CE but had its period of greatest productivity in the fourth century CE with the brothers Asanga and Vasubandhu. All Three Turnings had profound impacts on every school of Buddhism that came after them.

The Madhyamaka school, although critical of Early Buddhism in many ways, nonetheless transcends and includes many of its foundational teachings, while criticizing those notions it finds partial, limited, or incomplete. And many Yogachara schools attempted to integrate and synthesize all Three Turnings. This was an ongoing, cumulative, synthesizing unfolding, as if Buddhism was plugged into the great evolution of Spirit itself.

In other words, many adherents of Buddhism had a view that Buddhism itself was unfolding, with each new turning adding something new and important to the overall Buddhist teaching itself. My point can now be put simply: many contemporary Buddhist teachers, agreeing with psychologists and sociologists that the world itself, at least in several important ways, is undergoing a global transformation, believe that this transformation will affect also Buddhism, adding to it yet newer and more significant truths, and resulting in yet another unfolding, a Fourth Great Turning, of Buddhism itself. (Some people view the rise of Tantric Buddhism, or occasionally Vajrayana Buddhism, as a Fourth Turning, and from that perspective, we are speaking of a possible Fifth Turning. But generally we will remain with the more common Three Turnings and take it from there.) This Fourth Turning retains all the previous great truths of Buddhism but also adds newer findings from fields as diverse as evolutionary biology and developmental psychology—but only to the extent that they are in fundamental agreement with the foundational tenets of Buddhism itself, simply extending them to some degree, as it were. Known by various names—from evolutionary Buddhism to Integral Buddhism—the Fourth Turning, like all the previous turnings, transcends yet includes its predecessors, adding new material while retaining all the essentials. And what is so remarkable about this development is that it is completely in keeping with this general understanding of itself that Buddhism has grasped—namely, that Buddhadharma ("Buddhist Truth") is itself unfolding, growing, and evolving, responding to new circumstances and discoveries as it does so. Even the Dalai Lama has said, for example, that Buddhism must keep pace with modern science or it will grow old and obsolete.

A brief glance at Buddhist history will show what is involved. Original Buddhism was founded on such notions as the difference between samsara (the source of suffering) and nirvana (the source of Enlightenment or Awakening); the three marks of samsaric existence; that is *dukkha* (suffering), *anicca* (impermanence), and *anatta* (no-self); and the Four Noble Truths: (1) life as lived in samsara is suffering, (2) the cause of this suffering is craving or grasping, (3) to end craving or grasping is to end suffering, and (4) there is a way to end grasping, namely, the eightfold way—right view, right intention, right speech, right actions, right livelihood, right effort, right mindfulness, and right unitive awareness.

The ultimate goal of Early Buddhism was to escape samsara—the manifest realm of life, death, rebirth, old age, suffering, and sickness—entirely, by following the eightfold way and attaining nirvana. "Nirvana" means, essentially, formless extinction. The prefix "nir-" means "without," and "vana" means everything from desire to grasping to lust to craving itself. The overall meaning is "blown out" or "extinguished"—as if a lit candle were handed to you, and you leaned over and blew out the flame. What is extinguished or "blown out"? All the typical marks of samsara itself—including suffering, the angst that comes from craving for permanence, the separate-self sense, or self-contraction (often called "ego"), and its inherent fear, anxiety, and depression. The state of nirvana is sometimes said to be a state similar to deep dreamless sleep, in which, of course, there is no ego, no suffering, no hankering for permanence, no space, no time, no separation—if anything, there is simply the boundless peace or vast equanimity of being liberated from the torture of samsara and its suffering-inducing ways. According to some schools, there is even an end limit, or "extreme" form of nirvana, called *nirodh*—complete cessation—where neither consciousness nor objects arise at all, and that might be thought of as an infinite formlessness of pure freedom. Be that as it may, the goal is clear: get out of samsara and into nirvana.

According to Buddhist history, Gautama Siddhartha ("Buddha" is not a name but a title, and means "Awakened," and was added to his name after his Enlightenment) was raised as a prince, with all the princely affluence of palace life, and with a father who protected him closely, so that he wouldn't be exposed to the typical horrors of everyday life in India at that time. But then one day, Gautama escaped from the palace walls and, in wandering around the surrounding city, saw three sights that severely disturbed him—a very sick person, an old and decrepit person, and a dead person. "These are something my palatial life cannot protect me from," he thought, and he promptly left the palace and began a six-year search, studying under various holy men, looking for an answer to life's problems that he had witnessed wandering in his city. But after six years, nothing proved satisfactory, and, exhausted and frustrated, he sat down under the Bodhi tree and vowed not to arise until he had discovered the answer.

Early one morning, glancing at the starry heavens, Gautama had a profound experience. "Aha! I've found you! Never again will I be deceived!" he exclaimed, as much with utter joy as complete exhaustion. What did he find? Whatever it was, it converted him from "ignorance" to "Enlightenment." Different responses as to what he saw and understood have been given by various schools, all of them believable. One was the "twelvefold chain of dependent origination," a profound understanding of the completely interwoven nature of all reality and the inexorable role of causality in tying them all together— all of which conspire to inevitably cause suffering when driven by grasping. Another was the three marks of existence itself (impermanence, suffering, and selflessness) and the eightfold way to end their hold on the human being. According to Zen, Gautama had a profound *satori*, a deep awakening experience, awakening to his own true Buddha-nature and his fundamental oneness with the entire Ground of Being (or Dharmakaya), ending his separate-self sense, and with it, suffering. Whatever exactly it was, it did indeed soon become formalized in the three marks of existence, the twelvefold chain, and the eightfold way. Gautama Siddhartha had sat down under the Bodhi tree an ordinary individual and got up from it an Enlightened or Awakened being, a Buddha. When Buddha was asked if he was a God or supernatural being, he replied, "No." "What was he?" "Awakened," is all that he replied.

Such was the basic form of Buddhism as practiced for almost eight hundred years—until, that is, Nagarjuna, who began paying attention to this strange duality between samsara and nirvana. For Nagarjuna, this duality tore Reality in half and didn't produce liberation but subtle illusion. For him, there is no ontological difference between samsara and nirvana. The difference is merely epistemological. That is, Reality looked at through concepts and categories appears as samsara, while the very same Reality looked at free of concepts and categories is nirvana. Samsara and nirvana are thus not-two, or "nondual." And this caused a major revolution in Buddhist thought and practice.

Gautama Buddha had discovered the "emptiness," or ultimately illusory nature of, the separate-self sense; but he had not discovered the emptiness—the *shunyata*—of *all* of what is usually called "reality" (including not only all subjects, or selves, but all objects, or "dharmas"). Buddhism had just taken its second major Turn in its illustrious history, adding a novel and profound element to its already accepted discoveries.

Nagarjuna relies on the "Two Truths" doctrine—there is relative, or conventional, truth, and there is absolute, or ultimate Truth. Relative truth can be categorized and characterized, and is the basis of disciplines such as science, history, law, and so on. That a molecule of water consists of two hydrogen atoms and one oxygen atom is a relative truth, for example. But ultimate Truth cannot be categorized at all (including that statement). Any category or quality or characteristic makes sense only in terms of its opposite, but ultimate Reality has no opposite. Based on what is known as the "Four Inexpressibles," you can't, according to Nagarjuna, say that ultimate Reality is Being, or not-Being, or both, or neither. You cannot say it is Self (*atman*), or no-self (*anatman* or *anatta*), or both, or neither. You can't say it's implicate, or explicate, or both, or neither. You can't say that it's immanent in Gaia, or that it transcends Gaia, or both, or neither. You can't say it's a timeless Now, or a temporal everlastingness, or both, or neither. And so on for *any* category or quality. The reason is, as we were saying, that any concept you come up with makes sense only in terms of its opposite (liberated versus bound, infinite versus finite, something versus nothing, implicate versus explicate, pleasure versus pain, free versus limited, temporal versus timeless, good versus evil, true versus false, and so on), yet ultimate Reality has no opposite. As the Upanishads put it, "Brahman [ultimate Reality] is one without a second" and "free of the pairs"—the pairs of opposites, that is—and thus can't be categorized at all (including that statement, which would also be formally denied). Nagarjuna says, "It is neither void, nor not void, nor both, nor neither, but in order to point it out, it is called the Void." The Void, shunyata, or Emptiness. It's a radical "neti, neti"—"not this, not that"—except "neti, neti" is also denied as a characteristic.

Now what this does mean is that Emptiness, or ultimate Reality, is not separate from anything that is arising. (Technically, even that statement would be denied; but we are now talking metaphorically to get across the general gist of Emptiness—because the main point is that although it cannot be said, it can be shown, or directly realized.

More on this as we continue.) Not being separate from anything ("not having a second"), it is the Emptiness of *everything* that is arising. Emptiness isn't a realm separate from other realms, it is the Emptiness, or Transparency, of *all* realms. Looked at free from conceptualization or categorization, everything that is arising is Emptiness, or Emptiness is the Reality of each and every thing in the manifest and unmanifest world—it is their very Suchness, their Thusness, their Isness. Looked at through concepts and categories, the universe appears as samsara—as built of radically separate and isolated things and events—and grasping after those things and attachment to them causes suffering because, ultimately, everything eventually falls apart, and thus whatever you're attached to will sooner or later cause suffering as it falls apart. But looked at with *prajna* (or *jnana*)—nonconceptual choiceless awareness—the world of samsara is actually self-liberated nirvana. (In the word *jnana*, the root "jna," by the way, in English is "kno," as in "knowledge," or "gno," as in "gnosis.") Jnana is a nondual, unqualifiable knowledge or timeless Present awareness, the realization of which brings Enlightenment or Awakening. Awakening to what? The radical Freedom or infinite Liberation or radical Luminosity-Love of pure Emptiness, though those terms, again, are at best metaphors.

Since there is no radical separation between samsara and nirvana (samsara and nirvana being "not-two," or as the *Heart Sutra* summarizes nonduality, "That which is Emptiness is not other than Form; that which is Form is not other than Emptiness"), liberating Emptiness can be found anywhere in the world of Form—*any* and *all* Form is one with Emptiness. It is not a particular state of mind or state of consciousness but the very fabric or "isness" of consciousness itself.

A commonly used metaphor to explain the relationship of Emptiness to Form is the ocean and its waves. Typical, limited, bounded states of consciousness—from looking at a mountain, to experiencing happiness, to feeling fear, to watching a bird in flight, to listening to Mozart's music—are all partial states and thus separate from each other; they all have a beginning (or are "born"), and they all have an ending (or "die"). They are like the individual waves in the ocean; each starts, has a certain size (from "small," to "medium," to "huge"), and eventually ends, and, of course, they are all different from each other.

But Emptiness—the Reality of each moment, its sheer transparent being, its simple "Suchness" or "Thusness" or "Isness"—is like the *wetness* of the ocean. And no wave is wetter than another. One wave can certainly be bigger than another, but it is not wetter. All waves are equally wet; all waves are equally Emptiness, or equally Spirit, or equally Godhead or Brahman or Tao. And that means that the very nature of this and every moment, just as it is, is pure Spirit—Spirit is not hard to reach but is impossible to avoid! And one wave can last longer than another wave, but it is still not wetter; it has no more Suchness or Thusness than the smallest wave in the entire ocean. And that means that whatever state of mind you have, right here, right now, is equally Enlightened; you can no more attain Enlightenment than you can attain your feet (or a wave can *become* wet). Enlightenment, and the "Big Mind/Big Heart" that reveals it, is absolutely ever-present Presence; all you have to do is recognize it (about which, more later).

But this being so, one no longer has to retreat to a monastery—away from the world, away from Form, away from samsara—in order to find Liberation. Samsara and nirvana have been joined, united, brought together into a single or nondual Reality. The goal is no longer to become the isolated saint or arhat—looking to get off of samsara entirely—but the socially and environmentally engaged "bodhisattva"—which literally means "being of Enlightened mind"—whose vow is not to get off samsara and retreat into an isolated nirvana, but a promise to fully embrace samsara and vow to gain Enlightenment as quickly as possible so as to help all sentient beings recognize their own deepest spiritual reality or Buddha-nature, and hence Enlightenment.

In one sweep, the two halves of the universe, so to speak—samsara and nirvana, Form and Emptiness—were joined into one, whole, seamless (not featureless) Reality, and Buddhist practitioners were set free to embrace the entire manifest realm of samsara and Form, not to avoid it. The vow of the bodhisattva likewise became paradoxical, reflecting both members of the pairs of opposites, not just one: no longer "There are no others to save (because samsara is illusory)," which is the arhat's chant, but "There are no others to save, therefore I vow to save them all!"—which reflects the truth of a samsara and nirvana paradoxically joined, no longer torn in two.

The Madhyamaka notion of Emptiness henceforth became the foundation of virtually every Mahayana and Vajrayana school of Buddhism, becoming, as the title of T. R. V. Murti's book has it, *The Central Philosophy of Buddhism* (although "philosophy" is perhaps not the best word for a system whose goal is to recognize that which transcends thought entirely).[1]

But there were, nevertheless, still more unfoldings to come, as evolution continued its relentless drive. Particularly by the fourth century CE, the question had become insistent: granted that the Absolute cannot be categorized literally in dualistic terms and concepts, is there really nothing whatsoever that could be said about it at all? At least in the realm of conventional truth, couldn't more systems, maps, and models be offered about Reality and how to realize it?

Already, in such brilliant treatises as the *Lankavatara Sutra*, the answer was a resounding "Yes!" The *Lankavatara Sutra* was so important that it was passed down to their successors by all five of the first Ch'an (or Zen) Head Masters in China as containing the essence of the Buddha's teachings. In fact, the early Ch'an school was often referred to as the Lankavatara school, and a history of this early period is entitled *Records of the Lankavatara Masters*. (Starting with the sixth Head Master, Hui Neng, the *Diamond Sutra*—a treatise solely devoted to pure Emptiness—displaced the *Lankavatara Sutra*, and in many ways Zen lost the philosophical and psychological sophistication of the *Lankavatara Sutra* system and focused almost exclusively on nonconceptual awareness. Zen masters were often depicted tearing up sutras, which really amounted to a rejection of the Two Truths doctrine. This was unfortunate, in my opinion, because in doing so, Zen became less than a complete system, refusing to elaborate conventional maps and models. Zen became weak in relative truths, although it brilliantly succeeded in elaborating and practicing ultimate Truth. I say this as a dedicated practitioner of Zen for fifteen years, before I switched to a more Integral Spirituality, which included, among others, Vajrayana, Vedanta, and Christian contemplative approaches. We'll see what all this means as we proceed. And, as we'll also see, one can belong to any traditional religion, or no religion at all, and still adopt an Integral Spirituality, which is really an Integral Life Practice, incorporating what humanity has learned, East and West—and in premodern, modern, and postmodern times—about psychological growth, development, and evolution.)

The Yogachara school came to fruition in the fourth century CE with the brilliant half brothers Asanga and Vasubandhu. Asanga was more a creative and original thinker, and Vasubandhu a gifted systematizer. Together they initiated or elaborated most of the tenets of what came to be known as the Yogachara ("Practice of Yoga"), or Chittamatrata ("Nature of Mind Only"), school of Buddhism, and Buddhism had taken another evolutionary leap forward, the Third Great Turning of the Wheel of Dharma.

What all schools of Yogachara have in common is a continuing and intensifying of the drive to see and fully realize the union of Emptiness and Form, to integrate them in the here and now. Given the fact that Emptiness and Form are not-two, Emptiness itself is related to some everyday aspect of Form that the ordinary person is already aware of—in this case, pure unqualifiable Awareness just as it is. All schools of Yogachara either equate directly Emptiness and unconstructed pure Awareness (*alaya-jnana*), or at least equate them relatively as a useful orientation and metaphoric guide for practitioners.

Yogachara extends this notion of unconstructed fundamental awareness into the idea of eight (or nine) levels of consciousness, each a "downward" transformation of foundational luminous awareness (alaya-jnana). The first transformation gives rise to the storehouse consciousness, or the *alaya-vijnana* (the added "vi" to "jna" means "dualistic, separated, fragmented"—and thus this is the beginning of samsara as illusion, if one is ignorant of the prior all-encompassing alaya-jnana). But this storehouse actually contains, as collective memories, the resultant experiences of all human beings (and according to some, all sentient beings in toto), and the seeds for all future karmic ripening.

This is a particularly brilliant approach to what the Greeks would call *archetypes*—the very first forms of manifestation to be produced by Spirit as it begins to emanate or manifest the entire world. Archetypes were often conceived, by various Great Traditions around the world, as everlastingly fixed ideas in the mind of God or Spirit, and thus left no room for evolutionary input. But the more evolution became understood, the more it appeared that virtually everything had some sort of evolutionary origins or at least connections (including what Whitehead called "the Consequent Nature of God," although not what he called the "Primordial Nature of God," itself unchanging; these two dimensions of God—Consequent Nature and Primordial Nature—are quite similar to evolving Form and timeless Emptiness, both ultimately nondual).[2] Archetypes as traditionally conceived also had the inconvenience of being described only in premodern terms by the traditions, leaving out modern and postmodern characteristics— did that mean God Itself was unaware of the coming modern and postmodern eras? Not a very far-sighted God, that. But the *Lankavatara Sutra*'s version of the storehouse consciousness bypassed all those problems entirely, because the storehouse—as the ongoing product and accumulation of actual human actions—was itself created in part by evolutionary processes, inasmuch as human actions themselves underwent change, growth, development, and evolution. An added benefit of deploying the notion of the storehouse consciousness is that it helps explain what the Great Traditions mean when they speak of involution/evolution in a narrower and more specific sense (for example, what Plotinus called Efflux and Reflux): Involution/Efflux is the production of the manifest world via a successive manifestation or "stepping down" of Spirit into lesser and lesser versions of itself. Using Christian terms, Spirit goes out of itself (*lila* or kenosis) and steps downward to produce a reduced version of itself called "soul"; soul then goes out of itself and crystallizes into a lesser version of itself called "mind"; mind then reduces itself to produce a lesser form called "life," or "living body"; the body then sediments downward to produce the lowest and densest form of Spirit called "matter"; thus matter, body, mind, and soul are all forms of ultimate Spirit, but increasingly reduced or lesser forms. Once involution/Efflux is complete—and blows matter into existence with the Big Bang—then the reverse process of evolution/Reflux occurs. At first, there is only the physical or material universe; but then eventually body emerges and evolves out of matter; and then much later, mind emerges and evolves out of body; and later still, soul emerges and evolves out of mind; and finally, Spirit is recognized as the Source and Suchness of the entire display—a state of "Enlightenment" or "Awakening" or "metanoia." The archetypes—being the *first forms* of involution to be produced, and thus having an impact on all subsequent and lesser forms (one of the meanings of "archetype" is "forms upon which all other forms depend")—are thus crucial to all lower levels of being and consciousness. But instead of being "everlasting fixed ideas in the mind of God," the *vasanas* of the *Lankavatara Sutra*'s storehouse—the stored memories of human interactions, which could easily be interpreted to include Kosmic memories or habits, or morphogenetic fields—would manifest the effects of evolution itself, since evolutionary memories are part of what is being stored in the storehouse. In other words, the archetypes of the *Lankavatara Sutra*'s storehouse are constantly changing and evolving with the Kosmos itself, and thus affecting, via involution, all of the lower and denser levels of being and consciousness. Thus the vasanas (or the archetypes), instead of being fixed ideas preventing evolution, become one of the very carriers and distributors of evolution itself, not only allowing but encouraging evolutionary change. The universe, in one stroke, moves from a fixed, deterministic, causal machine to a creative, living, responsive, conscious Kosmos. This is still a profoundly useful notion.

To continue with the original involutionary story for the *Lankavatara Sutra*: The first "downward" manifestation produces the "tainted" alaya-vijnana storehouse out of the "pure" alaya-jnana (Primordial Wisdom and pure Emptiness). The second downward (or involutionary) transformation is called by the *Lankavatara Sutra* (and many Yogachara schools) the *manas*, which arises out of the storehouse and becomes (when misunderstood) the self-contraction and self-view, which then looks at the alaya-vijnana and misinterprets it as a permanent self or soul, and causes the alaya-vijnana to become even further tainted (beyond containing the first forms of manifestation or samsara itself, when misunderstood). The third transformation "downward" creates the concept of objects and the senses that perceive them, of which, in standard Buddhist psychology, there are six—the five senses, plus the mind (which in Buddhist psychology is treated as another sense, the *manovijnana*, whose objects are simply conceptual), giving us eight levels of consciousness (or nine if you count the original, pure, unconstructed alaya-jnana, or primordial nondual Wisdom Mind). This overall view gives us a chance to work not only with manifestation, involution, or Efflux, some version of which all Great Traditions possess, but also evolution, emergence, or Reflux, which is found in an evolutionarily workable version in relatively few places, including the

Lankavatara Sutra, thus giving Buddhism a truly profound approach to this issue faced by all the Great Traditions: "If Spirit is the only ultimate Reality, then why, and how, did this relative manifest world show up? What's the actual mechanism of that?" The notion of involution/evolution, Descent/Ascent, Efflux/Reflux in all its various forms, some version of which is found in virtually every Great Tradition, is the attempted answer to that question; and some version of that—such as the *Lankavatara Sutra*'s—is still viable today whenever that question is sincerely asked.

It's important to realize that, for Yogachara, it's not phenomena (or manifest events or the elements of samsara) that cause illusion and suffering, but rather viewing phenomena as *objects*, viewing them through the subject–object duality. Instead of viewing objects as one with the viewer, they are seen as existing "out there," separate, isolated, dualistically independent, tearing the wholeness of Reality into two realms—a subject versus objects. This product of the dualistic self-contraction of the manas and the tainted alaya-vijnana converts Reality in its Suchness or Thusness or pure Isness into an illusory, broken, fragmented, dualistic world, attachment to which causes bondage and suffering.

This state of bondage, itself illusory, can be seen through by "a sudden revulsion, turning, or re-turning of the *ālaya vijñāna* back into its original state of purity [alaya-jnana]. . . . The mind returns to [or is recognized as] its original condition of non-attachment, non-discrimination, and non-duality [pure alaya-jnana]"—in other words, by recognizing the ever-present state of nonduality, or the union of Emptiness and Form.[3] Although most Yogacharins insisted that the end state of Emptiness of Madhyamaka is the same as in Yogachara, there is an unmistakably more positive tone to the Yogachara—certainly in the concept of the nature of Mind, but also in how nonduality is conceived. For Madhyamaka, nonduality is virtually an utter blank, at least to the mind's conceptions, although that blankness is actually seeing Reality exactly as it is, in its Suchness or Thusness, without names, concepts, categories, or prejudices. While Yogachara wouldn't specifically disagree, it more positively sees Emptiness and nonduality as "the absence of duality between perceiving subject and the perceived object," which allows for the grand radiance, or luminosity, of Emptiness to be better recognized in the very midst of manifestation.

Again, it's not phenomena that are illusory or suffering inducing, but seeing phenomena as *objects*, as items set apart from awareness or the subject and existing as independent entities out there. Once they are separated from us, then we can either desire them or fear them, both eventually causing suffering, alienation, and bondage.

Now this slightly more positive view of Emptiness, not to mention its connection to ordinary awareness (as Zen would put it, following the *Lankavatara Sutra*, "The ordinary mind, just that is the Tao [or 'the way of Truth'])," acted to unify Emptiness and Form in an even stronger way than Madhyamaka's revolutionary nonduality. When Emptiness and Form are truly seen to be one, then Form itself is seen as the radiance and luminosity of Emptiness, and all of reality becomes a rainbow of luminous transparency, whole and complete, free and full, a realm of joy and celebration. The union of Emptiness and Form becomes the union of Emptiness and Luminosity, and playing with radiant luminosity—in the form of our own immediate Presence and brilliant Clarity—becomes a direct, daily occurrence.

All of this had a direct hand in the creation of Tantra (and its close cousin, Vajrayana Buddhism), the real flowering of the Third Great Turning. (As already noted, a few Buddhists, in fact, count Tantra/Vajrayana as a Fourth Turning, although this is not as well known. But if we do so, then of course this volume would be talking about the possibility of a Fifth Turning. But since this is less well known, we'll stick with the standard Three Turnings as presented here, and then go to discuss a possible Fourth Turning.)

Tantra was especially developed at the great Nalanda University in India from the eighth to the eleventh centuries CE. For Tantra, what Early Buddhism (and most other religions) considered sins, poisons, or defilements were actually—precisely because of the union of Emptiness and Form—the seeds of great transcendental wisdom. The poison of anger, for example, instead of being denied, uprooted, or repressed, as in so many other spiritual approaches, is rather entered directly with nondual Awareness, whereupon it discloses its core wisdom, that of pure brilliant clarity. Passion, when entered and embraced with nondual Awareness, transmutes into universal compassion. And so on.

Thus, in Tantric initiations, it was common to use the "Five M's"—five items that most religions considered totally sinful (such as alcohol, meat, and sex)—and directly introduce them in the initiation ceremony in order to emphasize that all things, without exception, are ornaments of, and fully one with, Spirit itself.[4] This nondual realization applies as well to all of our own "sinful" qualities—all of our feelings, thoughts, and actions, no matter how apparently negative, are at heart nothing other than Godhead or nondual Spirit, and are to be seen and experienced exactly as such.

Where the First Turning was the way of renunciation, denying negative states as part of despised samsara, and the Second Turning was the way of transformation, working on a negative state with wisdom until it converted to a positive transcendental state, the Third Turning and its Tantric correlate was the way not of renunciation or transformation but of transmutation—of looking directly into a negative state of Form in order to directly recognize its already present state of Emptiness or Primordial Wisdom. The motto here is "Bring everything to the Path." Nothing, absolutely nothing, is taboo; food, alcohol, sex, money—all are to be deeply befriended and lovingly embraced (within, of course, sane limits) as being ornaments of Spirit itself, direct manifestations of the ultimate Divine. There is *only* Spirit. There is only *Tathagatagarbha* (womb of Suchness). There is only *Svabhavikakaya* (Integral Body of Buddha). And all of this is because the sacred and the profane, the infinite and the finite, nirvana and samsara, Emptiness and Form, are not two different, separate, and fragmented realms, but co-arising, mutually existing, complementary aspects of one Whole Reality, equally to be embraced and cherished.

Looking at the nonduality of Emptiness and Form, we can say that Enlightenment "transcends and includes" the entire manifest world. With Emptiness, the entire world is transcended, is let go of, is seen through as a shimmering transparency, is understood to have no separate-self existence at all, is seen as a seamless (not featureless) Whole—and thus we are radically free from the torment and torture of identifying with partial, finite objects and things and events (including a small, finite, fragmented, skin-encapsulated ego), all of which are typically and normally seen as separate and "other." As the Upanishads put it, "Wherever there is other, there is fear."[5] Samsara is being caught in the hell of others (as Sartre might say). It is identifying with various ornaments of the Divine but without an awareness of the Divine itself—being in a genuine heaven but without a genuine Spirit (Emptiness) anywhere to be found. But recognize Emptiness, and then one's identity with any particular, separate, isolated thing or event evaporates instantly, leaving an identity, not with the small, separate-self sense, but with the entire world of Form. Since Reality is the union of Emptiness and Form, to discover Emptiness is to be free of any specific or isolated Form, and instead to become one with ALL Form, a radical Fullness that is the Form side of the radical Freedom of Emptiness—with infinite and finite, nirvana and samsara, Emptiness and Form, Freedom and Fullness, all nondual. You no longer look at a mountain, you are the mountain. You no longer hear the rain, you are the rain. You no longer see the clouds float by, you are the clouds floating by. There is no "other" here, because there is no longer anything outside of you that could hurt, harm, or torture you, or that you could crave, lust after, or hungrily grasp. There is simply the entire timeless Now, the ever-present Present, containing the entire manifest world, and you ARE all that. To quote the Upanishads again, *Tat Tvam asi*—"Thou art That"—where "That" is the divine Wholeness of the entire universe. In Emptiness, radical Freedom; in Form, radical Fullness—and both are "not-two."

Now, when it comes to the manifest world, where evolution is so prominently on display, Emptiness itself does not evolve. It has no moving parts, and thus nothing to evolve; it is the absence of absence of absence (if anything), and thus, again, nothing concrete to actually evolve. It is not apart from samsara or Form; it is the emptiness (or transparency or "wetness") of all samsara and Form. A sage who, two thousand years ago, directly realized Emptiness would discover and "possess" the same, identical Freedom as a sage who experienced Emptiness today, even though the world has evolved considerably in the meantime. But when it comes to Form, to the world of Form—well, that is exactly where evolution has occurred. And the world of Form has indeed evolved over the last two thousand years, becoming (as all evolution does) more and more conscious, more complex, more caring, more loving, more creative, and more self-organized, containing higher and higher Wholes (as we will see in more detail).

And thus, more truths have emerged. Two thousand years ago, humanity thought the earth was flat; slavery was taken to be part of the natural, normal state of nature; women were largely treated as second-class citizens, if citizens at all; there was no understanding of, say, brain neurochemistry and neurotransmitters such as dopamine, serotonin, GABA, acetylcholine, nor medical advances that have added an average of forty years to the typical lifespan. Likewise, new psychological and sociological truths have emerged and evolved, advancing considerably our understanding of what it means to be human. The world of Form, in short, has become considerably more complex and Full, and although an experience of Enlightenment—of the unity of Emptiness and Form—is no *Freer* today than it was two thousand years ago (Emptiness is the same, then and now), it is most definitely *Fuller* (Form has most definitely increased, grown, and evolved). Evolution itself operates by transcending and including, transcending and including, transcending and including—and thus a human being today transcends and includes most of the fundamental emergent phenomena going all the way back to the Big Bang. Humans today *literally contain* quarks, atoms, molecules, cells, a photosynthetic Kreb's cycle, organ systems, neural nets, a reptilian brain stem, a mammalian limbic system, a primate cortex, and—as its own "transcending" addition—a complex neocortex (which contains more possible neural connections than there are stars in the known universe). All of this is "transcended and included" in a human being.

Likewise, across the board with goodness, truth, and beauty. The world today has access to all of the great premodern Wisdom Traditions (and their meditative access to ultimate Truth and Enlightened Awareness) plus all of modernity's staggering advances in the natural sciences (physics, chemistry, biology, medicine, hygiene—stretching from a cure for polio, to putting a human on the moon, to the invention of radio, television, and computers that now contain more information than the sum total of all human brains) plus all of postmodernity's sophisticated understanding about the contextual and constructed nature of relative truths, and the central role of perspective in all relative ideas. Shouldn't the world's Great Wisdom Traditions keep up with the modern and postmodern additions to our knowledge and understanding? After all, what is it that is evolving in all of this? Why, of course, Spirit! Evolution is simply Spirit-in-action: Brahman, Tao, Buddha-nature, Godhead, Allah, YHWH, the Great Perfection, Ati, the Ground of all Being, One without a Second. Whitehead, we noted, divided Spirit into two dimensions: the "Primordial Nature of God" (timeless and unchanging; for us, Emptiness) and the "Consequent Nature of God" (the sum total of all evolution to date; Form). And while the Primordial Nature of God has not changed one iota from the Big Bang and before, the Consequent Nature of God has grown magnificently and substantially. There are commonly understood truths now that would have simply staggered the premodern mind, from the nature of brain activity (a brain that, as noted, has more neural synaptic connections than there are known stars in the entire universe) to the extraordinary unfoldings of a self-organizing and self-transcending evolution, to the nature of the Big Bang itself in its first nanoseconds. Not to mention the Singularity that is in all likelihood bearing down on us now in technology and will change the world more than any other single change in human history.

Should spirituality be left out of all of that? Should spirituality remain fixed in the premodern worldview? Or should not only Buddhism, but all Great Traditions, leap forward through their own First, Second, Third, and now—yes—Fourth Great Turnings?

If so, what exactly would be involved?

2

What Does a Fourth Turning Involve?

So, what of a possible Fourth Turning of the Wheel? After Vajrayana and Tantra, where we bring *everything* to the path, what else is possibly left to bring to Buddhism that it doesn't already have? Is this for real, or is it just some inflated, arrogant nonsense?

An "Integral" View

Well, we certainly want to be aware of that arrogant possibility and that danger; never underestimate the egotistical tendencies of humankind (including yours truly). But I mentioned that numerous individuals (and a number of studies) indicate that a small but significant percentage of the human population is going through a profound transformation, in many ways, a global transformation—"global" not just because it is affecting people around the world, but because individual consciousness itself is developing global dimensions; no longer egocentric or ethnocentric, it is becoming worldcentric and even Kosmocentric[1] in its identity, motivations, desires, viewpoints, perspectives, and capacities.

Nothing like this global interior consciousness has ever existed before in human history—at least not on any sort of widespread scale. Its impact simply cannot be overestimated. To give one quick example of what's involved: One of the pioneering researchers of this development and evolution of consciousness was Clare Graves. Graves found that human consciousness moves through around 8 major stages or levels. The first 6 are referred to as "1st tier," or what Abraham Maslow called "deficiency needs"—motivations based on lack and scarcity. These 1st-tier levels are all variations on what pioneering developmentalist Jean Gebser called archaic (or instinctual), magic (or egocentric), mythic (or traditional), rational (or modern), and pluralistic (or postmodern), which are also the major stages/epochs that humanity on the whole has gone through, up to and including today's postmodern era.

Now what Graves found about these 1st-tier levels is that people at each level think their values and truths are the only real values and truths in the world—all the others are infantile, loopy, mistaken, or just plain wrong. With any of those levels in place—which at this particular time in history covers 95 percent of the world's population—humanity is destined to disagreement, conflict, terrorism, and warfare. But then Graves found an astonishing fact about the next basic level of development. A very few people at the pluralistic/postmodern stage began giving responses that were radically new, unprecedented, literally unheard of before, and that surprised and confused every major developmentalist who started discovering evidence of this wildly new level. Graves ended up calling it "systemic," and others have called it "holistic" or "integrated" or "integral." But these levels were so staggering in their qualities and characteristics—and so completely new and novel—that Graves said of this transition that "an unbelievable chasm of meaning is crossed," and that it was a "momentous leap" (which I, in turn, like to paraphrase as "a monumental leap in meaning").[2] The leap is simply that the integral level—called "2nd tier" to emphasize its difference from all 1st-tier stages—finds some value and partial truth in all of the preceding levels, and so it includes them in its overall worldview. It is the first stage to include all the other stages, while all the other stages include only themselves. This is a huge and radically different transformation, unlike anything even vaguely seen in all of previous history. At this stage, consciousness has indeed become global and all-inclusive in its dimensions, including insights and truths from all cultures, all religion, all science, and sees a profound importance and value in all previous levels—archaic, magic, mythic, rational, and pluralistic. Put simply, it is a massively different type of thinking, an extraordinarily different type of consciousness.

This integral level or levels (some researchers have found 2 or 3 sublevels here; for the time being, we'll continue to refer to just one major overall level, realizing that we can subdivide it whenever needed) is indeed something radically new in human evolution. While some brilliant pioneering geniuses have demonstrated integral thinking— Plotinus, Shankara, some Yogachara thinkers, a few German Idealists, among others—never before in history has more than one-tenth of 1 percent of the population reached these levels. But over the past several decades, various thought leaders in virtually every field of human endeavor have developed these 2nd-tier, integral qualities, what Maslow called "Being values"—values based on abundance, embrace, and inclusion (as opposed to deficiency, scarcity, and lack, as are all 1st-tier stages). Up to 5 percent of the worldwide population has now reached these integral levels, and some developmentalists see this increasing to 10 percent within the decade.

This 10 percent turns out to be an important "tipping point." What researchers have found is that, during human history, *whenever the leading edge of evolution and development becomes around 10 percent of the population*, major, profound, and extensive changes occur throughout the overall population, as these newly emergent values begin to populate and saturate the culture, even though only 10 percent of the population is actually at this leading-edge stage. For example, and using the aforementioned major stages of archaic, magic, mythic, rational, pluralistic, and integral, when 10 percent of the population in Europe reached the rational level (the era that Will and Ariel Durant called "The Age of Reason and Revolution"), about three to four hundred years ago, there occurred the French and American revolutions; the rise of representative democracy over monarchy; the abolition of slavery (in a one hundred-year period, roughly 1770 to 1870, every major rational-industrial society on the face of the earth outlawed slavery, the first time that had ever occurred in humankind's entire history; even 15 percent of tribal societies had slavery); the rise of virtually all of the modern sciences (modern physics, modern chemistry, modern biology, geology, sociology, psychology, anthropology, medicine, among others); the early forms of feminism; the shift from mythology to reason as the premier form of knowledge; and the interest in universal human rights, not just the rights of a "chosen people"—to name a few. Now all of those are driven by reason or rational values, not mythic values, but only 10 percent of the population actually possessed those values—and yet all of the above still occurred, as those values began to permeate, and in some ways saturate, the culture. Likewise, in the 1960s, over 10 percent of the population had quite rapidly moved from rational/modern to leading-edge pluralistic/postmodern values, and we had the student revolutions that rocked that era around the world, beginning in May 1968, Paris; the extraordinary and profoundly far-reaching civil rights movement; the rise of personal and professional feminism; the major beginnings of the entire environmental movement; hate-law legislation; and so on. Again, only a small percentage (10 percent, eventually 20 percent) were actually at those levels, but their values began to permeate and saturate the culture. And now, today (2015), we are on the verge of a tipping-point of 10 percent of the population reaching this "monumental leap of meaning," the emergence of this entirely new tier, the emergence of the Integral levels—capitalizing "Integral" to reflect this "monumental leap."

And this, beyond doubt, would change everything. As a universally present growth level, it is a stage to which and through which every human being the world over is destined to grow, if continue to grow they do. This isn't just a simple concept, which you can learn or not learn, as you wish, or a mere theory, which you can take or leave (like, for example, Jacques Derrida's "deconstruction"), but rather, it is an inherent, universally present stage of human development, like Maslow's stages of safety, belongingness, and self-esteem (or Gebser's magic, mythic, and rational). In other words, the human race, *for the first time ever in its history*, is heading toward at least the possibility of a world beyond major and deep-seated conflict, and toward one marked more and more often by mutual tolerance, embrace, peace, inclusion, and compassion. And all we have to do for this to happen is just continue to grow!

Just as an acorn goes through several universal stages on its way to becoming an oak tree, and an egg goes through several universal stages on its way to becoming a chicken, so a human being goes through several universal stages on its way to maturity, a maturity not characterized by deep-seated conflict and aggression, but one that is now in progress of becoming characterized by deep-seated care and integral loving-kindness.

All religions, like all other disciplines, will be affected by this profound transformation. And, unlike the earlier interpretations and approaches to this worldwide transformation (for example, *The Greening of America, The Aquarian Conspiracy, The Turning Point, Education for Ecstasy,* and so forth), this is a much more nuanced view, based on significant research and evidence, and one that doesn't simplistically divide everything in terms of "old paradigm" versus "new paradigm" notions but instead sees at least a half-dozen previous transformations that humanity has already undergone—and the biggest one of all is lying just ahead of us! (In other words, this view tracks all of those 6-to-8 major levels of Growing Up, and not just two simplistic shifts—"old paradigm" and "new paradigm.")

In those earlier approaches, various Boomer writers, themselves part of the first generation to be raised under the roof of an ongoing, recent, profound transformation—namely, from that of rational/modern to pluralistic/postmodern, or from industrial to informational—noting all the major and far-reaching changes that such a transformation brought in its wake (for example, as we mentioned, the revolutionary civil rights movement, the environmental movement, feminism, greater social equality, and so on), understandably concluded that this one, single transformation ("old paradigm" to "new paradigm") was going to keep going and would eventually sweep through the entire world, replacing the one and only, previous, older paradigm, which was usually referred to as the "Newtonian-Cartesian" or "mechanistic materialist" worldview, with the amazing, single, world-sweeping, transformative, new paradigm, usually called "quantum," "holistic," "organic," "partnership," "Gaiacentric," or "ecocentric" (the old paradigm was "egocentric").

Thus, virtually all of these books had (and still have—they are still being written) a diagram with two columns, the first called something like "the old paradigm" and the second called "the new paradigm." Under the "old paradigm," which was blamed for virtually every one of humanity's problems throughout its entire existence, from nuclear threat to eco-despoliation to warfare to tooth decay, were items like "the Newtonian-Cartesian paradigm," "analytic-divisive," "patriarchal," "sexist," "racist," "rational-divisive," "abstract disenchanting," "deterministic," "fragmenting," "hierarchical," "rigid structure," "mechanistic," "disembodied," "ranking," and so on. And under the "new paradigm," credited with being able to solve every human problem in existence and bring joy and ecstasy to the entire human race (that's not an exaggeration), were items like "systems inclusive," "process oriented," "partnership," "holistic-integrative," "Web of Life," "feeling over thinking," "egalitarian rather than ranking," "uniting," "harmonizing," "eco-centric not ego-centric," "inclusive," "Gaiacentric," "coming from the heart (not the head)," "fully embodied, not disembodied," among others.

What wasn't realized is that the transformation the Boomers had just undergone—namely, modern/rational to postmodern/pluralistic—was simply one of at least a half-dozen major transformations humanity had undergone in its overall history, and it wasn't even the most profound (that was just beginning to emerge, the Integral 2nd-tier transformation). Further, taking all the half-dozen or so previous transformations (archaic, magic, magic-mythic, mythic, and rational) and smooshing them all together into a single previous paradigm—the rational-analytic "old paradigm"—and seeing the novel, emerging, pluralistic "new paradigm" as the great, grand, ultimate transformation now taking over the globe, contributed to their failure to see that the pluralistic transformation itself was simply one of numerous transformations humankind had already undergone (and was NOT itself the truly integrative paradigm that was actually sought—that belonged to the newly emerging next stage).[3]

By mushing all of these half-dozen transformations into two major worldwide changes—the "old paradigm" and the "new paradigm"—they missed all the subtle changes that had occurred stage to stage and pushed them all into just these two columns ("old" and "new" paradigm), thus failing dramatically to see just what problems, and solutions, each major stage actually brought.

As only one example, the postmodern writers blamed most social ills, including slavery, on the modern "old paradigm." In books like *A Light Too Bright*, the modern rational transformation was blamed for virtually every single problem introduced by all of the previous transformations combined (since these writers had only two basic choices— "old" or "new" paradigm—and the problems certainly weren't caused by their wonderful "new" paradigm), and thus slavery, for example, was blamed on modernity (and the modern Enlightenment).⁴ As one scholar put it, "If I was a minority, I'd get as far away from the Enlightenment as I could." (To which one perceptive critic responded, "Just where exactly would you go?")

In blaming modernity for slavery, these approaches missed the fact that modernity *ended* slavery, cured slavery, and for the first time ever in history. Most of the problems blamed on modernity, in fact, were problems created by premodernity and were ones that modernity itself was halfway to fixing. But, damn the facts, to these postmodern/pluralists, with their limited historical choices, modernity and its "old paradigm" just had to be the cause of all of humankind's problems. The solution these postmodern/pluralists thus came up with was politics (mostly the New Left) disguised as allegedly profound philosophy (for example, deconstructive postmodernism), which proceeded by disfiguring and dismantling ("deconstructing") virtually everything invented before the Boomers came along and "finally" got it right.⁵

The net result—after getting a fine start with the healthy version of the pluralistic stage (and bringing in everything from civil rights to environmentalism, much to their credit)—was that, after everything was "deconstructed," all that was eventually left over was nihilism and narcissism, that tag team from postmodern hell. Nobody had any value systems left that they could wholeheartedly believe in (since anything they could deeply believe in had long ago been totally deconstructed); and besides, if you passionately believed in this one thing, it meant that you didn't passionately believe in these other things, and what's wrong with them? Are you making a value judgment here against them? How dare you judge and rank other peoples' values like that! (As we will see, the rejection of all hierarchies—including growth hierarchies, and not just dominator hierarchies, which I will soon explain—is a hallmark of the pluralistic approaches and goes hand-in-hand with their sharp rejection of all "ranking" schemes.)

So the next generation, the "slackers," simply gave up believing in anything and spent their lives vegged out on the sofa blankly watching TV—or such is the stereotype. And as for this approach inherently increasing narcissism, studies show that the most recent graduating class of 2014 Millennials in the United States has more narcissism than any class since testing itself was begun! It's estimated to be two to three times the amount of narcissism of their Boomer parents—and Boomers were named the "Me generation"! (So some critics have labeled this recent cohort the "me-me-me" generation—in some ways unfair; like the "slackers," there is much to admire about these youngsters; the downside is directly traceable to the narcissism of their parents, as "the sins of the fathers are visited even unto the seventh generation.")

But much finer, more accurate, more granular stage-conception models showed that humans didn't have just these two major stages—"old" and "new" paradigm—but that they underwent a whole spectrum of developmental stages. Here's a brief overview of some of these stages, the stages of Growing Up—and we will be returning to these in more detail as we go along; this is simply to give an introductory sense of what is involved:

1. An original fusion state (Gebser's "Archaic"). Historically, the transition from the great apes to humans; today, the child's first year of life or so, Piaget's basic sensorimotor drives, Maslow's "physiological needs," and so forth.

2. An impulsive-fantasy stage (Graves's "animistic," Gebser's "Magic," Jane Loevinger's "impulsive"). This stage governed much of the original hunting and gathering societies, where, for example, a rain dance was done to "magically" make nature rain, and today, children from ages one to three or four—for example, they will put their head under a pillow, and because they can't see anybody, think that magically nobody can see them either.

3. The "Magic-Mythic" stage, Maslow's "safety" needs, Loevinger's "self-protective." Once the self has fully differentiated itself from its environment, it feels vulnerable and becomes concerned with its safety and security, and in defense develops a strong set of power drives, or what Spiral Dynamics (a developmental stage-model based on the work of pioneer Clare Graves, and covering—that's right—8 major levels of development, essentially the same generic ones we're pointing out now, but specifically regarding values) colorfully calls "PowerGods," a strong belief in superpowerful beings who could provide safety and security if approached correctly with prayer and ritual or other superstitiously enticing actions. This power stage governed

humanity's first major military empires that began to spread across the globe, facilitated by the invention of early farming that freed people from the almost constant demand to forage for food and allowed them to engage in other activities, such as fighting each other; their leaders were considered literally to be Gods—and they were, "PowerGods."

4. Gebser's "Mythic" stage, Lawrence Kohlberg's conformist "law and order," Maslow's "belongingness" needs, Loevinger's "conformist" stage, "mythic-membership," and so forth. A more conformist, group-oriented stage, where people still believe in supernatural beings of a decidedly mythic (but concrete-literal) sort, and believe that mythic-religious books are the literal truth of a supreme Being—the Bible, the Koran, the Pentateuch, some Pure Land sutras. James Fowler called this the "Mythic-literal" stage, since the myths are believed *literally*: Moses really did part the Red Sea, Elijah really did go straight to heaven while still alive, Lao Tzu really was nine hundred years old when he was born, and so on. This is still largely the basis of fundamentalist traditional religious beliefs; also the source of much prejudiced thinking and a great deal of terrorism (all done, of course, in the name of a chosen "God").

5. Gebser's "Rational," Piaget's "formal operational," Durant's "Reason and Revolution," Fowler's "individuative," Loevinger's "conscientious," and Maslow's "self-esteem." This stage is characterized by the emergence of a world-shaking reason and a more scientific and evidence-based approach to truth, because an individualistic sense of self, capable of 3rd-person reason, is developing out of the previous 2nd-person conformist and mythic-membership stage. Spiral Dynamics calls this new stage "StriveDrive," since the drive to progress and achievement becomes central. With the development of "reason, individuality, the modern sciences, and progress," this stage is accompanied everywhere by the emergence of what we now recognize as *modernity*, particularly focused on the Western Enlightenment.

6. "Pluralistic," Graves's "relativistic," "multicultural," "Gaiacentric," "ecocentric," "nonmarginalizing." A stage where people believe that "there are more things in heaven and earth than are dreamt of" in your rational philosophy and science, and there is a switch to multicultural, socially constructed, and therefore culturally differing beliefs; in short, what we now call the *postmodern* era, first announced in the student rebellions of the sixties, then spreading widely. This is a largely

"egalitarian" level, where all people and all cultures are seen as being equally valuable and equally true; no ranking, no hierarchies, no judging. This is the highest commonly available stage yet to emerge, where it is in a constant "Culture Wars" with the previous two stages—thus, postmodern multicultural values (#6) versus modern, rational, progressive, scientific values (#5) versus traditional mythic religious values (#4), all fighting for supremacy.

7. "Holistic," "integrated," and "Integral" stages, collectively called "2nd tier"; Graves's "systemic," Loevinger's "integrated," Gebser's "aperspectival-integral," Maslow's "self-actualization" needs. Finally, on the leading edge of today, we find the actual emergence of unified and integrated stages, where people believe that there is some degree of deep significance and importance to all of these previous stages, if for no other reason than that they become components of the higher stages themselves. This level (or levels) sees wholes everywhere and strives to bring the world together in interwoven unified harmonies. It is the very cutting edge of evolution today and is responsible for the majority of breakthrough discoveries now occurring at accelerated rates in all the major disciplines. At this point, only around 5 percent of the world's population has reached this level, but it promises to be a game changer in every way. It also marks an end to the "Culture Wars," precisely because it is the first level to see value in all previous levels. And it (and the next stage) has a major hand in the creation of Integral approaches to various fields, including Integral Spirituality.

8. "Super-Integral" stages or "3rd tier" stages; Susanne Cook-Greuter's "ego-aware" and "unitive," Jenny Wade's "transcendence and unity," Maslow's "self-transcendence" needs, and so on. Right now, a likely possibility (since evolution never stops) is the emergence of even yet greater stages where one's identity actually shifts to higher, supraindividual, transpersonal, spiritual sources (and here join up with higher "states," as we will carefully explore).[6]

No need to remember any of those now—we'll be going over everything we need at the appropriate time; this is just a quick overview, by way of background, for these 6-to-8 major levels of development (or "Growing Up"), which are generally agreed upon by virtually all of the modern developmental schools. In fact, I wrote a book called *Integral Psychology*, which had charts that included over one hundred different developmental models. As much as they differed, what was so amazing is that virtually all of them had somewhere between 6 and 8 of the essentially same levels of development, easily recognizable and summarized here; some had a few less, some a few more, but the same 6-to-8 basic levels kept showing up time and time again.[7] The evidence for them is simply overwhelming. And we will be directly exploring what these levels mean for spirituality in particular, and our general approach to our world overall. These newly understood stages of Growing Up are a monumental discovery, and they truly change everything. Among many other things, they demonstrate how much more detailed and sophisticated these maps of development that scholars have produced are compared to the simplistic "old paradigm" versus "new paradigm" (more about all of these as we continue).

The point is that any society and culture—and any of the subcultures in it—are going to be much more of a "layer cake," with different percentages of the population at each of these major stages of development. And each of these stages sees the world in a very, very different way, and it is simply impossible to approach any problem or issue without taking this elemental fact into account, something which is virtually never done at this time, with disastrous results. Everybody is still born at square one (at "Archaic" or sensorimotor) and begins their growth and development from there, passing through each major structure-stage until growth slows or ceases, with individuals indeed generally stopping at a particular level/stage at some point along the way (in each multiple intelligence, as we'll see). In the modern West, for example (and these numbers vary somewhat depending upon how they are measured, and they don't add up to 100 percent because they overlap), we find about 10 percent of the population at Magic, 40 percent at Mythic, 40 to 50 percent at Rational, 20 percent at Pluralistic, 5 percent at Integral, and less than one-tenth of 1 percent at Super-Integral. Individuals' structure center of gravity (their overall average or most-often used stage of development) will generally be at one of those major levels, and accordingly they will tend to hang out with others at the same basic level ("birds of a feather flock together"), including working in similar jobs (criminal types at power-drive stages; fundamentalist believers at Mythic-literal; businesspeople and scientists at Rational; people working in humanistic, nonprofit, human services, and at most NGOs at Pluralistic; integrative and systemic thought leaders at Integral, and so on). Each of these stage/levels has healthy and unhealthy versions; each brings new problems as well as new solutions; and it is still generally true, as the massively overquoted snippet attributed to Einstein has it: "A problem cannot be solved from the same level that produced it."

So each culture can be profiled by the "layer cake" that its population-percentage breakdown gives us. But let us immediately note that these "levels" of consciousness development are *not* levels of human beings; they are levels of complexity of thinking (or levels of consciousness) that humans can use, and any individual human can be at virtually any level on the overall spectrum of structures of consciousness (the same is true of *states* of consciousness as well, as we will see). The point of creating a composite map or Framework of these different levels (such as Archaic, Magic, Mythic, Rational, Pluralistic, and Integral) is not to pigeonhole, judge, label, or develop a prejudice about people. The point is to help us understand and communicate better with people who are using different worldviews, as individuals grow and develop through the entire spiral or spectrum of stages, and thus help us to increase our understanding, care and compassion, and capacity to communicate with people who are at stages different than the ones we might be at ourselves. It is also to help each of us get a sense of just how much further we ourselves can grow and evolve if we choose to do so. And, in fact, research shows that simply studying any developmental model accelerates that person's growth through the various structure-stages of development. Learning those models, like learning AQAL, is *psychoactive*—it has a direct and powerful capacity to activate and accelerate one's own growth and development through these areas, or through any of the dimensions in the AQAL Framework. ("AQAL" is short for "All Quadrants, All Levels," which itself is short for "all quadrants, all levels, all lines, all states, all types," which is the version of Integral Theory and Practice that I am involved with. I'll be explaining each of those dimensions as we go forward—again, no need to memorize any of those; I'll explain as we proceed.) The point for now is that this general framework is itself psychoactive for virtually all of its elements and dimensions. So if you are occasionally—or often!—bored with any of this "stage/level" or "composite map" stuff, please hang in there; research suggests that learning about it is powerfully opening channels in your brain that will make room for increasing growth, development, and expansion of your own awareness. It won't force you to believe anything; it will simply open up other, and new, possibilities in your own life.

Although the world is not on the verge of a staggeringly huge shift from a single "old" paradigm to a single "new" paradigm, it is on the leading edge of having 10 percent of the population jump from 1st-tier stages to 2nd-tier stages—that "monumental leap in meaning"—and this will "saturate" the culture with the Integral values of inclusion, nonmarginalizing, systemic holism, cultural harmony, human inter-connectivity, and higher, "nonmythic," contemplative forms of spiri-tuality (which we will continue to explore and elucidate as we discuss "Waking Up," and which, of course, is one of Buddhism's major strengths).

This transformation from 1st to 2nd tier can be expected to have a profound impact on every major discipline now in existence, including religion and spirituality. And as G. K. Chesterton once quipped, "Christianity and Buddhism are very much alike, especially Bud-dhism."[8] Something, however you look at it, is a bit special about Buddhism. For Buddhism, we have seen, was one of the few religions that from the beginning was marked by evolutionary and integrally inclined thinking, all the way up to the synthesizing Yogachara and Tantra. As one source put it, "Yogachara discourse surveys and syn-thesizes all Three Great Turnings." Buddhism is uniquely poised to be among those disciplines that consciously take the next major step, in-fused by the coming global, Integral, tipping point and transforma-tion, and make its own evolutionary leap forward with a Fourth Great Turning of the Wheel of Dharma and Truth, making that "monumen-tal leap of meaning" into the spiritual stream.

Now, I want to emphasize that the kinds of truths that would be included in any Fourth Great Turning are truths that can and, in my opinion, should be included in any and all of the world's Great Wisdom Traditions (shaped and molded, of course, by their own surface struc-tures, past history, and essential identifying elements). But the truths that we are talking about here are fundamental, basic truths of the human being-in-the-world itself, and should be included, in one form or another, in any system of human self-understanding (from spiritual to psychological to sociological to philosophical and more). If, follow-ing the common terms for 2nd tier, we refer to this as Inclusive or Integral Spirituality, then we would want to see, in addition to Integral Buddhism, an Integral Christianity, Integral Hinduism, Integral Kashmir Shaivism, Integral Judaism, Integral Taoism, Integral Islam, and so on. (See my book *Integral Spirituality* for a treatment of these basic themes.)[9] Not to mention Integral Medicine, Integral Business, Integral Education, Integral Politics, Integral Economics, Integral Law, Integral Relationships, and so on.

What kind of common truths would this Fourth Turning include? This is what we will be discussing in the coming chapters. Many of these factors are unknown to a larger world, but virtually every single element that I am going to present, as part of this "monumental leap in meaning," has numerous knowledge communities (if not widely well known) that have themselves provided, overall, a staggering amount of evidence, proof, and documentation of the existence and significance of these elements. Not one of them is doubted in the communities that actually study them. These are not vague, fantasized, oddball, or goofy beliefs, but evidence-drenched, data-loaded, communally verified, profoundly important ideas, elements, and factors, and the only odd thing about any of them is how relatively unknown they remain. Integral Theory has looked the world over for significant truths and ideas that should be included in any knowledge of a Human 101 course, and these significant elements (which it calls "quadrants," "levels," "lines," "states," and "types"—or, as mentioned, "AQAL," for short) have been drawn together into a metatheory that makes room for all of them. This metatheory, which I promise I will do my best to present in the simplest and most accessible way that I can— showing you exactly what it can dramatically offer your own life— will act as the background for our updating interpretation of an Integral Spirituality and Fourth Turning Buddhism, just as, to repeat one final time, it has already been used to create an Integral Medicine, Integral Education, Integral Economics, Integral Art, Integral History, Integral Transformative Practice, Integral Politics, Integral Architecture, Integral Business, Integral Leadership, and close to sixty other major human disciplines, all of which have been reinterpreted using the AQAL Framework to include these incredibly important but rarely known elements, facts, and ideas (the basic "AQAL" elements), which, on the whole, have a staggering amount of supporting evidence backing them—and thus include each of those disciplines in the tent of this "monumental leap of meaning." The peer-reviewed professional journal in this field—the *Journal of Integral Theory and Practice*—now has articles in over fifty-seven major disciplines that have been reenvisioned using the AQAL Integral Framework, and the result in every case is a more comprehensive, fuller, richer, and more effective discipline, with literally no exceptions to date.

The reason, I believe, that this endeavor has been so successful is that "Integral" is not just the name of a theory or metatheory—which, like any idea, you are free to believe or not believe—but when it refers in part to an actual stage of development itself, it is a *very real* territory of the Kosmos—namely, a real stage of evolution, growth, and development, which means that individuals don't get to merely accept it or not; as an actual stage of human development, each and every individual, to the extent that they continue to grow, will grow into and through this stage, this real territory in reality. It's the unalterable reality of this territory, its undeniable concrete realness, not the take-it-or-leave-it nature of a merely speculative idea, that is driving the extraordinary success of this Integral approach, which grounds itself in this real stage territory.

One of the major advantages of this AQAL Framework is that every one of its major aspects is something that is fully and immediately present in your own awareness right now. As you will discover in the following pages, you can gain access to these extraordinary facts just by learning where to look in your own consciousness, your own awareness, your own being. Astonishingly, since many of these AQAL elements are so rarely known to the rest of the world, right now you might not even suspect the existence of these aspects in your own being, even though all of them are present right now and are fully active. But once they are pointed out, they are usually met with one of those, "Ah! Why didn't I see that sooner myself? It's so obvious!" And yet you will never look at the world—or yourself—in the same way again.

Freedom and Fullness: WAKING UP and GROWING UP

By way of introduction, recall that for Buddhism, reality is nondual, a not-twoness of samsara and nirvana, finite and infinite, subject and object, Form and Emptiness. (As promised, I will soon give some exercises that will point out both Form and Emptiness in your own awareness, including exercises for realizing "ultimate unity consciousness.") We already noticed that Emptiness, being void of characterizations (including that one), hasn't changed since the time of the Buddha (in fact, since the Big Bang and before). The experience or recognition of Emptiness is a simultaneous realization, metaphorically, of infinite Freedom, Release, the Great Liberation—liberation from the binding conflict between subject and object and all the torment and torture they inflict on each other. We also saw that if the experience of Emptiness is one of Freedom, the experience of Form is one of Fullness. And while Emptiness has not changed from the beginning of time, Form has. Form, in fact, has undergone a ceaseless process of evolution, with each stage of evolution adding more and more complexity of Form to the universe: from simple strings to quarks to atoms to molecules to cells to multicellular organisms, with organisms themselves evolving into ever more complex forms, from single-celled organisms to photosynthetic plants to animals with perceiving neuronal nets, to instinct-driven reptilian brain stems, to emotion-generating limbic systems, to logic-capable triune brains, whose synaptic connections, we noted, number more than all the stars in the known universe.

The same complexification occurred interiorly. Humans, for example, evolved from simple Archaic, to 1st-person Magic, to 2nd-person Mythic, to 3rd-person Rational, to 4th-person Pluralistic, to 5th-person and higher Integral. These ordinal numbers refer to the number of overall perspectives an individual can simultaneously keep in mind. A 1st-person perspective can be aware only of the individual's own personal perspective, or "I" (as with egocentric Magic). A 2nd-person perspective can "take the role of other" and thus add a 2nd-person perspective—a "you" that added to an "I" becomes a "we" or "us" (as with ethnocentric Mythic). A 3rd-person perspective adds a perspective that can objectively be aware of both a 1st- and 2nd-person perspective, or "all of us," and thus also discover objective, universal, 3rd-person truths (as the modern sciences do—modern physics, chemistry, biology, medicine, and so forth—as with worldcentric Rational). A 4th-person perspective can keep in mind a 3rd-person view of a 2nd-person view of a 1st-person view (and hence comment on and criticize previous views, as postmodernism does with modern ideas; thus the postmodern Pluralistic and "deconstructive" view. Likewise a 5th-person Integral perspective, transcending and including previous perspectives, thus becomes even more and more holistic and integrative—the synthesizing Integral, and so on. And where Pluralistic has enough cognitive power to see all the real differences in various ideas and cultural notions—hence "multiculturalism"—but not, alas, enough to see their commonalities or universal similarities, and thus ends up fragmented and disjointed, the next higher Integral can see all those differences, but it also has the power to begin to see all the commonalities as well, to see all the "patterns that connect" individual cultures around the world, such as the 6-to-8 major levels of development found in all cultures worldwide. Developmentalists have traced stages up to a 7th-person and even higher perspectives (Super-Integral). The point is that each of these major stages of human development and evolution adds a new perspective, a new and larger degree of consciousness, and thus consciousness itself continues to grow, expand, and become "larger" and "larger," more and more "whole" (as does any genuine evolutionary sequence—atoms to molecules to cells to organisms, for example, with each of those being "larger" and "larger" or more and more "whole"), and this "greater wholeness" grows along with one's greater and greater capacity for love, care, identity, concern, morals, compassion, creativity, and so on.

The universe of Form, in other words, is becoming Fuller and Fuller via evolution. Thus, to reach Enlightenment in today's world—to experience the unity of Emptiness and Form—is not to have any more Freedom than the great early sages (East and West), since Emptiness is the same, but the Enlightenment *is* Fuller, since the universe of Form has continued to grow and evolve, adding more and more complexity, more Form and Fullness, more Wholeness at each point.

This greater complexity means that, among many other items we will be examining, more and more conventional truths have been discovered, and those need to be taken into account in any Fourth Turning. In the Buddha's time, for example, people—including the Buddha—really did think that the earth was flat. And how could these early sages possibly have known about neurochemistry, about dopamine, serotonin, and acetylcholine? Or about the limbic system and its role in emotions, or the reptilian brain stem and its instinctual drives? But in looking for the cause of human suffering, how could any complete account leave any of those out? Likewise, the actual interior stages of growth and development, such as those discovered by Jean Gebser, Abraham Maslow, James Mark Baldwin, or Clare Graves, should also be included in such an account: for example, the stages of human needs —physiological, safety, belongingness, self-esteem, self-actualization, and self-transcendence, to use Maslow's nested growth hierarchy. (These are simply another version, this time emphasizing specific characteristics or "lines"—in this case, the needs or motivation line— of the standard 6-to-8 stages that we've been summarizing.)

These particular types of developmental stages are a modern discovery, part of the new complexity that evolution brought with the modern era. Of course, we find stages in meditation, stages that are 1st-person, or direct *state* experiences (a term I'll explain in a moment), and these were clearly mapped out by the great contemplative traditions East and West (for example, St. Teresa's seven mansions, the ten ox-herding pictures of Zen, the stages of Early Buddhism so clearly systematized by Buddhaghosa, the stages outlined by St. John of the Cross, the six major stages of Mahamudra, and so on). But the more recently discovered developmental stages, which are stages of *structure* development (a term that I'll also elucidate momentarily) discovered by modern researchers such as Piaget, Baldwin, Kohlberg, Gebser, Graves, Loevinger, Maslow, and so on, can't be seen by introspecting, as 1st-person meditative *state*-stages can be, because they are 3rd-person *structure*-stages discovered by studying large groups of people over long periods of time under experimental conditions, and then drawing conclusions about the mental patterns involved—something you can't see merely by "looking within." This is why states, such as the waking state, or the dream state, or states of joy, happiness, sadness, anxiety, fear, perhaps a sense of oneness with nature, and so on, which can indeed be seen simply by looking within, were discovered by the earliest shamans, explorers of interior states, at least fifty thousand years ago, whereas James Mark Baldwin gave the first description of a structure a mere one hundred years ago. Structures are much harder to detect (they are, recall, like rules of grammar), and are thus found nowhere in any meditative system the world over. Most meditative systems are at least a thousand years old, and since structures were first discovered only one hundred years ago, no meditation school had time to include them—until now, that is.

For those of you a little rusty on grammar, let me point out that "1st person" means "the person who is speaking"—namely, an "I" or "me," and "2nd person" means "the person being spoken to"—namely, a "you" or "thou." A "you" plus an "I" gives us a "we," so this is sometimes referred to as the "you/we" or even just the "we" dimension. The "3rd person" means "the person or thing being spoken about"—namely, a "he," "her," or just "it,"and to say something is "3rd person" is generally taken to mean that it is objective and universally the case. All natural sciences, for example, are called "3rd person"—the idea being that, for example, if you want to know if it is raining outside, you go to the window and look, and if you see it's raining, you conclude, "Yes, it's raining." But you might be confused or mistaken, so just to make sure you invite a second person to look out the window, too, and so this person looks out, and sees it's raining, and says, "Yes, it's raining out there." Now if you want to make absolutely sure—you two might be suffering a mass hysteria and hallucinating the rain—you invite yet a third person to look, and he or she does so, and yes, sure enough this person also says, "I see it's raining, too." That third person's agreement is generally taken to be enough proof that, basically, "It is raining now (and here)" is a universally true notion that essentially every healthy person on the planet would agree to if they looked (now, at this place). So it's not a 1st-person opinion or taste; it's not a 2nd-person collusion or game; it's a 3rd-person fact or truth.

So, states (as in, states of Waking Up) are immediate, obvious, 1st-person realities, something you can directly experience for yourself (they might be true for others, too, but you'd have to check that out before claiming so; as it turns out, meditative states have been checked with subsequent practitioners, and often for hundreds, even thousands of years, so they are considered to be essentially very real realities, at least for those who study them). But the point is that, when you are in one of these meditative states, since they are 1st-person realities, you are *directly aware of them*—if you experience universal love, or being one with all things, or being drenched in infinite bliss, you definitely know it! So as you proceed through any meditative sequence, you will be aware of the states and their state-stages as they immediately present themselves to your awareness, no problem. And most of the world's great meditative and contemplative systems, East and West, have mapped out the generally expected stages that you might go through as you practice their particular form of meditation (and, as we'll see, there is a great deal of similarity to the maps of these state-stages wherever they have appeared around the world, which adds to their credibility).

But 3rd-person structures are different (for example, all of these 6-to-8 stages of development that we are discussing, since they are not 1st-person states but 3rd-person structures). Not that there aren't many general similarities between the various maps and models of these 6-to-8 stages—for there are—but that when you are experiencing any of these stages, you don't generally know it. They are not a direct 1st-person experience, and so they remain largely hidden. They are not something you are looking *at*, they are something you are looking at the world *through and with*—the frameworks and "hidden maps" that you use to make sense of your experience and your world, and without which reality is just a "blooming buzzin'" confusion.

This is why these frameworks are, as I earlier pointed out, very much like the rules of grammar. Every person growing up in a particular language-speaking culture, say, an English-speaking one, will grow up speaking that language quite correctly, for the most part: they will use subjects and verbs correctly, they will use adverbs and adjectives correctly, and on balance will put all the words together correctly following the English rules of grammar. But if you ask any one of them to write down those rules of grammar, virtually none of them can do it. They are all following these rules perfectly, but nobody knows what the rules are!

Structures are like that. Each of the major 6-to-8 levels of development has a structure—that is, a pattern governed by rules like grammar—and when people are at that structure-stage of development, they will almost perfectly follow the rules of that level, but have no idea that they are doing so. Moreover, they can't see these rules by looking within or introspecting; all they would see are various words, symbols, signs, and concepts, but not the hidden grammar rules governing them (just as you cannot look within now and see the rules of grammar that you are nonetheless following perfectly and that control the composition of virtually every sentence you speak). In order to discover the rules of English grammar, you would have to study numerous English-speaking people, examine how they speak, and laboriously deduce the rules they are following. This is why, although 1st-person *states* (being immediately available by introspection) were discovered at least fifty thousand years ago, 3rd-person structures, as we noted, weren't discovered until around one hundred years ago. And since most meditation systems are several hundred to several thousand years old, not one of them anywhere around the world has a knowledge of these 6-to-8 stages of normal development. You can look at meditative or contemplative texts the world over and never find a sequence such as archaic to magic to mythic to rational to pluralistic to integral to super-integral. You will find many maps containing the *stages* of *states* of meditation, but none of them contain *stages* of the *structures* of growth.

So we're calling these *structure*-stages the stages of GROWING UP, since they occur to all human beings as they grow and develop into mature humans. We're calling the *state*-stages of meditative development leading to Awakening or Enlightenment the stages of WAKING UP, because these are the fairly rare meditative stages leading to an experience of what is said to be ultimate Reality, ultimate Truth, a Great Liberation, a Supreme Identity (of the self with this ultimate Reality).

And whereas stages of GROWING UP are simply given to all humans if they continue to grow and develop, stages of WAKING UP generally occur only to those who voluntarily take up a meditative or contemplative or spiritual practice that allows their Wakefulness, or their pure Awareness, to move through the natural states of consciousness (such as waking; dreaming; deep dreamless sleep; pure empty awareness, or witnessing; and nondual "unity" consciousness), resulting in an awakening of their ultimate, nondual, radical Great Perfection or True Nature, unborn and undying, uncreated and unlimited, timeless and eternal, spaceless and infinite—the world seen in its pure Thusness, Suchness, or Isness.

Just as the many maps of GROWING UP generally give variations on the same basic 6-to-8 levels of growth and development, so, as we'll see in more detail in just a moment, the many different paths of the Great Liberation, or WAKING UP, generally give the same broad stages of meditative development, usually based on the essentially universal nature of those 5 major natural states of consciousness I just listed (gross waking, subtle dreaming, causal deep sleep, empty witnessing, pure nondual "unity"). What Integral Theory has discovered is that human beings actually have *two very important, but very different, axes of growth and development*: (1) the natural growth and development sequence through 6-to-8 levels of *structures* of consciousness, each with its "hidden maps" or rules of grammar that cannot be seen by those structure-stages themselves (that is, GROWING UP), and (2) the meditative growth sequence through 5 or 6 levels of states of consciousness, each state-stage here being not a naturally occurring stage of growth for all humans, but the result of a voluntary set of actions taken by a person to grow through all of his or her state possibilities, ending (hopefully) at a full awakening and awareness of all of the basic states of consciousness, including ultimate nondual "unity" consciousness (a Supreme Identity of the individual with ultimate Spirit)— a WAKING UP, an Enlightenment.

So the strange fact that all humans are facing today is that virtually every one of the major models of GROWING UP (mostly Western) have *no idea whatsoever* about any of the state-stages of WAKING UP—and thus no awareness of Enlightenment, Awakening, moksha, metanoia, satori, the Great Liberation, the Supreme Identity. Nothing. And yet of all the extraordinary Wisdom Traditions and the Paths of the Great Liberation (mostly Eastern), not one of them anywhere has any understanding, or even any mention, of the major levels, or stages, of typical GROWING UP (and they don't because although they are masters of introspection, you can't see these levels, these "hidden maps" of grammar rules, by introspecting). So humans have two major paths of incredibly important growth, *and yet never in humankind's history have they been brought together in one place.* This means that humanity, up to this point, has been training itself to be partial, fragmented, and broken. And the history of humanity to date is a history of a broken humanity. Bringing these two together, not only in theory but in actual practice, has been one of the major contributions of Integral Theory and Practice and is, I believe, part of what should be included in any genuinely Integral Spirituality, including any Fourth Turning. This is a truly revolutionary development.

Spiritual Intelligence versus Spiritual Experience

When these two different streams of development and evolution begin to refer specifically to spirituality, it means that humans then have two very different types of spiritual engagement possible for them. The first is a direct, immediate "experience"—via 1st-person *states* of consciousness—of spiritual realities (spanning a gross nature mysticism, a subtle deity mysticism, a causal formless mysticism, a mirror-mind witnessing mysticism, and a nondual "unity" mysticism). This is the spirituality of WAKING UP. More than a belief system, or a series of narratives about the relation of the human and the Divine, or a set of mythic stories about how to please a great Divine Being and get its boons, this type of spirituality is a direct *psychotechnology of consciousness transformation*, a set of actual practices, injunctions, exemplars, or paradigms (in the correct sense that Thomas Kuhn gave that word, which is not a "big theory" but an "exemplary social practice"—so many people kept misinterpreting "paradigm" as an overall big theory that Kuhn changed the name of paradigm to "exemplar," that is, an exemplary injunction to be followed, not a big theory to be believed). Although relatively little of St. Paul's teachings actually come from this first type of spiritual approach, when he says, "Let this consciousness be in you that was in Christ Jesus, that we all may be one," he could have been saying, "Let this consciousness be in you that was in Gautama the Buddha, that we all may be Awakened as one," and that would be right on the mark. The point is that this is an approach of *direct spiritual experience*[10]—leading ultimately to a nondual or "unity" consciousness with the ultimate Divine and the universe at large—and refers to the Waking Up dimension of our spiritual possibilities, the first major type.

The second major type of spiritual engagement is, on the other hand, simply a set of narratives, a series of stories and tales, often magic or mythic, purporting to explain the relation of the human and the Divine. It concerns not so much our direct experiences of the Divine but what we think or feel about the Divine. It concerns not our *spiritual experiences* (in Waking Up) but our *spiritual intelligence* (in Growing Up). That is, as we will explore in more detail later on, human beings don't have just one type of intelligence, often called "cognitive intelligence" and measured by IQ; rather it seems that evolution has equipped humans with many types of intelligences, each specializing in an important area of life that humans are likely to encounter—in addition to cognitive intelligence, there's emotional intelligence, moral intelligence, intrapersonal intelligence, aesthetic intelligence, musical intelligence, mathematical intelligence, kinesthetic (bodily) intelligence, and spiritual intelligence, among others. Integral Theory often refers to these *multiple intelligences* as *lines* of development, because as different as they all are, they all move through the same basic 6-to-8 *levels* of development that we've been discussing. In other words, different lines, same levels.

But notice that these lines develop relatively independently, so you can be highly developed in some lines, medium in others, and quite poorly in yet others (think Nazi doctors—very high in cognitive intelligence, very low in moral intelligence). This makes every person's growth and development a wildly individual and idiosyncratic affair, with a virtually unlimited number of possible combinations.

The important point here is that when it comes to spirituality, we can either directly experience it (in Waking Up), or we can think about it, ponder it, and intellectualize about it (in Growing Up). When we do the latter, it is usually (according to scholars from Paul Tillich to James Fowler) an attempt to answer the question, "What is it that is of ultimate concern to me?" As a multiple intelligence,[11] or line, spiritual intelligence grows and develops through the same major 6-to-8 levels of Growing Up that all the other lines do—it's just that it views these levels in spiritual or religious terms, according to the characteristics of the spiritual line or spiritual intelligence itself (which again, *thinks* about Spirit but doesn't directly *experience* or *realize* Spirit). Of course, as I'll eventually emphasize, both of these engagements with spirituality are incredibly important but have never both been included in any single approach.

And of crucial importance is that although the form of religion that most Westerners are familiar with (Catholic or Protestant Christianity) started with an emphasis on immediate states of consciousness and Waking Up, under the Church's hands, it increasingly became a religion of Growing Up, and—this is the crucial part—a spiritual line that became *arrested at the Mythic-literal level* (in the overall sequence Archaic, Magic, Mythic, Rational, Pluralistic, Integral, Super-Integral). It's thus ethnocentric, as the Mythic stage in general is (thus, it is the "in group," the "chosen peoples," the ones who have the one and only true way to salvation; all others are "heathens" or "infidels," and it's not a sin to kill an infidel—as a matter of fact, it looks pretty good on your religious resume). All *fundamentalist religions* come most basically from this level of spiritual intelligence (Mythic-literal), whether or not they have any stages of Waking Up, and this includes, of course, Jews, Muslims, Hindus, and—yes—we will see schools of fundamentalist Buddhism originating at this level.

The crucial part of this account is that there are *higher* levels of spiritual intelligence than the Mythic-literal (a level that, for example, takes all of the myths of the Bible as the absolute and literal word of God). As the modern rational Enlightenment began to emerge, most of the early scientific pioneers of the day were not atheists or agnostics; they were Christian believers, however they interpreted Christianity from the next-higher level, the level driving the Enlightenment itself, namely, the Rational level (the rational spiritual belief was called "Deism"). And there are still people continuing to interpret Christianity from the Rational level (such as the Jesus Seminar), as well as from even higher levels, including the Pluralistic (such as the well-known Marcus Borg) and the Integral (see Paul Smith's wonderful *Integral Christianity*).[12]

So the disaster of modern Western religion or spirituality is thus twofold: (1) it has tended to lose any extensive and exuberant connection with states of Waking Up (and thus a real "Christ consciousness" is largely out of its reach), and (2) it has been involved with spiritual intelligence and thus what one must believe (not what one must experience) in order to be saved, and worse yet, its spiritual intelligence is in a case of arrested development at Mythic. (Various rationalizations have been brought in to prop up the mythic beliefs, under the catch-all rationalization given by Tertullian: "I believe *because* it is absurd." Well, the absurd part is right.) Westerners have increasingly rebelled against this prison of spiritual limitations. An astonishing 20 percent of Americans now identify themselves with the phrase "I'm spiritual but not religious," where "spiritual" mostly means Waking Up—direct personal experiential realities, bypassing any and all dogma, and not Growing Up, stuck at Mythic-literal (a dogmatic series of myths that one must believe in order to be saved). Integral Christianity has caused a minor sensation simply because it provides both higher levels of spiritual intelligence (all the way to the Integral and Super-Integral levels in the spiritual line) *and* has reopened Christianity to its mystical, Waking Up aspects, which are extensive, profound, and beautiful.

The Church began moving away from direct mystical-state experience of Waking Up and toward narrative legalistic mythic terms because mystical states couldn't be easily controlled and monitored. And, since "nobody comes to salvation save by way of Mother Church," less and less could personal mystical states be tolerated—not to mention a fact that truly alarmed the Church—namely, mystics had that nasty habit of moving from an exclusively 2nd-person belief in the Otherness or "Thou-ness" of God and Jesus to the Unity or even Identity of the individual soul and God/Christ in Godhead, an identity supposedly allowed only to Jesus of Nazareth. The Spanish Inquisition was particularly charged with rooting out anything that looked like that belief and experience, and mystics everywhere had to begin walking a very thin line. Some, such as Giordano Bruno, stepped over the line and were simply burned at the stake; others, such as Meister Eckhart, had their theses condemned, though he was allowed to live (giving the strange result that, as Eckhart presumably now lives in heaven, his theses are burning in hell, giving him nothing whatsoever to think about).

These two different types of spiritual engagement—spiritual experiences in Waking Up and spiritual intelligence in Growing Up—can be seen whenever we look at scholars who compare and contrast different approaches to spirituality and the different types of maps of the journey they give of the process. Those who study the world's meditative systems (the systems of Waking Up) compare the various states of consciousness that each major stage of the particular meditative system gives, and more often than not, they find that the various approaches, in addition to having several important differences and different surface structures and cultural backgrounds, also have numerous central items in common, so that the maps of the major meditative systems overall have a great deal that they share. The work of scholars such as Daniel P. Brown give 5 or 6 major state-stages of meditative development and offer evidence of the basic similarity of those state-stages worldwide.[13] That's simply one example; I'll give many more as we proceed.

On the other hand, researchers focusing on the more typical stages of spiritual engagement that men and women go through (as opposed to the meditative state-stages that will be experienced only if you voluntarily take up a meditative or contemplative practice and work diligently at it for several years) end up focusing on the structure-stages of these 6-to-8 major levels of development as they appear to the spiritual dimension of humans—that is, they end up focusing on the stages of *spiritual intelligence*: What is it that is of ultimate concern to me? What is it that means more to me than anything else in my life? What is the nature of ultimate Reality or Spirit? Who or what am I really? People such as James Fowler, in his pioneering study *Stages of Faith*, found that people progress through 6 or 7 major levels in their own spiritual thinking (or spiritual intelligence).[14] And this thinking doesn't have to be overtly "religious" to be part of one's actual spiritual intelligence. At the Rational level, for example, people could be atheists, agnostics, or believers—the only thing that matters is that they are using a rational level of cognition to think through those issues of ultimate concern (the fact that they are thinking about ultimate realities and ultimate concern shows that they are using the multiple intelligence or the developmental line of spiritual intelligence, and the fact that they are approaching it using reason shows that they are at the rational level of that line).

The major point here can be directly seen in the following fact: Brown's composite map of the 5 or 6 major stages of Waking Up (which are *states* of consciousness) don't contain *any* of the 6-to-8 stages of Growing Up (which are *structures* of consciousness), and Fowler's stages of faith (which are stages of spiritual intelligence, or the 6-to-8 levels, or structures, of Growing Up as they appear in the spiritual line) don't contain *any* of the 5 or 6 stages of Waking Up. *These are clearly two entirely different axes of development.* But for anybody who takes up a meditative or contemplative practice, both of these sequences of growth are occurring—the naturally occurring Growing Up and the voluntarily occurring Waking Up—and any genuinely Integral or comprehensive approach would definitely want to take both of those into account; not to mention the fact that these two major but very different streams of spiritual engagement are available to every human on the planet, and any even vaguely complete survey of human potentials would want to include both.

So, as a quick summary of this truly important notion, Integral Theory discovered that humans actually have, not one, but at least two, major streams of growth and development. These two growth processes, such as Gebser's or Maslow's on the one hand (for example, archaic, magic, mythic, rational, pluralistic, integral), and the meditative stages on the other (for example, the stages that Evelyn Underhill's classic and brilliant *Mysticism* finds that mystics go through in one form or another—gross purification, subtle illumination, void or dark night, and nondual unification—or whatever meditative map we wish to use) actually refer to *two different growth axes in humans*.[15] The first refers to what are called *structures* of consciousness; the second refer to what are called *states* of consciousness. And a second important item that Integral Theory discovered is that things like 1st-person meditative *states* are actually *interpreted* according to the 3rd-person *structure*-stage one is at. For example, Buddhism can be—and today actually is (as we will see)—interpreted at Magic, Mythic, Rational, Pluralistic, and Integral levels. In a coming chapter, I'll give real and specific examples of Buddhist thinkers and entire schools that are each coming from one of these different levels.

So both Growing Up and Waking Up are crucial components of our overall spiritual development. Waking Up gives us direct experiential access to dimensions of Spirit itself, and Growing Up helps determine just how we will interpret those spiritual experiences. Later on, *I will give some exercises so that you can directly experience each of these developmental paths and its major stages, and thus be able to make up your mind for yourself.*

Summary

Allow me to draw a few conclusions from the major points discussed till now. Forgive me if some of this is repetitive; it's just that these ideas are somewhat new to most people, yet it's important that we grasp their essentials if we are to move forward from here. The rest of the book depends upon having at least a general familiarity with these basic concepts, and if you don't get them now, the rest of the book won't make much sense. So allow me to give a brief rundown here, and if, at any point in this section, you feel familiar enough with the material that its repetition is annoying, by all means skip to the next section, "Understanding the 'Culture Wars.'" Here are some of the crucial points:

Part of the understanding of any new and Integral Fourth Turning—or simply any truly comprehensive spirituality (or even any full-fledged view of Life itself)—would include the fact that *we actually have two major axes of spiritual development*: states and structures. The first, with regard to spirituality, is meditative *states of consciousness*, and we will soon be going through these with a straightforward clarity and simplicity, but for now we can simply summarize them by saying they start with gross egoic thoughts, move through subtle illumination and insight, then often include a causal formless absorption, and culminate in a nondual Great Perfection or Godhead (the union of Emptiness and Form, or Emptiness and Luminosity, or the individual and ultimate Spirit). And second, we also have the growth of *structures of consciousness* (for example, magic to mythic to rational to pluralistic to integral, with a different view of spirituality *at each level*). And—a very important discovery—people will largely interpret the meditative *state* experience according to the *structure* of the major stage of development they are at (in other words, they will interpret their Waking Up experience according to their Growing Up stage—and we will soon see exactly what this means and why it is so important).

To give a very quick example now, take *savikalpa samadhi*, which is just a technical term that means "meditative absorption or prayer with form": there is a Magic interpretation of savikalpa, a Mythic interpretation of savikalpa, a Rational interpretation, a Pluralistic interpretation, and an Integral interpretation, each more and more inclusive when it comes to its actual form. It is the same state but interpreted and experienced according to different structures. We'll later see examples of each of these differing interpretations, including entire schools of Buddhism being interpreted from a particular structure level, and thus see that this truly has an enormous significance in spiritual understanding.

Structures are also responsible for the patterns of our major multiple intelligences. "Multiple intelligences" is a term made famous by Harvard developmentalist Howard Gardner, who pointed out that we don't have just one kind of intelligence—cognitive intelligence—as was often commonly assumed (and measured by the all-important

"IQ").[16] Rather, we have several intelligences, including cognitive intelligence, emotional intelligence, moral intelligence, kinesthetic or somatic, intrapersonal, aesthetic, spiritual, and so on. Of significant importance, we have found that although these multiple intelligences are quite different from each other (they are subsets of what are often called "developmental *lines*"), they all nonetheless grow and evolve through essentially the same basic levels or rungs (often called "developmental *levels*" in contrast to the developmental *lines* that are moving through them). I have been summarizing one version of these basic levels as Archaic, Magic, Magic-Mythic, Mythic, Rational, Pluralistic, Integral, and Super-Integral, which is just one version of the names of these ubiquitous 6-to-8 common levels of Growing Up. We'll look at the considerable evidence for these levels in just a moment.

But what this means is that humanity has finally discovered BOTH Waking Up and Growing Up, and these developmental pathways hold true for any discipline—medicine, law, politics, education, spirituality, and so on. For the first time in humanity's history, we not only know of these two important pathways, but we also have a very profound understanding of the major steps, or stages, or levels that they each grow through, and therefore—for the first time—humanity can begin to train itself to be whole, to be unified, to be integrated, and not to be partial, fragmented, and broken. This is truly a revolutionary discovery.

And one of the things we have also learned—if we focus for the moment on developmental levels and lines—is that as different as the various *lines* are (for example, cognitive, emotional, moral, spiritual, and so on), they all move through essentially the same basic *levels* of development (for example, archaic, magic, mythic, rational, pluralistic, integral, super-integral, and so forth). Although the lines, or streams, are quite different, the levels, or waves, are essentially the same—hence, different lines, same levels (so we have magic cognition, mythic cognition, rational cognition, pluralistic cognition, and integral cognition; and we have magic emotional intelligence, mythic emotional intelligence, rational emotional intelligence, pluralistic emotional intelligence, and so on). AND, because of that, one can be at a fairly different level of development in each of the lines of development: highly advanced in some lines, mediumly developed in other lines, and poorly developed in yet others (I suggested, for example, Nazi doctors—high in cognitive development, poor in moral development). Overall development is thus far from a linear, lockstep, staircase unfolding, but is richly multidimensional and differs from person to person in an almost infinite number of different combinations (although the overall levels or waves are similar in each).

In short, structures are how we GROW UP; states are how we WAKE UP. Structures give us greater and greater inclusiveness, wider and wider identity and embracing and enfolding (from egocentric to ethnocentric to worldcentric to Kosmocentric—we will see what that means very shortly); states give us greater and greater timeless Presence, moving deeper and deeper into the very Suchness, Thusness, or Isness of this and every moment (unfolding deeper and deeper realms, from gross to subtle to causal to nondual). Any Fourth Turning would want to take both of these forms or axes of development into account. The more we discuss each of these, I think the more you will see the incredible importance of both of them. Considerable research over the years has shown that both of these forms of growth and development are occurring—or can occur—in every human, and so to leave out either of them is to profoundly miss out on a full understanding of human growing up and human waking up, and hence to fail to fully actualize one or both of them, which is simply disastrous for a human being's development and overall evolution.

The peculiar thing about both of these developmental sequences is that neither can be seen in the same way that the other is seen or discovered. That is, the way we see the 5 or 6 major stages of Waking Up is by introspecting, by looking within, and simply keeping track of what kinds of experiences tend to unfold at what point in meditation. But we can't look within and directly see the 6-to-8 major stages of Growing Up. These are like the rules of grammar, and although individuals at a particular stage of Growing Up will follow its hidden maps quite accurately, they nonetheless have no idea that they are doing so, just as they follow the rules of grammar very accurately but can't in the least tell you what they are. So the stages of Growing Up are very hard to spot in detail and thus weren't discovered by humanity until around a hundred years ago. Right now, you are almost certainly following a set of rules, a hidden map, that is governing almost all of your thought and behavior, and unless you have studied a developmental model, you will almost certainly have no idea what those rules and hidden maps are. (*Stay with the presentation, however, and you will find out exactly what those rules and hidden maps are, which ones you are likely following, and what you can do about it.*)

As modern Westerners were studying these hidden levels of development, they didn't tend to see any state-stages of Waking Up, not because those states are themselves hard to see, as structures are, but because the number of individuals who had actually awakened to many of these higher states was quite small. As we noted, most people won't become aware, or conscious of, states like deep dreamless sleep unless they engage in a serious meditation practice for several years. And so as Western researchers looked at typical, normal people as they grew and developed, they saw few if any stages of Waking Up, and so virtually no major Western developmental models have anything like Awakening, Enlightenment, moksha, satori, the Great Liberation, the Supreme Identity. This, of course, is disastrous (and yet it applies, essentially, to the entire Western world). *At the same time*, because the stages of Growing Up can't be seen by merely looking within or introspecting, none of the great meditative or contemplative systems anywhere in the world (East or West) include these profoundly important levels of development, levels of Growing Up.

And so, astonishingly, throughout humankind's entire history, never once were *both* of these incredibly important sequences of development spotted simultaneously and included in an overall map, or practice, of growth, or made part of a general cultural awareness. Humankind, up to today's point in its history, has been condemned to move through only one or the other of its two most basic systems of growth, development, and evolution. Thus we have had, throughout our history, the history of a broken humanity, East and West, and nothing *but* a broken humanity.

Further, you can experience virtually any state at virtually any structure level—for example, you can be at the mythic level and develop through all states completely, from gross to nondual unity consciousness, becoming one with the world, but the world you will be "one with" includes *only* levels up to the mythic. Over your head—and not included in your union of Emptiness and Form—are levels of Form that are Rational, Pluralistic, Integral, and Super-Integral. Those levels of existence or Form are *not* included in your unity consciousness, because they haven't emerged yet in your case, and you can't be one with something that you don't even know is there. So your unity consciousness is not actually a wholeness that includes everything, just a wholeness up to the mythic level. For example, you can be at an ethnocentric mythic level and yet still develop through all the major states and become a fully transmitted Zen master. But you would still have aspects of your personality that are ethnocentric, even racist. You might be strongly authoritarian and hierarchical, homophobic, sexist, patriarchal, xenophobic—all the characteristics of the ethnocentric mythic level, even though you experience yourself in a deep oneness with all of that. I really don't mean this in a harsh way, but Enlightened nerds are not only possible, they're common.

So these are two of the items—structures of consciousness and states of consciousness, Growing Up and Waking Up, Fullness and Freedom, particularly as they apply to spirituality (which they both do)—that would be an important consideration for the list of elements in any new and Integral or Fourth Great Turning.

Understanding the "Culture Wars"

Levels, waves, or structure-stages of development apply across the board to human activities and affairs. Take the famous "Culture Wars," for example, which is a zealously overheated argument as to which system of values is the one true system. There are generally agreed to be three major contestants in these Culture Wars: the traditional, often fundamentalist, mythic-literal, religious believers, advocates of God's truth as literally revealed in the Bible; the modern, rational, scientific believers, advocates of progress and achievement; and the postmodern, multicultural, sensitivity believers, advocates of nonmarginalizing attitudes and ecological sustainability. These three value groups are present not only in the United States but worldwide, and in some cases they are behind the breakout of actual warfare (although that also often involves even lower levels, such as Magic-Mythic power drives).

What few people seem to realize is that these three value groups are almost exactly three of the major structure-stages of human development and Growing Up that we outlined: the *traditional* religious fundamentalists are at Mythic-literal, the *modern* scientists are at formal Rational, and the *postmodern* multiculturalists are at postformal Pluralistic. The values being promoted by each of these groups can be read almost directly from the structures of these three major stages. All of these stages—Mythic, Rational, and Pluralistic—are referred to as "1st-tier" stages, because all 1st-tier stages believe that their truth and values are the only truth and values that are real. All the others are infantile, misguided, loopy, or just plain wrong—hence, the Culture Wars. And if these three groups are not in actual warfare somewhere on the planet, they can certainly be found on TV and radio programs and in most editorial sections of every major newspaper—not to mention the many books they author—arguing vociferously as to why they are right and the others are totally wrong. The rational scientists—and "new atheists"—believe the "sensitive, caring" postmodern Pluralists are loopy and "woo-woo," and that the traditional religious fundamentalists are archaic, childish, and dangerous. The postmodern Pluralists think that both the Rational scientists and the traditional fundamentalists are caught up in "socially constructed" modes of knowing, which are culturally relative and have no more binding power than poetry or fashion styles; this "knowledge" gives the Pluralist an enormous sense of superiority (although in their worldview, nothing is supposed to be superior). And the traditional fundamentalists think that both the modern Rational scientists and the postmodern Pluralists are all unbelieving heathens, bound for an everlasting hell, so who cares what they think anyway?

The simple study of virtually any major developmental model will show the origin and relation of all three of these groups to be three stages in the overall growth and development of human beings, all of them appropriate for a particular period of growth but inadequate, by themselves, at higher stages. But as the three latest levels of human evolution to emerge yet (aside from the just beginning, very recent Integral), these three stages are still fighting for supremacy—they are fighting for control of education, politics, civic values, "America's values," religion and spirituality, parental practices, life values themselves, and on and on.

This is why the emergence of comprehensive Integral values is such a revolutionary development, radically new in all of history. Integral stages go one step further and ask, "What partial truths do each of those 1st-tier truths have to contribute to a fuller view of humankind?" and then work on creating integrating frameworks, such as AQAL, to pull all of these fragments together to more accurately reflect the Whole of reality and all of its various interpretations. The result is often called a "2nd-tier approach," and it is indeed a radically novel evolutionary emergent that promises to transmute every one of those areas just mentioned, plus many, many more. This is behind the massive excitement and wild optimism about a worldwide "global transformation" to a truly unified worldview; *but*, we must remember that there is not just one transformation—from the "old paradigm" to the "new paradigm"—but there are, and have been, at least six to eight major transformations in history, and only the very latest one, the emergence of Integral, which involves at this time only about 5 percent of the population, is the huge game changer that the "global transformationists" present it to be. But it has indeed begun, and it is indeed a game changer. Using more sophisticated maps, such as Integral, gives us a much better picture of the actual steps that are involved and what we can do to accelerate this revolutionary transformation.

And we will be taking the same approach with spirituality at large.

Shadow Work

Including the personal repressed unconscious or "shadow" would be an important consideration for any new Turning. Discoveries about the personal repressed shadow elements in human beings are largely a modern discovery. Meditation can loosen the repression barrier and make access to the shadow easier. But this isn't always a good thing, and in some cases makes the situation worse. Most meditation, for example, works by helping us dis-identify with or detach from the body and mind, from merely personal thoughts, feelings, and emotions (for example, meditation manuals instruct students to simply and neutrally "witness" all that arises, realizing in each case that "I am not this, I am not that"). But much psychopathology stems from a premature or overdone detachment or dissociation or dis-owning of specific thoughts or feelings. Anger, for example, can be dissociated or dis-owned, which frequently then causes feelings of sadness or depression. In meditation, if I am dis-identifying with whatever arises, I will simply further dis-identify with and dis-own this anger whenever it arises, making my depression worse. The only advice the meditation teacher has for me is "Intensify your efforts!" which really makes it worse.

Regrettably, it's still the case in many religions and spiritual systems that if you have an emotional problem or shadow issue, the prevailing belief is that you simply aren't practicing hard enough. Either you aren't practicing enough vipassana, or you don't believe fervently enough in Jesus, or you haven't found the right relation to Torah, and so on, and for that reason you have emotional problems.

Adding some simple and widely accepted psychotherapeutic techniques to meditation practice can not only help handle many shadow elements, but also make meditation itself cleaner and more efficient and effective. Thus, some simple shadow-work procedures, too, would be a welcome addition to any Fourth Turning (several examples of which I will give in later chapters). Dr. Roger Walsh, a psychiatry professor at UC Irvine, and also a Buddhist teacher, says that, during meditation retreats, when he meets personally with students, about 80 percent of the questions he gets are best answered, not with meditation responses, but with responses based on basic psychotherapeutic techniques. If he's anywhere near right, this means that the average meditation teacher (assuming that the teacher lacks any psychotherapeutic background) is giving less than adequate responses to his or her meditation students 80 percent of the time, responses that are not addressing the real issues directly. This can't be good. A simple inclusion of some basic, general psychotherapeutic ideas and practices would be a very worthy consideration for any Fourth Turning.

Concluding Remarks

In the coming chapters, I will discuss these "3 S's"—structures of consciousness, states of consciousness, and shadow elements—and show how their inclusion would almost certainly be a beneficial component of any Fourth Turning for any Great Tradition (not to mention any Life philosophy in general). I will also cover several miscellaneous topics that seem just as important and are certainly worthy of at least consideration—such as subtle energies; polarity therapy; "we-space" practices; the relation of science and spirituality; an integral semiotics, or a new language for spirituality; the future of religion; state and structure pathologies and treatments; the real nature of evolution, an integral view; your own Integral Life Practice; networks; Artificial Intelligence and computer science; integral mindfulness; among others.

Before we get to those issues in more detail, allow me a few last introductory comments. Most contemplative forms of spirituality are fully aware of states of consciousness—that's their stock in trade, their fundamental currency. The Great Traditions generally give 5 natural states, as I mentioned—gross waking, subtle dreaming, causal deep dreamless sleep, formless Witnessing, and ultimate nondual Unity or Suchness. The typical human being starts out with Wakefulness, or pure Awareness, identified with the waking (physical) state. The goal of meditation, however stated, is to move Wakefulness from its limited identification with the gross waking state, through all 5 states, resulting in Enlightenment, Awakening, Liberation, or Nondual Realization, an identity with the Union, or Nonduality, of Emptiness and All Form—what the Sufis call "the Supreme Identity," an identity with unqualifiable Spirit itself and the entire manifest world—in which the entire world arises *within you*, the deepest You, your pure and True selfless Self and Suchness. *And I will be giving several clear experiential exercises that will help you directly realize these higher states so you can decide for yourself.*

As I've suggested, all the maps of the general stages of meditation made by the great contemplative traditions the world over, East and West, tend to have variations on these same 5 major stages of meditation (which I have been calling "*state*-stages"—such as gross, subtle, or causal—to distinguish them from "*structure*-stages"—such as magic, mythic, or pluralistic). These state-stages all start out with the typical, common, ordinary mind, identified with the ego and the "monkey mind"—a mind of incessant internal chatting and yammering and subvocal talk. As a bare attention, or bare Witnessing, is brought to bear on this internal thinking and feeling, it begins to slow down, relax, and become subtler and subtler and subtler, as Awareness or Wakefulness moves into more "subtle" dimensions of Consciousness. (The "subtle" dimension is experienced each night in dreams, but also during waking with vision, creativity, emotions, higher thought, and other subtle internal activity.) As meditation deepens, the "causal" (sometimes called "the very subtle") domain comes more to the fore, and thought and personality can be completely suspended, leaving only a timeless Now awareness. When this deepens into a direct experience of empty Witnessing awareness itself, Consciousness reverts to its pure, unblemished, unconstructed, timeless, spaceless, and objectless nature, and one's identity with the separate, isolated, individual organism drops altogether, leaving an infinite identity with pure Awareness/Being/Nothingness itself. Finally, even the empty Witness itself collapses into everything witnessed, into ALL objects (gross, subtle, or causal), and we have the pure, nondual union of Emptiness and Form in the groundless Ground of all Being, the pure and simple Suchness, Thusness, or Isness of this and every moment, where you and the universe are "not-two."

Now, as we briefly discussed earlier, states like these (and hence the states of *Waking Up*) have been understood by humankind for upward of fifty thousand years, going back at least to the early shamans and their "shamanic voyaging" through various states/realms of consciousness.[17] But, as noted, *structures* of consciousness (and thus the stages of *Growing Up*) are only a recent discovery—the first definition of a psychological structure was given at the beginning of the twentieth century, much too late to be included in any major meditation system, most of which are a thousand years old or older. And you can tell that the stages that *states* go through and the stages that *structures* go through are dramatically different just by looking at the names that these two sequences have generally been given over the years. As I mentioned, Evelyn Underhill, as just one example, maintained that all (Western) mystics go through the same 4 or 5 major stages: after an initial awakening experience, there is gross purification, subtle illumination, causal dark night and infinite Abyss, and ultimate nondual Unity. Those stages don't sound even remotely like, say, Gebser's *structures*: archaic, magic, mythic, rational, pluralistic, and integral. And indeed they aren't. They are two very different dimensions or axes of development of the human mind and spirit—they have different forms, follow different paths, use different injunctions or practices for evoking them, and possess different stages. And, as I suggested, one of them (structures) leads to GROWING UP, the other (states) leads to WAKING UP. And any integral or complete spirituality (or simply a complete Life path) would want to include both.

And right there is the problem. It comes in two forms: bad and worse. The bad case consists of the schools of spirituality that are fully in touch with states and state-stages of development in various types of meditation, contemplation, and centering prayer (stages of Waking Up, such as gross, subtle, causal, and so forth) but are ignorant of the various structure-stages, or levels, that are present in up to a dozen different multiple intelligences, or lines, each of which can be practiced, grown, and developed, leading to more and more inclusiveness, creativity, care, embrace, and so on (as one moves through the 6-to-8 common levels or structure-stages of Growing Up). Most Eastern (and Western contemplative) traditions are in that camp (that is, they have states but no structures)—and that's the bad case.

The worse case consists of the schools of spirituality that are in touch with *neither* states and state-stages (of contemplation or Waking Up) *nor* structures and structure-stages (of multiple intelligences or spiritual Growing Up). Or, rather, they are identified with a genuinely low or junior structure-stage of spiritual intelligence, relying mostly on magic or mythic-level narratives and stories—for example, Moses parting the Red Sea, God raining down locusts on the Egyptians, Elijah rising straight to heaven while still alive, Christ being born from a biological virgin, the earth resting on a serpent resting on an elephant resting on a turtle, and so forth. Most Western (and noncontemplative Eastern) traditions are in this camp.

So examine each spiritual tradition itself. Is it aware of the various states and meditative state-stages that lead from the isolated self-contraction, doomed to torment and torture in its set-apartness, to a full realization of the Supreme Identity of the self with the ultimate all-pervading Divine, a union of Emptiness and all Form, Infinite and Finite, One and Many, Spirit and individual—and thus aware of WAKING UP? And is the tradition aware of the various structures and structures-stages in over a dozen multiple intelligences (including spiritual intelligence), structures that will determine the very way that its practitioners will experience and interpret meditative and spiritual states in the first place—so they are capable of spiritually GROWING UP? Or will its practitioners continue to interpret their spiritual experiences in infantile, childish, or at best adolescent ways (that is, through magic and mythic-literal structures)? How many mystics (or meditation teachers) do you know who have a wonderfully deep state realization (perhaps even traditionally Enlightened?) but still show a remarkable narrow-mindedness when it comes to other realities (covered by structures and multiple intelligences)—such as morals, emotional capacity, psycho-sexual maturity, interpersonal openness, and so on? How many do you know who perhaps might be xenophobic, patriarchal, sexist, imperial-ist, authoritarian (and rigidly hierarchical), racist, homophobic, or who even advocate war and homicide? (If you think Enlightened teach-ers are incapable of this, just read *Zen at War*.)[18] If you're like me, there are more of these types (deep states, shallow structures) than you'd care to admit.

And while we're at it, does the particular spirituality leave room for shadow work, so that in addition to WAKING UP and GROWING UP, individuals can also CLEAN UP? That is, does it acknowledge that individuals need to clean up their repressed, unconscious shadow material that shows up when they project the shadow onto others and then spend their time shadowboxing their way through life? Alas, few if any spiritual systems do. (Here's a typical example of shadow behav-ior: a recent study of antihomosexual zealots, who spent considerable time trying to outlaw or otherwise get rid of gay and lesbian activity, showed that when they were exposed to gay sexual images and gay erotica, these zealots were actually much more sexually aroused than the average straight male. In other words, these individuals themselves have gay-shadow tendencies that they have projected onto actual gays, and thus they spend their time trying to eradicate their own shadows by eradicating homosexuals. This is classic shadow projection and its resultant shadowboxing. But it can happen with any quality, charac-teristic, need, or drive—positive or negative, and at virtually any struc-ture or state—whereupon one shadow-hugs or shadowboxes one's way through life.)

Such individuals are often drawn like a magnet to religion or spiri-tuality, in hopes of getting rid of their shadow elements, and their en-tire approach to their spiritual practice is drenched in shadow-avoiding moves. Any truly inclusive spirituality would offer an alternative: re-own the shadow, withdraw the projection, and grow in the process, CLEANING UP one's act at the same time.

And what about the constant warfare between science and spiritual-ity? Despite a spate of recent books (and films like *What the Bleep Do We Know!?*) purporting to show the similarity between sciences like quantum mechanics and things like spiritual mysticism, the gap is still largely unclosed, mostly because these "unifying" approaches make several fundamental mistakes—in both physics and mysticism—in their efforts. The first is a confusion of the *means* that are used to disclose quantum truths and mystical truths. Quantum mechanics, as a physical science, works with 3rd-person approaches—objective, empirical, mathematical approaches (and a knowledge of reality by *description*); the mystic works with 1st-person, experiential, direct and immediate interior states of consciousness (and a knowledge by *acquaintance*). When you look at quantum mechanics you do not see a unified reality, but instead a very long, abstract, analytical string of very complicated Schrödinger partial differential equations—that's it, that's all you see. The claim is that, in some instances, these equations can show "entanglement"—that is, that two particles, having once been in touch, stay in touch subsequently, no matter how far they are actually separated, thus purportedly showing the interconnected oneness of the entire universe. But quantum mechanics doesn't cover ecology, sociology, history, art, morals, aesthetics, music, logic, mathematics, psychology, psychiatry, psychotherapy, cultural studies, film and movies, or dozens of other fields—and it does nothing to show that these fields are "entangled." Further, as for being the "leading edge" of modern physics, quantum mechanics is a century old now—it was first proposed in 1905 by Max Planck—and has long been complemented by things like string theory or M-theory as the leading edge in modern physics; and far from showing a "unified" world, those new theories postulate the existence of literally hundreds of different universes or "multiverses," all disconnected and with little in common. Hardly an example of "nondual unity consciousness."

Moreover, mystical truths are found by looking within, focusing Awareness, and following Awareness back to its Source, there to awaken to *a unity with the ALL*. Quantum mechanics can't show a unity with history, poetry, art, psychiatry, logic, an ecosystem, language, and so forth. Also, when people claim that quantum mechanics shows the same reality as mysticism, they then enthusiastically describe that reality, and thus immediately violate Emptiness, or the non-conceptuality of all ultimate Reality; what quantum mechanics is giving us, in other words, is not ultimate reality but a small slice of relative reality. (We already saw that Spirit or ultimate Reality cannot be described as being, not-being, both, or neither—exactly what these "unifying claims" violate.)

This is a union of bad physics with bad mysticism, and this is supposed to show us all of ultimate Reality. Where's biology, chemistry, geology, neurochemistry, structures, states, shadows, sociology, politics, medicine, literature, psychology, history, and on and on and on? In covering only two electrons—which is what quantum mechanics does at most—is it perhaps leaving a tad out? Somehow, equations describing two electrons are meant to stand in for all of God, Primordial and Consequent. Does that even make sense? And if quantum mechanics really did show us a mystical unity, then every professional physicist alive would be installed in a profound mystical state, whereas in fact almost none of them are, which contrasts with, say, the number of long-term meditators who experience mystical states. To master quantum mechanics is not to master mysticism, or to prove it, or even necessarily to be accurately acquainted with it.

I edited a book called *Quantum Questions*, which was an anthology of the best writings on spirituality of all of the original founding relativistic and quantum physicists—people such as Einstein, Heisenberg, Erwin Schrödinger, Max Planck, de Broglie, Eddington, Pauli, and Jeans, and *not one* of them believed that the new science—quantum or relativistic—proved spirituality in any fashion at all.[19] As Eddington summarized the overall view, "For my own part, I am wholly opposed to any such attempt."[20] We'll return to this point later, but for now, the only reason I'm harping on this is that there is, in fact, a proof of Spirit's existence, but it's based, as we will see, on direct immediate experience, not indirect mathematical abstractions, and as long as we look to the latter, we'll never even consider (nor therefore discover) the former—sad indeed. At best, these new sciences are arguing for systematic relative reality instead of atomistic relative reality, a view I gladly (and already) accept, but a view that still proves nothing about ultimate Reality or Emptiness or does anything to give a person a direct experience of that ultimate Reality—even sadder, relying only on that.

But this is another item that any inclusive spirituality would want to include: not a method of doing science (although meditation can be thought of, in a sense, as an interior science), but simply showing a relationship between science and spirituality that acknowledges fully the importance of both and also the important ways in which they differ. (Something like the Two Truths doctrine might be a start here, with science covering relative truths and spirituality accessing ultimate Truth.) We'll later use something called "the 4 quadrants" to show a precise relation between the various sciences and the various types of spirituality, allowing room for each and all of them. If this works, this would put an end to one of the most acrimonious and hostile (and unnecessary) debates humans continue to engage in. Using and including all 4 quadrants, as we'll see, is a way of SHOWING UP for all of the major and important dimensions of reality—relative and ultimate— that are already available to human beings.

So Growing Up, Waking Up, Cleaning Up, and Showing Up—these are some of the minimum requirements that any new Integral or Fourth Turning Spirituality would want to embrace. The rest of this volume is dedicated to make that as clear and as believable as possible.

All of the world's Great Traditions came into existence at least a thousand years before the discoveries of modern science, and so of course none of them contain ways to fit these two most important endeavors together. But one thing is certain: any spirituality that can't pass muster with science will not make it past the modern and postmodern tests for truth, and any science that doesn't include some component of testable spirituality will never find an answer to the ultimate questions of human existence (à la the Two Truths). Would not a genuine Fourth Turning take all of that into account?

Let's see.

Part Two

States and Structures
of Consciousness

3

The Fundamental States
of Consciousness

We have been talking about the three major turnings of the Wheel of Dharma that Buddhism itself recognizes. The First is Early Buddhism, the original teachings of the historical Gautama the Buddha. Generally thought to be represented today by Theravada Buddhism, it is particularly prevalent in Southeast Asia and has recently found fans in the West, particularly with its practice of "mindfulness." The Second Great Turning is represented by Nagarjuna and the Madhyamaka school of Buddhism, which presented the notion of nondual Shunyata or Emptiness, a profound elaboration of the nature of ultimate "nondual" Truth that became fundamental to virtually every subsequent school of Buddhism, Mahayana and Vajrayana. The Third Great Turning, that of Yogachara, or Vijnanavada, Buddhism, is associated with the half brothers Asanga and Vasubandhu and is sometimes referred to as the Mind-only, or Representation-only, school, which was particularly influential in the Vajrayana and Tantric traditions.

As these three unfoldings developed, there was an increasing drive to integrate or synthesize all of them, and some fairly successful attempts ensued. Buddhism has always had a strong synthesizing tendency, and there are today a growing number of Buddhist teachers and students who feel enough new truths have emerged that need to be integrated into Buddhism that we are now on the verge of yet another unfolding, a Fourth Great Turning of the Wheel. What follows is the continuation of a few thoughts on some of the more important items that might be included in this new synthesis. And let me emphasize that these suggestions apply not only to Buddhism, but to any spiritual system that wishes to become more Integral, comprehensive, complete, or inclusive—indeed, to any life practice in general. These are fundamental facts of Human Existence 101, facts that apply to each of us in our lives, our jobs, our relationships—a Growing Up (into genuine Fullness), a Waking Up (into radical Freedom), a Cleaning Up (into real Flourishing), and a Showing Up (into Full Functioning). This Integral Framework amounts to a *user's guide to the universe*—including a user's manual for a human being-in-the-world.

States and Structures

As we began to explore in the last chapter, and will continue to explore in more detail in the following four chapters, *structures* of consciousness and *states* of consciousness are two of the most important psychospiritual elements that humans possess. There is a developmental spectrum in both, reaching from the least amount of consciousness to the most amount of consciousness. Further, when the self-sense, or self-system, is growing, developing, and evolving, it will successively identify with increasingly higher structures (creating higher and higher Views of the world) and also increasingly higher states (creating higher and higher Vantage Points on the world). These 4 items are the 4 most important aspects, or 4 basic vectors, of growth and development (that is, structures and their Views, and states and their Vantage Points).

Since these 4 vectors of evolution are quite well understood by the (relatively small) community of experts who study them, but are otherwise unfamiliar in any sort of detail to most people, in this chapter, I would like to briefly outline both structures and states and discuss the general issues of states and their Vantage Points. In chapters 4 and 5, I focus on the characteristics of each of the major states, and in chapters 6 and 7, I discuss structures and their Views. In part 3 (chapters 8–13), I delineate the pathologies or dysfunctions of both structure/Views and state/Vantage Points—what can go wrong at each and every one of these developmental milestones in both Growing Up and Waking Up. I hope this will give you a sense of some of the pitfalls to keep an eye out for in your own growth, development, and evolution, as well as some of the effective treatments for these dysfunctions (in other words, things you can do right now to help with any of these things that can "go wrong"—that is, how to "fix" them!). Few, if any, single approaches anywhere include all of these dysfunctions in both states and structures, but if we combine all of them in our "composite map" or Integral View, we get a fairly complete picture of all the things that can go wrong in our overall evolution, and promising remedies we can take in each case. I hope this comes across more clearly than it sounds! But all 4 of these vectors (structures and their Views, states and their Vantage Points) are so crucially important that I want to approach them—briefly—from several different angles, to help convey, I trust, a genuine understanding of each and why they are so important in your life as a whole.

Remember, in all of humankind's history, never have *both* of these developmental sequences (that is, Growing Up structures and Waking Up states) been recognized and consciously included—leaving, indeed, a broken and fractured humanity, both East and West, at every point in history up until today. This broken, fractured state of affairs in the human condition has been reflected in every single activity, East and West, of all humans with no exceptions. Evidence of this deep fracture can be found in virtually any direction we look, in our social, political, philosophical, spiritual, educational, governing, legal, and environmental views and behaviors. This has been the case, at least up until now, the second decade of the twenty-first century, when the emergence of a genuinely "Holistic/Integral" stage of development—a "monumental leap in meaning"—is bringing both of these crucial components together in a more comprehensive, inclusive, and effective fashion.

So, to begin: *states of consciousness* have been generally known by humankind for thousands of years—probably, as we noted, for at least fifty thousand years or so (from the time of the first major shamans, particularly their explorations of "overworlds" and "underworlds" via various states, often plant entheogen assisted).[1] As 1st-person, direct, immediate experiences, states of consciousness are open to introspection, meditation, vision quest, peak experiences, and other direct experiential modes—not to mention the simple nature of this moment's experience itself, which is a state. *Structures of consciousness,*

on the other hand (one simplified version of which we have been calling "archaic," "magic," "mythic," "rational," "pluralistic," "integral," and "super-integral"), are the implicit, embedded, 3rd-person
mental patterns or forms ("hidden maps" or "grammars") through
which the mind views and interprets (and thus experiences) the world,
including states. States are something we can *look at*; structures are
things we *look through*. (Multiple intelligences are made of consciousness structures, and thus each multiple intelligence—such as cognitive,
emotional, moral, aesthetic, interpersonal, and so forth—will go through
the same general developmental levels or structure-stages of archaic,
magic, mythic, rational, pluralistic, integral, and super-integral, with
higher stages yet down the evolutionary road. We'll return to this
important concept momentarily.) Things such as present experiences
(states of happiness, joy, sorrow, anxiety, fear, dread, enthusiasm, and
so on), day-to-day feelings, spiritual/religious and peak experiences
(spiritual visions, ultimate unity consciousness, God-unity experiences,
and so forth), altered or nonordinary states (out-of-the-body experiences or "astral travel," cosmic void experience, and so on), and meditative states (savikalpa samadhi, or "meditation with form"; *nirvikalpa*
samadhi, or "formless meditation"; *sahaja*, or nondual awareness;
and so on) are made of, well, states.

There is no doubt in my mind whatsoever that if structures and
their stages were understood during the Axial period—the middle centuries of the first millennium BCE, when most of the world's Great
Religions were first created—every major world religion bar none
would give them central emphasis for understanding their major
dharma, dogma, gospel, in the same way that all of their meditative,
or contemplative, branches give states a central and crucial role. *The
world looks different at every stage*—in both states and structures—
and that is an overwhelmingly important notion for understanding
virtually any topic that humans encounter, certainly including both
science and spirituality. As we will see, there is a profoundly different
form of spirituality at every state—and at every structure—and this
realization profoundly alters how we look at religion and spirituality.
What an extraordinary discovery!

So we'll start with a quick overview of states, then states and their
Vantage Points, then structures and their Views. Neither states nor
structures are mere academic niceties. Although a bit of intellectual

understanding is required to grasp them, please bear with me here, because both states and structures, as I keep saying, are incredibly important, and both are very active in your own awareness *right now*. And please let me emphasize: each state and each structure that I will discuss will be accompanied by direct experiential exercises that will give you a direct and immediate experience of them, so you can directly see for yourself what I am talking about. At no point is this merely an intellectual talking-head game!

Further, you always experience both a major structure and a major state together—states determine *what* you see (gross objects, subtle objects, causal objects, and so forth), and structures determine *how* you see it (mythically, rationally, pluralistically, and so on). And, most importantly, as we will continue to see, structures are indeed how we GROW UP, or mature through any stream, line, or intelligence that we have; and states are how we WAKE UP, or become more and more present to the Presence of the Present, its depth, profundity, and ultimacy—leading, ultimately, to the Great Liberation and the Supreme Identity.

And allow me to emphasize one more time that if you are uncomfortable with religious terms and mythic-literal concepts, and never had a chance to experience a direct spiritual experience in Waking Up, then please take all religious terms lightly until you have a chance to do some of these exercises and experience directly the spiritual realities I am referring to. The problem with so much of Western religion, as I earlier pointed out, is that it is largely bereft of Waking Up and is developmentally arrested at very low levels of spiritual intelligence— such as magic and mythic—and so of course it can tend to appear fairly silly to most moderns; and in those forms, it usually is. So please hang in there.

States of Consciousness

The Natural States of Consciousness

The great contemplative traditions generally list 4 or 5 major, natural states of consciousness, available to all humans virtually from birth forward. These states of consciousness (or "minds" in the most general sense) are said to arise correlatively with a particular "mass-energy" substrate (or "body" in the broadest sense). These 5 major state/realms, found explicitly in Buddhism, Vedanta Hinduism, Kashmir Shaivism, and in several Western Neoplatonic schools, and implicitly in virtually every mystical school East and West) are:

1. The *waking state of consciousness* and its correlative gross/physical body (or physical mass-energy). Overall, the "objective," material, sensorimotor world of Form and the simple awareness of it. (The body or "mass-energy" aspect of this realm is known in Buddhism as the *Nirmanakaya*—the Form Body.)

2. The *dream state of consciousness* and its correlative subtle body (or subtle mass-energy). The traits of this "subtle realm," while experienced every night during sleep, can be experienced in the waking state itself, including its libido or bioenergy; its mental capacities, images, and feelings; and its higher mental insights and intuitions—the overall realm of the typical "mind" and the subtle biological energy supporting it. (The body or "mass-energy" aspect of this realm is known in Buddhism as the *Sambhogakaya*—the subtle Transformation Body.)

3. The *deep dreamless state* and its "causal" (or "very subtle") body. This is the home of the very first forms of manifestation that emerge out of Emptiness, formlessness, or nirguna Brahman (ultimate Reality beyond all forms) and the "causal" mass-energy body correlated with them—forms that the Greeks called "archetypes," which are stored in the Akashic record that is found in many traditions or the "storehouse consciousness" of the *Lankavatara Sutra*. This state, as we will see, is often combined with the next state, "turiya," or the pure empty Witnessing Awareness, at which point this combined state, *treated as one*, becomes the home of one's True Self, one's Original Face, one's deepest True Nature (which is technically confined to just the turiya state itself); and inasmuch as the True Self is radically unqualifiable, this is also the "home" of Emptiness taken as radical Formlessness or Limitlessness. (The causal body aspect of this realm is called in Buddhism the *Dharmakaya*—the Truth/Emptiness Body.)

One has to be careful when one sees terms like "causal" or "Dharmakaya," to determine whether the narrow sense of "causal" is meant (that is, the first and subtlest forms of manifestation, which is the narrow, technically correct definition), or whether it is being joined with the higher state of "Emptiness/Truth" (which results when the "narrow" causal is combined with the Empty Witnessing, or turiya, state). Unfortunately, this can end up being quite confusing, but I hope what's going on here is clear enough. (That is, is "causal" being used to mean the "highest and subtlest of all forms" OR the even higher state of "no forms at all"? Both uses are common. I will try to be careful and let context clearly help determine which is meant—highest of all forms, or totally formless.)

4. *Turiya awareness* ("turiya" literally means "the fourth," as in the fourth state after the first three already listed—gross, subtle, and causal—which is exactly how it got its name). This is the pure empty Witness or unqualifiable pure Awareness, itself without an object but ever-presently capable of being Aware of all objects (gross, subtle, or causal), along with its supporting body or mass-energy. This is pure ultimate Awareness that itself is Empty, free of thoughts, objects, and things in any realm (gross, subtle, and causal) but capable of Witnessing all of them with the purest equanimity or mirror-mind awareness. It is usually equated with Purusha (True Self) or the *Nirvana Sutra*'s Mahatman (Great Self) and is what Ramana Maharshi called the "I-I," since it is the Awareness of awareness, or the great Observing Self (the first "I") witnessing the small, finite, object self (the second "I," or "ego"); "I-I" thus equals "Great Self-ego"—or that in you right now which is aware of yourself, as we will see in great detail in a moment. Since it is free of all objects, it can integrate all of them; hence its supporting body, or mass-energy component, is sometimes called in Buddhism the *Svabhavikakaya*, the Integrative Body. And finally:

5. *Turiyatita awareness* ("beyond the fourth"). This is sometimes referred to metaphorically as "ultimate unity consciousness." Specifically, it means the union of the Empty Witness with ALL objects witnessed (gross, subtle, and causal), the union of Emptiness and all Form, the collapse of the Witnessing Self, or True Seer, into everything that is seen, the result being a pure, selfless, ultimate nondual ("not-two") state of pure Suchness, Thusness, or Isness, a union of finite and infinite, subject and object, Emptiness and Form (or Emptiness and Luminosity), or soul and God in Godhead—or Ayin ("Nothingness") and all Form in Ayn Sof (or "the One"). Thus, it is pure nondual, or "unity," consciousness, the Supreme Identity, the summum bonum of all being and existence, the highest rung in the ladder of evolution (pure transcendence) *and* the wood out of which the entire ladder is

made (immanence), thus transcending and including the entire universe. Its supporting mass-energy, or body, is known by various names, including "Vajra Body," the Indestructible or Diamond (timeless nondual) Body. This is ultimate Enlightenment or Awakening, by any standard, East or West.[2] (Although one point that we will be following carefully is that as structures of Growing Up are added to the scheme in an Integral account, the actual "wholeness" of this ultimate state becomes more and more whole, the higher the structure of Growing Up that has also been reached. Since all experiences and states are *interpreted* by structures, the more "holistic" the structure that experiences the turiyatita state, the more "holistic" that Enlightened state will be. I'll return to this point and explain it carefully as we go along.)

One last technical point: in the preceding descriptions, I referred, at each level, to both "realms" and "states." "Realms" refer to the sum total of the phenomenological entities existing in each of those particular worlds (gross, subtle, causal, and so forth), and "states" refers to the awareness, or consciousness, of any of those specific phenomena. In a sense, realms are "ontological" and states are "epistemological," with the understanding that Integral Theory does not divide those two into separate, divorced, siloed dimensions, with one being more real and the other being grounded in it (idealism privileging epistemology or mind and realism privileging ontology or body). Rather it sees these as two dimensions of an underlying Wholeness. "Realms" consist of actual bodies, actual entities, actual phenomena with their concrete mass-energy (although the energy exists along a spectrum of gross to subtle to causal, as do the states themselves). Thus, the traditions have a very sophisticated way of handling the mind/body problem—namely, every mind has its body, or every state of consciousness (or "mind") has a corresponding mass-energy (or "body") realm. It's like a radio signal. If you're listening to a radio station, and music is being played, there are actually two items here: you are hearing the actual radio program, whether it's music or a talk show or whatnot (the "information" or "mind" component of the program), but then there's also the radio signal itself carrying the program to your radio (the concrete mass-energy radiation wave, or "body" component, that is carrying or "supporting" the content). According to the traditions, each mental or conscious state is similar to that: it has a content or information or mind-component (like the actual music you are listening to), and that content is being carried, or supported, by a particular mass-energy wave (like the radio signal that carries the music), which is in a particular "body realm." (Had the traditions been aware of brain physiology, they likely would have identified at least some of these mass-energy waves with brain waves "carrying" thoughts, but with neither consciousness states nor brain states reducible to the other—what we will be calling the "Upper Left quadrant" and the "Upper Right quadrant," respectively.)[3]

Thus, for the traditions, "minds" (or "states") and "bodies" (or "realms") always go together, so that what you really have are the gross body-mind, the subtle body-mind, the causal body-mind, and the ultimate nondual body-mind. We will also see that the "bodies or realms" are what we will be calling the Upper Right quadrant, giving us a *spectrum of energy*: from gross energy to subtle energy to causal energy to witnessing to nondual energy; and the states or sheaths (and structures) are what we will be calling the Upper Left quadrant, giving us a *spectrum of consciousness*, a spectrum of nonconcrete "minds," "states, or "sheaths": from—using "states"—the waking to dreaming to deep sleep to witnessing to ultimate nondual states, or—using the "sheaths" from Vedanta and Yogachara—from the level of the 5 senses to the level of the thought-mind (manovijnana) (often thought of as a sixth sense) to the level of the existential mind (manas) to the tainted storehouse consciousness to the pure, or Alaya-jnana, or Wisdom Mind, consciousness. (Again, all this will become much clearer as we proceed.) The simple point is that the "mind/body" problem is not a real problem for Buddhism or any of the nondual traditions, because every mind has its body—two interwoven dimensions of the same whole event, with no "problem" about how they fit together (any more than we have a problem figuring out how a radio signal and its content fit together).

Meditative States of Consciousness

At birth, consciousness or Wakefulness starts out largely identified with the gross waking state—that is, basically the physical world. The goal of meditation is to eventually discover pure Emptiness, the void Godhead, Ayin, pure Nothingness, or the Plenum/Void, one's own highest and unqualifiable True Self, or Great Self, or Original Face, or

True Nature, or Unique Self—by whatever name—and thus cease to identify with the small, finite, mortal, skin-bounded ego; and then take the further step of identifying that empty Witness or True Seer with all things witnessed and seen, combining Emptiness with All Form (gross, subtle, or causal) and thus finding instead what the Sufis call our Supreme Identity, Buddhists call nondual Suchness or Thusness, and Christians call Christ/Godhead Consciousness. This is the ultimate Condition of all conditions, Nature of all natures, and nondual Spirit that is radically free from an identity with any particular finite thing or event whatsoever. Or, put from another angle, is one with absolutely *every* finite thing and event, one with the entire manifest and unmanifest realm, radically One with the All, One with the entire Ground of Being. Identified with no single thing, or Nothing, it is identified with *all* things, or Everything, the Whole. Our True or Real Self, being one with everything, has literally nothing outside of it that we could want or desire, nor anything outside of it that we could smash into. Thus there is no fear, no anxiety, no angst, no other. The entire objective universe is seen as arising *within you*, so that both objects and subjects disappear into pure, simple, nondual Suchness—the transcendence and union of subject and object, nirvana and samsara, Emptiness and Form, heaven and earth, Divine and human, right here, right now. As the Upanishads say, "Wherever there is other, there is fear,"[4] but when we are one with the All, there is no Other (that isn't a texture of our own true and Real Self and Suchness), and thus we are liberated, enlightened, freed from all torment, suffering, agony, and torture and instead Awakened to ultimate Goodness, Truth, Beauty, and Reality: Unborn and Undying, Unbound and Unlimited, fiercely Free and wildly Alive, joyously One and blissfully All, radiantly Infinite and timelessly Eternal, radically Open, Free, and Full—a state known variously as Enlightenment, Awakening, moksha (liberation), metanoia (transformation), *wu* (transparency). Such is the nature of our True Self when we are intimately one with the ultimate state of being (namely, nondual spiritual Suchness or Thusness—moving from turiya to turiyatita, from Unique Self or Absolute Subjectivity (as Zen master Shibayama calls it) to pure, radical, radiant, ever-present nondual Suchness.

Between our original starting point, where our Consciousness or Wakefulness is exclusively identified with the gross waking state and gross physical body, and our final liberation, where our Wakefulness is identified with pure Empty Suchness or nondual Unity, there are those 4 or so states of consciousness that we just described that are less than fully Awakened. Each of those states constitutes an identity that is, so to speak, deeper and higher and closer to the ultimate nondual Supreme Identity, but not quite there—although, again, each state gets a bit closer and closer. The aim of meditation is to move through *all* of these states via Awareness or Consciousness or Wakefulness—transcending and including all of them—or moving through each, first identifying with it in Wakefulness, and then transcending or dis-identifying with it as we move to the next deeper or higher state, until we have transcended or *moved beyond* all of them to the ultimate Nondual state, and yet also *included all* of them in our awakened Awareness. So we have transcended or moved beyond *all* of them—we are identified with nothing, absolutely nothing, or pure Emptiness; and we have included or identified with *all* of them—we are both nothing and everything, Emptiness and All, radical Freedom and overflowing Fullness, zero and infinity. We have "transcended and included" all, and thus have discovered our Real Suchness, one with Spirit—the Supreme Identity—which is the Suchness of the entire Kosmos as well. We have, indeed, come Home.

Every mature meditative tradition the world over has major maps of these 4 or 5 natural states of consciousness (as reflected in, and molded through, the surface structures and cultural features of the society in which they occur). And, most importantly, each of those natural *states* (which are, in their deep features, universal, and in many cases anchored directly in universal biological realities—all humans wake, dream, and sleep, for example) becomes a major *stage* in meditative development or the process of Waking Up (each state becomes a "state-stage"). (The same kind of thing happens, of course, in the process of Growing Up, where each major structure of development becomes a sequential stage—a "structure-stage"—in the process of growth and maturation of the human organism, or the overall process of Growing Up. We will focus on that process in chapters 6–7.) The fact that many of these natural states are biological givens (anchored in biology but *not* reducible to biology) is probably part of what accounts for the fact that the meditative state-stages found throughout the world's great Paths of Liberation show so much similarity. (In evolution's "return to Spirit," or Reflux, these states of consciousness—waking, dreaming, deep sleep, and so forth—co-evolved and co-developed with the biomaterial brain states, and thus both of them show similarities wherever they appear. This is not to anchor meditation in mere biology, but to anchor biology in what we'll be calling the 4 quadrants, with meditation in another of its dimensions, all co-correlated, as we'll see.)

As we'll also see, although a *state* of consciousness and its realm, such as waking, dreaming, deep sleep, or ever-present nondual, is a permanent feature of human awareness, as we begin to meditate and move through those states (with, as noted, each step in that process referred to as a state-stage, to distinguish it from a structure-stage), the self-sense exclusively and temporarily identifies with the particular state-stage, an identification that produces a particular view of the world as the self looks at the world predominantly *through* that particular state—and thus will see a gross world, a subtle world, a causal world, and so on. These specific views, created by exclusively identifying with a particular state/realm, are referred to as *Vantage Points*, to distinguish them from the similarly created *Views* that are also being generated as the self-sense exclusively identifies with a particular *structure*. So structure-stages produce Views (archaic, magic, mythic, rational, and so on), and state-stages produce Vantage Points (a gross Vantage Point, a subtle Vantage Point, a causal Vantage Point, and so forth). The general idea is the same in each: when the self-sense exclusively identifies with a particular structure or a particular state—what I call its *dual center of gravity* (since the self is always identified with *both* a structure and a state)—the self will be looking at the world predominantly and primarily *through* and *as* that particular structure and that particular state. Eventually the self arrives at turiyatita—the nonduality of samsara and nirvana, Form and Emptiness, finite and Infinite. But even though consciousness is no longer exclusively identified with any of the states, the major state/realms themselves will still remain and continue to exist—even Buddhas wake, dream, sleep, and certainly have nondual Awareness. It's just that their identity has passed through all of those states and thus is fundamentally free of them and their limited, partial, broken identities.

In Integral Theory, there's something we refer to as the self's "center of gravity," which I just briefly mentioned. As noted, the self has at least two of these—its "*structure* center of gravity" and its "*state* center of gravity." Its structure center of gravity is where, on the overall spectrum of structures and their growth, or "structure-stages" (archaic, magic, magic-mythic, mythic, rational, pluralistic, integral, and super-integral, to give the version we've mostly been using), the self is averagely most identified at any given point in its overall growth and development in any particular line of Growing Up. For the structure center of gravity, we usually focus on the self-line, since it indicates the most general identity of the overall relative or conventional self-sense. And then the self also has a *state* center of gravity, which is where, on the spectrum of major states and one's growth through them, or "state-stages" (gross, subtle, causal, empty witnessing, ultimate nondual), the self is averagely most identified at any given point in its overall state growth in Waking Up. So, in structure development, the Growing Up process, one's self-sense might be mostly at the mythic level, while in state development, the Waking Up process, one might be mostly at subtle. One's dual center of gravity, then, would be indicated as (mythic, subtle). And so on with (rational, causal), or (integral, nondual), or (magic, gross), and so forth.

It turns out that both of these centers of gravity—both structure and state—are fairly easy to recognize, once one becomes familiar with them, and there are numerous tests that individuals can take to help determine them. They are simply two growth processes on two very important axes of development and evolution—structures and states—with each stage in both becoming more and more conscious, inclusive, and caring. In fact, once you have finished reading this book—assuming, of course, that you do—you will have a fairly good understanding of each of these structure-stages and state-stages, where you are in each growth scale, and what you can do to further your own growth and development in either or both, should you decide to do so. Understanding these two growth scales will explain much of what might have seemed puzzling in your behavior, as well as that of others, too—the world at large, in fact. Now one thing that these scales are not is a way to pigeonhole people—these are not levels of human beings, but levels of consciousness open to each and every human being alive, and from which virtually anybody can function should he or she choose to do so. Seeing that these stages are open to all people simply helps us, among other things, better understand, communicate with, and care for, people. Finally, understanding the enormous positive possibilities available at higher stages in each axis, structure and state, gives us a reason, a motivation, to continue to GROW UP and to WAKE UP, thus giving a real meaning and purpose to life. And all of them are grounded in the highest state possible, ever-present ultimate Suchness or Isness—as you are, exactly as you are, right now.

The Stages of Meditative States

So I was saying that every major meditation tradition recognizes these 4 or 5 major states of consciousness, and likewise has maps of the 4 or 5 major correlative state-stages, or meditative stages, for moving through them, transcending and including them as they go. Significant research has demonstrated that although the *surface features* of each of these traditions and their state-stages differ considerably from culture to culture, their *deep features* are in many ways significantly similar. In fact, virtually all of them follow variations on the 4 or 5 major natural states of consciousness given cross-culturally and universally to all human beings—gross (waking), subtle (dreaming), causal (dreamless sleep), witnessing (pure awareness), and suchness (nondual union). (I'll give specific examples of each of these in a moment.) As I mentioned, in the book *Integral Psychology*, I give charts of over one hundred systems worldwide of both structures of development and states of development, and about one-third of those charts include various systems of states and state-stages of meditative development— and, indeed, what is so astonishing is that virtually all of them are recognizably similar, dealing with the same fundamental states and state-stages of contemplative development. This is a testament to the essentially universal nature of this state axis of development and its major state-stages, just as the other two-thirds of the charts, dealing mostly with structures and structure-stages, and also showing a stunning similarity, are a testament to the essentially universal nature of the structure axis of development and its major structure-stages; all-in-all, this is overwhelming evidence for all 4 major vectors of development that we are discussing—states and Vantage Points, and structures and Views.

Instead of giving a huge number of examples of the similarities in deep features of the stages of meditation in the world's meditative traditions, I'll just give three or four taken randomly from around the world.

First, let's look at an overview of what's involved in general state development. No matter what *structure* center of gravity a person has when he or she starts meditation (a structure center of gravity that can be anywhere from magic to super-integral), the individual almost always will start with a *state* center of gravity at the gross waking state. This is because everybody is born at square one in both states and structures, and although, in the natural course of GROWING UP, a person will have moved several structure-stages beyond archaic before he or she begins to meditate, few people naturally move to higher states of consciousness without meditating, and so most, not all, people will start meditating at the gross state. (The particular structure center of gravity is indeed important, because it will largely determine how the various meditative state-stages are themselves interpreted and experienced. But we'll come back to that. Right now we're simply tracking states and state-stages in their most general terms.)

In terms of states, at the gross waking realm, the individual is identified with the physical body and the gross-reflecting mind—the gross, chaotic, "monkey mind"—the stream of thoughts, feelings, emotions, and sensations centered on the "wild" egoic state and reflecting the material realm and its desires. (If you want to know what "monkey mind" or "wild egoic state" means, just close your eyes and follow your internal dialogue for a few minutes, and note how chaotic it really is.) In mindfulness forms of meditation (and Western forms such as centering prayer), the person is told to simply witness this stream of events, without judgment, condemnation, or identification. After several months of this, the monkey mind will begin to calm down, and one's awareness will open to subtler dimensions of mind and being— perhaps subtle states of loving-kindness, states of luminosity and almost infinite illumination, stretches of profoundly peaceful stillness and mental quiet, or experiences of expanding beyond the ego into deeper and deeper states of I AMness. (In the gross stage, I generally refer to the self as the *ego*; at the "subtle" stage, I often refer to the self-sense as the *soul*; in causal/witnessing, I refer to the True Self or Real Self; and at nondual, I refer to pure "unity" or nondual Suchness, Thusness, or Isness.[5] A note to Buddhists on the use of the word *soul*:

the soul in the subtle realm, like the ego in the gross realm, or the True Self in the causal, is not an ultimate reality; it is only a conventional, relative reality. But as a conventional entity, it has a *relative* realness, as Nagarjuna explained.)

As meditative awareness deepens into the causal/Witness itself, stretches of pure awareness free of thought altogether can increase; states of transpersonal identity or True Self or infinite I AMness can increasingly occur; universal love, bliss, happiness, and joy can arise; identity with the finite body-mind can drop altogether, to be replaced with anything from Christ Consciousness to Buddha-mind to Ayin (a Kabbalah term for "Emptiness"). And if awareness deepens even further, from causal Witnessing to ultimate Unity or Nonduality, the sense of subject–object duality—the sense of a Looker witnessing phenomena—drops out entirely, and instead of looking at a mountain, you *are* the mountain; instead of feeling the earth, you *are* the earth; instead of being aware of clouds floating by in the sky, the clouds float by in *you*, in your own Awareness. As a Zen master put it upon his awakening, "When I heard the sound of the bell ringing, there was no bell and no I, just the ringing." When that state becomes more or less permanent, one's state center of gravity has gone from gross to subtle to causal/witnessing to nondual Suchness—and you *are* the Supreme Identity—one with Spirit, and one with the entire manifest world (whatever it is that the world consists of for you, which, as we will see, changes and expands from structure to structure to structure).

Evelyn Underhill, in her classic book *Mysticism*, points out that virtually all Western mystics progress through the same general 4 or 5 major state-stages on their way to permanent realization—and these state-stages are, of course, variations on the standard gross, subtle, formless causal, and nondual unity. But let me first point out that state development, unlike structure development, is much looser and less rigid. Structures are, well, more structured—they emerge in an order that cannot be changed by social conditioning. Also, you can't skip structure-stages, and you can't peak experience structures higher than a stage or so away (unlike states). Somebody at the mythic stage, for example, can't peak experience a pluralistic thought. But somebody at a gross state can peak experience a causal or even a nondual state. For example, mindfulness meditation has you start out by identifying (or at least trying to identify) with Witnessing awareness itself (the 4th state).

With that in mind, Underhill's stages are as follows:

1. Purification (gross). One works with purifying and releasing identity with the physical body and its desire-laden thoughts.
2. Illumination (subtle). One is introduced to subtler dimensions, luminosities, and higher emotions or feeling-awareness of the soul.
3. Dark night (causal). One discovers a formless cloud of un-knowing, a liberation from finite bondage, a taste of real "heaven." One often suffers terribly as this vast Freedom is lost because realization is not yet permanent—the "dark night" is not all the agonies you suffer because you haven't yet found God but all the horrid pain and suffering you experience from having once found God, then losing that awareness of God's presence.
4. Nondual Unity consciousness. Soul and God disappear into ul-timate Godhead.

The whole process is often initiated with a peak experience of awakening, or metanoia, a glimpse that shows one the paradise of ul-timate Reality and sets the soul on the path of state-stages and Waking Up.

In *Transformations of Consciousness*, Jack Engler, Daniel P. Brown, and I included a chapter by Harvard theologian John Chirban, who showed that the early church desert saints went through around 5 state-stages, all variations on Underhill's 4 or 5 basic stages (again, in our terms: gross, subtle, causal/witnessing, and nondual).[6]

Daniel P. Brown, one of the coauthors of *Transformations of Consciousness*, also of Harvard, has spent the last thirty years of his life studying the meditation systems of the world, focusing on one of the most sophisticated and complete systems ever devised, the Maha-mudra system of Tibetan Buddhism. Working originally with fourteen root Mahamudra texts, all in their original language, he showed that they each went through the same essential 5 or 6 stages of develop-ment (stages he was the first to call Vantage Points).

We'll return to Brown in just a moment and outline his important findings in some detail. But first I want to repeat the notion that a View is to a basic structure as a Vantage Point is to a state/realm. I want each of these to be as crystal clear as possible, because taken together, these give the 4 main vectors of overall human development, and all 4 are absolutely crucial: (1) structures and their (2) Views (or structure-stages), and (3) states and their (4) Vantage Points (or state-stages). Both basic structures (in Growing Up) and state/realms (in Waking Up) *remain in existence* in development once they have emerged, but Views and Vantage Points are transcended and replaced as development continues. Hang in here with me, and I think that very quickly you'll see both what is involved and why it is so important—especially for any human development and evolution (including, of course, any Fourth Turning or Integral Spirituality). We're going to look into this important notion for a moment, and then continue with our claim that the great Paths of Liberation—the major meditative and contemplative systems worldwide—all present essentially similar maps (the 4 or 5 major state-stages) of the overall axis of meditative spiritual development.

Transcend and Include

The general point is simple. Let's start with structures, and then pick up states. For structures, let's take as examples of the enduring basic structures, the major chakras, of which there are traditionally said to be seven fundamental ones:[7]

1. The root chakra, at the base of the spine, governing the "sheath made of food"—that is, the physical/material body (the "Archaic" or sensorimotor structure-stage).
2. The emotional-sexual chakra, located in the general genital region, and governing basic emotional-sexual energy and fantasy thinking (the "Magic" or "impulsive" structure-stage).
3. The hara chakra, or the "gut chakra," located in the gut region below the navel, and governing power ("He's got guts!"), due to the intentionality introduced by the emergence of concepts at this stage (the "Magic-Mythic" or "power" structure-stage).
4. The heart chakra, located at the heart region, governing belongingness, compassion, and beginning love, at first in very concrete, conformist, mythic-literal forms (the "Mythic-literal" or "mythic-membership" structure-stage).

5. The throat chakra, located at the vocal box, and governing self-expression in both self-esteem (the "Rational" or "achievement" structure-stage) and beginning self-actualization (the "Pluralistic" or "postmodern" structure-stage).

6. The "third eye," located slightly behind and between the eyes, governing high integrative mental power verging on paranormal capacities (the "Holistic" and "Integral" structure-stages, or 2nd tier).

7. The crown chakra, located at and beyond the crown of the head, and representing self-transcendence and the Real Self (3rd tier or super-integral structure-stages).

Now, the chakras are fairly good, if indeed somewhat crude, correlates of basic structures. I say "crude" in that, like "sheaths" or "koshas," they are structures of consciousness, but because they are disclosed by 1st-person introspection, not 3rd-person science, they have none of the granularity that Western models of basic structures possess. (The Western models, of course, totally lack states, and thus catastrophically lack any notion of Enlightenment or Awakening. But, as we've often pointed out, the contemplative traditions were themselves weak, if not totally lacking, in actual structures.) For example, modern structuralism discovered that the sheath called the *manomayakosha* ("sheath" meaning roughly "structure," in this case, "the mind structure"), which was taken as one basic sheath by the traditions such as Vedanta, contained at least five major structures—upper magic, magic-mythic, mythic, rational, and pluralistic. And modern structuralism found six substages of sensorimotor intelligence in what was taken as one chakra, chakra 1. Likewise, modern structuralism found that the throat chakra, which had been taken to be a single structure, contained at least two genuinely different structures, rational self-achievement and pluralistic self-sensitivity—two dramatically quite different structures. But until we discuss structures per se, the chakras will work—they do indeed exist, and they are fairly good examples of the energy correlates of the basic structures.

Development via the basic structures/chakras proceeds generally as follows in the developmental process of Growing Up. The self-sense is born consciously identified with chakra 1, the food/material chakra, the alimentary chakra (oral and anal). As chakra 2 begins to develop—the emotional-sexual chakra—the self-sense will eventually *dis-identify* with chakra 1 and switch its central, proximate, main identity to chakra 2, then identify with chakra 2, and integrate chakra 1 into its overall self-system. After the self-sense has been centrally identified for two or three years with chakra 2, the next higher chakra—chakra 3, the conceptual mind and its power drives—begins to emerge, and the proximate or central self will eventually dis-identify with chakra 2, "move up" and identify with chakra 3, and then integrate chakra 2 in its overall self-system.

Let's pause here and note a few crucial items. First, the preceding describes healthy development. In unhealthy development, when the self is centrally identified with, say, chakra 2, and some aspect of that chakra is deemed dangerous, bad, or just "wrong" for any number of reasons, then aspects of that level can be dissociated, repressed, or disowned. The impulses that are repressed at a particular chakra-structure—in this case, emotional-sexual impulses—do not thereby simply disappear, but are pushed into the personal unconscious, where they exist in dissociated or "shadow" forms. Most commonly, they will then be projected onto others, finding them, for example, terribly oversexed, while I am pure, innocent, and clean of virtually any of that nasty sex stuff. A good example of shadow projection can be seen in the recent research that I mentioned earlier showing that males who are extreme zealots in outlawing or otherwise trying to get rid of homosexuals, when exposed to homosexual images and gay erotica, are more sexually aroused than the average straight male. In other words, these zealots themselves had a fair amount of homosexual impulses, but they had dis-owned and banished them to their unconscious, from whence they projected their own shadow impulses onto other men and then tried to get rid of their shadows by getting rid of homosexuals. This is utterly typical shadow dissociation, dis-owning, and projecting—with its resulting "shadowboxing" behavior.

This type of pathology or "dys-ease" can occur on virtually any structure-level (as well as any state/realm) of consciousness, and two types of general problems typically occur when that happens. If the central self-sense does not fully dis-identify with a particular level (such as chakra 2, or the magic structure) in order to make room for the next higher level, then the person develops a *fixation* to that level (a shadow grasping), and hence creates a subpersonality that has an *addiction* to that level's needs, drives, and wants (in this example, sexuality); the person in this case might become a sexual predator. If, on the other hand, differentiation goes too far and the central self-sense doesn't appropriately dis-identify with a particular level but instead dissociates from it, it will *dis-own* facets of that level, develop a shadow *alienation*, and hence often create a subpersonality that this time is avoided, unwanted, and hence causes an *allergy* to that level's needs, drives, and desires. Thus, a person, in whom such a pathology occurs at chakra 1 (that is, alimentary, archaic, food) can develop either an addiction to food (for example, overeating) or an allergy to food (for example, developing bulimia, anorexia). At chakra 2 (that is, magic, emotional-sexual, fantasy), the person can develop an addiction to sex (for example, becoming a sexual predator, developing a sexual addiction) or an allergy to sex (for example, becoming puritanical, or sexually repressed). At chakra 3 (that is, magic-mythic, concepts, power), the person can develop an addiction to power (for example, becoming excessively egocentric, narcissistic, craving power over others) or an allergy to power (for example, developing a weak self-sense, becoming dis-empowered). At chakra 4 (that is, mythic, love-belongingness) a person can develop an addiction to love (for example, becoming a hopeless romantic, surrendering all power to relationships) or an allergy to love (for example, becoming uncaring of others, self-enclosed, unkind).

Food, sex, power, love . . . and so it can go. In later chapters, we'll follow these types of dysfunctions "all the way up" into the higher structures themselves; right now we're actually focusing on state development, but by way of a quick introduction, are using structures, since development there is so obvious and easy to see. All levels (structures and states) can develop fixations/addictions or dissociations/allergies, virtually all the way up. Pathology formation does not, contra Freud, stop in childhood but can continue throughout life, all the way up the spectrum of structures and states, simply because growth and development in both axes continue all the way up, and wherever growth occurs (the process of differentiation, dis-identification, higher identification, and integration), misgrowth or malformed development can also occur (poor dis-identification = fixation/addiction; poor integration = dis-owning/allergy). This is a major reason that any truly comprehensive, Integral, or Fourth Turning Spirituality should want to include shadow work in its basic framework.

The second important item to notice about the developmental process (in addition to unhealthy development and "what can go wrong") is what happens in healthy development when "it goes right." That is, in healthy development that involves "transcend and include," what exactly is transcended and let go of, and what is kept and included? Ever since Hegel pointed out that "to supersede is at once to negate and to preserve" (that is, "transformation or development is at once to transcend and include"), researchers have wondered just exactly what is negated and transcended, and what is included and preserved.[8] The answer now appears quite clear: the basic structures (for example, chakras) are preserved (included and integrated); the limited Views from those structures are negated (transcended and replaced). And likewise with states: the major states are preserved (included and integrated); the views from (or the Vantage Points of) those states are negated (transcended and replaced). This occurs with each and every major stage of growth in both structures and states—basic structures are included, their limited Views are let go of; natural states are included, their limited Vantage Points are let go of.

Let's return to the chakra/structures and continue the developmental story, showing exactly what this means. We saw that when the self starts out its developmental and evolutionary growth, it is centrally identified with archaic chakra 1 (oral and anal). This means that its *exclusive* identity is with chakra 1, and thus it sees the world almost entirely from chakra 1 alone. To Freudians, these are the oral stage and the anal stage, where the libidinal self is identified first with the oral region of the body (the infant gets most of its pleasure from eating and putting things into its mouth), and then with the anal region (where it first learns to control the body's otherwise spontaneous activities; so-called "toilet training").

Now, if everything goes well at these stages, the central self will dis-identify with the oral region, and then with the anal region, and then—with the emergence of chakra 2 (*pranamayakosha* or emotional-sexual energy)—the central self will finally let go of its identity with the food stage (the alimentary canal, oral and anal, chakra 1) and start to switch its central identity to the genital region, to chakra 2, the emotional-magic structure. This structure is called "magic" because the cognitive processes at this stage are indeed "magical": the self believes that mommy can turn the yucky spinach into candy if she wanted; or, to think something is to magically make it happen—for example, if I want my father dead and he actually dies, I caused it. Thought itself is ruled by magical displacement and condensation, what Freud called "the primary process," because it is one of the first or primary forms of thinking. So the self will switch its exclusive, or central, identity from chakra 1 to chakra 2, and now, exclusively identified with chakra 2, it will look at the world through the eyes of chakra 2—that is, its View will be the View that comes from the second or magical chakra. It will think, for example, that by hiding its head under the pillow, so that it can't see anybody, nobody will be able to see it either, much to the delight of the adults who are sitting around staring directly at the child with its rear end sticking in the air. So the child is no longer exclusively identified with chakra 1, nor does the child see the world from chakra 1. So although it no longer has the chakra-1 View (an oral View or an anal View), *it still does have chakra 1 itself*—it still eats and defecates. So the basic structure is *preserved* and *included*, but its View is *negated* and *transcended*, to make room for the View from the next higher chakra, chakra 2. And, in fact, if the self still has some of the View from the earlier stage, the chakra-1 stage, therapists will say the child has a fixation—in this case, an oral fixation or an anal fixation. ("Anal fixation" is one of the few psychoanalytic terms that almost everybody understands. We say, "That person is really anal," and we all know that it means "really uptight," "tense," "controlling." According to analysts, something went wrong during the anal stage, and the child became fixated on overcontrolling its body, and hence developed an "anal character.")

You get the point. In development, with each major transformation upward (or each stage of growth), the self dis-identifies with its central or exclusive identity with the present structure (or state), lets go of that structure's limited View of the world, and identifies instead with the next higher structure, and hence now *sees the world through the eyes* of that structure's View. The earlier structure remains and is included and preserved, but the View from that level is let go of in order to see the world from the next higher View of the next higher structure-stage.

It's very much like climbing a real ladder—as you move from rung 1 to rung 2 to rung 3 to rung 4, all of the rungs themselves are retained (indeed, the ladder would collapse if they weren't). Yet you can only see the world from the highest rung you are presently standing on—say, the View from rung 4. Each previous View was let go of as you stepped off one rung and onto the next higher one. At whatever the highest rung you're at—rung 4 in this example—you have all lower rungs present, but only the View from the rung you are currently standing on. And if you have any parts of the Views from lower rungs, it means that something went wrong—some part of you got stuck on a lower rung. Maybe you lost an arm or a leg on a lower rung (to stretch the metaphor)—you have shadow material still stuck to a View from a lower stage, and that shadow material still has all of the characteristics, traits, and desires of the lower and earlier age/stage, with all its immaturity, childishness, and impulsive desires.

Now, although you are seeing the world through the View at rung 4, you still have all the other rungs under you. Just as, at chakra 4, you still have all the lower chakras (1 through 3) available to you, likewise you have all the lower basic structures still present and still available to you. But you are no longer *exclusively identified* with any of those lower structure-rungs, and therefore you won't see the world from the Views of those lower rungs. You're no longer actually standing on them, so you can't see anything from them alone. You can definitely put your attention on those lower rungs, perhaps pay more attention to the energy as it moves up and through those rungs, but you can't see the world *exclusively* or *only* from those lower rungs, such as chakra-rung 2, without actually climbing down the ladder from chakra-rung 4 to chakra-rung 2, which would really be a massive regression. In real life, to move your central identity from chakra 4 (Mythic, concrete operational) to chakra 2 (Magic, early preoperational), you would have to lose all access to language, all access to conventional thought and emotions, all access to concepts and concrete thinking, and end up, silent and mute, at chakra 2, wallowing in magical thinking and primitive emotions. In real life, this happens only with severe brain damage, advanced Alzheimer's, and so forth.

So, in real growth and development, we retain the earlier structure-rungs (and state/realms) and we have access to those structure-rungs, but we no longer have an *exclusive identity* with those lower rungs and thus no longer can see the world only from a lower rung—we have the rung, but we no longer have its View. And when we do contact a lower rung, which is certainly possible at almost any time, we will do so from and through the present View or perspective that we have. If we are at structure-rung 4, for example, and we contact structure-rung 2, or our sexual energy, we will do so through the View of structure-rung 4. We may contact our sexual energy, perhaps even do therapeutic work on it, but we will do so from the View of rung 4. We will still possess language, conceptual thinking, and higher emotions, and thus we will not be seeing the world *just* from structure-rung 2—we no longer have the View that was created when we were ONLY identified with structure-rung 2. That, like all junior Views, will have long ago been negated, let go of, and transcended, as higher growth and development continued.

So we can contact an earlier and lower rung from a higher one, but without some sort of significant regression, we will not be contacting the lower View from that rung. If any lower Views remain centrally part of the self, then we have a pathology, a dysfunction (either an addiction or an allergy to parts of that View). We are supposed to retain the oral food drive but not have an oral fixation.

Subjects Becoming Objects

We come now to perhaps the single most important point about development. As Robert Kegan, of the Harvard Graduate School of Education, put it, "I know of no better way to summarize development than that the subject of one stage becomes the object of the subject of the next stage."[9] That might sound a little abstruse at first, but it's actually a very simple and straightforward—and incredibly important—notion.

We can see this by looking at what we have already covered about development. The relative, finite, conventional self, or self-sense, started out its developmental career by identifying almost entirely with chakra-rung 1, the archaic sensorimotor (or alimentary food) level. It identified its very core being, its self or subjectivity, with that stage. It couldn't see that stage objectively, because it was then identified with it—it was *looking through* that stage; it couldn't look *at it*. That stage was a *subject* of awareness, not an *object* of awareness. But as chakra-rung 2 begins to emerge (the magical emotional-sexual stage), then the self-sense dis-identifies with chakra-rung 1 and switches its central identity to that second stage. That is, it ceases identifying its self, or subjectivity, with chakra-rung 1 and switches its subjectivity to chakra-rung 2. This means that chakra-rung 1 is no longer a subject, it's an object. It's no longer the seer; it's something that can be seen. The new subject is now chakra-rung 2, and the self is identified with that. Now it can't see that stage or level: it's the self's new subject, not an object; something it looks through, not at. It doesn't have this stage, this stage has it. As chakra-rung 3 begins to emerge, the magic-mythic power stage, the self lets go of its exclusive identity with the previous chakra-rung 2, dis-identifies with that level, and switches its identity, its subjectivity, to this third level. Now it can see the previous level as an object. That level is no longer a subject of awareness but an object of awareness, but now it can't see the present level, precisely because that is now its subject, its self—something it looks through, not at.

So in each case, the subject of one stage becomes the object of the new subject at the next higher stage, and this continues until all subjects have been made objects, until all subjects have been transcended and let go of, and there is only pure Subjectivity that can never become an object, a pure or radical Awareness, or True Seer. (This is what Zen master Shibayama called "Absolute Subjectivity"—the ultimate Subject, or True Self, that is the Seer of everything but is not itself seen as an object. It is instead pure Emptiness.) If, at any stage or level, some aspect of that level remains identified with—that is, if some aspect of that level remains a hidden subject that can't be seen as an object— then exactly that is shadow material, hidden, split-off, and dis-owned material that forms a hidden subpersonality, a hidden "sub-subject" or "sub-self," which is indeed often projected onto others, so that they appear to own this self-material, trait, or desire, and you appear free of it. But, of course, you're not free of it; you are secretly identified with it but deny that fact, and thus dis-own this material as shadow. If this happens at, say, archaic stage 1, the material/food level, you will have not just the basic rung itself (the alimentary need to eat), the *oral drive*, but instead you will have an *oral fixation*—a hidden self-identity, a subject of awareness that refuses to become an object of awareness, and thus is split off as a hidden subject, a subpersonality that remains identified with the previous stage, where it sends up neurotic symptoms and painful dysfunctions, indications that part of your awareness is still identified with a lower, infantile, or childish need, drive, desire, or quality. The subject of one stage has not adequately and fully become the object of the subject of the next, but rather remains stuck as a hidden subject that is dissociated from the main self, or main center of subjectivity, and hides out as a denied shadow component.

Put this all a different way, and perhaps the importance of this fact will become clear: the very key to your growth, development, and evolution is to make your present subject an object—that is, it is to look *at* your present subject instead of using it as something through which to view the world (and thus remain identified with). As long as you are identified with your present self, your present subject, you can't let go of it and make room for the next higher subject, or relative self, and thus you derail your chances of reaching your Absolute Subjectivity, or Real Self and True Nature, let alone your Supreme Identity (as you remain identified instead with a small, finite, relative subject or self).

As we'll increasingly see, one of the things that makes practices like mindfulness meditation so powerful is the capacity to introspect, to look within and see whatever subjects are present, and in doing so, make them into objects of awareness, objects of mindfulness, thus accelerating the person's own growth and development in the process. The advantage of combining both Growing Up and Waking Up is that, precisely because the actual nature of these subjective selves—with their "hidden maps" and structures that can't be seen by merely introspecting or looking within—is that you can use Western models of Growing Up (or simply use the Integral Framework) to precisely spot the nature of these hidden maps and hidden structures, and having done so, *then* you can use mindfulness meditation to focus on these subjects, making them object—or transcending them, letting go of them, and moving beyond them to the next higher stage of developmental unfolding. This is what we call "integral mindfulness," because it uses the Integral Framework (which includes developmental studies) to spot the level of hidden structures and hidden maps that you are presently identified with (without knowing it), and then uses standard mindfulness (which itself cannot spot these hidden maps but can indeed focus on them directly once they have been pointed out) to make those hidden subjects of awareness into fully conscious objects of awareness, objects of mindfulness practice, thus transcending them, clearing them, and hence making room in awareness for the next higher level of development to emerge—accelerating dramatically your own evolutionary growth. (We will be returning to this point throughout this presentation, with specific examples and instructions on how to proceed with this integral mindfulness, thus rapidly accelerating your own evolution.)[10]

The same general points are true of states and their Vantage Points. As the central self-sense moves from state to state, the self will exclusively identify its central identity with that particular state, creating a state-stage, or a particular Vantage Point, where it will view the world primarily through the state-stage, or Vantage Point, that is created when the self looks at the world ONLY through that state. All lower states remain available, but all lower Vantage Points are let go of.

So let's now look more carefully at states of consciousness and the Vantage Points that are created as the self moves from one state to the next (with each state-stage possessing, of course, it's specific Vantage Point on the world).

Next, I will give a simple overview of state and Vantage Point development (from the point of view of 2nd-tier or integral thinking). Then I'll give some summaries of the overall characteristics of the various states, characteristics that different structures will interpret differently, and thus each structure will experience each state somewhat differently. This is why adding structures and their developmental stages to an overall view of meditation is so important for any truly comprehensive spirituality. From an integral perspective, each of the following states (and state-stages) is *seen and experienced differently by Magic, by Mythic, by Rational, by Pluralistic, by Integral, and by Super-Integral* structures. So keep that in mind as we proceed.

States and Vantage Points

We've already mentioned several systems that present the same basic 4 or 5 major states and their developmental state-stages (including John Chirban's summary of the early Christian desert saints, Evelyn Underhill's representation of the Western mystics in general, the systems charted in the book *Integral Psychology*, which represent over one hundred developmental systems, East and West, and Daniel P. Brown's representation of Tibetan Buddhism). To give another quick example of these major meditative stages by yet another spiritual scholar-practitioner, let me offer these successive state-stages as outlined by the well-known Tibetan Buddhist Mahamudra teacher Geshe Kelsang Gyatso (Mahamudra, along with Dzogchen, is generally regarded as the highest of the Buddha's teachings), who gives the following 6 stages of basic Mahamudra meditation:

1. Identifying our own gross mind
2. Realizing our gross mind directly
3. Identifying our subtle mind
4. Realizing our subtle mind directly
5. Identifying our causal/nondual mind
6. Realizing our causal/nondual mind directly[11]

The Tibetans actually recognize all 5 major states and bodies. This teacher uses the simple "Trikaya" scheme, with the three higher states all collapsed into one (which, as I explained when introducing these 5 states, is often done). The point is that all 4 or 5 major state/realms are fully recognized by this tradition, and it sees them generally unfolding, during meditation, in that sequential fashion.

Let's turn now to the more detailed and sophisticated work of Daniel P. Brown, and the state-stages he found in *all* of the Great Traditions that he studied in detail. (I will focus here on Mahamudra, due to its comprehensiveness; Brown has also examined Theravada, Patanjali's *Yoga Sutras*, and several Chinese and Christian sources, among others.) To more clearly represent Brown's most recent work as it relates to Integral Metatheory, I draw from my good friend Dustin DiPerna's *Streams of Wisdom*.[12] DiPerna and Brown worked closely together to ensure that the outlines of their work are up to date and hold integrity with the lineage.

Viewing Brown's work using an Integral lens, it is clear that Brown starts with the gross waking state, where the average person is exclusively identified with the gross physical body and gross thoughts and feelings. After various preliminaries and meditation practice gets under way, the first major shift is from the gross state-stage and its Vantage Point to the subtle state-stage and its Vantage Point. Here, one is no longer exclusively identified with the physical body and thoughts, or the gross realm in general (although, like basic rungs, this major state/realm remains in existence), but the central self is now identified with the subtle realm and its Vantage Point, which is no longer the gross ego but what Brown refers to as personal identity (a "subtle personality" that the Christian contemplatives call the "soul"). Brown calls this stage "Awareness," since it is the first stage free of gross rambling thoughts and emotions, and is more in touch with pure Awareness.

At the next state-stage after the subtle—namely, the causal state-stage—the subtle personality, soul, or Vantage Point is dismantled (although the subtle realm itself stays in existence), and what is found at this stage are the very subtlest (or "causal") forms of manifestation itself—particularly space and time. (Recall, these are what the Greeks called "archetypes," which means the "basic forms on which all other forms are based." The archetypes included things like fundamental geometric forms, space, and time—Whitehead includes colors. But the point is basically the same: "What do you have to have before you can have anything else?" Space and time would clearly fall into this category.) Brown calls this causal state-stage "Awareness-itself."

As development continues from the causal into the next state-stage, that of pure Witnessing awareness, one ceases to identify exclusively with the causal and its Vantage Point, and instead transcends causal space and time to find a pure timeless Now—and an Awareness that focuses on the pure Present. Brown calls this state-stage "Boundless Changeless Awareness." It's also at this point that three sublevels of nonduality begin to emerge: recognizing the nonduality of Emptiness and a particular object (1) after the object arises, (2) while it arises, and (3) before it arises—only the last one of which is Awakened Nondual Awareness (or Suchness), which sheds the subject–object duality that subtly remained with the Witness (a subject–object duality that the Witness Vantage Point, which Brown calls "individuality," possesses, because it always "stands back" from everything it witnesses and sees it as an object that arises "in front"—whether it be a causal object, a subtle object, or a gross object). This "individuality" is why the pure Witness is often referred to as the True Self or Real Self or Unique Self, which finally must itself be transcended for ultimate Nondual Unity, or pure Suchness, to be Recognized. When this happens, the world is seen as a seamless (not featureless) Wholeness, or nondual Reality, where a person's Awareness is one with all gross, subtle, and causal phenomena, but exclusively identified with none of them. Those realms continue to exist and arise (they are preserved and included), but there is *not* an exclusive identity or attachment to any of them (those limited views or Vantage Points are negated and transcended). So a person at this Awakened Nondual Awareness stage could, for example, explore the subtle realm, since it still exists and still arises (and the person will still go through the dream state each night, whether he or she is lucidly dreaming or not), and could continue to develop techniques and skills addressing the subtle realm—but he or she will see that realm from a nondual Awakened perspective. As with lower structure-rungs, one will not go back and experience the world from ONLY a lower state-stage, losing all access to the higher-stage perspective. Those lower viewpoints have long ago been let go of and transcended, while their realm—or their rung—remains in existence and continues to arise. It is the job of awareness at the Awakened Suchness "no-level" to integrate all of the previous junior state/realms into an integral Thusness or Isness. This task can still be mismanaged, producing various dysfunctions, as we will see in part 3.

Brown's research is extremely important, because it shows how detailed and widespread these 4 or 5 major states (and their state-stages) are. The Tibetan system is generally regarded as the most complex and most sophisticated meditative system found the world over, and the fact that its very highest schools are in fundamental agreement with these 4 or 5 major state/realms is simply further evidence that these states (and their Vantage Points) should most definitely be included, in one form or another, in any truly comprehensive, Integral, or Fourth Turning Spirituality.

Finally, to give a concluding, postmodern example of these state/realms, we have the American adept Adi Da, who maintains, "To Realize Most Perfect Divine Enlightenment, the ego must be transcended through three distinct phases—first at the [gross] physical level (the level of 'money, food, and sex'), then at the subtle level (the level of internal visions, auditions, and all kinds of mystical experience), and finally at the causal level (the root-level of conscious existence, wherein the sense of 'I' and 'other, or the subject–object dichotomy, seems to arise in Consciousness)."[13] The fourth phase for Adi Da is the Realization of "Always-Already Truth," the ever-present nondual Goal,

Ground, and Condition of all existence, high or low, sacred or profane, manifest or unmanifest. Thus, gross, subtle, causal, (implicit root-witnessing), and nondual—all 5.

As I noted earlier, these universal similarities are likely rooted in, or at least correlated with, the natural states of consciousness that the brains of all human biological organisms are born with—gross waking, subtle dreaming, causal deep formless sleep, plus ever-present nondual awareness, source and support of them all. Postmodernists who try to explain away all universals have a hard time explaining away these universal brain states. Trying to maintain that Buddhists have culturally constructed major brain states that are massively different from Jewish brain states that are different from Hindu brain states just doesn't make sense. Our biological brains and their states are similar in deep features wherever humans appear, and hence contemplative and meditative stages—which move through those states as stages—also take on a universal character (again, in their deep features, whereas their surface features differ from culture to culture and often individual to individual).[14]

As I also noted, and it is worth repeating, what is rarely—in fact, almost never—understood is the importance of both Views and Vantage Points in determining human experience, what is seen, how it is seen and interpreted, and therefore how it is actually experienced. These Views and Vantage Points are every bit as real as cultural and social factors, and they can give rise to entirely different worldspaces (spaces with differently perceived meanings as well as ontological features).

States and their Vantage Points, gross, subtle, causal/witnessing, and ultimate nondual, determine the types of phenomena in general that can arise to be experienced in the first place (or "*what*" arises, gross phenomena, subtle phenomena, causal phenomena, or nondual phenomena), and *structures and their Views*—with their "hidden maps" and grammar rules—determine *how* these phenomena are interpreted and therefore experienced. The same phenomenon (meditative state or otherwise), seen through a different View, will result in a virtually different phenomenon fundamentally. (This is not an example of the "epistemic fallacy"—the notion that epistemic ways of knowing determine the actual ontological realities of what is known. Nor is it an example of the converse, the "ontic fallacy"—the notion that the given ontological reality of an entity determines the status of epistemic knowledge of it. Both of these fallacies are based on a prior split, fragmentation, and fracturing of the realms of being and knowing, ontology and epistemology, feeling and thinking, into separate, isolated, siloed realms, whereas they are in fact two correlative components of the same underlying Wholeness, related to each other, not by "grounding" or "correctly representing" or "molding" each other, but by a *mutual resonance* of meshing or interfitting. More on this as we proceed.)[15]

As to the point at hand (the effect of structure-rungs, or "hidden maps," on the interpretation and thus the experience of an entity or event), take, as an example, a person in a dream state. This is a subset of the subtle realm, and the subtle is a realm of wild creativity, largely free of the determining constraints and limitations of the gross physical realm, so a person can dream of everything from flying through the air to seeing a unicorn to a figure with ten thousand arms to an important new application of an existing technology. But how a person interprets the dream will depend in large measure on his or her View (or level of structure-rung development). Let's say the person is a Christian, and has a dream of a radiantly luminous being of light and love. He or she might very likely see this being as Jesus Christ himself. If the person is at the conceptual/intentional mind, the egocentric and power-driven mind (structure-rung 3, Magic-Mythic, "power"), the person might see himself—and only himself—as actually being Jesus Christ, because the Magic-Mythic View is indeed egocentric or capable only of a 1st-person perspective (this View is totally self-focused, and in its dysfunctional forms, is common in schizo-paranoid phenomena). If we move up a stage to the Mythic traditional View, which can adopt a 2nd-person perspective and thus expand its identity from "I" to "we" or "us" (a group-centered View called "ethnocentric"), we find people who believe that the Bible is the literal word of God; true believers are "the chosen people" (while all others will burn in hell); the miracles recounted in the Bible are all literally true (from Moses parting the Red Sea to Noah and his ark saving all living beings to Christ being born from a biological virgin). Such a person might see this being of light that is Jesus Christ as the savior of all true believers, the savior of the chosen people (while all those who do not accept him as their personal savior are bound for everlasting hell). At the next higher View, that of the Rational or objective mind, the individual can adopt a 3rd-person, critical, and reflective attitude, which treats all people fairly, regardless of race, color, sex, or creed (a View called "worldcentric"), and will thus examine the Bible for alleged truths that made sense two thousand years ago but just don't make sense today (for example, not eating pork, not speaking to menstruating women, stoning to death those who commit adultery, and so on). When Thomas Jefferson sat on the steps of the White House and, with a pair of scissors, began to cut out all portions of the Bible that he felt were mythic nonsense, he was expressing a rational point of view. A person at this stage would likely experience this Jesus figure, not as the literal sole son of an anthropomorphic God born from a biological virgin, but as a renowned world teacher of great love and wisdom who still has important things to say to the modern world.

We have the same phenomenon—a being of radiant light and love—and yet three completely different interpretations and experiences of that phenomenon, depending on the subject's structure-stage or View. Now imagine meditation reaching a particular stage of illumination and insight—say, a subtle/luminosity state-stage. The subtle realm and its Vantage Point will determine what types of phenomena can arise in the first place—in this case, luminosity and insight—insight that might include awareness of impermanence and selflessness, just as the dream subtle realm determined the being of light and feelings of love in the previous example. But beyond that, in meditation, imagine the difference in actual experience and understanding of a Magic-Mythic View (egocentric power), a Mythic-literal View (ethnocentric belonging-ness), and a Rational View (worldcentric equality). At that particular point in meditation, the meditation tradition focuses on the particular state-stage itself and the Vantage Point of that stage, which, in its deep features, is essentially the same for all three of them—luminosity and insight. But the actual texture, the specific nature, the extent, the detailed interpretation, and the perspective will differ in many significant ways among these three individuals, depending in large part on their actual View, which in turn depends on the structure-stage and basic rung of the individual's structure center of gravity—seeing that meditation stage from a 1st-person perspective, from a 2nd-person perspective, and from a 3rd-person perspective is to see it very differently in many, many ways. As we've seen, the Vantage Point is one of the important factors that determines *what* we see (in this case, subtle luminosity and insight), but the View is one of the most important factors for *how* we see it (in this case, egocentric, ethnocentric, or worldcentric), the very lens through which we look at this and every experience—how we frame it, how we interpret it, and the meaning we give it, and thus how we experience it.

The point is that individuals are, today, already going through meditation practice from different structure-rungs of development, with different Views—not to mention that there are entire schools of Buddhism that are coming from different Views (as we'll see)—and taking both structures and states into account can only have beneficial results in numerous ways. Otherwise, if the teacher is at, say, a Pluralistic View, and is interpreting each stage of meditation from a Pluralistic View, then individuals at different Views will have their meditation experience interpreted in ways that often make little sense to them. Often their own experience of a particular meditative state-stage will actually be correct for the particular structure-rung they are at, but the meditation teacher will announce that it is being incorrectly seen and understood. In fact, the meditative state-stage could even have been experienced by the student from a higher structure than the teacher is functioning with—say, an Integral or Super-Integral View. The teacher's interpretation may severely damage the student's spiritual development and profoundly misinterpret the higher reaches of Buddhism itself. This happens much more often than is realized. As we'll explore later, this was especially common with many Eastern teachers, who, particularly in the 1960s and 1970s, arrived with a very highly developed state axis—often causal or nondual—but a rather poorly developed structure axis, often reflecting the traditional ethnocentric and Mythic-structure View of the traditional culture they came from. When they interacted with their students, the majority of whom were often from the higher structure of, say, the postmodern Pluralistic View, the results were often severely confusing, even disturbing. The teachers' advice when it came to states was often brilliant, and the students were appropriately blown away; their advice when it came from their structure View, on the other hand, was often embarrassing, being ethnocentric, homophobic, xenophobic, patriarchal, sexist, highly authoritarian, and rigidly hierarchical. Until both structures and states are taken into account, students will be left in these types of utterly confusing situations, and spiritual development itself will often be dysfunctional.

So we have briefly examined states and their state-stages (or Vantage Points). We found that all humans are born with 4 or 5 major states of consciousness (waking, dreaming, deep sleep, unqualifiable witnessing, and nondual unity) as well as their correlative "ontological" realms (or the sum total of objects that can occur in those individual states). And each of those "minds" or "consciousnesses" possesses a correlative body (or concrete mass-energy form—gross body, subtle body, causal body, integrative body, and nondual body), so that each mind has its body: a gross body/mind, a subtle body/mind, a causal body/mind, a nondual body/mind (and thus a mind/body duality is never a problem here).

Consciousness or Wakefulness starts out identified with the waking state (and gross body), and yet it will (mostly unconsciously) "cycle" through all major states at least once every twenty-four hours (moving from waking gross to dreaming subtle to deep-sleep causal, while resting in ever-present witnessing/nondual). But unless a person specifically takes up a practice such as meditation or contemplation, he or she (or the self's *state* center of gravity) will likely remain identified with the gross waking state (at least until significantly later in life, usually midlife or later). The main reason is that as a person's self-sense passes from one major state to the next, it will "pass out" or "go blank" (as when it passes from waking into dream or deep sleep) and so it will not know—while it is in that different state—that it has changed states at all. The self will happily dream away, almost completely unaware that it is asleep, unconscious, and dreaming at all— until, of course, it wakes up ("Wow, that was just a dream!"). Several years of meditation—which trains the Witness or Wakefulness to remain aware as it changes state—will usually be required for the self to be able to remain aware during sleep and thus experience "lucid dreaming"—being in the subtle dream state and *knowing* that you are in that state. But once that begins to consistently happen, you start to realize that, not only are you not identified with your gross waking ego, but there is something that remains Aware and Awake in you, even in the dream state—so you are not identified wholly with the dream state either. There is something in you, some deep center of

Awareness or Wakefulness, that remains Aware through both the gross waking state and the subtle dream state. Who or What is that?

As meditation continues, your Awareness, while awake or asleep, will begin to open onto vast, seemingly infinite stretches of Consciousness itself, plugged into what seems like all of space-time—vast, open, spacious, utterly dark yet suffused with infinite luminosity. At times it will appear completely unmanifest, a pure endless Abyss, out of which the subtlest of the subtlest of forms seem to emerge—subtle geometric forms, subtle sounds, audible illuminations, the very matrix of space-time itself, colored forms—pouring forth, "outward" and "downward," to create the entire manifest world, with all its causal, subtle, and gross objects. All of this pours out of your own Consciousness, the creative nexus of your own pure Self and infinite Will, often suffused with a radical Joy, pure Love, infinite Beauty, and unlimited Freedom. When this happens, then while asleep, you will often pass into the deep, dreamless sleep state; yet a tacit, utterly subtle Awareness or Wakefulness will also remain present, a thread of this deep center of Awareness or Consciousness that increasingly is seen as your own truest, deepest, fullest, most open Self, or pure I AMness.

This is pure vast Self, or empty unqualifiable I AMness, comes fully to the fore at the next state-stage, the pure, empty Witnessing Awareness. With a sudden shock of Recognition, you realize that this is your one and only True Self, the Self you had before your parents were born, the Self you had before the universe was born, the Self that is before anything is born because it is before time itself is born—or more accurately, the Self that simply never enters the stream of time in the first place but lives only in the timeless Now, the pure Presence of the pure Present—"Before Abraham was, I AM." This pure I AMness is the deep, clear Awareness in you that right now is simply, spontaneously, and effortlessly Witnessing all that is arising—this page, this computer, this room, this landscape—and yet is identified with none of it: "neti, neti," "I AM not this, not that, but rather its simple Witness." This I AMness, this Witness, this silent, clear, Observing Self realizes that "I have sensations of those objects—the cars, the house, the airplane—but I am not those objects; I have sensations, but I am not those sensations; I have feelings, but I am not those feelings; I have thoughts, but I am not those thoughts." In fact, "I have a body, but I am not that body; I have a mind, but I am not that mind; and I have a soul, but I am not that soul." Those are all objects that can be seen, but the true Self is the pure Seer, not anything that can be seen. I can no more see the Seer than an eye can see itself or a tongue can taste itself. If I try to see the Seer, or feel the Feeler, or know the Knower, all I will find are more objects, not the true Subject, the true Seer, or Real Self. Rather, all I will find as I rest in this pure Witness or True Self is a vast sense of Freedom, of Liberation, of Release, of Vast Expanse, of infinite Depth—a Freedom from identifying with all of these small, finite, puny objects (gross, subtle, or causal; sensations, thoughts, or feelings) with which I had mistakenly identified my true and infinite Self. This still, silent expanse of infinite depth and freedom, a vast equanimity, is often called "the mirror mind," because, just like a mirror, it simply reflects all that arises without identifying or grasping at any of it. Chuang Tzu says, "The Perfect Person employs the mind like a mirror —it receives, but does not keep; it allows, but does not grasp." Ramana Maharshi called this Real Self, or I AMness, the "I-I," the pure Observing-Self "I" that is aware of the small-object self "I" (or ego). When you are aware of yourself right now, the self you are aware of is the small-object self (or ego), and the Self that is aware of it is the Real Self, or true Witness. But I trashed my Supreme Identity with Spirit, with the Divine, with superconsciousness, and identified instead with this pitiful, bounded, finite, mortal, skin-encapsulated ego, which separated me from the rest of the All, and left me partial, limited, fragmented, torn, and broken—and therefore constantly open to suffering, torment, torture, terror, and tears. What I have called "me" all these years is a case of colossally mistaken identity.

Instead, my True Self or Original Self is a vast Freedom, a sense of radical Emptiness or Openness. "I have feelings, but I am not those feelings"—and thus I am Free of feelings. "I have emotions, but I am not those emotions"—and thus I am Free of emotions. "I have thoughts, but I am not those thoughts"—and thus I am Free of thoughts. "I have a body, but I am not that body"—and thus I am Free of body. "I have a mind, but I am not the mind"—and thus I am Free of the mind. This radical Freedom, pure Emptiness, transparent Openness, is my one and only True Seer and Real Self, the pure I AMness that is ever-present, all-inclusive, radically embracing. It is the mirror mind that, with unshakable equanimity, witnesses every thing, object, and event that arises in its pure no-boundary Awareness, the unborn and undying Original Face that I had before my parents were born, before the universe was born, before space-time itself was born and defined the texture of this particular universe. "Before Abraham was, I AM." Indeed. This pure spacious Awareness is nothing I can see as an object—it is simply a clearing, or space, an opening, or spaciousness, in which all objects arise moment to moment, a clearing or open space in which that mountain is arising, those clouds are arising, this room is arising, that building is arising, this book is arising. Free of all objects, it is the space or clearing in which they all are arising, moment to moment to moment.

As I rest in this infinite space of radical Emptiness and pure Freedom, the very sense of being a Witness, of being an Observing Self, of being a Looker, will sooner or later itself completely collapse. As Zen says, "The bottom of the bucket breaks"—and the sense of being a Self witnessing the objects around me completely dissolves: the Seer becomes one with all things seen, the subject and object become "not two," the world "out there" and the world "in here" reduce to a single experience of one taste. I no longer witness the mountain, I am the mountain; I no longer feel the rain, I am the rain; I no longer hear a distant waterfall, I am the waterfall; I no longer see the clouds, I am the clouds. I am no longer stuck on this side of my face, looking at the world arising moment to moment "out there." There is only the world arising moment to moment, and I am all of that. Every thing and event arises of-itself-so, and is self-seen, self-existing, self-liberating. It is no longer an object perceived by a subject, even by an Absolute Subject or Self, but is self-seen in and as its own pure Suchness, Thusness, Isness. I no longer see this table; this table sees itself. The Empty Witness has become one (or nondual, not-two) with all objects—gross, subtle, and causal—so that Emptiness and Form are truly "Nondual," or, as Zen says (in order to avoid qualifying the ultimate), they are "not-two, not-one." The same is true of self and Spirit, finite and Infinite, Form and Emptiness, relative and ultimate, samsara and nirvana, manifest and unmanifest, you and the ultimate Divine. You have, indeed, recognized a Home you have never left. (I will, in a moment, give some specific exercises to help you directly experience the real Seer or True Self, and beyond that, the pure nondual open Suchness, or Thusness. So please stay tuned for that.)

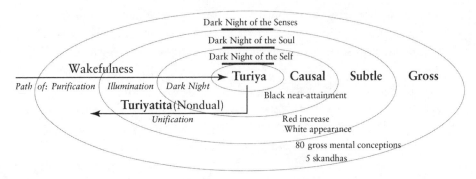

Figure 3.1. Major stages of meditative states.

Before we look at these states in a bit more detail, there's a simple diagram that summarizes them, which might be useful (see fig. 3.1). This figure contains gross, subtle, causal, turiya (which, we saw, literally means "the 4th," as in the 4th major state of consciousness—that is, the pure, unqualifiable, or Empty Witness, the Real Self, pure I AM-ness), and turiyatita ("beyond the 4th," the pure, Nondual union of Emptiness and All Form—gross, subtle, and causal—in pure Suchness or Isness). On the left of the diagram, representing the West, are Underhill's major stages, and on the "southeastern" line, starting with "five skandhas" (or five forms of gross awareness—form, sensation, impulse, concept, and egoic self-sense) are the stages from Highest Yoga Tantra, representing the East ("black near-attainment" is causal "luminous darkness," occurring right before Enlightenment, which, again, is the nondual union of Emptiness and Form). Each of the major realms—gross, subtle, and causal—has a "dark night" listed at its edge, which involves the death of the self at that state (or the release of the exclusive identity with that state/realm), which is necessary for the next higher state-stage to occur. When all deaths have been died—including the Higher Self of causal and the True Self, or Real Self, of turiya Witnessing—then the result is ultimate Nondual Suchness or Thusness, Reality *just as it is*, in its naked Isness, right here, right now.

We have seen that virtually any of these states can be experienced by virtually any structure and that structure will determine in large measure *how* the state is interpreted and largely experienced. This is indicated in a diagram called "The Wilber-Combs Lattice," named

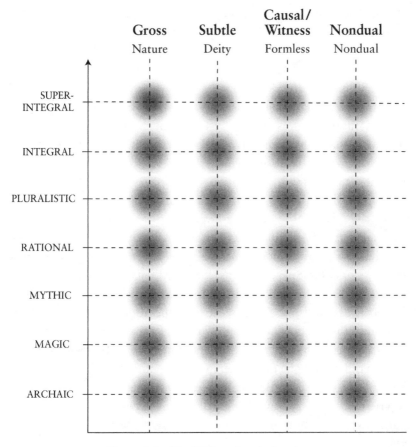

	Gross	Subtle	Causal/ Witness	Nondual
	Nature	Deity	Formless	Nondual

Figure 3.2. The Wilber-Combs Lattice.

after myself and Allan Combs, who hit upon essentially the same idea independently (see fig. 3.2). We put the major *structure-levels* (of any major line, or multiple intelligence, using any psychological developmental model you wish), running up the vertical left-hand axis. In figure 3.2, we're using our standard Archaic, Magic, Mythic, Rational, Pluralistic, Integral, and Super-Integral (which are variations on the Views especially from the worldview line, particularly as given by Gebser). Across the top, we place any of the major *states* that are being highlighted (in this case, 4 of our standard 5 states: gross, subtle, causal/witnessing, and nondual). Under each of those labels, we place the type of spiritual experience that occurs in peak experiences in that state/realm, when an expanded, nonordinary state of identity with the phenomena in that realm is experienced. (This expanded sense of identity, in any state, can run from "communion" to "union" to "identity." With a subtle deity form, for example, one can experience a communion with this deity form, a union with it, or a direct pure identity with it.) Thus, oneness with all the forms of the gross realm, or the natural world, is nature mysticism; oneness with a major deity form in the subtle realm is deity mysticism; oneness with the formlessness of the causal/witnessing realm is formless mysticism; and oneness with the ultimate union of Emptiness and Form is nondual Unity mysticism. This figure gives us two of our four major vectors of development—the "vertical" structure-levels and the "horizontal" state/realms. What is missing (as the figure is now drawn) is the dual center of gravity—that is, which structure-stage and which state-stage the self-sense or consciousness is most identified with at any given time. If we circled the former on the figure (to indicate which structure-stage the self is at), and put a square around the later (to indicate which state-stage the self is at), we would have all four vectors, and of course that's necessary to fully map any individual's dual center of gravity and overall development. The important point this figure makes is that, indeed, how a particular state/realm is actually interpreted and experienced will vary considerably depending upon the structure-rung that is experiencing that state, and thus taking both into account is crucial.

As we've seen, you could be at a mythic ethnocentric level of structure development and yet still complete state training and become a fully transmitted Zen master, because the traditions are tracking only state development (from gross to subtle to causal and nondual), not structure development (from 1st person to 2nd person to 3rd person to 4th person, and so forth). Thus they miss these crucial perspectives embedded in the "hidden maps" through which their states are being viewed and experienced, which guarantees a superb Waking Up but often a mediocre, even nearly primitive, Growing Up. We all know teachers like this, wonderfully awakened to very deep state development and yet poorly developed in structure capacities and multiple intelligences, victims of hidden maps at ethnocentric and even egocentric levels—and thus who are authoritarian, xenophobic, rigidly hierarchical, often sexist, patriarchal, sometimes racist, ethnocentric, absolutistic, often homophobic, and strictly conformist with regard to their tradition. They may believe in every sort of "magical" capacity of ancient enlightened Masters (for example, that they can fly, heal all illness, possess omniscience, perform every variety of miracles themselves, and so forth). These features—often including ethnocentrism, sexism, homophobia, authoritarianism—are unfortunately embedded in their teachings as they attempt to communicate dharma or spiritual truth, giving many people an overall rather negative opinion of "spiritual" realities in general. The modern and postmodern world will officially accept realities coming only from worldcentric or higher levels (this is why worldcentric modernity aggressively rejects *all* forms of ethnocentric religious fundamentalism, East or West); hence the only way to guarantee that spirituality has an honored place in the modern and postmodern world is to train its teachers and students to progress through not only the states of consciousness, from ignorance to Enlightenment, but also the structures of consciousness, from immaturity to full maturity. And the only way to do that is to include both Growing Up and Waking Up in any truly integral, comprehensive, inclusive spirituality, Fourth Turning or otherwise.

Now, it's time to give a more detailed analysis of the major natural states, including exercises for directly experiencing the two very highest states available—turiya and turiyatita, or true Witness and ultimate nondual Suchness.

4

The Gross and Subtle States
of Consciousness

This chapter provides a more fine-grained description of the first two natural states, the gross and subtle states of consciousness, fleshed out with some concrete examples, and chapter 5 does the same for the three remaining states, causal, witness, and nondual. But be strongly forewarned: exactly how these states are seen, interpreted, and experienced will depend in large measure on the structure center of gravity of the self doing the seeing, interpreting, and experiencing. As we will see in convincing detail in the chapter 6, a Magic experience of a subtle state is dramatically different from a Pluralistic experience of the same subtle state; a Mythic experience of a causal state is profoundly different from an Integral experience of the very same causal state. So the following discussion of the natural states (which continues into the next chapter) is a bit of an amalgam—a bunching of characteristics that are usually, but not always or necessarily, experienced by all structure-levels of the self. Further, I combine the "state" of consciousness, the "knowing" aspect, with the "realm" component, the types of ontological phenomena that can generally be found in each state. Same important warning: the "ontology" of a realm is not pregiven, not fixed and set in concrete, but is enacted and co-created by the subject doing the knowing and experiencing, and that will change during development. A Magic subject, with only a

1st-person perspective, will see some very different things than a Mythic subject, who additionally possesses a 2nd-person perspective. And those will vary dramatically from what a Rational subject, who adds a 3rd-person perspective, will see in this state, or a Pluralistic subject, with 4th-person perspective, and so on.

Thus this discussion in chapters 4 and 5 provides a *generic* presentation of these 5 major natural states of consciousness, the very core of the human being, who, upon realizing them from start to finish in a process of WAKING UP, discovers or recognizes the ever-present core of the Divine that is the ultimate Goal, Ground, Condition, and Suchness of each and every human being—indeed, of each and every sentient being (which means each and every individual holon in the entire Kosmos). The ultimate nondual State or Suchness *is* what is now reading this page, looking at this room, listening to those birds. In fact, it is not only reading this page in all its immediate Thusness, but it also wrote this page as well. *You*, the one and only *you*, the one and only Divine in each and every sentient being in the Kosmos at large, you, your own deepest *You*, as your own core I AMness, which you can feel, and are feeling, right now is the true and ultimate Author of this book and the entire universe at large, top to bottom. Feel that simple feeling of *being You* and recognize its ever-present, all-pervading nature, moment to moment to moment. Nothing, really, is more obvious or more present—or more real.

You will generally pass through these 5 major states of consciousness on your way to more fully and permanently realizing this ever-present nondual I AMness in its simple Suchness, Thusness, Isness, just as it is, exactly as it is, now to now to timeless now—the Present is the only thing that has no end.

The Gross (or Physical) State

The gross realm, technically for the traditions, refers strictly to the purely material realm, the physical realm, the sensorimotor realm, which is all of the levels of existence up to (but not including) the emergence of life (or the earliest cells). It corresponds to the first chakra (material) and to the first sheath (the *annamayakosha*, or the "sheath made of food"—that is, the physical sheath or level). But it is also very common to refer to several higher levels as being those that are most tellingly defined as "reflecting" the gross realm. Thus, for example, although the ego is technically part of the subtle realm, it is common to refer to the ego as the "gross-reflecting ego" and place it, loosely, in the gross realm, because the ego itself grows up in the world predominantly defined by the material or physical realm itself, and many of its drives, needs, and characteristics reflect those items most readily found in the gross realm (or at least having a significant gross dimension)—food, money, fame, fortune, cars, houses, and so on. Also, the realm that virtually all egos consider to be real, without question, is the physical, sensorimotor realm—for example, "scientific materialism," which acknowledges *only* this realm as real—hence, the "gross-reflecting" ego.

In the same way, it is common to find the first six chakras referred to as "gross-reflecting" chakras, and when this is done, the subtle realm (which technically begins with life, the second chakra, *prana*, or the emotional-sexual level) is instead said to begin at the seventh chakra, above the six lower "gross-reflecting" chakras (you see this done, for example, in Adi Da's *The Paradox of Instruction*).[1] But the highest this can be done (referring to something as "gross-reflecting") definitely ends around the Integral level (if it hasn't been ended earlier, which is most common). But by that time, the first eight structures ("Integral" being the eighth—after archaic, magic, magic-mythic, mythic, rational, pluralistic, holistic) have "objectified," "transcended," or "made object" virtually all of the types of phenomena that can be categorized as "gross-reflecting," and thus the next highest structure-level, the transglobal, or para-mind (the first of the Super-Integral structure-rungs or levels), completes objectifying essentially the entire gross realm (at least as it exists at this point in history or evolution). Thus there is nowhere else to go, with reference to states, except "upward" (or "to the right" in the Wilber-Combs Lattice)—that is, to the subtle realm, if the self hasn't already done so (that is, if it hasn't already shifted its state center of gravity from gross to subtle, which it can do, beginning, perhaps, as early as Magic or Magic-Mythic).[2] One of the effects of the para-mind's "objectification" of the gross realm is that it will often have experiences of the gross realm (including all of nature's forms) in either a communion, or a union, or even an identity fashion (this continuum is one that is found in every state; it refers to the relationship between the self-sense of that state and the overall phenomena of that state—it can be a communion, a union, or an identity). The latter (identity), in this gross/natural state, is an experience of identity or oneness with all of nature, as in "nature mysticism." But whatever the degree of union with the gross/nature realm (communion, union, or identity), the para-mind begins to display an understanding that the world is not just physical, it is psychophysical, whether that is understood in virtue of the role interpretation plays in all ontology, the inherent union of epistemology and ontology, the role concepts have in co-creating the perceived world, or the general understanding that every phenomenon in the world inherently possesses both interiors (consciousness) and exteriors (material form)—hence, it is psychophysical. In the 3rd tier in general, this insight becomes paramount, to the extent that it is understood that the 1st tier's separation of epistemology and ontology is an unnatural breaking, fracturing, or fragmenting of that which is actually an inseparable Wholeness. At 3rd tier, knowing becomes, not the given representation of an object by a subject, but a "mutual resonance" of all 4 quadrants "vibrating together" when "truth" is present, and failing to vibrate when "falsity" is present. "Truth," in any of its forms in any quadrant, is a matter of mutual harmonic resonance, not the static "representation" or "grounding" of epistemology in ontology or vice versa, which itself is the result of nothing but a prior fracturing of these correlative and mutually dependent dimensions. We'll pick up this topic, as well as finish the discussion of all the structures, including 3rd tier, in chapter 6.

One final point about the gross, physical realm. As I have pointed out several times elsewhere, one of the major problems with how the ancients viewed the material or physical plane is that, unaware of all the discoveries that modern science has made about the "micro" dimensions of matter, from brain physiology to molecular biology to neuroanatomy to bodily functioning to the triune brain and its functions, the ancients put *all* of the physical dimension on the very lowest level of the "Great Chain of Being." (The "Great Chain of Being" refers to the 5 major state/realms that virtually all Great Traditions recognized—namely, in Christian terms, matter, body, mind, soul, and spirit, with "Spirit" being both the highest level and the groundless Ground of all of the levels. That is, Spirit is both the highest rung of the ladder, and the wood out of which the entire ladder is made, so

Spirit both completely transcends and completely includes the entire manifest universe.) According to the ancient version of this scheme, the "feelings" of a worm, which exist on the living-body level, level 2, would be higher than the physical triune brain, which is a purely material, or level 1, reality. Something is clearly a bit off with that part of the scheme, when the feelings of a worm (no offense to the worm) are ranked higher than the triune brain of a primate.

What Integral suggests, as modern science has continued its onward march, is that *matter* is not the *lowest* level in the Great Chain of Being but rather is the *exterior* dimension of *every* level in the Great Chain (as Prakriti, Mahamaya, or Mahashakti is the exterior, manifest, material dimension of the Divine itself). This is what the 4 quadrants do (which we'll soon explore more; see fig. 4.1). They place all the material or physical forms of reality in the two Right-hand quadrants, in both individual forms (Upper Right quadrant) and collective forms (Lower Right quadrant). The individual material, or exterior, forms of atoms, molecules, cells, organisms, organisms with neural nets, with reptilian brain stems, with limbic systems, and with neocortexes are in the Upper Right quadrant, and collective exterior forms, from galaxies to Gaia, including, for example, the "objective" techno-economic base of a society—foraging, horticultural, agrarian, industrial, informational—are in the Lower Right quadrant (see fig. 4.1). All of the levels higher than matter in the traditional Great Chain of Being are now seen as the Left-hand *interiors* of the beings (individual and collective) whose correlative Right-hand, or material, *exteriors* were just outlined. Thus, the correlative *interior* structure-levels to the *individual exteriors* just given—atoms, molecules, cells, and so forth—are prehension, irritability, sensation, and so forth, and the correlative *interior* structure-levels to the *collective interiors* just given—foraging, horticultural, agrarian, industrial, informational—are the cultural worldviews of archaic, magic, mythic, rational, and pluralistic. Again, see figure 4.1 for one version of a 4-quadrant diagram. In this diagram, we have fourteen major levels; in other diagrams, we present five, sometimes twelve, sometimes more. It is simply a matter of how much detail we want to present at any given time, nothing more.

The 4 quadrants, which we will return to in more detail in a later chapter, represent four of the most basic and irreducible perspectives

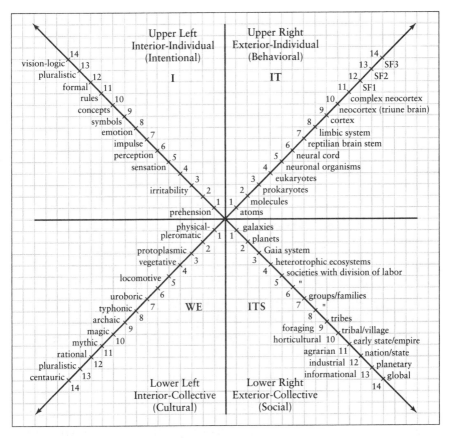

Figure 4.1. Some details from the 4 quadrants.

available in all reality: the interior and exterior of the individual and the collective, giving four irreducible realms (the interior of the individual, or the "I" space; the interior of the collective, or the "we" space; the exterior of the individual, or the objective "it" space; and the exterior of the collective, or the systems "its" space). All four of the perspectives from these quadrants need to be included for any truly comprehensive or inclusive account—and the same is true of spirituality, as we'll see. Each quadrant has different but equally important truths, phenomena, validity claims, methodologies, perspectives, objects and events, and so on, and each is so important that virtually every major human discipline, from medicine to law to spirituality to history to art, among hundreds, has attached itself to how its discipline looks from a particular quadrant and argues for the reality of that quadrant alone and the unreality or unusefulness of all the others—what we call "quadrant absolutism." One of the most important things an Integral approach has done is argue the irreducible and utterly significant importance of each of these quadrants for a genuinely comprehensive and inclusive approach. We will see many examples of this as we proceed.

This means, among numerous other things, that states of consciousness and their phenomena (gross, subtle, causal, and nondual) are no longer viewed as existing somewhere "up there" in the sky, totally divorced from the organism or nature and existing in some sort of metaphysical supernatural heaven, but are rather the conscious *interiors* of the *exterior* material states of objects—not *above* nature but *interior* to nature, not *beyond* but *within*. For example, each consciousness state in the Upper Left quadrant has a correlative brain state in the Upper Right quadrant (as only one type of example, "brain/mind" machines, using technologies such as binaural beats, will induce, in the brain—in the Upper Right—specific brain-wave states, and these will in turn induce specific consciousness states in the Upper Left). Neither can be reduced to the other; neither can exist without the other. This makes room for all of the states and structures of consciousness (in the Upper Left) without having to reduce them to merely material or physical phenomena (brain states in the Upper Right), although it finds that the two are correlative, mutually arising, mutually influencing, and mutually evolving (tetra-evolving, actually: evolution in all 4 quadrants).[3]

What modern science has found—and an Integral approach can certainly accept—is that *evolution* has resulted in a constant complexification of gross matter, whose objective *exteriors* (the phenomenon looked at from the outside in an objective fashion, individually and collectively) become *more and more complex*, while their subjective *interiors* (the phenomena looked at from the inside, from within their interiors, individually and collectively) become *more and more conscious*. This is Teilhard de Chardin's famous law of "complexity and consciousness"—namely, the more of one, the more of the other.

This allows us to connect what was previously viewed as "other-worldly" or "metaphysical" or "super-natural" with "this world," the natural and material world, as being the interior and exterior of the

same Wholeness of the Real and not split them apart into two antagonistic, separated, and disjointed realities (for example, heaven and
earth, transcendent and immanent). By seeing that neither can be dispensed with nor reduced to the other, we prevent the reduction of
spiritual (interior) realities to material (exterior) phenomena, and we
likewise realize the importance of the material plane as the vehicle
through which higher, interior, mental, and spiritual realities are able
to manifest and communicate themselves. The subtle dimension, for
example, can never be reduced without remainder to particular brain
states, but every time you are in a subtle state, your brain will show
certain brain-wave patterns; you can count on it. The 4 quadrants are
all like that—none can be reduced to the others; none can be dispensed
with. All are equally important—they arise together, develop and
tetra-evolve together, and die together.

So the "gross realm" has at least these two quite different meanings,
due to the ongoing evolution of our own knowledge about the universe and its constituents (yet another reason that the worldviews of
the ancient systems need to be constantly updated, while still retaining
their central features). The gross realm is the correlative *exterior* of all
the *interior* dimensions of every level in the traditional Great Chain,
and it also means the "lowest" of both those dimensions (exterior and
interior). "Exterior" is defined simply as the Right-hand dimension of
any phenomenon (that is, the phenomenon seen from an objective,
outside view). And "gross" as "lowest" means all of the levels of evolution and reality, in any quadrant, leading up to the emergence of
levels that possess life, or possess what the Eastern traditions call
"prana" or bioenergy, the emergence of which marks the end of the
gross realm considered as "the lowest" and the beginning of the first
level of the next higher state/realm, the overall subtle, whose very first
sublevel, which accompanies the first living forms, is often called "the
etheric"—for example, a cell has an etheric component, an atom
doesn't. Technically, this means that the cell is in the subtle realm
(though much more commonly classed as "gross-reflecting") and the
atom is in pure undiluted gross realm.

In short, the "gross realm" consists of, in the first instance (that is,
as the "lowest level of all reality"), the actual physical-material level of
reality (up to the emergence of living cells) in the Upper Right, along

with the Upper Right energetic support of that level (which involves the standard energy forces of physics—strong and weak nuclear, gravitational, and electromagnetic). In addition to that meaning, which we still use, we have the other, newer sense of "exterior" or "Right-hand" correlates, where "gross" means the exterior of every major level in the Great Chain, top to bottom (with, of course, the exception of all formless or unmanifest realms and the groundless Ground itself, which is the simultaneous Suchness of all 4 quadrants, symbolized by the paper on which the diagram is drawn).

Finally, we have the sense of "gross-reflecting," which means that any level up to around Integral 2nd tier, even though technically it is itself in the subtle realm (starting, again technically, with Magic, or chakra-rung 2), can take as the primary objects of its awareness, personality, and characteristics items that reflect or are reflecting the gross, physical, sensorimotor realm. Within that gross-reflecting stance, these levels can be more or less specifically materialistic (for example, when 2nd-tier vision-logic focuses solely on the Lower Right "material-exterior" quadrant and its interobjective systems and uses systems or complexity theory to frame all of reality). (The same thing happens when the first six chakras are referred to as the "gross realm" or, more accurately, as the "gross-reflecting" realm.) The point is simply that they all have, as their predominant background context, the gross physical realm. This realm has undergone by far the most evolutionary expansion in terms of our knowledge, going from being the very lowest level in all of reality, to being the exterior form of *all* (except unmanifest) levels of reality—quite a promotion![4]

The Subtle State

The Wisdom Traditions typically divide the subtle realm into three main areas, which we can call low, middle, and high subtle. These areas are often given specific characteristics, patterns, or forms. But it's important to realize that these characteristics and forms are not structures (in the technical sense we use that term) but are simply some of the basic features of those subtle areas, considered in a general sense. Of course, these characteristics will change significantly depending upon which actual structure is really doing the seeing or experiencing of the state/realm (as with the Wilber-Combs Lattice).

The Low Subtle

The low subtle is the beginning of the subtle realm and the subtle body itself, the body that (in its entirety) supports the dream state, various meditation states, thoughts and emotions, and the bardo realm (the realm said to exist between death and rebirth), among others. The first, lowest, or most junior subtle energy is often called "the etheric," which is the energy field that surrounds the first living holons (that is, viruses, bacteria, cells).[5] This subtle "life energy" is an energy that exists in addition to, or along with, the four standard energies or forces recognized by conventional physics (strong and weak nuclear, electromagnetic, and gravitational). Some theorists maintain that life energy is the energy that creates the "self-organizing" drive found in all living beings. (Although note that many avant-garde theories of evolution, including that of Integral Theory, view "self-organization" as a drive that is present in all beings or all manifest holons whatsoever and goes all the way back to the very beginning, the Big Bang. Integral Theory identifies this drive, among other things, as "Eros." If "self-organization" is seen as a drive present in all holons, then "etheric subtle energy" is a drive present in the first living holons.) In any event, "etheric subtle energy" is something that cells have and atoms don't. It is an *emergent* quality of evolution, and as all emergents do, it "transcends and includes" its predecessors.

The next major level of prana, or subtle life energy, is often called "the astral," or the "emotional-sexual." As the last name implies, this is found in all complex living animals that have a sexual reproduction system and drive. Viewed from the interior, this is an actual feeling, drive, or energetic motivation; viewed from the exterior, it is a system of hormones and glands and brain areas woven together into a complex system of behavioral signals and responses. It's included in the subtle because it can be experienced in the dream state; and theorists such as Freud saw it as the major drive in the dream state itself (as in much of the waking state in general).

In the typical traditional map of states and sheaths (where sheaths are the "layers" of reality surrounding and expressing the True Self and are correlated with the bodies or energies that support them), the first sheath is the annamayakosha, or "the sheath made of physical food"—that is, the gross realm and gross body per se. The second sheath is the pranamayakosha, or "the sheath made of prana, or subtle energy." The next higher sheath is the manomayakosha, or "the sheath made of mind." Now the tricky point is that the "sheath made of mind" (as well as the next higher sheath, the sheath of higher mind) is listed as being *within the subtle body*, or the pranic body (or supported by the subtle pranic body). This is common in many Great Chain theories, where a level is listed that really represents, not just that level alone, but the beginning of that level's traits and qualities that continue to exist on several higher levels. This is certainly true of prana, or subtle-body energy; it starts in the low subtle (with the first life forms of "etheric" energy) but defines the whole subtle realm (etheric plus emotional-sexual/astral plus mind plus higher mind). So that needs to be kept in mind. And to make things even slightly more confusing, several traditions introduce something like the notion of a "cosmic prana," which means a fundamental energy underlying *all* of manifestation and present in the gross, subtle, and causal domains. (Cosmic prana is thus similar to "shakti," or the total manifesting energy of the Divine, usually identified with its feminine forms—an energy quite similar to "the Holy Spirit" as used by Christian contemplatives.) In the same way, "subtle energy" itself is sometimes used to cover all the types of energy found in the gross, subtle, and causal domains (even though, technically, each of those domains is said to contain a different type of energy—gross energy, subtle energy, causal energy—which is what distinguishes them in the first place). So welcome to the world of jumbled semantics that comes from recognizing so many realms and dimensions beyond the simple sensorimotor. As with terms like "Dharmakaya" (which, we saw, can represent three of the highest five state/bodies, two of the highest five, or just one of the highest five), you have to let context help you to determine which meaning is being indicated.

Integral Theory, at any rate, sees the spectrum of bodies in the Upper Right—the gross body, subtle body, and causal body, for example—as being a spectrum of subtler and subtler energies (hence the definition of a "body" that we gave earlier as the "mass-energy" component of a level), and this *spectrum of energy* (or "bodies") in the Upper Right is correlated with a *spectrum of consciousness* in the Upper Left.

The Middle Subtle

The middle subtle supports a sheath, or level, known as the *mano-mayakosha* in Vedanta and the *manovijnana* in Buddhism. The common syllable in both of those terms is "mano," which means the conceptual mind. Now because the Great Traditions didn't have access to some of the more modern developmental methodologies that explore these types of dimensions in great detail, what both Vedanta and Buddhism count as one major level—the "mano-mind"—modern Western developmentalists see as actually containing anywhere from three to five levels, occasionally more. The mano-mind is a single sheath that contains what developmentalists would call the upper reaches of Magic, plus the Magic-Mythic, Mythic, Rational, and Pluralistic levels (according to the location of the "mano-mind" given by the traditions themselves—namely, it consists of all of the levels between the prana-mayakosha, or the sheath of bioenergy, or emotional-sexual level [Magic], and the vijnanamayakosha, or the sheath made of higher mind, which generally corresponds to 2nd tier). But between those two levels are in fact the higher reaches of Magic, plus Magic-Mythic, Mythic, Rational, and Pluralistic, and precisely because these structures can't be seen well or at all by introspection, they were often lumped together as one level, the "mano-mind." This provides yet another reason why the more accurate structure maps of Growing Up need to be included with those of the states of Waking Up. But in any event, all of these basic structures (whether considered as the single mano-mind or as all five of the more detailed mental levels of developmental models) are supported by the (middle) subtle body.

We can see why these levels would still be referred to as "gross reflecting" by many of the traditions. Buddhists, for example, view the conceptual mind (the "mano-mind") as actually being a sense like the other five senses, and its objects are simply thoughts and concepts—thus, six senses altogether. The very notion of the mind reflecting its objects just as the other five senses reflect their objects gives a strong sense of mind reflecting the gross realm, the way most other senses do.

Notice that these Great Traditions are giving us a phenomenology of the types of structures and levels that the subtle body can and is supporting and that can therefore, for instance, also appear in dreams.

They are giving the structures that can appear in various states. Because the West tended to refine structuralism, it found many more structures and levels than the traditions found (and to repeat, these structures can't easily or fully be seen by introspection, which is *the major tool used by these traditions*). But by placing the mano-mind within the general realm of the subtle body, the traditions give us precious information that we can flesh out with a fuller structuralism. When we do so, we find that the mano-mind really refers to a large area running from Magic to Pluralistic.

As for the subtle realm itself, this middle-range subtle includes such phenomena as developed emotions (anger, grief, happiness, sadness, joy); various mythic religious images, impulses, "beings," and beliefs; logical thoughts and concepts; and pluralistic perspectives and multiple views. Many of the ancient traditions interpret the beings experienced in the overall subtle realm as being ontologically real entities. In the high subtle, which we will turn to next, these entities include *Devas* (elemental deities with their energetic shaktis), such as Indra (thunder), Chandra (moon), Surya (sun), Vayu (wind), Agni (fire), and Prithvi (earth); *Asuras* (power gods), such as Bali, Prahlanda, and others; *Rakshasas* (demons), such as Ravana, Shumbha, Chanda, and Munda; and various local deities (gods and goddesses of various local places). Recall that the phenomena of the subtle (as for any state) is in large measure the co-creation and enactment of the particular structure that is experiencing it—in this case, those beings are at least likely to be the enactment of the Mythic-literal level, as is much of the narrative context of the Great Traditions.

Let me give a quick but very concrete example to make this point as clear as possible, since it's significant. Take the dream state, an example of a subtle state. When a nine-month-old infant (at the late Archaic stage) dreams, the contents of the dreams are, at best, cascading images, some crude symbols, and primitive emotive states—images of the breast, the mothering one, intensely affecting environmental objects and events, and raw emotions of rage, fear, and desire. By the time the child has reached age seven or eight, at the beginning of the Mythic-literal stage, dream images include beings and events with distinctly mythic images—horses, unicorns, warriors, power figures and "PowerGods," along with strong feelings of peer pressure and beginning concerns about conformity and being left out or rejected. At the middle of adolescence (emergence of Rational), the dream starts to contain some segments that are very logical and ordinary, a previewed list of things the individual is planning on doing tomorrow, necessary tasks for the upcoming prom, getting that new car from Dad, maybe a date with Susie or Bobbie, new sneakers, a new dress, that new basketball, plus any number of holdover magic and mythic figures, all cascading all over each other in displacement and condensation. Let's just stop here and notice how differently the same dream state—the same subtle state—is being seen and experienced, according to the structure that is doing the experiencing. Except for the common, broad-range characteristics of each of those dreams, based on core characteristics of the subtle itself, the actual contents and contours of the subtle dream state are provided by the particular structure that is experiencing the dream—the Archaic in the infant, the Mythic in the seven- or eight-year-old, and the Rational in the adolescent. Of course, there are some core characteristics of the subtle that are also present, such as being a realm of nonphysical entities, however else they might appear; being experienced in a body of imagery and visions, occasionally light infused; containing various luminous and "larger-than-life" entities and figures; immediate wish-fulfillment (to wish for a thing is to immediately see it as a dream content); instant transformation (one item can transform into another instantly); most phenomena being attached to emotional states of a broad range of intensity; and of course any common biological factors, such as theta brain waves. The content is supplied as much by the structure as by the state. This is significant, in that an individual always experiences both a structure and a state together and simultaneously; thus, present experience is more accurately referred to as a structure/state event. This is why bringing an awareness of the structure-stages of Growing Up to the state-stages of Waking Up is so important. The various stages of meditation development that we previously gave, for example, would more accurately be referred to not as gross, subtle, causal-witnessing, and nondual but as, for example, mythic/gross, mythic/subtle, mythic/causal-witnessing, and mythic/nondual, or pluralistic/gross, pluralistic/subtle, pluralistic/causal-witnessing, and pluralistic/nondual. This is a much more accurate view of what the individual meditator is actually experiencing, and these differences are real and crucial. Without an understanding of what the structures bring to the picture, those structures remain completely "hidden maps," rules of experiential grammar that people follow perfectly but have no idea whatsoever that they are doing so. We go through the meditation stages being completely unconscious and unaware of the hidden maps through which we are interpreting our experiences, thus getting a very lopsided view of dharma and truth indeed. So, with that general consideration in mind, we can return to the following point.

We were discussing the common tendency in many traditions to interpret the luminous forms found characteristically (or generically) in the overall subtle (recall that this stage is Underhill's general "illumination" stage) as being distinct, real, ontological beings. But in the cases of these "ontological beings," it is at least possible, perhaps likely, that these beings are simply various luminous subtle events as interpreted by the Mythic-literal structure. These states *can* be experienced by higher structure-levels, and when they are, their interpretation less often includes actual ontological beings, and more often archetypal patterns of the Mind and Awareness itself, such as vasanas or images in the storehouse consciousness. So I suggest keeping that open as at least a possibility. (But you are, of course, free to interpret these any way you like that makes sense to you.)

The subtle, in general, is also said to be the basic realm of the overall *bardo* state, which in most Eastern and some Western traditions is the realm between death and the next rebirth. The bardo experience itself is said to occur in three phases, which actually represent directly, first, the causal Clear Light Emptiness, which appears immediately upon death; then the subtle realm proper (with both peaceful and wrathful deity forms); and finally, the intimation of the gross realm (where the reincarnating soul sees its future parents making love, and, jealous, steps in to separate them, whereupon it is instantly conceived by those individuals as its parents, and finds itself in the womb of that particular mother). A person who has, while alive, practiced techniques such as dream yoga—and learned to "lucid dream"—will also, it is said, be able to control the events of the bardo realm, since it is basically the same subtle dream state, in the same subtle body, and possessing the same subtle energy. Just as somebody who is lucid dreaming can choose almost anything he or she wants and it will almost instantly materialize in the dream, likewise someone who is proficient in dream yoga can choose where and when they will be born, what their race and sex will be, who their parents will be, and so on, simply by holding that intention in mind. It's the same process, in the same subtle body, as a lucid dream.

But keep in mind that the bardo realms are also said to be precisely what is happening to a person in each moment of his or her waking life. At the beginning of each moment—of *this* moment—we are all directly immersed in the Clear Light Void, the vast, pure, infinite, open, clear, deep Mirror Mind, or pure Emptiness, or clear I AMness. If a person recognizes this, their pure Buddha-mind, Real Self, or ultimate Godhead, then they remain in that Awakened state. If not, they will "microgenetically" move down from this ultimate causal/nondual state and into the next highest state, the pure subtle. If they recognize that state, they will remain there, living a "heavenly" life largely free from pain, suffering, and torment. If not, they will once again contract and move down, to the lowest state possible, the gross, egoic realm, and there they will live the life of a typical human—some happiness, much sorrow, some joy, great suffering—until and unless they take up a spiritual practice and rediscover the higher realms of their own being, ultimately WAKING UP to their vast, pure, deep, spacious, Nondual Awareness or Clear Light Void, thence to assist others in their own Waking Up.

The High Subtle

Where to draw the upper limit on the high subtle—and thus begin the next major state/realm, the causal—is somewhat arbitrary. According to Vedanta, this region (the high subtle) energetically supports a structure or level ("sheath") known as the *vijnanamayakosha*, which is often translated as the level of the higher mind. This means that it would cover at least all of 2nd tier (the Holistic and the Integral mind) and possibly as high as the meta-mind (the second level, after the para-mind, in 3rd tier or the Super-Integral realm). This would mean that the meta-mind would mark the end of the highest the subtle state can reach (which also means that the meta-mind is the highest in development one can go without fully objectifying—transcending and including—the subtle). But this is part of how we have defined the meta-mind, as being the highest in development one can proceed without integrating the subtle dimension in toto. In other words, the meta-mind is the structure where the subtle state becomes conjoined with it (if the subtle hasn't been previously realized).

As a bit of a historical accident, the "high subtle realm" is usually what "the subtle realm" itself is taken to mean, because when syntheses of Eastern and Western maps were first attempted, there were only so many words to go around, and so "the subtle" simply came to be identified with what is really the "high subtle." (It wasn't often applied to, for example, emotions—they were so common, and the "subtle" was often so high even though technically emotions are supported by the overall subtle body.) In fact, because of that, the "high subtle" itself was often subdivided into low and high, or early and late, dimensions—with both of those often referring to different levels of the meta-mind (even though the subtle is a state, not a structure). (This was all occurring before the Wilber-Combs Lattice was developed and before there was an understanding of the profound difference between states and structures, so they were often identified. Hopefully all of that is not too confusing.)

Integral Theory usually stays with the convention of identifying "the subtle realm" with "the high subtle"—the state, not a structure—simply because what we are interested in with these states are, more often than not, altered states, nonordinary states, transpersonal states, or spiritual states. And experiencing the energy supporting the emotional-sexual level, the mythic level, or the rational level—even though technically all of these are being supported by the same subtle body—just isn't very interesting. People are experiencing mythic and rational levels all the time; but rare indeed is a full-blown experience of the meta-mind. Thus, unless otherwise indicated, "subtle states" generally mean "high subtle states." This is certainly true enough; it just leaves out the lower and middle range of subtle states; or, more accurately, it simply counts those as being in the "gross-reflecting states," which is also certainly true enough by convention.

Notice that the overall subtle state can be prepersonal, personal, or transpersonal, because, as with states and structures in general, almost any structure can experience that state, and each structure will interpret it differently—including prepersonal, personal, and transpersonal interpretations/experiences, depending on the actual nature of the structure itself that is doing the interpreting/experiencing. A preper-

sonal structure will usually interpret/experience the subtle as prepersonal; a personal structure will usually interpret/experience it as
personal; and likewise with a transpersonal structure. These three types
of structures often coincide with the distinctions of low, middle, and
high subtle. But more importantly, this is also closely related to the
degree of development that has occurred in the structures. At birth,
when the infant is in strictly prepersonal structures, it can still have
subtle-state experiences (such as being plunged in the subtle dream
state every night). But it would be less than meaningful to say that the
infant is experiencing a transpersonal dimension in that subtle state,
simply because, as Jack Engler put it, "You have to be somebody before
you can be nobody"—that is, you have to develop an ego before you
can transcend it, and this the infant has definitely not done. All of an
infant's state experiences (gross, subtle, and causal) will thus likely be
prepersonal, because his or her structures are prepersonal (and the
structures, or "hidden maps," do the interpreting). As the child's ego
begins to develop, and as its structures begin to move into approximately Magic-Mythic (Fulcrum-3, chakra 3, conceptual mental structure) and a separate self ("person") therefore begins to emerge, the
greater the possibility that the self can then be at least temporarily transcended in subtle or causal (and possibly even nondual) peak experiences or states. Prior to that point, the infant's experience of both subtle
and causal (and nondual) states will almost always be prepersonal.
And this means that these states are not inherently prepersonal, personal, or transpersonal—an important point that I'll repeat often.

As the self-sense continues to grow and develop (from prepersonal
to personal), and its structure center of gravity moves into, for example, Rational or Pluralistic, the dream state will typically take on a
primarily personal tone and content. If you wake a person who is at
those levels—say, a typical adolescent—from a dream, where the infant's dream state consisted mostly of prepersonal physiological impulses, images of the mothering one, breasts, oral desires, and so forth,
the typical teenager's dream is about high school, peer relations, overblown sex and power, performance and test anxiety, and other primarily personal needs, elements, and desires. But because the individual
has indeed formed an ego (or has entered into a "personal" range of
development), he or she can also be open to at least the occasional
"transpersonal" experience, and regions of the high subtle and causal

(and perhaps nondual) are made to order for transpersonal interpretations, and thus those types of dream contents become more common, in additional to the typical personal contents (and the occasional regressive elements from prepersonal realms).

If you wake people whose self-sense has developed to Integral and who stand on the edge of 3rd tier and para-mind from a dream, they will often report experiencing a personal/transpersonal twilight zone: walking in nature and tending toward having feelings of oneness with it, and images of light and luminosity, or simple "brightness." Occasionally, they report the presence of various beings that seem, in some cases, "otherworldly" in origin; also sporadic, intense emotions and affects of bliss, or sex transmuting into extreme transcendental pleasure, or love of all humanity; also fairly common, flying bodily to locations all over the world; premonition dreams, which have been empirically demonstrated to be true with a much more than chance frequency; angelic beings or spirit guides (sometimes a spirit animal); oneness with all plant life, all animal life, or all of nature itself. Sometimes they report lucidly dreaming. All of these contents have a strong transpersonal component or dimension to them—again, reflecting the structure that is interpreting and experiencing them. Virtually every structure can experience every state (see fig. 3.2, the Wilber-Combs Lattice), and the resultant structure/state (and individuals are *always* experiencing both a structure and a state) will reflect the elements from both. Most of the types of dreams just mentioned become more and more common the further into 3rd tier the individual develops.

This has caused a lot of theoretical confusion, usually of the pre/trans fallacy type—that is, where some infantile states are misinterpreted as being *trans*-egoic, simply because they are *non*-egoic, whereas they are usually just *pre*-egoic. This is the essence of the "pre/trans fallacy," the confusion of "pre" and "trans" because both are "non"—for example, the confusion of prerational and transrational just because both are "nonrational" or the confusion of preverbal and transverbal because both are nonverbal. Thus, many of the "dharma bums" of the Beat generation engaged in actions and behaviors that they were convinced were evidence of transpersonal and transrational liberation, whereas they were just prepersonal and prerational whoopee. This just goes to show again that *most of the states are not inherently prepersonal, personal, or transpersonal*, unlike structures, which can definitely and clearly be determined to be prepersonal, personal, or transpersonal. The reason, again, is that states are interpreted/experienced by structures; thus, prepersonal structures will most often experience states as prepersonal; personal structures will usually experience states as personal; and transpersonal structures will usually experience states as transpersonal. There are several exceptions, of course, because as states become more and more subtle, they have a tendency to become more and more transpersonal, but the final experience of such will be significantly influenced by the particular structure itself.

Which structures are prepersonal, which personal, and which transpersonal? Generally, Archaic to Magic are *prepersonal*; *personal* begins to emerge at Magic-Mythic and runs to Integral; and 3rd tier (para-mind to supermind) are *transpersonal* (or have beginning transpersonal aspects or components).

Why isn't Integral fully transpersonal? Individuals at Integral will say things like, "The earth is a single organism with one mind," and they will feel interconnected with that "single organism" but not fully one with it, and thus they themselves are not actually transpersonal. However, at the next level, at para-mind (the beginning of 3rd tier and Super-Integral), individuals often feel a direct unity with Gaia, or Nature, a direct nature mysticism, a psychophysical mysticism, and hence have a transpersonal experience of some degree. They will certainly feel such a direct unity at the union and identity degrees of the spectrum of degrees of relationship running from communion to union to identity. If they are at the communion degree of relationship (the most common), they will feel an incredible closeness with Gaia, but no direct unity, and thus there is not yet a direct transpersonal component, though it is verging on it. The next stage—meta-mind—has a clear and definite transpersonal component of one form or another.

Thus, para-mind is the dividing line between the earlier personal levels and the higher levels, all of which, past para-mind, always have a transpersonal component. That is, these higher aspects or elements supported by the subtle are all ones that can *potentially* be experienced as transpersonal, depending in large measure on the nature of the structure experiencing them.[6] As for the dividing line between prepersonal and personal, it is, as noted, generally at Magic (Fulcrum-2, chakra 2, emotional-sexual), specifically at what Margaret Mahler called "the rapprochement subphase." Prior to that point, the infant has separated its physical body from the physical environment (at the "hatching subphase," around four months) but has not yet separated its emotional self from the emotional environment (particularly the mothering one); this happens at the "rapprochement subphase," Fulcrum-2, or the Magic mind, usually around eighteen months, a subphase which is often therefore called "the psychological birth of the infant." Prior to that is prepersonal; after that it is personal (however tentatively).[7]

The high subtle includes all of the *potentially* fully transpersonal aspects, phenomena, and events of the subtle realm (which can be "peak experienced" fairly often to some degree with personal structures—as "higher," transpersonal, transrational states or elements or events—but only fully experienced with transpersonal structures themselves; otherwise these high, potentially transpersonal subtle elements are experienced, or translated downward, into personal or prepersonal experiences). These generally transpersonal elements in the high subtle include a transegoic self often called "the soul" (which gives way to the "Witness" or "True Self" at the causal/turiya state and the overmind structure, which itself gives way to nondual Suchness at the "unity" state and supermind structure); universal, almost infinite, feelings of love, bliss, joy, clarity, and happiness, as well as divine-like rage, extended hatred, even jealousy. The high subtle also supports a large number of holistic or systemic phenomena, including imagery of entire worlds, and emotions embracing all sentient beings; intense, sometimes even painful, states of illumination, light, and luminosity; and audible illuminations. Beings, events, or forms of radiant light are common, and the ancient traditions often interpret them, we noted, as actual beings, including angels, spirits, gods and goddesses, devas, asuras, and rakshasas. (The same caveat about structures and their interpretations applies here: many of those beings are likely subtle luminous phenomena interpreted from a Mythic personal structure-level.)

To recognize the subtle is to recognize a *within* to the Kosmos, and in many cases, a within that goes beyond, as each dimension transcends and includes its predecessors. That is why, as we noted, human beings contain, literally within themselves, enfolded in their own being, every major element that has emerged since the Big Bang itself. Humans fully include and enfold in themselves quarks, subatomic particles, atoms, molecules, cells, multicellular organisms (including forms of plant biochemistry), reptilian instincts, paleomammalian emotions, mammalian cortexes, and primate neocortexes. And each and every one of those contains their own interiors, their own prehensions, their own little ray of the Divine, *as* the Divine, sparks of their own unique individuality, Divine radiance, and inherent Truth, Goodness, and Beauty. Is this not a miracle of the first magnitude?

5

The Causal, Empty Witness, and Nondual States of Consciousness

The Causal State

Involution/Efflux and Evolution/Reflux

The causal realm is one of the most difficult to define because the causal is sometimes forced to do double or even triple duty, with the definition changing each time, depending upon how many states are being included in the system—usually 3, 4, or 5. If the tradition focuses on all 5 of the major natural states found in the traditions—gross, subtle, causal, witnessing, and nondual—then the causal always means "the most subtle" of all manifestation: the first state in finite manifestation out of the creative, infinite Abyss, which contains (by whatever name) what the Greeks called "archetypes," or the primordial forms that are required for all other forms. The archetypes are the things you need to get a universe going in the first place (time, space, forms, color, and so on), and thus are the things that are the first to emerge in "involution" or "Efflux." If the tradition focuses on just 3 of those 5 states, then the upper 2 states (empty Witness and nondual Suchness) are collapsed into the causal, and then the causal is forced to include not just the narrower but technically most correct definition ("the most subtle forms") but also the purely empty Witnessing and Nondual dimensions, so "the" causal ends up including 3 states smooshed together. If only 4 states are included, then the causal usually is combined with the empty Witnessing and thus includes 2 states smooshed together; here, the emphasis is almost always on the "emptiness," "formlessness," or "dreamlessness" of the state, and its empty or unqualifiable Awareness. Worse, many traditions do all three of those things—sometimes including all 5 states, sometimes just 4, sometimes just 3, and the terminology ends up being nightmarish.

Here, we are discussing just the technically correct, narrow, single-state version of the causal, which is the first state of phenomena to emerge from Divine Emptiness, creative Nothingness, Divine Being, Spirit itself. The causal state thus contains the earliest forms in all of manifestation, the archetypes, the primal forms that all other forms will be based on.

There is something crucial to understand about these archetypes and the causal realm itself. "Archetype" is a term made quite popular by Carl Jung and his followers; many people who know nothing else about Jung know that he uses the term "archetypes." But the way Jung uses the term is not at all the way the traditions use it, so if we want to understand the traditions correctly, we need to go into this briefly. According to the traditions, the causal archetypes are the first forms to emerge in *involution*, not the first or earliest forms to emerge in *evolution* (as Jung tends to use the term). So what does this mean, and how is the tradition's use of the term so strongly different from Jung's use?

According to most of the traditions, East and West, Spirit has a dual movement with relation to the manifest world. The creation of the manifest world occurs by (to use the terminology of the Christian version of the Great Chain) Spirit going out itself, stepping down and reducing itself to a lesser version of itself called the "soul." Then the soul itself sediments, or condenses, and again steps down and contracts to create a lesser version of itself—the "mind." Then the mind likewise condenses, crystallizes, and contracts into a lesser version of itself—the living "body." Finally, the living body sediments or condenses downward into the lowest, densest, insentient, lifeless version—matter, or the physical realm (where "matter" here means, not the exteriors of all levels, but the lowest of all levels).

So all of these realms are versions of Spirit—there is Spirit-as-

Spirit, Spirit-as-soul, Spirit-as-mind, Spirit-as-body, and Spirit-as-matter. Each level is simply a reduced version of Spirit, with less consciousness, less being, less Spirit, but all being Spirit nonetheless. To use the wooden ladder analogy, Spirit is both the highest level or rung on the ladder (its transcendental dimension) and the wood out of which the entire ladder is made (its immanent dimension). This entire movement "outward" and "downward" to create a universe is called involution. Plotinus referred to it as Efflux (the superabundant "overflow" and "outpouring" of Spirit).

When this involution or Efflux first occurs, each step downward is bought at the price of unconsciousness. As Spirit steps down into soul, it forgets it is Spirit and only recognizes soul. As soul steps down into mind, it forgets it is soul and only recognizes mind. As mind steps down into body, it forgets it is mind and only sees body. And as body finally steps down into matter, it forgets it is body and only knows the material world, which then blows into existence with the Big Bang, producing a universe of *nothing but* lowest-level matter (with all the higher levels being forgotten, unconscious, and not seen or manifest but existing as unconscious *potentials* of the universe). This explosion of the Big Bang into a purely material world is exactly what happened, according to the latest scientific theories: nothing but physical, material objects blew into existence—there was as yet no life; no living bodies had yet emerged, and hence no minds or souls either (although according to Integral Theory, there were *interiors* since the 4 quadrants go all the way down, starting with simple prehension in the lowest fundamental particles). But once the material world blows into existence—the result of the overall involution/Efflux movement—then the entire process begins to reverse itself. This reverse movement of matter back to Spirit is called evolution. Plotinus referred to it as Reflux (the "return" of Spirit, to Spirit, as Spirit).

In evolution or Reflux each successively higher level emerges from, or through, the previous lower level, and thus appears as a significant leap forward, often hard to explain. Out of matter, living bodies emerged ("How did *that* happen?"). Then out of living bodies, minds emerged ("*How?*"). We are now at the point in return evolution where, according to this traditional view, a significant number of people are starting to awaken to the fact that they possess souls, or—by whatever name—a spiritual component that goes quite beyond the mental ego. And that's speaking collectively. Individually, anybody can take up meditation or contemplation and successively awaken to all of these higher levels—not just soul, but all the way to Spirit—that were forgotten in the prior involutionary process but continue to exist in the higher unconscious. These levels are realms awaiting our own recognition, remembrance, or awareness, and hence our own WAKING UP (to switch to more Eastern terms, the process of evolution is not matter to body to mind to soul to Spirit but the essentially similar gross to subtle to causal to witnessing to nondual unity).

Now, as I was saying, the causal archetypes are the first forms that occur during involution, not evolution. The first forms in evolution—that is, the forms that came into existence with the beginning of the Big Bang—were, according to various physics theories, strings, quarks, or some other fundamental particles or phenomena. According to the traditions, those subatomic forms would be the *last* forms that were sedimented during the involutionary process, and they are based ultimately on the causal archetypes (which gave rise to soul forms, then mind forms, then body forms, and finally the matter forms of the Big Bang). Therefore, as the last forms in involution, they are the *first* forms to emerge in the reverse process of evolution or Reflux. Whatever you might think of this theory of involution/evolution, or Efflux/Reflux, it certainly solves the problems of where the Big Bang itself came from, and how higher forms manage to emerge from lower forms, a perpetual puzzle to philosophers and scientists alike. "You can't get the higher from the lower" is a common refrain you hear when philosophers and scientists discuss this issue, but this theory takes care of that problem: the higher emerges "out of" or "through" the lower in evolution because it was put there in involution, which is the creation of "the lower from the higher," which involves no theoretical problems at all.

Integral Theory takes the idea of involution/evolution and reduces to a minimum the number of forms said to be created during involution (in a metaphysical realm existing prior to the Big Bang) and leaves more of their form and content to being created during evolution (after the Big Bang and in *this* realm). This reduces the amount of "metaphysics" in these theories—"metaphysics" meaning, in this case, the postulating of eternal, pregiven forms and patterns created in the mind of God or Spirit, which then simply show up at the appropriate time in evolution, a notion that's just impossible to prove with any sort of evidence acceptable to modernity or postmodernity. Thus, Integral Theory postulates a bare minimum of forms and events that were created during involution and sees most forms instead as produced by the forces and processes of evolution itself, which are open to evidence and scrutiny. This "postmetaphysical minimalism" is aided by the fact that many of the forms previously thought of as "metaphysical" or "supernatural" can be demonstrated by more earthly methodologies—from structuralism to hermeneutics to ethnomethodology to systems theory to modern physics, among others. For example, the "levels of mind" thought to be metaphysical by the traditions can be demonstrated by developmental structuralism, which has discovered many of the structure-levels in many developmental lines or multiple intelligences. We don't need metaphysical "proofs" or notions to identify these numerous levels and lines; straightforward developmental structuralism and basic research based on *actual evidence* will do the job nicely—with the added benefit that this is a methodology accepted by most schools of modernity and postmodernity, whereas none of them accept metaphysics of the "eternal-idea-in-the-mind-of-God" variety. Hence, an Integral Methodological Pluralism gives rise to an Integral Post-Metaphysics. A few "metaphysical" items are still required, but as we said, we try to keep these "involutionary givens" to a minimum—a metaphysical minimalism.

Most of the "metaphysical" forms of the traditionalist theory of involution/evolution are extremely strict—involution created *everything* on every level of existence: physical particles; all forms of cells, and all forms of plant life, and all forms of animal life, with all their physiological processes; all forms of human culture, and all of its products, including all types of technologies and technological products, medicines, types of architecture, forms of law, types of poetry; all the "beings" in all the realms (gods, goddesses, asuras, devas, elemental spirits); all the books ever written; all the languages ever produced; every form of mathematics and logic; and so on and so on and so on. ALL of those were produced during involution and hidden in the higher unconscious, and evolution is nothing but an unfolding of those already created forms that are lying in our unconscious, or in Spirit, and awaiting their turn to emerge. In this view, evolution is just a rewinding of the involutionary videotape—nothing comes out in evolution that wasn't put in there by and during involution. But not only more modern forms of science but higher integral forms of thinking themselves have suggested that evolution is a much more creative process than previously pictured by the traditions, and that much of what was thought to have been created by involution is actually created by and during evolution. We only need original causal archetypes for the fundamental forms and processes that are necessary to get a universe going in the first place—things like space, time, and basic form, and instead of a specific number and types of levels of being, just one large force stretching from matter to Spirit, a force called "Eros" and responsible for the pull of the reverse trip from matter to Spirit. Eros is a self-organizing force responsible for the ceaseless drive to higher and higher wholes, which are created by evolution itself, not involution. This process is rather like what happens when one lets go of a rubber band with a rock on one end that has been stretched to its limits. The rock will, through an unpredictable swinging motion, slowly return to its original position. So too, the forms that emerge through evolution will slowly return, through all the grades of separation to Spirit itself, with the actual details of these many unpredictable swings determined by the numerous forms, processes, and patterns created by the return swings, by evolution itself, which Erich Jantsch defined as "self-organization through self-transcendence," an excellent definition. We don't *need* involution to create all these forms; evolution can do it itself—*and* this theory is one that can be accepted by modernity and postmodernity.

This Eros, or evolutionary drive, when combined with fundamental forms like the 4 quadrants, the form of holons, and space-time itself, creates a "transcend-and-include" movement to ever-higher, ever-more conscious, ever-more complex holonic forms—interior and exterior, individual and collective—from matter through life through mind through soul to Spirit itself. The original force in the stretching of the rubber band (an "involutionary given") will provide all the force required to create the different characteristics (forms on all the different levels) of each swing of the returning rock.

This explanation also allows us to account for the different forms that many otherwise similar phenomena take in different cultures and different individuals. Take something like angels, to use a traditional example. Luminous beings of light, sometimes with two wings, are common in the mystical literature of the West. But in not one single Western mystical text can you find the existence of a luminous being with ten thousand arms. Yet in Tibet and other Eastern countries, this is an extremely common icon—the being with ten thousand arms is identified as Avalokiteshvara, the bodhisattva of compassion (of which the Dalai Lama is said to be an incarnation). Both angels and Avalokiteshvara are high-subtle phenomena (as are many other luminous beings of intense light). What's real in each is the subtle dimension, which would have been created in one of the swings of the rock on its Refluxing, evolutionary return. But different cultures—possessing different surface features in all 4 quadrants—evolve slightly differing forms of the same basic pattern (different minor variations on the return path of the rock at the same altitude of return), which is something that evolution allows (due to different variations in the 4 quadrants affecting the actual path of the rock's return in different areas) but involution generally doesn't, since involution is traditionally thought to be one given sequence, the same wherever it appears in all cultures.

Thus you don't need to postulate such pregiven, eternally fixed, metaphysical elements anyway—whatever the phenomena are, evolution could have produced them just as easily as involution, but without all the metaphysical ontologies and otherwise unprovable assumptions.[1]

But what did exist in the unconscious of the Kosmos by the time the Big Bang blew into existence were all of the truly fundamental causal archetypes—all the fundamental patterns, forms, and processes necessary to get any sort of universe started in the first place. These I refer to as "involutionary givens"—that is, those items that were truly given or created by involution, and therefore showed up with the material universe, when it first showed up (that is, with the Big Bang), with a few elements and forms awaiting emergence down the line. On this view, most phenomena are produced by evolutionary forces obeying, or following, the relatively few original involutionary givens. Even conventional physicists acknowledge that some items had to be in place already before, or at least concomitant with, the Big Bang in order for the physicists themselves to be able to know about the Big Bang, such as a physical universe patterned in ways that could be represented by mathematics. That is, some sort of Logos (in this case, mathematics) was an involutionary given, because the existence of the Big Bang depends on a series of intricate mathematical equations and formulas, and these had to have been in place and working from the start or physicists wouldn't have even be able to postulate a Big Bang at all; that postulate depends on an already functioning mathematics to determine any of the universe's characteristics at all, including all the equations that tell us what happened in the first nanoseconds of the universe's coming into being. None of that would be possible without an already functioning mathematics. No, some form of Logos is an involutionary given, and thus it showed up with the Big Bang. However, it's not necessary to postulate as already existing in the involutionary unconscious all the items that mathematics would be applied to. Those would emerge as evolution itself brought them into existence. Thus, an Integral Post-Metaphysics drops all those items from involution but keeps a minimal Logos.

So the high causal contains the fewest and most condensed fundamental forms or phenomena that first emerged when the universe was manifesting out of Emptiness, or Spirit, in its descending, involving, Effluxing movement—where Spirit becomes *involved* in the coming-into-being material universe. The low causal, which I will summarize momentarily, contains the slightly less condensed, and more numerous, forms that emerge from the high-causal forms, as involution itself starts to pick up steam. And keep in mind the basic, nonmetaphysical definition of the causal realm itself: when you are in a pure, formless, unmanifest state of meditative absorption (the supracausal Empty Consciousness, or turiya) and you start to come out of it, *the very first forms you see, feel, and hear are the causal archetypes.* There are as many variations on these forms as there are individuals, but they all share certain deep-feature characteristics; although, again, the precise nature of the experience of these forms will depend upon the actual structure of consciousness that is doing the experiencing. A mythic experience of the causal is considerably different than an integral experience of it.

Now, how did Jung conceive of the "archetypes"? He was also looking for primordial forms that were, in a sense, the first forms to be produced for humans and thus forms upon which all subsequent forms would rest. But he was looking for early forms in the sequence of evolution, or Reflux, not the early forms in the sequence of involution, or Efflux. Although Jung tended to wobble somewhat in his definitions (because of certain inadequacies in each), he always returned to the

essential idea that fundamental forms found in the world's great mythologies were the fundamental forms, or archetypes, that the psyche
had inherited and that tended to be the most fundamental forms in the
human mind through all subsequent evolution. (At other times, he
more widely defined archetypes as "forms devoid of content," thus
attempting to handle criticism that his archetypes weren't really that
universal, since some cultures had them and others didn't. But he always, when he let his mind run free, was struck by the near-universal
forms found in most of the world's great mythologies, and so they
came front and center as his "archetypes.")

So Jung was primarily trying to trace some of the earliest and most
influential of forms in the mind that emerged and evolved as humans
continued their collective growth, development, and evolution. As we
might expect from what we've seen about the basic universal levels of
development, these early forms would indeed be magic and/or mythic.
Recall that the mythic-membership level has, as a basic rung, the "rule/
role" mind, the mind that can create concrete rules (such as addition,
subtraction, and multiplication) and that because it can take a 2nd-
person perspective, it can "take the role of other," thus creating numerous and varied roles that members of society can adopt. Jungian
archetypes often include many of these very earliest roles—things like
the warrior, the king, the queen, the prince and princess, the jokester,
the wise old man or woman, the trickster, and so on. Thus, if you pick
up a book such as Jean Shinoda Bolen's *Goddesses in Everywoman*,
based on Jung's notions, you will find a list of almost a dozen roles that
each woman is said to potentially have within her, and Bolen suggests
that a woman can become more developed and fulfilled if she gets in
touch with these roles in herself. Notice that these roles are all largely
prerational (literally, the mythic-role stage preceding the rational
stage); they are certainly not transpersonal or transrational (that is,
they are not real goddesses, or real transpersonal Spirit dimensions)
but simply some of the earliest, and therefore most fundamental (if less
significant) roles that humans learned to play. Getting in touch with
them can help us get in touch with our roots (but not our leaves, or
transpersonal branches).

The tendency among Jungians is to confuse *collective* with *transpersonal* or directly *spiritual*. But there are collective prepersonal, collective personal, and collective transpersonal elements. The fact that

something is collective does not necessarily mean that it is transpersonal collective. We all inherit ten toes, but if I experience my toes, I am not usually having a mystical transpersonal experience. Jean Bolen's archetypes, or "goddesses," are simple, early, prerational roles such as nurturer, lover, mother, warrioress, queenly ruler, and so on. The tradition's archetypes lie precisely at the complete opposite end of the spectrum, the earliest forms upon which all subsequent forms in manifestation depend, not some of the earliest and most fundamental forms that humans experienced in their evolution or Reflux.

The High Causal

First I'll give my view of the high causal, then some of the ancient traditions' interpretations. The high causal contains the very first, absolutely fundamental forms, patterns, and processes necessary for the existence of this particular universe (of the many potentially possible universes). These include the potential for space and time itself; the potential forms of color (Whitehead's "eternal objects"); the potential form of holons (which are the constituents of every structure and state of existence); the potential form of the 4 quadrants (the potential form of the inside and outside, or subject and object, and the potential form of the individual and collective, or singular and plural—the four primary *perspectives*, perhaps the most fundamental of all fundamental archetypes). The high causal also includes the beginning of the stretching of the "rubber band" of existence, which creates the morphogenetic gradient of the manifest Kosmos that tilts the Kosmos toward greater and greater being, consciousness, complexity, beauty, morality, and aesthetics, among others, in every realm and domain of the Kosmos. This "stretching" powers the drive of evolution to return to Spirit, and is fitly called "Eros."

This high causal is often experienced as a kaleidoscopic display of space-time geometric-like patterns emerging from a point of intense white light and cascading over each other, endlessly, timelessly. The experience is often accompanied with universal-Kosmic emotional affects, such as an almost infinite love, joy/bliss, compassion, and feelings of timelessness, spacelessness, and an utter inclusiveness or Wholeness. Audible illuminations are also possible, or the most subtle sounds imaginable, all taking on various colors and shapes, and massively love satisfying, as if the soul were drenched in chocolate.

The ancient traditions tended to see the high causal as the very most subtle (that is, causal) form, or as a potential for that form, often a trinity of various sorts of high gods and goddesses, or qualities, issuing forth from the Godhead, or Empty Consciousness as Such. One version of this, of course, is the trinity of Father/Mother, Son/Daughter, and Holy Spirit of contemplative Christianity. Hinduism (in some ways similar to Kashmir Shaivism and Vajrayana Buddhism) sees a holy trinity emerging out of the first potential Godhead Ishwara containing, in one version, the male/female deities of Brahma/Saraswati (a creative force), Vishnu/Lakshmi (a sustaining force), and Shiva/Kali (a creatively destroying force). These deities tend to be viewed as "forms of the formless," since the high causal is sometimes viewed, not directly as the first forms of manifestation, but as the potential for these forms—the forms as they are coming to be, not as they are fully formed (which happens in the low causal). When divine qualities are referred to here, they tend to be things like Being-Consciousness-Bliss, or Love-Truth-Beauty-Goodness.

Integral Theory sees this trinity/quaternity as the form (or potential form) of the "Big Three" (or the 4 quadrants, with the two outer quadrants—"it" and "its"—treated as one major "it-ness"). Thus, the Father/Mother is the Divine Thou (or 2nd person); Christ (the Son/Daughter) is the divine "I-I," or radically highest Self (1st person); and the Holy Spirit is the transformative power or energy ("it" or 3rd person) that connects the individual self with the ultimate Divine, and is the "substance" or "matter" (Prakriti or Mahamaya) of the entire universe. In Buddhism, this trinity is the "Trikaya"—the three bodies of gross, subtle, and very subtle (causal)—which in this context also means the ultimate divine Emptiness of the Dharmakaya, the historical individual form of the Nirmanakaya (the historical Gautama Buddha), and the transformation body connecting the two in Enlightenment (the Sambhogakaya, or "transformational body"). Integral Theory in general sees the "beings" or "Lords" as versions of the quadrants, which are the fundamental forms, or primordial perspectives, of I, you/we, and it. If their potential form is here in the high causal, their first fully manifest form is in the low causal. (Spirit in the 2nd person is a reality of the Lower Left quadrant; it is a "person" in the sense that a person is "being plus intelligence," and the universe certainly has that; it is important to clear out any of the lower structure-levels' interpretations of this "person" dimension, particularly the Mythic-literal, which sees it as the "gray-haired gentleman sitting on a throne in the sky"—which is entirely inappropriate unless you are actually at that stage in your own development, which occurs in today's world, around age seven.)

In the traditions, this dimension is often said to include an "archetypal universe," or the potential forms of *all* the lower forms in the universe that will be formed in later stages of involution. This is one of the areas that Integral Post-Metaphysics is likely to reduce dramatically in scope, since it believes most of these forms will be produced by evolution, not involution. In general, Integral Theory interprets most (though not all) of the "beings," "gods," and "goddesses" given by the traditions as fundamental involutionary givens, or primal causal archetypes, that have been interpreted as beings by the Mythic-literal structure of consciousness, but are actually primordial forms or perspectives (all 8 of them—the 4 quadrants each viewed from within and from without, giving 8 primordial perspectives or "zones"), as well as morphogenetic fields and forces, primal higher qualities of Kosmic reach (creativity, consciousness, love), or some aspect of the 20 tenets (which I will discuss in a moment).

I have often referred to the high causal as "final God" or "final Spirit," because it is the highest actual, beginning manifest form of Spirit, or God, or ultimate Reality. All of the other various archetypes originate from, and return to, this dimensionless, spaceless, timeless singularity, a point of Clear Light from which all other forms, colors, patterns, and processes emerge, first in their potential, congealing form (in the high causal), then in their first, actual, manifest forms (the low causal). The Clear White Light itself emerges from and as pure Emptiness, or pure Godhead of the supracausal Empty domain.

The Low Causal

The low causal contains, in addition to the actual manifest versions of all of the just-mentioned potential archetypes, several new archetypes, which are "lesser" in being, but not in importance. These include what I have called elsewhere the "20 tenets," which are some of the most basic and fundamental patterns we find in this particular universe. These patterns include the four drives of all holons: (1) to be an individual whole—a "whole drive," autonomy, or agency; (2) to be part of a whole—a "part drive," a "relationship drive," communion; (3) to reach down and embrace, or integrate, its various subholons—"Agape" (love of the higher for the lower); and (4) to reach up and become a subholon in an even greater superholon—"Eros" (love of the lower for the higher). The fact that holons, with their perspectives, four drives, and 8 zones, are archetypal in nature means that such forms will be fundamental to all the forms and networks found in returning/Refluxing evolution. This is part of the consciousness/being (the union of epistemology and ontology) that is given from the start, along with Logos and Eros, in this Kosmos.

The *Lankavatara Sutra*, as mentioned earlier, has a very sophisticated, and still quite useful, notion of a collective storehouse consciousness and a "nonmetaphysical" version of how it arises. The storehouse consciousness is not a storehouse of metaphysically unchanging ideas in the mind of an unchanging God but instead contains a memory trace of every thought, feeling, deed, and action of every human since the very beginning, and in some versions, of every sentient being (which would include strings, quarks, atoms, and molecules, because the 4 quadrants go "all the way down," which means that even these earliest individual holons have interiors or "prehensions"). These collective traces are called *vasanas*, and they amount to the substance of all of the Kosmic habits or Kosmic grooves throughout the universe. Here, in the low causal, is where all these Kosmic habits and morphogenetic fields are stored, and they form the basis of all of the structures and states found in all quadrants in all beings throughout the Kosmos. The nice thing about the *Lankavatara Sutra*'s version of this collective storehouse is that the forms in it—the vasanas (its archetypes)—are the products of evolution, not involution. They are the products of actual history, not eternal forms that are unchanging ideas in the mind of God, and thus their actual pattern and content depend upon real history, not eternal unchanging ideas. (If these archetypes derived wholly from everlastingly unchanging forms, then why can't we find any of the modern and postmodern ideas in the premodern texts? These patterns are evolved habits, not unchanging laws that are the product of involution.)

The 4 quadrants start to take on actual forms here in the low causal, after beginning to congeal in the high causal. For the traditions, this often means that each of the quadrants—I, we, and it/its—takes on an actual being, or deity. Thus, the Upper Left, or "I," becomes Purusha, Mahatman, or Christ consciousness; the Lower Left, or Great Thou, becomes the existing manifest Lord, or manifest Ishwara (Brahma/Vishnu/Shiva), Jehovah, or Allah; and the it/its realm of objective exteriors ("the physical") is Mahamaya (the creative capacity of the Divine) and Prakriti (the actual material stuff—or "exteriors"—of the manifest universe).

Along with all the potential and actual archetypes, the 20 tenets, actual forms in the quadrants, and the beginning traces in the storehouse consciousness, a genuinely manifest universe is coming to be, here in the low causal. At the same time, during involution, these archetypes are rendered "unconscious" and impart their influence through unseen "downward causation" that is interpreted differently at each structure (the creative tetra-enaction and interpretive cocreation of each phenomenon). Looked at from a 3rd-person perspective, we are starting to see a type of "Indra's Net," a multidimensional network of "jewels" (holons), each one reflected in all the others, an infinitely interconnected network of a Kosmos, with each holon interconnected, one way or another, with each and every other holon. This interconnection doesn't have to occur, and in fact, doesn't occur, in a one-to-one fashion but more often in a holarchical or nested hierarchical fashion. In the manifest world, for example, atoms, molecules, cells, and organisms are interconnected but not in fully equal ways. In all cases, *all of the lower is in the higher, but not all of the higher is in the lower*. Thus, all of a molecule is in a cell, but not all of the cell is in a molecule; all of an atom is in a molecule, but not all of a molecule is in an atom; all of Magic is in Integral, but not all of Integral is in Magic. Each higher or senior dimension "transcends and includes" its junior, and that tenet ("transcend and include," which is the dynamic of evolution and Eros) is one of the 20 tenets.

The Supracausal Empty Witness or Consciousness as Such

The 4th major state, "turiya," which literally is Sanskrit for "fourth," meaning the 4th major state of consciousness after the first three—gross, subtle, and causal—namely, that of Empty Witnessing, is viewed in several different ways by the traditions, depending largely on how strictly they take "Emptiness," "Shunyata," "Ayin," or the Creative Plenum/Void. In the strictest sense—taken by, for example, Nagarjuna in the Second Turning—absolutely nothing whatsoever can be said about this state of Emptiness (including that). The "four inexpressibles" apply to every quality imaginable: ultimate Reality is not Being nor not-Being, nor both nor neither. It is not Self, nor not-Self, nor both nor neither. It is not God nor not-God, nor both nor neither. It is not implicate nor explicate, nor both nor neither. It is not infinite nor finite, nor both nor neither. It is not a timeless Now nor a temporal everlastingness, nor both nor neither. And so on forever!

The reason this strict stance is taken is that these systems want to make absolutely sure that one's awareness and realization of Spirit is ultimate, immediate, direct, unbiased, unfiltered, uncaused, and not-two or nondual (and thus they would deny all of those qualities as well). Clearly, we can talk only metaphorically here, and the reason— put metaphorically!—is that any concept that we can form makes sense only in terms of its opposite, and yet Reality has no opposite, and thus is radically unqualifiable (beyond all thoughts, concepts, feelings, notions, ideas, qualities, or characteristics). But the fact that it cannot be conceptualized doesn't mean it can't be directly realized or recognized. It's just that it requires, not the typical mode of knowing (which is called *vikalpa* or *vijnana*, where the *vi* in both cases means "dualistic knowing," or knowing via concepts that generate dualistic opposites), but rather a contemplative mode of nondual knowing (referred to as *jnana* or *prajna*—the *jna* found in both words is, in English, "kno," as in "knowledge," or "gno," as in "gnosis," which is how nondual mystical awareness is often known in the West).

In order to realize jnana, prajna, or gnosis, the mind has to be completely cleared of any and all obstructing concepts. And so this "dialectic" ("it neither is nor is not, nor is both nor neither") is used to clear the mind of any and all concepts with which one might be trying to grasp Spirit or ultimate Reality. That clearing, generally combined with meditative practice, will open awareness to a pure, direct, immediate, unbiased, unfiltered awareness, which brings a recognition of ultimate Reality itself, or the world cleared of concepts, thoughts, and feelings and instead seen immediately in its Thusness, Suchness, or Isness—just exactly as it is, now, without judgment, condemnation, identification, or grasping. Just the pure immediate THUSNESS of this and every moment. "Thusness" (*Tathata* in Sanskrit) is taken as synonymous with "Shunyata," or Emptiness; the Thusness of this moment is the Emptiness, or Transparency, of this moment.

The capacity of the mind that can do this (and, for the moment, I'll continue to speak metaphorically, meaning that these words cannot be understood merely by reading them or thinking about them but only by a direct realization of their authentic meaning via jnana, or gnosis, usually invoked by meditation) is referred to as "the witnessing mind," or "pure, clear, naked awareness," or "the observing mind," or "consciousness itself without an object," or "choiceless awareness," or "the mirror mind," or "the unqualifiable witness"—"unqualifiable" meaning "Empty," or ultimately devoid of any characterization at all (including that one). Therefore some meditation systems, such as the Third Turning Yogachara, will, at least metaphorically, identify Emptiness and Witnessing Awareness, or Emptiness and pure Consciousness (Wisdom Mind), or Emptiness and pure ordinary mirror mind (as when Zen says, "The ordinary mind, just that is the Tao").

So what is this "ordinary mind"? Take this, for example. Suppose I ask you, "How do you feel right now from the *physical* point of view?" You think about that, and arrive at various answers. Then suppose I ask, "How do you feel right now from the *emotional* point of view?" and you think about that and also come up with a few responses. Then I ask, "How do you feel from the *mental* point of view?" and again you mull it over and come up with some answers.

Now what if I ask, "How do you feel right now from *all* of those points of view at once?"

Most likely your mind will become utterly still and quiet for several seconds. All interior mental chatter stops. There is just a lucid, still, silent, open awareness, with no real content at all. That's the ordinary mirror mind or the ultimate conceptless Witness. The same type of state will often happen if somebody jumps out and scares you. He or she goes "Boo!" and for a few seconds, your mind goes crystal clear and electrically still, becoming quiet and unmoved—just a vast ocean of radiantly unmoved still awareness, and then your heart starts pounding, you start breathing hard, and you say, "You nearly scared me to death!" But before that, in those few radiantly silent and electrically clear moments, you were directly in touch with jnana, with prajna, with gnosis, with the ultimate Witness, the pure Observer. And all of the great meditative traditions maintain that *each and every moment* your mind actually starts out that way—fully and nakedly present, focused on the timeless Now, being fully present in the Present. And *then* you start thinking, analyzing, judging, condemning, grasping, feeling, and separating—at once you exist on this side of your face, looking at the world "out there" as it smashes into you and generally begins to make your life intolerable, full of anxiety, suffering, despair, torment, tears, and terror. Identified with this small, finite, separate self or ego, we have forgotten our true, clear, vast, open, deep, empty, and pure Self, the pure Witness, the pure infinite Observer. That is the case of mistaken identity we discussed earlier, and that is the dismal state of affairs that Enlightenment or Awakening is meant to reverse. With Awakening, we are no longer *involved* in and as this world; we have *evolved* from and through it; we are in the world but not of it; we transcend and include it.

And all of that rests, most squarely and fundamentally, on this first step where we dis-identify with the ego, the self-contraction, the separate-self sense, and recognize and re-identify with our True Self, Original Face, Christ consciousness, Buddha-mind, pure Witness. There are higher states yet to come (such as Nonduality itself), but it all starts right here, right now, by resting in that which is looking at this page, and not with something in you that you can look at (like the separate-self sense or ego). Resting, that is, in the pure, silent, observing Witness, or turiya.

So let's do it. Right now, simply become aware of yourself, become aware of whatever it is that you think or feel is your genuine self. Where is it? What is this self feeling right now? Where is it located? (Many people think of it as between and slightly behind the eyes.) What job does it have, what relationship is it in, how old is it? Simply notice this self of yours, be aware of it, look at it, feel it, think about it. You might describe it thus: "I am this old, I'm this tall, I weigh this much, I work at this job, I am in a relationship with so-and-so, I have this degree, I belong to these clubs, I like this type of music, I enjoy these movies, I like working on the computer, I belong to these social networks, my dream job is such-and-such, I have these friends," and so on.

But notice that there are actually *two* selves involved here. First, there is the self that you just described, the one that you are looking at, feeling, and thinking about—I am this person, I am this tall, I weigh this much, I'm this old, and so on. But second, there is the self, or Self, that is doing the looking, that is actually being aware of all this—the actual Looker, the true Seer, the Observing Self, the Witness, which is seeing your objective self, or noticing it, or being aware of it. In short, be aware of that Self that is being aware of your self. Ramana Maharshi called this the "I-I," because it is the big "I" that is aware of the small "I." So, again, notice that when you look at yourself, there are at least two selves involved: the one you are looking at, and the one that is doing the Looking. There is the observed self, and there is the Observing Self. There is the witnessed self, and there is the Witness itself. Simply be aware of them both. One is an object, and one is a subject—or more accurately, one is an object (and sometimes a subject), and one is an Absolute Subjectivity (as Zen master Shibayama called it) that can never be an object or a subject, but is aware of both.

Notice that when you are aware of this pure subjective Witness, you aren't seeing anything in particular. If you see anything, that's just another object (or another subject, which, if you look at it, you'll notice is also really just another object—because you're looking at it!). So as you rest as this true Subject, or true Self, or pure Witness, notice that you don't see anything in particular. All you notice is a sense of Freedom, a sense of Release, a sense of Vastness, of Depth, of Timeless Expanse, and of deep clear Transparency. In that moment, you are no longer identified with the conceptual ego, the self-contraction, the painful separate self, the little seen self, but rather are resting in the infinite field of unqualifiable Openness, Spaciousness, Vastness, and Emptiness that is your own truest, deepest, most Real Self. There is no inside and no outside here, just the present now as it arises, moment to moment to moment. There is just an open clearing, a space, a spaciousness, in which everything is arising, timeless Present to timeless Present. There is no boundary to this still, quiet, radiant, luminous Awareness, just the clear, deep Isness of each and every moment as it arises, stays a bit, and passes, or as it comes and goes.

But what does not come or go is your own pure Witness, or True Seer, or unmovable Real Self. That center of pure, imperturbable, unwavering I AMness has never come and will never go, but is simply always already the case. You can never remember a time that you weren't I AM (seriously, try to remember a time when there was not an I AMness present). "Before Abraham was, I AM." "Tell them, I AM has sent you." There is one and the same I AMness in each and every sentient being in the entire Kosmos. What you most deeply are, and what I AM as well, is looking out of the eyes of each and every being in the entire world: every ant, deer, lion, Mexican, German, Canadian, Russian, Iranian, Israeli, all one and the same I AMness, one Spirit, one Self. As Erwin Schrödinger, cofounder of modern quantum mechanics, put it, "Consciousness is a singular of which the plural is unknown."[2]

It is *you* who were here when the Big Bang occurred. It is *you* who were present as atoms came together into the first molecules. It is *you* who watched as molecules became the first seeing cells in the first complex organisms. You were the one who saw organic molecules first turn the sun's rays into food, and you witnessed the first great forests as they rose and populated the earth. It was you who watched the chain of animals arise and arise and arise, becoming more and more complex, more and more whole, in their forms and functions. It was you who first came down from the trees and populated the plains of Africa, and you who built the first world empires and watched humans fight for their control. It was you who watched Christ lose his blood on the cross, Buddha awaken to his own mind under the Bodhi tree, Lao Tzu realize the oneness of the world driven by the Tao, and it was you who whispered into Confucius's ear what the word "humanness" meant. You spilled your blood in both world wars, saw your families shed tears at your illusory death, reawakened as you rocketed to the moon, saw the cultural revolution of the sixties, and realized the one that is now upon us all. You, and only *You* (your own deepest I AMness, just as it feels right now), were not just the Witness but the Author of all of that.

And yet now, as Philosophia whispered to Boethius in his distress, "You have forgotten who you are." So let that forgetfulness, that involutionary amnesia, end right here, right now. Rest in the Self that is aware of the self, and let your identity likewise expand from the skin-encapsulated ego to the ends of the Kosmos itself, all by resting in the Witness, the pure Observer, the true Seer, pure naked Awareness itself. Have done with this painful self-contraction—let it come and go as it pleases, giving it no heed, merely Witnessing it as it comes and goes like everything else, resting instead in the mirror mind of an I AMness that itself neither comes nor goes, but is and only is right now, right here, timeless and spaceless, open and empty, free and full.

It is not a question of how to bring this I AMness into being. The question is whether you have ever really been without it. You probably can't remember what you were doing last month, but one thing is certain—this same I AMness was there. You probably can't remember what you were doing last year—but I AMness was there. You can't consciously remember what you were doing ten years ago, or one hundred years ago, or a thousand years ago, or a millions years ago, or before the Big Bang—but this timeless I AMness ever was and forever is, simply because it is *timeless* Presence.

Zen says, "Show me your Original Face, the Face you had *before your parents were born*." *Before your parents were born?* Zen means that very seriously. There is a real, literal, definite answer to that question—before your parents were born, I AM. And not because I AMness is everlasting in time, but because it doesn't enter the stream of time at all—you Witness time go by, but the Witness itself is timeless. Feel the Witness right now; it doesn't move at all! It lives only in the timeless Now; the present is the only thing that has no end—and likewise no beginning—and thus is Unborn, Undying, Unmade, Uncreated, Unbounded, Unlimited. This timeless Now, this timeless Present moment, is the true meaning of eternity. As Wittgenstein said, "If we take eternity to mean not infinite temporal duration but timelessness, then eternal life belongs to those who live in the present."[3]

The Witness lives only in the timeless Present, the pure Now moment. Think of a past event: all you are really aware of is the present memory of it, experienced in the Now; when that event actually occurred, it was a Now. Think of a future event: all you are really aware of is the present thought of that, experienced in the Now; when it actually happens, it will be a Now. ALL you are actually ever aware of is this timeless Now.

And thus, "Before Abraham was, I AM." Literally! Before my parents were born, I AM. Before the universe was born, I AM. I AMness is the only constant in your entire life—and before it, and after it, an always already Isness, Thusness, I AMness, moment to moment, just as it is, *exactly* as it is, right here, right now. The ever-present, simple feeling of being *you*, right now, just as it is, and *before you are anything else*, not I AM this tall, not I AM this old, not I AM in this relationship, not I AM a fan of movies, but the simple immediate feeling of Being, the simple feeling of I AMness before it is any of those specific things—just *this*, nothing more.

Thus, I AM says, "I see objects—mountains, trees, cars, buildings—but I am not those objects; I have sensations, but I am not those sensations. I have feelings, but I am not those feelings. I have thoughts, but I am not those thoughts." Even, "I have a body, but I am not that body. I have a mind, but I am not that mind. I have a soul, but I am not that soul." The Witness has no fear; it is the Witness of fear. The Witness is not the victim of life; it is the Witness of life. Being the Witness of sensations, it is radically Free of sensations. Being the Witness of feelings, it is radically Free of feelings. Being the Witness of thoughts, it is radically Free of thoughts. Being the Witness of suffering, it is radically Free of suffering. The pure *Emptiness* of Witnessing Awareness is the radical *Freedom* of Witnessing Awareness.

"Let this consciousness be in you that was in Christ Jesus, that we all may be one." But, you see, that is the *only* consciousness you have *always* had ("consciousness is a singular of which the plural is unknown"), the only consciousness you have always *already* had. The simple feeling of Being, the simple feeling of *you*, is 100 percent of the Enlightened mind—just *this*, nothing more.

Which brings us to the Nondual state.

The Nondual State

Describing the Nondual is also somewhat difficult, for the same reasons that describing Emptiness is. One of the simplest statements about Nonduality is that it is the union of Emptiness and Form (as the *Heart Sutra* famously put it, "That which is Emptiness is not other than Form, that which is Form is not other than Emptiness"), but then exactly what that union is depends upon the strictness of your stance toward Emptiness, which is half of the formula, and that can run the gamut from very strict to much looser and metaphorical. And, just as important, it depends upon exactly what Form you now have, because each stage or level-rung of development produces a different Form, a different hidden map with which you will interpret and experience the world of Form altogether. And while Emptiness is timeless and unchanging, the world of Form most definitely *evolves*, and thus Enlightenment, as the union of Emptiness and Form, also evolves in some important ways . . .

The Experience of Nonduality

Let's first look at what is involved with Nonduality by way of some simple experiential exercises. Get in the state of the clear Witness ("I have sensations, but I am not those sensations; I have feelings, but I am not those feelings; I have thoughts, but I am not those thoughts"—I am the clear, pure Witness of all of those), and then Witness, say, a table sitting in front of you (or a mountain, a building, a chair, a glass, any object, but an object that stands out easily). Get a clear sense of the difference between the pure Witness and the object that is now being witnessed, an object that you are not. Get a sense of the Witness as the pure Looker, or Seer, of—for example, the table. Now let that sense of there being a Looker or Seer completely dissolve, leaving only the sensation of the table arising in awareness—not in your awareness, just arising in awareness, of itself-so. The table is self-seeing, self-existing, self-arising. There is only a table arising, and the awareness of that table is coming with the table itself. There are no subjects and no objects anywhere here, just the table arising—and you are *one* with that. What you call the "table" and what you feel as your Awareness of it are *one and the same feeling*. Feel what you call your self, your Looker, the Watcher, and notice that the table is arising exactly where that feeling is!

Now use Douglas Harding's simple exercise.[4] Notice that the table is right where you thought your head was—the table is resting on your shoulders, right where your head used to be. Notice the same for the rest of the world around you—simply see it all arising on your shoulders, right where your head used to be. There is no head; there is no subject looking at all those objects out there; there are just all those things arising, and they are arising on your shoulders, in the space where your head used to be. There is not the world "out there," on the other side of your face, and the world "in here," on this side of your face: the whole world "out there" is actually arising on this side of your face, is arising *within you*, within your headless awareness, right here, right now. Allow the immediate, direct awareness of the world to exist all on its own, pushing out any sense of a Watcher or Looker; there is simply this thing and this thing and this thing, all arising right here within me, arising in the open clearing, or space, where a Watcher or Looker once was. The very feelings of a thing "out there" and a watcher "in here" are directly and immediately the very same feeling—to feel the space where my head once was is to directly feel the world itself arising in that space. I can taste the sky; it's that close. Looking at the Pacific Ocean, I can pick it up in my fingers and hold it there; it's that close. Looking at a mountain, I can *feel* it arising *exactly in the space* my head used to be; it's that close! There are not two worlds—subject versus object—there is just *one taste*, and you ARE that; it is all arising *within* your very being.

Chögyam Trungpa was once asked what Enlightenment felt like, and he said, "The sky turns into blue pancake and drops on our head."[5] It sounds funny at first, but that's exactly it: the sky is actually arising in the space immediately on top of your shoulders, right where your head used to be—the sky has "fallen" where your head was, collapsing the feeling of the sky and the feeling of you into one feeling. Just as when the Zen master said, upon his Enlightenment, "When I heard the sound of the temple bell ring, there was no I, and no bell, just the ringing." Exactly! You lost your head and gained the entire sky.

In other words, subject and object are one in a pure state of nondual awareness. Now that state of headless oneness between you and what you are looking at can become more and more profound, including more and more items—in the gross, subtle, and causal realms—until the entire Kosmos itself is sitting on your shoulders where your head used to be, is totally one with your unadorned, empty, deep clear Awareness. The world of observed Form and the clear open Emptiness of your Observing Self have become one—or better, are seen to have always already been one (or "not-two"), the very definition of Enlightenment.

But notice one very important thing. You can be in this headless awareness state, seeing everything arise within you, and yet you will still be at a particular structure-level of development (for example, magic, mythic, rational, pluralistic, integral). You can be at any one of those levels and still have this perfect nondual or unity-state experience. And notice, when you are in that headless oneness state, it doesn't carry any information about what your actual structure-level is; that is, it remains a "hidden map," something that will never simply arise in your awareness for you to see and inspect and come to know. It remains a "hidden map" unless you have an overall framework or developmental view that will allow you to determine what your structure center of gravity is and its basic characteristics. Then, with that awareness, you can spot those characteristics in your thoughts, feelings, actions, and behaviors that reflect the particular "hidden map," and thus you will be able to make that subject object, thereby transcending it and making room for the next higher stage of development. You can remain in this headless oneness state, and each "hidden map" will emerge and govern how you actually interpret your experience and the meaning that you will give it, but you will have no idea that this is happening.

Thus, I might be at an ethnocentric Mythic-literal stage of development, and if so, and a worldcentric thought, feeling, or event happens to arise, it will be "over my head"; it will arise, but I won't be able to see it, because I have developed none of the tools for noticing and interpreting it, and so it won't really cross my headless unity awareness at all. I can't be one with something I don't even know exists. "Over my head" means "out of my awareness," and that is why all of the meditation systems worldwide that know this headless unity state very well are completely unaware of the many "hidden maps" that pass through it and govern how it will interpret, see, and understand the world it is otherwise one with. So, for this example, in this headless oneness state, I will be fully one with all of the stages up to, and including, the Mythic space, but I will be completely unaware of, and therefore *not* one with, the rational worldspace, the pluralistic worldspace, the integral worldspace, and the super-integral worldspace. All of these are "over my head," are *not* an actual part of my otherwise unity consciousness (so that my unity consciousness is actually partial, but in ways I will never be able to see or determine without an orienting framework that includes these hidden maps).

So we see again the crucial importance of including both Growing

Up and Waking Up, even with something as profound as the Enlightened nondual unity state.

The 1-2-3 of Spirit

The world either has an origin, a creative matrix, or the Big Bang is just a great big "whoops!" Out of absolutely nothing, for absolutely no reason, the material of this entire universe just blew into existence. Or, alternatively, it has some sort of creative matrix, which we, as humans, could at least be expected to have some sort of minimal contact with, since we, too, after all, are products of this creative matrix, and the creature would most likely have some sort of sense of the Creator or creative matrix itself.

Historically, individuals have often identified this creative source with one of the 4 or 5 major state/realms of consciousness, across a spectrum of degrees of connectedness that we have seen runs from communion to union to identity. Seeing the entire gross nature realm as Divine is Nature mysticism. Seeing the subtle realm as Divine results in various forms of Deity mysticism. Seeing the empty causal/Witness realm as Divine results in types of Formless mysticism. And seeing the Nondual realm as Divine results in various Nondual/Unity mysticisms. Integral Theory acknowledges, at the very least, the phenomenologically real experiential nature of each of those spiritual experiences, and adds that the details of those experiences and the interpretations of them will depend in large measure on the structure of consciousness (and its 4 quadrants) that is doing the experiencing. Virtually any of those state/realms can be experienced by virtually any structure-rung (with an emphasis simultaneously being placed on any quadrant), and that combination produces a wide variety of possible spiritual and religious experiences.

But Integral Theory does side with the "*not*-a-whoops" side of the argument. It does so, not because some sort of creative matrix solves the problem of where the Big Bang came from. (That would just replace that question with the equally unsolvable question, "Then where did the creative matrix come from?") Rather, like the entire spectrum of being and consciousness itself, this conclusion is the result of direct, immediate, repeatable human experiential evidence. If there is a Spirit, then, in the manifest realm itself, Spirit, like all manifest phenomena, would exist in all 4 quadrants (or the Big Three—what we call the 1-2-3 of Spirit, or Spirit looked at through 1st-, 2nd-, and 3rd-person perspectives). There are ways to approach the existence of Spirit in all 3 or 4 quadrants, but only one of them—soon to be discussed—possesses an actual proof of Spirit's existence.

Let's start by looking at the 1-2-3 of Spirit itself, or how Spirit looks from all three fundamental perspectives. Recall the grammatical basis of our terminology of 1st-person, 2nd-person, and 3rd-person perspectives: The 1st person refers to the person who is speaking—"I" or "me." The 2nd person refers to the person being spoken to—"you" or "thou"—and a "you" plus an "I" is a "we," so sometimes this view is referred to as "you/we" or just "we." And the 3rd person refers to the person or thing being spoken of—an objective "he/him," "she/her," "they/them," or simply "it" or "its." The view from the 1st-person "I" is the Upper Left quadrant; from the 2nd-person "you/we" is the Lower Left quadrant; and from the 3rd-person "it/its" are the Right-hand quadrants—giving us an "I," "we," and "it" perspective.

The 3rd-person, objective, or "it" view of Spirit is as some sort of objective Great Web of Life, a Gaia, or entire universe, that in its Totality is Divine. It doesn't really offer a proof of this; rather, it simply intuits that some sort of divine Spirit exists, and it equates that existence with the sum Total of the manifest world, generally conceived as a great interlocking order of all manifest reality, a Great Web of Life, Nature, or total cosmic substance or system. Some who are more scientifically oriented have looked at the general direction of evolution itself—toward greater and greater material complexity, higher and higher Wholes, more and more consciousness, greater and greater moral embrace—and concluded that this universe is headed toward an Omega Point, where all beings awaken to their oneness with this divine totality or system. Teilhard de Chardin's version of this Omega Point is, of course, perhaps the most famous, but it's a fairly common point of view among nature mystics, avant-garde scientists, and those with shamanic orientations. There is nothing specifically wrong with this view, except that (1) it doesn't necessarily follow that greater advances have to culminate in one, huge, final, big step (they could go on forever), and (2) it still doesn't prove Spirit, since what it maintains is that because all things must have some sort of cause, then the Big Bang must have had some sort of ground or creative source. But if that's true, then the creative source itself must also have had a cause, and you just get an infinite regress (or else you could accept something like Aristotle's "uncaused cause"—but the Big Bang itself could be that, so nothing much is gained here).

But if we accept Spirit's existence for whatever reason, Spirit in the 3rd person becomes a real and significant dimension of Spirit—namely, its objective, interwoven, material Form, or Manifest Existence—and the Great Web of Life needs to be included in any comprehensive spiritual system as the way Spirit appears when looked at in a 3rd-person objective fashion.

The 2nd-person, intersubjective, or "you/we" approaches to Spirit see Spirit as a Great Other or Great Thou, and many of them maintain that they know God or Spirit exists because they have a personal relationship with that ultimate Spirit. That relationship can also run the gamut from communion to union to identity, and often does, turning—at the identity end—into 1st-person approaches that see an identity, or oneness, or nonduality, between Spirit and one's own highest Self, but the reasons given for that here are distinctly 2nd person (rather like the movie in which Peter O'Toole believes he's God, and when asked why, he replies, "Because I find, each night when I say my prayers, I'm talking to myself"). But, in general, Spirit in the 2nd person reminds us that Spirit can be viewed as a living, conscious, vital relationship with everything in existence, including humans, and thus humans can develop a personal, living, conscious relationship with this great Spirit. Even if the "conversations with God" that I have are actually how formless Empty Spirit is felt to be communicating with me (interpreted via the structure-rung I'm at), it is nonetheless a viable and genuine means of connecting to (or resonating with) Spirit itself. Now, Integral Theory, of course, believes that all three of these perspectives are real (because they are versions of the 4 quadrants, themselves archetypal "involutionary givens" of this universe); and this 2nd-person perspective reminds us that dialogue is a viable form of Spiritual awareness, and conversation is the sincerest form of worship.

As for the actual "2nd-person" part, "person" is defined as "being with intelligence," and the universe certainly has being, and it certainly has intelligence, and there's no reason whatsoever it can't be approached as such. What 2nd-person approaches bring to the spiritual arena are all the qualities that one would like to think are involved with any ultimate Spirit, but are also ones that exist when there is relationship, such as compassion, love, gratitude, forgiveness, and so on. These qualities require relationship, such as Martin Buber's I-Thou relationship, in order to truly exist. You can't get them out of monism, not believably. Moreover, just thinking of the trillions of choices that went into the unfolding of evolution at large is to realize the staggering Intelligence that is present in the being of this universe (if nothing else, simply as the self-organizing and self-transcending drive of Eros, or Spirit-in-action), and to realize that you can approach that Intelligence and directly resonate with it is a profound and powerful spiritual path. Further, a path of devotional surrender to this Intelligence (or simple awe and wonder at this infinite Mystery) gets at the egoic self-sense in a way that other approaches just can't: you can take up a 3rd-person view of Spirit as the Great Web of Life and still retain your ego; likewise, you can imagine a 1st-person view of Spirit as your own True Self, but that always allows the self in any form (including the small egoic self) to remain stuck in the picture somewhere; but devotionally surrendering the self to this Intelligence is, well, to surrender this self in every way, if you're actually doing the practice right, and that gets at ego in a way that the others just can't.

What stops many people from acknowledging a 2nd-person approach to Spirit are the rather childish ways that earlier levels of spiritual intelligence picture this Spirit (for example, the proverbial gray-haired gentleman in the sky). But there are many higher levels of spiritual intelligence and thus many higher-level interpretations of Spirit in the 2nd person, which use highly evolved cognition such as that of 2nd tier and interpret the Intelligence of the Kosmos as a multidimensional, all-pervading, radiant, dynamic Pattern or Logos, manifesting the entire universe within its own all-encompassing Embrace, with that Totality of the All exquisitely and hypersensitively responding to each individual holon in that Totality. How could the Totality of All Interwoven Things not respond to any one of them? Why wouldn't you interpret any response to you as a direct relationship with you that the response involves, since that is in fact what it is? How could the Whole not respond to you since you are absolutely a member of that Whole? By definition, the Intelligence of the Totality is going to respond to you as an intrinsic part of that Totality; the sum Total of things is going to relationally respond to any particular thing in that totality, so begin engaging it in relationship as soon as you wish!

Now, on the other side of the I-Thou relationship is the "I" itself. So let's look at the 1st-person approaches.

These approaches maintain that divine Spirit is ultimately one with, or even identical with, the very highest Self in each and every sentient being, and can be directly known through practices like meditation. These meditation practices have what certainly could be seen as a generally scientific approach. Like all scientific experiments, they start with certain injunctions, practices, exemplars, or paradigms (using "paradigm" in its correct sense, not as a supertheory, but as a social practice or action, as Kuhn repeatedly explained). The injunction, practice, or paradigm is that of meditation practice itself, which has specific rules or injunctions, based on years—sometimes centuries—of trial-and-error experimentation about how best to do it. If one accurately completes the experiment, one is presented with certain data, experiences, or phenomena. This illuminative data culminates in what is known as satori, metanoia, or Enlightenment—the direct experience of what the Sufis call "the Supreme Identity," which is experienced as the transcendence of the separate-self sense and the unity or identity with a divine, nondual Ground of all Being. But as with all science, this data must be checked with others who have successfully completed the first two strands (the injunction and the data gathering). This third stage is a direct, sometimes fierce, communication and debate with the teacher and the community of students, who make sure that the data that a particular student gathers is consonant with the entire community of knowledge-holders in the particular practice. Incorrect or inaccurate data and their interpretations are soundly rebuffed by the community of interpreters, according to standards that represent, as we said, hundreds, sometimes thousands, of years of trial-and-error testing. This is no "believe the myths and you are saved" type of religion, but a profound psychotechnology of consciousness transformation—a personal, experiential, experimental approach, involving scientific testing, data collection, and confirmation/rejection by a community of knowledge-holders.

Give one hundred PhDs in science this direct experience of satori or

Awakening and ninety-five of them will agree that they have just experienced something like an ultimate Reality. This is the closest thing that we have to a direct proof of the existence of Spirit. It's no more real than any other type of science—but that, indeed, is saying quite a bit. According to Integral Theory, 1st-person approaches provide something like a proof of Spirit. Specific interpretations of the experience will depend, of course, on the structure-rung of consciousness that had the experience and on whether one is using 1st-, 2nd-, or 3rd-person perspectives on Spirit. Integral Theory recommends that a truly complete or Integral Spirituality have all three perspectives (or all 4 quadrants), along with practices in each to help growth, development, and evolution in each quadrant reach the highest levels possible for that person. Buddhism's own "Buddha, Dharma, Sangha" is an example, with "Buddha" representing the Upper Left quadrant, or consciousness (1st person), "Dharma" representing the Right-hand quadrants, or the "Thusness" or "Suchness" or "Isness" of phenomena (3rd person), and "Sangha" representing the Lower Left quadrant, or community (the "you/we," or 2nd person). And each of these quadrants has evolved. (Even "Buddha" has evolved, because its "nondual nature" includes Emptiness, which has not evolved, and Form, which definitely has evolved—hence, the union of Emptiness and Form, or Buddha-nature, has evolved too.)

In the Western traditions, Nonduality is generally represented by the union or identity of the soul with Spirit, and nondual Spirit is the union of Father/Son/Holy Ghost and unmanifest Godhead—so, in a sense, with nondual Realization both the soul and God disappear into Godhead (the "God beyond God" of the Gnostics). In the Eastern traditions, Nonduality is generally represented by the union of Emptiness and Form (although they lack an understanding of Form's ever-evolving, developmental-level nature), or in Tantra, by the more celebratory union of Emptiness and Luminosity. In some Eastern traditions, these higher state/realms are also identified with various God/Goddess figures (Samantabhadra/Samantabhadri, Shiva/Shakti, and so forth), and sometimes with various high qualities (Being, Consciousness, Bliss, and so on). Thus, Aurobindo follows a common example of identifying ultimate One Reality with *satchitananda*, literally "being-consciousness-bliss," as do some Vedantins (although others, being more on the "strict side" of the street, think that being-consciousness-bliss belongs to *saguna* Brahman, or Brahman with manifest form and qualities—that is, the causal realm, not the pure Nondual itself). Some think that ultimate Reality is nondual, but that Nonduality "contains" both Paramashiva (supreme, supracausal, absolute consciousness) and Shiva/Shakti (which can be thought of as an actual potential of what is Nondual—in this case, the masculine Shiva, or pure Empty Consciousness, and the manifest, luminous, feminine Shakti, or the energy/content of absolutely every manifest thing and event in the entire universe, with Shiva/Shakti always sexually united as divine consorts in every being). For Integral Theory, these deities are one interpretation of Spirit in 2nd person at these high levels.

The basic idea of all of the Nondual approaches is, generally speaking, a profound emphasis on Wholeness. (This Wholeness is so whole that "wholeness" itself is denied, since that is only one-half of a pair of opposites, the other being "partness." And we can't say, "Okay, include both," since that would create a reality that denied both. And so on, and so forth, à la the strict version of Nagarjuna's Emptiness.) But (yes, metaphorically) the drive to Wholeness is so strong that those types of intense "not this, not that" investigations are undertaken, and virtually any sort of dualistic, oppositional, or divisive version of Divinity is denied—as the Upanishads say, the Divine is "one without a second" or "free of the pairs"—the "pairs" being all pairs of opposites. So that refers to *any* pairs—timeless and temporal, finite and infinite, spiritual and material, conscious and unconscious, sacred and profane, subject and object, mind and body, inner and outer, past and future, one and many, transcendent and immanent, heaven and hell, love and hate, being and nonbeing (nothingness), sentient and insentient, masculine and feminine, implicate and explicate, good and evil, pleasure and pain, happiness and sadness, joy and sorrow, liberated and bound, awakened and ignorant, enlightened and unenlightened. At the most, the "law of three" is brought into play, where, given any two opposites, one of which is generally considered desirable and the other despicable, a triangle is created with the two opposites on the bottom two points of the triangle and a new quality—the desirable quality but now with a capital letter—occupying the top point of the triangle. Thus, love and hate are united by Love; good and evil are united by Good; enlightened and unenlightened are united by Enlightened; spiritual and material are united by Spiritual—and so on. And then the Divine is identified with all the capitalized words (Love, Good, Being, Consciousness, Bliss, and so forth). But even that is considered by the "strict" side to be a simpering concession to the weak willed, and ontologically, it makes room for a fourth term—the despised quality with a capital letter (Hate, Evil, Sorrow, Maliciousness), which solves nothing.

But I think you get the essential idea. There is an awareness or consciousness ("experience" is sometimes used but has the disadvantages of suggesting both a subject and object and a beginning and end, none of which pertains to this awareness) that is so Full, so Overflowing, so Superabundant, so radiantly All-Inclusive, that it cannot be captured by any words, thoughts, concepts, feelings, or ideas. Yet recognizing that awareness or consciousness (which cannot be described but can be directly realized with a different mode of knowing—"jnana" or "gnosis") seems to answer every puzzle or question that has plagued humans from the start: Who am I? Why am I here? What is the purpose of life? What value do I have? Where did this world come from? Why is there something rather than nothing? Awaken this Awareness, and it all becomes as crystal clear as a bright summer day at a cloudless beach.

In the last three chapters, I have presented the 5 major natural states of consciousness and a summary description (via an Integral interpretive lens) of each of their corresponding realms. I have also summarized the development of the self's *state* center of gravity through each of them, with each state-stage producing a specific Vantage Point (much as each structure-stage produces a specific View). The overall result of this voyage of Wakefulness or Consciousness through gross, subtle, causal, and turiya (empty witnessing) states is a final awakening to Nondual Ultimate Reality, a union, or "not-two, not-one," of Empty Witnessing with all Form—gross, subtle, and causal—or the ultimate suprawitnessing Supreme Identity state of turiyatita, pure nondual Suchness, Thusness, Isness.

This Full, Awakened, Complete Awareness is an immediate, direct, personal "experience," and it presents itself as the most certain of all human experiences. (Several of its advocates—from Descartes to Augustine to Shankara—maintain that this Awareness cannot be coherently denied. You can imagine your senses deceiving you, by presenting objects that aren't really there. But you can't imagine this Awareness being deceived as to its existence, because even to imagine that it doesn't exist requires this Awareness to imagine that. Thus, whether you believe in it or not, you can't get rid of it coherently. Of course, you can imagine states in which your Awareness seems not to be present—such as being anesthetized for surgery. But individuals who have had several satoris and have a state center of gravity at nondual maintain that they retain a very subtle Awareness during that anesthetized state. I can testify to being in a clinically confirmed coma for four days, and yet "Big Mind"—this nondual Awareness—was present every moment. There is the recently much reported experience of a Harvard brain surgeon—Dr. Eben Alexander—who had his neocortex temporarily decommissioned completely, and yet he reported not only continuing to be Aware, but to be in the most real state by far that he had ever experienced, an ultimate Reality if ever there was one—which he called "an infinite darkness suffused with light"—in other words, a perfect description of the causal realm, *Awareness itself*. How about actual death? Well, most of the meditation systems worldwide maintain that death is simply the death of this particular gross body-mind, with the subtle and causal body-minds going through a bardo realm on the way to being reborn in yet another gross body-mind. This thing called "consciousness" is starting to look much harder to get rid of than standard scientific materialism imagines—the general point being that awakening to it comes with a certainty that cannot coherently be denied.)

If we add up the thousands of years of realizations of the higher realms and states of consciousness, we find a staggeringly similar set of assumptions found wherever humans have existed, and for as long as they left records, although its clarity continued to unfold and evolve in greater and greater degrees: there is an ultimate Reality to this world (a world that, conceived without this ultimate Reality, is merely illusory); this Reality is so vast that it is unqualifiable (Emptiness); at the same time, it is so Whole that it includes all possible pairs of opposites in its All-Inclusive embrace; it is the Creative Source of this universe, and is present as the ultimate Suchness as well as the evolutionary drive (Eros) of every holon in existence anywhere; it threw itself outward (kenosis, lila, involution) to create the Big Bang and to remain as the creative capacity (Eros, evolution) of every element in existence, bar none, while being also the Condition of its condition and the Nature of its nature; humans and all sentient beings are one with this ultimate Reality in an ever-present, full, complete, and timeless fashion; this oneness ("not-two, not-one") can be directly realized in Awareness, through an alternate state of knowing (jnana, gnosis, satori, metamorphosis), bringing an awe-inspiring and stunningly overwhelming recognition of this ultimate Reality, and an end to all dilemmas, puzzles, sufferings, angst, tortures and torments, and a direct realization of one's Supreme Identity with this Ultimate Estate. The net result is that there is *nothing but* Spirit in any direction. Seeing this is Spirit; not seeing this is Spirit; understanding it is Spirit; not understanding it is Spirit. Spirit is not hard to achieve, realize, see, or understand; rather it is utterly impossible to avoid.

• • • • •

Before you know anything, you know *this*. Before I AM anything, there is simple I AMness, in and of itself, just so—and you are aware of that I AMness right now, yes? Before you are aware of anything, you are aware of *this*. Before you feel anything, you feel *this*. It is constantly unknowable, this knowledge of All. It is forever undoable, this already accomplished isness of All. It is too complex to be known; too simple to believe; too present to be grasped; too here to be felt. All events are in its embrace, knowing that Suchness is where all beings converge in the Presence of each other's hearts. It will fulfill your being, explode your mind, ground your soul, repair your Self, and realize your Spirit. The entire universe is arising within you, and deny it as you will, it always has. Just look: you are not in this room, this room is in you. (Feel it arising *within* your headless awareness?) Likewise, you are not in this Kosmos, this entire Kosmos is in you (where your head used to be, yes?). Supernovas are exploding in your heart; the sun is radiating from within your brain; the moon is your own shadow late on a summer eve's night; the earth is your feet as you walk on air; the stars are the neurons of your night, whenever you look at all; the rain is the rushing of your own beating blood, drenching the world with your Life.

And this is what and who you really are and always already have been.

6

The Hidden Structures of Consciousness

The Importance of Structures of Consciousness in Spirituality

Our review of the states of consciousness and their development high-lights the fact that, for whatever reasons, most Western models of development don't include major states, and thus—rather disastrously—don't include things like Enlightenment or Awakening or metanoia. Most Western models map out *structures* of consciousness and their structure-stages, or Views, which govern how we Grow Up, not how we Wake Up. It's not totally clear why Western researchers ended up focusing on structures of consciousness and their development—and excluded states. Perhaps it was because most religions in the modern era, when modern Western psychology arose, had long ago largely given up contemplative state development, and thus few people were at any state-stages higher than gross, or perhaps subtle at most, and without some very strong practice like meditation or contemplation, there was little chance that they would develop much, in terms of states, during the time period that states were being researched and studied for any developmental stages that they might show. Structures, on the other hand, although they cannot easily be seen by mere introspection, phenomenology, meditation, or contemplation (and thus they were rarely found, we have noted, in any Great Wisdom Tradition), nonetheless do show up clearly and quite obviously when studied by—say, developmental structuralism. They jumped out at modern researchers using those tools, because, almost without exception, all human beings naturally and universally begin their life at something like an Archaic stage (sensorimotor, physiological/alimentary, indissociation/fusion), and then begin to develop and unfold through several quite different structure-stages as they move into Magic, Magic-Mythic, Mythic, Rational, and higher. Consequently, if a developmentalist is looking for stages of development, these levels (in all lines) will rather forcefully announce themselves, and will be found in *every* human studied. State development, on the other hand, as we have often seen, is generally a voluntary, chosen development. You must specifically decide to take up a practice or series of practices in order to shift your state center of gravity (from gross to subtle to causal, and so forth), and relatively speaking, very, very few people actually undertake those arduous practices. Thus, unlike structure growth, which always and naturally occurs in the typical course of normal maturation, state growth is rare, sporadic, and often idiosyncratic. Since structure growth occurs in every human being, whether he or she chooses it or not, every population that the developmentalist examines will definitely contain several different structure-stages, but few, if any, state-stages. Hence the preponderance in modern Western growth models of structure-stages (or developmental levels) through which move various multiple intelligences (or developmental lines)—lines through levels, or horizontal aptitudes through vertical altitudes. These were everywhere the developmentalist looked, and so naturally their models, maps, and theories focused almost exclusively on them.

So it wasn't that Western models were antispiritual, or aggressively secular, or wanted to avoid transpersonal stages, but that few, if any, of the populations they studied were at any of those higher levels. They were certainly not in higher states, as just explained; nor were they at higher structures, either. When researchers evaluate people using methodologies such as dynamic structuralism, they find that most individuals stop their adult development somewhere in 1st tier (mythic fundamentalist religion, modern rational scientific materialism, or postmodern multiculturalism). It's very rare for individuals to develop into 2nd-tier Integral, let alone 3rd-tier Super-Integral structure-rungs of development. As a matter of fact, research based on Clare Graves's work suggests that about 5 percent of individuals are at 2nd tier at this time, and those at the upper level of the 2nd-tier stage (high vision-logic, late centaur, Fulcrum-8) are not much more than 0.5 percent, which means, one in every two hundred people. The number at 3rd tier is a *tenth* of that, if that high. Consequently, when researchers investigate the average population, very few of which are long-time meditators, they will find very few people who have developed into 2nd tier, let alone 3rd-tier, transpersonal, Super-Integral, or spiritual structure-levels of development.

So again—and it's worth noting—it's not that Western researchers were intentionally antispiritual in their research, it's just that few of the people they researched were engaged in any sort of practices that would yield either higher states (beyond gross or subtle) or higher structure-stages (beyond 1st tier). Therefore, very few of the people they investigated were anywhere beyond prepersonal and personal realms of consciousness, and so transpersonal, transrational, genuinely spiritual—as opposed to prerational mythic religious—realms did not show up for them. Although it is worth recording that many Western developmentalists, seeing the obvious and clear direction of evolutionary development—from prerational to rational to even higher, apparently transrational, levels—*postulated* that, beyond their highest, usually 2nd-tier structure-level, there were higher, transpersonal, spiritual-mystical levels. Lawrence Kohlberg, for example, postulated that beyond his highest level, level 6, there was a seventh level, "universal-mystical." Abraham Maslow postulated, beyond his self-actualization level (2nd tier), an even higher level, "self-transcendence" (3rd-tier, transpersonal). Susanne Cook-Greuter expanded Jane Loevinger's ego development spectrum beyond 2nd-tier centaur to specifically look for several 3rd-tier stages, and she found them, as did Jenny Wade and Clare Graves.

But for the most part, "East is East and West is West, and [apparently] never the twain shall meet." The Eastern (and Western contemplative) systems, working with states and state-stages of development, were working with WAKING UP (in communities of those who had voluntarily taken up meditative or spiritual practices and thus engaged otherwise rare higher states of consciousness, which were carefully mapped out), and hence they included higher states of Enlightenment,

Awakening, and Liberation. The Western developmental systems, on the other hand, were working with structures and structure-stages and thus focused on GROWING UP, but they rarely covered the higher and highest stages of GROWING UP itself (the 3rd-tier, Super-Integral, transpersonal levels). Thus Western developmental theories were doing a terrific job of presenting relative truth but had no understanding of ultimate Truth and Awakening or Liberation, while Eastern systems did fine with absolute Truth and thus ultimate Enlightenment and Awakening but had a very poor and partial grasp of relative truth and its structure growth.

And thus, for literally all of humankind's history, these two incredibly important developmental sequences—the sequence of states in Waking Up and structures in Growing Up—were never, not once, brought together, understood together, and practiced together. Sadly, humanity—East and West—has thus been deeply and demonstrably broken for its entire history to date. And you can see evidence of this fundamental brokenness in every area you look—philosophy, psychology, theology, meditation, government, legal systems, educational systems, family systems, business and finance arrangements, sex and gender relations, you name it. The history of humanity has been the history of a brokenness.

One of the apparently important roles of Integral Theory is to help to begin uniting both of these utterly crucial axes of development. This activity is aided by the descent and emergence of integral 2nd-tier levels in general, for they are primed and predisposed to engage in exactly these sorts of wholeness endeavors.

States and structures are both very important, but for different reasons. States open us to deeper and deeper realms of Reality, deeper and deeper sweeps into the Thusness of Presence, each one getting closer and closer to ultimate Emptiness, absolute Reality, and the Great Liberation itself. The most fundamental phenomena that are arising—gross objects, subtle objects, causal objects, nondual objects, and so on—are determined by the deep features of the state/realms themselves—the very *what* of manifestation is state determined. Growing through states, we become more and more present to the Presence of the Present, the very core of Reality as it is, in its Suchness, its Thusness, its very Isness. Structures, on the other hand, provide the core of *how* any experience—including meditative and state experiences—will be interpreted and largely experienced. A peak experience—of, say, the high causal—will carry with it the bare features of the deep structures of that state/realm, but many of its specific details and particularities will be supplied by the structure that is doing the experiencing (in all 4 quadrants). As I've often noted, a mythic experience of the causal is considerably different than an integral experience of the causal.

Likewise, a religious mythic-fundamentalist (for example, Islamic; I don't mean to "profile" Muslims here, but Muslim fundamentalists have been in the news quite a bit lately for just the following reason and are thus obvious examples) who has a mythic-fundamentalist peak experience of the ultimate Nondual realm will indeed experience that realm as an all-inclusive, unitive, infinite, and eternal ultimate Reality (a union of infinite unqualifiable Openness and finite manifest Form), but in this case, "the entire world of Form" that will be united in this "unity consciousness" will include (given the nature of the ethnocentric Mythic structure doing the experiencing) *only* objects that have manifested, or come into existence, up to and including the Mythic level; other Forms, whether Rational, Pluralistic, Integral, or Super-Integral, will be "over the person's head" and thus forms that he or she cannot become one with, since they don't exist anywhere in the awareness of this person. Further, for this individual, the limited and narrow ethnocentric nature of this interpretation means that others might have a similar Nondual experience and *think* that they are liberated, but unless they accept Allah, they are just kidding themselves. And so the Mythic "Nondual" experience will be *one* with everything in the Kosmos *up to and including Mythic*, but it will NOT include Rational, Pluralistic, Holistic, Integral, or Super-Integral worlds, Forms, and phenomena. And since this level is indeed a strictly limited and particular "us" versus "them," individuals at this stage cannot accept other mythic-literal versions of spirituality—in fact, they often find them the most threatening (precisely because of their similarity—hence historically the extremely widespread prevalence of "holy wars"). That limitation is combined with the fact that there is no way for the fundamentalist to be one with the higher structures either (and their corresponding worlds), since they don't yet exist in the mind, or reality, or space of the mythic believer. The essentials of the Nondual *state* (a feeling of unity or wholeness) will be real and for the most part genuine enough for this person. As we saw in the example of the headless unity state, the unity is a real, felt experience. But within that state, the person experiencing it could be at any number of hidden structure-levels without knowing it; *nothing in the headless unity state gives the experiencer any indication of anything like these "hidden maps" or structures.* And in this case, the structure interpretation of the state will be considerably less than full or complete, actually *excluding* everything beyond Mythic (as well as any alternative, competing myths). Thus this particular "unity state" is actually less than a full Unity or real Wholeness—even though it is directly felt to be—because of the fractured, limited, partial structure interpretation it is being given (and this is without the person even knowing that this partiality is being imposed by a "hidden map"; everything feels perfectly "Whole" to them!).

This is why it's almost impossible to change the mind of fundamentalist mystics about their views of God. The structure component of their unity experience might indeed be inadequate, incomplete, and partial, but the state component is so real and so utterly convincing that they focus on that, and it's impossible to budge them there, which in a certain sense is perfectly understandable. This, incidentally, is essentially the same reason why schizophrenics, who are undergoing an altered subtle-state experience so intense that it is actually being hallucinated, combined with a structure-response that runs from electric bliss to abject terror, will *not* surrender the belief in the experience: the state component is so utterly real and certain (which is largely true), but the psychiatrist tries to talk them out of both the state experience (which is real) and the structure-response (which is fractured and "wrong"), and the schizophrenic flatly refuses. So the psychiatrist tries to burn it out of the schizophrenic's brain with electroshock or drug it to death, which is essentially the same way you'd have to handle a fundamentalist mystic, and for basically the very same reason—a real state plus fractured structure experience, with the overall complex given utter reality and certainty by the very real state.

This is one of the many reasons that spiritual systems need to understand not only states of consciousness (which many of their contemplative branches do) but also structures of consciousness (which, so far, not one of them does), because it is the structures that will be experiencing and interpreting the meditative state experiences. Of course, Western orthodox researchers just as badly need to understand states and state-stages if they want to have the slightest understanding of WAKING UP and the Great Liberation itself. (To overlook the one and only ultimate Reality in the universe is not exactly something to be proud of. Given the Two Truths—relative and ultimate—imagine not being aware of one of them, and the ultimate one at that! Talk about a total, complete, utter cultural disaster!)

But of immediate concern for any Fourth Turning or Integral Spirituality—given the fact that the contemplative branches of most traditions are fairly well aware of states and their state-stages or Vantage Points—is the rather complete lack of understanding of structures and their structure-stages or Views (with their "hidden maps" and the extraordinary impact that they have on our thoughts, feelings, ideas, actions, and behavior). So in the next two chapters, we will focus on structures (or levels of development) and multiple intelligences (or lines of development), along with the Views that occur when the self-sense is exclusively identified with a particular structure-stage in any particular line.

Ladder, Climber, View

As we briefly outlined in chapter 3, in structure development, we have what we call "ladder, climber, View." The ladder is the spectrum of basic structures of consciousness, or the basic rungs in the ladder. Once they emerge, most of their features stay in existence (they are "enduring structures"). The climber is the self-sense or the self-system. As it climbs the basic rungs of existence (the levels or rungs of the developmental ladder—although Integral Theory does not view these as rigid rungs but as general probability waves),[1] it temporarily and exclusively identifies with its present rung and sees the world through the eyes of that rung. In other words, its View of the world is determined by its present rung and that rung's characteristics (just as when you climb a real ladder: at rung 3, you see the way the world looks from the third rung; at rung 6, you see the way it looks from that rung, and so on: ladder/rungs, climber, View).

For example, when the self identifies with the concrete rule/role mind (rung 4), it sees the world from the ethnocentric, concrete, mythic-literal View. When it identifies with the rational mind (rung 5), it sees the world from the modern, worldcentric, rational, scientific, or objective View. When it identifies with the pluralistic mind (rung 6), it sees the world from the postmodern, pluralistic, multicultural View. When it identifies with the vision-logic mind (rung 7), it will see world from the Integral View, and so on.

In short, each structure-rung in the ladder generates a different View of the world around it (just as if you were climbing a real ladder). With each next-higher stage of development, the self steps off the previous structure-rung, *loses the View of the world from that previous rung*, steps up to the next higher structure-rung, and begins to see the world from that new and higher View. Again, just as when climbing a real ladder, the climber (or self-sense) *loses the View from the previous rung—but the previous rung itself remains in existence* (all the way back to the first rung). Thus, development is "transcend and include," or "negate and preserve"—the successive Views (or structure-stages) are negated and transcended (as the self steps up to the new and higher rung and its View), but the structure-rungs themselves are included and preserved (all rungs remain in existence).

Before we continue, we need briefly to discuss a technical point. We have already seen that the human mind contains perhaps a dozen multiple intelligences—cognitive intelligence, emotional intelligence, moral intelligence, interpersonal intelligence, intrapersonal intelligence, kinesthetic intelligence, logico-mathematical intelligence, spiritual intelligence, aesthetic intelligence, and so on. However, as different as these multiple intelligences, which we also call *developmental lines*, are from each other, all of these *developmental lines* move and grow through the same basic *developmental levels* (or basic structure-rungs), whose general Views we have been referring to as Archaic, Magic, Magic-Mythic, Mythic, Rational, Pluralistic, Integral, and Super-Integral (using 7 or 8 major developmental levels or basic structures in general).

But we have to be very careful in how we name these basic developmental levels. Precisely because they are the same for all of the different developmental lines or multiple intelligences, the terms for the developmental levels or basic structures themselves can't be terms that inherently favor just one or two developmental lines, which is a constant problem for developmentalists. It's like a mountain with twelve paths going up it (each path representing a developmental line or a multiple intelligence)—including a path up the north side of the mountain, the east side, the west side, and the south side. Now the Views from these paths are clearly quite different—you wouldn't want to use pictures from the east path to describe the Views from the west path. There are, in fact, few characteristics, or Views, that are common to all the paths (so finding names or terms that fit them all is quite difficult). But there is one thing that all the paths and their Views share in common—and that is *altitude*. So you can definitely say things like, "All four people on the north, east, south, and west paths are now at 5,000 feet," or "All are now at 7,000 feet," or "Two are now at 3,000 feet and two are at 4,500 feet," and so on. As long as all paths start at the bottom and end at the top, positions along different paths can be at the same altitude—altitude doesn't apply more to one path than to another—and so altitude will work as a way to name the degree of development up any and all paths, with no prejudice or bias.

These path altitudes, which stand for the *degree of development* "up" any path or line, are represented by Integral Theory with colors (taken basically in the same order as a natural rainbow), since colors do not privilege any particular path or View.[2] You can see these colors in figures 6.1 and 6.2, which run up the left side of the graph, representing how "far up" any of the developmental lines have grown or developed. But since anybody unfamiliar with the system won't know what the colors mean, we are occasionally forced to use names or terms for the general developmental levels or basic structures, in order to get some introductory points across, as I have been doing up till now (for example, using terms such as Archaic, Magic, Mythic, and so forth). Some researchers use terms like "opportunistic" (Magic-Mythic), "diplomat" (Mythic), "expert" (Mythic-Rational), or "strategist" (Holistic) for these levels, which is fine, but the problem with those terms is that they all sound like they are levels that the same typical rational person could be at, whereas these developmental levels, or structures of consciousness, are profoundly different at each level (cognitively, an "expert" is at amber/orange, whereas a "strategist" is at teal—they could hardly be much different). Saying that somebody is "opportunistic" (red) sounds like it could apply to any rational (orange) businessperson with a ruthless competitive edge, which neglects the fact that the "opportunistic" or power level, when it was first developing in a child, was occurring during the preoperational, magical-like stage of development, and there is nothing "rational" about it. Many developmental models name these stages as if they were adopted by a rational-level cognition, instead of, as Gebser, for example, does, reporting how they actually appear in themselves in a prerational form. "Magic-Mythic" captures this reality; "opportunistic" doesn't.

Integral psychographs are diagrams that list vertically the major developmental altitudes or *levels*, and list horizontally several developmental *lines*, or multiple intelligences; see figures 6.1 and 6.2. In these two figures, I have used standard Integral Theory colors and provided twelve major levels. I have then presented, in each figure, around a half dozen major developmental lines, or multiple intelligences, and you can see how their various levels, structures, or stages (and their corresponding Views) stack up compared to each other. In the second diagram, figure 6.2, I have included the meditative states circular diagram (from fig. 3.1) at the far end of the lines, to indicate that virtually any of those meditative states can be experienced at virtually any of those structure-levels in the various lines, a crucially important insight.

I have found that the best terms to use in a very general sense—keeping in mind all the problems with using any terms at all—are the variations on Jean Gebser's terms that I have been using to name the Views from these general developmental levels, or basic structures—archaic, magic, magic-mythic, mythic, mythic-rational, rational, pluralistic, integral, and super-integral (technically, these are terms for Views in the worldview line). Gebser's terms at least give a real sense of major differences between levels—"magic" and "rational," after all, don't sound very similar—and they're not. But please keep in mind that when we are discussing the general developmental levels of altitude, or the basic structures of consciousness themselves, we could use an extraordinary variety of terms to describe them, simply because they refer to basic levels that must apply to ALL of the developmental lines or multiple intelligences, which range, of course, from cognitive terms to emotional terms to moral terms to aesthetic terms and so on. And, naturally, when we look at a particular level—say, the red level—in each of the actual lines, it will have a different name or term applied

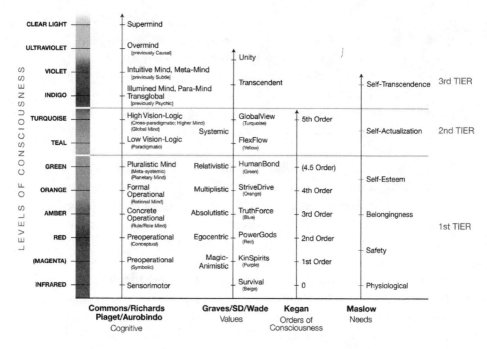

Figure 6.1. Some major developmental lines.

to it, taken from that line itself, because now we are referring to a specific developmental level (red) not in general terms but in the precise terms of *that particular and specific line or intelligence.* Thus, red (with a Magic-Mythic View) cognition (Piaget) is called "preoperational," red values (Graves) are called "egocentric," red morals (Kohlberg) are called "preconventional," red "orders of consciousness" (Kegan) are called "2nd order," red "levels of ego-self" (Loevinger) are called "self-protective," and so on. They all have different specific features, but they are all at the "red" altitude.

Thus, we are perfectly allowed to use the names of colors to refer to the same degree of development or consciousness in cognitive, emotional, moral, and aesthetic development (as well as all other lines), because "red" favors no line at all, whereas names taken from a particular line are often not only just narrow and limited but often flat-out wrong. For example, referring to "formal operational cognition," a correct term taken from the orange level in the cognitive line, as

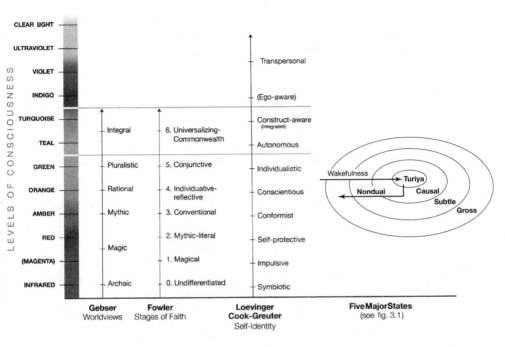

Figure 6.2. Some further developmental lines (plus meditative states).

being "postconventional" or "postconformist," terms taken from the moral line, at first seems to make sense because formal operational cognition does support postconventional morality. Unfortunately, somebody with formal operational cognition can have postconventional morals, OR conventional/conformist morals, OR preconventional morals, and so using "postconventional" to name that overall general level of development—orange—would be very wrong and confused. This is exactly the problem with naming the general levels with terms taken from only one line—it doesn't easily apply to ALL lines, which is what we want, and it is a requirement that altitude and colors meet. Further (and we will be exploring this in detail), Integral Theory points out that the different developmental lines are relatively independent from each other, so a person can be at very different levels in various different lines.

So keep in mind that when we use terms such as "magic" or "mythic," we are referring, respectively, to the magenta developmental level or basic structure and the amber developmental level or basic structure, as it appears in any developmental lines or multiple intelligences.

Of course, another way to refer to the various levels, which doesn't privilege the characteristics of a particular line, is to simply number them—and I often do that, too, as do many developmentalists. The number of levels will then often vary, depending on how much detail we need to convey. Sometimes we refer to three levels; sometimes five; sometimes seven; sometimes ten; sometimes twelve; sometimes sixteen; sometimes more. Each time, of course, we have to indicate what those numbers are actually referring to in terms of the color labels, and since this generally varies from numbered system to numbered system, we always have to be careful here, too.

As for altitude itself, what else can we say that it represents, other than the general level, or degree, or stage of development itself? For Integral Theory, altitude represents empty Consciousness. Consciousness is not a thing, process, event, or system, but the opening or clearing in which things, processes, events, and systems appear or arise. Consciousness, in its *ultimate* sense, is the *empty* clearing or opening in which manifestation occurs. *Levels* (in structures or states) *of consciousness* therefore represent the "amount" of opening or clearing in which various phenomena can appear. As for structures of consciousness specifically, the "higher" the level (or structure), the "more" phenomena that can arise within it. Levels of altitude, in that sense, are paradoxically the "amount" of "nothing" in which "something" can arise. The greater the nothing, the greater the space for the something. Each higher level is an opening or clearing in which not only its own specific phenomena can arise, but, via "transcend and include," this space also includes the previous levels' opening (and thus includes the space for their enduring phenomena as well); hence "transcend"— open or clear, and "include"—make room for or preserve.

In a sense, this is quite similar to the Yogachara/Madhyamaka view, where ultimate Consciousness (*chittamatrata*) is itself ultimate Emptiness, Spaciousness, or Openness. "Relative consciousness" is any *specific level* of Consciousness (red, amber, orange, green, and so forth), that is, a particular "amount" of "nothingness," which allows a particular amount of "somethingness" to arise. Again, the greater the opening of relative consciousness, the more phenomena and more types of phenomena that can arise or appear. This relationship is reflected in the increase in the number of perspectives that higher levels can take—each perspective being a new and greater amount of relative consciousness. Thus, levels up to red can take a 1st-person perspective ("egocentric"); amber can take a 2nd-person perspective ("ethnocentric"); orange can take a 3rd-person perspective ("worldcentric"); green, a 4th-person; teal, a 5th-person; turquoise, a 6th-person; super-integral, a 7th-person and higher ("Kosmocentric"). "Relative consciousness" is also closely related to the degree of complexity, for what we find in evolution is that the greater the degree of complexity of a holon (or individual phenomenon or organism), the greater is that holon's awareness or consciousness. Hence consciousness increases as we move from atoms to cells to plants to reptiles to mammals to primates to humans, and continues to increase in humans from infrared to magenta to red to amber to orange, and so forth. This is Teilhard de Chardin's famous "law of complexity and consciousness"—namely, the more complexity, the more consciousness. (This is what we find in the 4-quadrant view as well; as a glance at figure 4.1 will show, as material complexity in the Right-hand quadrants increases, the degree of consciousness in the Left-hand quadrants correlatively increases.)

Now, what we were discussing is the general pattern of development, where the self-system (or climber) steps up to a new and higher structure-level or basic rung of development (a new and higher level of relative consciousness or openness). This happens with each and every multiple intelligence or developmental line. But instead of going through each line and showing the actual structure-stages involved, we can just use the generically named levels (magic, mythic, and so forth, or simply colors) and show what is involved in the generic case, with the understanding that a similar type of process occurs with each multiple intelligence or line.

This "generic" development is always occurring in the various lines; there are no "levels development" without them occurring in some particular line. The "lines" are where the "levels" actually appear; these levels never occur on their own in thin air: they are levels of some line. And to say that each line of development is always expressing a particular level of development is to say that the line's expression is always being governed by that level's "hidden map" or "hidden grammar." In other words, a level's basic structure governs the stage of any line that is at that particular level, that is, any line using that particular "hidden map" or basic altitude (or color) structure as its guidance system. So, in short, levels are always levels in a particular line. Likewise, although not as common, if we refer to levels in state-stage development—and it's perfectly fine to do so—the level is always of a particular state-stage stream.

Table 1 provides an abbreviated list of basic rungs or basic structures and a few of their corresponding Views (the way the world looks when a structure becomes a structure-stage; in other words, when the self identifies with a particular structure-rung, it becomes the self's structure center of gravity, the major structure or "hidden map" *through which* the self looks at, and interprets, the world). The self "climbs," rung by rung, the rungs of the developmental ladder, in each case generating a particular View of the world (that is, a worldview) from that specific rung—the one it is standing on—which it then jettisons as it moves up to the next higher rung. The self climbs up the ladder in order to adopt the View from the next higher rung—while still keeping the previous rung in existence as part of its overall being. (Of course, actual development is not nearly as chunky and clunky as this ladder metaphor suggests; Integral Theory sees these structures as "probability clouds"—the probability that the self-sense will be found at a particular altitude—and these unfold loosely through the various altitude stages. To get this looser meaning across, Integral Theory often refers to "levels and lines" as "waves and streams." But these three elements—probability clouds, self-system, and identified worldview—are captured graphically with "ladder, climber, view," and so it is useful for that reason.)

Table 1 presents an abbreviated list of both the basic structures or rungs (the "probability clouds") and the correlated structure-stages or Views from those rungs. "Fulcrums" refers to the *stages of the self-line* as it develops vertically through the basic structures or rungs. Fulcrums, in other words, are the structure-stages of the self-sense line, the core "location" of the structure center of gravity. They become of paramount importance when it comes to the creation of dysfunctions, or shadow elements, as we'll see).

Table 1. Basic structure-rungs and some of their supported views

Climber	Rung (structure)	View (structure-stage)
Fulcrum-1	sensorimotor mind / basic physiological	Archaic, fusion, symbiotic
Fulcrum-2	fantasy mind / emotional-sexual / images and symbols	Magic, immediate / gratification, impulsive
Fulcrum-3	conceptual or intentional mind	Magic-Mythic, power drives, / safety, "PowerGods," / opportunistic
Fulcrum-4	concrete rule/role mind	Mythic, conformist, / traditional, belongingness, / diplomat
Fulcrum-4/5	abstract rule/role mind	Mythic-Rational, expert
Fulcrum-5	formal or rational mind	Reason, multiplistic, modern, / achiever
Fulcrum-6	pluralistic mind	Pluralistic, postmodern, / planetary, individualistic, / sensitive
Fulcrums-7 and 8	low and high vision-logic / 2nd-tier mind	Holistic, systemic, strategist / Integral, global, construct-aware
Fulcrums-9 (3rd-tier)	para-mind (super-integral)	Transglobal, ego-aware
10	meta-mind	Visionary, ironist
11	Overmind	Transcendental
12	Supermind	Nondual, Transcendent-Immanent

During the course of structure and structure-stage development, as the self or climber steps from one stage to the next higher stage, two important things happen: the previous rung is retained, and the previous View is dropped. That is, *the self drops or loses the View from the lower structure-rung it was just on, and replaces it with the View from the next higher structure-rung it steps onto, while retaining the basic structure-rung itself—hence "transcend and include."* Obviously, when you're climbing a ladder and you move from, say, the third rung to the fourth, you no longer look at the world from the third rung—that View is gone—instead you look at the world from the fourth rung. But the *third rung still remains in existence*—you're just no longer standing on it. So in each stage of structure development, the basic structure-rung remains in existence and is included, but the View from that rung is lost, transcended, or negated, and is replaced by the View from the next higher rung as the self exclusively identifies with that. This is what we mean when we say that development transcends and includes, or negates and preserves.

We'll finish this section by repeating the crucial point: structures interpret states (including meditative states), and thus the structure-rung that an individual is identified with at any given point plays a large role in how the individual will interpret—and thus experience—the world that is arising, including any particular state or meditative state that is arising. Without including structures of consciousness, we can never fully understand states of consciousness.

7

The Structure-Stages
of Development

Types of Spirituality

First, a brief summary and quick review of the two major types of spiritual awareness available to humans, since we want to be clear which one we are now going to be examining. As we saw in chapter 2, there is a spiritual awareness that is based on structures (also known as *spiritual intelligence*) and one that is based on states (also known as *spiritual experience*). *Spiritual experience*, or a 1ˢᵗ-person state, is what we have been discussing in terms of meditation and its major state-stages (summarized in fig. 3.1). These are important, because it's how we WAKE UP—how we have direct and immediate experience of the Divine dimensions of reality—whether it be nature mysticism of the gross realm, deity mysticism of the subtle realm, formless mysticism of the causal realm, or ultimate unity mysticism of the nondual realm (see the Wilber-Combs Lattice, fig. 3.2). These are direct, immediate experiences of the Divine Ground of Being as it appears in the various state/realms—gross, subtle, causal, and nondual.

Spiritual intelligence, on the other hand, is less experiential and more intellectual, or intelligence oriented. It is, in fact, one of the multiple intelligences. (See fig. 6.2, where Fowler's work, which is one of the first, and still most important, studies on the developmental levels of spiritual intelligence, is summarized.) It is oriented to the values and meanings of the Divine Life. For spirituality, it is how we GROW UP.

From Paul Tillich to James Fowler, spiritual intelligence is especially indicated by how we answer the question "What is it that is of ultimate concern to me?" For someone at rung 1, archaic, it's food and survival. For someone at rung 2, magic, it's sex and emotional pleasure. For someone at rung 3, magic-mythic, it's power and security. For rung 4, mythic belongingness, it's order and belonging. For rung 5, rational, it's achievement and excellence. For rung 6, pluralistic, it's sensitivity and caring. For rung 7 and 8, 2nd tier, it's loving embrace and inclusion. For 3rd tier, it's pure self-transcendence and wholeness —including possible conjunctions with gross, subtle, causal, and nondual. And remember, a person can be at virtually any of those levels or structures while being at virtually any state or realm, because of having a dual center of gravity—that is, they are at both a structure-stage (of Growing Up) and a state-stage (of Waking Up); that is, they both have a View and a Vantage Point.

So let's look at spiritual intelligence and its growth and development in a little more detail. These levels/stages of spiritual Growing Up need to be added to the levels/stages of Waking Up for a fuller, more comprehensive view of the Divine Life (or an Integrally meaningful life in general).

Spiritual Intelligence and Development in 1st and 2nd Tiers

"Spiritual intelligence" has been given many different meanings, most of them focusing on particular *aptitudes* or *skills* that a spiritual intelligence would likely show—including love, compassion, wisdom, how to apply spiritual insights to daily problems, and so on. (I might particularly mention the work of Cindy Wigglesworth. See her website Deep Change, www.deepchange.com.) But here I am going to focus, not so much on *aptitude* as on *altitude*, on the vertical stages of the growth and development of spiritual intelligence, because these structure-stages and their corresponding Views are what all spiritual traditions, contemplative and otherwise, are missing, and what we are recommending as a crucial addition to any Fourth Turning. This applies, of course, to all multiple intelligences and their structure-stages. But since spiritual intelligence is itself a multiple intelligence, we can hit two birds with one stone by focusing on spiritual intelligence as an example of structure-stage growth in general and how its corresponding Views likewise grow and evolve, while focusing on the spiritual View in particular. This will give us a generic understanding of *levels* of vertical growth, or altitude development, as well as a particular example of that in the spiritual intelligence *line* of development.

Much of this is in sync with James Fowler's monumentally pioneering work, first presented in his *Stages of Faith*.[1] Humankind has known for hundreds, even thousands, of years that spirituality, or religious orientation, depends in part on states of consciousness and state-stages (or Vantage Points). But Fowler was one of the first to show, with substantial evidence and research, that a person's spiritual orientation also depends on structure-stages of development (or Views). These, of course, are variations on the standard, general levels of development that we have already outlined—archaic, magic, magic-mythic, mythic, rational, pluralistic, and integral (these are *exactly* the stages that Fowler found in the development of spiritual intelligence). But his actual research and reams of data relating specifically to spiritual development made his efforts pioneering.

Further, after giving a few details from some of the more important developmental levels or structure-stages (especially relating to spiritual levels), I'll give specific examples of entire schools of Buddhism found at each stage or level. These are real eye-openers for many people, I think, because you can so clearly see how different interpretations of Dharma are given by different levels of development, and yet the individuals involved with this have no idea that they are doing it (that is, "hidden maps" really are hidden).

Fowler calls the magenta *Magic* View (supported by the emotional-sexual, fantasy mind, genital chakra-rung 2) "intuitive-projective." It's focused on safety, security, and survival, and magical charms to both secure survival and ward off evil spirits. It's very anthropomorphic and superstitious. Fantasy thinking, which equates and confuses wholes and parts and equates all wholes with similar parts—for example, if one Asian person is dangerous, all Asian people are dangerous, in other words, prejudicial or biased thinking, is common. The image of an object is not clearly differentiated from the real object (for example, people believe that if you stick a pin in a toy doll representing a person, then something bad will happen to the real person). Because of this tenuous differentiation of self and surroundings, "animism," which ascribes human characteristics to entities in nature ("The volcano erupted because it's mad at me"; "It's flooding because our tribe offended spirit elements"; "The flower is blooming because I'm in love") is common. It's not its ascribing of awareness or intentionality to nature that is the problem with animism (nature has plenty of both in reality), rather it's the ascribing of *human* characteristics to nature, providing an "anthropocentric" interpretation, that is problematic. Anthropocentrism occurs because the human self has just barely separated and differentiated itself from nature, and its boundaries with nature still overlap and are often confused. Ancestor worship starts to become common, and is often the source of petitionary prayers (ancestors are a source of primary spiritual wisdom, and are to be called on whenever help is needed). Tales and legends are a common source of community bonding. The basic rung at the Magic View (magenta, impulse, fantasy, images and symbols, emotional-sexual) is largely limited to a 1st-person perspective ("egocentric"), so the individual is more concerned with his or her own salvation than that of others.

Fowler calls the red *Magic-Mythic* View (supported by the conceptual/intentional mind, gut chakra-rung 3) "mythic-literal." The difference between magic and mythic lies in where the source of miracle power is located. In *magic*, the source of miracles is the self—I do a rain dance, and Nature obediently rains; I stick a pin in a doll, and the real person is actually hurt. In *mythic*, the self has surrendered the illusion that it can intervene in nature and history and miraculously change it; but if it can no longer perform miracles, God can (or Goddess or some other supernatural being). This Magic-Mythic stage marks the transition from a previously omnipotent *magic* self to an omnipotent *mythic* God or Gods—a stage Spiral Dynamics accurately calls "PowerGods." There is a concomitant emphasis on, and belief in, miracles. I can't do them, but God can (or so can any superpowerful, supernatural figure, like mommy, who could change the yucky spinach into candy if she wanted). And if I ritualistically approach God in a way that pleases Him, then He (or She) will perform a miracle for me (thus, magic is transferred to mythic bigger-than-life beings—hence the name "magic-mythic"). Mythic narratives begin to develop, and magical incantations are believed to put one in right relationship to Divinity, which will then be more likely to intervene in nature and history on my behalf (to ensure the hunt, cure my illness, give me a child, make the crops grow). The basic rung supporting this View—the conceptual, representational, vital mind (red)—is still largely limited to a 1st-person perspective ("egocentric"), and so narcissistic power is a major concern (both in oneself and in Divinity—"PowerGods"). The self has just succeeded in differentiating itself from the surrounding world, and thus its own vulnerability is a serious issue—several developmental schools refer to this stage as one whose major concerns are "safety" or "security." Reflecting this threatening environment, God is powerful, wrathful, vengeful, and very unpredictable. The self generally experiences a survival-of-the-fittest, dog-eat-dog world that is "red in tooth and claw." This stage is still superstitious, self-centered, and animistically infused.

Fowler calls the amber *Mythic* View (supported by the concrete operational, rule/role mind, heart chakra-rung 4) "synthetic-conventional." It is "conventional" because the basic structure-rung can take the role of other—can adopt a 2nd-person perspective—and hence one's View switches from *egocentric* to *ethnocentric*, one's identity expands from the individual self to the group (the clan, tribe, religion, political party, community, nation), and one's capacity for love and care extends from oneself to a variety of others (in Carol Gilligan's model, from "selfish" to "care"—as with the "heart" chakra). One's morality likewise shifts from egocentric to strongly group oriented, usually conformist—"my country, right or wrong; my religion, right or wrong; my group, right or wrong." A basic "law and order" stage. Strong boundaries are drawn between "Us" and "Them," and religiously, my group is God's "chosen people." My life might become devoted to jihad, by whatever name, or the desire to either convert or kill nonbelievers. Killing nonbelievers is not a sin; it's a religious promotion. There is a strong desire to understand God's absolute truth (Graves calls this stage "absolutistic"), a truth that is often contained in one book (the Bible, Koran, *Pure Land Sutra*, Mao's *Little Red Book*, and so forth), which is often a mythic narrative taken to be absolutely and literally true (Elijah really did ascend into heaven in a chariot while still alive; God really did rain locusts on the Egyptians and kill all of their first-born males; the earth really is resting on an elephant that is resting on a serpent that is resting on a turtle, and so on). Those who believe in God's word are destined for heaven, or a Pure Land, those who don't, everlasting hellfire (or some other equally unpleasant series of reincarnations). The concrete operational, or rule/role, mind supporting this View makes both the rules and one's roles very important, to be rigidly followed. Breaking the rules or violating the roles can lead to damnation (and, if this stage is institutionalized, excommunication). Rigid social hierarchies and religious hierarchies are common, such as the caste system or the Church. For those within the chosen group, love and compassion are recommended, since these are all God's chosen children. For those outside the group, conversion, torture, or murder are a few of the options. For more moderate believers, charity and good works are common, since the implicit belief is that the recipients are at least potential converts to the chosen group. The amber Mythic level, with its ethnocentric capacities, marks the first great, major civilizations in humankind's history, each spreading across most of the known world in their time. And the Mythic-Literal stage formed the foundation of many of the world's Great Traditions that are still alive and influential to this day—Jewish, Christian, Hindu, Islamic, Shinto, and so forth. The ethnocentric nature of this level/stage is one of the things that make religion in the modern and postmodern world such an ambivalent force—on the one hand, preaching love, compassion, and concrete morality; on the other, calling for jihad, or holy war, on all those who do not accept its view of Divinity—an ambivalence that has made religion so hard to understand for modernity: how could something that preaches so much love have been the cause of so much human suffering, torture, and death, all in the name of God? And the answer is, God itself is ethnocentric, or God is *my* group's God: believe in and accept my version of God, and we love you; disagree, and we will kill you. And so it was in historical fact. Moving religion from this amber ethnocentric level to versions of its own orange worldcentric stage is a major task of the modern and postmodern world, and a primary aim of the "conveyor belt," as we will see.

Fowler calls the orange *Modern-Rational* View (supported by the formal, rational, 3rd-person mind, throat chakra-rung 5) "individuative-reflective." It is "reflective" because the basic rung of formal operational mind (orange) has added a 3rd-person perspective, from which an individual can take up a more reflective, objective, critical, even skeptical view of his or her experiences and beliefs. "Rational," as the general name of this View, doesn't mean dry, abstract, distanced, or viciously analytical. Rather, it means that it can understand conditional worlds, "what if" and "as if," and thus begin not only to question the literal truth of mythic religious beliefs, but also to read them with more symbolic and metaphoric meanings. Beliefs tend to be based on evidence and universal reasonableness, instead of mythic revelation. All individuals are treated fairly, regardless of race, color, sex, creed, or religion. In terms of spiritual intelligence, atheists, agnostics, and religious believers can all be at the Rational level, as long as they have reached their conclusions through logic, evidence, and reflective considerations, including the perfectly logical conclusion that logic alone is not necessarily the only form of knowledge, and that other, more intuitive modes deserve equal consideration. Again, when Thomas Jefferson sat on the White House steps and furiously cut up his Bible with a pair of scissors, he left in those sections that passed these rational tests and rejected the others. When Bishop John Shelby Spong did essentially the same thing with his Bible, he was changing his religious beliefs so that they were based less on childlike myths and more on reason and evidence, and he still came out the other side as a strong and devoted believer in the essentials of the Christian faith, as seen through the Rational and Pluralistic Views. Buddhism, from the start, has been at the least a Rational View, based not on dogma, authority, or mere faith—and possessing few if any gods, goddesses, or spirits, and no mythologies—but instead on directly checking with one's own experience and reason (although not all Buddhist followers lived up to those levels, as we'll see), a reason, of course, connected with realizing states of consciousness (a spiritual intelligence connected to Waking Up, which is given primary emphasis).

Fowler calls the green *Postmodern-Pluralist* View (supported by the pluralistic-relativistic, 4th-person mind, throat chakra) "conjunctive." (Orange rational is also correlated with the throat chakra since both Views are "vocally self-expressive," but this is rung 6.) Supported by the basic structure-rung of the pluralistic mind, it is devoted to taking as many perspectives as possible (an endeavor that reaches a real fruition at the next stage, the holistic-integral). Although it is still a step away from the genuine holism of 2nd tier, this View is deeply interested in wholeness, reconciliation, and nonmarginalizing. There's not just a passive tolerance of other religions but often an active embrace. This View doesn't just abide other Views, but often actually seeks to understand them and incorporate them into its own worldview. (It is ultimately hampered in this approach by the fact that it is still 1st tier, and so still believes that this pluralistic stance itself is the one and only true stance there is, which itself is a contradiction that postmodernism has never managed to navigate adequately, believing that its view is superior in a world where it also believes that nothing is supposed to be superior.) With this "almost Integral" or "half Integral" stance, if you will, the Pluralistic View sees important truths in all religions, even if it feels most comfortable in its own, and often seeks to incorporate aspects of other religions into its own (if spiritually oriented; it might also be atheistic or agnostic and still be at this level of spiritual intelligence). In any event, it deconstructs traditional hierarchies, speaks out strongly for the oppressed and disadvantaged, has a strongly planetary and environmental ("ecocentric") sensibility, and is particularly open to nature mysticism and spirit in the 3rd person as the Great Web of Life and the Universe Story. It is socially engaged, actively supports minority rights and feminism, and advocates for sustainability in all walks of life. This is a relatively new View, with its supporting basic structure, the pluralistic mind, having itself evolved to any significant degree only beginning with the revolutions of the 1960s, which were themselves driven largely by this stage.

One of its most notable characteristics is its denial and condemnation of every form of hierarchy. In this, it fails miserably to distinguish between dominator hierarchies (which are indeed loathsome) and actualization, or growth, hierarchies (which are the form of most growth processes in nature, including humans). In dominator hierarchies, with each higher level, the few dominate and oppress the many. In actualization or growth hierarchies, each higher level is more and more inclusive. For example, a fundamental growth hierarchy in nature is the hierarchy of atoms to molecules to cells to organisms. In this hierarchy, or what Arthur Koestler calls "holarchy," which might be a more accurate name, each higher level literally includes and embraces its junior level; it doesn't oppress it—molecules don't oppress or hate atoms—if anything, they love and embrace them!

The most commonly used evidence to condemn all hierarchy is Carol Gilligan's book *In a Different Voice*, where she suggests that men and women think differently: men emphasize rights, justice, autonomy, and hierarchy, and women think more in terms of relationship, care, communion, and nonhierarchy (as themes).[2] Feminists assumed that since most rottenness in the world is patriarchal, and all men think hierarchically, and since dominator hierarchies are bad, then all hierarchies are bad—all hierarchies must be dominator hierarchies.

But Gilligan made a second point in her book, a point studiously overlooked. She pointed out that although men think hierarchically and women nonhierarchically, *both men and women develop through the same four major hierarchical stages* (her terms). In women, Gilligan called these hierarchical stages "selfish" (egocentric), "care" (where concern expands from self to group—ethnocentric), "universal care" (concern for all peoples, regardless of race, color, sex, or creed— worldcentric), and "integrated" (where both men and women integrate the contrasexual mode—our Integral). In other words, *women's nonhierarchical thinking develops through four hierarchical stages—* that is, it's a growth hierarchy. In cutting out all hierarchies, feminists cut out all women's growth. An unfortunate move, to put it mildly.

But that's what the pluralistic View does—it cuts out all hierarchies, or flattens them, as the current phrase has it. And thus in heroically deconstructing all dominator hierarchies, postmodernism catastrophically deconstructed and destroyed all growth hierarchies as well, a cultural and spiritual disaster. The denial of all hierarchies, or rankings, is one of the surest indicators that you're dealing with the pluralistic level of development (green) and the conjunctive stage of spiritual intelligence.

Fowler calls 2nd tier, or the teal/turquoise Integral (supported by synthesizing vision-logic, forehead chakra, rungs 7 and 8), "universalizing," and it puts us right at the very edge of today's evolution, at least as far as structures are concerned. Although rare Integral pioneers can be spotted a thousand years ago or more, 2nd tier only reached more than 1 percent of the population in the 1970s, and more than 5 percent at the turn of the millennium (with best guesses putting teal Holistic today (2015) at about 4 percent and turquoise Integral at about 1 percent). Wherever it appears, there is a concomitant drive to find patterns that connect, the unities under the diversities, the wholeness that goes with every partness, the oneness alongside every manyness. The emergence of the Integral mode—even at today's 5 percent, let alone at the prophesied soon-to-be 10 percent—is a monumental turning point in evolution itself, whose impact simply cannot be overemphasized.

Recall some of the characteristics of the Integral stages, rungs 7 and 8, supported by low and high vision-logic (teal and turquoise): they cognize wholes, connections, and unity-in-diversities (metaparadigmatic and cross-paradigmatic). (Note that, in our overall summary of "6-to-8 major levels," we have combined these two levels, since both are 2nd tier, into one basic level, "rung 7." This is simply a matter of convenience; whether we count them as two separate levels or one general level, the essence of this overall stage is its inclusive, all-embracing, integral nature, the first of its kind anywhere in history.) First and foremost, this is 2nd tier; unlike each 1st-tier View, which believes its truths and values are the only real truths and values in existence, 2nd tier sees important contributions made by all the previous stage-rungs and Views. If nothing else, each junior level becomes a component, or subholon, in each succeeding senior level, as each stage of evolution transcends and includes its predecessor. A whole neutron becomes part of an atom; a whole atom becomes part of a molecule; a whole molecule becomes part of a cell; a whole cell becomes part of an organism. Each stage is a whole/part, or holon, and the resultant nested hierarchy is a growth holarchy. The Integral stages intuit this, and thus see the importance of every preceding stage of development, not just in humans, but in the Kosmos at large, going all the way back to the Big Bang. The Integral View sees itself as intrinsically interwoven with the entire universe, an interconnected, seamless, vital, living, creative, and conscious Kosmos. The fundamental, intrinsic, evolutionary drive of the Kosmos to evolve higher and higher wholes is the same force that produced mammals from dust and Integral from Archaic—a drive that Whitehead called "the creative advance into novelty" and Integral calls "Eros." Integral levels themselves are creative and highly conscious; each moment is new, fresh, spontaneous, and alive. It is the first stage that integrates, or better, recognizes, the already existing prior union of knowing and feeling, consciousness and being, epistemology and ontology. It does not fracture them from each other and then try to "ground" one in the other, but rather sees and feels them to be complementary aspects of the same seamless Whole of reality, operating not by disembodied reflection or representation but by embodied mutual resonance within all 4 quadrants. "Truth" is not the grounding of a siloed epistemology in a realist ontology, or a representational/propositional match with an objective phenomenon, but a 4-quadrant mutual resonance between knower, known, and knowing, all tetra-enacted.

Thus, unlike the previous Pluralistic View, the Integral View is truly holistic, not in any New Age woo-woo sense, but because it sees itself as part of a deeply interwoven and interconnected and conscious Kosmos. The Pluralistic View, we saw, wants to be holistic, all-inclusive, and nonmarginalizing, and even calls itself "The Integral Culture," but with its typically 1st-tier attitude, it despises other levels and their values, and thus can hardly include them. It loathes the modern Rational View, absolutely cannot abide the traditional Mythic View, and goes apoplectic when faced with a truly Integral View. But the Integral stages are truly and genuinely inclusive. All of the previous structure-rungs are literally included as components of the Integral structure-rung, or vision-logic.

Views, of course, are negated, and so somebody at an Integral View does not directly include a Magic View, a Mythic View, a Rational View, and so on (although the Integral rung, vision-logic, does include *all* of their underlying rungs—from images and symbols to rule/role to formal operational). By definition, it is impossible to include all Views, since they are created by *exclusively* identifying with, and seeing the world through, a particular rung (just as with a real ladder, you stand on just one rung at a time; even though all the lower rungs are still present, you aren't standing on them). You can't *exclusively* identify with ALL rungs—any more than you can stand on all the rungs in a ladder simultaneously.

All *rungs* are "included" and "preserved" in each higher rung, as actual components, but "exclusivity" Views tend to alternate between *contradictory* stances, which can't themselves be included. They can only be let go of, because they don't fit together; in fact, they are often mutually contradictory—for instance, in moving from the egocentric power View to the next stage's conformist law-and-order View, you can't be both a wildly individual power seeker with rabid anticonformist drives AND a nice, sweet, totally conformist person following religiously all the rules of your culture! Nor can you include both a mythic, conformist law-and-order View and a rational individuality View—these don't fit together either, although, again, their underlying rungs do; yet another reason why rungs are included, but Views are negated. Remember that a View is generated when the central, or proximate, self *exclusively* identifies with a particular rung of development and looks at the world primarily and solely through that rung. Somebody at a Rational View is exclusively identified with the corresponding rung at that stage—namely, metarule or formal operational mind (see table 1). For such a person to have direct access to, say, a Magic View, which means the View of the world when it is looked at exclusively through the impulsive-fantasy, or emotional-sexual, rung, the individual would have to give up the rational mind, and give up the concrete mind, and give up the representational or conceptual mind and all linguistic capacities, and regress totally to the impulsive mind (something that doesn't happen without severe brain damage, advanced Alzheimer's, and so forth). The Rational person still has complete access to the emotional-sexual *rung* (or structure) but not to the *exclusive* View from that rung (because he or she is no longer exclusively identified with that rung and is no longer standing on just that rung in the ladder of development). Thus, rungs are included; Views are negated.

So a person at Integral doesn't directly, in their own makeup, have immediate access to earlier Views (archaic, magic, mythic, and so on), but they do have access to all the earlier corresponding rungs that supported those views (sensorimotor, emotional-sexual, conceptual, rule/role, and so forth), and thus can generally intuit what rung a particular person's center of gravity is at, and thus indirectly be able to understand what View, or worldview, that person is expressing (magic, mythic, rational, pluralistic, and so on). The Integral levels actively tolerate and make room for those Views in their own holistic outreach. They might not agree fully with them (they don't do so in their own makeup, having transcended, negated, and let go of junior Views), but they intuitively understand the significance and importance of all Views in the unfolding sweep of evolutionary development. Further, they understand that a person has the right to stop growing at virtually any stage and its View, and thus each particular View will become, for some people, an actual *station in life*, and their values, needs, and motivations will be expressions of that particular View in life. And thus a truly enlightened, inclusive society will make some sort of room for traditional values, modern values, postmodern values, and so on—understanding that every *stage of development* is a potential *station in life* for large numbers of people, and thus room must be culturally and socially made for that.

Everybody is born at square one and thus begins their development of Views at that lowest rung and continues from there, so every society will consist of a different mix of percentages of people at different rungs and Views on the overall spectrum—an archaeological "layer cake" of all of the major level-rungs of existence (and their Views) that have emerged and evolved thus far, starting with the first and moving to the highest-to-date in that culture.

And yet only an Integral View possesses that understanding, which means, as evolution continues to move into Integral levels, society is poised for perhaps the most momentous transformation in its entire history—a profoundly and truly *inclusive* orientation (what Graves called that "monumental leap in meaning"). There's been nothing like it before in history because there has never been a *tier* transformation before, certainly nothing like this one. All previous transformations were stage transformations. But the transformation from the Pluralistic stage to the Integral stage is also and simultaneously a transformation from 1st tier to 2nd tier—and that, *that*, is epic, revolutionary, and utterly unprecedented. We don't even have any examples of how to construct a radically inclusive, all-rung, all-View society, where all Views are given a voice, perhaps differently weighted, but a voice nonetheless, as each stage of development becomes a welcome station in life.[3]

The Integral stage (turquoise), or Fowler's "universalizing," is the highest structure-stage Fowler's research presents. He has no Super-Integral, 3rd-tier stages; nor did his research cover states or state-stages, because so little spirituality in the West has any state-mystical development in its teachings, and so little of it showed up in his research. The Integral Institute gave Fowler the first "Integral Spiritual" Achievement Award for his truly pioneering research into the structure-stages of spiritual intelligence—the first of its kind anywhere in history—and when I spoke to him about structures and states, he said that the existence of both of them made perfect sense to him and solved a lot of puzzles he had been considering, particularly the relationship between spiritual intelligence, or stages of faith, and Enlightenment and Awakening, or stages of states. But he could hardly have been expected to research that which is rarely there anymore, and thus shows up in few if any research populations. As for the lack of 3rd-tier structure-stages, this is likely for the reasons we discussed at the beginning of chapter 6. The percentage of people at turquoise is around 0.5 percent (or, at any rate, less than 1 percent); the percentage of people at the next stage, indigo or para-mind, would almost certainly be at most less than a tenth of that. So there just aren't enough of them to show up in most research populations.

But this is slowly changing as evolution continues its relentless "creative advance into novelty." Turquoise, and then 3rd tier, are, in the meantime, literally the "growing tip" of humanity's consciousness and culture—the small, pioneering, exploratory, growing apex of the developing plant, reaching for the sun, which the entire body will soon follow as growth continues.

Spiritual Intelligence and Development in 3rd Tier

We can discuss these 3rd-tier structures (and their spiritual intelligence) in terms of certain common features they possess, tentative as any such conjectures might be (although there is a modest amount of research starting to trickle in about these stages). Integral Theory postulates at least four levels of 3rd tier at this time. Aurobindo, for example, had four major levels in 3rd tier (the para-mind, he called "the illumined mind"; the meta-mind, he called "the intuitive mind"; and then what he called "Overmind" and "Supermind," which are terms I have borrowed from him but define somewhat differently).

Each level of 3rd tier has three fundamental characteristics: a transpersonal component or aspect, a direct sense of wholeness, and an "awareness of awareness."

First, being 3rd tier, they all have (or certainly at least the higher ones have) a direct transpersonal aspect, component, or dimension to them. This means that the person has started to recognize or intuit some version of his or her Higher Selves. (If the subtle realm is involved, the "soul" is felt; if the causal realm, the "Higher Self"; if the Witnessing realm, the "True, or Real, Self"; if the nondual realm, the

Witness-less, Selfless, Subject-less "Suchness." The specific form of each of these depends in part on the specific structure that the state is being conjoined with—for example, the "soul" in the gross-oriented Nature mysticism realm is of a somewhat different structure than the soul in the subtle-oriented Deity mysticism realm, since the structure/ state complex has shifted significantly.) In any of those transpersonal events, the individual feels a deep and abiding current that begins to run quite beyond the personality, and, at the Supermind, beyond "individuality" itself in any form. At 3rd tier, one's sense of *Kosmic connection* is thus wide, deep, profound, and immediate. A sense of Wholeness is directly experienced (and expands at each successive level), and is connected with the transpersonal dimension of identity that is present at each level. The "transcend and include" nature of structure development has made structure upon structure upon structure more and more aware, so that an "awareness of awareness" is now inherently present at each level (or an almost constant Awareness of the fact that one is aware). This is not necessarily a highly self-reflexive awareness—"I am always Aware that I am aware"—but simply, even when the separate-self sense or "I" is arising, there is the ever-present sense of a background Awareness of a much vaster, broader, deeper contextual Consciousness in which the "I" and all other manifest objects are arising. It is closer to a type of "I-I" Awareness, whose actual realization is an increasing aspect of 3rd-tier levels, until "I-I" directly manifests in Overmind and disappears into the Suchness of Supermind, at which point "awareness of awareness" ceases to be associated with any individuality at all and is felt rather as an intrinsic quality of the nondual Kosmos itself in all dimensions. This transpersonal "awareness of awareness" is directly connected to the particular type of Higher Self being experienced at the particular level (for example, the soul, the Higher Self, the True Self, or nondual Suchness).

3rd tier is marked by being essentially a specific union of states and structures. All structures are always arising in a particular state (that is, every experience is a "structure/state" experience), but at 3rd tier, the particular state becomes an intrinsic part of the structure itself. For example, indigo is often the union of the para-mind structure and the objectified gross state (that is, minimally, the gross state; higher-state unions are possible). Violet is marked by the union of the meta-mind structure and the subtle state (again, minimally the subtle state—which means, structure development cannot proceed beyond this point without including an objectifying of, and conjoining with, the subtle state; higher-state conjunctions are possible, and the subtle-state conjunction can happen earlier, but development cannot proceed beyond this point without at least this degree of subtle-state conjoining). Ultraviolet is marked minimally by the conjunction of the Overmind structure and the causal/Witnessing state. And white or clear light is marked minimally by the conjuncture of the Supermind structure and the Nondual state.

The 3rd-tier structures are also marked primarily by their perception of wholes: indigo, by directly *seeing* wholes; violet, by directly *feeling* wholes; ultraviolet, by directly *witnessing* wholes; and clear light, by directly *being* wholes. This sense of wholeness began, of course, with 2nd tier, but this wholeness enters 2nd-tier awareness in a conceptual manner, and also somewhat sporadically—now present, now not, always a background possibility but not always a foreground given. Most importantly, 2nd-tier wholeness is a wholeness that is largely conceptualized—2nd tier constantly thinks of itself and its world as a vast interwoven and mutually interdependent dynamic series of things and events that are intimately interconnected with each other in an almost infinite number of ways. But with 3rd tier, the "awareness of wholeness" is fairly constant, along with an "awareness of awareness," and most significantly, this wholeness is directly experienced, not merely thought; one's self, at whatever 3rd-tier level, is a wholeness interwoven with various aspects of the Kosmos at large, and in a direct and immediately experienced fashion.

Those specific sequential relations to wholeness (seeing, feeling, witnessing, being) can vary, although those are typical averages, and they are consistent with Aurobindo's descriptions of them—"seeing" with "illumined mind," "feeling" with "intuitive mind," "witnessing" with "Overmind," and "being" with "Supermind"—but what doesn't vary is the "awareness of wholes" in general that marks each 3rd-tier level, along with its transpersonal aspect and its "awareness of awareness" component. "Thinking," to the extent that that word has any meaning in 3rd tier, occurs by moving from one prehended whole to the next whole to the next, concluding with a concrescence of wholes completed by that process. These wholes can be seen gross wholes (indigo para-mind), felt subtle wholes (violet meta-mind), witnessed causal wholes (ultraviolet Overmind), or nondual wholes (white or clear light Supermind), with the caveat that these state unions are only the minimal ones required to move beyond that structure; higher-state unions are possible with all of them. Each level of wholeness "transcends and includes" the previous levels' wholes, with the net result that, at Supermind, there is a Whole Reality with no major structure or state left out (at least at this point in evolution)—an ultimate, superhuman, Super-Integral Awareness by any standard. Supermind's electric awareness is a *coincidentia oppositorum*—a union of all possible opposites, excluding no aspect of Reality. It is the ultimate, leading edge of evolution itself at this time, and thus is a major input-influx station where Spirit itself enters the manifest world via new and novel manifestations, which find their way down the overall great spectrum of structures and states via ceaseless "downward causation" (or involutionary imprinting), which affects the very nature, process, and course of evolution itself.

The stunning new discoveries and evolutionary alterations awaiting humans at this point in history are not to be found so much in the Upper Right quadrant, with its nano-, robotic, and genetic breakthroughs, stunning as they are, and that are already threatening to completely redo the three-hundred-year-old "humanistic" definition of humans—which has, one way or another, dominated both the modern and postmodern foundational self-image of what it is to be human—and to do so by redefining what "human" and "consciousness" themselves mean in relation to advanced technological breakthroughs and possibilities. Instead, bigger, more profound breakthroughs await in the Upper Left, where the increasing number of people developing into 3rd-tier supramental capacities will redefine the human self-image by redefining the profound role highly developed consciousness can play by having a direct impact on evolution itself. This has already begun to happen with 2nd tier, where highly evolved people already have the capacity to help co-create the newly emerging world via their tetra-enaction in all 4 quadrants, but this will become greater and greater as more and more individuals move into 3rd tier and its evolutionary leading edges, especially that of Overmind and particularly Supermind. This will be a supramental, superconscious singularity in which human intentionality directly intervenes in evolution (by way of involution/Efflux), not via mere computational power artifacts—as with the prophesied technological singularity—but unswervingly via human (or superhuman) intentionality directly and immediately altering the networked structure of the Kosmos itself.

Each 3rd-tier structure has some aspect of its identity that is transpersonal—that is, it is directly beyond the isolated, individual body-mind. This begins tentatively in 2nd tier, where the self begins to think of itself as irrevocably interwoven with systems within systems within systems surrounding it, so that "individual" begins to dissolve into "global systems." But in 3rd tier, this moves from being a thought to being some variety of direct experiential awareness—a directly seen or felt wholeness. Again, this is one of the differences between the wholeness of 2nd tier, where wholeness itself is first fully disclosed and becomes fundamental to awareness, and the wholeness of 3rd tier, where wholeness becomes more directly interconnected and intermeshed with individual identity itself in a complex interweaving. Further, the "transcend and include" nature of structures, at 3rd tier, reaches such a degree that "awareness of awareness" becomes a constant and intrinsic feature of most 3rd-tier structures. That is, the individual is almost constantly conscious of being aware of Awareness itself, of the Awareness that is co-creating the Kosmos itself. The "reflexivity" of the "awareness of awareness" is brought by the degree of "transcend and include" in the 3rd-tier structures, or the degree of wholeness of each succeeding 3rd-tier level, as each structure continues to "transcend and include," "transcend and include," "transcend and include," until the archaeological layering is so thick and rich that "awareness of awareness of awareness" is inherently sewn and interwoven into the very fabric of 3rd-tier structures. Also the "depth" of the consciousness is increased by the degree of state inclusion in each succeeding level, which also contributes to the degree of wholeness in each senior level.

Supermind, at this point in evolution, seems to be the highest structure of consciousness yet to begin to emerge, and it is combined with the highest state of consciousness yet to emerge (nondual Suchness). The result is a seeing/feeling/witnessing/being interwoven stream of Whole after Whole after Whole after Whole, which instantaneously present themselves to the mind's eye, or nondual Awakened Awareness, in a spontaneous, effortless, dynamic fashion—while Supermind is also able to concentrate on individual particulars at any point, and to do so in the timeless Now, while also including the entire history of a holon all the way back to the Big Bang. All of this is a constant feature of Supermind consciousness—the entire Kosmos is aware of the entire Kosmos, in the Kosmos, through the Kosmos, as the Kosmos. It is an Indra's Net electrically hypercharged with superhuman capacities in its every movement, as human and Divine become increasingly hard to tell apart, both dimensions seamlessly entangled with each other, as each other. This is different from Big Mind alone, which can be experienced at virtually any lower level, and is itself defined simply as the nondual (or turiyatita) state. But Supermind is Big Mind *plus* every single structure or level of evolutionary development going all the way back to the Big Bang. As the highest structure-rung in the human, it contains all of the previous holonic levels that humans contain (all the way back to the beginning of evolution itself): strings, quarks, atoms, molecules, cells, organisms, as well as the fundamental properties of life forms, from plant biochemistry to fish to amphibians to reptiles to mammals to primates. These forms are fully enfolded in a human being at birth—we literally contain and include the essential elements from each and every level of existence in the entire Kosmos. Supermind also contains all of the human holonic structure-levels as they evolved and developed: the sensorimotor rung (with its Archaic View), the emotional-sexual (with its Magic View), intentional concepts (with its PowerGods View), the rule/role mind (with its Mythic View), the abstract rule/role mind (with its Mythic-Rational View) the formal operational (with its Rational View), pluralistic (with its Pluralistic View), vision-logic (with its Holistic and Integral Views) para-mind (with its Transglobal View), meta-mind (with its Visionary View), and Overmind (with its Transcendent View). Finally, we have Supermind and its utterly Unitary Wholeness Nondual View, which is Big Mind state PLUS *all of those previous structures*. It is the action of nondual Big Mind working in conjunction with the entire evolutionary Kosmos that makes Supermind the most superhuman structure/state that exists anywhere, capable of a "personal omniscience" that, due to its access to every previous structure-rung in the human being, has access to every world that has yet emerged and evolved anywhere in the Kosmos. This is the Kosmos seeing itself through the Kosmos, and resonating with each and every element in every manifest world that exists, a thunderously staggering Kosmic space that is beyond the wildest imagination, even when you're in it.

The 3rd-tier "union," or even "identity," between states and the structure-levels of para-mind, meta-mind, Overmind, and Supermind brings the deep potentials of states into the evolutionary stream of structures, and for the first time in a relation of necessary interwovenness. In contrast, in 1st and 2nd tier, states and structures always exist together and are always interacting, but they are relatively independent of each other (both are *always* present as a structure/state complex, but there are hardly any constraints on which structure is present with which state). You can be at orange rational and have a peak experience of a nondual state; you can be at green pluralistic and have a peak experience of a subtle state; and so on. You can also be at virtually any structure (beyond red) and experience the entire sequence of state development, all the way to traditional Enlightenment—although you will interpret those states according to the structure-stage you are at (such as amber or green).

If "Big Mind" is used as a synonym for the nondual state, you can be at, say, teal, and have a Big Mind experience (which you will interpret in teal terms). But notice: you cannot be at teal and have a peak experience of Supermind. Supermind is a structure, not a state per se (although it is conjoined with the nondual state), and therefore, in its structural dimension, Supermind must be grown and developed. Integral Theory says, "States are free, structures are earned," which means that most states can be peak experienced, or plateau experienced, by virtually any structure, because these states are already present in some degree in everyone, just as an infant wakes, dreams, and sleeps (or goes through gross, subtle, and causal realms), but structures themselves have to grow, evolve, and unfold in a developmental fashion, "transcending and including" their predecessors. So you can't be at, say, a Magic structure, and peak experience a Pluralistic structure. The highest structure you can peak experience is only one level higher than the one you are at, two at most (and that rarely). So Rational can peak experience Big Mind—or virtually any other state—but it cannot peak experience high vision-logic, para-mind, meta-mind, Overmind, or Supermind. Those have to grow and develop on their own; they have to be "earned."

This is why Supermind is so important—it's Big Mind PLUS all of the previous structures, infrared to ultraviolet. As the highest structure that we are aware of that has emerged so far, and being "in union" with the nondual state, which is the highest realized state to date, Supermind is especially the point where state potentials enter directly into structural potentials, and thus Supermind is the ultimate growing tip of evolution itself. Now this doesn't mean that other structures can't or don't contribute to evolution. They do, especially those that are just being laid down now as Kosmic habits or Kosmic grooves, which means, roughly, any structure at, or higher than, turquoise (and to some degree, teal). These structures are newly emergent features in the Kosmos, and thus individuals at those structure-levels have a significant impact on how those (and higher) structures are actually formed and shaped as they continue to emerge and settle into the specific Kosmic structure-pattern (or habit) that they will eventually have on a relatively permanent basis. You, in your very thoughts, actions, and behaviors, with your obvious interest in Integral, are contributing to the very form of tomorrow, the very structure of the leading-edge patterns of consciousness, culture, and evolution itself. Welcome, indeed, to your place in history—you are, right now, contributing to its very shape.

This is a major difference in how Integral Theory views evolution compared with the standard Neo-Darwinian synthesis. In the standard Darwinian view, for evolution to occur, you need genetic material (DNA or RNA), and you need a random or chance mutation in this genetic material in an extremely rare form that is not lethal—because virtually all of them are—and further, one that actually contributes to the organism's capacity to successfully reproduce. This also means that you need this same incredibly rare mutation (or a series of them) to occur in a male organism *and* a female organism simultaneously, and—even more unlikely—they have to find each other and then mate. (What if one is in Siberia and the other is in Mexico? Even the notion that "similar regions produce similar mutations" is worthless, because some bioregions are the size of four states—what if the male is in Wyoming and the female is in Nebraska?) Finally, they must tend the offspring until it can mate and pass on the "evolved" material. All in all, an unlikely story.

For Integral Theory, every moment is a Neo-Whiteheadian "prehensive unification" (or what Integral Theory calls a "tetra-prehension," to indicate that this prehension, or "feeling," of the previous moment by the newly emerging moment occurs in all 4 quadrants). The point is that every moment, in every quadrant, passes on its basic form and qualities to the next moment, which embraces and enfolds those items (the "include" part of "transcend and include"), and then adds its own new or novel or creative aspects (the "transcend" part of "transcend and include"). As long as this new moment "fits" in all 4 quadrants ("tetra-prehension"), then it will be selected and carried forward in evolution, along with its new and more creative aspects. If it doesn't fit well in all quadrants (through "mutual resonance"), it will be extinguished, or become extinct, and simply cease to exist.

One of the ways that Whitehead views this is that each moment comes to be as a subject (a holon with prehension or protoconsciousness or protoperspective), and as it does so, it "feels" or "prehends" the previous moment's subject, which therefore becomes an object of the present moment's new subject. This new subject feels, embraces, or "includes" the previous subject (now as object), which is the "determining" aspect of the past on the present. As the new subject includes, prehends, or enfolds the previous moment, now as object, that previous moment obviously has an impact, a "causative" impact, on the new present moment. According to Whitehead, the present moment then adds its own new, novel, and creative components to "transcend" that previous moment and thus, to some degree, to "transcend" the previous moment's determining influence and bring something new into the Kosmos. (Without this novel or creative addition, nothing new would emerge anywhere in the universe, since the present would be totally determined and caused by the past.) Thus, moment to moment, on a microscale, the subject of one moment becomes the object of the subject of the next moment. Yet this is also the form of development in human stages, on a mesoscale. As Kegan put it, in human development, "the subject of one stage becomes the object of the subject of the next stage."[4] The same fundamental movement of "transcend and include," which Integral Theory maintains occurs in every region of the Kosmos, is how a present moment actually fits with a succeeding moment; it's what has to happen for that to occur. This happens not just in microholons (Whitehead) and mesoholons (Kegan), but also in macroholons, such as collective or social holons, where the intersubjective nexus-agency becomes a subcomponent of the next moment's nexus-agency—again, the same "transcend and include" is the operative dynamic. This "transcend and include" is thus one of the basic 20 tenets, or fundamental "involutionary givens," of this particular universe. That is, this "transcend and include" did not itself evolve but had to be present from the Big Bang forward, already operating from the first moment of the emergence of this universe, or this universe itself could not have moved forward at all.

But this is another reason that you—your thoughts, actions, feelings, communications, interactions, and behaviors—can directly contribute to evolution in all 4 quadrants, simply by adding something new and novel that hasn't existed before (including thoughts, feelings, ideas). If your addition is occurring on teal or turquoise (or higher), then it is open to becoming part of the very structure of that level of consciousness (Left Hand quadrants) and complexity (Right Hand quadrants). You don't need to have sex and pass on some fluky genetic mutation to somebody else who also had the same fluky mutation in order to contribute to evolution. If that were so, where did all the novelty and newness come from in the universe during the millions of years before sex was invented? (Atoms, after all, gave rise to molecules, a massively new and novel emergent, Eros in action, and molecules gave rise to living cells, a stunningly creative emergent, all without genetic mutation and natural selection but rather in a "transcend and include" in mutual fit in all 4 quadrants.)

And doesn't that standard Darwinian view really mean that, for instance, today's geniuses who aren't sexually active, or those who have same-sex partners, or those whose profound mutations occur only in themselves and in nobody else are not going to contribute to actual evolution in the slightest? Another moronic story.

No, simply think the highest thoughts you can; feel the deepest love you are capable of; reach up or down to the highest, or deepest, Divinity that you can experience; treat others with the tenderest of kindness and the most caring of compassion that you possibly can; and if you are anywhere near the leading edge of evolution (which you certainly are if you are interested in the subjects found in this and similar books), you will directly, immediately, and instantly contribute to what Whitehead called "an ultimate of the universe"—namely, the "creative advance into novelty." In other words, you will contribute to evolution itself. Indeed, welcome to your place in history.

So let's look at each of the higher 3rd-tier levels in more detail. Again, these are to some degree hypothetical; but whatever we decide about them, they are profoundly important: they represent the actual future of humanity.

Indigo Para-Mind

At the para-mind (indigo, Fulcrum-9, Transglobal View), the person tends to drop the typical egoic body-mind identification and starts to experience a much broader, wider, vaster sense of individuality, reaching out and beyond the mind (or "aside" from the mind, which is what "para" means), sometimes expanding to the entire realm of nature, or the entire gross realm (occasionally further). It is at this level that the gross realm must be conjoined with, or fully objectified, if development is to continue (and this "conjunction" can occur across the broad spectrum of communion, union, or identity). This level (as with most others) is also capable of including subtle, causal, and nondual state/realms, depending upon the developmental history at previous structure-stages and what states they have already included (or the individual's state center of gravity). In any event, knowing and feeling—consciousness and being—are felt as deeply interconnected, two aspects of the same Whole event.

Because of that, the universe is seen, understood, and felt, not just as a physical realm, but as a profoundly psychophysical realm. The very concepts and ideas one uses to frame the world are seen, for the first time, to have a profound impact on how that realm appears and is experienced. This is different from the Pluralistic level's view about the importance of interpretation in unpacking experiences, because the latter is simply a view about how a separate epistemology affects, or helps to determine, a separate ontology (which, in its more extreme versions of social constructionism, does commit the standard version of the epistemic fallacy—all things are said to be nothing but "social constructions"—the world is *entirely* created by one's mode of knowing). But this 3rd-tier view is not a recognition of how two separate realms (knowing and being, or epistemology and ontology) affect each other but a direct experience of the underlying Whole that unites them both as correlative dimensions of the same Whole event, which can't be separated into two realms in the first place (which all 1st-tier levels do). These dimensions are rather two different ways of viewing and feeling the same fundamental reality. What we call "perception" (of "objects") and "conception" (of a knowing "subject") both issue from a deeper, more organically Whole dimension than either of them alone. When an epistemic proposition is said to "represent" an ontic object accurately, what is actually happening, at a deeper level—as revealed at 3rd tier—is that a single, prior, reverberating Whole reality is resonating at both poles (inadequately labeled "epistemic" and "ontic"), giving the impression, to 1st-tier perception, that two different realms have been brought together, or that one has been "grounded" in the other, or that one "represents" the other. In fact, a single Wholeness is vibrating, or resonating, in tune, and if the Whole is real or true, the proposition will appear to "match" the object via mutual resonance in what are inadequately called "subject" and "object," and if not, not. But it is the Wholeness, not the split representation, that is real. This is why what "ex-ists" at any given level is a co-enaction of them both (along with the particular methodology, a single Wholeness of "who," "how," and "what" that are mutually interwoven—in other words, a 4-quadrant resonance), and thus what arises in consciousness is the result of this deeper Wholeness as it simultaneously tetra-arises in and through all 4 quadrants. The world is not physical; it is psychophysical, all the way up, all the way down— every single Right-hand event in the world has a correlative Left-hand dimension, bar none.

This means that epistemology, methodology, and ontology are all intimately interwoven as different correlative aspects of this same Whole Event (or "who," "how," and "what"). Change any one of them, and the *experienced phenomenon* is changed to a significant degree: integral pluralistic subjects or epistemologies, or "whos"; *and* integral pluralistic methodologies, or "hows"; *and* integral pluralistic objects or ontologies, or "whats"—overall, Integral Pluralistic Enaction. "Truth" is determined, not by having one of those "reflect," "represent," or "be grounded" in any of the others, but by a mutual harmonic resonance of all of them in all 4 quadrants (the 4 quadrants are inherently present in each anyway, as four intrinsic dimensions of the same Whole Event). This means that one "feels" truth as much as one "knows" truth and "enacts" truth—all simultaneously resonating with each other when truth is present, and not resonating when truth is lacking (or "falsity" is present)—and the phenomenon being "felt/known/enacted" is as well a manifestation of a state and a structure (the dual center of gravity). This might sound like an inordinately complex affair, but it is actually incredibly simple and immediate; what makes it sound complex is 1st tier's prior tearing apart of all of those dimensions in the first place. (Or, more accurately, it is that 1st tier does not have enough cognitive power to see the Whole to begin with, and thus instead it actually experiences each of them as being separate, set-apart, fragmented partialities. So 1st tier genuinely and honestly believes that the areas it is trying to bring together—such as epistemology and ontology—are actually separate, independent, "smashing-into-each-other" dimensions. Only by 2nd tier are they cognized as unified, and only at 3rd tier are they directly experienced as unified. (See chapter 3, note 15.)

Compassion, at 3rd tier (and beginning immediately with indigo, with intimations already present at turquoise), starts to include not only all humans ("worldcentric") but all sentient beings as well ("Kosmocentric"), particularly if actual "nature mysticism" is present (and even if not, because every individual holon is a sentient being—every "physical" event is really a "psychophysical" entity, via "panpsychism"—and thus including all sentient beings means including the entire manifest universe, down to the sentient beings that are quarks and atoms, whether called "Nature mysticism" or not). Wholes are readily *seen*, and "thinking" (to the extent that that word has any meaning in 3rd tier) occurs primarily by moving from one prehended whole to the next prehended whole to the next. At indigo para-mind, those wholes are delivered primarily by the next cognitive stage up from vision-logic, which is, namely, not vision-logic but pure *vision* (what Aurobindo called "the illumined mind"). Spirituality here, as noted, is often of a "nature mysticism" variety (although higher forms are available), but that just means that spiritual intelligence at this level is profoundly psychophysical in its nature, understanding the deeply interwoven (and mutually enactive) character of consciousness and Kosmos at all levels.

Further, all forms of spiritual intelligence at this indigo level (whether communion, union, or identity) have a strong focus on *the communion of all being*, or the interconnectedness and "oneness" of all sentient beings at all levels. That is, Indra's Net takes on a real four-dimensionality (which began at 2nd tier, but flowers at 3rd), which means that the universe is not merely *holographic* (a view common in green cognition, which is a particularly nonhierarchical *flatland* form) but also *holarchical* (which adds a developmental depth dimension). "Holographic" means that "all things are contained in all things," whereas "holarchical" means that "all of the lower is in the higher, but not all of the higher is in the lower." Evolutionary sequences are obviously holarchical—for example, atoms to molecules to cells to organisms: all of an atom is in a molecule, but not all of the molecule is in an atom; all of the molecule is in a cell, but not all of the cell is in a molecule; all of the cell is in an organism, but not all of the organism is in a cell; and so on. Each level "transcends and includes" its predecessor, which is the only way that one moment of the universe can exist with the next moment of the universe. This gives a genuine vertical *depth* to the universe, not a flatland equivalency everywhere, and accounts for the undeniable "increase in complexity" (and consciousness) that the universe has been bent on displaying since day one.[5] The Kosmos is thus not merely holographic (with no degree of depth recognized anywhere), but is rather holographic and holarchical—an interwoven interconnectedness, psychophysical in nature, that holographically networks innumerable holarchies (where, in each case, all of the junior is in the senior, but not all the senior is in the junior). These holarchies, multileveled, multinetworked layer cakes of holons, are the result of Spirit-in-action's, or Eros's, "transcend and include" movement for some 14 billion years, going all the way back to the Big Bang, transcending and including, transcending and including, transcending and including. Wherever you hear an account that speaks of the Kosmos as just "holographic," you're hearing a green View, and worse, in its truly flatland version, one that lacks any vertical depth.

Such views also are incapable of supporting a truly developmental or evolutionary view, since there is no gradient, no room for Eros, just a flatland view of every point containing every other point, endlessly and equivalently—with nowhere at all for evolution to go. If evolution ever produces one real emergent—something that is present now that was not present yesterday—then a holographic universe is impossible, since in a real hologram, each part contains the entire whole, and if new wholes are emerging, they clearly aren't part of the earlier hologram—and so the model and metaphor collapses.[6]

Aurobindo says of this level that it "works not through thought but primarily through vision"—a point we already agreed with but arrived at somewhat differently than did Aurobindo—and this *vision* "affects a powerful and dynamic integration by illumining thoughtmind with inner vision, imbibing the heart with spiritual sight, and the emotions with spiritual light and energy." Note the emphasis on "integration," or Wholeness, seen with inner vision. When this indigo level claims that it is agnostic, what it almost always means, to the extent that it is truly indigo (or 3rd tier), is that all of the typical and traditional notions of God are inapplicable here; and given the typical notions of God that are available—most of them magic or mythic-literal of one variety or another—being agnostic, or even atheistic, is completely understandable. But what is actually occurring in the indigo awareness is an infusion of consciousness with transpersonal elements that can be interpreted as multisystemic interconnections with virtually all beings in existence, an experience of the Great Web of Life as being interwoven with one's own indigo Self as if it were the skin on one's expanded body, the realization that one is not merely an individual person but part of an incredibly extended system or network (or "Great Web") of life and being (which is *thought* at turquoise but *experienced* at indigo)—so that one begins to feel that way, as one's own expanded identity. The psychophysical nature of all Reality gives every thing and event in existence a radiance, an almost inner glow, as subject and object grow increasingly more interwoven and "closer" to each other, reflecting two poles of an underlying Wholeness, directly seen or perceived with the para-mind. The self has indeed begun to step into realms that are increasingly transpersonal, and the net of its own identity is thus expanding into more and more dimensions of a genuinely Kosmocentric nature.

Violet Meta-Mind

The violet meta-mind, as a structure, likewise transcends and includes all previous basic structure-rungs, and thus there is a profound felt understanding of the holarchical nature of all previous levels, their knowledge and substance and interconnection with the surrounding

Kosmos. The meta-mind (violet, Fulcrum-10) works primarily with a cognition of *feeling-awareness* (and felt Wholeness), which is capable of focusing on the timeless Now for certain stretches, while also capable of tracking long reaches of historical, or evolutionary, time. Feeling-awareness is particularly a unity of intellect and feelings, knowing and being, in an unbroken, seamless conjunction, with epistemology and ontology so tightly bound as to rarely even be distinguished, although the distinction is available to the meta-mind (though rarely used; hybrid terms such as "perspective/dimension" are often substituted). This is a type of culmination of the union of knowing and feeling that first began in 2nd tier, where, for the first time, epistemology and ontology were understood as two conjoined aspects of the same Whole Reality (and thus were likewise conjoined with methodology, or the "how" of the tetra-enaction process, involving all 4 quadrants in mutual harmonic resonance). The immediate "touchness" of feeling-awareness is similar to what Aurobindo meant when he called this stage "the intuitive stage," with "intuition" implying the immediate "touchness" that is so characteristic of feeling-awareness (although, as we'll see later, "intuitive" is perhaps not the best name for this level, since it implies "intuition" is not available at lower levels, which simply isn't true). The "immediateness" of feeling-awareness is a product of such a rich and thick history of "transcend and include," going all the way back to the Big Bang, that this level begins to bring all of the previous structures under its umbrella via this feeling-awareness, which is extraordinarily all-encompassing, or wildly inclusive—inwardly touching all of these rich previous structures, but doing so in an accelerated, immediate fashion; one "feels" their "Wholeness" in a single grasp, Wholeness after Wholeness after Wholeness. It is the "meta" part of this meta-mind level, the "moving beyond ordinary mind," that contributes to its being able to embrace, to "include," these previous levels in its feeling-awareness, as if the Erotic process of "transcend and include" has gone on for so long that both the "transcend" part, seen in the "meta" aspect, and the "include" part, seen in the "feeling," or "immediate touch," aspect, have both become nearly superhuman. This is a process that is headed straight to Supermind, which is, in itself, nothing short of what indeed could be called "superhuman," and that is now indeed an aspect of humanity's own future—that is, its own genuine "superhumanity," a combination of evolution into the superhuman dimensions of all 4 quadrants—from Upper Left state Big Mind, to Lower Right technological Singularity, to Lower Left cultural transformation, to Upper Right cyborg brain/computer/consciousness connections, to Upper Left structural Supermind itself. We will return to this extraordinary possibility when we discuss Supermind.

Various deep features at this meta-mind stage include rapid data-scanning capacities; feeling-awareness of "felt Wholes"—where thinking proceeds immediate felt Whole by immediate felt Whole by immediate felt Whole, delivering up, at any moment of direct attention, the particular "Wholeness" being discerned at that point in the scan; luminous "visionary" awareness (with "visionary" defined as "beyond 1st- and 2nd-tier phenomena"); profoundly creative processes (due primarily to the release of feeling/knowing from being bound to gross dimensions and restrictions, and transcending lower tiers); feelings of "shimmering," "gleaming," "incandescence," and "radiance" due to "luminous visionary" components; spirituality felt as especially "fecund" and "superabundant" (connected with widespread "creativity"; "the mother of all worlds"); and a profound sensing of the surrounding environment as being one's own body, one's own skin.

Some of these luminous/radiant forms and patterns (as with those in the actual subtle realm) are often interpreted, especially by lower levels, as real beings infused with profound luminosity (for example, angels). The "radiant or luminous patterns" are partly why spirituality here often tends toward a "deity mysticism" variety (where "deity," at this level, is often interpreted—*by this level itself*—as the Intelligence of the Kosmos, the creative power, or force, of bringing forth whole worlds, a nonanthropomorphic view of Spirit in 2nd person), which is also in keeping with the general visionary nature of the meta-mind. ("Meta" means going quite beyond the "gross" mind as well as the lower 1st and 2nd tiers, and thus the meta-mind is unanchored directly in the sensorimotor or gross-mind realm, and is hence free to roam the "imaginal" or "visionary" realm with great and fluent ease. This is demonstrated particularly in the subtle dream state itself, where merely to think an object is to see it materialized, and images cascade all over each other, transforming at whim into other images and other objects, stretching from the timeless Now to vast stretches of real time.)

If the form of spirituality here involves conjunction with the subtle (a direct "deity mysticism"), we find a communion/union/identity with Divine forms (occasionally higher); but apart from that, the spiritual intelligence at this stage is in most cases focused on realms of awareness that are not merely gross or gross oriented, or 1st- and 2nd-tier bound (that is, a spiritual intelligence that focuses quite *beyond* "the Great Web of Life," to items such as the Intelligent Metacreatrix of the Great Web itself), and tends to the "imaginal" or "visionary" as related to divine forms of felt Wholeness, moment to moment, along with an "awareness of awareness" that is common to all 3rd-tier levels. As I noted, the "felt Wholeness" is what Aurobindo called "the intuitive mind," since "intuitive" has a sense of immediate feeling or touching, which is what "feeling Wholes" or "feeling-awareness" possesses—although, in one sense, this term is a bit misleading, as it implies that "intuition" is available only here, at this level, whereas intuition per se is simply an *immediate apprehension*, and thus intuition itself can be experienced at many lower levels. See, for example, Frances Vaughan's *Awakening Intuition*, which points out that intuition can be present at physical, emotional, mental, and spiritual levels (that is, there is physical intuition, emotional intuition, mental intuition, spiritual intuition).[7] The type available at the meta-mind is a variety of spiritual intuition. But "intuition" itself simply means a direct, immediate perceiving or feeling; all phenomena on all levels of consciousness—structures and states—are known first by intuition, whether they are images, symbols, concepts, rules, metarules, vision-logic, or vision. The various phenomena simply present themselves, immediately, to awareness, no matter what complex preconscious processes went into presenting them. Then, depending on the level and its type of cognition, secondary processes swing into gear that are deductive, inductive, representative, iconic, and so forth, and are generally "nonintuitive," or "mediate." But all knowing is, in its initial conscious stage, intuitive: it is simply "given," even though that "givenness" is almost always a preconscious 4-quadrant production. In short, Awareness itself is initially and primarily intuitive: it simply and immediately ("without mediation") sees the given phenomenon; it doesn't perceive a phenomenon, then reason about it, think about it, and name it before it then actually sees the object. It sees the object first, immediately and intimately, and then it may or may not reason about it, think about it, label it, and so on.

But the whole point about "feeling-awareness" is that it is the beginning of the union of the slightly "heady" Witnessing capacity with the more "bodily" feeling capacity, a union that will continue and come to final fruition in the nondual Supermind. In the meantime, it means a "warming" of Witnessing, a "thawing" of Witnessing, a "feeling Witness," which starts to relax its typically "stand-offish" stance of standing back, in a merely distancing fashion, and simply Witnessing all that arises, while resting in its own unfeeling Emptiness, and instead moves toward "touching" or "feeling" what it is Witnessing, thus bringing "heady" Witness and "bodily/feeling" Form that much closer together. This also means that subject and object themselves, primordially divorced in 1st tier, and starting to become a unified Whole in 2nd tier, continue their coming together here, on the way to a fully nondual Supermind. This is part of the intimate "feeling" nature of this level—subject is so close to object that they "feel" togetherness as part of that mutual resonance that determines truth value (once the "representational," or "epistemic privileging," mind, on the one hand, and the "ontic privileging" mind, on the other, are transcended).

Aurobindo, again through a slightly different process but one that results in many similar conclusions, states, in reference to this subject–object closeness, that this awareness "is nearer and more intimate to the original knowledge by identity." This occurs when

> The consciousness of the subject meets with the consciousness of the object . . . and feels or vibrates with the truth of what it contacts [compare our "mutual resonance"]. This close perception is more than sight [hence more than "vision"], more than conception [hence "meta-mental"]: it is the result of a penetrating and revealing touch which carries in it [transcends and includes] sight and conception as part of itself. [Meta-mind] sees the truth of things by a direct inner contact [feeling-awareness], not like the ordinary mental intelligence by seeking and reaching out for indirect contacts through the senses.

This is part of the ongoing and increasing intimacy of subject and object that evolution itself brings via its constant "transcend and include" dialectic toward more and more unified, more and more whole, less and less fragmented and divisive consciousness. The sky is becoming more and more of a big blue pancake getting ready to fall directly on your head, known immediately by the touch of "one taste," and not merely as a temporary or prolonged state, but as a real structure and Kosmic groove cut deep into the universe itself, as evolution's own self-transcending and self-organizing processes bring more and more naked intimacy into its own unfolding miracles.

Ultraviolet Overmind

The Overmind (ultraviolet, Fulcrum-11) is the first structure that is almost entirely supramental (a process that begins with the previous meta-mind). When conjoined, it operates with Higher Self forms of awareness (causal), and, in its even higher reaches, the Witness becomes conjoined (if it hasn't already), bringing the turiya state and its ultimate Real Self forms of awareness, along with the standard structural "awareness of awareness" and direct "Wholeness."[8] In any event, Overmind is beyond what is typically called "mental" forms of awareness or knowing/being. Large stretches of transcendental dimensions (with few if any immanent correlates) tend to open up (more so even than with the meta-mind), and one of the common pathologies here is a tendency to "float" away from earth-bound relations and instead be absorbed in almost infinite stretches of love, light, luminosity, insight-awareness, audible illuminations, and structurally upward yearnings (not to mention the "Emptiness" aspect of the empty Witness that can be conjoined with this level). Consciousness can become fascinated with itself and spend inordinate stretches absorbed in its own being, drawn to its own Source (the structureless, stateless ultimate Emptiness that can be directly conjoined with this structure). Thus Emptiness can exert an attractor allure, one that can totally entrance the Overmind, drawing it away from any of its immanent aspects and into an endless exploration of, and sometimes an actual addiction to, its transcendental, Erotic dimensions. In rare cases, when other shadow elements are present, this can slide into psychotic depersonalization (as can the state of Empty/Witnessing itself); in many cases, it shares a great number of characteristics with similar causal/ Witnessing-state dysfunctions, such as "split-life goals," where the individual can't decide whether to withdraw from the world entirely and pursue spiritual goals alone, or try to follow the path of "a monk in the world" and attempt to unite his or her transcendental awareness (of "heaven") with its immanent aspects (of "earth"). This dilemma is less likely to be resolved if it is generated predominantly by the causal/ Witnessing state itself instead of the Overmind. The difference is that the causal/Witnessing state, as a state, is unanchored in many, if any, structures, and hence tends to float in its own direction unencumbered, whereas the Overmind, as a structure (even if conjoined with the causal/Witness), transcends and INCLUDES all previous structures, and thus, in spite of its tendency to transcendental wandering, it is anchored in all the previous structures (going back, in fact, to the Big Bang itself) and thus usually finds its way back to uniting "this world" with any "other world," simply by virtue of the sheer gravitas of its own structural weight and makeup pulling down on its ankles.

When the Overmind actually emerges and comes online (relatively rare as that is at this point in evolution), it becomes the grand transition between the Supermind and all lower forms of mind and knowing/being, and thus plays a crucial role in both involution and evolution.[9] When awakened, Overmind begins operating to translate the implicit knowledge of the Supermind to the lower levels; it also receives "upwardly" the results of evolutionary habits into the storehouse consciousness (where it works in conjunction, again, with the causal state, the actual "location" of the storehouse consciousness). Overmind is thus a genuine "gatekeeper" between the Primordial Nature of Spirit and the Consequent Nature of Spirit (previously governed only by actions in the higher states).

Forms of spiritual intelligence with Overmind include ones that are "transcendental" in tone, "luminous," "radiant vibrations" of consciousness, even reaching into the pure "formless mysticism" that can come with the conjoined Emptiness/Witness. But there is a real difference: namely, this is a formless "object-less" awareness that, right at its edge, runs into all of the previous levels' Forms (as structures that are "transcended and included" in the Overmind itself), and this allows the Overmind to "oversee" all lower knowledge/being/ideas/feelings, giving a particularly strong sense of "Fullness" as the Overmind reaches into all lower levels and infuses them with clarity, consciousness, sublimed feeling, and universal love-bliss. Also possible, due to the close connection to Supermind (which can be in various degrees of "beginning to emerge," thus affecting Overmind directly to varying degrees), is thus a tentative access to the nondual union of Emptiness and all Form. And with Overmind and Supermind, "Form" includes ALL types of Form that have evolved since the Big Bang, because *all* of them are transcended and included in the human compound individual, and thus the "Fullness" aspect of these highest levels is the greatest Fullness of any structure and state available anywhere, enfolding in itself the entire Universe Story in all 4 quadrants—a fuller Fullness does not exist.

Overmind can likewise find temporary unity with either Emptiness (formless Abyss, Consciousness without an object) or Form (luminous superabundance) for extended periods. When the emphasis is on Emptiness, the spirituality tends toward various types of "formless mysticism," when on Form, various types of what might be called "superabundance," "overflow," or "spontaneous Presence" mysticism. If the Witness is conjoined here (and, if this hasn't already happened, this is the latest structure-stage at which this must happen for development to continue), the spirituality is open to various types of formless mysticism and "non-earth-bound" awareness. This is where the aforementioned problems such as "split-life goals" can become a serious issue, with the utter infinity of Freedom of the formless dimension becoming an Erotic fixation, available for endless hours of radical, unlimited, unborn, undying, never-ending Release, Liberation, Self-Exultation, and Self-Exuberance. It is only the sum total of all Forms lying on the very edge of the horizon of Overmind Awareness that calls out and, via the allure of the Life force itself, draws Awareness back toward its native "transcend and INCLUDE" orientation.

The Overmind, in its more theoretical possibilities, is a massive Big Data crunching machine. Having transcended AND included all possible Forms in the manifest universe (all the way back to the Big Bang), it is capable of "touching" or "prehending" the types of phenomena present at each and every one of the major, previous, evolutionary levels of being and consciousness (again, all the way back to the Big Bang) and thus can "know" (via intimate awareness) information in virtually any realm, discipline, or area of human knowledge—information that is, in lesser structures, known through a subject–object dichotomy in which there is some distance between the subject and object that has to be closed, whereas here it is known

through an intimate resonance of the Wholeness underlying them—
a type of Divine overview of all types of data or information presented to it. It doesn't automatically know all of these details on its
own, but if presented with any of them, it automatically "feels," "understands," or "resonates with" that information, understanding the
phenomena from the inside out, as it were. The "Witnessing" that it
brings at this level (with the conjoined Witnessing state) is even more
of a "feeling Witness" or "warm Witnessing" than the meta-mind,
since it is even a step closer to Supermind. This feeling Witness loves
Big Pictures and is constantly scanning for ways that "heaven" (its
"transcend" Awareness) can make sense of, or comprehend ("together prehend"), the facts and details of "earth" (its "include" component).

The Overmind, as the great conjoiner between absolute and relative
truth, finds that all of its knowledge is "intermixed," and sometimes
has a hard time telling the difference between what is absolutely true
and what is relatively true. Its spirituality is thus sometimes of a confusing variety—now ultimate, now relative. As the Witnessing state/
realm is the first initiator of dualities in the state realms (with what
Daniel Brown calls "individuality"—a very subtle and beginning self-
sense or subject–object dichotomy), so the Overmind is the first great
initiator of dualities in the structural realm. In particular, the Overmind initiates the subject–object duality in the structural realm, a duality found only in potential in the Supermind. It also has the
singular–plural duality, which too is present only in potential forms in
the Supermind, which together give rise to the 4 quadrants.

If the causal/witnessing Awareness is conjoined here at Overmind,
then the Overmind becomes conjoined with the storehouse consciousness of the causal, and this becomes one of the most important junc-
tions in all of consciousness, combining as it does the stored Kosmic
grooves of all lower levels (structures and states) with its own profound, novel additions, or the "transcend" part of its "transcend and
include." This—an even deeper holographic/holarchical networked
Network than the meta-mind—is the major junction point, via the
storehouse consciousness and the (implicit, possibly soon to become
explicit) Supermind—a crossroads between involutionary/downward/
Effluxing causation from the already formed vasanas and morphogenetic fields and Kosmic grooves (as well as the Primordial Nature of

Spirit) and the evolutionary/upward/Refluxing reception from all the newly forming Kosmic grooves (anywhere in the Kosmos) and newly forming vasanas and morphogenetic fields (received "upwardly" into the storehouse consciousness as part of the Consequent Nature of Spirit, henceforth available for the "downward causation" of involution to, for example, govern the form of folding proteins, the form of a tadpole development, the form of orange emerging through amber, and so on). This ceaseless downward/upward, involutionary/evolutionary, or Effluxing/Refluxing is the way that newly formed Kosmic habits, or Kosmic grooves, become permanently stored and thus available, henceforth, to govern the growth and development of all similar forms anywhere in the Kosmos. This is how "habits of Nature" become "laws of Nature" (which are simply deeply set habits with a vanishing probability of changing, so that they appear to be eternally fixed laws instead of evolutionary habits hard-set).

The online Overmind, as a Kosmic junction between ultimate and relative truth, between unmanifest or formless Spirit (or Emptiness, Primordial Nature) and formed-characteristics Spirit (or Form, Consequent Nature), as well as between "leaving" and "arriving" Forms of the storehouse, is a Kosmic network cross-juncture if ever there was one. This is another reason that, although this stage can be experienced as a great simplicity, it is also a stage where there can be much confusion and dysfunctional, fragmented development, until the primordial "punching through" to the Nondual Supermind.

Aurobindo emphasizes these two conflicting aspects of the Overmind—the fact that, in itself, as the next-to-highest level so far in existence, next to Supermind, it is a grand, boundless, Kosmic consciousness; but also as the first structure that is "removed" from Supermind, it is the beginning of the dualistic, illusory world (when perceived apart from Spirit/Supermind). Thus, to take the latter point first, the Overmind, says Aurobindo,

is the line of the soul's turning away from the complete and indivisible knowledge [of Supermind] and its descent towards Ignorance. Overmind is the beginning of the separation of aspects of the Truth, and forces their working out as if they were independent truths [such as trying to figure out the relation of "epistemology" and "ontology" as if they were separate realms], and this is a process that ends . . . at lower levels, in a complete division, fragmentation, separation from the indivisible Truth above.

Still, the Overmind itself, despite containing the first dualisms (or more accurately, not the first dualisms in involution, but the last dualisms to be overcome in evolution's Refluxing to the supramental Spirit, since the Supermind is not produced by involution but by evolution),[10] is the next-to-highest level that Spirit's own evolution has produced to date, and is thus a structure of almost infinite grandeur. Says Aurobindo, "But the Overmind is still a power of [K]osmic consciousness, a principle of global knowledge, a delegated light from the supramental Gnosis. When the Overmind descends, the predominance of the centralizing ego-sense is entirely subordinated, lost in largeness of being; a wide cosmic [again, Kosmic] perception and feeling of a boundless universal Self and movement replaces it. The source of revelation is not in one's separate self but in the universal knowledge."

Aurobindo mentions the word "Gnosis." As we've pointed out, the "gno" in "gnosis" is the same as "kno," as in "knowledge"; and in Sanskrit, it is "jna," which shows up in the extremely important terms "jnana" and "prajna," both terms taken by various Buddhist traditions to mean "ultimate nondual knowledge," "knowledge that is unto Liberation." Notice that Aurobindo says that this Overmind Truth knowledge is "delegated"—meaning that it is one step down from Supermind. "Gnosis" or "jnana" is traditionally sourced from the state of turiyatita, or "beyond the fourth" (beyond the Empty Witness—namely, nondual Suchness, or Thusness). This gnosis, when present in Supermind, is due to the conjoined nondual state.

There is another type of nondual awareness—more profound than gnosis, although, as it were, "containing" gnosis as an aspect of itself. But this "higher gnosis" is not merely a state gnosis, but a structure and state gnosis—the nondual gnosis of the Suchness state (the unity of Emptiness and Form) added to a structure comprehension that is literally the fullest of the fullest of all Form possible (because the Supermind has "transcended and included" every structure since the Big Bang). Typically, when gnosis descends, it is through the filter of whatever structure, whatever "hidden map," is present as a lens at whatever level the individual happens to be when the gnosis is activated—it could be mythic, it could be rational, it could be integral, and so forth—and the person enters a "headless, thoughtless, unity" state of consciousness, but always as interpreted through its particular hidden map. But at Supermind, the "hidden map" is, for the first time, the absolute leading edge of evolution itself—the fullest of the fullest Form anywhere in existence—and thus is, moment to moment, the most complete knowledge available to consciousness in general. This "all-structure gnosis" reverberates throughout the known world with a thunderous and electric inclusivity, sweeping up every single thing and event in the known Kosmos into its all-permeating embrace. This is a gnosis unlike any that have ever appeared before (although, indeed, there have been various types of "leading-edge gnosis" in the past, which occurred whenever the structure-level experiencing gnosis, or jnana, was also the highest structure-level that evolution had achieved at that time—whether it was mythic or rational or pluralistic, and so forth). But Supermind is today's ultimate leading edge, and thus the level that holds this honor in today's world. And—to return to the specific point at hand—the Overmind, as one mere step away from Supermind, shines via a "delegated" (or one-step-down) version of such. This means that certain fundamental dualisms are in place, in particular, as noted, the dualisms of the 4 quadrants (subject versus object and singular versus plural), which, when seen as Spirit's own ornaments, become the abundantly creative forms through which a Kosmos is manifested, but when viewed apart from Spirit, are the root sources of maya, illusion, and delusory finite awareness. Overall, the difference between "ignorance" and "Enlightenment" at the Overmind level is relatively small indeed; especially when conjoined with the Empty Witness state, the resulting "jnana samadhi" (True-Self awareness) is but a small step from "sahaja samadhi" (nondual spontaneous Suchness awareness). With the Overmind, the big blue pancake has already collapsed and is in the process of falling straight for your headless condition at a very accelerated rate.

One of the most notable features of Overmind is its almost constant "awareness of awareness" (which becomes a 24/7 given at Supermind; and again, not necessarily as a highly self-reflexive, constant self-staring, but as an ever-present background Consciousness embracing All). This close to "constant consciousness" is due to the thickness, the richness, of structure upon structure of consciousness on consciousness, an endless prehension of prehension (again, all the way back to the Big Bang). That virtually the complete history of the entire universe is *literally* enfolded in a human being at this level is an astonishing fact to ponder. When experienced, it is as if one's True Self (one's immediate feeling of empty, open I AMness) were indeed the absolute All, in a fullness of superabundance that is radiant, infinitely on fire, glowing and gleaming, a luminosity arising from an infinitely deep ocean of radiance, bubbling up as an unstoppable, unquenchable happiness, or love-bliss, overflowing in all directions without a single thing or event outside of it. And due to the conjoining of the Empty Witness with this structure (which has to happen for development to continue, and in virtually all cases that I am aware of, it has definitely happened), this Mirror Mind effortlessly and spontaneously embraces/ reflects every phenomena, in every world, in every universe, in this Kosmos (much as, right now, you already hear the sounds around you, you already see the sights in front of you, you already feel the objects in your awareness—you don't have to try to do any of that; it is already happening—spontaneously, effortlessly, and of-itself-so). This Witness is the "warmest" Witness imaginable, the "loving embrace Witness," where everything on the mirror of awareness is embraced with an infinite love and tender encircling, a "holding" of the entire universe in the palm of your hand—*you*, its ultimate Author and Creator in the depth of your infinite I AMness ("Tell them I AM that I AM has sent you").

Susanne Cook-Greuter (who, with Terri O'Fallon, is one of the few researchers actually investigating 3rd-tier levels) writes that, referring specifically to a slightly lower 3rd-tier stage but in a sentence that could well apply to this stage of development, "Individuals become non-judgmental Witnesses to the being-becoming of a self in moment-to-moment transformation with a constant awareness of behavior, feeling, and perception." Note the Witnessing, and the "constant awareness [of awareness]." With Supermind (as well as with turiyatita), a "constant consciousness" descends on individuals that anchors them in that which is aware of *all changes of state*—aware of that which is aware in waking, in dreaming, in deep sleep—the constant (as in "timeless," Now-moment, eternal) awareness that is spontaneously "conscious of everything."

In relation to exactly that, Ramana Maharshi made a very disturbing statement, which became a genjo koan (a spontaneously arising koan, or ultimate issue) for me for over a year: "That which is not present in deep dreamless sleep is not real." Well, that took out pretty much everything in my life—in yours too, yes? He wasn't saying that something not present in deep dreamless sleep had *no* reality—things not present in deep dreamless sleep have plenty of *relative* reality, just not *ultimate* reality. And why not? For Ramana, that which is not ever-present cannot be ultimately real; the ultimately real is not something that can have a beginning in time, since that would make it strictly temporal, not timeless or eternal; and that which is not eternal is not ultimately worth seeking or desiring, since it will eventually decompose one way or another, leaving its holder deeply disappointed and unhappy. But the Real Self, Ramana's "I-I" (pure, empty, open I AMness, the pure Witness), is present in all three states—gross, subtle, and causal, or waking, dreaming, and deep sleep—and thus is a truly ever-present, timeless, eternal Realness. Being "present in deep dreamless sleep" isn't about the dreamless state itself, it is about timelessness, about eternity, about an ultimate Ground of Being and the Source of entire worlds, about who and what you really are before you are anything else, about something which, when re-cognized or re-membered, opens you to that which is indeed Unborn and thus Undying, Unbeginning and thus radically Unending. If you let your awareness drop into the space of your Heart and listen from its very center, you will discover that the entire Kosmos is arising in that silent Awareness, with every single thing and event in the universe arising within that radically open, spacious, clear, deep Heart Space, as if that Space were the box in which the entire universe came wrapped. Beyond thought and feeling, in the very Center of the Kosmos, in the perfectly unlimited openness of that Heart Space, in that gorgeously Silent and elegantly Still clearing, arise all manifest worlds—that bird over there, that building here, that automobile across the street, that person pulling a cart, that cloud floating right there—all within that opening, or clearing, that is spontaneously aware of everything, always, here and now, moment to moment to moment. With the gentlest embrace and most tender mercies, you reach out and literally enfold the entire universe within you, within your Heart Space, your loving Heart-Witness of this and every Present, and likewise its loving Feeler, Knower, and Seer—always Unborn and forever Undying.

You *already know* this immediate I AMness, yes? You are *already* aware of this ever-present simple feeling of I AM, right? And with the Overmind, this I AMness becomes the Observing Self, not merely at whatever level it happens to be intuited, but nearly at the leading edge of evolution itself, and is thus able to reach out and embrace virtually every level of every thing and event that has emerged in the entire history of evolution itself. At this level, I AMness reverberates throughout an entire Kosmos of its own ultimate Thusness—the Kosmos knowing the Kosmos through the opening in your own Heart Space, the Universe touching the Universe in your soon-to-be fully headless Condition, with you mindlessly, headlessly, out of your mind and into your Real Self and Suchness, a homecoming to a place that you have never left and a destination with no actual beginning (that which has a beginning in time is strictly temporal; we are talking about something you have *always already* known, in your own purest Heart Space of spontaneously ever-present I AMness).

When you recognize, or remember, your pure Witnessing Self, you realize that it was actually present all along, yes? Whether in the past you realized it or not, this Witness was always the Presence that was aware of whatever was arising, existing, coming to be and leaving. This Witness, in other words, in reality has no beginning—as far as you can actually tell, it has always been there, always Witnessing this present moment. When you fully recognize it, it always has the sense of, "Oh that! How could I have missed that? *That* has been here all along!" When I was studying with my root Dzogchen teacher, students would always come in and say things like, "Wow! I finally got it! I was sitting and meditating, and all of a sudden this feeling of absolute love and care and oneness descended on me, and I disappeared into this incredible cloud of all-embracing awareness. I finally got it!" And he would always say, "Did this wonderful experience have a beginning?" "Yeah, yeah, like I said, I was just sitting there—about an hour ago— and this thing hit me!" "That's very nice, but that's not your real Buddha-nature. Go back and sit until you can show me something that does not have a beginning."

What doesn't have a beginning is this ever-present Witnessing, as your Real Self and ultimately Suchness. Once you have spotted it (your ongoing sense of I AMness), you realize it has been there all along, silently but ever-presently and all-pervadingly Witnessing every thing and event that arose in your world. *This* has no beginning; *this* has no end; *this* has no time; and eternal life belongs to those who live in its ever-present Present.

And, of course, according to the traditions, this Witness is aware of all the various states—gross, subtle, causal—so this Witness, or Real Self, is aware of, not only your waking state, but your dreams as well (and you can realize this if and when you start lucid dreaming). Likewise, in deep dreamless sleep—when literally *every object of the manifest world has disappeared*, and there is only vast Emptiness, a vast Nothingness, a pure Formlessness—the Witness is present in that state as well, as a very tacit, very subtle Awareness, which is why when somebody asks, "How did you sleep last night?" you often respond quickly with something like, "Oh, I slept great!" You know that because your Real Self was actually there, "sleeping great." In that deep dreamless state, the only thing that is present—since all phenomena are completely gone—is this tacit Witness, this Real Self, this ultimate Reality; and, as you realize when you experience it directly, it has always been there, spontaneously aware of all that was arising. *That* is what is present in deep dreamless sleep, and since that is the only ultimate Reality (especially when one with Suchness), that is why "that which is not present in deep dreamless sleep is not real." Yes—see that?

You can *never* remember not being I AMness, can you? Think hard! You can't because you never have; this is the face you had BEFORE your parents were born! Not the face that you discover today or tomorrow in time. It has always been just so, and you *know* it, because it is the *all* and *only* thing that is ever-present in your awareness, and it always has been, even before your parents—and the universe—were born. Think hard! Can you *ever* remember not being *just this*? *Ever*?

White Supermind

The Supermind (white or clear light, Fulcrum-12) is, as far as we can tell, the highest structure and View yet to emerge in evolution in any degree at all (and it is preciously rare). This makes it both the most infinitely complex and the utterly most simple occasion in existence.

As the Supermind becomes awakened and comes online, it is busy translating the fundamentals of the Ultimate Nondual Reality "downward" into the manifest realms and receiving the evolving natures of the manifest realms "upward" into its own Consequent Nature (with most of them stored in the causal storehouse, which is transcended and included in Supermind). The Supermind, as a structure (and as conjoined with the Nondual state), transcends and includes all junior structures of each individual in their entirety, and thus the Supermind is a type of individually unique "omniscience" for each being, since it "knows" all there is to know about the ongoing events on any and every level for that individual. This is to truly "Know Thyself," in and through every level conceivable, a radically new and unprecedented type of Self-knowledge (and quite beyond Big Mind satori, because this is Big Mind PLUS every evolved structure in the universe). This includes the same type of "omniscient resonating" with all Kosmic levels that the Overmind begins to possess, but Supermind takes a final step further, resonating with all data as seen in an ultimate, infinite, nondual fashion, and not just in a conventional, finite, relative fashion, no matter how high. (This is possible with the nondual state in general, which can be experienced on virtually any lower level; but then the Form component that is understood when that happens includes only Form and data up to the level at which this occurs. Supermind is the only level that includes *all* levels—at least, all levels to date in evolution—but this in itself makes it unprecedented.)

We could refer to this as a "Unique Self," as the manifest Witness is, because this is indeed a unique structure/state for every person, but only if we remember that there is nothing that feels like a "self" at this altitude, because there is nothing that feels like a subject or an object, or an inside or an outside—those distinctions can be recognized, but there are no inherent self-identities attached to them. This is, if anything, not so much a "unique Self" as a "unique Suchness."

This is the structure-level at which the Primordial Nature of Godhead (or Nondual Great Perfection) enters the being of the individual, not just as a Ground (which it can as a state realization at almost any level), but as a Ground inherently receiving/embracing all evolving new and novel events (including new structures) into its Consequent Nature. Again, it is not just Big Mind, but Big Mind inherently united with all previous structures of existence going all the way back to the Big Bang, in the most comprehensive and inclusive form imaginable, up to the radically leading edge of evolution itself—the white altitude Supermind. It is the radical Freedom of the purest Emptiness plus the fullest of the fullest of the world of Form. It transcends absolutely ALL, in purest Freedom, and includes absolutely ALL, in the utter sum total Form of unmatched Fullness. Put bluntly, it transcends and includes the entire universe to date. That is, Supermind enfolds into its ongoing Consequent Nature the entire universe as it has unfolded till now, and then includes each future moment as a new and in some ways novel and creative moment. (How long Supermind will be able to do this until a new and yet higher structure is needed and thus begins to emerge is literally impossible to say, being part of the irreducible Mystery of Spirit's own emergent evolution.)

Supermind is the radical crossroads where absolute and relative truth are not just exposed to each other, as with the Overmind, but are deeply and intrinsically one (or not-two) with each other, a "feature" of the Nondual state itself when joined with all previous structures (which is what Supermind does). It is one of the most difficult nondual realizations for human beings to master since it's not just that "eternity is in love with the productions of time," but in a deeper, more mysterious fashion, eternity and time are the same, or not-two.[11] Also, Supermind requires not only the end limit of Waking Up in nondual Suchness, but the end limit of Growing Up in white altitude—an exceedingly rare accomplishment, and something that in itself is an endlessly ongoing journey that is its own self-liberating goal. Thus, as the radical leading edge of evolution itself, combined or conjoined with the highest state realization, Supermind is the upper limit of both Growing Up and Waking Up (and hence, Showing Up). These most primordial and significant growth and development processes in humans are now radically unified at their very end limits—a superhuman condition if ever there was one.

Supermind—because of its "transcend and include" of the Overmind/causal realm—has the most penetrating insight into, and understanding of, the storehouse and its Kosmic grooves and habits of every structure yet to have evolved in any realm. By the time a significant number of humans have consciously reached Supermind, and there is a culturally significant amount of art, morals, and science emanating from it, those activities (for example, science) will scarcely be recognizable in today's terms. Indigo truths, violet truths, and ultraviolet truths will already have gained a major purchase in culture at large.

The relative truths associated with white Supermind might, as only one example, have already turned into a "trans-"transhumanism, with the "exterior" matter of the "interior" spirit having evolved into silicon instead of carbon, but with an understanding, now totally lacking in transhumanism, that there are levels of consciousness and that our cyber-awareness will have to be built at the highest level possible—not rationality, as transhumanism now thinks, but the supramental Supermind. If this were so, Supermind would itself instantly reprogram the digital platform to include rules and capacities for including—and inducing—even yet higher evolution, since being at a fixed level of development for all eternity would be the closest thing to an antinatural, antiliving, death-inducing boredom possible, not to mention its being out of touch with the governing reality of this universe, or an evolutionary Eros of some sort. Other "trans-"transhuman possibilities include robots doing virtually all of the manual labor of any type (and economically paying humans for the work they do on their behalf); the remaining humans would have been "enhanced humans" for quite some time, with genetic alterations set to dispose humans to evolve to the highest levels yet understood in all lines (perhaps to violet meta-mind, or ultraviolet Overmind, or even white Supermind; although by that time even higher levels would have become available); reaching toward and occasionally into the Overmind/Supermind would give humans the capacity, in some moderate ways, to alter physical laws, which, after all, are psychophysical habits (which means nothing that can't be redrawn with a sufficiently powerful impulse); any human bodies remaining would have been rendered in effect "immortal," with 3-D xeroxing machines simply reproducing any part of the body that begins to wear out; wormhole space travel might have disclosed dozens, even hundreds, of alien forms of life, and new "Integral maps" would have been drawn with higher relative levels of awareness including planetary, interplanetary, galactic, intergalactic, transgalactic, universe, transuniverse, multiuniverse, unitary; early intergalactic warfare would have been replaced by galactic federations; nondual ultimate realities and Supermind superrealities would be on the map, with educational standards typically set with those as goals; and multiple universes will have been recognized, with black holes the entryway to those universes and white holes receiving matter and dark matter from them (and transuniverse travel a looming possibility). All of these could be potentials (and some, actualities) already produced by an evolving Kosmos and lying in the storehouse, awaiting a sufficiently evolved mass of human consciousness in order to disclose themselves. And by the time 10 or 20 percent of the population reaches the level of Supermind, perhaps there will be another four, perhaps six, or even more, new and higher levels beyond Supermind to which humans would be open to discovering if they continued their own growth, development, and evolution.

For now, in any event, Supermind directly realizes itself as a consciousness/being Whole, after being Whole, after being Whole, a timeless/temporal Now after timeless/temporal Now, after timeless/temporal Now. The entire history of each timeless Now is part of the timelessness of each Now, and there is no difference felt or known between the Present and all time, each event being experienced sub specie aeternitatis. This gives the feeling, vis-à-vis time, that you are not moving through time, but rather time is moving through you (that is, through your awareness), with your being not moving at all. It's like sitting in a movie theater and, without moving from your seat, having the entire scenery move past you (and if the you is "headless," then *in* you).

This "timeless/temporal, being/Wholeness" gives Supermind a direct feeling of being the same Awareness looking out of the eyes of every sentient being everywhere, no matter what level (since it is looking out of the eyes of every rung in existence). This is a common "mystical" experience of several different unity states—the oneness of all being—but it is present here for a completely novel reason: because here the actual rungs of all the lower levels are cascadingly available to Consciousness, there is accordingly a feeling that all the lower rungs, not just the Big Mind available on all lower rungs, are fully and directly available, which profoundly emphasizes the 100 percent present-everywhere nature of omniscient Consciousness at this level.

The spirituality of this level is clearly hard to describe "accurately," and might best simply (and metaphorically) be called "nondual holonic": it recognizes (via beingness) the wholeness and the partness of every event everywhere, the infinity and the finitude of every phenomenon, the oneness and manyness of every event, the subjectness and objectness of every subject and every object ("the subject-knows-the-object knows itself"), the involutionary and evolutionary direction of every movement. Its Nondual state component provides many of the standard nondual dimensions of its being, and its "transcend-and-include"-all-structures component amplifies the Fullness of that nonduality through a holarchical interwovenness of unimaginable proportions. It is the 1st-, 2nd-, and 3rd-person faces of Godhead, before they are faces, as Godhead continues to create a manifest world and reabsorb it into Itself.

Supermind, for most individuals, lies in the emergent unconscious, pulsing patiently to emerge (in the simple Forms that have already been laid down by a small number of intrepid pioneers). These features will flesh out considerably as evolution continues and more and more people enact—and co-create—this structure. It is an event startlingly new to the Kosmos, as the widest of the wide, the deepest of the deep, the highest of the high, ready to emerge and refashion the world, sitting on the edge of the profoundest of secrets ever divulged to the human heart, waiting to flood the human mind with no less than the mind of God, right here and now in this living moment and timelessly for time to come. The radically infinite, empty openness of Spirit and the radically full wonders of history cross at every moment in its very own being, a singularity of sorts that fashions time, space, history, and becoming with its own beacon of luminous omniscient Thusness. You can feel the universe coursing through your veins, see the Kosmos as how your headless brain feels from within, know the stars as neuronal firings of your own eyes letting the world in, every living being nothing but the beating of your very own Heart, unfolding in your very own Heart Space—now and now and now—the earth itself your very own feet as you pace the Kosmos made of your very own breathing, in and out endlessly. Evolution and history are nothing but an impertinence if they are anything other than the story of your own unfolding Suchness—the Tree of Life being your own body, the Web of Life your own skin.

The possibilities of Supermind are hard to even imagine, given the infinite depth of feeling that it brings, the unending horizon of knowing it possesses, the unlimited connectivity it feels with the Kosmos as its own inner Being and Divine Thusness. The center of your own Awareness is a Big Bang, where out of purest Emptiness a Kosmos arises moment to moment, and evolves within your own Awareness through every grade and level of being up to your own True Self and beyond to unfathomable, utterly obvious Suchness.

There are endless tales in the traditions of extraordinary evolutionary developments such as the Rainbow Body, a body of pure Light lying on the other side of Enlightenment, a transfiguration of one's own Being into a pure Spirit Realm of Radiant Light, leaving behind teeth and nails, not much more, a translation of the human being, while alive, into a Heavenly Estate beyond all description. Aurobindo imagined the material body refashioned into a body of Spiritual Light, transfiguring every cell and system into a radiant source of Spiritual energy, reforming the body in every way imaginable, shining out from each and every one of its cells to a radiant Infinity. And so the stories go.

But the thing to remember about the Supermind that makes it different from all of those is that the Supermind is the Rainbow Body (however you might wish to conceive that) PLUS every structure of consciousness, being, and awareness that has emerged from the very beginning of this universe, some 14 billion years ago. That is what sets it apart from Big Mind and every nondual form of Being and Awareness ever known or described. That is not to say that those extraordinary adept-inhabited kayas or bodies (for example, the Rainbow body) don't exist; it is to say that the traditions were not tracking the structures of consciousness that may or may not have accompanied them, and thus just as a Zen master can be fully transmitted as having traditional Enlightenment and yet still be at a Mythic-literal structure-stage of development, so a Rainbow Body could exist at who knows what lesser levels of actual structure development. It becomes the realest of the Real only at evolution's leading edge—the Rainbow Body of the Supermind level. That, by any definition, would be humanity passed into superhumanity, the evolutionary emergence of the Superhuman, marking a shift into realms of being and awareness hardly conceivable by today's standards, and yet if you simply look at the direction of overall development and evolution from the Big Bang until now, from strings to quarks to atoms to molecules to cells to multicellular organisms, each of these shows an increase in the universe's own sensitivity, an increase in the ways that the universe can become aware of its own being. In other words, starting with matter itself and then moving into simple photosynthetic plant forms and moving into the earliest animal forms, into fish, amphibians, and reptiles, and from early mammals into primates, every one of these shows an increase in the sensitivity of the universe to its own existence; each one is more sensitive, complex, unified, whole, conscious, and aware. From there we move to humans, and thence from infrared to red to amber to orange to green, which marks the birth of the universe having become self-reflexive and fully self-conscious, evolution having become shockingly aware of itself. On to teal and turquoise, with evolution having become self-whole, with its sensitivity moving into inclusive, comprehensive, embracing forms, and from there into what can only be called superconscious and superhuman realms, a sensitivity of the universe to the wholeness of the universe itself, the universe looking at itself and seeing the wonder of what it has wrought, all through its own stunning self-organization and self-transcendence. Given this overall, absolutely unmistakable direction to greater and greater wholeness, greater and greater sensitivity, greater and greater consciousness—whether this is an inherent tendency of the universe itself or the product of chance and necessity doesn't matter, just look where it is obviously headed! (to more of the same, surely, with something like a superhuman Supermind looming on our collective horizon, whispering into our ears, "Just keep coming, the Kingdom is at hand")—how can we doubt the simple record of what Whitehead calls "the creative advance into novelty," with each new creative step pushing more and more in this utterly obvious direction?

Aurobindo tends to assume that Supermind is the source of *involution*, giving rise to Overmind, which then gives rise to all lesser structures. In contrast, I believe that Supermind is the summation of *evolution*, created by evolution in the course of its creative tetra-unfolding, not pregiven as the source of involution and merely rediscovered and remembered by evolution. Involution begins, in each moment today, with nondual Suchness, which gives rise to every lower state as well as every structure that has arisen thus far in consciousness. The higher structure-levels that have not yet emerged remain merely potentials, having no solid Form but awaiting tetra-evolution to co-enact and co-create them, at which point they may enter the involutionary/evolutionary, Effluxing/Refluxing movement. When Supermind arises and conjoins with the nondual Suchness state, Suchness is, for the first time, arising in conjunction with an interpretive framework that includes every level of being and awareness in the entire universe, which is what makes Supermind such an extraordinary emergent unlike any other 3rd-tier structure. Perhaps, more accurately, it should be thought of as 4th tier, but in any event, it is a historically unprecedented emergent, clearing the way for a future so radically different in every quadrant that, again, "superhuman" is the only term that comes close to hinting at it.

But, in the meantime, it awaits all who manage to complete the evolutionary and developmental process of Growing Up conjoined with the developmental process of Waking Up (along with whatever Cleaning Up and Showing Up is required). Imagine sitting in a theater, watching a film. As you sit in your chair, your relation to the events on the screen is beyond motion and stillness—both motion and stillness are occurring in the film, but you are impartially Witnessing them; you are yourself neither of them. Then imagine the screen turning into that big blue pancake—in this case, a big kaleidoscopic rainbow-colored pancake—and falling on your shoulders where your head used to be. The entire world (of the film) is arising within you, on this side of your face, in the headless opening or clearing where your head once was. You yourself, your own Suchness, Thusness, or nondual headless oneness, are embracing both motion and stillness as parts of the world arising within you, but at the same time you are exclusively identified with neither; they are simply arising in your awareness, in your open Heart Space, staying a bit, and then passing on, as the next world scene arises within you and unfolds whatever it has to bring, eventually also passing on and making room for the next event.

Now take it one step further. By way of analogy, imagine a fence with one vertical board missing, so that when you sit on one side of the fence, you can look through that slit and see things passing by on the other side. A cat walks pass the opening—you see its head, then its body, then its tail. Out of your sight, the cat turns around and begins to walk past the open slit again. And once more, you see its head pass by, then its body, then its tail. You might naturally think to yourself, "Ah, the head is causing the tail!"

Because you can't see the wholeness of the cat, you see it only in partial, temporal segments, one segment after another. The entire world seen through this slit thus appears in a linear, temporal fashion even though if you were to get up and sit on top of the fence, you would see an entire world of Wholes, all simultaneously coexisting together.

Imagine that the film world—unfolding in the headless space of one taste—is now seen not in a one-at-a-time fashion that gives the illusion of temporal linearity (with the future emerging into the present and moving into the past) but instead in an "all-at-onceness" of pure wholeness or unity. Imagine that instead of looking at the film one frame at a time, you cut up all the frames, stacked them on top of each other, and then put the stack in front of a light and looked through all the frames simultaneously. Of course, in actuality, all you would see is a blur; so you have to imagine being able to see each frame individually, while also seeing them all together as a single, whole, simultaneous event.

So there you are, in the theater, headlessly one with the entire film, and the film itself is seen as a whole event arising in your headless, one taste, unity state. In the timeless Present of the moment, the whole film exists within you, all of it at once, in a timeless unity state that also includes the entire past of the present event (the entire film). You are seeing the film without the subject–object duality (in your headless unity state), and you are seeing it as a whole in the timeless Present (with all frames being seen at once, as a whole). You yourself are neither moving nor still, dark nor light, inside nor outside, past nor future, but contain all of these within yourself, as the entire film world arises within your headless oneness or unity consciousness.

As for all time existing in the timeless Now—it already does, as do all ultimate realities. All you ever know is the timeless Now, and that's already true in this very moment. You don't have to work at, or "practice," keeping your attention focused in the now moment, as some spiritual practices would have you do, because it's always already fully in the Now, come what may. The past is not actually occurring now, you can't directly be aware of it, and your attention is *never* aware of it, is never actually in the past. All that you are aware of now are thoughts of the past, and all of those thoughts are a present, Now experience; they exist only in the Now moment. When the past actually occurred, it was nothing but a Now moment. Likewise, you can't experience the future at this moment, only thoughts of the future. Your thoughts are never actually in the future; they are occurring and exist only Now. When the future actually happens, it, too, will be Now. The timeless Now is not hard to attain but absolutely impossible to avoid! As are all ultimate realities. All are ever present, whether we realize them or not. From spaceless and non-subject–object headless unity to eternal, timeless Nowness, ultimate Reality is always already an always already reality! The Great Liberation is never a case of bringing something that doesn't exist into existence—a strictly temporal, non-eternal action—but is simply recognizing an ever-present and already, and always already, existing reality, just as it is, just as it always or timelessly is, everywhere and everywhen. As my Dzogchen teacher said, "Come back when you can show me something that does not have a beginning in time."

So see the entire world around you like that—always already in a headless, one taste, unity consciousness, with the present timeless Now and all actual time already being one single Present moment, a vast and single Wholeness arising within you, moment to timeless moment, present Wholeness to present Wholeness—and that would be close to Supermind's Awareness.

Aurobindo says, of the supramental Supermind, that it is "a principle superior to mentality and exists, acts, and proceeds in the fundamental truth and unity of things and not like the mind in their appearances and phenomenal divisions." It is a Unity and Wholeness beyond all the fragmentations of subject versus object, past versus future, good versus evil, pleasure versus pain, inside versus outside, being itself "beyond the pairs," as the Upanishads put it, meaning beyond the pairs of opposites altogether, what is also called "one without a second." This is a Wholeness beyond ideation, beyond comprehension, superabundantly overflowing into every nook and cranny in the entire Kosmos, filling it with a pure Awareness beyond thoughts and feelings and existing as the simple opening, space, or clearing in which the entire universe is arising right now, timeless moment to timeless moment. It is a "Consciousness," says Aurobindo, "always free from Ignorance." Imagine every vacancy, every hollow, every barren spot anywhere in your existence, and imagine them flushed with a radiant superabundance that engorges them with the utter Fullness of a radical infinity, overflowing to the utter ends of the universe itself, constantly bubbling over in an effervescent Kosmic Fulfillment with no boundary and no barrier, just bubbles of infinity tickling your being top to bottom. Imagine, at the same time, that every heaviness in your world, every solid, dull, and gravity-drenched item anywhere in your existence evaporates into a gleaming, glowing, Transparent Emptiness, a radiant, shining, brilliant Brightness that is lighter than Light and unobstructed as the sky on a summer morning's dazzling daybreak. You are as Full as you could possibly be, and as Free as you could possibly imagine, and it is all in the very Nature of your ever-present own true Thusness.

In this moment, it all comes to rest. In this present, it is all fully given. In this now, it all radically exists. As this Kosmos, your own Suchness arises moment to moment. When you feel the *deepest you* or I AMness "in here" and you feel the *entire universe* arising "out there," they are directly one and the same feeling—one taste—with both of them arising in the clearing, the opening, the space where your head used to be but that is now seen and experienced as the One Taste of All That Is. You can drink the Pacific Ocean in a single gulp; taste the sky's deliciousness; inhale the sun till it fills your lungs with a radiant luminosity; step into the earth as your body's own skin, even for all eternity; feel a snowfall as your own being covering the world in a blanket of your gentle softness; greet each sunrise as the eternal return of the Light of your own Self-Realization. Truly, what is not given? When has this ever not been known? What could we ever possibly *want*? How could we ever possibly *fear*? Where could we ever possibly *go*? When could we ever possibly *arrive*? Why pretend *anymore*?

Part Three

Dysfunctional
Shadow Elements
in Development

8

Shadow Work

As I have mentioned, few, if any, spiritual systems have any extensive or sophisticated understanding or models of shadow material—that is, personal, repressed, dissociated, dis-owned, unconscious material. There is awareness of negative emotions and their effects, various defilements, even a storehouse consciousness that anticipates Jung's collective unconscious by over a millennium.[1] But aside from this general understanding in the traditions of certain shadow-like elements, that there are specific defense mechanisms that generate types of the psychodynamically repressed unconscious is by and large a discovery of the modern West.

One can certainly argue that psychotherapy and spirituality are two completely different things and that they shouldn't be confused, and so there is no need to integrate them. One can experience an Enlightenment state condition no matter what one's therapeutic condition, and one can certainly undertake most typical forms of therapy without experiencing Enlightenment or Awakening. (There are an increasing number of leading-edge shadow treatments that incorporate a recognition of nondual Reality, or Enlightened peak or plateau experiences, but now I want to talk about the reverse: not including spirituality in therapy but including therapy in spirituality.) I grant that they can be considered independently, and, in a certain sense, they are independent of each other; but when it comes to the actual, day-to-day, pragmatic steps and stages of spiritual practice, one invariably—and that means *always*—runs into some degree of shadow material, making it an inherent, intrinsic aspect of the overall spiritual dimension and the path itself.

Dr. Roger Walsh, as I mentioned, is a psychiatrist and a Buddhist teacher. When he teaches meditation retreats, he often has daily sessions where he meets with individual students one-on-one and addresses the issues that are coming up in their meditation practice specifically and their life in general. And he says that around 80 percent of the issues that come up are mostly psychotherapeutic, not spiritual or meditative, and so he responds with therapeutic techniques and suggestions, not meditative or spiritual ones. If he's anywhere near typical, then meditation teachers in particular (and spiritual teachers in general) who are not also using therapeutic techniques are giving responses to their students that are off the mark 80 percent of the time, and thus not ultimately helpful, or not as helpful as they could be. This is just scary, and certainly doesn't constitute a very effective *upaya*, or skillful means. It thus appears that shadow work is a legitimate issue that should be included in any Fourth Turning (or in any Integral Spirituality in general, or Integral Life Practice, for that matter).

The shadow exists most basically because of the actual nature and form of the developmental or evolutionary processes that the psyche goes through—in both structures and states. We've seen that the core dynamic of development (in individuals as well as in the universe at large) is "transcend and include," or "negate and preserve"—each present moment preserves the essentials of what went before and then adds its own creative, novel, transcendent elements. And something can go wrong with either one of those (transcend or include) at virtually any level or stage (in both structures and states), producing a specific type of shadow issue in each case. It's actually quite straightforward, and very predictable, in a sense.

Addictions and Allergies

We saw that in each developmental sequence (structure or state), the central or proximate self first identifies with a basic structure or major state, thus seeing the world through that structure or state, hence generating a View and a Vantage Point. While at this structure or state (chakra/sheath/structure or state/body/realm), the self needs to embrace and integrate all the major features of that dimension—all of the qualities, thoughts, feelings, needs, and drives of that structure or state. If the self fails to adequately embrace any of those elements, it will either remain fused with, and embedded in, those elements (a failure to transcend, to differentiate)—thus creating a *fixation* or *grasping* or *addiction* to those elements (in the gross: food, sex, power, money, and so forth; in the subtle: luminosity, prana, soul-elements, insight, illumination, and so forth; in the causal: archetypes, Now-moment, blissful feelings, Higher Self-aspects, and so on) or, on the other hand, it can dis-own and dissociate from those elements (a failure to integrate, to include)—thus creating an *avoidance* or *dissociation* or *allergy* to those same elements (food, sex, power, soul, Higher Self, and so on).

It is especially at each developmental junction, when moving from one structure-stage to the next-higher structure-stage (a "fulcrum") or from one state-stage to the next-higher state-stage (a "switch-point"), that these types of dysfunctions are most likely to occur. In moving from the oral to the next-higher stage, for example, if the self fails to differentiate adequately from oral drives, it will remain identified or fused with those drives, thus developing an oral fixation or oral addiction, constantly substituting food to satisfy other needs and using food to generate comfort. If, on the other hand, differentiation and dis-identification from the oral stage—which is supposed to happen— goes too far into dissociation and dis-owning, then the self generates a food allergy, and ends up with eating disorders such as bulimia or anorexia. In either case, an infrared food subpersonality is often created, which lives in the submergent unconscious and sends up constant symptoms and symbols, reading food into much of its interactions and relations. What is supposed to happen, of course, is that the oral realm will remain, but the exclusive identity with the oral, its View, will be let go of and will pass—with no oral fixations or dissociations, no oral addictions or allergies. *One still has the capacity and the need to eat.* One still has the basic structure-rung of food, chakra-rung 1, the oral realm, but one no longer exclusively identifies with it or sees the world primarily or only through that lens. One retains an oral drive (the structure), but not an oral fixation or dissociation. Structures remain, Views pass; states remain, Vantage Points pass.

A subpersonality is a subject at one stage that refuses to become an object of the next. As we saw, Robert Kegan defines development as "the subject of one stage becomes an object of the subject of the next."[2] I would put it more specifically that the "I" of one stage becomes a "me" and eventually a "mine" of the "I" of the next stage.[3] A subpersonality is an "I" that won't become a "me/mine," and thus either remains embedded in the central "I" (as fixation) or splits off as a sub-"I," or subpersonality (dissociation), both of which are unconscious, or not a proper object of awareness (that is, a subject at that stage that fails to become an object of the subject of the next stage, and thus distorts and tears the developmental process itself, keeping parts of the "I" arrested and attached to elements of the earlier stage, and ripping off parts of consciousness that should be continuing their "transcending and including" growth and development to even higher and wider stages of awareness). In this situation, either the "transcend" or the "include" part has become busted, broken, torn, or misnavigated, leaving only roadkill in its wake).

The same thing happens with states, especially at their switchpoints (that is, as the state center of gravity moves from the gross to the subtle, or the subtle to the causal, and so on). For example, as the self moves from the gross to the subtle, its center of gravity shifts from the gross ego to the subtle soul, where the soul is the self primarily identified with the subtle realm and its Vantage Point (though still aware of the gross realm, just no longer exclusively identified with it—the state-realm remains, the Vantage Point is replaced). Now as the self prepares to move from the subtle into the causal, it must let go of its subtle soul (or die to its subtle soul) in order to do so. If it fears this death, or avoids it, the self might remain secretly identified with, or attached to, the soul—a soul addiction—and this soul addiction will skew its understanding and true grasp of the causal realm. Awareness-itself (as Daniel Brown named this causal state-stage) will become significantly distorted. Awareness-itself will not be free of the (subtle) personality but will be intimately attached to it and identified with it (and thus will possess an unconscious soul fixation). On the other hand, if this differentiation and dis-identification goes too far into dissociation and dis-owning, a soul allergy results, where the person doesn't transcend the soul but instead splits off parts of it as an unconscious soul subpersonality, which it dis-owns and loathes, while also loathing the soul in general wherever it shows up—in theology, in psychology, in other people, in other religions, in itself. What it loathes, of course, is its own subtle soul, which it has not properly transcended but dysfunctionally dis-owned.

The 3-2-1 Process

Most of these dissociated and dis-owned parts of oneself began as part of the self (a 1st-person quality, thought, feeling, trait, or characteristic), which was then pushed away—by a defense mechanism *made out of the same material* as the basic rung, or major state, that the self is at when the dysfunction occurs. Here quickly are some examples of dysfunctions arising at various fulcrums: introjection and projection by the fundamental self–other boundary of the sensorimotor realm (magenta Fulcrum-2), dynamic repression by the conceptual mind at the intentional-power stage (red Fulcrum-3), rule/role dysfunctions and problems with socially "fitting in" with the rule/role mind at the mythic-membership conformist script stage (amber Fulcrum-4), self-esteem and other dysfunctions at the formal operational/introspective mind stage (orange Fulcrum-5), pluralistic aperspectival madness (among others) at the pluralistic stage (green Fulcrum-6), and holistic severing by vision-logic at the Integral stage (turquoise Fulcrum-8). In each case, some part of the self is pushed away by a rung-specific, state-specific defense mechanism into an "other," a 2nd-person element in the unconscious, and then this is often pushed even further away into a completely alien 3rd-person element (an "it" often projected onto a "him," "her," or "them").

The dysfunctional process of shadow creation, in other words, proceeds from 1st person to 2nd person to 3rd person—or 1-2-3. Therefore, the 3-2-1 process developed by myself and the Integral Institute reverses that process, moving the alienated 3rd-person "it" material to a directly faced 2nd-person "you" element to a fully re-owned and re-identified 1st-person or "I/me" material. Let's say, for example, that George has a significant degree of anger (a 1st-person impulse), but for various reasons (for example, the anger is unacceptable by his parents, religion, or culture), he dissociates from the anger or pushes the anger out of his awareness (into a 2nd-person "other" in his mind), and then projects it further onto exterior others (a 3rd-person "him," "her," or "them"—in general, a 3rd-person "it"). Since everybody now seems angry at him, George develops a considerable amount of fear, and perhaps depression, in response. Perhaps this fear (projected anger) keeps showing up in nightmares as a devouring monster, or as a feeling that his boss is always upset with him for no apparent reason (he projects his anger onto the boss, so that now the boss always appears angry *at him*).

The 3-2-1 process starts by identifying the 3rd-person item that one is most reactive to, either in life or in dreams (the monster, one's boss). This material, by the way, can be positive or negative—if positive, one overly admires, vastly overrates, or hero-worships the person onto whom one's own greatness or other valuable positive qualities have been projected; if negative, various individuals in the environment seem full of that negative quality, often directed right at you—in this example, one's anger. So, after identifying the reactive element in one's mind, one then faces this other person, creature, or thing and talks to it in the 2nd person. "Who are you? What do you want? Why are you here?" and so on, for several minutes or more, creating an I-thou dialogue with this 2nd-person material, converting it from a 3rd-person absence into a 2nd-person presence. After really getting to know, and especially, feeling, this 2nd person, one then takes the role of this 2nd person in the dialogue and identifies with this person or creature, speaking not *to* them but *as* them, until one has thoroughly re-owned, and re-identified with, the quality, feeling, or characteristic that this projection was holding, thus returning it to the 1st-person element that it really is.

Let's return to George, who dreams that a monster is attacking him. As George speaks *as* this monster and starts identifying with it in the dialogue (talking to his regular self as the other member of the dialogue), he will immediately feel that the monster—and that he *as the monster*—wants to annihilate his regular self. As the monster, he's furious, enraged, and hostile as hell to this poor regular-self guy. The more he feels the monster, the more he feels his own aggression; the anger and aggression will no longer be able to be denied, dis-owned, repressed, and projected. Once he identifies with the monster, instead of directing the aggression at himself, he will aim it outwardly at somebody or something else, somebody other than himself. It was only aimed at him when he dis-owned the aggression/monster, thus, in effect, turning his own aggression inward on himself. Reidentifying with his aggression/monster, the anger can now be redirected outward. Toward what? This is where the original meaning of *aggression* comes to the fore. The etymology of *aggression* is "to move toward." Aggression itself is not bad or unhealthy. Aggression is not the same as hostility (the meaning of *hostility* is "to move against." Aggression is not hostility; aggression is actually a healthy, useful, skillful approach. Thus, we say that the president's committee on waste management "is moving aggressively to handle this issue." That doesn't mean that the committee is mad at, or feels hostility toward, the issue; it just means that the committee is proactively moving with much energy to handle the situation. Similarly, if a stag is on its way to a salt lick, and there is a bramble-bush blocking its way, it will lower its head, flare its nostrils, stroke its hooves on the ground, and aggressively charge the bush, knocking it out of the way. The stag isn't mad at the bush, it doesn't hate the bush; it is simply mobilizing energy to remove a blockage. That's what aggression does: it is the energy that overcomes obstacles and barriers. But if aggression in general is confused with hostility or nasty anger, then it might indeed be judged bad and thrown out of the self-system, and then that unblocking energy becomes aimed directly at the self, as if the self were something that needs to be knocked out of the way, and so of course the self reacts with fear, depression, and so on. If the self can effectively re-own this energy, then it can be turned outward once again (or directed inwardly if it is needed there), as the force of removing barriers and obstacles. This is a very powerful, very useful 1st-person drive.

If there is actual hostility that is being projected, a genuine hatred of a person or thing in the individual's world, it is almost always itself due to a prior projection of some aspect of the individual that the individual loathes—just as the antigay zealots hated their own homosexual tendencies, projected them onto gay men, and then experienced enormous hostility to gays, which they saw everywhere. In these cases, one has to do the 3-2-1 process with the despised quality first. Identify the person, thing, quality, or trait that one hates "out there," and then 3-2-1 that element, returning it to its rightful owner.

When the process is done correctly, there is usually a great sense of relief and release when finished. If the attribute was experienced as a negative quality, which is often how positive qualities are experienced when dis-owned and projected, re-owning it will return it to its inherently positive, joyous qualities—a terrific relief, converting this frightening "it" to a happy "I"!

Freud himself was on to this basic process of shadow creation and shadow cure. Most people don't know that Freud never once used the terms "ego" or "id." Those Latin terms for "I" and "it," respectively, were used by his translator, James Strachey, to make Freud sound more "scientific." The terms Freud always used were directly the German pronouns *das Ich* ("the I") and *das Es* ("the it")—and they were written just like that. So he would say things like, "If we look into the mind, we immediately notice two regions. The I is a directly available, conscious region open to our will and easily seen. But then there is a larger region, dark and inaccessible, and this it region is largely unconscious to us and quite mysterious. The it remains largely unknown." Thus, one of his most famous statements, which he gave when asked what the goal of psychoanalysis was, is always translated as "Where id was, there ego shall be." The literal translation of what Freud actually said is "Where it was, there I shall become"—a rather perfect description of the 3-2-1 process. Thus, "The desire to eat—it is just stronger than me, I can't help it" becomes "I am choosing to eat too much, and therefore I can stop it." This converts the dis-owned "it" to a re-owned "I," where I can control it. It's like if I were to pinch myself: I pinch myself, then deny and forget that I am doing it—"It's just happening, I don't know why, it really hurts, and it won't stop." I go around complaining about the pain (or anxiety, depression, guilt, obsessions), but I don't know what to do about it; it seems out of my control—and it is, as long as I'm dis-owning it. But once I see that *I am directly pinching myself*, I won't ask how to stop—I'll just stop. (If you are pinching yourself, and you really know that you are pinching yourself, do you ever ask how to stop doing it?) Until I re-own and re-identify with this pinching activity, it will indeed remain an "it," and I will be baffled. But once recontacted and re-owned, the process is once again open to "I" control. If I'm actually pinching myself now and know that I am, I am perfectly free to simply stop. Asking "How can I stop it?" just means that I haven't yet seen that I am doing it myself—when I see *that*, it will stop. 3-2-1.

So the steps in 3-2-1 are: Find it, Face it, Talk to it, Be it.

Step One: Find It. Locate the symptom, pressure, pain, image, person, or thing that seems to be the core of the problem—the fear, anxiety, depression, obsession, jealousy, envy, anger. Locate it, and notice everything about it—the symptoms themselves (the uncomfortable feelings generated by the problematic person, place, or event). Notice its location in your body (for example, head, eyes, chest, breasts, arms, shoulders, stomach, gut, genitals, thighs, lower legs, feet, toes, perhaps single muscles or muscle groups, sometimes bodily organ systems—digestive, urinary, reproductive, respiratory, circulatory, neuronal). Notice its general size, color, shape, smell, texture (whatever comes to mind when you think any of those elements). Notice what seems to most trigger it, what seems to soothe it, and activities that often accompany it (for example, increased heart rate, increased breathing, particular muscle tightening, headaches, difficulty swallowing, sexual inadequacy or disinterest). Don't judge them as good or bad, positive or negative. Just pretend that you are videotaping them, taking pictures of them, exactly as they are, not as you want or wish them to be—you are aiming for just a simple, comprehensive mindfulness of them. Get a lot of plain neutral videotape on every aspect of the problem. Get it fully in your awareness as an object.

Step Two: Face It. Once you have a good deal of videotape of the problematic item, then face it. If the symptom seems to be triggered by a particular person, then locate that person in your mind, and face him or her (or them). It might help to sit in a chair and put another "empty chair" in front of you. Put the problem in the empty chair—the person, monster, image, event, or simply the symptom itself (depression, anxiety, fear, envy).

Step Three: Talk with It. Ask it numerous questions, and listen carefully to what it has to say. "Why are you here?" "What do you want?" "Why are you doing this to me?" "Where did you come from?" "How long have you been here?" "When did you start?" If it doesn't know the answer to any of these questions, ask it to guess. "Well, you say you don't know why you're here. Why do you *think* you're here?" When it asks you a question, answer it, and see how

262 | Dysfunctional Shadow Elements

the problematic person or entity responds; you might even ask the problem issue what it (or he or she or them) thought of your answer. Get to know it directly as a living, breathing, creative, next-door neighbor, a person addressed in the 2nd person, converting it from a 3rd-person "him," "her," "them," or "it" directly into a 2nd-person "you" or "thou." The more you do each of these steps, the more likely you will already notice a certain diminution of the symptom itself. Then finally:

Step Four: Be It. Now, switch roles entirely. When it responds, you sit in its chair, and *you* yourself become the problem (person, monster, issue, and so forth). Identify with it. Speak in the dialogue *as* it, not *to* it. And speak to your regular self, sitting in the chair in front of you. Feel what it is like to be this symptom that is intentionally causing another person—the person sitting in the chair in front of you—these problems. It is here that you have to be the most observant and the most open. When the person (the regular you) sitting in front of you (as problem) asks, "Why are you doing this to me?" you have to be able to step into a role of someone who might be extremely mean-spirited and demeaning: "Because you're a stupid little moron, and you deserve to suffer." "You've always been a huge disappointment to me because you can't do anything right."

A good way to explore those kinds of responses is to ask, "Just whose voice is *that*? Mom's? Dad's? A sibling's? An early friend's?" This is the opposite of projection, called "introjection," the internalizing of an alien, false voice into your mind as if it were yours. In these cases, you don't re-own that voice; you toss it out! So keep that possibility in mind as well. Most people have extensive nets of introjections—internalized opinions, directives, commands, drives, or notions—that they got from their parents, early teachers, close friends, and especially the culture at large. These internalized networks, part of what we call "the embedded unconscious," are just that: embedded opinions and directives, whose internalized nature we are totally unaware of, but that tell us insistently what to think about virtually everything out there, and "in here" as well, and a significant part of shadow work is directly looking for the elements of this embedded network of introjections and then ejecting—dis-identifying with—these embedded introjected notions.

"Flourishing" and Journaling

If you want to take shadow work seriously, keeping a simple journal is a good idea. Use it to record brief summaries of your 3-2-1 sessions or actually conduct the 3-2-1 sessions in handwritten (or computer-written) dialogues in the journal itself. I'm going to mention something here very briefly that is actually quite important, and I don't want the brevity of the discussion to be mistaken for the topic's being of lesser importance, because it's a very significant subject. It's something called "Daily Entries." If you are doing shadow work, or if you are meditating or practicing contemplative prayer—or engaged in any sort of Integral Life Practice—it's a very good idea, each morning when you wake up and before you get out of bed, to do a brief 3-2-1 with any significant elements in the night's dream, and then make a "daily entry." This daily entry is a three-page entry (no more, no less) about anything "personal" that you want to write down at all—it could be about last night's dream, today's coming events, something that happened to you in the past, any thoughts that happen to cross your mind, on any topic, right now, or some particularly striking event or insight in yesterday's meditation. If you can't think of anything to write, then write about that ("I can't think of a single thing. Why am I doing this, anyway? It's incredibly boring, I don't see the point, how idiotic can you get? Write, write, write, big deal . . ."). The point is to bring mindfulness—a pure, neutral, judgment-free Witnessing—to bear on each sentence that you write, making that subjective statement into a clear object of awareness. So bring a pure, clear, Witnessing awareness to bear on every sentence that you write. This three-page entry becomes the place where you make mindfulness/Witnessing a permanent habit in mind, thus building into your psyche the single essential element found in all developmental and evolutionary processes: the subject of one moment becomes the object of the subject of the next. This is what the awareness that you develop when you do a "daily entry" in effect does—it inscribes on your mind the essential spirit of evolution; it makes growth and development a Kosmic habit, a Kosmic groove, in your own being, and not only unconsciously (which is what typically happens) but also consciously.

Some people find that their "daily entries" start to take on specific forms or directions. Some people find themselves starting to write plays, novels, or screenplays. Others find themselves increasingly jotting down their ideas on specific human issues (for example, in philosophy, psychology, or religion), commenting on world events, or starting to write books. Any of these are fine. If you start to go over three pages, it's best to stop writing in the journal and start writing the particular piece as a separate work—that is, actually start writing a screenplay or a running news commentary or a book on philosophy or religion. The only requirement for the "daily entry" is that it is "personal," and that simply means that it is something that comes to your mind when you intentionally write out three pages of anything. Whatever is in your subjective mind, you are going to make object. You are, that is, going to grow, to evolve—whether you want to or not!—because this is the very essence, the very core, of growth, development, and evolution.

If you are doing other, specific practices, such as the 3-2-1 process, you can include those in your journal. You can even start the screenplay or the book in your journal, but if you do, clearly mark it off from the day's three-page entry; you want writing that three-page entry to become a habit in and of itself, so you don't want to confuse writing it with other activities. But you can include anything else in your journal that you want to—not only 3-2-1 sessions but notes on your meditation practice, what is happening with it, what actual practices you are doing, and so on. If you are doing an Integral Life Practice,[4] you can track all of your modules in your journal. If you're taking a Web course, such as "Full Spectrum Mindfulness" (www.fullspectrummindfulness.com), you can track that in your journal.

You might also take up something like "Positive Psychology," which is an important movement that emphasizes not only fixing what is wrong with oneself, but enhancing and extending what is already right with oneself. Don't just fix what's broken, but make use of, and enhance, what's working. (For this, a book like Martin Seligman's *Flourish* is a good place to start.[5] Take the "signature strengths" test in the book, or on his website, and proceed from there.) This "flourishing" or "thriving" is the positive aspect of Cleaning Up emphasized by Integral Theory—along with Growing Up, Waking Up, and Showing Up. Shadow work involves the "negative aspect" of Cleaning Up, or fixing what is broken. But emphasizing what is working is also an important part of any Integral approach to life and practice, and we do such exercises whenever we practice Witnessing Awareness or Nondual ("Headless") Awareness, which takes both of those strengths, which are ever present in everybody, and practices enhancing them.

Other positive practices that are extremely useful—and recommended—include practicing *gratefulness* and *forgiveness*. These are two astonishingly and deceptively powerful practices. To practice gratefulness or gratitude, consistently set aside a few minutes each day to make a note in your journal, or just in your mind, of things that you are grateful for. One version of this is Positive Psychology's "Three Positive Things" exercise (which again, you can do in your journal or in your imagination). Each evening, make a brief note of three things that happened that day that you are grateful for, that made you happy, or that went well. Evolution has tended to build into the brain a habit of looking for hazards and things that can signal danger or trouble; there is much less drive to notice things that are positive, that we should be grateful for, that make our lives better or happier. So we have to build that in as an added habit, and "Three Positive Things" is one way to do exactly that. If you make it a daily practice, just set aside a small amount of time each day—five or ten minutes will do—and write down (or simply review) three items that happened to you that day that you are grateful for. Start by doing it for one week—but whatever happens, don't miss a day for that one week. Then see if you can't tell, after just one week, that there has been a genuine shift in how you are feeling—basically, toward being happier. Almost everybody who does this (and there is actual research attesting to this) feels noticeably happier in just one week![6] If you feel happier, then you'll have a genuine, tried-and-tested reason to continue with this practice. (For the importance of gratitude in a spiritual view, let me recommend Brother David Steindl-Rast's website, A Network for Grateful Living, www.gratefulness.org, and any of his books.)

Forgiveness is an attitude recommended by many of the Great Traditions. The separate-self sense tends to be built out of a handful of basic, negative emotions (or emotions that we think are positive but have overall negative effects). Forgiveness is an antidote to regret and resentment and is a powerful ego-transcending attitude. It works especially well with gratitude, both of them together covering the negative and positive sides of the street. I certainly recommend practicing them together. The wildly popular set of self-help spiritual lessons called *A Course in Miracles* is built almost entirely on practicing forgiveness, with quotes such as "Forgiveness is how I remember my Higher Self" and "God is the Love in which I forgive."[7] If you take up a practice of forgiveness, again, just a few minutes each day is fine, as you begin to lay down another habit of mind. Try "One Thing a Day," where, for a few minutes—five minutes is fine—each evening, pick the event that most irritated you that day, and practice forgiving the person—the other person, or perhaps yourself—most responsible for it. It's also a good idea, at least in the beginning, to spend a few minutes with "One Thing Each Yesterday": begin a list (keep it in your journal) of all the things and people that you can think of—from your past—whom you are angry with, blame something important on, or deeply regret knowing because of something they did to you (or you suspect that they did). For some people (such as your parents), this will likely be a list of things that you resent. Directly and genuinely practice forgiving that person (or yourself) for each specific item until it really "takes." You will know when it takes when either one of those *A Course in Miracles* quotes kicks in, and you feel either a closer presence of Spirit's Love, or a more direct contact with your own Higher Self (however you conceive it). Each time you genuinely forgive somebody whom you believe wronged you (including yourself with various issues), you will feel the separate-self sense uncoil just a little bit more, relaxing more and more into the vast All Space that is its own truest and most self-liberating Nature.

One of the things that is particularly valuable about keeping a journal is that it will help you, with more and more precision, spot exactly where you are in the processes of Growing Up, Waking Up, and Cleaning Up (as well as Showing Up, if you want to track that). You will, for example, in your "Daily Entries," start to see evidence of which particular level/stage of "hidden maps"—the particular developmental altitude—your central self is presently located at. Your "entries" will embody a particular set of assumptions, values, purposes, and traits, all of which will largely be determined by the "hidden map" of whatever your present structure-stage is. As you continue to learn more about each structure and its View, you will be able to very easily spot exactly where you are on the overall spectrum. Evidence shows that individuals who learn the basics of a developmental map end up progressing through those stages at a measurably faster rate, so simply learning the Integral model and applying it to your own productions will accelerate your growth through these stages (that is, the Integral Framework is, indeed, "psychoactive"). Add to that the fact that, with each "entry," you are making subject object, and you have the basis of a truly accelerated growth and development process at your disposal. Welcome to a tomorrow that is deeper, higher, and wider, and a present that is more Present.

More on Shadow Material

You might discover as you continue work like the 3-2-1 process that a particular "neurotic problem" that might be bothering you is that you did something that was in fact morally wrong. "I'm hurting you because of how you treated your mother in your last trip home," or "For how you treated your best friend when he was in the hospital." Before we cover those cases, it is worth emphasizing that in many or even most cases, it is a trumped-up charge, related to some sort of event interpreted via infantile or childish fantasy: "Because of how silly you looked wearing braces for three years. What an idiot you were—and still are!" But the point, remember, is that in each case, *you* are the actual source and cause of these ideas, impulses, and judgments. They might have originally come from your parents, a childhood friend, or a teacher, but you internalized or introjected them and made them a part of your own self, and if you are not to blame for the original impulse, you are to blame for continuing to act on it. Somewhere during step three or four of the 3-2-1 process, you will run into the basic and major reason that you dis-owned the quality, characteristic, drive, impulse, or fantasy in the first place, *why* you are repressing or otherwise defending against it. Whether that cause is a younger, didn't-know-any-better you, or someone in your world who had authority over you and whose voice you introjected, in any event, become fully aware of that repressing voice and—for these trumped-up charges—then eject it, get rid of it, toss it. It's keeping you tied to a false self-image and diminishing the likelihood of the emergence of a real, genuine, authentic self-image (an accurate, conventional self through which your True

Self or Witness can view the world with the least amount of distortion, and through which it can communicate to the world with the least amount of dysfunctional noise).

And when you spot the cause of the particular repression, the fundamental response, in almost every case, is the same: you need to forgive yourself for whatever it is that you are or did, think you are or did, were told you are or did, or fantasized you are or did. Another reason that practicing *forgiveness* is so important—and worth practicing daily—is that it is the fundamental key to ending the repressing, defending, dis-owning drive in yourself. If you projected a positive quality, forgive yourself for not living up to it, then give yourself permission to step into *your own greatness*, and not simply project it onto others (perhaps use repeated affirmations: I fully deserve this *greatness*; I give myself permission to live my own greatness!). We live in a culture of "specialness" and "greatness," where everybody is supposed to acknowledge how special and great they are; but it's surprising how few *honestly* do so—there are plenty of fake "greatness" claims, but very few honest recognitions of the utter specialness of being a sentient being with an irreducibly unique perspective. Maslow called the fear of our own greatness "the Jonah complex," and many of us have some degree of that—so give yourself permission to discover, re-own, and step into, your own authentic greatness! If you are projecting a genuine negative quality, forgive yourself for having it, and promise yourself to work on cleaning up that quality, whatever it is. Many symptoms are due to unfair childhood, or unfairly fantasized elements; forgive others who may have been involved, and forgive yourself for buying into it.

Now, as we started to note, occasionally symptoms are due to a real conscience attempting to call attention to a real and unethical misdeed you actually did, not a trumped-up charge but a truly immoral act. Here you need to truly assume responsibility for it, forgive yourself for the misdeed, and definitely work on changing whatever aspect of yourself engaged in the deed in the first place. *Your shadow symptom won't fundamentally go away until you delete the unethical element in yourself.* Get rid of it, and then forgive yourself.

Note that, in our "no blame" society, it's common to assume that whatever problem you have is not your fault; somebody else is to blame—your parents, peer group, partner, kids, work, society itself.

We live in a "victim mentality" and "victim chic" culture that teaches ethical and moral irresponsibility at every turn. Eastern traditions are brought in and used to "live merely in the Now" so as to avoid any ethical obligations or "shoulds." But that, in every case, is a misreading of Eastern traditions. Buddhism, for example, summarizes its entire teachings in three major strands: *shila*, *dhyana*, and *prajna*. The first foundational item is *shila*, which means "ethics." *Dhyana* means meditation (it's a Sanskrit term, which, translated into Chinese, is *channa*, and that translated into Japanese is *zenna*, or Zen). The third is *prajna*, which we have seen as pro-gnosis, the Awakened awareness of Enlightenment that is the aim of the whole sequence. But the sequence can't even get started without shila, without ethics, without normative *shoulds*. No ethics, no Awakened awareness, no Enlightenment. The problem with a "therapeutic culture" such as ours is not getting an awareness of the shadow into the culture (a version of which is virtually everywhere: nobody's to blame for anything because their shadows made them do it!). The problem is to get a correct and not overblown version of it, an overblown version that sees every misdeed I commit as the result of something Mommy did to me, or schooling did to me, or society did to me, not something that I did to myself. Even if I am not to blame, or am not responsible, for the original introjected material that became the shadow that led to the misdeeds, I am responsible for how I *now* continue to handle it—and that starts with assuming responsibility for it (and only *then* forgiving myself).

So although the shadow and shadow material are often created by forces over which you had no control, the actual dis-owning or denying of the shadow material is a lie that you tell yourself about your own constitution—the shadow is the nexus of the lie. You know somebody has a great deal of this nasty material, but since it can't be you (the lie), it must be somebody else—anybody else—and suddenly the world is full of nasty shadow villains, most of them, for some strange reason, aiming their hostility at you (simply because that's where it really belongs). So a delicate mixture of "tough love" for yourself is necessary in dealing with these issues—be tough, be responsible, stop blaming others for your ills (and forgive them if they truly had a hand in it), re-own your own shadow, and, healed and wholed, rejoice in the blissful thrill of a genuinely authentic self! The formula is simple: false self + shadow = authentic self. Your "overall self" is your True Self (or

Witness) plus your conventional, relative, finite self, and that finite self can be a false (inaccurate) or an authentic (accurate) self-concept. The choice is truly yours . . .

The 3-2-1-0 Process, or Spiritual Transmutation

There is an extension of the 3-2-1 process that we call the "3-2-1-0" process, and it involves the extra practice known as "transmutation of emotions." We have seen that the Tantric view of Nonduality is particularly powerful and doesn't renounce negative emotions or work to gradually transform them, but rather steps directly into the emotion with nondual Awareness, which almost instantly transmutes the emotion into its corresponding transcendental wisdom (anger, for example, then arises as the *brilliant clarity* of nondual Awareness).

In order for this process to work correctly, the original emotion has to be an authentic emotion—meaning, the negative emotion that one is working with must really be in its true form, and not some displaced, repressed, denied, or distorted form of a negative shadow. But that is exactly what repression, dissociation, and dis-owning do—they fundamentally alter even a negative emotion into a false and misleading form. Thus, in our example of dis-owned anger appearing in the dream as a monster: the monster is likely to generate emotions of fear, not anger. And it's not obvious at all that this fear is the result of a projected anger—thus it appears as real, genuine, authentic fear. When I see the monster coming after me, I feel *fear*, not anger! Therefore, if one is working with transmuting emotions, one will understandably work with fear, and work to bring nondual Awareness to bear on fear. But fear is a nonauthentic emotion in this case: it's not real, it's not the actual emotion that was originally generated (rather, anger is), and thus transmuting this inauthentic emotion will create only an inauthentic wisdom, a wisdom that is not being generated by the real and accurate energy of the original emotion, but a twisted wisdom resting on a twisted emotion and distorted energy. This can actually be fairly damaging, not liberating, because a false emotion is being elaborated and blown up to transcendental proportions.

But if one performs a 3-2-1 process on this fear first, it will fairly quickly return to its original, authentic form of anger. And *then* if one performs the transmutation of emotions on that authentic emotion of real anger, a genuinely authentic transcendental wisdom will result (namely, brilliant luminous clarity). We call it "3-2-1-0" because, with nondual Awareness, the subject–object duality is overcome (at least temporarily), and thus the "1st person" is transcended into "no person" or "no subject" (no subject–object duality), or "0 person." (If this practice sounds appealing, *Integral Life Practice* contains a chapter on the 3-2-1 and the 3-2-1-0 processes.[8] Numerous books are also available on the Tibetan Buddhist practice of emotional transmutation, and those can be consulted—just make sure that you've first done a 3-2-1 or similar such practice to make sure you're working with the original negative emotion and not an inauthentic, reactive emotion to a projection.)

Most meditators find this process easy and enjoyable. It can be done for just a few minutes each morning, with the most attractive or disturbing elements in the night's dream, or done a few minutes before sleep, with the most admirable or irritating person during the day (both sessions can be included in your journal). This is just one short example of shadow work, but this 3-2-1 or 3-2-1-0 process is often enough to handle a great deal of shadow material. (If more work is indicated, a professional therapist or various self-help books can be consulted.) And also notice, if one is doing a version of the 3-2-1-0 process, then the last step (the returning to original nondual Awareness) can lead right in to one's basic meditation practice, which can pick up from there. Likewise, if one is doing a 3-2-1-0 process during meditation, reaching the "0" step will return one to pure nondual Awareness itself, which is a genuine help to almost any form of meditation practice available.

Doing a 3-2-1-0 process with meditation becomes a type of "double relaxing": The first relaxing occurs when any intense positive or negative emotion is returned to its original form; one relaxes from the intensity of a dissociated and projected feeling (anxiety, fear, depression, obsession, and so forth) to a smoother and more relaxed state. The second relaxing happens as one meditates on the self-contraction itself (the practice of meditation) to return it to pure, open, nondual Awareness, a second and most profound relaxation into the openness and spaciousness of nondual Mirror Mind. Whichever contraction arises in any moment—the contraction of a false, inauthentic feeling (cured with a few minutes of 3-2-1 in the course of meditation) or the self-contraction itself (cured with nondual meditative awareness, or a 3-2-1-0)—one is returned to the open, transparent, clear, empty, deep spaciousness of Buddha-mind.

Shadow elements can be generated from virtually any View (at any structure-rung) and any Vantage Point (at any state-realm). No matter how otherwise healthy one's structural development is or how successful one's meditative state development is, a shadow malformation can completely gum up the works. We know from long, hard, bitter experience in meditation from its introduction to the United States some forty years ago, that meditation (and spiritual work in general) won't cure shadow issues and often inflames them. We all know meditation teachers who are often superb state teachers but structurally are shadow-ridden neurotic nuts, to put it as politely as I can. Don't be a victim of your own shadow, but include at least a little shadow work along with your meditation.

Remember, even if the relative, finite, conventional self is not the ultimate, infinite, Real Self (or pure Suchness), it is the vehicle *through which* the Real Self and Emptiness must operate in order to communicate with the conventional world, and if you have a True Self trying to express itself through a finite false self, instead of a finite authentic self, then you really are not going to sound very enlightened. At best, an enlightened neurotic. Work on converting your false selves to authentic selves, as a way to honor and serve your own highest Self and true Suchness.

9

Dysfunctions of the 1st-Tier Structure-Views

Overview

In chapter 3, I briefly traced out the typical shadow issues involved with the first four major structure-stages (or what we're referring to as their general correlations, the chakra-rungs). In this chapter, I am going to outline the typical types of shadow dysfunctions that can occur through the *entire* spectrum of first-tier structure-stages (or chakra-rungs) of Growing Up. Then, in the next two chapters, we'll cover 2nd- and 3rd-tier shadow elements, and then move on to state-stages and their shadows. You are more than welcome to use these chapters as "diagnostic" aids in helping determine where you might have any shadow elements. Some people find this rather uncomfortable, and tend to shy away from the issue entirely. But looking for one's shadow elements is actually a profoundly useful and deeply helpful endeavor. It's like having a Geiger counter that will buzz wildly whenever it gets near the prized uranium. Finding shadow material will set off a type of interior Geiger counter in you, and far from that being a bad thing, it indicates where the treasure is located. Because your hot uranium elements—your shadow material—indicate exactly the areas where you can grow. They indicate places where you have lost track of, and dis-owned, your own potentials, your own "goodies," and running away from them is like running away from where the Geiger counter goes off—you're running away from the treasure. So I urge you to just suck it up a bit and move on through this material—I truly believe you will find it ultimately most liberating and freeing.

To give some indication of the type of things that we will be going over, let's very briefly review what we saw with the first four major structure-chakra stages and their problems. There's no need to remember any of these; I'll bring them up and summarize them whenever needed. After this brief introduction, I will go over the entire spectrum of structure-stages (and then state-stages), so you will have a complete, if simplified, guidebook to your hidden sources of uranium. We're quickly reviewing these first stages and their dysfunctions because these earlier and lower structures are some of the most basic, primordial, primitive, and fundamental levels of consciousness that humans have. Some are so primitive, in fact, that they are, in essence, "prehuman" or "subhuman," and addictions/allergies to these levels cause some of the most disturbing, distorting, torturous, and yet relatively common problems that humans face. Worse, given their "commonness," many of them constitute what has been called a "normal neurosis"—that is, a typically, widely shared sickness taken as normal, to-be-expected, nothing unusual. Further, there are two dysfunctional tracks with these earlier stages, something we deeply find nowhere else. First, things can go wrong with the phenomena that are most centrally emerging at each stage—for the first three stages (Fulcrum-1 [F-1], Fulcrum-2 [F-2], and Fulcrum-3 [F-3]) these are, respectively, food, sex, and power (things held in common with many animals, hence, again, "prehuman"). Second, there are things that can go wrong with the formation and creation of the conventional self itself, the creation of its own self–other boundary, which is not present at birth, but comes into being slowly and haltingly through developments at these first three fulcrums. Something can go possibly wrong at each stage, which gives rise, in each case, not just to a different dysfunction, but to an entirely *different type* of dysfunction, from the severe psychoses (F-1) to the intermediate borderline/narcissistic disorders (F-2) to the more typical standard psychoneuroses (F-3). So these earlier "subhuman" stages are the scene of an extraordinary amount of developmental, evolutionary action, leading up to the first truly human level, the heart chakra-rung of beginning love and belonging (F-4) and care for sentient beings other than oneself.

At the first basic structure with its Archaic View (oral/anal, root chakra, Fulcrum-1, sensorimotor, infrared), the dysfunctions are either allergies or addictions to food (and *physiological needs* in general). If the self-line and self-boundary themselves are involved (along with factors in the other three quadrants), the results are the serious psychoses, as a weak or nonexistent self-boundary allows flooding by states, particularly the subtle state in actual hallucinations (which are dreams occurring in the waking states).[1] Psychoses are distinguished from neuroses in that, as typically defined, psychoses are a problem with being in touch with conventional reality itself—people "see" and "hear" things that "aren't there" (voices, hallucinations, the entire world trying to kill them ["paranoid schizophrenic"]), every event is centered on their self and its centrality to the entire universe ("delusions of reference"), and so on. The psychotic is "living in another reality," and that reality, for Integral Theory, is actually a state—almost always, the subtle state—that is flooding the waking-state self, due to the porous self-boundary, in such a vivid way that it is directly perceived, a real "dream" is occurring in the waking state. It is the genuine reality of the subtle state itself that makes the psychotic so utterly convinced that his or her hallucinations, and condition in general, are absolutely real. Neurotics, on the other hand, are in touch with "normal or conventional reality," but then have various repressions, denials, inadequate cognitive interpretations, or other problems that nonetheless make some sort of sense to a conventional understanding. And "borderline" conditions are those that are borderline between psychoses and neuroses.

Notice, then, something that movies always get wrong: Schizophrenia, which is a form of psychosis, as its name (somewhat misleadingly) implies, is taken by almost all films as something usually called a "split personality" (which is what "schizo" seems to mean)—that is, somebody with multiple personality disorder—for example, the lead character in *The Three Faces of Eve*. In films, the character's psyche is fractured into several subpersonalities, one of which is usually portrayed as a cold-blooded serial murderer. Such an individual is labeled as totally "schizo" or as a "split personality." But real multiple personality disorder (a genuine "split psyche" condition) is actually a neurosis, a severe neurosis, to be sure, but each of the personalities is fully in touch with conventional reality—there are no hallucinations or waking-dream fragments. (In movies, if the murderer is indeed hearing voices and "obeying" them—usually to kill or torture somebody—that person is rarely presented as having multiple personality disorder. The person's whole psyche is screwed, not just one of a number of "split" personalities.) Real "split mind" is a neurosis, not a psychosis, because all of the "split sections" are still in touch with conventional reality, however poorly the psyche itself is doing. Should any of those fragments start hallucinating—bingo! Psychosis.

At the second basic structure with its Magic or impulsive View (emotional-sexual, genital chakra, Fulcrum-2, the emergence of images and symbols in fantasy, magenta), typical shadow issues, particularly at the higher reaches of this stage as it moves into red, involve addictions or allergies to sex itself (which, according to the traditions, is focused on this chakra-rung, even if it matures later in life),[2] as well as significant disruptions of emotional well-being in general, or prana (which, as the pranamayakosha—the "sheath/level composed of prana or élan vital"—is said to be localized at this level, or chakra 2). These disruptions of basic bioenergy or early emotions (anger, desire, pleasure, wishes, joy, and so forth) can generate primitive anxiety, depression, stress, reactive rage, or fear; plus, if the *self-boundary itself* is involved, they result in the narcissistic/borderline conditions, dysfunctions that involve the newly emerging self–other boundary.

Remember the point that is crucial here and is worth repeating: at these first three major structure-stages, the conventional self itself is just beginning to emerge from an original undifferentiated and embedded state, where subject and object are fused and confused—the infant can't tell where his or her body stops and the chair starts—and out of this original fusion state, the self–other boundary slowly emerges. In this process, something can go wrong with any of the specific elements emerging at those stages—food, sex, power, and so on—but something can also go wrong with the formation of the self–other boundary itself. If that happens—in conjunction with factors in the other quadrants, including family dynamics in the Lower Left and brain chemistry in the

Upper Right—then, at chakra-rung 1, the earliest and most primitive stage, a failure to form the self–other boundary accompanies the most severe forms of dysfunction, the psychoses. At the next chakra-rung, or rung 2, problems with the self-boundary, now approximately "half formed," as it were, result in narcissistic/borderline problems, where either the individual hasn't yet differentiated self and other, and thus treats the entire world as an extension of himself or herself, in other words, the narcissistic personality disorders, or the boundary has started to form but is still very weak, and thus is always being threatened by a porous self always being overpowered and annihilated by the world—the borderline syndromes. With chakra-rung 3, the self–other boundary is finally in place, if all has gone well, and so the standard neuroses caused by a strong self repressing bodily feelings can now occur. In treating something like the Fulcrum-2 borderline conditions, the therapist's goal is to get the individual's self-boundary to be strong enough that it *can* perform Fulcrum-3 repression for the first time—repression would be an improvement! So with these first three stages and three fulcrums, there are not only the major elements emerging at each stage, each of which can become dysfunctional (F-1 food, F-2 sex, F-3 power) but also the class of dysfunctions set in place by the growing self-boundary (F-1 psychoses, F-2 narcissistic/borderline, and F-3 standard psychoneuroses).

At the next major basic structure (egocentric, gut chakra-rung 3, Fulcrum-3, emergence of the intentional or conceptual mind, red), with its Magic-Mythic View (also called "PowerGods" or "opportunistic"), common pathologies involve addictions or allergies to power and power drives in general, problems with safety and security (since the self is just forming, and worrying about its existence as it does so), as well as classical forms of repression of bodily states and feelings (sex, aggression, desire, wishes, élan vital) by the newly emerging conceptual mind and its repressive power (which, we just saw, results in most traditional psychoneuroses caused by actual repression or similar defense mechanisms, such as classic anxiety, depression, obsessions, displacement disorders, and so forth). Here we are at the more standard and typically understood stages of development, with a relatively strong self–other boundary in place, and conventional forms of defense mechanisms and dysfunctions. The earlier stages are all forms of *pre*-differentiated realms, which are pre-(subject–object) and *not* trans-(subject–object), or prepersonal and pre-egoic, *not* transpersonal and trans-egoic. Many theorists confuse these early stages of *adualism* (totally lacking emergent dualisms, undifferentiated) with very high spiritual states of *nondualism* (transcending and including dualisms), infantile states that are said to be recontacted in a "mature" form to issue in Enlightenment, but they are really nothing of the sort. They don't integrate subject and object, self and other, organism and environment; they simply can't tell the difference between them in the first place. A "conscious form" of that would be nothing even vaguely similar to Enlightenment, but rather a conscious experience of chaotic fusion and massive indissociation, a more painful and un-Enlightened state one could hardly imagine. So try and avoid this simple form of the "pre/trans fallacy."

Keep in mind that the pre/trans fallacy applies specifically to recognized developmental sequences—such as prerational to rational to transrational, or preconventional to conventional to postconventional, or preverbal to verbal to transverbal. It doesn't apply specifically to states, such as gross, subtle, or causal, since states can be experienced and in some ways developed in all sorts of different sequences. As we earlier saw, no state is inherently prepersonal, personal, or transpersonal—that distinction is largely supplied by the structure that is experiencing the state (although the subtler the state, the more it tends to be interpreted transpersonally if there is a structure that can do so). Thus, the infant's experience of the causal, which can be quite extensive, is virtually always of a prepersonal, pre-egoic causal state (and a prepersonal delta brain-wave state), because the infant's structures are all prepersonal; none of them are yet transpersonal. So whether we are talking structures or states, the infant's experience is *not* one of a nondual spiritual Ground or transpersonal awareness or any potential form of any of those. It is largely a state of prepersonal indissociation, fusion, and embeddedness, often uncomfortable and painful (just as the child will soon be "teething," or cutting its emerging teeth, so the child is "selfing," or cutting its emergent self—and both are mostly not pleasant, not happy occasions), and so the infant spends a good deal of its time crying, as it struggles to develop the rudimentary tools necessary to adapt to the gross sensorimotor world.

As we arrive at the fourth basic structure (concrete rule/role, heart chakra, Fulcrum-4, beginning love and belongingness, amber), with its Mythic and Mythic-membership View (and usually "Mythic-literal," or mythic absolutism and fundamentalist forms), typical shadow issues involve allergies or addictions to love and belongingness, and newly emerging social-fit issues (such as peer grouping, conformist "fitting in" with appropriate roles, and rule/role "games people play"), among others.[3] In a certain sense, this is the first "human" stage of development, displaying characteristics—especially the capacity to take the role of other, to adopt a 2nd-person perspective—found in no other animal species. Of all the definitions of "human" provided over the ages—from the "political animal" to the "symbolic animal"— probably the most accurate is the "role-taking animal," the capacity to see not only what one is oneself seeing but to put oneself in the shoes of an other and see the world as that other is seeing it. This is an astonishing capacity, and begins to play on what can be legitimately viewed as deeply transpersonal dimensions of humans, however tentative at this early point. (With Schopenhauer, for example, humans are capable of a moral response—or treating another person as oneself— precisely because they ultimately share One Self: how else, seriously, can you explain it?) There is something about the heart chakra that the traditions find specifically and uniquely human. Of course, precursors to love exist at many earlier levels (and as nonreflexive forms of Eros, all the way back to the Big Bang, it's the drive to higher unions, higher wholes, which marks every major stage of vertical evolution bar none). Darwin certainly saw forms of love in many other animal species— birds, for example. He almost never referred to the "mating season"; he always called it "the season of love," and he meant it seriously. And the previous human stages—the first three fulcrums—are all marked by forms of unreflexive self-love, or egocentric love. But there is something about love become reflexive, something about love reflected through the capacity to see another being *by seeing the world as that being sees it* (that is, one "I" adopting the view of another "I," and thus able to form a true and genuine "we," arguably for the first time), that is unique, and it emerges uniquely starting with this structure-level of development. The truly human levels of being, for the first time in history, are awakened and come online. With this development, individually and collectively, our entire history entered a radically new and unprecedented sphere of being and becoming, a world under whose umbrella we are all still partially sheltered.

So much for a brief review of these crucial, early chakras (and basic structure/Views) along with their correlative shadows—in food, sex, power, and love, essentially. Next I will go through all of the structures, starting with the lowest but this time moving all the way to the very highest structures in all of development, the extraordinary Supermind, in a very pragmatic and easy-to-grasp fashion, particularly emphasizing ways that you can easily spot these stages (and their shadows) in yourself, and thus in effect act as a real test, a real metric, in helping you determine what your own altitude or structure-level really is, the particular "hidden map" that is making so many decisions for you right now about what you want, what you value, what you see in life, and how you want to get it. These are the hidden maps that no spiritual systems anywhere can or will show you. And yet simply spotting which one is most influencing you right now will, by making that hidden subject an aware object, act to free you from that limitation, transcend that partial View, and open you to the next-higher, wider, and broader level/stage of consciousness, with increased capacities for love, care, concern, and creativity, as higher and higher dimensions of your own being start to radiantly emerge, come online, and remake your life from the inside out.

Now all of this is particularly important to be generally aware of because, not only do all humans have a full spectrum of structure-stages (and state-stages) available to them—although sadly very few are aware of this fact—but something can go wrong at each and every one of these stages. Because each of these stages is built by a set of Kosmic habits (such as "transcend and include" or "differentiate and integrate"), each of those components can malfunction, and that will create a problem, a pathology, a dysfunction, that will mildly to severely disrupt normal functioning and subject the individual to various, often quite painful, disorders. Every evolutionary stage of creative emergence is also the emergence of a possible pathology, and truly, for anything resembling an enlightened society, it behooves us to be aware of both of these—both our different structure-levels (and state-stages) of evolution and the numerous things that can go wrong with each. Lamentably, virtually all cultures now in existence are desperately ignorant of both. But there is no reason whatsoever for you to be. So for the next few chapters, here is a guide to what can go right—and wrong—with your own growth and development.

One final point needs particularly to be emphasized. There are several dozen developmental models now available. Virtually all of them focus on one or two developmental lines (cognitive, emotional, aesthetic, moral, interpersonal, spiritual, and so on), and then study human beings as they grow and develop through those lines. They usually create tests or metrics that they administer to people to help determine where they are at in this development, and then they attempt to discern the structure or pattern of the various stages through which all people seem to move (the various levels in the particular line). They arrive at their models by studying and testing real humans and theorizing from there.

That is an important approach, but it is not the approach that Integral Metatheory takes. Rather, Integral takes all of the major developmental models and puts them all on the table, and then compares and contrasts them all. From that, it creates a model of all these models, or a map of these maps—a metamodel, a metamap—using all the models to fill in any gaps in any of them. The result is a supermap, a supermodel, a composite or integrative map or model covering all of the bases touched on by each of them, and leaving out none of the fundamental elements. In *Integral Psychology*, I list over one hundred different models that are all used to create the Integral Metamodel. And this means that this model is definitely inclusive and comprehensive. Unlike any single model, it covers all the central bases.

Now this doesn't mean that individual models aren't important or useful; they most definitely are. And Integral Metatheory often uses one or more (or several) individual models when investigating any specific occasion. And you can see in the Integral Psychographs that I gave (see fig. 6.2) that numerous individual models are included in them. But if you are using Graves's model, you won't get Piaget's stages; if you are using Loevinger's model, you won't get Kurt Fischer's stages. The Integral Metamodel uses—and includes—them all.

So what I have been giving (and will generally continue to give) are the overall general summaries made by this Integral Metamodel of each of the major structures and states of development. General characteristics from across all of the various lines are generalized when we speak of any given "level" (even though, when we want to study a specific line in a given individual, we will usually use a specific model that was originally developed with that line in mind—such as Piaget for cognition, or Maslow for motivation, or Loevinger for self-sense, and so on). But by giving the "composite description" of each major structure-level, we are covering all of the bases, making sure to touch on every significant element, something that no individual model can or will do. This is why, to give only one example, Roger Walsh, in his new book on wisdom, uses the Integral Metamodel as a guiding framework. He states, "Currently, the most comprehensive of all metatheories is Integral Theory, which was created by a remarkable polymath named Ken Wilber. Even among metatheories, Integral Theory is unusually, or even uniquely, comprehensive."[4] The same meta-approach is taken in virtually all the other topics covered in this book, which guarantees a certain sturdiness to the conclusions. But be that as it may, here is a quick metamodel overview of the major structures and their possible shadows—and remember, you can't get this from any individual model.

Infrared Archaic

As always with development, the basic rung remains, and the View from that rung is negated and is replaced with the View from the next-higher rung. So the self starts out identified with chakra-rung 1 and its alimentary drives (oral, anal, physiological). If all goes well, the self will dis-identify with its exclusive attachment to that chakra-rung and move on to the next higher one, chakra-rung 2, which is the beginning of emotional-sexual proper, élan vital, and emotional well-being in general. If, however, the self remains attached to some aspect of rung 1, the self will retain or keep, as a hidden subject (or "sub-subject" or "subpersonality"), some part of the View from rung 1; it will retain an oral or an anal fixation, and part of the self (as a subpersonality) will continue to see the world through that alimentary View. Parts of the View of rung 1, in other words, remain as parts of a subject that cannot or will not be seen as an object (an "I" that won't become "me/mine"), that will not be negated, transcended, and let go of, but remains instead identified with the subjective self-sense (and its "hidden map") of, and colors its View from, a lesser, narrower, shallower, junior rung. It's a rung-2 self with a rung-1 fixation or addiction. The self-sense should have stepped cleanly and entirely off rung 1 and onto rung 2, and begun to see the world from the View of rung 2 (or "View 2"). But if part of its self-system remains stuck at rung 1, an oral or anal fixation (or a basic physiological, infrared, need dysfunction or misnavigation problem with this stage in general), then this will distort and limit the "amount" of consciousness that is able to grow and develop from rung 1 to rung 2. Rung 1 itself was definitely supposed to remain in existence—the self still has the capacity and the need for food and the full ability to eat—but the self was supposed to no longer *exclusively identify* with that rung and look at the world only with its oral View; that View was supposed to have been dropped as the self stepped up to rung 2 and its higher, wider View. But with fixation or addiction, part of the self is still looking at the world through the lens, or View, of rung 1, thus limiting, distorting, and twisting rung 2 and its View. The self doesn't just retain the need to eat or a healthy *oral drive*; it is stuck with an *oral fixation*, an addiction to eating (or to satisfying some other physiological needs).

At the other extreme, the self or consciousness can go too far and not simply dis-identify with rung 1 but dissociate or dis-own aspects of it (oral or anal, material, physiological), and thus split off parts of the View of rung 1 and develop an *avoidance* or an *allergy* to those (or any related) aspects. Again, the rung wasn't cleanly retained and integrated, it was dissociated and dis-owned, and thus its View wasn't cleanly let go of, but split off as part of a subpersonality that now distortedly continues to view the world largely through rung 1, and not straightforwardly through its present stage of rung 2 and its new and higher View. One doesn't retain a natural food drive in a well-fed body, but instead develops an allergy to, and avoidance of, aspects of eating, or, in general terms, one has problems with aspects of fundamental well-being, or being safely well-fed in a secure bodily being, and instead creates a pathological dysfunction that results in anything from bulimia to anorexia to undereating and body-image problems to, in severe forms involving the self-line, near-psychotic-like insecurity about the gross body and the gross realm itself. Typical female versions of this kind of dysfunction hover around "I'm not beautiful, I'm fat!" no matter how skinny and beautiful they actually are.

As for being actually "fat," recent studies show that a staggering 60 percent of the American population have weight problems. Now realize, this means dysfunctions going all the way down to this Archaic level—one's relation to something like food—a relation that itself marked the very first emergence of the very first primitive forms of life on earth: life is a process of taking in higher-structured nutrients and releasing lower-energy "waste" products ("Life lives on negative entropy"—that is, it takes in order, releases chaos). And two out of three Americans are disrupted at this earliest, most primitive, most archaic level of their entire being. The whole culture is disrupted at this level; it is now a "normal neurosis" that is epidemic. You can't even get to higher-level criticisms of American culture—from racist to sexist to greedy capitalist to socially alienating to pornography pushing—without starting at this lowest of all possible levels: we are a culture deeply misrelating to the foundations of Life itself. You cannot get more foundationally messed up than that.

This also illustrates something that, although I have not been focusing on it in this particular discussion, is never insignificant nor should ever be forgotten—namely, the effects of the other quadrants on the development of dysfunctions in each, since the quadrants all arise together, evolve together, and are mutually interwoven in all ways, including health and sickness—in this case, the immediate and direct effects of, for example, the Lower Right quadrant on the Upper Left quadrant dysfunctions, social factors such as poverty, lack of basic nutrition, lack of basic human health care, material-level disruptions/scarcities, and the lack of extension of the basic rights of decency and universally recognized human rights.[5] And add to that the networks of artifact exchange and transfer, specifically those dealing with food and nutrients, that are distorted and broken in many fundamental ways, so that many Americans are facing problems generated on higher levels—income disparity, racist and sexist atmospheres, male "success object" demands, female "sex object" drives, lack of cultural meaning and purpose—and, in recompense, are downing "comfort food" at an alarming rate. We are an all-mouth culture, because of failings at higher levels that we are simply not addressing and a wholesale regression to the lowest levels possible, and we shore up safety and security at those lowest levels by eating ourselves into satiated numbness. For the first time in history, the generation born now can expect to have shorter life spans than their parents, because of the ill-health consequences of a childhood where over half of them will be overweight. This "turn to comfort food" has become institutionalized in the Lower Right, as part of the very network of social exchanges and social institutions now embedded in this society.

Other profound impacts on the Upper Left quadrant from other quadrants include those from the Lower Left, where such things as family dynamics and skewed family values have direct effects on the self and its pathologies in the Upper Left (including its archaic food pathologies). The family is an almost endless source of so many significant others, mother, father, grandmother and grandfather, all sorts of siblings, brothers to sisters, not to mention aunts, uncles, cousins—and today's multisourced families of stepfathers, stepmothers, half brothers and half sisters, lord knows how many half-related ex-stepfathers, ex-uncles, ex-aunts—all having a inordinate impact on Upper Left emotional health. The further impact of the interpersonal emotional atmosphere surrounding jobs, bosses, paternal concern about money and income, being able to care for the child's safety and security, not to mention college and general expenses, all have a huge Lower Left impact on Upper Left emotional well-being. One of the problems with a green "postmodern culture" is that, with its pluralistic "nonjudgmental" and "hands-off" attitude to every sort of individual behavior, no matter how dysfunctional or pathological, we're not even allowed to make judgments about a person being "dysfunctional" or "healthy"— who are we to judge about what is right and not right for any individual? How arrogant, how oppressive, how dominating is that?! If Junior wants to stuff his face with Twinkies for breakfast, who are we to say "No"? (And that is exactly what Junior, in many different ways, is doing. This puts parents in a real bind. In some states, children have actually sued their parents for trying to impose "discipline" on them. "Children are people, too" is a common, green-driven sentiment behind this entire catastrophe.)

In a "therapeutic culture," such as ours, where nobody is to blame for anything that they do, "shame" has all but disappeared from the cultural fabric. This got started with a small percentage of the population, neurotically burdened with an overactive superego or internal critic, and suffering inordinate amounts of shame for almost anything they did. Therapists noticed this and began circulating theories that shame, in any form, is bad, is neurotic, and that we need to get rid of it altogether and promptly. Well, we did. Shame, which is a crucial part of the fabric of any well-functioning culture, acting, as it does, as a filter between the lower, "subhuman" drives of a person (for food, sex, and power) and the higher drives of love, care, tenderness, courage, and presence (by making people appropriately feel shame when they act primarily on one of those lower drives to the detriment of their fellows), has all but disappeared from the cultural landscape—and hence, from the individual psyche—and thus so has the major force stopping regression to earlier and more primitive levels (starting with food, moving to sex, moving to power), and accordingly our culture is now essentially overrun with all three.

These earlier drives—food, sex, and power—are essentially subhuman; they are not the drives of higher levels (or the goals of a life well lived) for love, meaning, authentic values, goals, and purposes, and holistic and embracing worldviews, let alone the transpersonal and spiritual dimensions of an individual. Satisfying these needs is a necessary—but by no means sufficient—condition for having higher-level drives; but in becoming an actual goal of life, life itself becomes subhuman. These drives deal with Maslow's "physiological" and "safety" needs, nothing higher—no "love and belongingness," no real "self-esteem," no "self-actualization" at all, nothing even near "self-transcendence." These problems with this culture, as I said, don't even get up to the standard level at which typical criticism kicks in, such as that we are victims of the "old paradigm," or the "Newtonian-Cartesian paradigm," seeing a deterministic, mechanistic, analytic-abstractions world. (If only we could get up to those levels!) These fundamental problems are much deeper, much more primitive, much harder to address, much more foundational. And they will likely not get addressed in any functional fashion, because, to mention just one reason, green will not allow the introduction of "shame," because green denies that there is anything that a human should be ashamed of. Since there is no universal "what is right" and "what is not right" for a human being, shame is altogether inappropriate. And with that aperspectival madness, we will continue eating, sexing, and greedily powering ourselves to death—all without any deeper or higher meaning whatsoever, all without the slightest redeeming social qualities, all without anything pulling us out of our subhuman dispositions into the light of a genuine humanity (at which point all of those lower drives positively blossom and can be wonderfully embraced!). But any individual wishing to attain even the modest goal of returning to a real humanity has the staggering weight of the Lower Right social institutional dimension and the Lower Left cultural dimension pulling him or her down by the ankles, making transformation upward indeed an uphill battle.

Worse, probably as significant as any quadrant on Upper Left emotional health is Upper Right genetics and brain neurochemistry, particularly taking into account the incredible rise (and often wildly overblown influence) of biological psychiatry, which believes that mental and emotional dysfunctions are due entirely to brain neurotransmitter malfunctions, and are treatable solely by biomedical means, predominantly medications. The dirty little secret about neurotransmitter medications is that, in over 50 percent of the FDA-approved antidepressant medications, they proved no more effective than placebo ("sugar") medicines.[6] Martin Seligman, founder of Positive Psychology, claims that this is a multibillion-dollar scam on the American people.[7] But despite the poor performance of psychiatric drugs, nobody doubts that problems in this quadrant are correlative with problems as they show up in other quadrants, and research is racing forward in this quadrant faster than in any other.

The point here is not one of blame but of compassion. What we're seeing is that strong pressures in all 4 quadrants greet anybody born in today's world with an almost overpowering drive to overeat and tendencies to being overweight, even of clinical proportions. Concern with our culture can start right here, with compassion for the individuals caught in this horrendous cross fire. Anybody who knows somebody who has had problems with being severely overweight (or anybody who has had these problems themselves) knows how little they feel their own willpower has a role to play in all this; the forces just seem overwhelming and beyond their control. And in many cases, that's exactly right. The factors in the other three quadrants—from institutionalized comfort food to cultural lack of control mechanisms to genetic/brain predispositions—are largely out of reach of the individual's control, and thus the "it" of these symptoms is incredibly hard to turn into an "I"'s control.

Almost all the books by change agents on these issues—problems facing our world and what we can do about them—claim to have a solution to the world's ills, and it depends on everybody on the face of the planet adopting their views (that is, everybody reading their book), the likelihood of which is nil. I'm terribly encouraged by the terrific growth in interest in Integral approaches across dozens and dozens of different disciplines and areas, but I'm not naive enough to believe that the world will simply adopt these views overnight. Rather, the forces in all 4 quadrants (or rather, in the overall AQAL Matrix itself) will play themselves out, with certain nudges here and there being helpfully given by more integral approaches, but by and large, they are forces that will answer to their own destiny, their own causes and contexts, their own karmas. All we can do is continue to add our voices to the mix and hope that those who have the eyes to see will begin to share in more comprehensive, more inclusive, more embracing perspectives. So I'll include, in an endnote, a brief summary of my 4-quadrant suggestions for this "comfort food" epidemic.[8]

In the meantime, one bit of at least slightly good news is that, given all the problems, the "transcend" part of "transcend and include" can, at least to some degree, and depending on many other factors, work to redress, via its own novel emergence, the problems handed to it from lower levels, hence accounting for the occasional emergence of extraordinary human beings from the worst possible social conditions. More typically, a malformation at a lower rung is, via the "include" part of "transcend and include," often carried forward and included in various forms in the next higher level, and that amalgamated malformation is included and carried to some degree in its succeeding level; but each stage-rung can also, via its "transcend" and "emergent novelty," act to balance and redress, as much as it can, the original malfunction. Often, within a few stages, the self-system has corrected to a fair degree the original problem and can return to a degree of functionality, although that is built on an archaeology of roadkill and scar tissue, ready to erupt at any time, and that ideally will be addressed via fairly genuine shadow work.

(For the use of mindfulness in dealing with any of these Fulcrum-1 physiological disorders, see *Integral Meditation* and the Web course "Full-Spectrum Mindfulness," www.fullspectrummindfulness.com; both of those also guide the use of mindfulness in helping to deal with shadow material across the full spectrum of stages.)

Magenta Magic

This brings us to chakra-rung 2 (the pranic, magenta, bioenergy, Fulcrum-2, emotional-sexual level, with the emergence of images and symbols in the fantasy mind), with its View as Magic, impulsive, exclusive body-pleasure, immediate gratification. We needn't get over-Freudian here, but Freud's basic point was that the infant starts out as "polymorphous perverse"—meaning that the infant gets pleasure from every area and activity of its entire body. (Woody Allen, famous long-time analysis client, became quite taken with this notion; the phrase "polymorphously perverse" appears in at least three or four of his movies.) But then this original and total bodily pleasure with life energy begins to narrow down and focus on various bodily parts, restricting its fuller possibilities. The infant first narrows this libido to its oral zone, then to its anal zone, and then here, at chakra-rung 2, to its genital area. If there are any specific and repeated traumas at any of these areas, the self can become either hyperattached to those areas or hyperavoidant of them. Later, as an adult, as these areas become more and more awakened and functional, any of these early repressions or fixations can come to the fore, creating what can be quite severe neurotic (or even psychotic) problems, as the original scar tissue inhibits full adult functioning.

For Integral Theory, these early childhood phases are when the original potentials for particular types of Kosmic grooves are being laid down—in all 4 quadrants—and they will significantly influence the subsequent unfoldings of these feelings, capacities, and bodily or mental areas later in life, as they continue to blossom. But one can dis-own aspects of any of these earlier chakra-rungs at any point in subsequent development, if one identifies with any of them and then dissociates (or fixates and attaches to) any of them. As the self steps up to chakra-rung 2 and identifies with it (and its View of the world), if all goes well during this period, a fairly healthy magenta structure-rung will be laid down, a healthy Kosmic groove will be set, and thus this structure and function will work smoothly throughout subsequent life, as is the case with all basic structure-rungs healthily laid down.

If, however, as the self begins its growth to the next higher chakra-rung, in this case, red chakra-rung 3, some aspect of consciousness remains stuck or fixated at chakra-rung 2, then that forms part of a subject that refuses to become object, part of a View that will not be let go of, part of a "hidden map" that the self continues to *look through*—as a subject—and therefore can't *look at* as an object, thus part of an identity that it will not dis-identify with (and thus this will ultimately jam some part of "neti, neti").[9] This part remains in the submergent unconscious as a shadow impulse or even a full-blown subpersonality (a "sub-subject"—that is, *not* an object), sending up symptoms and symbols of an emotional-sexual fixation and thus an addiction. In the young child, this shows up as numerous problems, some as simple as the self-sense remaining saddled with a tendency to "immediate gratification" and great difficulty delaying desire. Later in life, starting particularly in adolescence, as sexuality blossoms, it (sexuality) has no place to land except on these distorted, broken, and fundamentally scarred original Kosmic grooves, and if it is a fixation, the adolescent becomes sexually obsessive—sexually addictive—and his or her behavior begins to evidence sexual overobsession (even judged by the typically high sexual interest of adolescence). This sexual fixation is often accompanied by numerous mental or cognitive problems as well (generally short-circuiting cognition into immediate gratification forms) and can include difficulty in the early stages of fashioning an authentic self-esteem, problems with lasting romantic relationships, and "objectification" of the opposite sex. (This objectification occurs in both sexes, with males tending toward viewing excessive X-rated pornography and females toward entertaining intense romance-novel fantasies, where the male is objectified as the "success object," the "knight in shining armor" who comes to take her away from a life of abject misery and showers her with extraordinary wealth. Much of these types of fantasies, of course, are based on cultural factors in the Lower Left quadrant.) Further aspects of "fixated sexuality" include compulsory masturbation with feelings of "emptiness," "hollowness," and "barrenness" (and not in the Buddhist sense).

This sexual addiction is a surprisingly common dysfunction, especially among males (whose Upper Right quadrant and its intense load of testosterone predisposes males to all manner of hypersexuality). Studies show that the average college male has an explicit X-rated fantasy once every five minutes (!), whereas women have a "romantic fantasy," not X-rated but of a soft-lit dinner with her mate in front of a fireplace, walks on the beach, that sort of thing, around once every thirty minutes. Male sexuality is so wildly outrageous—as Nora Ephron put it, speaking of her husband, "The man is capable of having sex with a venetian blind"[10]—that when women hear the exact and actual details of male fantasies, they are totally, absolutely shell-shocked; male sexual fantasies appear so degenerate, obscene, brutal, disgusting, almost unimaginable (all I can say is, you should see them from this side). But for male sex addicts, none of their sexual behavior is truly satisfying, causing them to actually increase the behavior in a desperate bid for satisfaction, which is still deeply ungratifying in any deep way, and thus not really finding it, they are driven to more and more of the same type of hollow sex, trying to feel something authentic—failing again, they are driven yet deeper into meaningless empty-feeling-inducing sex.

In females, "sexual addictions" take the form more often of "oxytocin flooding," with oxytocin, known as the "relationship hormone" (acting as a "relationship drug") driving the woman from one hopeless romantic situation to the next. She is never able to get a sense of what she really wants, *or her own autonomy*, since that is totally buried in, and is constantly defining itself according to, her relationships and what she has to do to satisfy her partners in them rather than what she can *also* do to satisfy her own wants, drives, needs, grandest values, and deepest visions, and to do so in full partnership with her mate, not in an (oxytocin) "drugged" and mindless servitude to him. (This lack of autonomy can also be found in her other self-defining relationships: if she's a mother, she defines herself solely in relation to her children; if a wife, in relation to her husband; if in a romantic relationship, her lover; if she's a daughter, her parents, and so on.) And in her few off hours, she reads Harlequin romances about being taken away from all this, but since her autonomy/agency drive is out of whack, the "idyllic setting" that she imagines being taken to is the same type of setting she has now, only "much prettier"—the perfectly painted nice house with pink trim, an exquisitely mowed bright green lawn, children laughing and playing in the backyard on the swing set, a lovely white picket fence all around—and all of her jailers still present, husband, kids, parents, all smiling and waiting for her to serve them dinner. In short, she doesn't want to be the doctor; she wants to marry the doctor, which is totally fine, as long as it is not coming out of a barren, hollow sense of self but her authentic self and its genuine wishes. My point is that, with this ersatz ideal so deeply buried in the woman's embedded unconscious, it's almost impossible for her to know what she really, truly wants. I've given a deliberately caricatured picture here (more in line with the ideal of the 1950s), but the idea is that these types of "oxytocin (Upper Right) romances (Upper Left)" can tend to snarl women, since their "relational" strengths become overblown and hyperextended. In these cases, instead of the woman just expressing her own authentic self and deepest autonomy through numerous and abundant healthy relationships, feeling her autonomy expanded, shared, and enhanced by the joy of sharing it with beloved others (is any joy truly at its best unless shared with loved ones?), the relational strength goes too far into relational fusion and relational meltdown, and the woman, far from finding herself in her relationships, starts losing herself in them. The earliest tendency for such relational fusion can go all the way back to here, to the "emotional-sexual" chakra-rung or basic structure, with its "deep feeling-élan vital relational joy."

If, on the other hand, the requisite healthy differentiation and dis-identification from this stage goes too far into dissociation and disowning of emotional-sexuality and relational joy, then when sexuality blossoms, it has nothing to support it except this broken and fractured Kosmic groove. In this case, since the "sexual repressive" stance is an avoidance of, and hence an *allergy* to, deep feeling and emotional-sexual impulses in general, or to "élan vital relational joy," this joyous relational exuberance is blocked from being expressed and shared in sexuality. In other words, there is sexual avoidance, sexual dissociation, or sexual allergy of various types (from puritanical repressive zealotry to impotence to frigidity to feelings of everything from sexual embarrassment to sexual disgust). In the "emotional-sexual" equation, as its early lines are being developed here for the very first time, a general "emotional allergy" is slightly more common with males (an *allergy to feelings in general*, except aggression), and a more specific "sexual allergy" is slightly more common with females, where sexuality is almost always embedded in an overwhelming number of cultural, social, and psychological factors, often—still!—of a prohibitory and repressive nature. Superficial sexual images are everywhere; deeply satisfying sexual relations, much less common.

The so-called double standard in sexuality—related to the idea that women have only two basic archetypal roles: the all-good Madonna (or mother) and the all-bad sexually loose whore—is in part culturally constructed and worthy of abrupt dismissal; but there are a small number of grains of truth in it best understood through a limited use of evolutionary biology. By "limited," I mean realizing that it comes from, and only covers, the Upper Right quadrant; the other three quadrants provide a much-needed context that can counteract, mitigate, or even totally reverse the elements in the Upper Right. So remember, for Integral Theory, it is absolutely not the case that "biology (Upper Right) is destiny." That's a quadrant absolutism that feminists rightly rejected, but Integral Theory's point is that you don't have to throw out all of the insights of biology in attempting to understand sex and gender—biology is not totally useless, after all—you just have to set it in the entire context of a 4-quadrant, or better, full AQAL Matrix, so as not to overestimate its importance or impact. So, with that firmly in mind . . .

Let's go back perhaps two hundred thousand years ago in human history, when our sexual patterns were still being laid down and determined. When a woman was pregnant, she was absolutely certain of who the mother of her unborn baby was—namely, her, of course—and so she was utterly sure of being able to pass on her genes with this pregnancy; having more sex would *not* in the least increase her chance of passing on any more genetic material at all (which is the primary drive of humans according to certain Neo-Darwinians like Richard Dawkins and the "selfish gene" notion). She's already pregnant; she can't pass on any more genetic DNA by having more sex. For the next nine months, sex is not going to help her pass on any more of her DNA. Her primary goal at this point, rather, is to find someone, usually a man, and usually the father, who will protect her and her offspring when the bear is outside the cave threatening to eat them all, and she is in no condition to take up a warrior stance, sitting there with a belly the size of a 1958 Buick. The bear takes one look at that and says, "Buffet!" So she will be drawn to a powerful man (which also often means someone wealthy, at least according to the values of that culture, and that often means older, since older men tend to have accumulated the power in the culture), and she will want to stay close to him. And if he's the father, she will always assure him that the child is indeed his since, unlike the woman, who knows who the mother is, the father has no proof whatsoever that he is the father, and if he's going to spend all his time and accumulated resources protecting that mother and child, he better know that it's his DNA that he's working so hard for. However, as for his own capacity to pass on his DNA, there is no reason whatsoever for him to stop having sex with other women during this woman's pregnancy; in fact, *the more sex he has with other women, the greater his Darwinian advantage.* Unlike the mother, who has no Darwinian advantage in having sex when she's pregnant (she's already won the "pass-on-my-DNA" lottery), the man has every reason in the world to keep spreading his seed around.

In these circumstances, what the woman fears most about another woman is not so much her mate being drawn to having sex with her; that's definitely not good, but it's not the worst (and men being men, she's even slightly prepared for that). What she fears the most is that her mate will start to develop a close, personal, emotional, caring and sharing bond with another woman, sharing intimacies and emotional feelings with the other woman that he doesn't share with her, because that means that he might indeed develop an intimate bond with the other woman and eventually leave his wife for this new, exciting "person I can really talk to." If her mate were to leave her for another woman, it would strip her of all his protection (which ranges from his wealth used to help support her children to his physically attacking the bear when the woman is pregnant and can't protect herself or her children from predators or attackers). The man can't see anything wrong with this "emotional relationship," because, after all, he's not having sex (the one item that the male counts as serious), but for the wife or mate, this a four-alarm fire, pointing clearly and directly to the loss of everything that the wife counts on the male to provide for her and her child. She's alarmed. She finally confronts her male mate. And what's the first thing that she says to him? It's *not* "Did you have sex with her?" but the much more important "Do you love her?" All men have at least the tendency to stray with sex, and down deep, most women know it's meaningless (which it often is), but if he "loves her," that is a threat to everything the woman needs for her and her child's survival. If he really loves the other woman, he might choose to withdraw his protection, power, and wealth from his wife and transfer it to this new woman. (Again, we are talking about the ways things existed two hundred thousand years ago, as our genetics were being laid down; things are somewhat—not much—different today, but the point of evolutionary psychology is that many of these patterns, laid down over two hundred thousand years ago or more, are still with us in our brain structure. Don't worry, it's only one quadrant—the Upper Right—but that can be very useful in understanding some of the drives in our overall psychology, if balanced and interwoven with all the other quadrants.)

Men, on the other hand, have almost the opposite concerns. The man is hypervigilant about the slightest thing that indicates that his mate has had sex with another man, not love for him. He doesn't fear losing protection, wealth, or power (what the woman tends to look for) but indications that the woman's child (and its DNA) is not actually *his*. *That* is his concern. And you have to realize that there is absolutely nothing that the man can do to guarantee this (certainly not in those times—there were no paternal DNA tests, and so on). If some other man snuck into his wife's bed and they got it on, and she became pregnant, then the husband would be working his tail off to support and pass on the DNA of another male—exactly what his whole Darwinian nature is primed to prevent. This is why, in many cultures, such as Islamic cultures, a woman's sexual features—her body, her face—must be totally covered. And this is why a man being alone with a married woman was brutally punished. A woman who was even suspected of adultery was often stoned to death. (Christ's famous words "Let he who is without sin cast the first stone" were said exactly with reference to such a situation.) But men are like that—if it's not my DNA, kill 'em both (mother and child)! Married women out in the public sphere were always accompanied by a male bodyguard (in many cases, a eunuch—that takes care of that possibility, doesn't it?), or at the least several servant girls, to assure that the woman was not left alone to advances. And this is why, as was said of Caesar's wife, "She had to be above reproach." You can imagine the furor that would be caused if a Caesar's wife was carrying the DNA of somebody other than Caesar—this would be both blasphemy, since Caesar was God, and treason, since he was head of state. The man suspected of having sex with a Caesar's wife was put through unimaginable tortures (and the wife often simply murdered).

This is why, when a woman was suspected of infidelity, the only thing that the man wanted to know was *not* "Do you love him?"—farthest thing from the man's mind—but rather "Did you have sex with him?" "Did he ever see you naked?" "Did he touch you?" All of that possibly leads to sex and pregnancy, which means that the husband might not be the real father, the real owner of the DNA being passed on. He doesn't mind if they had hundreds of hours of the most intimate, emotional conversations possible—he couldn't possibly care less about that—the one thing the woman cares most about! Instead he wants to know, "Did he see your tits? Tell me the truth!"

So, due largely to the hormone profile of their Upper Right quadrant (testosterone in particular), men tend to "objectify" women as *sex objects* primarily meant to provide them with sexual release (and the release of their little DNA carriers), and women, with a million years of evolutionary psychology still burned in their brains, tend to view men as *success objects*, primarily meant to provide them with wealth, power, and safety to protect them and their children as the biological clock keeps ticking. (I once asked my sister-in-law, who was dating a man who had become a bounty hunter because "you can kill people if you want," why she was seeing him—so many people were alarmed with her choice—and she replied, "Because I feel safe around him.")

An Integral approach makes room for such findings and the data that supports them, but by seeing them as the results in *only* one quadrant—the Upper Right—realizes that the other quadrants can modify, tone down, lessen, and even reverse those drives. Biology is most definitely not destiny; but the advantage of this approach is that both men and women can scan their own psyches and see how much of this million years of evolution is still active in them, how much it speaks to them, and thus how much, or how little, they can choose to listen to it. It simply increases one's options; it doesn't narrow them in the least. In any event, sexual allergies and sexual addictions are two very common dysfunctional responses to this most powerful of drives.

As for the "emotional" part of the "emotional-sexual," we've noted that many traditions (such as Vedanta and Vajrayana) tend to locate the central emotional dimension here, at chakra 2, or in the second major sheath (or kosha), the pranamayakosha—"the sheath made of prana (bioenergy or emotional-sexual energy)." For Integral Metatheory, this chakra-rung 2 contains the first major flowering of the most rudimentary emotions (which begin in their most primitive forms in the previous chakra-rung 1): fear, desire, rage, frustration, irritability. But each new level or structure-rung adds a newly emergent class of more complex and sophisticated emotions or affects in general. So affects are confined to just this level, but there is a full spectrum of affects accompanying each and every level up to Overmind and Supermind. Thus, rage first tentatively emerges at rung 1; when images are added to rage (at rung 2), you get anger; when concepts are added to anger (at rung 3), you get hatred—and so on up the spectrum. Likewise with satisfaction to pleasure to joy to happiness to bliss, spanning all three tiers.

And with each new affect, there is the possibility of a new pathology involving that affect—a new addiction or a new allergy. We will be tracing some of these new developments as we continue, but this general fact is indeed worth keeping in mind.

Red Magic-Mythic

Similar dynamics, if not as strongly driven, are nonetheless still at play with chakra-rung 3 (the intentionality or power mind, red, Fulcrum-3, gut chakra) and its View (opportunistic, Magic-Mythic, or magic power in mythically heroic figures—"PowerGods"). Fixation to it leaves one not just with an empowered and healthily strong self but with an overblown drive to "power over" others. People with such a fixation are authoritarian, controlling, egocentrically dominating, and manipulative (a *power addiction*)—generally, overtly "opportunistic" (William Torbert's name for this type of leadership style/stage). In contrast, dissociation and dis-owning aspects of this level leave the self weak and disempowered, lacking healthy self-assertion, overly obedient and subservient, submissive, a "milquetoast," a "momma's boy" or "daddy's girl" (namely, a *power allergy*). Dysfunctions at this stage also include the whole range of the standard battery of classical psychoneuroses since the mind's newly emergent concepts and intentionality, along with its newly formed strong self-boundary, are now powerful enough to officially repress and dis-own virtually any of the body's feelings and impulses, and this includes feeling in general (resulting in the stereotypical dry, abstract, "heady" personality): lack of joie de vivre; repression of the drives toward food, sex, or power (or elements of its own and any earlier levels); classic anxiety and depressive disorders; obsessive-compulsive disorders; psychosomatic problems (circulatory, digestive, nervous, urinary, reproductive); disruptions of prana (subtle energy) in almost any of its systems and channels (for example, acupuncture meridians); lack of felt meaning (for example, see the work of Eugene Gendlin) and body aliveness in general.

In its healthy forms, we find this stage in the value line of firefighters, test pilots, astronauts, and members of rescue teams, where this stage's focus on the immediate present and its tendency not to inordinately think about tomorrow or worry about the future allows more "courageous" action in the here-and-now. In its unhealthy forms, with its excessive power drives and its need for relatively immediate gratification, it is common in members of criminal organizations such as La Cosa Nostra. (Mafioso members don't refer to themselves as "Mafia" members, they use the words "la cosa nostra"—which in Italian literally means "this thing of ours." So they won't say, "Here's our newest Mafia member," but they will actually say, "Here's the new member of this thing of ours," and maybe later, "Make sure you tell nobody about this thing of ours.") This is the major level where the mind can be at war with the body, with the mind's embedded judgments and beliefs (often introjected from parents, family members, early friends, culture itself, particular religions, individual philosophy) often at odds with various bodily feelings, impulses, and desires. The mind's general approach here is to simply seal out, split off, repress, or dis-own the questionable material, banning it to the submergent unconscious, thus turning an "I-impulse" into an unconscious dissociated "you-element," and often further projecting that entirely onto a 3rd-person entity—a "he/him," "she/her," "they/them," or simply "it"—and projecting that out of the self-system entirely, onto some individual or group of individuals, especially if they already have a fair amount of the alienated and projected material themselves, thus acting as a good "hook" for the projection. This is the last major stage where the repressing entity (mostly the mind) is battling the individual's body. Starting at the next stage, the battle switches from mind versus body to mind versus other minds—that is, with the emergence of the rule/role mind, the focus shifts to how my (mental) role fits into the larger social group of other roles, and how clashes between the various roles can cause conflicts and disturbances, just as clashes between the mind's judgments and the body's feelings cause conflicts at this fulcrum.

Amber Mythic

At the next major structure-stage, we find dysfunctions (allergies and addictions) occurring with chakra-rung 4 (the concrete beginning love and belongingness mind, the rule/role mind, amber, Fulcrum-4, concrete operational) and its View (concrete Mythic-literal, mythic-membership, ethnocentric conformist, fundamentalist, absolutistic, "diplomat"). One of the particular problems with chakra-rung 4 is that its concrete Mythic-literal or conformist View is "absolutistic." Not only does the Mythic View genuinely and deeply believe that its truth and values are the only real truth and values in existence (all 1st-tier stages share some degree of that belief) but it does so in an *absolutistic fashion*—for example, the Bible and its myths are all absolutely and undoubtedly true; there is simply no room for any doubt, of any sort, whatsoever. Further, there is the gravest retribution imaginable for denying and surrendering this particular absolute truth or View, a genuinely severe punishment (such as everlasting damnation, a string of horrid reincarnations, or two bullet holes through the head with La Cosa Nostra). Because one's deepest meaning and purpose is often connected with the View at this stage (absolutistically!), to be "excommunicated" from this "belongingness community" is the one of the worst things that can happen to one—for example, to be thrown out of one's fundamentalist Marxist group, excommunicated from one's Mythic-literal religious group, or tossed from one's fundamentalist feminist group, one's scientistic society, one's devotedly believed-in political group, and so on.

The typical form of conflict at this stage is, as just noted, not between the mind and body, but between the mind and other minds, between particular rules and roles, generated by the rule/role mind, which in their positive aspects help individuals move from an egocentric identity to an ethnocentric identity, an identity not just with one's own self, wishes, and desires but with a number of larger groups and their ethics, requirements, allotted roles, and specific rules to follow. This is, generally speaking, a new task for the self, so accustomed is it to being unable to "take the role of other" and thus assuming that whatever it was thinking is what everybody was thinking; first finding out that this is not always, or even usually, true is often something of a shock. All of a sudden, you become aware of the world of other roles—and people seeing the world through different perspectives than you do—which is a major growth in awareness, and requires a massive readjustment and accommodation. Recall that every holon (including each human holon) has two major horizontal drives—agency (or autonomy) and communion (or relationship)—and the task at this new level is learning to balance these two drives in a way that supports both and doesn't simply lead to unending turmoil. On the one hand, there is autonomy, or the drive to be a whole in and of it-self—self-defining, self-governing, self-determining. But the shocker about human individuals is that each autonomous human holon depends, for its very survival and existence (not to mention many of its deepest satisfactions and joys), on being part of a larger collection of other autonomous human holons. The individual has not only a drive to be a wholeness unto itself but also a powerful drive to be part of a larger wholeness beyond itself. It wants to be both a whole and a part; it has an agency drive, and a communion, or relationship, drive. Being one's own "wholeness" seems fairly straightforward, but how exactly do you be a "partness"?

Thus starts the human's lifelong journey into the extraordinary world of mutual relationships. All holons, at every level, exist in a se-ries of relationships, or have a Lower Left quadrant, but starting only at this level do those relationships start to be "mutual," "conscious," "reciprocally aware," or involve "taking each other's role." The peo-ple with whom we have these relationships include every variety: family, friends, schoolmates, colleagues at work, neighbors, political-party members, clan, tribe, or national members, romantic partners, various club members—not to mention relationships with other sen-tient beings, from pets to the local ecosystem (all of which have interi-ors, as the 4-quadrants go all the way down) to spiritual relationships with one's fellow practitioners, one's teachers, and perhaps even a great Thou (or Spirit in the 2nd person) that you feel a personal rela-tionship with.

As with all made, grown, or assembled things, any of these relation-ships, having been built up, can break down. Hence, we start to see the dysfunctions that begin to dog virtually all relationships, bottom to top, and things that one can do to help mitigate them. Relationships, of course, continue through higher and higher levels—there are lower quadrants at all levels, top to bottom. It's just that, at this stage, it has its first major breakthrough, since at this level the individual can "take the role of other" and thus start to enter relationships in a real, genuine, and consciously reciprocal fashion. Take a ball colored red on one side and green on the other, and place it between you and a four-year-old. Turn it several times so the child can see that each side is a different color. Then place the ball between you and the child, with the red side facing the child and the green side facing you. Ask the child what color it is seeing. The child will correctly say, "Red." Then turn the ball several times, and stop it with the green side facing the child and the red side facing you. Again ask the child what color it is seeing. The child will correctly say, "Green." Then ask the child, "What color am *I* seeing?" and the child will not say, "Red," which is the color you are seeing, but will say, "Green," the color the child is seeing. In other words, the child thinks that whatever color it is seeing, you must be seeing, too. Do the same thing with the child at age seven or eight, and the child will correctly say, "Red." In other words, because of the rule/role mind, the child can now take the role of an other—take your role—and see the world through your eyes, put itself in your shoes. This rule/role mind ushers the child into the world of role taking, which allows the child's identity to expand from being egocentric, being identified only with itself, to being ethnocentric, being identified with various groups and interacting with different roles in those groups, roles different than its own, as it now realizes for the first time in its life.

This "taking the role of other" is typical of the incredibly important *emergent* characteristics (the "transcend" part of the "transcend and include") that mark each and every stage of evolution and development, as that relentless "creative advance into novelty" continues. Historically, this allowed various groups to be brought together for the first time in any large and substantial way, and the first truly great civilizations and the first great feudal empires arose and spread across the face of most of the known world. The "Mythic-literal" View of this stage, wherever it showed up across the globe, created the core tenets of what still exist today as the world's great religions (Judaism,

Christianity, Hinduism, Shintoism, Islam, alchemical Taoism—along with their inner, hidden, esoteric, and contemplative branches).[11] What many of the exoteric Mythic schools had in common was an absolutistic, fundamentalist orientation, a Mythic-Literal approach that pictured its view of spirituality as being the "one true way" and not open to questioning or doubt; this fundamentalist strand is present to this day in many of the great religions and comes directly from the rule/role mind stuck in a 2nd-person ethnocentric perspective that is caught in strict conformist and absolutistic forms of thinking (and an amber altitude in the spiritual intelligence line).

In today's world, the child's "latency period" (around six to twelve years) is anything but "latent"; rather it is an incredibly active and alive stage where the young child is learning how to try on roles and make them mesh or fit with other roles, and gaining the social and emotional intelligence of being able to "fit in" with other people. Peer pressure becomes all important, since the incredibly strong drive to "be a part of" a larger group—to be liked, to be popular, to have friends, to fit in—is a crucial drive during this period of development (studies also consistently show that various peer groups have an influence equal to or greater than that of parents on personality development). This is also where "games people play" start to become important, as a variety of different games—and their payoffs—are tried out. "I'm always right," "I always screw things up," "Nobody ever likes me," "I can never finish anything I start," "Girls (or boys) always make fun of me," "My parents think I can never do anything right," "I'm king of the hill and things always go my way," "I'm not studying because I'll just flunk anyway," "I'd go out for sports, but I have no athletic talent at all, and I never had," "I asked my girlfriend to go steady, and I knew she'd say 'no.'" Dozens, even hundreds, of such "scripts" are played out by the rule/role mind, as the child moves through the dozens, even hundreds, of various new areas and roles that the child (and adult) will be asked to play in his or her life. Schools such as Cognitive Therapy, Rational Emotive Therapy, and Transactional Analysis have mapped out dozens and dozens of these types of scripts that lead to emotional, mental, and generally neurotic problems, and have demonstrated how almost all of them are based on false data and false conclusions, which generate an enormous number of painful symptoms and blistered feelings, and that the key to curing the symptoms is to dig up the scripts and expose them to the light of more reasonable and accurate information.

The basic theory here is that a typical emotional reaction is not just $S \rightarrow R$, where "S" is the triggering event, or stimulus, and "R" is the response, or feeling, it brings up, but rather is $S \rightarrow C \rightarrow R$, where "S" is the triggering event, or stimulus, "C" is the cognitive thought, or mental interpretation, or judgment, and "R" is the final response. In other words, between a triggering stimulus and the eventual feeling or response, there is how you interpret or judge the stimulus; and that interpretation or judgment has a huge hand in determining what you actually end up feeling ("R"). So if somebody offers you a job ("S"), and you think, "I never do anything right" ("C"), then you will respond with "No, I better not" ("R"). Instead, if you think, "Sometimes I do things wrong, but sometimes I do quite well" (which is almost certainly the more accurate view), then you might respond, "Sure, I'll give it a try, thank you very much."

Almost all of the "negative" games that I mentioned are based on what is called "catastrophic expectations," which assume that things will go horribly wrong in any event; and with that attitude, it's likely to become a self-fulfilling prophecy. So dig out all "Never" and "Always" statements (for example, "I never do well on tests or "I always make a fool out of myself on dates") and change them to "Sometimes" statements (for example, "I sometimes do poorly on tests, I'll do better this time" or "I have sometimes made a fool of myself on dates, but there's no reason I have to this time").

People who are depressed often have a habit of selectively remembering all the bad things that happened to them and forgetting the good things. So, as we mentioned with "flourishing" and "journaling," a simple exercise for such cases (try it yourself, it works!) is each night, for five or ten minutes, to write down "three things that went well today," or for which you can be grateful. They don't have to be earthshaking, just generally positive ("My friend called me out of the blue to wish me well," "My mate dropped by work just to give me a kiss," "My next-door neighbor found our dog, who has been missing almost a week"). And, if inclined, also write down why you think they went well (just whatever comes to mind; don't give yourself a hernia trying to figure it out). Do this every night for a week—three things that went well that day—and see if you don't start feeling noticeably happier. As I mentioned, research on this exercise shows that people feel much less depressed, and much happier, after doing this for only one week, and the results last at least six months (keep doing it, and the results continue as well).

All of these are examples of "script pathology" and "script treatment." Recognizing the ways in which we talk to ourselves makes a huge difference in how we actually experience our lives and our worlds. Many of these old scripts, if we look at them, go all the way back to childhood, often to this very stage where scripts were first learned, where we originally learned to take the role of other and interact with it. We picked up many silly, goofy, or just plain wrong things, and admittedly new to the game of role taking, we made some pretty silly mistakes. What's not so silly is that those scripts don't go away but are still there, in our subconscious, repeating those silly ideas and making us suffer for them. There's no need whatsoever for those "hidden maps" to continue torturing us—dig them up, make those subjects into objects of awareness, and replace them with much more accurate views.

One of the major problems with any views that are developed at the rule/role Mythic level is indeed their absolutistic, or intensely unyielding, nature. If this absolutism is hooked with a religious view, then the repercussions for not believing in the particular religious view are usually horrendous—in ancient times, such disbelief, if loudly and publicly announced, might be met with beheading, burning at the stake, being drawn-and-quartered, tortured in any number of barbaric ways, drowned, or imprisoned for life (if lucky). But even in today's world, the general motive that lay behind that type of treatment is still present in this stage itself—namely, that if you stop believing the major beliefs of your membership group, or your peer group, or, yes, your religious fundamentalist group, or any fundamentalist group (fundamentalist scientism, fundamentalist Marxism, fundamentalist feminism, fundamentalist men's movement), then you should be, in one way or another, excommunicated, that is, kicked out. And for somebody at the level of belongingness needs, which is another term for this stage, that is a traumatic experience, one to be avoided at all costs. In "mythic-membership," believing the myths is fundamental to membership.

This is one of the reasons that growth and development beyond this stage can be so difficult—the repercussions of giving it up, of surrendering its View, can be so difficult, so traumatic, so painful, especially if you are a member of a fundamentalist religious group. As the orange Rational modern stage begins to emerge, the sheer horror of being judged as less than "a true-blue believer" often leads the Mythic mind (if not properly dis-identified with) to repress that orange emergence with a fury, or at least try to. The Mythic-Literal religious View is ethnocentric, believing that there is one and only one True Way, and therefore it also believes in a "chosen people" who alone have this Truth—and thus the orange worldcentric (or what Graves called "multiplistic") View of the Reason-mind is utterly taboo. If I let go of this absolutistic Mythic View, it's not just an idea I am giving up, it's my immortal soul, and in surrendering that absolute Truth, I am headed for everlasting damnation, eternal hellfire, the loss of my very soul itself, everlastingly. This makes self-reflection and self-criticism almost impossible for this Mythic stage, and even if rationality manages to emerge, often my self-sense will remain basically at Mythic-Literal, and then I will simply use rationality to support and prop up the Mythic View with various sorts of spurious rationalizations (a stance called Mythic-Rational; see the discussion of the "expert" stage, in the next section). Many Intelligent Design arguments, for example, fall into this category. In some ways, these arguments correctly identify several of the inadequacies of the standard, modern Neo-Darwinian view. (I don't want to be obnoxious, but it's not like that's hard to do.)[12] However, it's one thing to elucidate inadequacies of Darwinism, it's quite another to conclude that those inadequacies *prove* the existence of my version of God, his Bible, and his one and only Son. How on earth do the acknowledged inadequacies of Darwinism prove that Jesus is the one and only Son of God? They prove only that a creative drive, Eros, or a self-organizing dynamic is inherent in the universe starting from the Big Bang.

This ethnocentric Mythic religious View is one of the greatest impediments to world peace and harmony now in existence. When people are stuck in a 2nd-person, ethnocentric, "us versus them," mythic-membership conformist View, it effectively prevents any understanding of anything worldcentric and universal, including universal tolerance, fairness, justice, and peace. In their place, by whatever name, is "jihad"—"holy war"—the idea, across a span of intensity, that the only correct approach to infidels or unbelievers is something along the spectrum that runs from voluntary conversion to forced conversion to death. And worse, today (in 2015) some 60 to 70 percent of the world's population is at the ethnocentric Mythic stage or lower, which bodes very poorly for a harmonious world anytime in the near future.

To combat this intolerance, the world religions need to become "conveyor belts" of transformation, by including a full spectrum of spiritual-intelligence Views of their own teaching, reaching from egocentric to ethnocentric to worldcentric to Kosmocentric (that is, by covering the entire spectrum of basic structures and each of their Views' version of their particular religious beliefs). Until then, stuck at a spiritual intelligence of Mythic ethnocentric, most of the world's religions preach love and compassion, while practicing intolerance and jihad. A fixation to this stage produces a Mythic addiction in individuals (Upper Left quadrant) that is nearly impossible to surrender, all the more so because it is usually intensely supported by a cultural surrounding (Lower Left quadrant) that fully encourages, embraces, and rewards a continuing belief in the particular Mythic View being promulgated.

To say it again, in the Left-hand quadrants, the ethnocentric Mythic religious View is perhaps the most dangerous and pernicious impediment to world harmony that now exists. Most of the world's present conflicts, wars, and terrorist acts have at least one foot in this ethnocentric level. But if the world's religions developed a conveyor belt of spiritual teachings, then individuals would realize that they can let go of their Mythic absolutism, intolerance, injustice, and jihad, and embrace a fully worldcentric spirituality that treats all God's children with equal fairness, regardless of their actual faith (or color, creed, or sex). The Mythic View should be properly acknowledged and even taught during a particular developmental period of the individual's life (at the Mythic level of the mind, myths are all it understands anyway, so of course the Mythic version of the spiritual teaching is presented at this stage). But it should also be set in a full spectrum of *levels and stages of belief*. If the religious beliefs and practices are taught in their Magic to Magic-Mythic to Mythic to Rational to Pluralistic to Integral *versions*—that is, the central tenets of that religion are interpreted through each of those major Views, with the appropriate version taught depending on the person's actual stage in life and development, then, with the particular religion's full blessings and encouragement, when the Rational mind begins to emerge in an individual, an appropriately worldcentric and reasonable (scientifically compatible) version of the religion is taught (replete with universal fairness and tolerance, and compatible with science—not scientism or scientific materialism, neither of which is scientific). Teaching religious beliefs in this developmentally graded fashion will directly help dismantle the ethnocentric belief in a "chosen people" and the beliefs that drive people toward jihad, and thus will mark the end of killing others in the name of God. Precisely because they have been taught that there are higher levels of the religion (and spiritual intelligence) that do not depend upon or fully endorse the Mythic-Literal version of its teachings, individuals of that faith realize that they can let go of their Mythic absolutism and yet still be fully in accord with the overall doctrine, dharma, dogma, or gospel of the particular faith, one that is fully backed by the particular church's highest authorities. Individuals would have the church's permission to let go of the absolutistic Myth (amber) and embrace a more reasonable and authentic version (orange and higher). In one stroke, this would, among so many other things, dismantle the vast majority of terrorists' primary motivation and justification for violence—that is, "The modern rational-secular world makes no room for my God, and therefore I have the right and the duty to blow it up," because now there *is* a modern reason-compatible (though not necessarily reason-driven; it might engage stages of Waking Up, for example) version of their faith, and it makes room, in 1st-, 2nd-, and 3rd-person perspectives, for all the God they could want (especially when state-stage development, or Waking Up, is added, something that any truly comprehensive or Integral Spirituality would include, it goes without saying).

At the same time, when developing through this Mythic stage, we don't want to dissociate or dis-own it, since that tends to cripple the self's capacity to form strong love and belongingness bonds, which begin flowering at this stage. For example, in Carol Gilligan's stages of moral development in women, she calls the first stage *selfish*, where the woman cares only for herself; this corresponds to our early *egocentric* stages. The amber Mythic corresponds to Gilligan's second stage, which she calls *care*, since the capacity for care and loving-kindness emerges here and extends beyond the egocentric self, but only for a particular group or groups—hence, our *ethnocentric* stages. She calls the third stage *universal care*, which corresponds to the emergence of orange rational care and widespread loving-kindness, which extends to *all* groups, or all humans, regardless of race, color, sex, or creed—our *worldcentric* stages. Why shouldn't religion likewise develop and Grow Up through those levels as well? Since the individuals believing in those religions definitely grow through those stages, how possibly could the religion not also? And likewise, she calls the fourth and last stage *integrated*, where each sex integrates the contrasexual attitude, which corresponds to our *integral* and beginning *Kosmocentric*, which includes an identity not only with all humans but all sentient beings, hence the entire manifest world. In dissociating from the emerging capacity at this Mythic stage to engage belongingness, love, and care, the self brutally hobbles its capacity to enter into caring and loving relationships in general, something that will likely cripple it for the rest of its life (and in its higher, wider forms, too). When this happens, the "communion" or "relational" component of the self-sense is thrown over for a dry, alienated, hyperagentic component, and a rather miserable loneliness, angst, and exaggerated sense of separateness descends on the individual's self-sense, or the sense of communion extends, at most, to the "chosen group" or "chosen people," although in a broken, distorted form. This antisocial personality, often driven also by a previous level's power addiction, is often behind the mass murders (usually machine-gun inflicted) that the Unites States (especially in its high schools, where adolescents, who are typically at this stage, are gathered in large numbers) has seen too much of lately.

These major stages of development, up to today's highest level that is generally available (that is, 2nd-tier Integral), have emerged during the previous stages of human evolution itself. Once a stage was laid down, its fundamental rung remained in existence (as it was transcended and included by each higher stage), and it emerges and unfolds in each human being in the same sequence in which it was created in the first place by evolution. And as it emerges, it generates the associated View from that rung, also in the same order. The great periods, or eras, of collective human development are very clearly marked by these major stages. We see the Archaic era emerge as humans began to evolve from the great apes (a million years ago). Then the great Magic tribal era begins as specifically human beings

(Homo sapiens) emerged, and began living collectively in tribal structures with an eco-carrying capacity (due to the necessity of hunting and gathering) of around forty or so people. With the emergence of farming in the Lower Right (creating a huge expansion in the amount of available food, which allowed a profound expansion in the size of human populations in a given culture), we see the emergence of the rule/role mind and its Mythic View in the Left-hand quadrants, and the first great towns, cities, and civilizations—including military empires—spreading across the globe (beginning in its earliest forms around 10,000 BCE, and flowering 2,000 BCE to 1,500 CE). This included the original Mythic forms of the world's Great Religions, which every civilization bar none produced. People born in one of this era's cultures began their life at Archaic, then developed to Magic, and then—if mature—to Mythic stages (and if an interior pioneer, then beyond the conventional stages and into early stages of Reason, as with some of the early Greek cultures, for example). The major conflicts in these cultures were between the Mythic conventional religious believers and "pagan" Magic believers (for example, in medieval Europe, Mythic religious organizations such as the Spanish Inquisition were responsible for the deaths of literally hundreds of thousands of Magic "pagan," or "witchcraft," believers). Then came the emergence of modernity and the "Age of Reason and Revolution" (around 1,500 CE), the beginning of the Rational stages of development, made utterly apparent by such historical periods as the Renaissance and the Enlightenment. With this development, the cultural conflicts now included not only the battle between Magic pagans and Mythic religious true-believers, but between modern Rational humanistic scientists and both those groups. In the West, this shifted into the "Culture Wars" when, during the 1960s, the pluralistic mind and the postmodern multicultural View emerged, and the three central value systems at war switched up a general stage to Mythic versus Rational versus Pluralistic—the "Culture Wars." And now (in 2015), with the leading edge of evolution moving into Integral stages, we face an evolutionary revolution greater than any previous emergence altogether, the emergence of the Integral Age. These specific stages of human evolution thus are fairly obvious in the great eras of human development.

The Amber/Orange Mythic-Rational

This is a stage that only some of the major models of human development include. It's present in Loevinger's, Cook-Greuter's, and Torbert's models but not present in Graves's, Spiral Dynamics', Wade's, or Kegan's. It's basically a transition between early reason and late mythic. I'll simply make a few comments in passing. Like Rational, it can perform early formal operational actions, but like Mythic, it remains narrowly focused and strongly identified with its area of interest. Torbert and Cook-Greuter refer to this stage as "Expert," since it takes its newly forming rational capacity and applies it diligently and narrowly to a specific field, becoming "expert" in that particular area. It's overall approach remains fairly rigid, unyielding, and specific. At one point, Torbert referred to this stage as "technician," again indicating its rational capacity, but narrowly and specifically applied. "Big Picture" thinking is still largely beyond it, and simply tends to confuse it, if not outright irritate it. It straddles "ethnocentric" and "worldcentric," with a beginning capacity for worldcentric rationality, but as applied almost ethnocentrically to its own chosen, narrow, specific field—and rarely any place else. Loevinger at one point referred to this stage as "conformist-conscientious" (hyphenating her name for the stage before it—"conformist"—with her name for the stage after it—"conscientious"), again indicating its transitional "straddling" of two major stages—for her, amber "mythic-conformist" was simply the "conformist" stage, and orange rational was the "conscientious" stage (with its strong awakening of rationality and its introspective and self-critical capacities), and hence this mythic-rational stage was "conformist-conscientious," a conscientious rationality used in almost mythic-conformist (even absolutistic) ways; or, again, "conformist-conscientious" is "ethnocentric-worldcentric," an almost ethnocentrically narrowed worldcentric rationality.

Likewise, for Kohlberg, who added this stage after his basic six major stages had been determined; he referred to it simply as "stage 4/5"—a transition (although real) between strong advanced amber "mythic-conformist" (in Kohlberg's scheme, stage 4, the "law and order" stage: "my country, right or wrong," "my religion, right or wrong," and so forth) and the orange worldcentric rational (for Kohlberg's moral line, stage 5, or the "prior rights, social contract" stage, marking the world's first great democracies, rising above ethnocentric "us versus them" and anchored instead in principled morals highlighting the individual's rights, no matter what race, color, sex, or creed—that is, clearly worldcentric). As is so often true with this stage, you can think of it as the highest of the preceding stage or the lowest of the succeeding stage. For Piaget as well, there is a "transition" stage listed at this point of development, which is the transition between the highest of (amber) concrete operational and the lowest of (orange) formal operational. He sometimes referred to this as "substage 1 of formal operational," where some of its basic principles are being laid down (versus substages 2 and 3, which constitute the core of formal operational cognition, or pure orange). Many people don't realize that after orange formal operational, Piaget had a final, higher stage—"polyvalent logic, systems of systems," or pure 2ⁿᵈ-tier vision-logic.

When a particular model includes "expert" as a separate stage, it often counts as members of this stage individuals previously seen as belonging at either the "mythic" stage or the purely "rational" stage. This stage is sometimes called "self-aware," since introspective awareness—generally so lacking in pure concrete-conformist modes—is starting to emerge. These are genuine novel emergents, and are the ones most responsible for researchers like Loevinger and Kohlberg introducing them as a separate, albeit transitional, stages.

Be that as it may, what is undeniable is that, in the general spectrum of altitude development, these various level/stages exist in an *ongoing continuum* of more and more complexity, more and more consciousness, more and more depth. Exactly *how* one slices up that stream is open to various interpretations, but none of them deny or question the direction of the overall stream and the increase in such fundamental characteristics as perspective taking, degree of differentiation/integration, amount of complexity and consciousness, breadth of identity, the capacity for love and care, and degrees of freedom.

But bring a group of dedicated "experts" together, and you're only barely higher than a group of mythic fundamentalists. They each have their own particular specialty or focused field, and they tend to understand (and accept) no other approaches. Their individual presentations will focus on their specific approach to a problem and make no attempt to include other approaches or other methods in their overall view. When they mention other approaches, they usually describe why they are not as accurate, effective, or efficient as their particular approach. When they do that, those are characteristics representing the "mythic ethnocentric" or "in group" side of their street. Within their particular approach, they are often very well informed, versed in its applications and areas of expertise, and full of very specific, non-context-dependent solutions for a particular problem. However, if their solutions run into difficulties when applied, this leaves them puzzled as to what to do next (except try the approach again).

When I don't specifically count this level as a separate level on its own, it is most often treated as "advanced Mythic," or the upper reaches of the Mythic stage as it is already beginning to be invaded by early rational, introspective, and multiple-perspective capacities. (In table 1, which summarizes basic structures and their views, this stage is referred to as "Fulcrum 4/5," and its basic structure is listed as "abstract rule/role," since "concrete rule/role" is the previous structure; the word "abstract" here indicates the beginning of formal operational cognition—again, a "concrete/abstract" transitional stage.) Those individuals who are beginning to rationalize the absolutistic myths are exactly the experts in that population; they are the first "scholastic experts," who spend an inordinate amount of time dragging out a massive body of detailed evidence that supports their explanations as to why all those myths are still literally and absolutely true. They often draw, as a last resort, on something like Tertullian's "I believe *because* it is absurd" (which, in its capacity for rationalization, is something like a Guinness World Record; with that attitude, you can rationalize any idiocy ever imagined, and the sillier it is, the more reason you have to believe it). It is the "experts" who make leaving the general amber, mythic-membership, ethnocentric strata so incredibly difficult to manage. The "experts" know it all, technically protect it all, expertly support it all, and altogether swallow it all. It is the religious experts in particular religions who engage most vocally and most fully in the Culture Wars, sometimes brilliantly and worldcentrically, rationally, poking holes in the accepted scientific materialist explanations—only to replace them with an ethnocentric, primitive, mythic Jehovah.

There are many dysfunctions that can beset the Mythic-Rational expert level, including various addictions and allergies to the emergent components first found at this level of development. But I'm going to focus on one, since it is so central and widespread here, and that is what might be called "loss of faith." The deeply ethnocentric, absolutistic nature of the previous Mythic-Literal stage of development makes it a stage that is just inordinately, incredibly difficult to surrender. This is especially true if it is hooked (as it often is) to a fundamentalist belief system (fundamentalist religion, fundamentalist scientism, fundamentalist feminism, fundamentalist Marxism, and so forth). Because in each case, the surrendering of the mythic belief means the total annihilation of the self's identity—it is excommunicated from, cut off from, forced out of, the community of the only ones who are truly saved, and nothing but various forms of withering damnation await it. Because of the importance of propping up the "truth" of the mythic belief, when rationality first emerges, it is immediately hijacked in service of providing new logic and extensive arguments to support the mythic belief. "Talmudic" is often used to mean an insanely extensive logical analysis and argument to support even a completely minor and trivial claim—mythical-rational at full speed.

And yet, if growth and development continues at all, sooner or later the simple inadequacy of a mythic-literal approach to God, life, and the universe becomes more and more undeniable. And this is the crisis point—this loss of faith—that can throw the self-system into a massive dysfunctional crash. Typically, the self heightens its strict adherence to the belief system—an addiction—or it totally tosses it overboard, disowning important partial truths and capacities in the process—an allergy. This "loss of faith" was, during the Middle Ages and up through the Renaissance and Enlightenment, probably the single largest psychological disturbance that humans faced. They believed they were being forced to surrender their very souls, and they did not go quietly into that dark night (just as "loss of self-esteem" became very widespread in the modern orange achievement era, and "loss of value" in the green postmodern).

The essential dynamic of this "loss of faith" dysfunction is simple and fundamental: any absolutistic belief inherently maintains that it is a restricted truth; that only a select "chosen" have access to it; that most others are cut off from it and therefore lack the knowledge that is unto salvation (religious salvation, scientific salvation, political salvation). What cannot be known, on this side of the transformation, is that the next higher, emerging level is actually an expansion of the reach of truth, an enlargement of those who have access to it, and thus an even freer and more liberated and more "saved" or "salvaged" awareness. The move from "us" to "*all* of us"—from absolutistic ethnocentric to multiplistic worldcentric—which represents an enormous leap in freedom, consciousness, morality, and care, looks to be, at the start, a simple oblivion, a death, an annihilation, because I have to give up this limited attachment to "us" (without realizing that "us" is *included* in "all of us," via transcend and include). With a truly severe loss-of-faith crisis (in any belief system), one's entire life can seem devastated, destroyed, annihilated, extinguished. There is no future left, only a past that is now thought to have been utterly and totally wasted and deceived (instead of being yet another higher step in the right direction), and a darkness beyond dark can settle on the soul for days, weeks, months, even years. But should the jump be taken (for example, if Christian, from "only those who believe in Christ as their personal savior can be saved" to "there are many paths to the Great Liberation, and the Christian works the best for me"; or if a scientician, from "only exacting science can give us anything resembling actual truth" to "there are numerous methodologies with their own distinctive and genuine truths, science being but one"), then there is a rebirth on the worldcentric, multiplistic, many-truths orange level, a genuine rebirth following the death of the previous, narrow, limited stance.

In today's world, this crisis is faced by any individual coming from a major, literal, absolutistic attachment to virtually any belief (religion, science, racism, sexism, politics) and discovering that "there are more things in heaven and earth than are dreamt of in your philosophy." More inclusive, more comprehensive, more conscious levels of reality await, and surrendering one's narrower, smaller, more limited and partial beliefs is a mandatory step in that Erotic direction.

Orange Rational

At the next uncontested basic structure beyond Mythic—namely, the throat chakra (Fulcrum-5, orange, formal operational, the hypothetico-deductive level), with its View (Rational,[13] self-esteem, achievement, conscientiousness, and excellence)—dysfunctions include problems with self-esteem, achievement, and accomplishment (either addictions or allergies to any of those characteristics). An overblown fixation to self-esteem needs leads to an almost constant checking that every decision is "true" to the self, that the self's needs and aims are the items most primarily being addressed, and that everybody around the person defers to his or her self's needs and requirements. People with such a fixation can't see a significantly important person anywhere in the world beyond themselves, except those responsible for getting them their entitlements. Most people find such types insufferable to be around—"Why are these people always thinking about themselves?"—and yet their dysfunction is, to a large degree, supported and encouraged by today's postmodern culture, where "my truth" is my truth and "your truth" is your truth and neither can be challenged. The educational system itself has been hijacked by the "self-esteem movement," which, with the best of intentions, attempted to get rid of any orange "merit" elements from the educational system that "ranked" people, so that nobody's self-esteem was harmed. Thus, "grading" or "judging" was removed wherever possible; everybody gets a gold star; everybody is taught to call themselves "special"; there is no valedictorian or "highest" ranked students, but instead, at graduation, every single student gives a speech (I have sat through more four-hour graduation ceremonies than I can tell you). Kids in the earliest grades are taught to sing songs—to the tune of "Frère Jacques"—such as, "I am special, I am special, look at me, look at me." The net result of this self-esteem addiction is that the graduating class of 2014 had the highest rates of narcissism ever recorded, since testing itself was begun!—*some two to three times higher* than their parents, the Boomers, who were already themselves known as the "Me Generation" (so that this newer generation is thus being called the "Me Me Me Generation"—despite some of its very admirable elements). As Joel Stein in a *Time* magazine cover story on this topic put it, "We found that teaching self-esteem actually teaches narcissism."

But the sad thing about narcissism is that it's actually broken self-esteem; narcissistic individuals have very low rates of successful relationships, very high job turnover rates, higher rates of depression and anxiety, and otherwise score poorly on general psychological health assessments. Nevertheless, polls show, they still expect to get promoted every two years, *regardless of actual job performance*. Truly a sad development, and largely the result not just of an orange "self-esteem" fixation but often a green dominance as well (which I'll cover next).

On the other hand, rejecting, dis-owning, or poorly navigating the self-esteem needs are the cause of many of the problems correctly claimed by the self-esteem movement; they just aren't as widespread as supposed, they are not the sole cause of all personal problems; and most importantly, real self-esteem results from actual accomplishments not self-told stories of specialness. But the lack of self-esteem indeed can lead to poor judgments in behavior (in the worst instances, leading to drug addictions, criminal activity, major underachievement in jobs, relationships, and life itself). Also common at orange Fulcrum-5 is the dissociation of the orange worldcentric form of any emotion or feeling (including worldcentric love, compassion, hatred, envy, joy). The emotions that arise on the orange level are indeed orange—that is, worldcentric emotions, focused on humans in general (which is why the "me-me-me" component of excessive self-esteem addiction, occurring on an orange *worldcentric* level, often includes, or reactivates, a red/*egocentric* regressive underbelly); but if any emotions are actually repressed *here*, they are worldcentric emotions and worldcentric repressions, truly problematic and often severe.

This simply illustrates that significant elements of almost any level, starting as soon as the self–other boundary is in place, certainly by red, can be split off, dis-owned, and banished to the submergent unconscious, and these split-off elements can sometimes take the form of a subpersonality. This subpersonality, this *sub-subject*, is a subject that refuses to become an object of awareness, but remains as a subject, an *unconscious* subject, that is, one not capable of being an object, and thus one that is unconscious; hence open to projection. This sub-agency, this sub-self, retains all the general characteristics of the level at which it was created—the same age, the same needs and desires, the same general qualities, and so on. Thus, a red subpersonality—where the red stage generally predominates around ages four to seven—will retain the psychological qualities of that age, with its similar needs and desires, its egocentrism, its power drives, and so on, even if the central self, or proximate self, is orange or green or higher, age twenty or thirty, and so forth. Contrary to Freud, who felt major repression ends with the red stage (since he was primarily tracking the early formative stages of libido, prana, or bioenergy, from its oral to anal to phallic to genital stages, ending with red at the "latency" period), it is definitely possible for subpersonalities (or simply shadow elements) to be formed all the way up to Supermind, simply because evolution—with its differentiation and integration (transcend and include)—continues all the way up, and something can go wrong with either of those aspects (differentiation or integration) at any point, producing addictions or allergies, and corresponding shadow and subpersonality factors.

A very common problem with the modern Rational orange stage is the allergy to all things green/postmodern, when green itself begins to emerge and descend on an orange Rational mind that is not yet ready for pluralism of that variety in any form. People at this stage sometimes even aggressively dis-own their own green Pluralistic perspectives, thoughts, and feelings (creating what I call "a repressed *emergent* unconscious," since what is being repressed is higher psychological material trying to come down, not lower material trying to come up—which would be the repressed *submergent* unconscious). As these green Pluralistic Views are dis-owned and projected, the orange individual sees, for example, the whole stance of postmodernism—its multiculturalism; its emphasis on "feelings" and "coming from the heart," not intellect and "coming from the head"; its emphasis on individuality and its unchallengeable truths ("What's true for you is true for you, and what's true for me is true for me, and neither can be challenged"); the antiranking, antihierarchical, antimeritocracy, and antiexcellence stance (for green postmodern pluralism, "merit" and "excellence" are actually bad; they involve judging somebody to be better than somebody else, and that kind of judgment is felt to be the basis of all oppression and social ills)—as an attack on civilization itself. Postmodernism's attempts to get rid of "hate talk" and "judgmental attacks" leads orange to scream that "the First Amendment's right to free speech has now been replaced by the right to not have your feelings hurt!" (As one orange comic put it, "What these people recommend doing is 'coming straight from the heart,' thus bypassing the obstruction known as their brain.") But this green, this extremely exaggerated anti-any-sort-of-judging, this extreme political correctness, has become so much the standard attitude of American universities that many comics, including

Chris Rock and Jerry Seinfeld, now say that they just won't play college campuses anymore, because humor there is dead.

In a similar vein, orange tends to see all green postmodern "sensitivity" trainings, "multicultural" classes, and "gentle male" workshops and seminars as being woo-woo, childish, and silly, and thus orange will never miss an opportunity to belittle them to anyone who will listen. It's not that some of orange's criticisms of green aren't true or shouldn't be made (many are very accurate and right on the money); it's when orange projects its *own* emerging green tendencies and impulses (as shadow elements) and then attacks green, for that reason primarily, that problems begin. When orange projects its own green, it then sees "double the amount" of green running around out there, and that would be enough to drive anyone crazy. (We'll return to this repressing of an *emergent* green Pluralism, and the fairly serious developmental problems that can result.)

Another very common projection of the orange level is of its own spiritual intelligence and spiritual qualities in general. Having just thrown off what now seems to orange to be the outrageously silly (and certainly irrational) nature of Mythic-literal beliefs—and yet still having an active spiritual intelligence, now capable of operating from the orange Rational level—orange individuals (still tending to see *all* spirituality as being Mythic-literal in nature, and having already judged all of that as pure twaddle) understandably but catastrophically judge *all* spiritual beliefs (including any of their own Rational spiritual beliefs) to be just as silly and irrational, and thus aggressively project any of their own spiritual impulses that might emerge onto others, particularly those who still believe in Mythic-literal fundamentalist forms of religion. Their resultant attack on all spirituality is thus vocal, vicious, and vehement. Often known as the "new atheists" (such as Richard Dawkins, Stephen Hawking, and Christopher Hitchens), they aggressively attack all spirituality as being the most dangerous and demented force on the planet. It's not that some of their points aren't true or don't need to be made; it's that the sheer vehemence with which they hold their views (not to mention the cherry-picking of spiritual items chosen to attack—how hard is it, really, to belittle myths like Noah's Ark or Moses's flight from Egypt?) are a tip-off, as always, to projected material. These attacks are *rabidly* antispiritual (and notice that when they do attack spirituality, virtually none of them attack meditation or contemplative spirituality—a new atheist like Sam Harris actually says that he is *not* referring to meditative forms, and, as a matter of fact, he himself meditates), and the "frothing at the mouth" nature of their attacks is a dead giveaway to the projected shadow material driving it. These individuals have repressed, and then projected, their own higher forms of spiritual-intelligence qualities and hence viciously attack anything that looks like spirituality "out there"—precisely like the antihomosexual zealots who spend all their time trying to get rid of their shadows by getting rid of those onto whom they have projected them. (I'm referring to the research showing that antihomosexual zealots, who have devoted their lives to antigay activities and legislation, when shown gay sexual images and homosexual erotica, were actually much more sexually aroused than the average straight male. That is, these zealots had considerable gay impulses themselves but had repressed and projected this shadow material, and were thus trying to get rid of their shadows by getting rid of homosexuals.) The antispiritual zealots are likewise trying to get rid of any nasty spiritual impulses that keep whispering in their ears, and to do so by getting rid of any "true believers" out there. This projection is the only thing strong enough to provide all the emotional juice driving the unrelenting vehemence of their attacks. Zealot antihomosexual, zealot antispiritual—same shadowboxing.

These individuals who are projecting their spiritual shadows end up shadowboxing their way through life, vocally and vociferously denouncing anything spiritual. (They usually see all spirituality as Mythic-literal, which, again, is not exactly a hard argument to win. As noted, it's not difficult to attack two-millennia-old myths and stories in light of today's knowledge.) What is unfortunate here is that in projecting anything that even vaguely smells spiritual or religious, these individuals are cutting themselves off from the higher, rational, and transrational (NOT prerational) forms of their own spiritual intelligence, thus cutting themselves off from issues of ultimate concern for them—and for the world. We need them to focus on higher, mature forms of spirituality and the solutions they offer to the major problems that the world now faces, not to spend their time attacking the childish form of a spirituality long ago surpassed by Spirit itself in its own evolution. (To be fair, I have already noted that I consider the Mythic-literal fundamentalist religious beliefs to be today's single greatest cultural threat to humankind; and with some 60 percent of the world's population at amber ethnocentric or lower, we need serious critiques of this problem to be constantly front and center, but these critiques should not proceed by completely distorting, and then destroying, absolutely all forms of spirituality, including higher stages of spiritual intelligence and the entire path of Waking Up. This would be to throw out an inconceivably precious baby with a ton of dirty bathwater.)

When orange is involved in repressing any form of its own attempting-to-emerge green Pluralism (and thus attacking things like "A Nation of Feelings!"), it's not that the specific criticisms aren't valid, it's that they are attacking not only a particular topic but also (knowingly or not) a particular type of thinking (pluralistic), and thus attacking an actual stage of their own growth. Occasionally this can end up causing severe cases of arrested development (as can a similar repression of the newly emerging Rational stage by Mythic, or at any level, for that matter), because, in this case, once the orange Rational mind has dysfunctionally embedded a set of deeply antigreen ideas and beliefs, these will act as a strong repression barrier to any further emergence of green material from this person's own emergent unconscious, and henceforth development will thus likely come to a slow halt. How can any of my own higher stages (which start with green when I'm at orange) even emerge, when green itself is so thoroughly loathed anywhere it appears? Thus, the problem is, in part, not just a *psychological* repression (for personal emotional reasons) but a *philosophical* repression (for principled ideals, however mistaken), and thus not just psychological shadow work but studied philosophical work will often be required to loosen this particular repression barrier and allow healthy forms of the higher, green, Pluralistic mind and its View to emerge. And so too is Pluralism's own common repression of the newly emerging Integral mind largely a philosophical repression, also requiring philosophical work to undo. As for green repression, many businesses and organizations attempted to address this repression with various forms of "sensitivity" and "multicultural" training, attempting to get Mythic and Rational individuals to expand their perspectives and horizons—or even develop—to the Pluralistic stage, with mixed results. Many individuals simply adopted the required pluralistic *behavior* (Upper Right) without changing their actual *attitudes*

(Upper Left), with the trainers never quite realizing just how difficult it can be to change levels of consciousness altogether. Not to mention the fact that Robert Kegan estimates it takes approximately five years to change genuine stages—certainly not something that a few sensitivity trainings can be expected to accomplish in a few weekends.

Right now, the orange formal mind, which has, for several hundred years now, been collapsed to its largely reductionistic, dysfunctional, and frankly pathological versions (from flatland scientific materialism to a greed-infested version of capitalism), faces perhaps its largest and most serious challenge to date: the global warming issue. This problem, in many ways, a result of orange artifactual and technological know-how commandeered by either lower levels of cultural moral development or by a pathological version of orange itself, is perhaps the most serious overall threat to life on this planet, in its many forms, that has yet been faced in all of humanity's history. In terms of what is amounting to a horse race concerning humanity's future, we have in the positive pan a Right-hand coming technological singularity and a Left-hand possible 2nd-tier global transformation; and, in the negative pan, a Right-hand global warming and drastic ecological despoliation and a Left-hand stationing of the center of gravity for 60 to 70 percent of the population at ethnocentric amber (that is, the center of gravity of most Nazis) or lower. This race, with the future of humanity at stake—either a glorious one headed toward humanity's highest potentials in general or a hellish nightmare of the torturous collapse of humankind's very means of survival—is, unfortunately, at this time too close to call.

Green Pluralistic

If consciousness does manage to continue its growth and development and move into the next major structure (green, chakra 5, Fulcrum-6 [sharing throat chakra 5 with orange Fulcrum-5, since both are self-expressive], pluralistic mind), and its View (postmodern, early self-actualization, "sensitive self," relativistic, individualistic), shadow issues often involve pluralistic impulses themselves (that is, multiple emotional feelings toward the same phenomenon, causing confusion, disorientation, and often, the repression or dissociation of several of the conflicting emotions). Difficulties with beginning self-actualization can also occur, either by hyperzealously jumping into it with an addictive zeal (for example, attending a growth seminar virtually every weekend while taking several online self-potential courses) or by phobically and allergically avoiding it (for example, belittling higher self-potentials and mocking any individuals involved in such, and likely also short-circuiting one's own higher potential growth and development).

A very, *very* common problem with green is the dissociation, disowning, and projection of its own remaining orange tendencies (including any qualities or characteristics associated with orange: the intellect, capitalism, business, rationality, profit, money, excellence, ranking, achievement, and merit)—creating, for this green, an intense orange allergy. The orange Rational stage is often known as the "achiever" or "meritocracy" or "excellence" stage, since orange seeks the very best and brightest in all things (part of the energy of its bursting out of amber conformity and monotony). The green Pluralistic stage, on the other hand, is known as "egalitarian," since it sees all people as being born—and remaining—essentially equal, and they are to be treated as such in all areas. Thus, for green, anything that is an "accomplishment" or "achievement," anything that is considered "best" or "excellent," is actually a bad thing, because it singles out certain people to be noticed and rewarded, while others are ignored; thus, any excellence is inherently oppressive. In effect, they make an intense judgment that all judgments are bad (another version of the standard performative contradiction rampant at green). This judgment is intense enough on its own; when some amount of orange remains unconsciously identified with but is then dissociated and projected, an extremely intense orange allergy results, with green's rampant egalitarianism running smack into its own projected drives for antiegalitarian achievement and excellence, and then recoiling from them in exaggerated and intense disgust. This orange allergy is absolutely rampant in green populations. Particularly orange items having to do with business, capitalism, profit, and progress are looked upon with near horror, and when somebody or something that actually has a normal amount of orange has a particular green's *projected orange* added on to them, then this "double dose" of orange sends green into paroxysms of rage, fury, and condemnation. Orange becomes the source of all the world's problems, from environmental devastation to nuclear war to oppression to tooth decay.

The individual caught in this pathology projects all of his or her own remaining orange qualities onto the world at large, and thus loathes those specific orange qualities and activities with a special passion, often joining sensitivity-oriented groups that are aimed particularly at reducing the influence of a specific orange quality in themselves and in the world. It's not that some of these orange phenomena are not worth reducing or removing entirely; it's that when one's own repressed and dis-owned versions of them are projected onto the real exterior versions, those exterior versions take on, as noted, a "double badness"—whatever badness they might themselves possess plus the now-added badness of the projected quality—overall, an evilness that is quite overblown and beyond anything that's actually happening, which leaves one with a distorted view of the "evil orange" world around it, and thus often less capable of approaching the problem in a reasonable and civil fashion. Any form of capitalism, profit motives, excellence and achievement, meritocracies, business in general—all are aggressively and relentlessly attacked, condemned, and judged as viciously heartless and mean-spirited. The morning after 9/11, green critics were online saying things like, "The copilot of those jets was capitalism; we got what we deserved!" Re-owning one's own orange impulses, and then transcending and healthily integrating them, is the only therapeutic remedy. (This is a particularly difficult therapeutic move, especially since the media, alerted to the small but significant number of genuinely corrupt businesses, reports these almost nightly, and they don't even have an idea of what a "conscious" or "decent" or "good" business would look like, thus making "corrupt business" a hugely alluring hook for one's orange projections. Who still doesn't know how rotten the "Enron" affair was—and how many years ago was that?)

As for green, in addition to the possibility of there being something that was once in consciousness but that has now been pushed into the repressed *submergent* unconscious (such as orange), there is the almost as common repression of something not yet in consciousness but that is trying to emerge—namely, the next-higher stage—in this case, the 2nd-tier Integral thoughts and feelings that are attempting to emerge at this green Pluralistic level, but whose dis-owning this time creates a "repressed *emergent* unconscious," composed of teal or turquoise qualities and attributes. The repression of these qualities and attributes results in a widespread and vehement "Integral allergy." This usually happens because both teal, the first emergent Holistic View, and turquoise, the first fully Integral View, include actualization holarchies (that is, nested growth hierarchies), and green has an inherent allergy to rankings of any variety (and that includes holarchies). So green generally loathes Integral 2nd tier altogether, repressing and dissociating it in itself wherever possible (as long as green is its structure center of gravity).[14] Since green does not, as yet, have an actual understanding of 2nd tier, it often (mis)interprets any individual teal or turquoise person or phenomenon as actually being a red, power-driven, egocentric entity, and responds in the same way it would to red, with loathing, judgmentalism, and negativism (even though it is not supposed to possess any of those qualities). Green Pluralism likes to think of itself as "integral," and even calls itself "The Integral Culture" because of its admitted dislike of, and attack on, marginalization, oppression, segregation, and judgment or rankings of any variety. But green absolutely loathes 2nd-tier teal and turquoise and condemns them at every turn, it cannot abide orange in almost any form and attacks it whenever it can, it utterly despises amber and speaks out about its dangers at every opportunity, and on and on. Like any 1st-tier stage, it thinks its View is the one and only true and valuable View there is, and all others are childish, inaccurate, silly, or just plain wrong.

Green has the cognitive capacity to see all the many differences between various cultural claims to truth (hence, "multiculturalism") but not enough capacity to see the many ways in which the various cultures also share certain similarities, or the many "patterns that connect" them all in a truly universal Integral fashion—a capacity that, as the name implies, first emerges at the next major stage, the Integral 2nd tier.

Green also takes a specifically "multicultural" view by maintaining that there are no Big Pictures, that there are no universal "metanarratives" (such as I am giving here about development and its universal stages, which Pluralism would consider pure oppression). And it believes that there are no Big Pictures or universal truths because it maintains (in densely worded, intentionally obscure arguments) that all truth is culturally constructed; all knowledge is context bound, and contexts are boundless; and all knowledge is likewise dependent upon interpretation, and interpretation is local, context determined, and hence relative. But Pluralism believes that every one of those claims is true for all people, in all cultures, in all places, at all times. In other words, it believes that all of them are most definitely universal truths—they are not culturally constructed, not a mere interpretation, not a local knowledge, but a pure universal truth, a real Big Picture, an authentic metanarrative. In short, it believes that it is universally true that there are no universal truths; it believes that its view is superior, but it also believes that there are no superior views anywhere.

This is called a "performative contradiction," because you yourself are doing what you claim you cannot or should not do. This view ranks ranking as being bad; judges judging as being oppressive; gives a very Big Picture about why Big Pictures are not possible; claims it is universally true that there are no universal truths; places hierarchies on the lowest level of its particular hierarchy; and claims its view is superior in a world where nothing is supposed to be superior.

The application of those claims—no universals, cultural construction of all knowledge, the nonmarginalizing, interpretation-bound nature of knowing—is behind one of the most widely adopted postmodern philosophies that ever came into existence, that of "deconstruction" (introduced by Jacques Derrida, who, in 1979, was the most widely quoted academic in the United States). Deconstruction, in effect, "deconstructed" (or disassembled, more or less destroyed) virtually all previous approaches to knowledge, by claiming that all of them missed their essentially constructed ("made up") and interpretive ("not universally true") nature, and only deconstruction got it right. But the net effect of deconstruction was to destroy the possibility of believing in any value at all. "Don't you know that value of yours has been thoroughly deconstructed? There's nothing believable left of it! Moreover, to enthusiastically believe in *this* value means that you don't believe in *that* value—and what's wrong with that one? Are you judging it as inferior? Are you being oppressive, marginalizing, repressive?" As this general attitude began to permeate culture, values and purpose and meaning-in-life likewise began to evaporate; all that was left was that tag team from postmodern hell: nihilism and narcissism (what else could you believe in?) Narcissism scores, we saw, skyrocketed; slackers saw no value in life at all, and didn't even pretend to look for it; millennials settled for some of the lowest values around—"money and fame"—hard to deconstruct those, and otherwise fobbed-off values (they didn't even go through a rebellious phase as adolescents, since there were no values worth fighting against—or for). Books like *The Da Vinci Code* and *The Purpose-Driven Life* each sold over 20 million copies, as people looked desperately for something to believe in. This whole stance—I call it "aperspectival madness" (the belief that no perspective has any value that is better than another one)—became perhaps the most common dysfunction of the entire postmodern age, as any believable value evaporated from the culture at large. (The only "believers" in any values who were still left were the amber religious-mythic fundamentalists, who still paraded their absolutistic values whenever possible—showing just how embarrassing values really were if you actually held them.)

This truly serious problem stops only when green consistently meets with failure in being able to translate the world coherently through its pluralistic structures, which, over time, become increasingly fragmented, partialized, broken, and fractured, tearing the self into partial, tormented fragments as well. Only as the inadequacy and failure of this View is consistently seen and directly felt—and nihilism and narcissism start to lose their flavor—does green let go of this limited Pluralistic View and take that "monumental leap of meaning" into Integral 2nd tier.

The very important, new partial truth that postmodern Pluralism was onto is that evolution actually touches everything. The postmodernists would say that there is "nothing but history." That is, there are no suprahistorical or foundational truths or "final words" about anything, but everything rather is the product of a ceaselessly ongoing historical unfolding and creating. From Nietzsche to Croce to Heidegger to Gadamer to Foucault to Derrida, the standard "given" or "discovered truths" (believed to have always been "true" and thus able to be discovered at some point) were all deconstructed into items that were not discovered but created, not given but invented, not perceived but interpreted, not facts but opinions. All we of today can do is understand that we are swamped and enslaved by ideas that are not true and eternal but that are essentially fictions that were created at some time in history and then taken to be genuinely true, whereas all they are is historically relative creations with no more validity than poetry or fiction (which are likewise merely created, and don't represent existing truths). The drive of most postmodernists was thus to find ways to escape these past fictions and instead act with a genuine autonomy or real freedom (but without postulating any suprahistorical truths that can do so, that can "save" them).

But even if "there is nothing but history (or evolution)," the postmodernists managed to come up with quite a list of things that they took to be very true (the constructed nature of all knowledge, the created/fictional nature of "truth," the interpretive/contextual reality of all knowledge, its having no reality beyond its relative-historical unfolding—and this is true for all peoples in all places at all times). If they tried to apply their own relativity to their own statements (which several tried), it simply contradicted everything they said. Thus: "There are no truths anywhere, and that applies to this statement as well, so it isn't true either, and so there's no reason whatsoever for you to believe anything I'm saying." That's not a very convincing philosophy, and it is here—after introducing some very important partial truths, that postmodernism fell apart, badly.

But there is an alternative to this sheer nihilism that still accepts many of the partial truths. Granted that there is nothing but history, nothing but evolution, starting with the Big Bang, nonetheless that history leaves traces, that evolution leaves tracks, they both leave habits. And these Kosmic habits create stable and enduring entities, regularities, "laws," and patterns. Those patterns can be discovered—and the postmodernists themselves discovered some of them (even if they often misinterpreted them). These patterns create the stable and enduring entities of the Kosmos (from atoms to molecules to cells to organisms), the stable laws of science, and the enduring stages and states of development that are nothing but the habits of past developments carried forward ceaselessly, as habits are. This view is similar to that of Charles Peirce, who saw "laws of nature" as "habits of nature," and it makes a great deal of sense. Further, seeing history as leaving enduring traces—seeing it as "genealogical" or "developmental"—gives us a way out of the chaotically incoherent and contradictory view of rampant nihilism that postmodernism left us with. Granted that there is nothing but history, but this history leaves habits, patterns of existing things, and these patterns grow and evolve and historically unfold—novel habit by novel habit by novel habit—leaving more and more habits as patterns that connect; and these patterns (including things like quadrants, levels, lines, states, and types) succeed in building up a manifest universe whose stable habits are the foundations of various genuine "truths"—which are discovered as these enduring pattern/habits are discovered. And this also means that new truths are continuing to be created, enacted, and laid down each and every moment. So where truth as habits are discovered, truth as emergents are newly created. We never have the "final word," because new historical entities and their habits are emerging all the time, and as long as they mesh with previous patterns, they will be carried forward, as new habits, in the ongoing growth and evolution of this Kosmos. And the human mind—another collection of evolutionary habits unfolded and interwoven historically—can itself start to understand this truth, especially when its own complexity reaches a level of existence that can comprehend these complex habitual relations. And that begins, most noticeably, at the level of development known as Integral 2nd tier and the monumental leap of consciousness to that level.

It's now time to examine that leap—and ones beyond even that—as well as what can go wrong with any of them. The shocking thing about shadow material is that it can be produced at virtually any level of being and awareness, and this can happen for the simple reason that evolution continues at all manifest levels, and something can go wrong in any of the evolutionary steps that are involved in each new emergent transformation (such as "transcend" or "differentiate," "include" or "integrate"), producing allergies and addictions to aspects of our very own selves, psychological and spiritual autoimmune disorders, from the very lowest to the very highest levels. Each new stage or transformative unfolding of evolution brings not only a new and higher consciousness but a new and more pernicious shadow possibility. And the brighter the light, the darker the shadow.

10

Dysfunctions of the
2nd-Tier Structure-Views

In the previous chapters, we looked especially at the earlier structure-stages of development, which are, in effect, humanity's past, humanity's yesterday. In this chapter, we look at humanity's future, humanity's tomorrow. The following stages have as yet been reached by less than 5 percent of the worldwide population. But the thing about established stages of development is that they are truly existing realities, actual Kosmic grooves, developments become ongoing habits, cut into the very being of the universe itself, and ready to unfold and flower as their time ripens. By looking at the psychospiritual models that have tentatively mapped the higher reaches of human becoming in real, existing individuals, then to the extent that these higher levels have actually been laid down to a substantial degree, however modest, we are in reality looking at the roads and paths to tomorrow that have already been cut, already been laid down, already been co-enacted and co-created and burned into the very contours of the Kosmos itself. "Nothing but history" has added new enduring habits.

At the same time, what is so exciting about this development is that, precisely because it is still being laid down in so many of its features and dimensions, it is still, in some significant ways, open to the co-enacting and co-creating that we—that you and I—actually bring to this process. Because these habits are not fully set in all their character-istics, they are still being formed. By our very thoughts, beliefs, endeavors, and actions, we are helping to lay down habitual Forms of the Kosmos that are stored in that Form-storage bin (and where the morphogenetic fields or developmental patterns of all manifest forms are contained, from the form of an atom to the form of the folding protein to the form of the amber level), wherever it might happen to be. And whether that is the Akashic record or the *Lankavatara Sutra*'s storehouse or some other outrageous dimension, one thing is for sure: it is a very real space in the very real world, constantly reaching down and hammering the sensorimotor world into its habitual patterns and forms and functions. And it is this very Form-storage bin that you and I are invited to help mold and create, slipping our own being and awareness into the developing stream of the Kosmos itself, having a hand in shaping and evoking the very structure of the universe as it will unfold tomorrow. The old saying from the traditions (reflecting the reality of involution/evolution) that "if you want to know what your thoughts were yesterday, look at your body today; if you want to know what your body will look like tomorrow, look at your thoughts today" is true for the shape of tomorrow's body in general—if you want to know what it looks like, simply look at your thoughts today.

Therefore, let us think wisely. Let us reach for the highest, widest, deepest, noblest notions we can possibly imagine; the highest, widest, deepest, wisest moral impulses we can possibly find; and the highest, widest, deepest, most courageous actions we can possibly take. Do you have any idea of how profound your responsibility is to this endeavor of humankind's future? If you knew, in your heart, the extraordinary impact that every thought, feeling, and action you take will have on the form of a tomorrow coming now into being, you would be radically electrified into your best and brightest at every single moment of every single day you live. You are in effect a God creating the world in six days—where a day is a hundred years—but think carefully here! It is truly up to you!—the deepest you, the highest I AMness, you can possibly find. That is the author of a tomorrow rising now—right over there!—just perceptibly on the horizon of the future's sunrise, its very rays starting slowly to warm your face.

In this endeavor, let us look closely at the maps of today that are following the leading footprints of the pioneers who have already gone down this small but widening road, leaving their footprints etched in the surface of the very face of the Kosmos. It is there that we can look for hints, there that we can find the early forms of a world being built with a greater care, higher consciousness, wider moral horizon, a deeper set of drives, a broader reach of identity, stretching from the skin-encapsulated ego to the radiant forms of a Supreme Identity calling out to us all. Step by step along that road we move— but we are on a speeding locomotive, and we are laying tracks at the same time that we run down them.

The following stages are hints, faint suggestions, distant calls of gossamer paths ever so lightly laid down in their early formative stages, and are quite open to being readjusted, redrawn, rerouted, or reconfigured by our very thoughts and actions themselves, today. The paths ahead are faint ghostly trails, awaiting our own footsteps down them to actually build them permanently, Kosmic habits not yet fully habit formed, but morphogenetic fields that will govern all that is created after them. At this leading edge of evolutionary unfolding, we are not so much being driven by the push of yesterday as by the pull of tomorrow, an Agape of the future's higher possibilities drawing us upward more than an Eros of the already pushing us up, our eyes riveted on a horizon of ever-increasing awareness, love, care, embrace, creativity, and enfolding. Start heading down that road consciously, and you are agreeing to take on the responsibility of the very contours of tomorrow's world in all of its dimensions, a nod to the God within who is in control of the genesis of the entire Kosmos arising out of the dim fog of a tomorrow yet to be laid down—*your* tomorrow.

Although many of the following stages have been laid down to a degree that is still quite tentative and diaphanous, they are still firm enough that major deviations from them are experienced as missteps, as dysfunctional dis-eases, as problematic misnavigations—as pathologies. The specific form and functions of these higher stages are yet to be fully formed, but the processes that are doing so—the general processes of evolution itself ("transcend and include")—are already fully operating in any event, or no unfolding at all would be occurring. Those processes can definitely be misnavigated, with quite standard problematic results (failure to transcend leads to fixation and addictions; failure to include leads to dissociation and allergies), and thus the major dysfunctions that can occur are already apparent even as the specific contents are as yet uncertain. This, of course, holds true as long as you hold the general features of Integral Theory itself to be true, in which case, the following might be quite useful; if you don't, you are most certainly invited to bring forth your own versions of how these stages and their dysfunctions will unfold and operate from there. But in either case, we are now walking down the faint, hazy path of an increasingly stark face of tomorrow coming directly at us.

Teal Holistic and Turquoise Integral

At these next major basic structures, that of low and high vision-logic (Fulcrum-7 and Fulcrum-8, teal and turquoise, 2nd-tier structures, both chakra 6—the "third eye" or synthesizing chakra), with their Holistic and Integral Views, dysfunctions include unhealthy relationships to systems and functional Wholes in general. Either the individual pathologically avoids them in many places that they occur (holistic/integral allergy), which at this stage is not just a *problem* (as it would be at lower levels) but a *pathology* because these levels themselves are now holistic in their very nature, and thus denying Wholes here amounts to a self-denial or an autoimmune disorder, or, on the other hand, the individual overzealously sees everything as holistically including everything else, leaving little or no room for individuality, self-expression, personal recognition, and holarchical asymmetry: holistic/integral allergy or holistic/integral addiction (and, of course, this can involve allergies/addictions to both the previous lower stage and the higher emergent stage—repressed submergent and repressed emergent).

A very common pathology at 2nd tier—perhaps even *the* most common—is a green allergy. With a green allergy, the 2nd-tier individual, sick and tired of the extreme green culture that he or she had to fight so hard in order to emerge into Integral, simply dissociates and disowns any and all of its remaining green impulses and qualities, and projects them onto the world at large, and then the "mean green meme" seems to be absolutely everywhere. As always, the projection of a shadow element makes the presence of that shadow element in the world seem enormously greater than it really is, and this certainly happens with the green allergy that 2nd tier often develops. The only cure, as always, is to re-own and integrate the green components of the self (via something like a 3-2-1 process), and then transcend and include them in a healthy 2nd-tier structure. Failure to do so can significantly slow, even stall, further development (into 3rd tier).

Green allergies have reached near epidemic proportions in Integral communities. Integral individuals with this dysfunction loathe and condemn green characteristics wherever they see them—in education, in business, in spirituality, in philosophy, in others, in themselves. They overlook the "many gifts of green" (including such things as the civil rights movement, the worldwide environmental movement, feminism, protect-the-handicapped legislation, hate laws, and so forth) and focus solely and merely on the "mean green meme" and its extreme versions with their undeniable maliciousness and nastiness. Such an individual often becomes hypersensitive to many typical green characteristics, including green's virtual incapacity to reach a conclusion about a course of action (for example, a meeting, with green, is considered a success not if a course of action is decided upon—since that would require denying other courses of action, a marginalizing and oppressive move—but if everybody gets a chance to stand up and share their feelings); green's superior attitude to virtually every topic it approaches (as if its way, and only its way, is the correct way to view things, even though every 1st-tier level thinks that way, and even though green professes to believe that there are no superior views anywhere); green's common tendency to confuse dominator hierarchies with growth hierarchies and then to charge a person possessing either of them with being an oppressive swine (in so many words); and so on, throughout a litany of green qualities, and explosively reacts to them all. A green-allergy individual uses "That person is being so green" (worded one way or another) as the ultimate put-down and reason to reject their views entirely, with no further discussion required, and otherwise reacts to normal green characteristics as somebody with a chemical-sensitivity syndrome reacts to even modest amounts of industrial agents. But this keeps a green component dissociated in the individual's own being, and this, as noted, can stall or even prevent higher development into 3rd tier. Green definitely needs to be *transcended*, but it also needs to be *included*.

Contrasted to green allergy is, of course, green addiction. This is also fairly common in Integral individuals, and the primary reason for this is that green itself is the major stage through which Integral must emerge—it's the ocean in which the Integral island stands. And making a clean break with yesterday is always hard. Green itself is so typically vocal about its opinions, and—given that it is usually the most common stage in any population from which Integral might emerge— Integral is typically used to having green's ideas and opinions forced on it, at least as background. Much like someone with "Stockholm syndrome" (where individuals who are kidnapped start identifying with their kidnappers), Integral can be kidnapped by green and retain a hidden green identity, or subpersonality—a green fixation/addiction.

When this happens, the Integral stage will often share a misconception that is rooted directly in green, namely, the idea that "Everything is connected to everything else." But that is actually true only in a very specific fashion. In any developmental nested hierarchy, or growth holarchy, all of the lower is in the higher, *but not all of the higher is in the lower*, and thus not all of the higher is connected to the lower in any truly direct or equal sense. Thus, all of an atom is in a molecule, but not all of the molecule is in an atom—hence, not all parts of the molecule are connected to the atom. And all of a molecule is in a cell, but not all of the cell is in the molecule. Likewise, all of a word is in a sentence (that contains that word), but not all of the sentence is in that word, and so on. This is true of all the vertical dimensions in all holarchies everywhere. So throughout the universe there are aspects of the senior that are not directly connected to the junior. Thus, the world is indeed intimately interwoven (holographically AND holarchically), and not in the flatland version of absolute equivalence that these types of Views (broken teal, typical green) assume.

This confusion of green with Integral is also made relatively easy in that, in many ways, green consciously and actually considers itself "integral"—some scholars have even called the green community, composed of "cultural creatives," the "integral culture." In reality, of course, green is not "the integral culture," it is what is preventing the integral culture, but it does have designs in that integral direction: green doesn't want to marginalize or exclude other values (although it does despise orange, amber, 2nd tier, and so forth); it loathes dominator hierarchies and their oppressing drives (even though it confuses these with growth hierarchies and thus has no real way out of oppression); and it believes that "everything is connected to everything else" (overlooking holarchical asymmetry, as explained); among others. So as Integral emerges, it is often encouraged by those around it to identify any of its green components as being "integral" or "nonmarginalizing" or "interconnected," thus creating a tendency for Integral to knowingly or unknowingly identify with green qualities. And if that is done unknowingly—unconsciously—then this becomes a "repressed submergent" element (that is, likely a subpersonality) that Integral remains identified with—in short, a pathology.

This type of fixation, or unconscious identity, often affects one developmental line (or multiple intelligence) more than others, so that the psychograph becomes quite dotted with spots of fixation. It is common, for example, for individuals to reach 2nd tier in their cognition, but have their proximate self-sense (or center of gravity) remain at green. It's easier to "talk" Integral than to actually "walk" Integral; and given that the cognitive line is usually necessary but not sufficient for the other lines, it's not unusual for the cognitive line to be a stage or two ahead of other lines. In that case, the "fixation" on green is not technically a pathology, just a matter of normal uneven development; it's when green is actively held on to beyond the period it could just as well be developmentally let go of or transcended that is a pathology, a green fixation, a developmental arrest in a particular line.

Green fixation (as either a real pathology or simply a normal uneven development, but in any event it involves green believing that it is integral) is extremely common in what is generally called "the Integral community"; it is probably, in fact, the most common of such dysfunctions. In one integrally oriented organization, it appeared that around 85 percent of the members had a 2nd-tier cognition and a green center of gravity (talk Integral, walk green), and the rest had 2nd-tier cognition and a 2nd-tier center of gravity (talk and walk Integral). In other words, 85 percent versus 15 percent; and that is rather common.

Right now, the general Integral movement is not only differentiated, but in some ways fragmented, based upon the amount of green allergy, green addiction, and "full" 2nd-tier Integral that can be found in it. The people in these organizations with much actual residual green (that is, green fixation/addiction) often have a standard psychograph that consists of 2nd-tier cognition (teal or turquoise) but a structure center of gravity, or general self-sense, still at green—so, as noted, they talk Integral, walk green. Those with a large amount of green allergy are generally more at the Integral stages themselves, but they have a fair amount of "repressed submergent" green elements, which are projected, and thus they focus on the "mean green meme" and have a great distaste for all things green. They have a particularly low opinion of the "talk Integral, walk green" organizations (and individuals) and generally make their opinions well known. A few Integral organizations are relatively clean, with their members' cognition and self both clearly at 2nd tier (or higher).

But these types of issues are to be expected with any movement such as Integral. Keep in mind, this is the first major stage where a fair number of individuals actually know it is coming and continue with an eye out watching for more and more of its signs. (Every truly Integral overview or framework has several developmental models that it is aware of and often uses, and every one of those models has at least one stage higher than green Pluralistic—namely, a systemic or integrative stage of one variety or another.) If you look at the 1960s, when the green postmodern Pluralistic stage first emerged on a wide scale and the various revolutions that such emergence brought took place, virtually nobody—from authorities to laypeople—had even guessed, in the 1950s, that those revolutions and their massive changes were headed directly for us. The student revolutions that began in May 1968, Paris, and spread to the rest of world, took almost everybody by complete surprise. But as those revolutions went into full force, the bulk of developmental studies was becoming more and more well known—even if it was just to have green and its antiranking condemn all of them. But all of those developmental models, without exception, showed a stage or two higher than the Pluralistic postmodern, which was presently driving the various revolutions (the higher stages were variously called, at the time, "systemic," "autonomous," "integrated," "integrative," "integral," "integral-aperspectival," "strategist"), and thus the coming Integral revolution was widely expected (even if by a relatively small number of people overall; and a good number of individuals are still tracking the emergence of Integral). And unlike the participants in the Pluralistic revolutions of the 1960s, who did *not* know that most of their basic assumptions were the product of a particular, specific stage of human development (a stage that was merely one of at least a half-dozen other stages), most of the people in Integral organizations are fully aware of developmental studies, and thus they have at least some

sort of self-reflective awareness that they are close to the edge of evolution itself—that unlike Mythic, Rational, or Pluralistic (whose values
are the traditional, modern, and postmodern values at the heart of today's Culture Wars; none of which is at the leading edge of evolution),
the Integral stages are indeed, generally speaking, the highest basic
stages that evolution itself has produced thus far, to any significant
degree. (It is true that 3rd-tier stages have begun to be laid down, but
most are as yet mere scratches on the face of the Kosmos.)

This leading-edge nature feeds into a self-reflection that can thus
reactivate narcissistic tendencies—"I'm at the highest stage in evolution!"—and thus reactivate all sorts of psychological dysfunctions.
(One of the best and most effective ways to handle this issue is by becoming involved simultaneously in some sort of genuine structure-stage
and state-stage development—thus, not just Growing Up but also
Waking Up—which helps to transcend ego and the separate-self sense
and keep humility as a constant characteristic of self-awareness. Other
than that, Cleaning Up, or specific shadow work—at the least, a quick
morning and evening 3-2-1 or 3-2-1-0 process—is almost mandatory
at this, and all higher, stages.)

In some of the fairly rare studies done on 2nd-tier stages, there are
indications that the first of the 2nd-tier stages, the teal Holistic, has a
fair amount of certainty and self-security. It is the first stage at 2nd tier
and has just emerged out of green's "aperspectival madness," has
started to grasp the many patterns that connect various cultures and
individuals worldwide, and is secure in this knowledge and its awareness. Turquoise Integral, on the other hand, starts to show a mild amount
of wobbling insecurity, even though it is "more holistic," more integral. One of the reasons for this is that it lies right next to 3rd tier, or the
first stages with a genuine amount of direct transpersonal awareness.
This transpersonal awareness, as its name indicates, means that awareness itself is clearly moving beyond the individual body-mind, or individual organism, and is not just thinking about the global interwoven
networks with which it is indelibly interconnected (as 2nd tier does), but
is starting to identify with, and directly experience, these transindivid-
ual networks and transglobal meshworks. And this means some degree
of death to its own individual self-sense. Of course, every level faces the
death of the self on its present level and its rebirth on the next, new, and
higher level; but for the first time, this death-and-rebirth involves the

death of a substantial personal self on the way to a transpersonal future (which becomes greater and greater with each new 3rd-tier stage). This is the same type of "dark night" faced by various state-stages as consciousness dies to a lower identity (gross ego or subtle soul) and awakens to a higher identity (causal Higher Self, or turiya True Self, not to mention ultimate Suchness).

If none of these serious types of "self-death" has occurred yet, it must starting with indigo, or the beginning of 3rd tier—turquoise Integral's own next higher stage. Turquoise Integral thus stands on the edge of the realization that its own future growth and development involves reaching into areas beyond its particular personal self-sense, which can infuse upper 2nd tier with a mild but insistent insecurity, as this death-including future seeps into its consciousness.

People sometimes imagine that since Holistic and Integral levels are just that—holistic, integral, whole, unified, inclusive—that they can't have any real problems; they can't have shadow elements because they are so unified. But as we saw with the dissociation and projection of their own green elements (that is, with green allergy), these stages are perfectly capable of fragmenting, splitting, breaking, and dissociating—it's just the nature of what is dissociated that is so different here. These stages, like all others, are the product of evolutionary unfolding, of "transcend and include," or "differentiate and integrate," and if something goes wrong with either one of those, we get either an addiction (failure to differentiate or transcend correctly) or an allergy (failure to integrate or include correctly). The major difference between teal Holistic and turquoise Integral is the degree of Wholeness in each act of their consciousness. With teal Holistic, Wholeness is perceived within several different areas being looked at, linking them in an overall holistic scheme (for example, paradigmatic); with turquoise Integral, Wholeness is perceived within but also across several different areas, finding Wholeness across several different holistic schemes ("a holistic of holistic," for example, cross-paradigmatic). In the following, I'll treat them both together as "Wholeness-perceiving" levels, since the important point here is essentially the same in both of them, but there are at least some significant differences that should be kept in mind, and they all center on the "degree of Wholeness" involved.

To word this slightly differently, the essential core of the dysfunctions at these 2nd-tier Integral stages is that what is dissociated, or split off, tends to be Wholes themselves. Now there are only whole/parts to begin with (holons), and so what is being "repressed" here are holons of higher and higher degrees of depth (or height, whichever metaphor you prefer). Orange cognition (such as formal operational cognition) can begin to form universal sequences of things, which accounts for its capacity to create "worldcentric" meshes. But there is disagreement as to whether formal operational can form extensive systems—some scholars say yes, some say no. It appears that Piaget added a new level of cognition that was beyond formal operational and was "systemic." But in any event, by the time we get to green, we have something like a systematic cognition (a cognition of real systems) or even a metasystematic cognition (a cognition of "systems of systems"). The leap to 2ⁿᵈ tier gives a definite teal "systems of systems" and a beginning of "systems of systems of systems," with turquoise cementing that capacity and opening even to "systems of systems of systems of systems." There is an enormous amount of variance in how different models view these higher levels of wholeness perception (and just how many "systems" are being perceived); what is not denied by any of them is that each higher stage brings a capacity for greater (higher, wider, deeper, larger) wholeness, for holons or whole/parts whose larger "wholes" have more "parts"—more inclusive by more inclusive by more inclusive by more inclusive.

Let me give an example of what "greater wholeness" ("larger holons") actually means, because we tend to think of "greater" just in terms of size, and so miss the increase in quality that is often involved. Take a child at the stage of early preoperational cognition (say, four years old), and show the child a ball colored blue on one side and yellow on the other. Place this ball between you and the child, and spin it several times so that the child can clearly see it is colored blue on one side and yellow on the other. Then place the ball with the yellow side facing the child and the blue side facing you, and ask the child, "What color do *you* see?" The child will correctly say, "Yellow." Then ask the child, "What color am *I* seeing?" And the child will say, "Yellow." In other words, the child cannot take the role of other, cannot put itself in your shoes, cannot even see your point of view. The child is, of course, still in the egocentric realm of development, and so the capacity to take the role of other has not yet clearly emerged.

Now take a notion like "Enlightenment," which is often defined as "the union of Emptiness and Form," or less technically, a "unity consciousness," a "oneness (or not-twoness) of subject and object." Imagine hypothetically that this child were Enlightened; what would be the actual nature of the "unity consciousness" or "wholeness" that this child would experience? The child would certainly feel a oneness between his or her perceptible form and your form—that is, a oneness of his or her body and your body and all the other "physical objects" out there. And that would be a genuine type of wholeness. But that wholeness would not include an awareness of your actual perspective, or of how you view the world. So you couldn't really say that this child was "totally one" with you, because the child is one only with your body; he or she can't see your mind, your perspective, at all. And this might not be obvious if we simply asked the child what he or she is one with, and the child pointed to all the objects around him or her—the child is one with your exterior, which is one of the objects the child sees, but is NOT one with your interior, or how you actually see the world. So the child's "wholeness" is fairly limited, even though the child would feel a "total oneness" with his or her world; but the child's world does not include any "others" at all since it does not include their interiors.

So "wholes" (and holons) are like that—qualitative aspects are increasingly parts of the "wholeness" of higher wholes, and yet this isn't obvious to mere sensory perception. The "other person" could be seeing systems, or systems of systems, or systems of systems of systems, and yet the child would see NONE of that in his or her "unity consciousness." A massive wholeness is "over the child's head"—it's just not something that is even capable of entering the child's awareness, even though the child is experiencing a type of "union of Emptiness and Form." But the "Form" is quite limited and less than the true fullness that the actual "other" is experiencing. This is an extremely important point, and it comes into play in an incredibly wide number of areas. For example, somebody at, say, amber mythic can go through the Waking Up stages all the way to turiyatita, or pure "unity consciousness," and yet still have just an ethnocentric unity—unity with just a particular group of people marked by a limited number of qualities—and yet this limitation would not be obvious to mere sensory awareness. The "enlightened" individual would still feel a "total oneness" with his or her world, but he or she would be not even be capable of seeing an actual worldcentric individual qua worldcentric, just other ethnocentric individuals similar to himself or herself. Zen masters who are at an ethnocentric level of Growing Up, yet experience a full "unity consciousness" in Waking Up, claim that they are "one with all sentient beings," and although they FEEL that way, they simply aren't. They cannot see the interior qualities of people at rational worldcentric, or multicultural pluralistic, or holistic Integral (or higher)—all of them are, in fact, "over his or her head." You can see many examples of this "ethnocentric Enlightenment" in *Zen at War*.[1] (That's one of the reasons we have to be sure to include Growing Up with Waking Up, or the "wholeness" of our "unity consciousness" will not be so Whole after all.)

Thus, all levels of development are composed of holons, and these holons run the spectrum from fairly "shallow" and "narrow" wholeness-and-partness, to higher and higher and higher wholeness-and-partness. And it's these holons, on any level, which have the qualities of that level, that are fixated to, or alienated from, and thus generate addictions and allergies—*with the characteristics of that level*. By the time we get to 2nd tier, we are working with a wholeness/partness that reaches up to "systems of systems" and higher, and it is those Wholes (or holons) that are fixated to or dissociated from. And by this point, this is such a significant degree of wholeness/partness (which I summarize simply by using the term "Wholeness") that the Wholeness itself comes to the fore as being the central core item alienated by the defense mechanisms of these levels. This is the shortest, simplest summary of dysfunctions at these stages. A typical example of this is many of the new atheists, who certainly have a 2nd-tier cognitive capacity, and who acknowledge the Whole of science, and embrace it with an abiding joy, but deny and dis-own the Whole of spirituality. They are deaf to their higher spiritual intelligence as it whispers in their ear, and as a result, in repressing the Whole of spirituality, they make science into their religion and believe it with a religious zealotry and furor. Their spiritual intelligence continues whispering in their ear, and they continue misinterpreting it as merely a scientific materialist whisper. This is a high-order dysfunction indeed.

As another example, when some item of teal (which can see at least "systems" and "systems of systems") is repressed and projected at this stage, it is not just, for instance, green as it appears in one person or one entity or one area, but green in numerous different areas, all united and treated as one by having the similar characteristic of "green-ness." It's not just a green person that is disliked, it's all green people as a whole (in other words, it's the "system" of green people—say, all American green individuals, or even the "system of system" of green people—for example, all green people worldwide, that is rejected). Likewise, if something like "love" is dissociated, it is love across several different areas that is usually denied and dis-owned. The person might cease to love in general; might refuse to love people in general; or might cease to love a particular type of work-related tasks or an entire type of music or movies (rejecting entire "systems of systems"). The psyche, used to handling Wholes (and whole systems) at these levels, can defend against them as well—and that's exactly what it does at 2nd tier.[2] Again, it is wholes (that is, holons, or whole/parts) at every developmental level that are fixated to (addictions) or dissociated from (allergies), but the "depth" or "height" of the holons becomes greater and greater and greater with each new stage or level of consciousness, and so the defense mechanisms of that stage operate on those "greater holons," which actually have the specific characteristics of the particular stage.

And since defense mechanisms, as we previously defined them, are the "locus of the lie" (the source of self-deception, of lying, of denying this quadrant's validity claim of truthfulness), the defense mechanism operates with untruthfulness, with lying, and that is what causes the problems. The result is that defense mechanisms end up bringing about exactly that which they were meant to ward off. When material that is defended against is *pushed out of the psyche* (by a defense mechanism), it *leaves a conscious gap or hole*, where the repressed material used to exist, and the defense mechanism then places in that gap or hole at least two items: First, it creates a *symptom*, a painful, distressful, neurotic or psychotic symptom, which is how the repressed material feels when it is repressed, distorted, and dis-owned (it's still there, in reality, and so the psyche continues to experience it, but now in a distorted, torn, and extremely uncomfortable fashion, the "uncomfortableness" due to the violence of crushing the repressed material out of awareness, like putting it in a car crash and having it writhe in crushed and crumpled agony). Second, also in that neurotic or psychotic gap is placed a *symbol*: a symbol that is the result of a lie in awareness. The deceitful material must now present itself to awareness not in its truthful, honest form but in a hidden, devious, lying fashion. Whenever things that in-volve the now-repressed material cross the psyche, the shadow func-tion lies about what that material is, creating a *symptom* and a *symbol*, or series of symbols (hidden meanings about what the verboten mate-rial really is)—this is what is left of the lie.

Various schools of psychotherapy all therefore do at least two things: they address both the painful symptom and the mysterious symbol present. They offer ways to fill that gap and its painful symptom with a different feeling or thought (through a specific form of therapy, exer-cises, practices, physically based treatments, or drugs), and they devise various theories on *how to interpret* that mysterious symbol, or series of symbols, that issue from that gap. Thus, a common "talk therapy" (Upper Left) theory is that depression (the painful feeling in the gap) is caused by repressed anger. Their theory is that SAD = MAD, and that is how they interpret feelings of depression. They then attempt to get the client to use that interpretive guideline to fill the gap with different feelings and thoughts—anger instead of depression. When the depres-sion is "correctly" interpreted as anger, the repression ends and symp-toms and symbols will therefore cease. Other theories on depression maintain that it is caused primarily by the malfunctioning of brain neurochemistry (Upper Right), and the symptom and symbols can be treated by medication. Other theories see the depression as "learned helplessness" and treat the symptom with learned effectiveness exer-cises, and treat the symbols by interpreting it as an untrue and false belief in helplessness—the belief that there is nothing that can be done, that they are stuck with this forever—clearly not true. Yet other theo-ries see the cause as being cultural (Lower Left), with marginalized in-dividuals becoming "identified patients" who are forced to be labeled as the primary example of the cultural shadow (which is a very painful assignation), and only by interpreting the symptoms and symbols as being such can the individual overcome them. Yet other theories, such as eco-psychology (Lower Right), see individuals as being part of a great Web of Life, or Gaia, and having split themselves off from that larger network, they suffer the pain of alienation and separation, and will get better only when they repair that rupture. There are around fifty major theories as to the cause of both major symptoms and their symbols, many of which have specific treatment modalities. (In this presentation, I am particularly focusing on the developmental aspects of the Upper Left quadrant, using orienting generalizations taken from dozens of the most successful and respected developmental models in existence, set in a philosophical background of Integral Metatheory. I occasionally make parenthetical or endnoted reminders that although I am focusing on the Upper Left, all 4 quadrants—with their own variations on levels, lines, and states—need to be taken into account for a fuller understanding, and indeed they must. But the material I am covering here is absolutely essential to this understanding and can stand on its own for what it covers.)[3]

To return to the "Wholeness" dysfunctions at 2nd tier: These "Wholeness repressions" indicate the nature of the material involved in shadow repression at each and every level. Each level can create shadow material (and possibly subpersonalities) by repressing or dissociating the elements found on that level itself. At orange worldcentric Rational, for example, we saw that it was worldcentric orange elements or emotions or qualities that were repressed and projected. If elements from a lower level attempt to come up and are repressed, those elements are kept at that lower level (that's what the repressed *submergent* unconscious is). Likewise, elements trying to come down from a higher level that are repressed remain at that higher level (the repressed *emergent* unconscious). Otherwise, the elements from the orange level itself that are repressed are repressed *at* the orange level; they are orange elements themselves that are split off at that level and retain that level's qualities and characteristics, even when they are repressed or projected. They are orange shadow elements or orange subpersonalities (functioning as *orange* elements). Likewise with green—at that level, shadow material was itself green pluralistic (along with submergent and emergent material at lower and higher levels). And now we see the same thing with 2nd-tier Wholeness-perceiving levels—it is the elements from *those levels themselves*, various types of Wholes, that become shadow or subpersonality material (along with any submergent and emergent material, both of which continue to retain the characteristics and qualities of the level from which they originate, as does the material from the Integral levels themselves).

Individuals can dissociate, deny, and dis-own elements of virtually any level that has emerged (or is about to emerge), and this is true all the way up to the white Supermind. We have already briefly examined spiritual intelligence as it moves through the four hypothesized higher levels of 3rd tier. In the next chapter, we examine how the shadow appears in those four 3rd-tier levels. And keep in mind that simultaneously with all of these shadow elements in the levels of Growing Up, there are shadow elements being created by any states and state-stages that are occurring in the process of Waking Up (or simply state material in general). *These state-shadows occur alongside the structure-shadow material simultaneously being generated.* We will look at this state-shadow material after we finish our account of structure-shadow issues.

How Many Levels Are There?

One last item quickly. I have often remarked that the number of stages/ levels—in either structures or states—is largely a matter of convention and personal choice (and random choices of initial measurements). In various presentations, I have given three levels, five levels, seven levels, ten levels, twelve levels, and sixteen levels (with hints of even more). As long as there is credible evidence for these levels, none of them is the only correct way to number the stages—it's simply a matter of how much detail you want and how granular you want to be in your presentation. And different specific problems will benefit from a different number of levels and detail.

The lower levels (certainly 1st-tier levels and mostly 2nd-tier levels) are fairly well demarcated and the total number of levels that are "actually" present is set, although these, too, can be condensed and summarized into any number of fewer stages for simplicity's sake (and different models of the different multiple intelligences will give a different number of levels). For example, even if we give twelve or sixteen stages of overall development, all of them can be conveniently summarized as moving from egocentric to ethnocentric to worldcentric to Kosmocentric levels—and that is perfectly acceptable.

As for the notion of "tiers"—"tiers" are unlike structures or states. Structures and states are actual features of the Kosmos; they are real components of the universe at large. They have been laid down as Kosmic habits, or Kosmic memories, or Kosmic grooves, and reside in that grand Form-storage basin, wherever it might be. But every now and then, developmentalists find that a newly emerging stage is so radically and wildly different from any stages that have come before, that they gather together these new stages and refer to them as a "tier" and distinguish the new tier from what is then called the "lower" tier that came before the newly emergent and higher level. We see this going back at least to Kohlberg—his moral stages, most of which are 1st tier, as Spiral Dynamics uses the term, actually have within them three major tiers, called preconventional (egocentric), conventional (ethnocentric), and postconventional (worldcentric). That is perfectly acceptable, and they can indeed be considered different tiers. If we include them with Graves's 1st- and 2nd-tier divisions, we would really have four tiers—preconventional, conventional, postconventional, and Integral. That, too, is perfectly acceptable. But a "tier" is just a way to gather together structures and states that have something very important in common and group them together.

I understand that Graves believed that 2nd tier would have six stages, too, like 1st tier; but because these tiers are not actual Kosmic grooves but simply human conventions, I found that several character- istics that could be considered a new tier (that is, 3rd tier) started much earlier; no need to wait another 4 stages to get to Graves's 3rd tier. In fact, "awareness of awareness," "transpersonal components," "direct Wholeness awareness," and "heaven/earth unities" were powerful characteristics that deeply affected those who moved into para-mind, meta-mind, overmind, and supermind. And so I began the start of 3rd tier—as a simple conventional designation—at indigo para-mind, right after turquoise Integral. There were just too many really signifi- cant differences between 2nd tier and 3rd tier as I presented them, and so I have gone with that. At the same time, I realize that this is a simple decision to adopt a convention, and I'm certainly open to alternatives.

As to the total number of levels: The 1st-tier stages are all so set in their forms, they are Kosmic grooves cut so deep into the Kosmos, that the chances of their changing their Forms is very slim indeed. But as I've noted all along, 2nd tier is still being laid down in many ways, and so it is still open to being formed and shaped by the thoughts, inten- tions, and actions of each of us right now. Because of the relative new- ness of 2nd tier, some researchers (for example, Jenny Wade) believe that there is only one stage at 2nd tier, the way it is presented today. What I have done in this case is divide 2nd tier into "low vision-logic" (teal holistic) and "high vision-logic" (turquoise Integral). If these turn out to be one major level, that's fine—that would be the vision-logic level, and we would adjust our maps accordingly; but I believe that the evidence is strong enough to recognize two levels here, and although I will often classify them both as "Integral," I believe that they are indeed distinct.

The same thing is especially true with the gossamer levels of 3rd tier. I believe that each of them has the potential of being divided into, for example, "low and high para-mind," "low and high meta-mind," "low and high overmind," and "low and high supermind." This would give us a total of eight 3rd-tier basic structures, and eight 1st- and 2nd-tier basic structures, for a total of sixteen major basic structures in the overall spectrum of consciousness. I believe that the evidence tentatively supports all sixteen levels, but it is definitely still (especially in its highest reaches) rather thin, and so I have taken the safer route of including just four major 3rd-tier levels and have not yet divided them into a "low" and "high" level; but I won't hesitate to include any number of those extra levels as evidence becomes stronger. I do not want to hear that this model includes only twelve levels; at a minimum, it includes sixteen; to be safe, I'm presenting twelve. (But note that the book *Integral Psychology* includes sixteen levels because there was enough evidence to do so; and there still is—except, again, it is rather thin in the upper reaches.) All of the models that I've seen that include eight major levels in 3rd tier are very promising but very tentative, and none are completely compelling. Given that models of higher development that clearly distinguish states of consciousness (Waking Up) from structures of consciousness (Growing Up) were introduced by Integral Metatheory only a few decades ago, we still need a substantial amount of research in order to say with confidence, for example, that violet meta-mind actually has low and high meta-mind as clearly distinct stages; and the same goes for the rest of the 3rd-tier stages. This shouldn't hamper individuals from proposing and claiming any number of higher stages—I fully support that type of research and theorizing. This Integral discipline is just a few decades old, and much, much more detail awaits our earnest discovery.

Finally, a word on "altitude." There are dozens of developmental models in existence, each dealing with a different developmental line or multiple intelligence (or grouping of them), and each having a varying number of levels. (*Integral Psychology* has charts that include some one hundred different developmental models and their major stages.) Many of them claim to be THE developmental model—that is, the one true developmental stream from which all other streams are branching, and thus the one true way to configure and number levels of development. Clearly they can't all be right—although, in another sense (the typical Integral sense), they are all right—it's just that they are indeed working with different developmental lines or intelligences or ways to group them, and they are each taking a specific perspective on the great Developmental River of being human; each is "true but partial."

But one thing is certain: if you take all of these models and put them next to each other (as the charts in *Integral Psychology* do), the *general* similarity in all their stages is just unmistakable. Integral Metatheory was one of the first, if not the first, to make the official claim that essentially all of the various developmental lines (including multiple intelligences) are moving through the same great morphogenetic developmental gradient, the same "tilt" in the Kosmos that drives development and evolution itself (that is, Eros), a "tilt" that Integral Metatheory formally calls "altitude" (which means the amount, or degree, or level, of general development in any line). This altitude gradient is what virtually all of the developmental lines have in common, no matter in what model. And further, this altitude gradient theoretically has a similar number of levels, although those are immensely variable because this overall gradient, like a tilted floor, can be divided into any number of "levels of tilt." But the point is: *different lines, same levels*—all the different developmental lines are running through the same altitude tilt or gradient.

What happens with each developmental line (including multiple intelligences) is that the specific characteristic defining the particular line (a given intelligence, capacity, quality, or skill) is set in the overarching context of this morphogenetic field, and that field places a "stress" ("a self-organization through self-transcendence"—or Eros) on the given line, and combined with factors in all 4 quadrants, the result is that the particular line is driven to undergo growth and development through a set of qualitatively distinct levels or stages or waves. Those stages appear differently in every line (given the different, defining characteristics of that line), and this is also why one model will not fully cover all lines. But what is not different is that those stages each proceed through a developmental gradient that is common to them all, and thus each stage's "altitude" can be identified, and in a way that allows direct comparison with all other stages in all other lines: again, different lines, same altitude levels. And this, indeed, is what we see.

You could thus display all of these on something called an "integral psychograph." Here, you simply take a given number of developmental lines or several different developmental models and you line them all up and present them together on the same graph, with "altitude" going up the vertical axis and the various different lines or models running along the horizontal axis. You can see examples of this in figures 6.1 and 6.2.

As one way (and only one way) to refer to degrees of altitude (or "levels" of altitude), Integral Metatheory followed the ancient practice (found in, for example, Yoga psychology) of giving each major degree or level a rainbow "color"—running, for example, from infrared to magenta to red to amber to orange to green to teal to turquoise to indigo to violet to ultraviolet to white (with subdivisions more than possible). The order of colors is important for the traditional psychologies, because each level is said to correspond to a subtle energy, which can also be found in nature, such as in a rainbow, so the order of the colors of levels of altitude, unlike those used by Spiral Dynamics, should match the order found in a rainbow. This is important because biomachines activating a given level would need to match the real color found at that level. Thus, as only one example, all of the traditions put "violet" or "purple" toward the very highest of levels, whereas Spiral Dynamics puts it at one of the lowest, and this would backfire badly when any actual energies were used.

The general characteristics of altitude presented in this manner make it different from the altitude as actually described or defined in any one given model. Any given model of development—Piaget's, Kohlberg's, Loevinger's, Kegan's, and so forth—has its version of altitude and stages of development (or levels of altitude), and the nature of what is being measured as development to begin with. Also, every single model in existence so far deals with one particular type of overall development—it focuses on a particular line, or a specific grouping of lines, and it divides them into different stages, or levels, and often tiers. The simple fact that they are all different—they might share some characteristics, and usually do, but on balance they remain fundamentally different models that do not strictly match other models—

means, again, that none of them are "the" one and only correct view of development. The differences in the models reflect the real differences in the characteristics of the specific lines being modeled.

Integral Metatheory, on the other hand, does put *all* of them on the largest potential integral psychograph imaginable. In various psychographs given in Integral Metatheory books (including this one), you can see psychographs with the developmental models of Piaget, Michael Commons and Francis Richards, Graves and Spiral Dynamics, and Jenny Wade, Kohlberg, Kegan, O'Fallon, Cook-Greuter, Loevinger, and so on. When Integral Metatheory gives a general summary of a particular level of altitude (or gives a particular name to a degree of altitude, such as "magic," "mythic," "pluralistic," "holistic," and so on), it is based on the general characteristics of that level that can be found in ALL of those models at any particular altitude level. What Integral Metatheory is most often working with, in other words, is altitude in general, not any specific line of altitude or version of altitude or model of altitude. It's presenting an overall "Integral Psychograph" whose levels, stages, degrees, characteristics, and qualities are drawn from any or all of some one hundred models of development (as shown in the charts of *Integral Psychology*).

In this way, Integral Metatheory believes that its version of altitude is the most sound version available; at the same time, it does not in any way deny specific versions or particular models or different lines (as formulated in different models). The whole point of a "metatheory" is that it is a theory of theories, or a model of models, and not simply a theory or a model, which all of the particular models themselves are (and they are appreciated for being just that!). When, for example, the term "orange cognition" is used by Integral Metatheory, it could be referring to the stage in Piaget's model that is at orange, or in Kurt Fischer's at orange, or the cognitive components of Kegan's at orange, and so on. Formally speaking, it's what all of them have in common— namely, a degree of developmental altitude along the altitude gradient through which all lines pass. If any of these models are definitely shown to be deficient, then fine, those models will no longer be part of any grand psychograph. But until such evidence is offered, if ever, they are viewed as part of the overall potential growth spectrum running through this altitude gradient.

Thus when, in this book, you hear the different levels being discussed in 1st, 2nd, and 3rd tier, you will know that you are getting the "best" of all the models that discuss that particular altitude level (and at the same time, you are strongly invited to check out any or all particular models that include that line at that level in their formulations—Integral Metatheory does indeed "include them all," or certainly those "true but partial" aspects of them).

11

Dysfunctions of the 3rd-Tier Structure-Views

Overview

Although each level of 3rd tier and its Super-Integral View (para-mind, meta-mind, overmind, and supermind—or indigo, violet, ultraviolet, and white, or clear light) is different, a few things can be said about the pathologies of 3rd tier in general. First of all, most of these levels have some degree or dimension of transpersonal awareness, and any aspect of that can be either fixated to (producing an addiction) or dis-owned and dissociated from (resulting in an allergy). Transpersonal *addictions* mean an addiction to a particular level's form of transpersonal awareness, thus failing to make room for the higher, newer version at the next higher level; this fixation often results because the transpersonal experiences addicted to are relatively so new, novel, extraordinary, unprecedented, and deeply gratifying, that the individual doesn't want to let go of them or die to them, not realizing that even greater forms of transpersonal awareness are available, at the coming stage, if he or she does so. A transpersonal *allergy*, on the other hand, is a direct dis-owning or dissociating of a specific level's transpersonal reality, which renders it largely unconscious. This usually occurs because the transpersonal experience involves a death of that level's self-sense, and the self, fearing that death, denies and dis-owns the experience itself, converting it into shadow.

In either case, this means, in effect, that the 3rd-tier self caught in such a dysfunction has a "smaller," "lesser" amount of genuinely transpersonal awareness than would otherwise be experienced, because consciousness has become split off to some degree, and thus has formed a transpersonal subpersonality that holds this repressed, split-off, dissociated, fixated, unconscious material. These fixations/dissociations (or addictions/allergies) can, if not addressed, be carried into virtually any and all higher 3rd-tier stages, significantly deforming those structures and distorting their Views, and severely limiting the amount of transpersonal awareness available at each. If severe, this can derail and arrest development altogether at that point.

Also common at these higher 3rd-tier structures are energetic allergies or addictions that arise in direct relation to the state subtle energies that accompany all 3rd-tier levels. Actually, this is part of the Upper Right quadrant mass-energy correlates that accompany all Upper Left consciousness states and structures (the Left-hand quadrants in general are "consciousness" and the Right-hand ones are "matter" or "mass-energy"), and any dysfunction in one is accompanied by a correlative dysfunction in the other. I have been focusing mostly on the Upper Left components in consciousness and the dysfunctions as they appear there, because the Upper Right energies are a particularly complex subject, which deserves a treatment all its own. However, the overall idea is straightforward, and once the general idea is grasped, the reader can apply it wherever appropriate. For the moment, I will simply note that the actual circulation of subtle energies through any of its major chakras, meridians, shunts, or veins (nadis) can be mangled, disturbed, or distorted, often due to a pathology or dysfunction of a particular Upper Left *structure* (this includes not only the lower structure-rungs but also the para-mind, meta-mind, overmind, and supermind) as well as a pathology in a particular Upper Left *state* (gross, subtle, causal, witnessing, or nondual). A disturbance in either structure or state (View or Vantage Point) affects the other quadrants, including the correlative mass-energy states in the Upper Right (which would include, for example, brain-wave patterns). And, of course, the Upper Right energy itself can be disturbed and distorted, which—as all malfunctions do—invades and disturbs all the other quadrants as well, particularly Upper Left consciousness.

Put slightly differently, this energetic dysfunction, like all the dysfunctions we are discussing, has both an Upper Left, or consciousness, component, and an Upper Right, or material or body/mass-energy, component. (Of course, it has a component in all 4 quadrants. As I've noted, I haven't been including these quadrant correlations since they can become quite complex and take us significantly beyond the scope of this book. But it should at least be kept in mind. Likewise, Lower Left cultural factors and Lower Right systems factors are particularly significant in the creation of psychospiritual dysfunctions and distortions, and I deal with them at length in the follow-up book to *Sex, Ecology, Spirituality*, volume 2 of the Kosmos Trilogy, which is nearing completion.

If these Upper Right energetic dysfunctions occur in higher structures or states and are persistent and intense, these disturbed subtle energy currents can be carried downward, via the "downward causation" of involutionary currents, and end up causing mental disturbances, emotional disturbances, or, at the material bottom of the spectrum, actual physical diseases (often located close to the chakra where the higher subtle disturbance occurred, or along a meridian, or nadi, where the subtle energy was contaminated, and so on). Western medicine has a particularly difficult time dealing with these illnesses, let alone curing them, because their cause and origin are not in the physical gross body itself, but in a higher subtle or causal body, invisible to typical orthodox Upper Right Western medicine. Many of them go by the names of "degenerative diseases" (or "diseases of aging") and include illnesses such as heart disease; certain cancers; type 2 diabetes; arthritis; liver, kidney, breast, and prostate problems; and brain/cognitive disorders, including some types of MS and Alzheimer's (although all of these have other causes as well and not all of them are due to subtle energy disturbances, a not-insignificant number are, at least according to energy medicine). Addressing these types of illnesses has been one of the major aims of complementary, alternative, and integrative medicine—not to mention Integral Medicine, which is even more "integrative" than "integrative medicine," inasmuch as it includes all the dimensions of the entire AQAL Matrix. (See the section "Energy Malfunctions" in chapter 13.)

Gross, subtle, or causal energy malfunctions are some of the Upper Right correlations of every structure and state dysfunctional development, top to bottom, in the Upper Left; but in 3rd tier, the states themselves—or the self's identity with these states—are starting to be transformed altogether and integrated with structures, and because of that their energetic components are often brought forth prominently.

Also common to 3rd-tier dysfunctions are various difficulties with the "transcend and include" process as it directly relates to the basic structures and Views of these higher levels. We have seen these specific types of problems before—that is, with "transcend" or with "include," which are the underlying causes of addictions and allergies, and we have seen these problems in virtually every level in 1st and 2nd tier. It's just that here, these problems can occur in relation to both the personal and the transpersonal components of these levels, making the dysfunctions particularly complex. In any event, again either an allergy or an addiction to the dysfunctional material is created.

By far the most common overall dysfunction in 3rd tier is a "splitting" between spiritual/"heavenly"/"otherworldly"/transpersonal 3rd-tier awareness and "this-worldly"/"earthly"/personal 1st- or 2nd-tier awareness. The expansive, free, transcendental, liberated, enormously open and spacious nature of transpersonal 3rd-tier awareness dwarfs anything in 1st or 2nd tier, and the possibility of a generalized attachment to 3rd tier and a "repression" of lower levels in toto sweeps into being. The individual simply wants nothing to do with conventional, ordinary, "earthly" existence, and spends his or her time in transrational structures or states, basking in the joy, love, freedom, and liberation drenching those higher levels. This can contaminate virtually any everyday arena: one can become bored with one's job (often quitting it, or simply showing so little interest that one is let go); bored with one's relationship (and if married, drift significantly away from one's spouse, and even children); bored with one's friends (eventually alienating them with lack of attention and concern); bored with one's possessions (they're "just things" and have no permanent self-being anyway; true enough, but the pathology here is more an active pushing away than a simple letting go); bored altogether with one's bodily being (food can lose its appeal; sex can lose its allure; feeling, however, might paradoxically gain in strength, especially if this particular splitting of upper and lower is caused by a pre/trans fallacy, with prerational feelings being elevated to transrational glory and being "wallowed in"—one can become lost altogether in the simple, pretemporal, passing present and immediate gratification, confusing it with the transtemporal timeless Present, which includes and embraces all time, but does not reject it, as the passing present does).

The causes of this splitting between "heaven" and "earth" (in structures or states; here I am concentrating mostly on structures; I'll focus on states in the next two chapters) are many and varied, and exist in any number of degrees, from mild to psychotic. In general, it is due to a "Wrong View" (and this is a very common cause, as we will continue to see)—that is, a less-than-Integral View. In contrast, an Integral View would instead correctly emphasize, from the start, the "transcend and include" nature of all levels of being and awareness, and put a strong emphasis on both negating and preserving the essentials of each level (thus fully including and integrating both the "heavenly" and "earthly" at every step of the way). In this splitting, on the other hand, there is an overemphasis on the "transcend" part (negating or repressing the lower or "earthly"—dis-owning it, not just dis-identifying with it) and a severe ignoring of the "include" and "integrate" part; that is, Eros degenerates into Phobos (fear), and transformation upward becomes not an expansion to "transcend and include" into higher Wholeness, but an active narrowing, contracting, and pushing away from the junior levels out of fear, escapism, or denial—Phobos, not Eros, producing not higher Wholes but broken Wholes.

The "challenge and support" recommendation for each developmental level in general means, indeed, a transcending (challenging) and including (supporting) of the essentials of every level of being and awareness. As development moves into the "heavenly," transpersonal dimensions of 3rd-tier unfolding, special attention needs to be given to the "include" and "support" aspect, so that "otherworldly" really does transcend—*and* fully include, embrace, surround, incorporate, permeate, and love—all "this-worldly" elements (of course, without forming an exclusive identity with any of them).

It's like when Hawaii became a state of the United States. In order to do so, what did the territory of Hawaii have to "transcend" or "let go" of, and what did it "preserve" or "include," as this smaller whole became part of a larger whole? The actual geographic territory of Hawaii itself remained unchanged, and it became an actual part of the

United States. But anything to do with an *exclusive identity* with that territory (that is, its own sovereignty), that had to go: it could no longer print its own money, have its own foreign policy, declare war, issue its own language, and so on—it was no longer a separate and independent territory. What remained or was included? The basic structure or territory of Hawaii itself—its actual land, its people, its fundamental day-to-day activities—those were all "included" and "preserved," while any *exclusive identity* with *any* of that was "negated" and "transcended." Basic structures endure; Views are transcended. Just so with each and every level as a new and higher level emerges. The lower level's exclusive identity, its sovereignty, its separateness (and the View from that sovereignty) is surrendered and let go of, but its basic structure, its actual territory, its rungs, are most definitely included, incorporated, embraced, and enfolded (into the greater sovereignty—and View—of the next higher level).

The same is generically true of all the lower levels that are primarily gross reflecting or "this-worldly" or "earthly" oriented and those that are subtle, causal, transpersonal, "heavenly," or "otherworldly" oriented (whether in structures or in states). Even at the upper limit of development, the very feeling of a transpersonally open, spacious, infinite, all-permeating, all-pervasive, all-inclusive awareness needs to have, as one of its very feelings, the feeling of the earth, of this world, of this body and its feelings and affects, of conventional realities, of sensorimotor realms. These are in no way "anti-"spiritual or "contra-" transpersonal, but are actual subholons in the new superholon, actual ingredients in the more inclusive, more expansive, more spacious dimension.

The problem is that there are *states* of consciousness that are themselves *only* formless, only infinite, utterly without objects (no "earthly" objects or otherwise; the pure Witness or Seer without anything seen; Absolute Subjectivity; "Consciousness without an object"; the states of nirvikalpa, nirvana, nirodh, infinite Abyss and Void, Ayin, and so on), and although these states are not *ultimately* Whole (they are Emptiness without Form, and hence are not fully nondual), they are nonetheless very real, very powerful, very alluring, and one can easily become addicted to them (and their gross-realm-transcending "bright-love-bliss-radiance").

And, further, on the structure side of the street, although every rung includes and incorporates its previous rung(s), the Views from a previous rung and the next-higher rung are often, as we have seen, contradictory and in strong disagreement—which is yet another reason why each junior View is negated and let go of in order to make room for the next-higher and senior View (a few quick examples as reminders: the impulsive, power-driven, egocentric View of red becomes a conformist, membership-oriented, belongingness, "fitting in" View at amber; which becomes a highly individual, stand alone, achievement-oriented, "stand out," worldcentric View at orange; which becomes a communal, sensitive, sharing-oriented, egalitarian View at green, and so on). Each of those Views strongly and inherently disagrees with its predecessor; but each of their underlying rungs—the red conceptual mind, the amber rule/role mind, the orange rational mind, and the green pluralistic mind—includes, incorporates, and enfolds its predecessor (as "operand"), no problem. But each of their Views are antithetical and do not get along well at all, because the rung that it is generated from is more limited, more restricted, less inclusive than its successor, and thus actual *identities* with those rungs (as well as their exclusive Views) *do not fit* with each other at all. Hence, they are the "transcended," "negated," "let-go-of" aspect of "transcend/differentiate and include/integrate," and their rungs are the "include," "preserve," or "integrate" part.

Because of that, if the Views of the junior level are not cleanly let go of, so that their rungs can be fully included without the accompanying contradiction and disagreement of their Views, then the lower level itself—in this case, the "earthly" realms altogether—is not fully included; aspects of it are sealed off, repressed, denied, dissociated (so that both the earthly Views and the earthly rungs are denied and jettisoned—or pretended to be jettisoned—with the rungs actually remaining in unconscious, distorted fashion, and the Views often projected). Heaven does not embrace earth, but heaven denies earth, and "My kingdom is not of this world." It is so *easy* to see how that can happen, which does not make it the less catastrophic.

So exclusive states of heavenly formless absorption, the general Joy of 3rd tier itself, and contradictory Views from lower earthly structures can combine in any fashion to produce a heaven not of this earth; a 3rd tier dissociated from (and often repressing) 1st and 2nd tier; a fear and denial of the lower (a fear that the lower's contradictory View will pull it down from its higher View, as Eros degenerates into Phobos); an "otherworldliness" that wants nothing to do with anything "this-worldly," a heavenly "transcendence" that is in reality an ugly turning away from earth and all its inhabitants and all its needs and rights.

This repressive splitting shows up in many ways: There is the Theravada teacher whom I heard say, when asked about the environmental crisis, "I don't care; I'm not coming back" (that is, he is getting off the earthly round of reincarnations altogether by staying in unmanifest nirvana—*exactly* what the bodhisattva vows *never* to do, and to combat this attitude is exactly why the bodhisattva vow was put in place to begin with). Or, there are the Mythic-literal fundamentalist interpretations of all this "heaven/earth" stuff, a common one of which is "I don't care about all your 'environmental crises,' which show only your unrepentant nature, not only because 'My Kingdom is not of this world' but because I'm headed for the Rapture, coming this way soon" (the Rapture is a point where God and Christ open heaven to all true believers, and the forces of righteousness battle all those left on earth, vanquishing them and sending them to everlasting damnation, while all true believers are transported straight to heaven in a wildly blissful rapture). Or, the thousands of little everyday turnings away from earth consciousness and its Life and Grounding reality, which causes even the flowers to weep.

As I said, some of the many varieties and versions of this dysfunction ("heaven/earth" splitting) are by far the most common malformations in higher development. Consciousness itself becomes light-headed, unrooted, lost in mind and supramind and unconnected to felt body and living vitality. Light is divorced from Life, amounting in many cases to an almost total disgust with conventional reality, conventional culture, and conventional society. This is a severe problem to remedy, because so many factors can contribute to producing it, and each of them needs to be addressed in order to fully heal the dysfunction. At the least, some sort of somatic plus integrative therapy usually needs to be introduced; and most importantly, a "Right View" of Integral Inclusiveness is mandatory—this splitting is a philosophical problem as much as a psychological or spiritual problem (although it is those as well). In general, awareness needs to be realized as a profound feeling-awareness; the Witness, a loving Witness; the Overmind, a prehensive Overmind. This is in keeping with the true nature of the higher structures and states themselves, which inherently "transcend and INCLUDE" their predecessors in reality and in any event; this "splitting" is just that—a splitting, a breaking, a fracturing of a Wholeness already actually in place and operating, and this integral reeducation is a simple re-cognition, re-membrance, and re-collection of, and a re-uniting with, that which is already deeply known and felt, just not acknowledged and lived. (It should be noted that a similar type of splitting can and does occur in states—in this case, between the gross/physical "earthly" and the higher, more "heavenly" subtle/causal/witnessing. The causes are somewhat different, but the results are quite similar. We'll explore this in chapters 12 and 13.)

"Right View" is the first and foundational step of Buddha's original Eightfold Way. The reason for this is likewise foundational: how we interpret reality governs, as much as anything, how we experience reality. This is not just the claim found in the therapies that we mentioned that work with $S \rightarrow C \rightarrow R$ (that between a stimulus "S" and a response "R" lies an interpretation "C") but the whole notion of co-enactment—that the very perspectives we hold about reality are co-instrumental in bringing forth the phenomenal realities that we experience. Virtually every model of psychological development that starts to track 3rd-tier levels reports stages where individuals come into a sharp understanding that their own theories and ideas help co-determine what they perceive "out there"—an inherent understanding that what we believe "subsists" is inseparable from what "ex-ists" for us, that what we take as a single, pregiven, ontological reality "out there" is actually co-enacted by our own awareness and perspectives, and every level co-enacts a slightly different world (whose accumulations become staggering). That there is a single "pregiven reality" just lying around passively waiting for all and sundry to see is the very first belief that every single 3rd-tier stage gets rid of, and fast. To hear somebody say that "You need a strong ontology in place so that your epistemology has something that it can solidly ground itself in" is to hear 1st tier speaking through this person's mouth. The "epistemic fallacy," as typically stated, is itself a fallacy. As I have noted several times, knowing and being, epistemology and methodology and ontology, are all mutually interwoven and inseparable processes, different dimensions of one underlying Wholeness, and they register "truth" through a process of felt mutual resonance, not isolated mental "representation." They are not previously separate, isolated dimensions that are brought together to ground or represent one another, or are otherwise brought into relationship with one other, but they are more like the north and south poles of a single magnet, setting up a vibratory field pattern of which each is an inseparable moment.[1]

The fundamental sensorimotor mind is not at all used to, or even capable of, seeing the interwoven networks and whole meshworks that actually constitute reality. These are items, like the good things that happen to us, that we have to train a habit of seeing, at least until the true nature of higher realities actually and fully kicks in, and then the first things those higher levels see are Wholes, and only secondarily do we abstract from those Wholes the notions of separate isolated things and events existing alienated in space and time. "Right View"— an Integral View—is thus crucial to any sort of harmonious and balanced growth and development, grounding us, from the start, in the View of the significantly higher levels themselves (and ultimately, grounding us in the View of nondual Supermind).

Most of the elements in the AQAL Framework—a fundamental framework for a more inclusive and comprehensive view of reality— are elements that the average person is not aware of at all. Most individuals don't know about the "hidden maps" of the 6-to-8 (or so) developmental stages that they go through in the process of Growing Up. Most are unaware of the Paths of the Great Liberation, and the state-stages leading from ignorance and bondage to Enlightenment and Awakening in the process of Waking Up. Most don't consciously acknowledge the 4 quadrants, even though they constantly use 1st-, 2nd-, and 3rd-person perspectives. And there is little chance that we are going to awaken to the higher—let alone superhuman—potentials that we have available to us unless we know to look for them in the first place. Without a good map of Bermuda, we just wander around the territory, lost, dazed, and confused. "Right View"—"Right Map"—is the utterly crucial step, the *first* step, in any growth and development process, or simply Life itself.

Another quite common problem at 3rd-tier structures (as well as higher states in general) is a losing track of, and hence projection of, one's own positive transpersonal or spiritual qualities or characteristics, which results in overidealization or hero-worshipping of various people onto whom the elevated material has been projected (this is particularly common with spiritual teachers who serve as the recipient, or "hook," of the projection). Failure to realize and own one's genuine spiritual/transpersonal qualities is due largely to a modern cultural devaluation of the spiritual, itself due largely to a mythic level/line fallacy. (A "level/line fallacy" is the confusing of a given level in a line—in this case, the mythic-literal level—with the entire line itself—in this case, spiritual intelligence—thus failing to see or appreciate that there are more sophisticated, higher, truer levels in that line, and thus rejecting the entire line itself—in this case, the spiritual. Because the mythic level in that line is rejected, the whole line is tossed, and spirituality on the whole is dismissed as "childish" or worse.) Once that happens, it is not uncommon to take any of these higher spiritual qualities, as they arise in oneself, and not recognizing them as one's own good qualities, project them onto others, which populates the world with overly admired and idealized individuals, built largely of one's own should-be-owned wonderful material. This is populating the world by *adding* material to it that is *subtracted* from one's own soul and spirit, leaving one's own interior inventory crippled and desiccated.

A simple way to begin addressing these issues is to notice anybody that you particularly admire, and then do a 3-2-1 or 3-2-1-0 process with them in mind—or in the empty chair. Get a feel for the higher qualities you might have projected onto him or her, and then start to take back and re-own those qualities in yourself. When, in the exercise, you are talking to, or as, the admired individual, really feel what it is that you admire so much about him or her—get as clear a sense of it as you possibly can—and then, realizing that "it takes one to know one," directly re-own these qualities; simply *take them back*. It is a particularly good idea to keep track of these in your journal as they unfold. The more "awesomely amazing people" you see out there, the greater the recovery project you likely face, so don't hesitate to get started . . .

Occasionally a genuinely transpersonal negative quality—an "evil" trait in transpersonal dimensions, quite frightening in general—can be projected, and then the individual begins to see and experience "demonic" presences in others. The "evil" nature of this material is sometimes created by a projection of one's own positive transpersonal and spiritual material, with the "evil" aspect itself created by the projection. This is because projection often "reverses" or "flips" various aspects of that which is being projected. For instance, if one has a large amount of anger—which is typically directed away from the self and aimed toward the world—and then projects that anger, it will usually "flip" or "reverse" direction and seem to be coming from the world and be aimed at the self (simply because the self is its true place of origin). This can cause anything from fear to depression to panic attacks. Similarly, if, say, a woman has a pleasant feeling of sexuality but projects that onto the world, then the world will seem populated with people who want to sexually approach, perhaps even attack, her— thus that "good" quality of delightful approach has reversed to a "bad" feeling quality of aggressive attack. Likewise, in some cases, a positive transpersonal quality, when projected, can give rise to "negative" or "evil" transpersonal qualities that are felt to be arising in the world and aimed at the individual (a 3-2-1 or 3-2-1-0 process will make this evident, if it's occurring, and correctly reverse it).

On some occasions, given that there are real, transpersonal negative qualities and emotions (for example, there are transpersonally oriented and driven anger, hatred, jealousy, envy, and so forth), feeling a major negative in the world might be a projection of a genuinely negative shadow, of negative transpersonal material in the individual, and needs to be dealt with directly as a real shadow issue (which can also be handled with a dedicated 3-2-1 process or similar shadow work, along with dedicated forgiveness).

Another possible result of the devaluation of spiritual or transpersonal realities caused by a widespread cultural level/line fallacy is that the denial and rejection of anything that even vaguely looks spiritual will cause many genuinely higher qualities, if and when they actually arise in oneself, to be judged negatively and projected onto the world as a negative shadow that now needs to be attacked and even destroyed "out there." Individuals of almost any spiritual stripe are thought of quite negatively; a type of "new atheistic" vehemence to anything "spiritual" springs into existence; the desire to rid oneself of any of one's "spiritual" qualities leads to a desire to rid the world of individuals who themselves seem to be spiritual. And there is usually little distinction made between genuine saints and sages, on the one hand, and simple fundamentalist absolutists who have jihad in their hearts, on the other—all of them are to be utterly rejected. This denial also tends to disrupt an individual's actual development into 3rd tier, since its "transpersonal" dimensions are equated with mythic-literal, regressive, fundamentalist silliness and sealed out of awareness, cutting off one's own growth and development into those higher dimensions as well. This is a genuine tragedy, and a tragedy quite common in today's higher-level developments, since we have so little positive, authentic, accurate interpretations of genuine transrational, transpersonal structures and states—all of them are dumped into the "childish religious" regressive garbage can and thoroughly dispensed with.

As previously discussed in some detail, when individuals manage to develop into the higher structures of 3rd tier, a very typical distress occurs as the person increasingly experiences transpersonal and transcendental qualities—"otherworldly" and "heavenly"—and wishes consequently to have done with typical "earthly" or "this-worldly" lifestyles altogether, thus wishing to leave the conventional world almost entirely (and take up, say, a cloistered life, literally or figuratively). This can be fine if it is based on a genuine desire to withdraw into a retreat situation for periods of concentrated growth and development, but it is quite another situation when it is due to an *inner fracture* between higher/spiritual realms and lower/earthly realms in the individual, a failure of integration that leads only and ultimately to horribly shattered dreams. Sadly, some people take years, even decades, to make this discovery of the lack of interior integration of their spiritual and earthly qualities. This can be headed off by careful attention to development itself (in structures and states), to making sure that both the "transcend" and the "include" part are given equal and adequate attention, resulting in a balanced and more harmonious transpersonal development (and this can be initiated, and guided, with a correct "Right View").

This inner fracture can parallel a common interior splitting of emotional and feeling states into, on the one hand, transpersonal/spiritual ones, which are felt to be "all good," wonderful, and exhilarating, and conventional/normal states, which are felt to be increasingly dull, negative, "all bad," boring, or even evil and demonic. If and when this happens, the individual is particularly open to substance abuse (that is, put plainly, drug addiction; I'll return to this possibility in just a moment). Also, this interior splitting process often reactivates earlier, similar dissociative problems (such as magenta Fulcrum-2 *splitting* or red Fulcrum-3 *repression*) and re-creates lower-level shadow material. This inner splitting is also headed off by a similarly careful attention to both the "transcend" and "include" components of Growing Up through the higher transpersonal structure-stages, especially as states (and Waking Up) are added to the mixture. This, again, is almost always a simple matter of the framework (and genuinely "Right View") in which one holds the structures and states and their many dimensions, with anything less than a truly Integral Framework being problematic and dysfunction inviting. The less-than-Integral or less-than-Inclusive maps open the door to interior splitting, dissociation, and dis-owning, because these much-less-than-adequate maps of the interiors leave out important aspects and dimensions, in particular, their seamless integration. In other words, these maps leave out a good deal of the real territory of being-in-the-world on the whole. Developing a "Right View"—a genuinely Integral, or Inclusive, Framework—is a core component of addressing these malfunctions.

In these cases, the common 3rd-tier dysfunction has to do with integrating spiritual (or transcendental) and material (or immanent) realms in general. (This, too, is often due to an inadequate "Right View" or less-than-Inclusive map of all the realms actually present in all individuals.) The spiritual realms of light, love, and blissful joy increasingly drift away from the ordinary realms of lackluster, conventional, increasingly "boring" events, which come to possess less and less meaning and value. Integrating the infinite and finite components of a human being—its Emptiness and Form aspects—is a crucial task of development in 3rd tier (involving both structures and states), and failure to do so is not uncommon.

As for drugs, in many ways they are made to order for killing the pain and massive discomfort of this interior splitting, as well as for artificially inducing "heavenly" feeling states that in some ways mimic the actual neurotransmitter profile of higher structures and states. With drugs (or misused prescription medication), one can—through manipulating the Upper Right brain to release huge amounts of neurotransmitters such as dopamine or serotonin—artificially put the

Upper Right brain in a state that tetra-arouses Upper Left consciousness to feel "totally good," "blissed out," "on top of the world," "never coming down." And for months, the individual can have a relatively decent chance of manipulating consciousness by manipulating the brain. As the lead character in *Drugstore Cowboy* puts it, "Most people don't know how they are going to feel moment to moment. A junkie always knows—all he has to do is read the label." And by reading the label, the substance abuser can maneuver his or her states of consciousness into almost always being in "heavenly" states—and that is exactly what they are, states of genuinely transcendental bliss, peace, joy, ecstasy, wild enthusiasm (from "en-theos" = "a god within"), frenzied elation. Eventually—a sad story, the ending of which everybody knows, including the addict—the nerve receptors become less and less sensitive to the drug, higher and higher doses are needed, the addict's life starts to become organized largely around, and then solely around, getting more drugs, and the poor soul ends up in one of only three ways: dead, in prison, or in rehab.

Rehab has a rather poor reputation—other than as a great place to meet celebrities—based on a rather sad set of facts: even the most successful of them claim not much more than a genuine rehabilitation rate of 25 percent, many much less. One of the problems with rehab the way it is usually conducted is that it is, well, considerably less than Integral. But recently, several Integral approaches to rehab have been initiated, and so far, they have had rather astonishing successes.[2] One of the things that the Integral approaches all do—in addition to addressing quadrants, levels, lines, and types—is pay strong attention to states, particularly meditative states, and through the use of either brain/mind machines or actual meditation or both, they teach the addict that higher, deeply peaceful, even blissful states are still possible, but through perfectly natural means, not artificially induced. For most addicts, the hardest part of surrendering drugs is realizing that they will never again feel as good, as "high," as they did on drugs—but that is not totally true, as they discover with these meditative states. So the old joke: A person asks another if he drinks, and he says "No." The first responds, "You mean, when you get up in the morning, that's the best you're going to feel all day?" The answer is no longer "Yes." This is a large part of these approaches' success.

Spiritual Bypassing

A typical side effect—or sometimes a direct cause—of various types of interior splitting is "spiritual bypassing," where ordinary, common, mundane problems are glorified by giving them a deeply spiritual meaning, which is supposed to show how evolved this person is (instead of how shadow swamped). Typical spiritual bypassing (which can happen at 1st- or 2nd- or 3rd-tier structures as well as higher states) can take many forms, such as interpreting an incapacity for deep emotional connection as being an example of a highly transcendental accomplishment—a spiritual "nonattachment"—instead of the broken "detachment" it really is. Or spending hours a day on spiritual practice when it is due not to a genuine push of healthy Eros (which it might be) but instead to a push of pathological Eros—that is, Phobos, a fear and running away from life, not its transcendence and inclusion. Or seeing an overly emotional "touchy-feely" connection with everybody as an example of loving Agape (which it might be), when it is actually a broken communion drive, a severe neediness, a meltdown, or fusion, with everybody, not their loving inclusion. Or a reliance on "feelings" and always "coming from the heart" and a concomitant exclusion of all "intellectual" elements as a drive toward nonconceptual awareness, gnosis, or prajna, which it might be, but it might also actually involve a "pre/trans fallacy," a regression to *pre*-rational states and stages and immediate feelings because those are confused with *trans*-rational states and stages. Note that the prerational states are also narcissistic and egocentric, often a tip-off to what is actually going on. Is this person becoming more self-involved (prerational) or less self-involved (transrational)? Does he or she use the word "I" *more* or *less*? And given the anti-intellectualism that is rampant in spiritual circles, that is a very common spiritual-bypassing dysfunction. Or viewing a refusal to make any negative judgments about anybody or anything as being the practice of all-embracing Love, which it could be, but it also might be an extreme addiction to the Pluralistic green stage and its antimarginalizing and "no ranking" drives (itself a confusion between growth hierarchies and dominator hierarchies). Or seeing a desire to have multiple sexual partners as being a deep spiritual nonattachment and nongrasping to sexuality (which it—very rarely—might be), instead of recognizing it as sexual addiction and sexual profligacy and immediate impulse gratification. Or seeing a failure to achieve excellence in any attempted activity as being a complete transcendence of self-promotion (which it might be), instead of its being a lack of genuine effort to achieve—a laziness, a commitment inadequacy. Or viewing paying no attention to outcomes in any activity one undertakes as being a deep practice of karma yoga (where one performs actions without thought of results—which it might be), instead of its being a simple inability to finish anything one has ever started. Or interpreting the deep feelings of emptiness and aloneness one feels as being the practice of Emptiness (which it might be), instead of its being a fairly serious borderline condition that experiences all of life as a barren hollowness. Or seeing an avoidance of all aggression whatsoever as being the practice of nonreactive awareness (which it might be), instead of its being a deeply confused notion that aggression itself is antispiritual. (*Aggression* is derived from the French for "to move toward," whereas *hostility* means "a deep-seated ill will toward something" and is reactive. Earlier I gave the example of a stag moving toward a salt lick, and finding a pile of bramble bushes blocking its way, its nostrils flare, it lowers its head and charges the pile, clearing a way. That is healthy, normal "aggression," the natural and healthy purpose of which is to overcome obstacles and barriers—the stag isn't "mad" at the bramble bush or angry and hostile toward it; this confusion of aggression and hostility is common in spiritual circles and simply blocks healthy attempts to remove obstacles.)

These are just a few examples of "spiritual bypassing," of the ways that ordinary, everyday problems can be rationalized as deeply spiritual virtues instead of the mundane dysfunctions they actually are. The cure, again, in most cases involves some sort of shadow work (a 3-2-1 process or some authentic shadow therapy).

The therapeutic shadow issues of 3rd-tier Super-Integral Views are definitely difficult issues to handle, especially in this culture, where spirituality is equated almost entirely with accepting a grand mythic narrative of a particular superman, whose extraordinary capacities and powers we can never actually attain (since he is the one and only Son of God anywhere in existence), but whose actions we are nevertheless supposed to copy and emulate, and compared to whom we are ultimately judged (guess how that comes off?). Even in spiritual systems that have a decent access to state development, they are almost always divorced from any understanding of structure-rungs of consciousness and their Views and development (the stages of Growing Up), and thus possess little if any understanding of the "hidden maps" governing people's lives or the shadow issues that can develop. Given also this culture's anemic understanding of higher, transpersonal, 3rd-tier structures (and transcendental states), finding a therapist that is aware of both conventional and transpersonal shadow issues is well nigh impossible. All one can do, until cultural understanding evolves further and starts to remedy this situation, is search the Internet for therapists or groups that seem genuinely alive to these issues and "spiritual emergencies" in an adequate fashion, and avail oneself of the good help available therein.

Next, I will provide some details about some common dysfunctions of the individual 3rd-tier stages themselves.

Indigo Para-Mind

One of the especially defining qualities of indigo para-mind (Fulcrum-9) is its understanding, in a concrete and palpable fashion, that the world is not merely physical but psychophysical. This means, in its broadest sense, that every Right-hand, exterior, "material" form or component has a Left-hand, interior, prehension or "consciousness" component. This manifests in any number of ways: that what arises moment to moment is dependent on the theories and ideas that I hold about reality; that what I "perceive" is deeply interwoven with what I "conceive"; that as it arises moment to moment, reality is actually a great unknowable mystery, and only as I label and conceptualize it does it take a definite form; that there is a mutual feeling interaction of the subject and the object—that is, of the subject feeling the object feeling the subject; the sense that every thing and event that is presently arising is directly arising in the field of my awareness and exists as part of that field; that while I am looking at objects, objects are looking back at me. Any one of these or dozens of other ways begin to break down the dichotomy and barrier between knowing subject and known object, since they are just like the north and south poles of a magnet—two end points of an underlying single reality of a Whole field. This is basically the level where the sky starts turning into a big blue pancake and begins falling toward your headless state (a fall completed in either the nondual state or the supermind structure).

And this is true "all the way down." Thus, when only atoms were in existence, they were still arising in each other's field of prehension. Each atom created a clearing, or opening, in which other atoms could manifest, and thus creation was a co-creation, a co-enaction, with each atom's subjective prehension existing in an intersubjective prehensive field—each atom mutually created a space or clearing in which the other atoms could arise. This subsisting "mutual creation" or "co-enaction" becomes a directly felt reality starting in 3rd tier.

There are numerous dysfunctions that can arise in regard to this psychophysical awareness. One is that there is an urgent drive to interpret the world in deeply unified holistic ways, even if they are reductionistic. Thus, interpreting the Kosmos as being one unified material substance is common at this level in our scientific culture. This "pan-materialism" (which is just an "all-Right-hand" quadrant world without any Left-hand qualities) seems to fit the unified feelings that a psychophysical awareness brings. Almost as common is a "pan-idealism"; the whole world is a single unified consciousness (without any Right-hand exteriors, just Left-hand interiors). Both of these fractured ideas are best handled with "Right View."

On the other hand, if indigo para-mind has any significant fixations left at 2nd tier, it will tend to hold on to this "unified system" as a mere idea (which is what happens at 2nd tier), and thus will not be able to clearly or fully switch into a *direct feeling* of this "unified system." Its head is in the right place, but its heart isn't quite there. "Unified psychophysical reality"—verging on a genuine Nature mysticism—remains a strong intellectual belief but not a direct conscious awareness (which is otherwise quite common at para-mind). And this particular splitting produces very noticeable sensations of what can only be described as feeling somewhat "odd" or "strange" or "not quite right"— one is thinking about all this unity but not really feeling it, so one's thoughts don't actually match reality. Something seems definitely wrong, but it's hard to place exactly, since what I'm thinking seems to be true (and it is, intellectually; it's just not translating into direct feelings, and so something is indeed "wrong").

This fixation to 2nd-tier perspectives is often due to difficulties in accepting the true death of the individual, personal self, a death that is faced when one moves into increasingly transpersonal 3ʳᵈ-tier stages. I just can't quite imagine myself in a tomorrow where I don't exist. I can't *see* that tomorrow. (And indeed the person can't, because the actual Seer, or Witness, doing the seeing is always ever present; the I-I will never die, it will just finally be seen as interwoven with nondual Suchness, and therefore I AMness can never coherently imagine a future where it is not.) But this simply highlights why it is important to have a healthy, fully functioning, highly developed, conventional or finite self (the "I") in place as a healthy vehicle through which the Witness or transpersonal Self (the "I-I") looks and communicates. The Witness itself is Empty, unqualifiable; and unless absorbed in a formless state, it is always conjoined with a finite, manifest, relative self-sense through which it will see the world that it itself creates, and through which it will communicate with that finite world. Starting with higher structures such as 3ʳᵈ tier and higher states such as causal (or earlier, if a path of Waking Up is adopted), it is important to begin to let go of the exclusive identity with that personal, conventional, finite self, and increasingly switch it to being one with the True Self and pure Suchness (while transcending and including the relative, finite self as a vehicle for the True Self). Remaining attached to 2ⁿᵈ tier (and certainly 1ˢᵗ tier) makes that switch in identity close to impossible.

Thus, in regard to this issue, the point for any individual is twofold: (1) to correct that fundamental case of mistaken identity, where one's True Self or Witness is *confused* and *identified* with the small separate-self sense, or where "I-I" is confused and identified with "I" and (2) to make sure that the small, relative, finite self or "I" is as fully functioning and as highly developed (in terms of altitude) as it can be, so the True Self or "I-I" has an increasingly larger, wider, higher structure through which to view its world and a healthy vehicle through which to communicate with the conventional world. Having a broken, false, inauthentic, conventional self *through which* the True Self is forced to speak is a disastrous situation. To enhance this always-occurring unified complex of "infinite True Self/finite relative self" is the entire rationale behind including Growing Up and Cleaning Up with Waking Up (where Growing Up and Cleaning Up relate to the finite relative self—making it as accurate and complete as possible as a vehicle for the

True Self to communicate with the conventional world—and Waking Up relates to actually putting one in touch with that infinite True Self and Suchness).

The 2nd-tier self is often called "centaur," after the mythic being where human and animal—mind and body—are a unified whole. As John Broughton's research discovered, at this Integral stage, "Mind and body are both experiences of an integrated self"—the centaur (teal and turquoise).[3] But having served its purpose, the centaur needs to step aside and make room for even wider, larger, higher, finite selves. Failing to let go of the centaur thus infects the indigo level with a 2nd-tier fixation, and this disrupts the field of awareness itself at this new level, producing, among other things, this "splitting" between thinking of the world as Whole and directly experiencing it as such.

What is required in these situations is a direct mindfulness practice on the centauric self-sense itself. That is, the individual directs pure open awareness to a feeling of his or her separate-self sense as it is arising moment to moment (a self that we are assuming, in this case, is centauric; but this practice works—and is recommended—for the separate self at any level, as a way to help make that subject object). Simply become aware of your self. Videotape it. That simple practice of directly being aware of (in this case) the centauric self converts that subject into an object, and thus transcends it, lets go of it, looks *at it* and no longer *through it*. Releasing awareness from its fixated attachment to 2nd tier allows awareness to jump almost immediately into an expansion with the entire psychophysical wholeness, in any of its forms of intensity (from communion to union to identity). Vision-logic is included as an operand of indigo vision, and healthy growth and development can continue.

Existing in relation with the "community of all being," another capacity that tends to come online at indigo, can also skew the person in dysfunctional ways. With 3rd tier, as I have often noted, evolutionary "transcend and include" has occurred so often and with such depth and richness that an almost constant "awareness of awareness" emerges at 3rd-tier stages. This presents the individual at indigo with a fundamental choice: to identify more with the increasingly obvious Witnessing awareness (the "awareness of awareness" itself) or more with the increasingly unified field of objects of awareness (including the community of all being)—more with the Subject (the awareness of awareness) or more with the Object (a unified Field that now contains the community of all being).

Of course, the ideal is to include both; but extremes either way are possible and are the stuff of indigo pathology. Identifying with the Subject, with the Awareness of awareness, when extreme, amounts to a dissociation with the manifest realm itself, and certainly with its community of all being. Both the horizontal autonomy drive and vertical Eros drive go pathological, and the individual ends up as an isolated, unfeeling, unmoving Subject of awareness (however experienced—as an immovable I AMness, a rigid but open clearing or empty field, or a "no-self" awareness); in any event it is fairly depersonalized rather than transpersonalized.

On the other hand, the individual can swing in the opposite direction and find not merely a communion/union/identity with the community of all being but a fusion, a meltdown, a collapse into it. Both one's horizontal communion drive and one's vertical Agape drive go pathological, and one loses one's Unique Awareness of awareness in a faceless, unending, overwhelming community of all things, events, beings, and phenomena, cascading wildly over each other, invading awareness with a jagged little pill of multiple "relatives," all "totally loved and embraced" in an unending horror-story family holiday. One of the few treatments that works, in either case, is an aggressive "Right View" reeducation process, focusing especially on a 4-quadrant felt-awareness training: feel your "I" (or "I-I") space; feel your various "we" spaces; feel the objective "it" space of material objects; feel the "systems"—feel the *relationships*—in your "its" awareness (for example, this table is part of all the furniture objects in my apartment; my apartment is part of all the apartments in my building; my building is part of all the buildings in this city; this city is part of all towns and cities in this state; this state is part of all states in this nation; this nation is part of all nations on this planet; this planet is part of all planets in this solar system; this solar system is part of all solar systems in this galaxy; this galaxy is part of all intergalactic systems in this universe).

In general, the problems that can develop at indigo para-mind have to do with its being the first major stage where actual transpersonal dimensions are included with personal dimensions in an individual's awareness and identity—and not just as a notion, idea, philosophy, peak experience, or spiritual belief, but in a direct, immediate, felt manner. This is a profoundly significant shift in consciousness, and is a major reason that this is indeed the beginning of an entirely new (and higher) *tier* of consciousness, growth, and development. (And, realized or not, it is headed straight toward superhuman Supermind.)

In the works of today's "thought leaders," one of the more advanced ideas that can be found is the notion that the new physics and new biology all point to a "unified" world or a genuinely "holistic" universe. If the "unified world" of these theorists includes just exterior material fields and physical events (following a holistic version of scientific materialism), the notion is often coming from the teal holistic level. If real interiors are acknowledged and included, and a real spectrum of consciousness is recognized along with the spectrum of physical matter, the notion is often coming from the turquoise level. If the "unified world" is something that is directly felt (a real psychophysical holistic prehension), this is often an indigo para-mind insight—the idea that is *thought of* at turquoise now becomes *directly apprehended* at indigo. Thus, a common statement at turquoise is "The world is a single organism with one mind," and that type of idea becomes *directly felt* at indigo (and not merely thought or intellectualized).

It should be noted that these ideas and feelings and prehensions of a "unified integrated world" are not due merely to accepting some theory from physics, which would actually be a serious form of subtle reductionism, but are due, to the extent that they are genuinely grasped, to directly apprehending the actual territory of the reality at one of those three major levels. But in order to be a truly correct and inclusive theory matching a real psychophysical apprehension, all of the other AQAL elements up to and including indigo would have to be included, and this is virtually never done in any existing work on "new paradigms" (outside of Integral theorists).

On the other hand, by far the most common "unified field theory" (as found in new paradigm, New Age, "new physics" notions) is an extremely flatland, exterior-only version of teal reality. It maintains that every single thing and event in the world is "interwoven, entangled, intermeshed, and unified" with every other single thing and event—this is a "holographic universe." This completely overlooks the genuinely developmental and truly evolutionary aspects of the universe that are holarchical—that is, where "all of the lower is in the higher, but not all of the higher is in the lower" (for example, all of an atom is in a molecule, but not all of the molecule is in the atom). A more Integral view of the universe sees holarchical dimensions of levels of development, with each level becoming more unified not because it is the same as every other level but because it "transcends and includes" its junior levels, while all of the elements on a given level are indeed holographically interwoven—thus, networks of holographic occasions interwoven through holarchic waves. (This leaving out of levels and nested hierarchy or holarchy is often due to the strong presence of green in most of these versions of a "unified" universe. And this typical version also tends to leave out the profound shift in consciousness or modes of knowing required to grasp a genuine Unified reality—a gnosis, jnana, prajna.) They give the impression that if we just read *The Tao of Physics*, or learn about the Akashic record, we will be fully Enlightened. But if learning the "new physics" were truly the same as awakening to ultimate unity consciousness, every professional physicist alive would be Enlightened, whereas virtually none of them are. Thus, the typical "unified universe" theories represent what is probably a genuine intuition of higher-state or structure unities, but interpreted in wildly less-than-Integral ways, resulting most often in the total reduction of the unified Kosmos to nothing but the Lower Right quadrant—dynamic systems of interwoven flatland its.

Violet Meta-Mind

The violet meta-mind stage (Fulcrum-10) is the home of the "dreamlike" meta-mental visionary processes, marked by both a greater degree of "transcendence" (demonstrated in, for example, the "dreamlike visionary" nature of awareness itself, indicating its capacity to see quite beyond phenomena of merely 1st or 2nd tier) and a greater degree of "inclusion" (demonstrated in the "feeling" or "touch" tone of the awareness itself, what I refer to as "feeling-awareness," which accesses a significant, if not total, capacity to be in touch with the timeless Now, or pure Presence). As usual, something can go wrong with either of these, resulting in various types and degrees of dysfunction.

As for the transcendence side, an overblown or exaggerated attachment to this quality contributes directly to the tendency of 3rd tier in general toward "splitting"—splitting heaven and earth, and drifting toward an embrace of heaven and a rejection of earth altogether (although the opposite extreme—becoming fixated and addicted to earth—also becomes quite possible at this level; see below). Heavenly attachment at this specific stage means an exaggerated visionary awareness, pushing beyond all conventional objects or phenomena and rising into the luminosity, light, radiance, and love-bliss of ascending, Erotic currents. This can result in intense bodily feelings of ecstatic, hypersexual, suprasexual sensations (with a possible reactivation of infantile polymorphous perversity); actual absorption states of luminous radiance and blinding clarity; contact with ultraimaginative "other worlds," including imaginal contacts with "alien" beings or "masters" or "guides" of this universe; total rejection of conventional culture and virtually all one's conventional relationships, which may be connected with a drive to vocally, vehemently, and outspokenly criticize present-day culture on a wide variety of social media; withdrawn, distanced, pathologically detached "witnessing" states shorn of affects or feelings entirely; supercreative displays in awareness, including wildly novel ideas and notions in any field of endeavor (business, art, medicine, philosophy, and so forth); states of hyperpainful bodily sensations whenever one steps out of merely detached "witnessing" states; substance addictions due to attempts to self-medicate the ongoing intensity of bodily sensations when they are allowed to arise in awareness; a general attitude of "my kingdom is not of this world," and the general repercussions that come with such a fragmented view. (And all of these are due directly to dysfunctions in structure-Views, not dysfunctions in state Vantage Points; those, of course, can also be occurring here, particularly the ones correlated with high-subtle states; see chapters 12 and 13.)

On the other hand, one can become overly attached to the "earthly" side of the street, which pulls one into states of hyperimmanence, with an exaggeration on the "feeling" aspect of feeling-awareness, and a radical, intense embrace of all things earthly. But in this case, which is what makes it distinctive, this is an embrace of earth driven by a power deriving from heaven, a fairly high form of which meta-mind is directly plugged into at the violet altitude, which results in a particularly severe form of earth distortion. Although professing a profound "love" for earth, this is the love of addiction, not open-heartedness. Here one is often pulled back into a fixation at the indigo level of the gross-Nature psychophysical wholeness; one isn't "transcending and

including" earth, one is merely "including" earth. This draws the visionary meta-mental processes down and into intense interrelation-
ships with the present conventional culture and world, and often into
a self-announced (or at least self-assumed) "prophetic" stance. The
individual regards himself or herself as being a significant guide and
change agent for today's global culture, speaking out on all issues of
global concern—and from an essentially regressive indigo perspective
with a fractured visionary awareness (which means merely trying to
change present culture as a substitute gratification for also actually
transcending present culture).

Under such circumstances, the individual presents himself or herself
as being an almost omniscient, always correct "visionary" about what
world civilization needs to do in order to save itself and survive. And it
is most assured that if the world does not take this advice, and quickly,
then it is headed for serious disasters of one variety or another, depending on which specific advice the world didn't take. But with absolute authoritative thunder, this individual holds forth, especially on
virtually all sorts of social media, on every major crisis now genuinely
facing humanity, and presents a definitive analysis of the causes of the
problem—which, given his or her downplay of the "transcendental"
and "visionary" aspects of this level (which would provide truly novel
insights) and instead favoring its immanent, conventional, fixated features, these analyses are often taken from any of a number of rather
widespread, almost clichéd, postmodern views and presented in a
dressed-up form. After holding forth on these various causes, this individual then presents a series of equally conventional/postmodern "solutions," often along the lines of what is called "the new paradigm"
(which is simply a formal statement of green values and Views couched
in scientific language). The key to this type of "fractured visionary
prophecy" is that the individual presents solutions that require every
single man, woman, and child on the face of the planet to learn the
solutions that this individual presents. The person is presenting their
view of a "wisdom culture," but it will work and take effect only if
everybody agrees with it and thinks the same way. Only if the entire
planet thinks the way this person thinks will any of the solutions actually start to kick in. The utter impossibility—indeed, silliness—of having 7 to 8 billion people agree with this person's ideas if we are to save
the earth and save humanity never seems to dawn on this individual,

because his or her viewpoint is (unconsciously) infused with a truly higher and wider meta-mental awareness that has access to truly higher and wider truths, but truths that are being seen and prehended through broken, dysfunctional, and regressive processes. If you think that you have all of the world's global issues figured out, you might indeed have a bit of this dysfunction. (You can also find a great deal of this type of "prophetic" self-evaluation at many lower levels, including amber, orange, green, and 2nd tier, but nowhere are they backed with the certainty and "bigness" of truly higher 3rd-tier awareness as they are here; this gives these types of prophetic deliverances, when they come from this level, a certain "crazed" intensity and authoritative roar.) Certainly a more balanced and inclusive View (as part of "Right View") is called for here, along with practices of "neti, neti" ("not this, not that")—mindfulness of, or dis-identification with, the present self-sense and its correlative, mishmashed View. (Journaling and "Daily Entries" can be quite helpful here.)

Given its close association with the subtle state, and its own structures that have several items in common with the subtle state (such as its very "visionary" or "dreamlike" meta-mental processes), how this level interprets "subtle phenomena" becomes a significant issue. My opinion, as integrally grounded as I can make it, is that the "beings" that might appear at this level (whether due to this level's structure itself or to the infusion of an actual subtle state), and that appear to be real, separately existing beings or entities (from angelic creatures to saintly figures to taken-for-real aliens to world masters and ascended guides) are primarily archetypal forms (in the technically correct sense of causal or subtle primordial forms upon which manifest creation is based), many of which are imbued with an inherent luminosity, creativity, and vitality, and hence can take on forms that appear to be specific individual beings. But the interpretation of these luminous forms as "alien beings," "angels," "discarnate spirits," and so on, is usually a reactivation of the earliest levels of interpretation at which such "beings" become a commonly perceived phenomena (real or imagined)—namely, the Magical or the Mythic-literal. Although the Mythic View has long since been let go of, transcended, and replaced by higher Views, the enduring structure of the rule/role mind that originally gave rise to the Mythic level (when exclusively identified with) is still present and active, generally being operated on by higher rungs (such as formal operational). Hence, it can be selectively focused on, regenerating a Mythic interpretation of whatever phenomenon it apprehends (although seen through the perspective of the self's center of gravity—in this case, indigo or violet). The intensity of the luminous forms at this level (whether state or structure) can be so overwhelming—one's mind is literally flooded with the light of a thousand suns, or the radiance of a supernova exploding in one's brain—that, just as the mind will assume that there is a "real person" behind a computer that is programmed to dialogue with humans (see the movie *Her*), so the mind will tend to impute real "intentionality" and "individuality" to these luminous forms. They genuinely appear as real ontological entities.

When this happens, the individual is faced with "higher beings" that are, in effect, channeling his or her own higher Intelligence, and thus appear to have extraordinary, novel, liberating insights into a person's problems and issues. "Ascended masters" are "contacted," communicated with, and usually obeyed. "Channeling" various entities from other galactic locations is a fairly common experience with this ("channeling" is very common at lower levels; the difference here is that a truly meta-mental wisdom is being channeled, and not merely, say, one's pluralistic mind). If Christian, "angels" are experienced; if Buddhist, various high bodhisattvas and buddhas themselves; if Hindu, a whole pantheon of Vedic gods and goddesses. These are virtually all, in my opinion, archetypal (subtle/causal) primordial forms being interpreted through a Magic-Mythic lens. (It's not that Spirit in 2nd person doesn't have any real meaning here; there is indeed a sense in which the Intelligence of the Kosmos contains areas that are beyond your own self-sense, and thus can be contacted as a Great Other or wondrous Thou. In other words, the 4 quadrants are always present in the manifest world, all the way up, all the way down.) These networks of "ascended beings" are thus, in reality, the ascended aspects (meta-mental) of one's own being and awareness, being viewed Mythically and thus as ontologically real and separate individual beings. What separates this from the much more common and prevalent "channeling" or "ascended masters" of lower levels is the genuine input from meta-mental Intelligence that is being funneled through these forms. If you look at most of the "channeled" material at the much more common lower levels—usually amber or green—it is almost uniformly of a mediocre, counterculturally clichéd material—

alien masters telling us that we have to "love mother earth or face extinction," "Love one another from the heart," and so on. Is that really all that hypergenius aliens have to say to us?

On the whole, the violet meta-mind is a real transition space from largely "earth-oriented" realms to the beginning of truly "heaven-oriented" realms, and this is what especially makes this level distinctive. And "heaven" does not mean a place anywhere other than right here and right now; it is simply present reality seen through a higher-dimension lens. Just as rationality is not located in a world that is physically "higher" than sensorimotor intelligence, but is the same world seen through a higher level of development and consciousness, so real "heaven" is not some pie-in-the-sky location away from this world entirely, but is simply a deeper interior to this world itself—not above but within this world. The meta-mind is a genuine transition to being anchored in that deeper (hence "higher") within. And the whole point of evolution is that each higher dimension embraces, includes, and enfolds the previous junior dimensions (unlike states, which can exist relatively independently). Evolution is in love—in love with all of its previous productions, and always (barring pathology) lovingly enfolding them in each of its higher productions (Agape in action). The net result is a Whole World that is an intensely interwoven, inter-meshed holistic network (with holarchical interconnections), where "eternity is in love with the productions of time,"⁴ and, indeed, embraces them with a cherishing care.

The "visionary" nature of the violet meta-mind is fundamentally due to the growing perception that the entire Kosmos is indeed a co-enaction of consciousness itself, and the present given universe, as normally perceived, is merely one of hundreds or even thousands (or more) of other worlds (and this, indeed, is one interpretation of the string theory of modern physics). On the one hand (from one perspective), these are all different aspects of One World; on the other (from another perspective), they are all completely separate and different worlds altogether. Individuals often have the sense that they can "penetrate" or "step into" one or more of these other dimensions—the world is just such a wildly open, transparent, diaphanous, sheer, gossamer, filmy place that one can walk right through it and into other worlds. And the Present moment itself is often the doorway; it is not by "transcending" temporal duration entirely that one can penetrate to an alternative reality but by entering into this Present with more and more Presence. One can step deeply enough into the timeless Now to step into another dimension altogether—just step right here, and push hard.

It's easy to get lost in those worlds, which are, at bottom, simply different dimensions and perspectives of one's own (violet) consciousness (although, as noted, from another angle, they are all real, ontologically different realms because they are each genuinely co-enacted by a different perspective in consciousness). Given that this stage is the first great transition from "earthly" realms to "heavenly" realms (as a permanent structural enaction), getting lost in these "higher worlds" is indeed one of the most common dysfunctions of this level. The deeply transcendental, otherworldly, electrically visionary nature of consciousness at this altitude makes fixation to this side of the street an incredibly inviting and alluring venture. This is likely to couple with the dysfunction, discussed earlier, of standing in heaven and giving a blistering critique of life here on earth, with all the semiprophetic pomp and pomposity that comes with it.

One of the things that often happens with these specific dysfunctions is that, after making some initial discovery of a timeless Now or pure Present (either in 3rd-tier structures or higher states), one can step into that Present and then step right through it into what seem to be endless, "deeper," "higher" realms altogether, a kaleidoscopic cascade of universes upon universes that at one point seem to be nothing but a slight wiggle in this moment's timeless Now, and then at the next explode into almost infinitely extending real realms that are all alive and invite exploration—with a sign on the door that says "Welcome to Heaven!" This is extremely common in high subtle and low causal states, but if it happens with structures, it tends to happen right here, with the violet meta-mind (due largely to its visionary nature).

In short, getting "lost in heaven" is the most common dysfunction of this level. As a dysfunction, it is—in terms of simple numbers— much more common as a result of a malformation in high subtle or causal states (given that subtle and causal states are much more common than this high altitude, and most states, and their dysfunctions, can be experienced at almost any structure-stage). But this problem is simply the living result of the enactive nature of the real world and the fact that consciousness can co-create an almost endless number of universes, any number of which one can become fixated or semiad-dicted to, with straightforwardly dysfunctional results.

Ultraviolet Overmind

The Overmind (ultraviolet, Fulcrum-11) is, as we saw in our previous discussions, something of a profound juncture, an interface between the Supermind (and its utterly Total Embrace of All That Is) and all the lower levels or structures, each of which is marked by, in its own way, being *less* than All That Is. This is therefore an extremely important interface. It is the juncture likewise between "ultimate truth" (in turi-yatita and in Supermind) and "relative truth" (in virtually all lower structures and states, except when blessed with a turiyatita peak expe-rience). It is the final juncture between an ultimate heaven and any remnants of a real earth (prior to their final union in Supermind). And it is a primary juncture between evolution reaching up (or Eros) and involution reaching down (or Agape). The Overmind can thus vibrate between an utter Simplicity (of consummate Wholeness) and a some-what confusing Complexity (with all these cross-currents running through its veins).

The essential "feeling" of this ultraviolet Overmind level is that of a warm, loving Witness (or pure caring I AMness). So try it: go ahead and rest in the pure Observing Self right now ("I am not this; I am not that; I am the pure open Observing Self"), combined with a feeling that what is being witnessed is the entire Kosmos—for which, simply picture all of the objects arising in your awareness right now as being parts of one large and inseparable Painting of All That Is. Everything that is arising in your field of awareness right now—the good and bad, the big and small, the inside and outside, the light and dark, the ani-mate and inanimate, the pleasurable and the painful, the hot and the cold—all of it, every single thing and event, with absolutely nothing left out—all of that is just one huge Painting of All That Is, and that is what you are aware of right now. You are not (yet) one with this Paint-ing (unless you have a state experience of turiyatita or unity conscious-ness); rather, you are its Witness, but a Witness that is in love with the entire Painting itself. As you picture every single thing and event aris-ing in your awareness as being an intrinsic aspect of this one, whole, indivisible Painting of All That Is, arising moment to moment in your field of awareness, allow your Heart Space to open, and imagine this entire Painting flooded—just literally flooded—with a warm, glowing, vibrant Love for this entire Painting. Nothing in this Painting is left out as unloved—not a single thing or event in your awareness is judged negatively, not included, or viewed harshly—but rather your Heart reaches out and puts its arms around this entire Total Painting, loving it with every ounce of energy it has.

One more step (and this is the slightly hard part, but it will move your awareness from a mere state experience closer to a structure experience of Overmind). Imagine that this Total Painting is like the cut-up frames of the film that we placed on top of each other and then witnessed as if each of the frames could be seen separately, as well as being part of the whole film. Imagine that each and every object in this Painting is actually a series of many individual paintings, each of which is a frame from a different time in the object's overall history, going all the way back to its beginning, and then unfolding all the way forward, through a series of smaller paintings, from the Big Bang up to today's Total Painting (or holons within holons within holons . . .). Each thing you are aware of has a history. In any way that you wish, simply picture that history lying immediately behind (and "one with") every thing in the Total Painting (lying just "behind" but also "within" the Painting as a whole).

The point is to simply imagine that each object in this Painting, arising right in front of you, has "behind" it earlier versions of itself, so that the Painting as a whole will go all the way back to the Big Bang (and imagine the Painting right after the Big Bang—nothing but zillions of quarks and atoms falling all over each other), and then, as evolution proceeds, the Painting becomes more and more complex but still whole, as novel entities are added to subsequent Paintings; molecules emerge and are added, cells emerge and are added, organisms emerge and are added, and so on. So generally, all you really need to do is imagine that the Painting arising in front of you right now goes all the way back to the Big Bang and that this Total Painting is not just the flat surface that it initially appears to be but actually has, behind it, an extraordinary developmental/evolutionary *depth* going all the way back to the beginning of this universe. Just see the Painting as it is arising now—the Total Field of Everything in your awareness right now—and then imagine behind it a single black point, and then imagine hundreds of Paintings behind this present one, becoming simpler and simpler, going all the way back to this black point, the Big Bang out of which they all ultimately issue.

So, your Observing Self is witnessing a single, indivisible, whole Painting of All That Is arising right now in your awareness (which includes absolutely *everything* arising in your awareness), and the Painting itself reaches all the way back to a black point of the Big Bang, some 14 billion years ago. Put all of these together—including your own developmental history—and welcome to a brief glimpse of your Overmind.

An individual at the Overmind can end up emphasizing any or all of these various aspects, and different types of dysfunction can center on each. If the Observing Self (especially conjoined with the causal/Empty Witness) is overly emphasized, there is the ever-constant possibility, already discussed in connection with the previous stage of meta-mind, of 3rd tier getting caught in various types of "splitting" (splitting of 3rd-tier "heaven" from earlier "earth" realms and tending to emphasize the ascending, Erotic components of a heavenly gaze). But this tendency to heavenly splitting is even more severe with ultraviolet Overmind than with violet meta-mind, because there is more of both "transcending" and "including," and hence a possibility for greater fixation to either. Vertical splitting in meta-mind tends to fixate on the "transcendental" and "visionary" aspects of the meta-mind, pulling into higher Forms of its own consciousness. Vertical splitting in Overmind tends to pull in even further into the completely "formless" dimension of consciousness (especially when conjoined with Emptiness/Witnessing). The "awareness of awareness" tends to focus on Awareness itself. Consciousness without an Object tends to vibrate with its own intentionality. The inherent bliss-thrill, titillating vibratory exaltation, and gorgeously infinite stretches of Consciousness as Such become their own objects, and the subject–object dichotomy is temporarily overcome with a consciousness/bliss monism; I become the infinite joy I feel. This makes virtually any conventional interaction completely lifeless, dull, boring, even irritating, as a "kingdom not of this world" is fully embedded in one's awareness, which wishes never to return.

But, in general, return it does, unless a severe dysfunction requiring treatment occurs. If so, the fundamental treatment includes, as do so many 3rd-tier pathologies, a corrective "Right View" that emphasizes the integral and nondual nature of Reality, both relative and ultimate, combined with turiyatita practices, or "headless" unity practice emphasizing the unity of both heaven and earth, and any Cleaning Up to help remove whatever shadow elements might be present in the earth realms and causing allergic reactions. This abandonment to another world often self-corrects at ultraviolet because of the sheer weight of the number of structures that are the "include" part of this level's "transcend and include." Outside of Supermind, Overmind has the fullest of the fullest Form in the entire Kosmos (literally); included in its inherent *structure* are structures going all the way back to the Big Bang (as does our Total Painting!). The sheer weight, the sheer gravitas, of these structure-rungs acts like "shackles" wrapped around the ankles of Overmind, pulling it back to earth.

This, of course, is one of the real strengths of the Overmind—its being plugged into every major level and dimension in existence, all the way back to the origins of this universe. It is this near-omniscient awareness and knowledge that makes Overmind the ultimate Big Data crunching, Big Data loving knowledge machine that it is. The state that is often conjoined with Overmind is the causal/Witness (True Self or I AMness), and as a state, I AMness often rests in pure silence and simply watches the world arise without comment, judgment, or attribution. If it thinks about the world that is arising, it does so using whatever structure that happens to be present with this state (which can be, as we've seen, virtually any structure-rung in the entire spectrum). But the Overmind is I AMness PLUS every structure going back to the Big Bang—it is, in its most common condition, constantly processing the information coming in from every level of existence all the way up to its own. This is why it's the Big Data loving, Big Data crunching machine that I mentioned. And whether this is a consciously engaged knowledge processing, or simply an intuitively felt prehension/love of the Total Picture of All That Is, it is Kosmically universal in its sweep.

Just like seeing every item in awareness as part of a single, huge, indivisible Total Painting (all the way back to the Big Bang), Overmind sees the entire Kosmos in all its possible depth (covering its entire history), with a prehending tenderness for each and every depth it reaches out and embraces. Overmind, in its intrinsic healthy nature, is helplessly, hopelessly, in love with the entire World. Its Heart Space is an opening, or clearing, in which the entire World, the entire Kosmos, is arising moment to moment, and Overmind tastes each and every phenomena in it with a delicious and contagious enthusiasm. When around people in whom Overmind has emerged, you feel a sudden, electric jolt of radical clarity; deep understanding seems to permeate every fiber of awareness, with all things included in this clarifying jolt. Rays of sunlike clarity radiate from deep within them to everything around them. Right behind that follows an influx of the intense Love that is actually behind this Witnessing Clarity, so that first your Head, then your Heart, seems to expansively respond.

When either the empty Observing Self (Subject) or the complex unified single Picture (Object) becomes especially focused on, the result is not necessarily a dysfunction, as we have been discussing them thus far. Either one, when not extreme and not dissociated from its complementary component, can become the basis of a type of "mystical" involvement (along the standard continuum of communion to union to identity). When the Subject component is highlighted, this results in various types of "formless mysticism" (especially when conjoined with the Empty Witness). This allows the Erotic component of evolution to come to the fore, and Eroticized awareness entertains the "being/consciousness/bliss" aspect of the manifest Divine. (With this emphasis, the Big Data crunching nature of this structure often leads to a Simple and Silent Presence, fully in the timeless Now, effortlessly and spontaneously floating prior to time.)

When the Object component is highlighted, this results in what I called "superabundance" mysticism, "overflow" mysticism, or "spontaneous Presence" mysticism. The textures of the entire Painting are embraced with an almost infinite Love and Loving-Kindness, and a Presence to the Present of the entire World comes strongly to the fore. Both of these are due to the inherent characteristics of the Overmental structure itself, and are not just an importation of state experience (although that is always a possibility, too).

The very complexity of this ultraviolet level—embracing as it does everything from the near-ultimate Real Self to the mutually interwoven Painting of the entire Kosmos (and its evolutionary depth all the way back)—along with its being the interface between the infinite and finite can sometimes cause problems. The individual at this stage can sometimes succumb to this complexity with a genuine confusion, a lack of Wholeness (and an inability to "witness Wholes"—that is, Observe the entire Painting, Whole after Whole after Whole, which, as we've seen, is the standard form of Wholeness experienced at this level). This results in various degrees of bewilderment, perplexity, puzzlement, and even turmoil, upheaval, and disorder. Part of the real problem is that this structure-level is so far beyond the typical center of gravity of the vast majority of human beings—and beyond the center of gravity of any major culture anywhere on the planet—that its Lower Left quadrant is virtually deserted (though it continues to house Divine Other/Divine We awareness). But among human culture, there are almost no real others in this space; there is no language or jargon anywhere that can signify the typical referents here (there's literally no widespread or commonly understood way to talk about this); the individual has the sense that he or she is making this all up (even though a deeper place knows that this is the closest thing to ultimate reality that he or she has ever experienced—which just makes the confusion all the worse). "It's lonely at the top" has never applied to anyone as much as it applies to those at 3rd tier (and particularly its own higher levels, Overmind and Supermind). It would be a different story entirely were experiences of this level even a little more common, so that there were at least some microcultures that had started to form and share their insights and understanding of this level of reality, and begun creating a semiotics so that humans could discuss what was happening—along with creating various maps and metatheories to help identify and signify all of the components of this otherwise overwhelming complexity. But barring that, "you're on your own" is another truism that is especially true for this level of development.

I've noted the vast complexity (and ultimate Simplicity) of this level, and some sort of dysfunction can beset virtually any of those aspects. All of the previous, lower levels are experienced as "earthly" (or a realm of Form), and the next higher (and ultimate to date) level is experienced as "heavenly" (or transcendental and Empty/Open). As usual, one can be addicted or allergic to either (creating a repressed emergent or a repressed submergent unconscious). The most common dysfunctions, in this uncommon structure, are allergic (submergent) earthly and fixated/addicted (submergent) earthly. (Problems with the emergent structure—which is Supermind—are much rarer given the rarity of Supermind itself.)

"Allergic earthly" is in some ways similar to "fixated heavenly" (although the specific dynamics differ, and the latter, as noted, is much rarer, involving the much rarer Supermind). With allergic earthly, the realm of Form itself is experienced as toxic, since one is generally recoiling from all structures, up to and including meta-mind. One is contracting away from, avoiding, or repressing the submergent, previous structure-stage realms. One's awareness tends toward Emptiness, or Consciousness without an Object (or the turiya state), and the entire realm of Form becomes an irritation, an inflammation, a suffering-inducing ongoing nightmare. This makes both the emergence of the Supermind-structure and the state-experience of nondual unity consciousness virtually impossible, due to its deeply dualistic nature. One denies one's own roots in the earth, and the feeling dimension of awareness itself becomes compromised. The Open, Empty nature of Consciousness itself becomes a constant attraction, and the Formless realm becomes a luxurious bath of relief (except that the repression of the lower spheres is causing a constant inflamed undercurrent). The infinite and earth-free (object-free) nature of Consciousness is totally embraced and endowed with a sense of ultimate and only Reality itself (overlooking the deeply dualistic nature of this condition). The circulation of subtle energy from Light (above) to Life (below) is badly disturbed and often contracted and enormously reduced, which can also lead to a large number of physical ailments. With even the visionary nature of meta-mind reduced or repressed, Consciousness contracts to a type of "numbed timeless Now" moment, a high-altitude version of the "passing present," which doesn't embrace all time as much as deny it. The loving nature of Witnessing Awareness is itself reduced, sometimes almost entirely, with the result being indeed a numbed Awareness of the Total Painting of All That Is, rather like having a generic frostbite to one's general sense of all Being.

Much the opposite, of course, occurs with "fixated/addicted earthly" —the attachment of Consciousness to the previous meta-mind structure and a resultant attachment to the entire realm of Form. Aspects of Witnessing Awareness (or Absolute Subjectivity) become infected with various objects; pure Witnessing Awareness itself is infested with the visionary mind of the previous violet meta-mind stage, which is the "addictive" aspect of this dysfunction. This produces a sense of, while Witnessing, actually being a subjective center of Awareness and not the pure Emptiness or Openness that actually is the real Witness (this "subjective center" is the aspect of the visionary meta-mind to which one is attached—a failure of the "transcend" aspect of developmental "transcend and include"). One remains developmentally fixated to the pleasures of the visionary meta-mind, with a sense of temporal ever-lastingness instead of actual timelessness. This has the effect of blocking the even greater Joy/Happiness of the Overmind itself.

White Supermind

What makes Supermind such an extraordinary development is that it is, basically, at the leading edge of evolution itself—*as* evolution itself—although in regions so far beyond where the average individual is today that the only thing that keeps it held up at that height is the platform prop of the inherent perspectival differences in each level of consciousness, and the fact that at least four levels—indigo, violet, ultraviolet, white—have emerged in 3rd tier, in however an ephemeral and diaphanous fashion, so that the repetition of four consecutive "transcend and includes" has left at least four higher stations (or levels) floating as gossamer possibilities beyond the most solid leading edge now available (namely, turquoise, which has around 1 percent of the worldwide population; 3rd tier in general has less than one tenth of that, *if* that).

But as the leading edge of evolution itself (uniting both the highest structure and the highest state in an ongoing, unfolding manner—fully bringing together Growing Up and Waking Up for the first time in all of Kosmic history), the Supermind is an embodiment and epitome of the outrageous miracle that evolution itself is: the single, greatest, all-pervading, driving force (Eros, Spirit-in-action) running throughout the universe in literally all domains; the one imprint that no existing phenomenon anywhere in the universe does not feel; the bright Brilliance of the nondual union of the ultimate, infinite Divine Reality with its everyday, ordinary, finite operations; the intersection of the unimaginably creative *involutionary* currents (creating Something out of Nothing) and the equally creative *evolutionary* drives (creating Something out of Everything), each serving the other in the most intimate of ways; the radical nonduality of an Absolute Truth in desperate love with the productions of Relative Truth, which themselves are in helpless adoration of their Lover; the very mechanism where, in a sense, the entire Kosmos reaches down (Agape) and pushes up (Eros) in the creation and manifestation of each and every single new entity and event; the Kosmic Address where can be found the perfect intersection of the Mind of God and the mind of Humanity as they become perfectly indistinguishable; and the cutting, biting, leading edge of an unfolding Humanity on the verge of moving into its own Superhumanity, a trans-transhuman superfuture in which an entirely new era in the history of the Kosmos begins unfolding, in which the two fundamental dimensions of Reality disclosed thus far—Absolute and Relative—come into a nondual binding junction that will henceforth be the always present, all-pervading, common unity-ground of each and every thing unfolding during that subsequent era (and hence allowing a new dimension, a new Ground, of all previous Grounds to come into actuality, and hence an entirely new and profound and even Greater Liberation).

In the meantime, there lies the gorgeous glory of the Supermind. As the union of the highest state and the highest structure, it is the place that, not alone but in particular, state phenomena enter the stream of the evolution of structures. And structures, with their "transcending and including" Eros, are how the Kosmos binds together all that it has produced and manifested. For example, the human holon, as I have often pointed out, transcends and includes all the major structures since the Big Bang—quarks to atoms to molecules to cells to plants to fish to amphibians to reptiles to mammals to primates, and from there, infrared to magenta to red to amber to orange to green to teal to turquoise to indigo to violet to ultraviolet to this, the white clear light altitude that is Supermind. Without the transcending and including action of evolution, all of them would be disconnected, segregated, randomly wandering, and inchoate isolated elements, knowing each other only in the random accidental collision. But in addition to all the 1st- and 2nd-tier unifications, beginning with 3rd tier, all states of consciousness are conjoined with particular structures of consciousness, allowing evolution's own "transcend and include" to pull them together into a genuinely Whole, holonic, and holarchic deep embrace. The two fundamental streams of human growth and evolution—structure development and state development—now become not just always simultaneously interacting but simultaneously conjoined and united into a single stream.

Thus, when the Supermind comes consciously online, it becomes, along with a conjoined nondual or turiyatita state, the starting source of involution itself in this individual, and as involution moves (in states) from nondual to witnessing to causal to subtle to gross, it simultaneously moves (in basic structures) from white to ultraviolet to violet to indigo to turquoise to teal to green to orange to amber to red to magenta to infrared, which then completes itself by moving downward through all the prehuman levels in that individual human being, paleomammalian to reptilian to fish to cells to molecules to atoms to quarks—that is, the specific structures that are presently enfolded in this particular individual—its paleomammalian limbic system, its reptilian brain stem, its organic Kreb's cycle, its cells, its molecules, atoms, and so forth. The reversing, Refluxing, evolutionary unfolding likewise starts at the bottom of both these chains and moves its impulses all the way to the top, to Supermind and the nondual state. And at any point along these two movements (upward or downward, in structures and states), any malformations, sticking points, or pathological knots will be regenerated moment to moment and create a gap, filled with symptoms and symbols, where an individual's specific dysfunctions and pathologies, wedged in these movements at the same point where the original malformation occurred, kick into gear. Thus, no matter what our highest center of gravity in structures and states, within those that have become operative in us, our pathologies become reactivated moment to moment, spewing their dysfunctional versions of the particular structure or state everywhere. For the same reason (the same original, ongoing, and reactivated miscarriage), we can address these problems directly and therapeutically (in one or more quadrants) and thus, with luck, effect something like a cure, or amelioration, of this dysfunction via Cleaning Up, which includes negative shadow work and positive flourishing practices.

With regard to Supermind, a dysfunction can develop in regard to either of the evolutionary or involutionary, moment-to-moment series of Effluxing/Refluxing movements and currents. With involution, this can present a significant problem, because the malformation created at white clear light can potentially be carried down the entire chain of basic structures, all the way to the bottom (in which case it tends to be a contributing factor to actual physical illnesses—heart disease to cancer to a host of lesser concerns).

What type of dysfunction might that be? The normal, healthy nature of Supermind, recall, is essentially an ongoing "stationary flow state" of "being/Wholeness" to "being/Wholeness" to "being/Wholeness," in an all-time/timeless to all-time/timeless to all-time/timeless Present Presence, or eternal "unmoving/ongoing" Now-moment of Suchness embracing all structures (the film frames cut and superimposed on each other for a "single Wholeness" film view). In other words, every single thing and event in our Kosmic field of Awareness, throughout its entire history (the "developmental depth" added to the Now-moment, fleshing it out), is the "content" of Awareness at this ultimate level. If *any* particular occasion, of any sort (in the entire Total Painting of All That Is), is repressed, denied, dis-owned, or dissociated, a lesion in consciousness develops; there is something in this Present moment that we won't look at, something in this pure Present moment (containing the past, present, and future) that we don't like, something that we are turning away from (whether that something actually happened in our past, is happening now in our passing-present field of awareness, or will happen in our imagined future), and that denial and dis-owning creates a "hole" in the present Kosmos, in present Suchness and Thusness, which manifests primarily as a malfunctioning, pathological functioning, or dysfunctioning of any thing in the vicinity of that hole. That dysfunction can be carried downward, via involutionary or "downward causation," to any number of lower levels, where it can erupt and disrupt normal functioning at that level.

It might, for example, erupt at indigo and disrupt the pure perception of psychophysical Wholeness (infecting it with a "hole" that cuts into the seamless Whole, creating a gap filled with rejected or avoided elements); or at green and disrupt the pluralistic perception of phenomena's many important differences (creating a "hole" of numbness to important differences that need desperately to be noticed); or at orange, and disrupt the truly worldcentric nature of perception there (creating a "hole" into which ethnocentric or egocentric impulses are instead dumped); or at red, disrupting the healthy function of power and converting it to one of its many pathological forms (a "hole" in healthy power filled with a drive of "power-over"); or at infrared, where it will contribute to the formation of any number of physical illnesses (via a "hole" in the organic systems' functionings required for healthy status). The original "leaving out," the "unwillingness to perceive," that "turning away" from something in the total Present consciousness/Kosmos—that "hole" in awareness—has traveled all the way down the "downward causation" chain and ends up creating, for example, a lack of blood flow to the heart or brain, causing a heart attack or stroke (this is one of the possible causes of at least 30 percent of illnesses that have no obvious discernable cause).

This highlights the importance of Cleaning Up for any and all higher structures. Once a higher structure has emerged, not only can that higher structure be invaded and infected by the problems at any lower structure (via "upward causation" in the holarchy), but the higher, more powerful structures can themselves exert a profound downward causation on all lower structures, infesting them with their own dysfunctions, problems, and shadows. It is this latter factor (the higher structures' power to deform lower ones) that brings such a profound Responsibility with each evolutionary transformation upward—a Responsibility to oneself and to one's world. Higher structures can not only deform your own capacities but can, by being turned outward in direct attack, cause enormous damage in the world. The higher the level, the more intrinsic power—for good or evil—that it has. At tribal magenta Magic, you can only do so much damage to the world with a bow and arrow; but with orange technology, from hydrogen bombs to gas chambers, your capacity for malevolence has increased radically. At a higher level, you can in fact be more moral, rising from egocentric tribalism or ethnocentric traditionalism to worldcentric and Kosmocentric loving embrace of all, or, with a malformed development, your capacity for evil can be increased by a similar degree of magnitude, moving from being able to kill perhaps another tribe of forty people to being able to kill an entire race in attempted genocide (something utterly beyond tribal capacity, but not because they were more moral) to being able to kill the entire human race (self-defeating but now possible with the tools that we have created).

Supermind is the epitome of Freedom—and Responsibility. You—and in the deepest sense, You Alone—become responsible for the entire planet and all of its beings. Immanuel Kant beautifully defined a "cosmopolitan" as one who feels that (paraphrasing) "when anyone anywhere suffers, I suffer"—a profound worldcentric awareness. And the ultimate Kosmopolitanism is when one feels that "when anyone or anything anywhere suffers, I suffer, because I AM them." Supermind is that type of all-inclusive, all-pervading, all-embracing Responsibility, and it starts with being able to hold the entire Kosmos in your Awareness without shutting out so much as a single little thing—absolutely everything entering your field of awareness (with no exceptions whatsoever) is fully and totally embraced, saturated with Love, radiating from the infinity of your own Heart Space, streaming from the radical Fullness of your very own Being, and reaching out to each and every thing and event in each and every direction to the known ends of the Kosmos itself. There is simply nothing anywhere, at any time, on the outside of this Awareness (it is "one without a second"), and having no outside, it has no inside either, but simply IS (just as when you first adopt a "headless" stance, everything "out there" appears on "this side" of your face, and then both inside and outside disappear into a headless one taste).

To contract at all in the face of this Undivided Wholeness Awareness (the Suchness of the Total Painting of All That Is) existing in this timeless all-inclusive Present is to set in motion the self-contraction, the separate-self sense, that latches on to the relative, finite, conventional, small self (or "I"—a necessary functional entity for this manifest world, created by the True Self itself, along with the rest of creation), and does so as if it were itself the True Self (or "I-I"), thus setting in motion the entire train of events known as Ignorance, Illusion, Maya, Deception, the Fallen World, the Dualistic World, the World of the Lie. That is transmitted to each and every lower structure present, and the radically Enlightened nature of the Supermind becomes lost and obscured in wave after wave of avoidance. And that avoidance rests on this, what can be called "Primordial Avoidance"—this very first, subtle "looking away." If we go back to the single indivisible Total Painting metaphor, there is some element, no matter how small or seemingly insignificant, that, for whatever reason, I don't want to look at, to be aware of, to notice, to allow into my awareness. That single, simple, primary turning away, looking away, moving away—that Primordial Avoidance—sets in motion the events that are, at this level, the dominant cause of the world of maya, illusion, ignorance, and deception. And every level, top to bottom, is infected with this delusion.

Primordial Avoidance—whether in the ever-present nondual state of unity or turiyatita consciousness, or in the Supermind (or both)—is the simplest of actions. This entire world is arising, moment to moment, and, as you see in higher states such as "headless" unity, the entire world is arising in your field of Awareness AS your Awareness. I AM-*That*. (At which point, there is neither a separate I AM nor a separate That, just the hyphen; as with the Zen master, "When I heard the sound of the bell ringing, there was no bell and no I, just the ringing".) You can practice that awareness now, by getting into the Witnessing stance, the stance of the pure Observing Self, and observing the entire Painting. Then let the Painting turn into that big blue pancake and fall on your "headless" nondual unity state—there is then just the entire Painting, in all its depth, arising moment to moment where your head used to be. Stay with that Total Painting Awareness, and look carefully to see if there are any items that you are shy of, reluctant to feel, or maybe laced with fear or anxiety about. Or perhaps you will discover a numbness hiding something you don't want to feel, which makes it much harder to spot, since becoming aware of numb areas is especially hard. You're looking for something that basically isn't there; numbness is a lack—it's a lack of feeling or seeing, something you can't, by definition, feel or see; so approach those possibilities with all diligence.

Almost certainly, sooner or later, you will find something that you turn away from, that you look away from, that you move away from. It might even be that your awareness gets lost in thought and you lose awareness of the Painting altogether. In any event, this is the precise moment when you drop Wholeness or drop the Totality—by either losing the whole Painting or simply losing just one of its smallest elements: by doing either you are already out of touch with the Totality, looking away and turning away and moving away. This will simultaneously throw you into a contracted space as well as a temporal time, as the emergence of the subject–object duality creates the distance or space between the seer and seen, and the "loss" of the timeless Now, or Present, squeezes the Present into the passing present, which then doesn't include the past and future but is *surrounded* by the past and future. Both space and time are the result of this Primordial Avoidance.

You look away, you turn away, and thus you move away. You look away in space, and thus you begin to move away in time—and out of the timeless Now and Present Presence. You find yourself lost in temporal musings, time wandering, past or future thoughts cut off from the Now moment, and with that, you are out of the Whole and into the spacetime world of finitude, isolation, suffering, separation, and death (separate entities come into being, and therefore separate entities can disappear from being—they can, that is, and for the first time, die).

The cure? *Watch that looking away, watch that turning away, watch that moving away.* Pay attention, give awareness, to that very first looking away, however it appears. Watch that turning away, and thus watch that moving away. Watch that Primordial Avoidance in its very subtlest, barely noticeable forms. Watch that Primordial Avoidance as it first turns away from, and leaves out, some element, however apparently insignificant, of the Total Present Painting—some looking away, some avoidance, some contracting. The very act of Avoidance puts us into a world of choices, usually in terms of opposites, with one of the poles positively sought and one negatively avoided: suddenly, we want pleasure, and to avoid pain; we want good things, and to avoid bad; we lust for grandeur, and turn away from the mediocre; seek fortune, fame, greatness, and despise destitution, ignominy, insignificance. We avoid or look away from some element, or aspect, of the Total Painting—we just don't like it, and thus we *contract, tighten, narrow* our Awareness. It's not that any of those choices are bad; they are "bad" when we don't simultaneously see the Total Painting of which each is a simple element. We forget the Whole, and grasp for parts. Only the Whole is Full (its parts are all pieces); only the Whole itself doesn't suffer (its parts all suffer); only the Whole doesn't die (its parts all die); only the Whole embraces all time *within it* (its parts exist only *within* time).

That very first, however seemingly insignificant, Primordial Avoidance of even the smallest thing, throws us out of—contracts us away from—a Total Painting Awareness and into a world of parts, a world of broken, fragmented, tortured, tormented, doomed-to-die *parts.* And thus, as Thoreau put it, the mass of humans "lead lives of quiet desperation."[5]

This points out one of the difficulties faced by many of the truly higher structures and states, namely, balancing and integrating ultimate realities with relative realities. How do we keep in mind both the ultimate reality of the simple Suchness or Thusness of any thing, as well as the relative realities of the Total Painting itself? The primary solution to this quandary lies in the real meaning of "nonduality," as contrasted with something like, say, pantheism. For pantheism, the "Total Painting" metaphor is taken as being the total truth. Spirit, the ultimate Divine, is simply the Totality—the Sum Total—of all manifest things and events. Pantheism might choose Gaia (meaning the whole universe) as its God or Goddess, which forms a Great Web of Life, with each individual thing and event being a particular strand in that overall Web. That version of Divinity does indeed face all the problems of "parts" and "the Whole" and how to give each its deserving due. And for each individual thing, there is the question, "What part of the Whole are you?"

But real nonduality doesn't work that way. For the nondual vision, 100 percent of infinity, being utterly dimensionless and spaceless itself, is fully present in and at each and every single point of space, or at each and every dimension of manifestation. All of infinity is present at each finite point, and thus, ALL of infinity is present right HERE. Likewise, 100 percent of eternity, being itself totally without time, is fully present at each and every point of time, so that ALL of eternity is present right NOW. (Thus Wittgenstein's point that "if we take eternity to mean not infinite temporal duration but timelessness, then eternal life belongs to those who live in the present.")[6]

So there isn't the awkward question "Just which part of the Whole am I?" For nonduality, every single point can say, "I am the full infinity, existing in a full eternity." The real timeless and spaceless—thus truly eternal and infinite—ultimate Reality, or Spirit, is not some stretch of time, however long, or some span of space, however big (and thus is not simply a Totality of all space and all time, like a pantheistic Gaia), but is rather 100 percent fully present in every single point of space and time anywhere and anywhen. This is why all of the infinite and all of the finite are nondual or not-two. And all of eternity and all of time are nondual or not-two. So you don't get in touch with the timeless Now by trying to restrict your attention to the passing present moment without thinking of past moments or future moments, just focusing on the immediate present, because that doesn't give you a real timeless eternity but simply the passing temporal moment. Real eternity includes present thoughts, past thoughts, and future thoughts —all of them are arising in the present timeless Now-moment, a Now-moment that doesn't exclude the past or future but embraces them.

The Christian mystics point out this difference with the terms the *nunc fluens* and the *nunc stans*. The former, the nunc fluens, the "passing moment," is the relative now moment, set apart from the past and the future; whereas the latter, the nunc stans, the "nonmoving moment," is the timeless Now inclusive of all past, present, and future thoughts, since all are arising in *this* Now moment, whether you realize it or not. So the passing present is definitely something you can focus on, get in touch with, be aware of, and many practices have you do just that (usually thinking it is the eternal Now that you are contacting); but the real eternal Now, the present timeless Now, is not something that you can contact but something you can't escape—all you are ever *really* aware of is an all-inclusive present Now-moment. (Thus, think of the past; that thought is occurring Now; and when the past actually happened, it was a Now. Likewise, think of a future event, and that, too, is a present thought; and when the future becomes real, it will also be a Now.) The *only* thing that you are *actually* ever aware of is a timeless Now, and in a headless space that embodies 100 percent of infinity. This is why the true Paths of the Great Liberation uniformly maintain that Enlightenment, or Awakening, is not something that you can attain; rather, all of it is fully, completely present in this here-and-now moment. (This is why the *Prajnaparamita Sutras*, the central texts of Mahayana Buddhism—and notice the "prajna"—repeat over and over that if the seeker could just understand that Enlightenment *cannot be attained*, that is itself Realization. And it can't be attained, because 100 percent of eternity is already fully present right NOW. How can you possibly achieve something that is already the case? Whether you know it or not, realize it or not, your present awareness is a headless, "unity," nondual, infinite and eternal and timeless Now awareness. Your Awareness is exactly like that, and has always been like that, even when you didn't realize it. This is ALL that is actually EVER really happening.)

The reason that Primordial Avoidance is the beginning of what is referred to by the traditions as the "illusory" world is that it isn't actually happening, it is not the REAL state of affairs. In reality, there is only the headless, nondual, Whole, timeless Now moment; we can pretend to Avoid that, but the results are not a real state or a real condition but a pretend state, an illusory state, a state that actually isn't even really there—as a simple correct looking has showed us on several occasions and in several different ways (your actual "headless" condition, the reality of only a timeless Now, and so on).

This Primordial Avoidance illusorily occurs in all individuals, whatever their structure-level (except for Supermind itself), and thus practicing being aware of it is a good idea for anybody at any stage (since looking directly at illusions dissipates them).[7] However you practice it, definitely spend some time paying attention to your Primordial Avoidance, your avoidance of the Present Totality of the Whole Painting of manifestation, and how you initially, very subtly, barely noticeably, turn away from something, look away from something, move away from something in the Fullness and Wholeness of the entire Painting of your overall Present. There is some impulse, some item, some something—a thought, a sensation, an image, a physical location, a person, a religion, an idea, a desire—that you simply do not want to fully look at, to openly let into your awareness. And thus, you look away, you turn away, you move away—and therein is the origin of your suffering. (This is a good practice to keep track of in your journal. People often find very specific things that they are avoiding and can often trace them to a series of repeating events in their past, usually with a series of very significant others—parents, siblings, friends, peer groups, teachers. Often, as one avoided element becomes conscious and embraced, a subtler one will emerge to take its place, and so on, as you move from state to a higher state to a higher state, which can also accelerate structure development.)

With Supermind, because of its all-pervading, all-embracing nature—which includes all the major structures all the way back to the Big Bang—you also have the sense that you are rather literally looking out of the eyes of all sentient beings precisely because the Supermind, unlike Big Mind, does indeed include all previous, lower structures, going all the way back, again, to the Big Bang. This is more noticeable when you rest on the Observing side of the street than the observed Painting side. Here, you're not looking *at*, say, a deer; you are looking *as* the deer—you are looking out of the eyes of the deer as it looks at the world. Your sense of I AMness and the deer's sense of I AMness seem to be one and the same feeling. And this is certainly the case for all human beings (but it's also true for all insects, all bacteria, and so forth). You look at another person, and you are yourself looking at yourself (that is, your Self looking at your Self). There's the distinct feeling that you are the I AMness that is directly each individual's own interior state. (And that happens to be literally true, in that the overall number of Real Selves or Big Minds is but one. As Schrödinger said, "Consciousness is a singular, the plural of which is unknown." There is one Big Mind = one Big Self = one Spirit looking through the multiple structures and eyes of finite, unique, individual minds and selves in all sentient beings.)

This type of "omnipresent" Awareness is common with both the Witnessing state and the Nondual state (and Big Mind states in general), but what is distinctive about the Supermind is that it is capable of feeling how Big Mind is experienced by each structure-level of consciousness itself. Thus the "Fullness" dimension of the Supermind is considerably "greater" than the Fullness aspect of Big Mind, since "Fullness" is determined by the amount of Form embraced by Emptiness in the nondual state and the "amount of Form" depends upon the actual altitude level of development of the structure doing the experiencing. Only at Supermind, with its "all-structure" resonance, is the Form absolutely Total, being the sum total of all manifest Form from the Big Bang to the immediate ongoing present—ALL is transcended and included in Supermind's ongoing evolutionary unfolding. Big Mind, experienced at, say, the orange level, is how Big Mind looks through orange at the world. Supermind's experience of Big Mind, however, experiences how Big Mind looks to every major level of development that has emerged to date, bottom to top—an "omni-omni-presence." This is why when, for example, orange has an experience of Big Mind and looks at a deer, it might indeed feel that its own I AMness is the same as the I AMness of the deer, but that experience is actually much closer to orange's I AMness than the deer's. The Supermind, however, can get much closer to how a deer itself is truly feeling its own I AMness. To the extent that such empathic resonating is possible, the Supermind will come the closest to being able to do so—and in its absolutely inclusive nature, truly does so.

So Supermind is indeed a union of formless Emptiness and the entire world of Form, but with Supermind, the world of Form actually becomes truly and fully Whole for the first time. All lesser structures still have levels "over their heads" that exist in the Kosmos. For example, although an experience of Big Mind at amber will indeed be a unity consciousness of Emptiness and the entire world of Form, nonetheless the Form in this case goes up only to the world of amber; all higher worlds of Form—orange, green, teal, turquoise, indigo, and so on—are all still "over its head." And you clearly cannot be one with something that doesn't even exist for you. So with any "unity consciousness" short of Supermind, the Big Mind is real, the pure Emptiness is real, but the Form is partial, limited, fragmented, and thus these actually represent, if we can put it this way, a "partial Enlightenment," or a "limited Enlightenment." Not so with Supermind, which, in transcending and including all levels of Form that have emerged to date, is a full and complete Wholeness, a genuine Unity, a real nondual Oneness, a union of Emptiness with the genuinely *entire* world of All Form.

Thus, in truly combining—or rather, in realizing the always already union of Emptiness and All Form—this is the realization of the *true* Total Painting of All That Is, including not only (on the absolute side) an unmanifest infinity and eternity at each and every point of the manifest Total Painting but also (on the relative side) a genuinely *total* Total Painting, with nothing whatsoever left out of manifest existence, because the Supermind directly knows all of existence, in all of its levels and dimensions, by acquaintance, by identity, by being, and not merely by description, by naming, by describing. This is a Wholeness of which there is no greater Wholeness, and each moment, as a new subject-occasion emerges and adds to that Whole, the new Whole is now embraced within Supermind's own self-liberating, ongoing, full and all-embracing Wholeness.

Whereas the infinity and eternity of this Wholeness is always already given and can never be attained, and the ultimate reality of the entire show is fully present here and now, the relative reality—the actual evolutionary structures and emergent realities and worlds of Form—has to grow and develop and evolve through time, intentionality, effort, and work. The pure Being is always already present and always already given; the temporal Becoming is the work of Spirit-in-action over time, and has to be engaged in as a genuine growth process. Big Mind is given; Supermind is earned (in significant part). And thus, whereas Big Mind is always present, Supermind is in part an emergent, a product not only of Being but also of Becoming, and uniting these two—Being and Becoming, eternity and time, eternal Emptiness and all temporal Form—is another side of Supermind's genuine Wholeness beyond Wholeness.

Experiencing one's own deepest I AMness (and true Suchness) as looking out of the eyes of all sentient beings is simply one of the ways Supermind's "all-structures" ("*all*-Form") nature is reflected in the manifest universe. (This "all-eyes" experience is sometimes had by Big Mind at a lower structure or level, but precisely because that level is lower or junior, it is significantly more limited than Supermind's, having, as it were, "less Form.") And as for Supermind itself (whose "all eyes" experience is actually backed with an "all-structures" awareness), this Awareness of "looking-through-all-eyes" becomes a good indicator of any sort of residual Primordial Avoidance—with "all total Form," even the slightest amount of Primordial Avoidance stands out like a sore thumb. With human beings, for example, if any racist or sexist or religious prejudices remain, however modest, they will show up in this Awareness as a reluctance to fully, totally, genuinely identify with the other person if he or she is being held in a biased manner (for a white WASP male, it might be an African-American, a Jew, a Hispanic; if a sexist male, any woman; if ageist, any old person; if antireligious, any Catholic, Muslim, or Hindu, and so on). One will subtly turn away, look away, and move away from people whom one holds prejudicially. The deep subconscious thought is "I don't want to look through that person's eyes; I'm not going to touch that person; I'm certainly not going to identify with him or her or how they see the world." This is the result, pure and simple, of fixations remaining at the amber (or lower) ethnocentric levels; prejudices that, in a full and normal development, would have been erased in the move to orange worldcentric awareness. (And, of course, a Primordial Avoidance can occur with dissociations at *any* structure lower than Supermind and prevent a Full Identity with any part of the Total Painting, fracturing the Fullness of the Supreme Identity.) But attached to, split off and rendered unconscious, these malformations have accompanied development at each and every one of its higher transformations (starting at the level of the repression itself and carried forward to every subsequent, higher level), clear and unmistakable proof of the capacity of lower-level deformations to remain in existence even into higher and wider and deeper forms of consciousness, malforming and distorting them in the process (often, in fact, giving the prejudice more power; as the higher level's more sophisticated cognitive powers come online, they are able to more aggressively rationalize and operationalize the bias). And this is also a perfect reminder, which can never be repeated too many times, that just because we have achieved a higher level of development and a higher level of consciousness, this does not in any way, in itself, guarantee that things have become better—they could have become *more powerfully* worse.

In short, Supermind looks and indeed directly feels like a superhuman capacity—seeing through all the eyes of sentient beings everywhere as an infinite and eternal Pure Spirit, as nondual Suchness, and as a reflection of its "all-structure" (all-Form) resonating capacity. "Seeing" isn't quite right; there is no sense of a subject seeing objects—there is simply a wide-open space with phenomena arising "within" it moment to moment, with no looker or watcher or seer, just things exactly as they are, self-arising and self-liberating, hanging in the air of Thusness, and interiorly resonating with each and every structure it encounters. Thus, Supermind reaches out and embraces every single thing and event in the entire Kosmos, known and unknown, though "reaching" and "embracing" are also not quite right, either; there is just the uttermost simplicity of a pure clear open spaciousness that already is indistinguishable from everything already arising in and as its radiant clarity, whose very interiors feel-radiate as infinity or open-to-absolutely-all. Infinity lines every finite event anywhere in existence: Supermind inwardly touches everything from the dark matter of the universe—which constitutes some 96 percent of this universe and is poorly understood, but no matter; in this case, infinity is still its Ground—to countless undiscovered and unknown galaxies, planets, and supernovas. All are touched and grounded and implicitly felt by Supermind—your own deepest *You*—as a direct texture of its own being and as a product of its own hyper-Full overflowing, which you can feel bubbling out of yourself all the way to the ends of the world, and through each and every structure, top to bottom. When functioning as Supermind, every distant supernova, galaxy, and solar system—not to mention your next-door neighbor, the far side of the globe, every sentient being on the planet, the planet itself—feels exactly the way your lungs, heart, hands, and feet now feel: as perfectly seamless aspects of your own you-ness.

The Supermind is the entire manifest Kosmos at one with, in union with, your perfectly Empty I AMness. This radical not-twoness spills out of your Heart as radiant Love, embracing all beings anywhere in existence, and, paradoxically, is devoted to the service of all of them. I say "paradoxically," because in terms of Being, no individual needs a single thing to be added to their makeup (each and every one, in their truest Thusness, is the Great Perfection, always already and eternally the case); but in terms of Becoming, the entire world awaits—and desperately needs—your service. And it is up to *you*—and in a special sense, You Alone—to provide enlightened evolutionary guidance for the entire planet. If not you, who? If not now, when? What is holding you back? Your ultimate reality is this deepest service—to occupy the planet, to *occupy the All*. This is genuine Kosmopolitanism. There is only one Spirit, one Self—who does it belong to if not *you*?

In reaching out and touching all, or better, in being the clear open spaciousness that all things and events, known or unknown, are always already arising in and perfectly one with—the very Nature of their natures and the Condition of their conditions, the Jell-O holding up all the pieces of fruit suspended in a jiggly gelatin fruit cup—Supermind electrically and shockingly interweaves seamlessly with all that is, in every dimension, in every realm, in every possible manifest universe. It is saturated with the existence of all that exists, and is shot through the eternal timeless moment that embraces every stretch of time and the infinite spaceless point that includes every stretch of space. Supermind is looking out of the eyes of anything anywhere that looks, flowing out of the structure of each and every being, at each and every level that has emerged to date. Its being is this ongoing endless Wholeness that includes all structures and all realms, joyously embracing absolutely all manifest qualities, which is another name for Love—*your* Love—which is the All that Supermind's utterly nondual nature is, everywhere and everywhen. Go to the very ends of the manifest universe, and you will there find your Love, holding everything together. Go to the very ends of time, and there is your Love, embracing all and carrying it forward. Go to the deepest interior you can find in yourself, or in any other, and your Love will be smiling back at you. Love, Eros as Spirit-in-action, is the very motor of this and every manifest world, the fuel on which the great machine of manifestation runs, and without which, things and events would merely hang in midair, with no push or pull to set them moving in any direction at all. But dose the scene with the perfume, the scent, of an all-pervading, all-permeating background Love, and watch them all begin to move and wildly dance, more and more insistently, all looking for but one thing: ways to come together into greater and greater Wholes, deeper and deeper Unions, higher and higher Ones, which leaves a stratified universe, a grand, layered, holarchic display of the degrees and depths of Love itself, from the infinitesimal to the infinite, culminating, at this particular time in historical unfolding, in Supermind, where you can feel the depths of your own Love holding the entire Kosmos together— beginning to end, top to bottom, inside to outside, and in all ways— moving it to greater and greater gorgeous glory and radiant embrace. This is the contagious Condition you could never have forgotten; this is the royal Reality that Primordial Avoidance only pretended to avoid (it lied about its lie of separation—it never really occurred); this is the Home you never left and the Return that is always already promised to you, any time at all you wish to reclaim it; this is the interior of the entire world and the wrapping in which the gift of the universe came when delivered to your door; and all as simple as the call of a whip-poor-will in its haunting, quiet song, penetrating the darkness of a late still eve on a moonlit summer's night.

In sum, dysfunctions at Supermind involve getting "wrong," or "incorrectly perceiving," any of the features just discussed. These include misunderstanding the nature of eternity and infinity; being caught to some degree, however minor, in Primordial Avoidance of the Total Painting; malformations in either "downward causation"/ involutionary currents or "upward causation"/evolutionary currents; a failure not only to fully integrate the structure component of this stage (which transcends and includes all previous structures all the way back to the Big Bang, and this includes correctly integrating "prehuman" levels as well, such as atoms, molecules, cells, the reptilian brain stem, the paleomammalian limbic system, the mammalian cortex, as well as human levels, infrared to white) but also to fully integrate those structures with all major states up to and including turiyatita, or Suchness (and this can be complicated by shadow material in either of them); misperceived "omni-omniscience" (not fully feeling one with the interiors—as well as exteriors—of all sentient holons); failure to cleanly unite Being (ever-present infinite and eternal) and Becoming (temporal evolutionary developmental unfolding) —the former is given, the latter is earned; not fully integrating heaven and earth, thus failing to disclose the radical Wholeness of this and every manifest world in existence, the one True and Real Condition of every thing, event, process, entity, realm, dimension, and Kosmos—and *your* real Nature, your real *you*.

Treatments for these dysfunctions can be summarized fairly simply, even if their application can be complex: attain a truly Integral Awareness, and uproot any action of Primordial Avoidance. "Integral Awareness" means Awareness attuned to both ultimate and relative realities —it is aware of the True Self and pure Witness and, beyond even that, it has a direct apprehension of genuine Suchness or Thusness, the ultimate Condition of all conditions, Quality of all qualities, and Nature of all natures. This True Self, or pure Witness, is "looking through" the eyes of the conventional, relative, finite self, and thus a genuine amount of Cleaning Up has ensured that the relative self is an authentic self, not a false self with shadow. Likewise, dysfunction inducing is a failure to fully acknowledge, grasp, and genuinely resonate with the 1-2-3 of Spirit (which is the first manifest Form of Spirit as it steps into manifestation—that is, the beginning of the quadrants that will run top to bottom, starting with the highest, the ultimate). It is also foundationally important to have a "Right View" that includes an intellectual understanding of at least all of the major elements of AQAL (quadrants, levels, lines, states, and types) because one's "experience" of ultimate nondual Reality is determined in significant measure by how one interprets that experience, and a genuinely *full* interpretation of Reality helps ensure a full realization of that Reality (and a full interpretation means a full AQAL conceptualization, or whatever full and Integral view one wishes—but it should be full and Integral, for sure). Each of the specific dysfunctions mentioned in the previous paragraph can be addressed by a specific set of therapeutic practices that are a mixture of the elements mentioned in this paragraph, and most readers will be able to deduce many of the specific aspects of such therapeutic endeavors from what has been said thus far. (Otherwise, I develop them in a book-length treatment—now in progress—with the working title "SuperView.")

The ultimate Freedom, radical Fullness—and compete Responsibility—of the Supermind are all literally unending. This is the central reason that Supermind needs to be fully Cleaned Up. I noted that higher structures, with their higher capacities and power, can be greater and greater sources of "evil," to use a strong but appropriate term. If Auschwitz is a product of orange technology (with red/amber morals), you can imagine what the products of Supermind might be if it were broken, twisted, or fixated to, or repressing, lower levels (up to and including itself)—an unprecedented degree of "evil." When truly unqualifiable Spirit manifests in a given universe, not only does it do so via the quadrants (and the AQAL Matrix in general), it also tends to do so via opposites in each of those elements. And that means, as but one example, that in addition to there being Spirit in 2nd person—or "God"—there are also manifested Demonic trends (not in the mythic-literal sense of an actual being or Devil but as negative, destructive currents such as Thanatos). One definition of "dysfunction" is "functioning in a Demonic fashion," and one should pay serious attention to, even "fear," the Demonic versions of Supermind. Simply imagine the dark side, the dark face—the twisted, distorted, deranged version of the most glorious Glory, beatific Beauty, falsehood-smashing Truth, thunderously sincere Truthfulness, fully resonating Mutual Understanding (which is Self-Understanding), and exquisitely functioning Functional Fit—those crushed and distorted are the Demonic Supermind.

Thus, each increasing level of development brings new capacities and new "evils." Just take any growth holarchy—matter to body to mind to soul to spirit, for example—and imagine both the "good" and the potentially "bad" versions of that level, and you'll see what I mean. And historically this is exactly what has happened. Early crimes were perpetrated on material goods—for example, theft and destruction, and living bodies—for example, slavery, rape, oppression. As mind emerged, new crimes emerged with each level of its development—for example (in ascending order), destroying another person's safety, be-longingness systems, self-esteem capacities, or self-actualization pos-sibilities. Today's leading-edge crime is cyberterrorism, the use of high-cognitive-powered technology skills to hack, steal, destroy, or infiltrate websites of everything from the Defense Department to edu-cation systems to corporations to private citizens. Even what to con-sider a crime at each new level is hotly debated (with regard to cyberterrorism, is Edward Snowden a treasonous criminal or a much-admired hero?).

A Supermind run amuck is a thing to be, yes, "feared" is probably the right word (fear is itself the product of self–other duality—as the

Upanishads put it, "Wherever there is other, there is fear"[8]—but as the Supermind goes dysfunctional, various types of "other" creep into it, and thus "fear" is indeed appropriate). Starting in the near future, we will be discussing the crimes of the Supermind for decades, as unimaginably Good and outrageous Evil both pour forth from its actions. At any point in development, the Darth Vader move is always possible. This is simply another reason why, along with Growing Up, Waking Up, and Showing Up, Cleaning Up needs to accompany each and every stage of development that humans endure. Truly, the lack of Integral views will be (and are) more and more destructive as evolution continues to higher and higher levels, with every stage truly being a Good News/Bad News story. Seriously, let us go with Integral and the Good News until the very duality of Good and Bad has lost all meaning in the pure Suchness of this and every moment—but a Condition that still embraces all Form and manifestation, and thus will always require some sort of Integral Framework for its most accurate interpretation.

Conclusion

We have been looking specifically at shadow elements in each of the major structure-rungs in development, and the general conclusion is that all of the levels of development, bar none, potentially possess some form of shadow material. Dealing with shadow material is the "negative" aspect of Cleaning Up, or working to fix what's broken, malformed, or dysfunctional in each structure and state. The positive side of Cleaning Up, the "flourishing" side, deals with strengthening and celebrating what's right, what's working, with every structure and state. (In a separate treatise, some colleagues and I are working on a full-spectrum Flourishing guide, where we outline and categorize the key selective strengths and positive virtues of every major structure-rung and every major state-realm in existence, along with practices and exercises that have been demonstrated to activate and cultivate each of these. Please stay tuned for that, tentatively titled "Integral Flourishing.")

What we learn from shadow material is that it is a direct result of the very form of evolution itself. Evolution is an ongoing process of *transcend and include* (or *negate and preserve*, or *differentiate and integrate*), in every realm it touches, and something can go wrong with either one of those core aspects of evolution, which each time produces a different type of shadow material specific to the particular structure or state where the malformation occurs. In general, if something goes wrong with the transcending or differentiating component, then the self fails to adequately let go of its present level or stage (in either structure or state), and some aspects of its own being remain fused with, or stuck to, elements of that level, producing a *fixation*, or an *addiction*, to those elements, which are now split-off from, and dis-owned by, the main currents of consciousness (and the proximate self) and relegated to the unconscious, as shadow impulses or even full subpersonalities, which are then often projected onto others. On the other hand, if something goes wrong with the include or preserve component, then the self fails to adequately integrate and embrace aspects of its own being, and an *avoidance*, or *allergy*, to those aspects is created, while those aspects —like those previously fixated to—are split-off from, and dis-owned by, the central/proximate self, or main currents of consciousness, and relegated to the unconscious as shadow impulses, or full subpersonalities, and from there often projected onto others.

The net result of these developmental miscarriages is that the central or proximate self (the functional, finite, conventional self-sense, through which the True Self, or pure Witness, views—and communicates with—the world) is reduced from an authentic self to a false self plus a shadow. This shadow—as material that one denies ownership of—creates a gap, or fissure, in the self (a perforation in consciousness), and that gap, or "hole," is filled with painful *symptoms* (the felt energetic components of a crushed and broken consciousness) and puzzling *symbols* (the conceptual lies, or defenses, meant to conceal the core material from awareness by presenting it as something other than it is). Both facades cover the real ingredients of the gap, namely, the now-banished shadow elements, excommunicated by a fundamental lie, an untruthfulness (which is a violation of "truthfulness," the main validity claim of the Upper Left quadrant)—the shadow is the nexus of the lie. This alienation of aspects of one's own being is carried out, at each level, by the tools of (and in accordance with) the capacities available at that level (so that each level's defense mechanisms are specific to that level, as is the actual shadow material itself). Thus, levels of consciousness = levels of defense mechanisms = levels of shadow material.

The "cure" is a direct reversal—carried out, however, in the space of the present day's consciousness and under its own features—so that, in essence: shadow + false self = authentic self. The ideal situation is that, at each level of development, the *Real Self* or *True Self* or *pure Witness* views the world through the eyes of an *authentic self* at that level. The pure Witness, or the essence of Awareness at each and every level of development, views the world through the relative self of that given level, and that relative self can be more-or-less *accurate* or *authentic*, or more-or-less *false* or *inauthentic*, in which case shadow material is present alongside the inauthentic self. Reuniting shadow and false self gives an authentic relative self, through which the ultimate True Self— the turiya, Witnessing Self—can view its enacted world.

Here we see another major difference between the meditative, or contemplative, traditions the world over (especially found in the East) and modern psychological models (especially found in the West). One difference that we've already seen is that the former deals almost exclusively with stages of Waking Up (or states) and the latter with stages of Growing Up (or structures). Another is the difference between what they hold to be the "most true self" versus the "false self" in humans.

For the Waking Up (and mostly Eastern) traditions, the True Self ("the most true self") is a state achievement, something discovered at turiya or Witnessing (or higher Suchness), where the True Self (turiya or nondual turiyatita) comes into full awareness. All other selves, with no exceptions, are "false selves," because they are all finite, conventional, and dualistic (no matter whether they're "healthy" or "unhealthy," "accurate" self-images or "inaccurate" self-images, authentic or inauthentic relative selves—they're all finite, and thus all illusory, period). This approach sees no major difference between the authentic self and the false self, because both of them are equally finite selves, and therefore equally unreal, equally illusory, equally maya-bound. They also don't make the distinction between the authentic self and the false self because they are generally unaware of the shadow itself, and thus don't see that, in the equation authentic self = false self + shadow, there is indeed a difference between these two selves. True, both are finite, and thus both are definitely not the Real Self, or true Being, which is why they are both treated the same, as illusory, but the *relatively real* differences between them are overlooked, and thus the advantages of having an authentic relative self over an inauthentic or false relative self are totally overlooked, and one's Enlightenment or Awakening to True Self can thus end up being expressed through a broken, partial, fragmented, inauthentic, false self. This view that regards both the authentic self and the false self as being merely and equally illusory selves, so that there is no real difference between them, is found in virtually all schools of Waking Up.

For the Growing Up approaches, on the other hand, there is no infinite Real Self or true Witness. The Growing Up approaches, having no access to Waking Up states, have no awareness or knowledge of the turiya or Witness or True Self state (or the turiyatita or Suchness condition). Rather, they track only the stages in finite Growing Up, and they notice, with key pioneering investigators such as Freud, how the development of the relative finite self can lead to various miscarriages and developmental malformations, tearing the relative finite self into even less real versions of selfhood, in this case, a false self split from shadow elements that are rendered unconscious. The aim of these approaches (focused on Growing Up) is thus to reunite the shadow with the false self ("Where it was, there I shall become"), with the goal of producing as healthy and as fully functioning a finite self as possible for a dualistic, relative, conventional self in the first place. This accurate self-image, this authentic self, is the "most true self" for these approaches. In contrast, the aim of the Waking Up approaches is to drop identity with any finite relative self at all, and whether that is a relatively correct self-image or a relatively false self-image doesn't matter in the least to them—both are finite, ultimately illusory, not-Real-Self (or not-Emptiness) entities and thus need to be rejected. One approach recognizes the authentic self; the other approach recognizes the Real Self. (The goal of Growing Up therapeutic approaches is "Where it was, there I shall become"; the goal of Waking Up approaches is "Where I was, there I-I shall become.") Neither approach does both. And so they constantly argue, when they manage to talk at all, as to which self is the ultimately highest self humans have access to—authentic self or Real Self. For each of them, the self of the other is purely "nonexistent" or "illusory."

Once again, we see that the Integral approach unites two different approaches, both of which have incredibly important truths to tell us, but both of which have rarely, if ever, been brought together before.[9] The whole point of working with as authentic a self as possible is that it is the vehicle through which the True Self (and ultimate Suchness) will express itself. And a True Self speaking with the voice of a false self rings deeply disturbed and inauthentic, even though in touch with an ultimate and infinite Self. But that Self is hobbled by the limited and broken vehicles through which it must express, communicate, and show itself. This is not good. When a True Self speaks through a false self, it's noticeable to almost everybody (even though they might be initially overwhelmed by the True-Self component, and only considerably down the road do they come to realize, painfully, the effects of the inauthentic-self aspects).

On the other hand, to have only an authentic self and not also a Real Self or True Self (let alone ultimate Suchness) is to hold a chimera, an illusory little thing, a finite bundle of subjects, all of which can be made objects and thus aren't even a real Subject, a Real and True Self. Parading an ultimately illusory product as if one had an ultimately astonishing and totally valuable thing to be sought after is to be deeply out of touch with any sort of ultimate Reality at all. The awakened ones shake their heads in slow sadness—while those who do possess an authentic self look in wonder at someone expressing such certainty (coming from his or her Real Self) through the mouth of such a false and fractured self. Both of them, as is so often the case, are right—both have some very true but very partial truths. Let those with eyes to see lovingly embrace them both.

12

Dysfunctions of the Gross and Subtle States

We'll now look at a few of the more common problems and dysfunctions that occur in the gross and subtle states and their Vantage Points. During state growth and development, the central or proximate self's center of gravity switches from one stage to a next higher stage to a next higher one, and what happens at each and every one of those switch-points (as well as fulcrums) can always be miscarried, poorly handled and poorly negotiated, leaving a pathology or dys-ease or dysfunction in its wake. In each case of healthy development (fulcrum or switch-point), the self dis-identifies with (or differentiates from, or transcends) the previous structure or state, then moves to the next higher structure or state, identifies with it, and then integrates it properly with its predecessor (surrendering/letting go of the narrower View or Vantage Point, and including/integrating the basic rung or realm). Problems at any of those subphases will generate pathologies (for example, failure to adequately dis-identify or transcend creates a fixation or addiction; failure to adequately integrate or include creates an avoidance or allergy).

Gross-State Dysfunctions

Gross and gross-reflecting state dysfunctions happen all the time, but they are not usually caused directly by state development, because all individuals start out at the gross state; they do not develop into it. Thus problems in the gross realm are often caused by problems in gross *structure* development, not state development (and thus involve infrared food, magenta sex, red power, amber love, orange self-esteem, green self-actualization, and so on). Since every experience is always a combined structure/state occasion, the structure dysfunction often inflicts the state—in this case, the gross or gross-reflecting state—with a conjoined dysfunction. Aspects of the gross or gross-reflecting state itself become compromised, misnegotiated, misnavigated, and misdigested, hobbling the state in various ways. We have already covered the essentials of the structure dysfunctions that can occur in the gross and gross-reflecting state (those structure dysfunctions can also occur with higher states, depending on which state the structure happens to be identified with when the dysfunction occurs; depending, that is, on the address of the dual center of gravity when the dysfunction occurs).

There are, nonetheless, a few gross-state problems that are created in relation to other, higher states, and those are worth mentioning, as they are rather common and can be quite serious.

Problems Involving Higher States

The first is simple psychic *inflation*—where the gross-reflecting mental ego is flooded by higher (usually subtle or causal) state material. For example, ego boundaries might loosen inappropriately and invite a dysfunctional version of Nature mysticism, flooding the ego with feelings of fusion with Nature that it cannot control or, in many cases, even understand. Instead of finding a prior oneness with Nature, the ego is simply inflated nearly to the size of Nature. This can happen to people involved in such movements as deep ecology, where the noble-enough goal of a Nature unity consciousness is derailed by an ego too eager to claim credit for the action itself, and thus not opening to the spaciousness of Nature but being invaded, flooded, and inflated by its grandeur. The ego takes credit for all of the cosmic glory of a starry night, a narcissistic inflation (common with boomeritis) that sees the ego as the necessary cause of creation itself (a typical confusion found in many "new paradigm" approaches, where, for example, the "measurement problem" in the collapse of the wave packet in quantum mechanics is ascribed to an action of the ego itself, thus making itself the sole creator of all manifestation). This is a structure dysfunction—a green central self fused with a red egocentric underbelly—that allows, even invites, invasion by higher, often transpersonal, states, and a possible inflation of ego.[1]

In some cases, the gross mental ego is invaded by subtle-state material—sometimes the subtle soul itself—whereupon the ego begins to confuse its own "earthly" powers with subtle "superpowers" and soul capacities (and it interprets this as "discovering who I really am, and for the first time!"). The only reason this can be a problem—since the individual does indeed possess soul powers—is that the ego itself does not possess soul powers, and its general functions and capacities may not have not evolved to handle higher, transpersonal soul capacities well. The negative results range from a near psychotic-level narcissistic expansion of the ego to more mundane feelings of being indeed something of a superman or superwoman, often with "secret" hidden powers (such as the ability to read minds, see the future, or cause harm or health to other people, or possessing omniscience or being a prophetic voice in global transformation, and, on the more manic or psychotic side, being able to fly, perform miracles, alter the weather, control the outcome of wars, and so forth).

One of the sadder sides of these types of pathologies is that orthodox therapists and psychiatrists misunderstand entirely the real cause of such dysfunctions. They do not understand the actual reality of the higher states that are partly involved, and thus instead of seeing the manic or psychotic components as being, in part, higher material trying to come down, they see them only as lower-id material trying to come up. The true aspects of these individuals' pathologies—the genuinely true aspects of the higher states themselves—are never acknowledged and given their due, and thus the "cure" in orthodox circles usually involves switching from mania to extensive depression, since all of the pathology—its true *and* false components—is interpreted as false, a humiliating and utterly depressing situation. Further, individuals experiencing these higher states know beyond a shadow of a doubt that some of them possess a genuine and undeniable reality, and thus when the typical therapist attempts to deny or talk them out of both the true and false aspects of these experiences—instead of acknowledging the true components and helping the individuals to see how they have misinterpreted those true aspects using the false aspects—the individuals immediately cease trusting the therapist, because the therapist clearly doesn't know what he or she is talking about (and in this respect, they don't). Acknowledging the true aspects or components of the experience of the higher state and then helping individuals see how they have misinterpreted and thus to some degree distorted them, helps those individuals move through these experiences in much more authentic and effective ways, and can even allow them to benefit from these experiences (since the higher states themselves often contain true, authentic, real transpersonal dimensions with real transpersonal wisdom and truth).

It is genuinely unfortunate that, in moderate to severe cases, orthodox treatment involves either burning the experience out of the brain with electroshock, or drugging the brain into oblivion with antipsychotics guaranteed to produce zombie-like effects in a matter of days. The major problem with such approaches is that the real component of these experiences cannot be so easily forced out of existence—reality is reality—and thus overtreatment is almost always part of any course of action, which decommissions vital functions of the brain until it's simply incapable of registering those realities at all.

Causal-state inflation is generally similar to subtle-state inflation, but it usually has stronger, often more negative, and hence dire consequences. The gross ego inflated with causal-state material will often believe that it, and it alone, is actually God or Spirit (not that its Real Self—and the Self of all sentient beings—is Spirit but that its individual ego or person is Spirit), replete with numerous extraordinary and Divine powers, such as being able to read and strongly influence the thoughts of others, or believing that everything that happens in the exterior world is actually focused on the self and is happening because it has deep meaning and messages for the self. (New Agers call this "synchronicity," and psychiatrists call this "delusions of reference." Synchronicity is real but rare; "delusions of reference" are common with "new paradigm" and New Age and *The Secret* approaches.)[2] The sad fact, again, is that occasionally some genuine siddhis or paranormal capacities are being experienced (see Michael Murphy's impressive *The Future of the Body*),[3] but this is happening inadvertently and without the real knowledge or meditative experience of how to control them, so that they run riot through the psyche.

Another very common gross-state dysfunction (in relation to higher states) is the creation of what I have been calling "the repressed *emergent* unconscious," where material from higher states (or structures), which could have emerged at the particular stage now present, is actively, dynamically, forcefully repressed, dissociated, and kept out of conscious Awareness (producing a "higher," even transpersonal or spiritual shadow, and a possibly quite developed shadow subpersonality—a so-called golden shadow). This is surprisingly common in this culture, where the identification of Spirit with the Mythic level of Spirit makes virtually anything associated with Spirit seem childish, silly, something to be embarrassed about, not sought after, denied. Hence, with this "embedded unconscious" belief, or antispiritual prejudice in place, anytime any genuinely spiritual or transpersonal material begins to emerge and descend, the present level of development—in this case, the gross mental ego—will often tend to repress and dissociate that material, sealing it out of its awareness at all costs. (This is much more common in states than in structures; structures have unmistakably transpersonal components starting only at 3rd tier, and less than one-tenth of 1 percent of the population is at 3rd tier, whereas polls show that some 60–80 percent of the population report "higher state" peak experiences or temporary mystical states.) If the repressed spiritual material has already emerged, it simply goes into the "repressed *submergent* unconscious," while if it is just beginning to emerge, it remains in the "repressed *emergent* unconscious," kept there, not by lack of growth (which is usual), but by active repression or aggressive dis-owning (hence "the *repressed* emergent unconscious"). In either case, the repressed transpersonal component generates shadow or subpersonality material, creating most often overblown allergies to anything spiritual and occasionally, strange and, to the individual, unexplainable attractions and addictions to spiritual material. In both cases (allergies and addictions), the individual suffering such repression might begin to feel numerous unpleasant symptoms (for example, severe headaches; energetic disruptions in the body—particularly circulatory/ heart and digestive problems; insomnia, anxiety, depression; or, if severe, bipolar disorders), as well as various symbols or symbolic expressions of the repressed spiritual material. (We have seen that projections might convert positive to negative qualities, so that demonic, evil, monstrous images might invade dreams or be perceived in those around one; alternatively, with repressions of the positive, brilliantly luminous and loving images and icons appear, but with no way to govern them or understand them; or they are projected onto other people, with concomitant hero worship and hyperadulation.)

Treating these "golden shadow" (emergent or submergent) dysfunctions can be very difficult, especially because the background cultural understanding of spiritual intelligence and its many levels and structure-stages is almost totally lacking (including the realization that some levels are infantile, some childish, some adolescent, some adult, and some extremely wise and mature), and instead the level of spirituality that is generally available is confined to the Magic-Mythic levels, which most grown adults find appropriately childish and silly. The result is a "level/line fallacy": the entire line of spiritual intelligence is confused and identified with only one of its levels—in this case, the Mythic-literal—and thus when the Mythic Level is dismissed, the entire line is dismissed with it. This is a very common cultural pathology in the West since the Enlightenment.

To help curtail all these hindrances, an entirely new and more comprehensive framework of spirituality needs to be almost muscularly learned by the affected individual (and it certainly wouldn't hurt if culture itself picked up some of these more accurate notions). Not to mention the difficulty of finding therapists or psychiatrists who are themselves aware of the transpersonal domains and have some experience with recognizing and treating them. This is one of the areas where a group practicing a classical meditative system can indeed be of help. Even though it will almost certainly lack an understanding of structure-stages and have no comprehension of the difference between structures and states, the simple presentation of a type of spirituality (meditation/Waking Up) that does not depend upon unwavering belief in a mythic-literal creed but instead seeks an actual change in the state of consciousness and Awareness itself can immediately offer a spirituality that is much higher on a general spiritual intelligence scale, thus bypassing most of the typical individual's qualms, reservations, and negative judgments about conventional religion. (This is also why an astonishing 20 percent of the population of the United States identifies with the phrase "I'm spiritual but not religious." "Spiritual" almost always means some form of direct, 1st-person, immediate, authentic spiritual experience; and "religious" almost always means the standard, institutional, mythic-membership, fundamentalist version of "religion." One poll, reported in the *New Monasticism*, showed an astonishing 75 percent of Millennials identified with that phrase. These are truths that are increasingly seeping into the culture at large, and all religions, sooner or later, will be forced to confront these very real issues.)

Necessity of a New Culture of Spirituality

I'm generally wary of consultant, or change agent, recommendations that require—as almost all of them seem to—when it comes to helping with global problems (global warming, financial meltdowns, warfare, terrorism, trafficking, nation-state inadequacies, worldwide ecological disruptions, disease epidemics, problems with capitalism and consumerism, and so forth), changes that, in order to actually work, involve virtually all people on the planet changing their way of thinking to agree with the changes the expert is recommending. In order to work, changing from the values of consumerism, greed, and profit, for example, to the values of love, care, and compassion, will have to be embraced by the vast majority of every man, woman, and child on the planet. How to do that is never explained. A snap of the finger, and suddenly all humans have changed in the ways the change agent recommends, and then the world is better. Um . . .

But it's hard not to get the notion that, particularly when it comes to spirituality and religion, the global village needs a worldview change. Consider what is happening with structure-stages themselves. If we look at the premodern tribal and traditional world, today's modern and postmodern world, and then the coming age (which I will describe in a moment), which we can refer to, respectively, as Worldview 1, Worldview 2, and Worldview 3, one feature stands out, almost above all others, as being prominently featured in each of them—and that is the relation of each of those eras to a Supreme Reality. In Worldview 1 (the premodern world), the relation is that God is everywhere; in Worldview 2 (today's world), God is nowhere; and in Worldview 3 (the coming world), God is everywhere again. This is a shocking, violent, utterly pandemic series of jerking changes, and they jump out at you wildly and unmistakably once you see them. And these are violent shifts that humanity actually had to (or soon will) undergo.

The premodern Worldview 1 was marked, almost without exception, by cultures that everywhere saw some sort of Higher Being, Intelligence, God, Goddess, Spirit, or Nature spirits as being the Source and Ground of all existence. A human being's job was to come into as close and compatible a relationship with that ultimate Being (or beings) as possible; and all disasters, bar none, were due to being out of correct relationship with this ultimate Reality (whether the tribal Great Spirit of Nature or the traditional Father Who Art in Heaven). This Reality was, in virtually all cases, of a Magic or Mythic-literal variety. (There was the occasional subtle or causal—possibly nondual—state experience, but otherwise this is a Magic-Mythic world.)

And thus, virtually the first thing that the modern Worldview 2 announced was "the death of God." The belief in magic or mythic beings, ultimate or otherwise, was rejected entirely and across the board, and a rational scientific materialism stepped in and dominated the greatest thinking minds—and the background culture—of the entire era (and still does at this time). A mythic, revelatory mode of knowing was replaced by a rational, experimental mode of knowing, and with people like Isaac Newton, suddenly "all was light." Evolution stepped into God's traditional role of creator and refiner of manifestation, and supernatural beings or forces of any variety were rejected in total. The entire human race went from believing that God was everywhere to believing that God was nowhere. It was literally and wildly that abrupt and that massive a change in human beliefs and values. Of course, everybody, even in the Age of Enlightenment, is born at square one, and must grow and develop through the level-stages that have emerged thus far, and so any individual in the modern and postmodern age begins at Archaic, moves to Magic, further grows to Magic-Mythic, and if development continues, moves into Mythic and then only into Rational and possibly even Pluralistic. Numerous individuals stop short of the highest Rational or Pluralistic stages, and thus various percentages of the population remain at Magic or Mythic stages. In the United States, for example, almost 60 percent of the population today is "churched"—hence likely at a Mythic or lower level (correlatively, Robert Kegan, in *In Over Our Heads*, estimates that 3 out of 5 Americans, 60 percent, are at Mythic or lower)—whereas in northern Europe, only 11 percent are churched. But the leading edge, in any event, and the mainstream cultural background philosophy, is Rational/Pluralistic, and NO GOD is its credo.

Yet what is awaiting us? Virtually every major developmental model that looks into that leading edge sees, beyond the further reaches of today's stages (somewhere around "integral" or "systemic" levels), stages that can only be called "spiritual" or "transpersonal" (from Kohlberg's highest "universal mystical" to Maslow's "self-transcendence" to Cook-Greuter's "transpersonal" and "unitive" to O'Fallon's "transpersonal" and "nondual"). These are definitely spiritual in the sense of "not religious," meaning not magic or mythic—definitely NOT *pre*-rational—but rather are superconscious and *trans*-rational (transcending and including reason). Humanity is headed, one more time, into a staggeringly monumental and wrenching transformation, this time from NO GOD ANYWHERE to another type of GOD IS EVERYWHERE. The whole point of calling these 3rd-tier transpersonal stages "structure-stages" is that they are not voluntary stages one may or may not take up (as Waking Up is), but rather are stages that everybody, like it or not, want it or not, will grow through, if grow indeed they do. Humanity will be growing into stages where superconscious, transpersonal, transrational realities are a given in any and every culture that continues its growth, development, and evolution. This is indeed a "God everywhere," but the experience of God here is now at the opposite end of the spectrum of growth, not at its earlier, infantile, and childish stages (prerational magic and mythic), but at its highly evolved, radically mature stages (transpersonal and transrational 3rd tier). Given the fact that developmental stages are recognized as stages only if they cannot be skipped or bypassed, and given that every developmental model that looks into it sees something like a transpersonal 3rd tier headed this way, then humanity on the whole is, virtually with no doubt whatsoever, moving directly into a GOD IS EVERYWHERE future.

And therefore, the religion of tomorrow will be a widely pervasive, thoroughly accepted, if radically different form of spirituality (including at least the aspects that we are covering in this volume). But that it will come into existence, whatever it may actually turn out to be, is something very close to a certainty, based on compelling, present-day, direct, developmental evidence.

One of the most profound problems imaginable with this development is that the only language widely available to discuss this transrational God comes from nothing but the prerational holdovers of a much earlier and less mature era. Virtually every word out of the mouth of anybody in Coming Age Worldview 3 will be exposed to various "pre/trans fallacies" —that is, confusing prerational and transrational because both are nonrational. And so here is my "globally sweeping (every man, woman, and child)" claim: we need an entirely new language, an entirely new semiotics, an entirely new way to talk about God, in order to describe the world that we are growing into. Without that, we are headed for a confusion-of-meaning epidemic that is of staggering proportions.

At first, people will be forced to use the signs and terms of the prerational traditions, speaking of "God" and "Goddess" and "Spirit" and "Ultimate" using the terminology well developed by those traditions and used not only by the entire human race for the totality of its first major era but also by large populations who remain at those stages in today's world. The meaning of those words will be, in many cases, almost the complete opposite of what 3rd-tier individuals have in mind when they use those terms; but what other terms will they have?

And so, yes, this is a plea that we start now by putting in place "conveyor belts" of spiritual intelligence in each and every major Great Tradition the world over (I know, the odds of that are close to zero), but I'm sure you can see the problem. With conveyor belts in place (which would interpret the main tenets of the given spiritual system in the specific terms of each of the 6-to-8 major levels of development), we would already have a system that recognizes the fundamental differences in spiritual and religious worldviews at each and every major structure-stage of growth (as well as hopefully working in state-stages of Waking Up), and thus, as humanity collectively gets closer and closer to transpersonal 3rd tier and the jerking changes that are headed our way as we move from a GOD NOWHERE culture to a coming GOD EVERYWHERE culture, we will already have large communities of individuals that have been, in collective human interaction and real pragmatic applications, developing entirely new languages and practices for these new and higher levels of consciousness and spiritual intelligence. Instead of a collision-of-meanings transition of monumental proportions—a fifty-car cultural Kosmic collision—we would have a relatively smooth shift from a world where God is nowhere to be seen or found to a world where God begins to look out of the eyes and hear with the ears of larger and larger numbers of people (not to mention the Kosmos at large), a shift that will change the values, meanings, goals, and purposes of every culture on earth.

This is happening, my friends. It is a tsunami headed our way. It will affect every single area of human existence and change it in ways that we can only begin to imagine. But headed this way it most certainly is. How shall we respond?

Structure-Related Problems

Finally, a few brief words on those dysfunctions in the gross and gross-reflecting state that are generated by problems in one of the major structure-stages and its development in that gross state. What these all have in common are fractures or lesions in a structure that leave open and invite, or even cause, higher-state elements to stream into the gross-state ego. I've already discussed a few of these (such as distorted Nature mysticism). A few quick observations on each structure-stage itself.

With the magenta Magic View self-sense (Fulcrum-2), some of the major dysfunctions here (in addition to sexual and impulsive disorders) are the borderline syndromes, where the self–other boundary is only tenuously formed, and thus is open to constant, overwhelming disruption by present experience ("too much experience, not enough structure," is commonly said of these ailments). Invasion by subtle-state material usually exaggerates this already difficult problem, placing more stress on the self–other boundary than it can already handle. If severe enough, this can push borderline syndromes into bipolar, possibly even psychotic conditions. Borderline conditions are already considered close to "incurable," and with subtle-state invasion, unfortunately this becomes even more the case.

At red Magic-Mythic, or the power stage (Fulcrum-3), higher-state infusion (subtle and occasionally causal) usually ups the amperage of the "power-over" drive, increasing the—it's hard to say it any other way—obnoxiousness of the dysfunction. This condition is already egocentric, and subtle-state inflation can reactivate Fulcrum-2 narcissism, making the power-driven person into a near Caesar, Christ, Napoleon, or some such (a "legend in their own mind"). That's what happens with a power addiction; if the person is in a power-allergy condition, the influx of subtle-state material often goes to the other side of the self-boundary, making the "other" even more powerful and the self even less powerful. Both of these, of course, make the Fulcrum-3 disorder even more difficult to treat and handle.

At amber Mythic-membership (Fulcrum-4), higher-state infusions become indelibly intermixed with the person's conceptions of the Great Other (God or Spirit) that they already "religiously" believe in. The absolutistic drive often becomes, if possible, even more absolutistic. There are real and higher energies pouring into one's conception of this Great Other, making it altogether "more Great" (and with, we have seen, partially true material). This makes the fundamentalist View, already well nigh impossible to budge, almost completely impossible to budge. If this happens, individuals are close to guaranteed to spend virtually all of their life at this Mythic-literal stage, driven as they are now by an ongoing infusion and transfusion of authentic subtle-state blood. These people often appear (and in some ways actually are) very much "at peace." They have an unshakable access to the one and only ultimate God in all reality, assured of His loving and caring protection of every element in their lives. What could possibly go wrong?

At orange Rational-achievement (Fulcrum-5), an influx of higher-state material charges the achieving self (or the desired-to-be-achieved goal) with an extra shot of energy and value. The state of excellence so arduously sought becomes almost Divine in its dimensions and desirability, driving the individual to even more overachievement and relentless seeking. An occasional (more rare) occurrence is the invasion of awareness by a causal formless condition, which can dismantle the entire value of the previously sought-after goal, as well as decimate the self-esteem that is sought (by decimating the self). This becomes quite difficult to handle because the factors contributing to it are so multivariate, and very few therapists have all the pieces of the puzzle available to them (all structures, all states, their characteristics and interactions, the exact nature of shadow material, the quadrant interfaces, and so forth). Generally speaking, as the causal-state experience fades more and more into memory, the achievement-state conditions slowly reconstruct themselves, though rarely with the same enthusiasm. Growth to the Pluralistic multiperspectival stage, should it occur, offers this individual a more peaceful station of life at which to rest.

With green Pluralistic-relativism (Fulcrum-6), invasion by higher-state material generally leads to a variety of confusing results and seemingly paradoxical stances. "Aperspectival madness," endemic to this stage, can, somewhat paradoxically, become relaxed, as the subtle (or occasionally causal) state certainty latches on to one or a small handful of perspectives and energizes those above all others, giving the Pluralistic individual some actual ground on which to stand and make a genuine decision of preference (instead of trying to hold all options completely open in egalitarian equality—with its resulting paralysis). A particular activity or job that the person is involved with suddenly becomes *valuable* and *meaningful*—that is, *better* than alternatives, not just different. Meaning can actually be reestablished in this individual's life, much to his or her satisfaction (if occasional confusion). Downsides can occur when a sudden influx of causal-state formlessness evaporates the already tenuously held multiple perspectives, leaving all of them even more "deconstructed" than before. It becomes almost impossible to reinstate any sort of value or meaning in these cases, since all perspectives are equally vacuous, and this is now further backed by a higher-state certainty. This isn't a true equanimity (such as with the mirror mind) but an aperspectival madness carried almost to infinity. Therapy is almost always ineffective here, since too many factors have to be lined up and knocked down for any traction to occur; hope, though slim, rests with continued growth into Integral 2nd tier.

Such a higher level—the teal Holistic (Fulcrum-7) and turquoise Integral (Fulcrum-8), which together constitute "the Integral level"—is already a bit of a transition zone, from purely "earth-bound" 1st tier to increasingly "heaven-bound" 3rd tier, and higher states can hit this zone with any number of quite different results. One possibility is that the positive influx of subtle or causal states lands on the vision-logic of Wholeness, and in doing so, simply stamps that Wholeness with even more believability. This occurs when the "peak-experienced" higher state is diffused evenly over and through this stage (with a "full fusion" or "embeddedness" type experience); if it remains as an astonishingly different and higher felt state, set apart from any present reality by its greater Presence and Allure, this actually cuts into the present level's feeling of Wholeness and posits a yet-higher realm existing somewhere beyond what present vision-logic can disclose. If this stage is fairly well along in its maturation, this can act as a genuine catalyst to "transcend and include" this stage by opening itself to yet-higher occasions. If, on the other hand, this stage is just being entered, such an experience can undermine the reality of the stage itself, making accommodation and adaptation to it more difficult. In these circumstances, essentially the whole of conventional reality is "demoted" by this sparklingly higher state/realm, and ordinary reality in general loses it luster, its allure, its believability. In some ways, this can be handled by a "Right View," so that the individual understands that although these higher states are real, they don't displace or deny the importance of ordinary structures and stages, so these shouldn't be dismissed cavalierly. At 2nd-tier levels, most subtle, causal, and nondual states are experienced with significant transpersonal elements, and if these are appropriately understood in their correct Integral context, these transpersonal experiences can lie in the storehouse consciousness and act as significant teleonomic pulls, or attractors, to both higher structures and higher states. On the other hand, as always, infusion from higher states can drive up any narcissism or egocentrism still remaining in the system, or, if severe, actually contribute to some degree of regressive activity. The centaur (the finite self at 2nd tier) is not transcended into soul or Higher Self but is invaded by, and confused with, soul or Higher Self, resulting in simple inflation of the self. This "inflation," in a variety of different forms, can occur at virtually any structure and any state, with a simple inflationary influx of any higher state.

Subtle-State Dysfunctions

The subtle state, which is capable of being developed (and thus exists as a state-stage with its particular Vantage Point),[4] can not only suffer the general types of dysfunctions that the gross can (though with different content), it can also undergo the typical problems that occur at any point in the overall developmental process itself (relating to differentiation/dis-identification/integration)—that is, there can be problems at any subphase of the switch-points as they move from gross to subtle, or from subtle to causal—in other words, problems with moving into the subtle space and problems with moving out of it. I'll start with the former.

Gross-to-Subtle Dysfunctions

We already saw that, according to many meditative systems, the growth from gross to subtle involves the dis-identification with an exclusive identity with the gross realm itself (and its qualities and traits) and a higher exclusive identity with the subtle itself (and its qualities and traits), which results likewise in a shift from a Vantage Point that sees the world (in terms of states) primarily through the gross lens to a Vantage Point that sees the world primarily through a subtle lens— that is, moving the self-sense from the ego to the soul.

The soul, in relation to the ego, is primarily defined by its "visionary" qualities, which in their various forms, move quite beyond the standard, ordinary, gross, sensorimotor, or physical realm. The ego, in all its actions—including even the way it uses the Wholeness of vision-logic—is always something in final reference to the sensorimotor realm. In its food drives, it is material; in its sex, it is physical; in its fame and fortune, it is in reference to the amount of gross sensorimotor goods it can purchase and consume—lots of money, many houses, numerous expensive automobiles, lots of women with attractive physical attributes (or many adoring men), global travel, and so on. It uses vision-logic to create vast networks of holistic systems (as vision-logic, by definition, does), but all the systems are composed of material sensorimotor bits (actual physical objects or physical digital data bits and bytes, and physically transmitted information streams). It is related, in its thoughts, actions, and deeds, to the Right-hand, exterior, sensorimotor *surfaces* of all things and events, and this is in keeping with its essentially gross and gross-reflecting nature.

The soul, on the other hand, is oriented to interiors. This includes a native orientation to Left-hand phenomena, both in itself and in other beings. The soul lives on vision and visionary elements (all the way up to the meta-mind and its visionary worldview). This means elements that, in themselves, are not directly related to the present, physical, gross sensorimotor realm but to today's wildest possibilities, highest reaches, deepest feelings, widest perspectives, grandest visions, most creative insights, and the greater grandeur of what tomorrow can bring, in all its wondrous possibilities and evolutionary innovations. According to many traditions, the soul is the aspect of consciousness that, composed of the same "subtle energy" as the wildly creative dream state and the bardo realm (the "in between" state following the death of the present gross body and the individual's reincarnation in the next life's gross body), is said to actually exist in a continuing fashion from one life to the next to the next (until final Liberation). The ego stores lessons we learn in this life; the soul stores ongoing lessons we learn from life to life. The traditions generally maintain (including many of the early schools of Christianity) that we are put here on earth to learn certain vital and central issues of existence itself, and as these lessons are learned, they are stored in what the Tibetans call "the eternal drop for all time." That is, there is an ongoing, reincarnating, life-to-life learning process, which stores our accumulated "wisdom" and "virtue." Thus, the soul doesn't contain specific memories of past lives—the memories of one's present life are stored in the organic brain of this life's gross body (and the Tibetans refer to this as "the drop for this life") and die when that brain and its body die. Rather the soul contains the general life lessons summarized as our "wisdom," which usually means understanding of ultimate Truth (Godhead, Emptiness or Suchness, absolute *bodhichitta*), and our "virtue," which usually means our understanding of relative truth ("good deeds" and compassion, relative bodhichitta). Remembering being "Cleopatra" or "Napoleon" is not what the soul is about; continuing to grow in wisdom and virtue, from life to life, is.

Let me stress that it is definitely not required that one believe in reincarnation or transmigration in order to accept Integral Theory. "Life-to-life" lessons can be interpreted as lessons in this life that are nonetheless "bigger than this life" and that reach "beyond my ego"—those are good definitions of "subtle soul" as well. But Integral Theory, as a metatheory, makes room for reincarnation as a possible *hypothesis*, and if we tentatively accept this hypothesis, I believe that as this subtle soul travels from life to life, we are born, in each life, with a given "developmental set point"—the highest general level of development that we achieved in our previous life, whether red, orange, turquoise, violet, and so forth. (There is also a state developmental set point; same basic idea but with reference to states.) Given this set point, all of our development and transformation in our new life, up to the set-point altitude, occurs relatively quickly and easily and with very few problems; once at the set-point altitude, the individual must then begin sincere and often difficult growth and consciousness transformation, often with great effort, since each new and higher stage of development (structure or state) is bought only by learning new lessons that are not contained in the soul's accumulated "wisdom" and "virtue" thus far (and included in its set point). So each stage that the self manages to attain in the new life, beyond the set-point stage, occurs by the self learning new and higher wisdoms and virtues, which are then stored in its "eternal drop" and become part of the new set point in its next life.

Whatever one thinks about reincarnation, it at least explains one of the most puzzling and confusing facts that developmentalists see all the time—and cannot satisfactorily explain: some individuals, placed in almost ideal circumstances with close-to-perfect parents, still develop in poor, retarded, dysfunctional ways, and others, exposed to the most wretched environments and circumstances imaginable, nonetheless develop quickly and in normal, sometimes even exceptional, ways. Margaret Mahler, perhaps the greatest developmental observer ever to appear, summarized all the evidence by saying—contrary to virtually every developmental model in existence—that "the lion's part of adaptation must come from the pliable, unformed infant,"[5] which is to say that despite what the parents might do, or the presence of reinforcing environments, or any of the other factors developmentalists always point to in order to account for development, said development is basically up to the child, period. The child—not parents, or schooling, or environmental factors—determines the basic course of development. At the least, the claim that the child comes with a previously determined "developmental set point" is in perfect agreement with that evidence. Parents with more than one child almost always instinctively know this—although they raised all their children essentially the same, the children usually end up with wildly differing personalities, despite being treated more or less identically, as if they came "preformed" in many ways, which, according to reincarnation, they most definitely do. Needless to say, I repeat, it is not necessary to believe in reincarnation in order to embrace Integral Theory; it's simply one of the possibilities to which the theory, as an inclusive overview, is open.

An early version of the soul self-sense can be intuited as early as red and kicks in at amber, but is more common in 2nd tier and beginning 3rd tier; it must engage at the latest by meta-mind. Its potential space is nonetheless experienced each night in the dream state, as well as being the self-sense that functions during the entire subtle-stage range of meditation practices. Daniel Brown defines the beginning of his stage of subtle-state *Awareness* as the dropping of an identity with the gross self and its thoughts and the emergence of the subtle "personality"— that is, the subtle soul. The soul experience is a sense of expansiveness in consciousness, of open, luminous, loving clarity; the soul has a sense of opening to higher and wider and inwardly deeper spaciousness, and has an intuition of its ongoing reincarnated nature as a feeling close to timelessness. (Thus, whether actually reincarnated or not, it is definitely getting closer and closer to its fully timeless Original Face, or the Unborn/Undying True Self of the empty Witness state, which, as the causal/Witness, is the state immediately "above the head" of the subtle soul, and is constantly intuited by it.) The ego sees the present physical world and its possibilities; the soul sees the possibilities of a whole evolutionary stretch of unfolding time, almost an infinity of "before" and "after," which it might interpret as stretching throughout lifetimes, temporarily focused on this one. (The reincarnated nature of the soul, whether realized as such or not, usually translates its lifetimes-of-experience nature into a feeling of vast spaciousness existing beyond this present physical self or ego. The soul knows it is more than anything the ego itself can see, and translates its "lifetimes-beyond-this-life" nature into a "consciousness beyond this present limited state and anything the ego can see," experiencing it as a vast, wider, higher, more open, more spacious, more divine, more luminous consciousness "above and beyond" its head—or within and beyond its Heart—and reaching to infinity (and hence this may, again, be interpreted as connected with an ongoing reincarnation, whether the reincarnation is actually real or simply the result of these types of interpretations of the expanded spaciousness of the subtle soul realm, which is most definitely real). Because the soul (for either reason) represents the "between lifetimes" enormous stretch of possibilities, it is always seeing beyond the present state or condition; always envisioning something higher, wider, deeper, brighter; always bringing a brilliance of creative insight to each and every moment; refusing to settle for what is and always asking "What can be?" It is the state (and the self-sense) immediately above the head of the ego (figuratively and occasionally fairly literally), and the ego is constantly intuiting this open brightness of possibilities, although deciding to act on it (by transforming its state center of gravity from gross to subtle) is a decision only the ego can make.

In short, the awakening of the subtle soul (from the gross ego) does not necessarily bring an awareness of past lifetimes (and awareness of specific past-life memories is not primarily what reincarnation is about, as we've seen); rather, soul awakening brings with it an expansion from gross states into subtle states, one of whose characteristics, according to many traditions, is the capacity to live in the subtle-awareness stream connecting one life to its reincarnated or transmigrated successor, but which, as I suggested, may instead be how it translates the immediate feeling of literal expansiveness, spaciousness, and openness, which reaches beyond the present limited gross condition and gross ego into higher, wider, deeper, even Divine awareness. The straightforward certainty of virtually all near-death experience survivors that "they will *never* die" comes from being directly embedded in this subtle (even causal) state that is "beyond," one way or another, this limited, gross body-mind and its Vantage Point. Zen describes nondual Suchness Enlightenment as "body-mind dropped!," and this subtle self or soul is the first great step toward that full "dropping," opening, as it does, onto a higher plane of greater awareness, wider consciousness, deeper love-capacity, and utter certainty that I AM more than this simple physical body-mind—in fact, much more. Of course, the traditions— mostly the Path of Saints—that focus merely, or especially, on the soul tend to interpret the highest spiritual state possible as one in which the soul lives on everlastingly, either from one life to the next to the next, or in some sort of everlasting heavenly realm, in either case never dying. This *everlastingness*, an endless temporal duration, is mistaken for *eternity*, a moment without time (the timeless Now or spontaneous Presence), and the highest self-sense is taken to be the immortal soul, while actually, we've seen, it is but a halfway house to True Self and ultimately nondual Suchness. Deity mysticism, which we've noted is the archetypal spiritual mysticism of the subtle realm, generally takes as its goals the awakening of the soul plus a recognition of, and "plugging into," its Divine Ground (via communion, union, or identity), which results in the *immortality* or everlasting existence of the soul, conquering "death" and living forever instead of surrendering to death and resurrecting on yet higher levels of greater Self and more Divinity. As a stage in Waking Up, awakening to the soul or subtle personality is invaluable and highly desirable; as the end point in Waking Up, it is an arrested development short of its own highest potential.

If during this developmental shifting from gross to subtle, there are any significant developmental snarls, these usually occur in one of two basic ways: The transforming self-sense remains stuck to, or in identification with, aspects of the gross ego, so that the soul emerges with a hidden "ego addiction." Or, at the other extreme, if the self-sense doesn't just dis-identify with the ego but dissociates and dis-owns it, the soul is saddled with an "ego allergy."

As for *ego addiction*, if there is a remaining attachment to the gross realm, then a common problem is that the self of the gross realm (the mental ego) becomes insinuated into the self of the subtle realm (the subtle soul) and thus the soul will remain attached and fixated (addicted) to various gross-realm desires, pursuits, and egoic goals (although the soul usually dresses up this "ego addiction" in subtle-soul terminology and disguises). This will infect the subtle stage's *Awareness* (Daniel Brown's term for this subtle state-stage) with remaining gross-realm thoughts, images, desires, and feelings. This hidden ego fixation or addiction will make it almost impossible to experience the Awareness (of the subtle realm) with any sort of purity or clarity. Where illuminative insight and clarity should begin to dominate consciousness, remaining gross-realm thoughts and emotions will invade it, obscuring Awareness with drives particularly common to the lower three chakra/realms—food, sex, and power (and all lower six chakras considered as "gross-reflecting"). The soul itself will be somewhat egocentric, meaning, in this case, that it will take on some of the characteristics and drives of the ego itself ("this-worldly" money, sex, fame, power). This is behind everything from a priest committing pederasty to a spiritual teacher spending students' money on a dozen Rolls-Royces.

With such an ego addiction (or hidden ego fixation), the soul will—to say the same thing in a slightly different way—develop a fixation or addiction to various egoic needs and drives. If the subtle is being experienced in its particularly spiritual forms—especially the common "deity mysticism" of this realm (with an emphasis on Spirit in 2nd person)—this addiction will directly affect the soul's approach to the Divine itself. For example, the soul may wish to extract from Spirit the objects of egoic wants (usually disguised and rationalized—if it has a desire for excessive wealth, for example, the prayer might be "In order to help spread your Word more effectively, oh Lord"), which is usually accompanied with "fighting" with the Divine over the often guilty conscience that results as it overindulges in egoic food, sex, money, or fame. If, on the other hand, the spirituality of this realm is fundamentally Spirit in 1st person, or Awareness per se, then Awareness will become contaminated with constant interferences of egoic thoughts and feelings (again, often relating to food, money, sex, or power, with the fixation this time to the self-sense or the subject that desires those). There is a constant interruption of the subtle meditation stages with gross egoic thoughts, images, desires, and feelings; no matter what the student does, he or she just can't seem to shake egoic inclinations, which often confuses the teacher as well (since the student might be doing everything right in the actual subtle stages—the problem is, those stages are *unconsciously* infected with egoic qualities from the moment of their arising).

On the other hand, if the soul is more consciously indulging in its egoic inclinations, meditation under those circumstances is then often taken up as a way to (explicitly or implicitly) increase the ego's access to these lower-realm objects and skills, because the soul usually believes that meditation will increase a person's power and capacity and aptitude to do so (which, in a certain sense, is true). Business leaders will take up meditation as way to "kill the competition"; athletes as a way to "bury their adversaries"; specific structure-stages in their gross-oriented forms can be fixated to, with their particular desires coming to the fore (a way to increase "absolute truth" in amber, "achievement" in orange, "sensitivity" in green, and so forth). Much of "mindfulness" training in the West is being sold to egos as a way to increase the ego's physical longevity, business prowess, athletic success, or financial gains, among an almost endless list of gross egoic desires.

At the other extreme, there is *ego allergy*. If there is a dissociation from the gross mental ego, then the soul will develop a dis-owning (and allergy) to various egoic drives and needs, and often to the ego itself in toto—an "ego allergy," in whole or part. The ego is then attacked wherever evidence of it is seen—in theology, in psychology, in oneself, in other people. The ego (often confused with *any* sort of self-sense or self-system at all, including a normal, healthy self-construct or authentic self necessary for conventional awareness) is demonized as the source of all sin, illusion, separation, and suffering—the "ego" becomes the devil incarnate. Every human problem—literally, every single human problem—is blamed on the ego. An allergy to egoic concerns prevents Awareness from attaining an even equanimity to all the contents of consciousness—it will subtly (and usually unknowingly) spend much time and effort avoiding any issues that remind it of the ego. Instead of owning the ego correctly, and *then* dis-identifying with it, moving up to soul, identifying with that, and integrating the gross realm into overall consciousness, aspects of the gross realm relating to egoic identity, function, or forms will be repressed, alienated, and disowned. While the soul is becoming the new God, the ego is becoming the new devil. As a consequence, both the soul—and Awareness—are deformed. (This is particularly a problem in Western Buddhism.)[6]

This dysfunctional negating of any or all things gross/egoic can result in a wide variety of very specific negations and repressions—for example, of food, leading to conditions such as bulimia or anorexia; of sex, with a Puritanical sex repression confused with sex transcendence (and inclusion); of money, where the correct spiritual attitude is taken to be a complete rejection of any financial motivations whatsoever ("money is the root of all evil"); of power, where the appropriate spiritual approach is held to be so noninvasive and "sensitive" as to amount to complete psychospiritual anemia; and so on, through any gross object, inclination, or desire (in essence, destroying the entire Nirmanakaya).

Or the egoic allergy can extend to the entire sense of subjectivity itself, especially in its anatta or "no-self" forms, where any sense of subjectivity is denied as it arises. On the one hand, that approach may, almost accidentally, lead to a genuine awakening of ultimate nondual Suchness (but only if the ultimate is not itself directly interpreted as being "no-self" as opposed to "self"—a deeply dualistic notion that will effectively prevent an authentic realization of nondual Suchness and lead instead to an experience of a relativized "emptiness"). But more likely this egoic allergy will undercut not only an awareness of any "I" but also of any "I-I." The individual recoils in the face of his or her own Real Self and true Witness (or the entire turiya state). The "I-I" is an important step on the way to pure nondual Suchness (or turiyatita), and automatically cutting off any subjectivity of any sort directly undercuts higher and the highest Absolute Subjectivity (Zen master Shibayama's term for Buddha-mind). It is from Absolute Subjectivity (or "I-I") that Absolute Nonduality (or Suchness or Thusness) is most directly, fully, and easily realized. Starting from the gross egoic realm and denying all sensations of subjectivity will directly and profoundly undermine that growth in Awareness. Denying any sensation of subjectivity is one of the easiest ways to derail Waking Up that there is, and when it leads to Waking Up (which is fairly rare), it does so almost "accidentally," because the person is undercutting subjectivity by accessing nondual Suchness without actually realizing what he or she is doing. "Right View" is *not* that there is only "no-self" in all domains, but that there is a relatively real and healthy authentic self (at every stage of altitude development), through which the true Witness or Real Self (and ultimately nondual Suchness itself) expresses itself and communicates with the conventional finite world. Denying such a conventional self (as egoic allergy does) does not get rid of the conventional finite self—because that is always present, liked or not—but merely relegates its development to the realm of the accidental; the finite self simply has to look after itself, with no help from the individual at all, and in most cases it fairly quickly degenerates into one or another form of false self (where shadow elements flourish because no responsibility is being assumed for this conventional self, and thus its boundaries become recklessly porous and poorly maintained, allowing shadow material to be easily generated). And it is with this false self that ultimate Suchness must express and communicate itself (disastrously, always).

Part of the difficulty in these cases is a mismanagement of the "transcend and include" drive of development and evolution itself, and this occurs because of the poorly framed relation of the spiritual realms (starting with the subtle) and the conventional realms (headed by the ego). Instead of surrendering an *exclusive* identity with the gross realm, the self believes it must surrender the entire gross realm itself, not merely an exclusive attachment to, or identity with it. That is indeed one of the main issues spirituality must address, but it does so by "transcending and including" the gross—not by "transcending and repressing" or "fixating and grasping." The former (allergy to the gross) and the latter (addiction to the gross) both malform the gross *and* the subtle in their own insidious ways. Consciousness, as it moves from gross thoughts and feelings to subtle Awareness, needs to equanimously let go of *exclusive attachment* to gross thoughts and feelings, while *preserving the capacity to think and feel*—and to neither fixate on nor dis-own any of them. Doing either one fundamentally distorts the very nature of the soul—and its subtle Awareness—as well as the mental ego (and its thoughts and feelings, all of which should become subsets, or objects, of a subtle self-awareness, not an addiction or an allergy of it). Ironically, by allergically avoiding and denying the ego, the ego remains embedded in consciousness, distorting both the subtle soul and subtle Awareness (or the overall subtle Vantage Point).

These are just a few of the major dysfunctions that can occur in the dynamic and developmental relationship between the gross realm (and its self, the mental ego) and the subtle realm (and its self, the subtle soul). As is generally the case, difficulty anywhere in the "transcend and include" ("negate and preserve") process will result in various dysfunctions. At this gross-to-subtle switch-point, problems with the "transcend" (or "negate") aspect usually mean a failure to do so correctly, leading to a fixation on the gross ego (or aspects of the gross realm), which results in various addictions to gross-realm phenomena (especially food, sex, money, power, fame, and material wealth). On the other hand, difficulties with the "include" or "preserve" component mean a failure to integrate the previous realm, and a phobic dis-owning of the gross ego (or aspects of the gross realm), which results in numerous allergies to the gross realm (allergies particularly to, again, food, sex, money, power, fame, and material wealth) or a general allergy and denial of subjectivity itself (which can derail the entire Waking Up process). In both cases, both the ego and the soul—and gross thoughts or feelings and subtle Awareness—are simultaneously deformed and misnavigated, resulting in numerous dysfunctions, pathologies, and incorrect (inaccurate) meditative or spiritual development—problems made all the worse by the positively anemic understanding in this culture of development in general and spiritual development in particular.

The subtle-state/realm is a particularly vulnerable location in the AQAL Matrix for pathological malformations, for the simple reason that it is the major transition realm between conventional material realms (gross) and higher unmistakably spiritual and transpersonal realms (causal and higher). As the transition point—the switch-point—between the finite and the infinite, it especially falls to the subtle to master the intricate dynamics of "transcend and include"—especially including or integrating both finite and infinite, earth and heaven, "this-worldly" and "other-worldly." The spiritual domain is, as we have seen, a realm of increasing paradoxes in which the "pairs of opposites" are ideally brought closer and closer together, in more and more harmonious, dialectical, and interwoven forms. This depends first and foremost on the developmental/evolutionary process of "negate and preserve" or "transcend and include." This is why, in most Great Traditions, developing the "Right View" is usually placed somewhere near the very beginning of the spiritual process, since having a correct understanding of actual spiritual development is crucial. This is one reason why including both states and structures (Waking Up and Growing Up)—or, in general, having a more Integral view—is so important to any new and inclusive Spirituality or Fourth Turning.

Subtle-to-Causal Dysfunctions

The subtle, I just noted, is an especially significant (and sensitive) switch-point in development, since it is the major transition point between more ordinary, conventional realms (gross and gross-reflecting) and senior, more spiritual realms (causal and higher). And things can go wrong in the subtle, as with most other states and structures, in one of two directions: problems dealing with the previous stage and material that has already emerged in existence, and problems with the succeeding stage and material that has not yet emerged but is in the process of doing so (that is, from the emergent unconscious, as well as from ongoing, creative, evolutionary emergence, Whitehead's "creative advance into novelty").[7]

I have already discussed the problems that the subtle might have with the already emerged gross. Problems with the yet-to-emerge (or just-beginning-to-emerge) causal are in some ways similar to all such emergent material: the present-stage self-sense has to die to itself in order to make room for the next higher realm, its self-sense, and its particular Vantage Point. Whether with respect to an emerging state or an emerging structure, this can be a very vexing, difficult, unnerving endeavor, and many of the problems of these soon-to-emerge higher states (or structures) involve the difficulty the present self has in dying, in fundamentally letting go of its being and its limited viewpoint (View or Vantage Point) and passing into a higher, wider, deeper sense of self, being, and Awareness.

For the subtle-to-causal relinquishment, this means the dark night of the soul—the subtle soul itself must die, must jump into the Abyss, must close its eyes to what looks like its entire life (only to discover a yet higher life on the other side of its apparent death). Of course, one of the simplest ways to face this issue (or pretend to face it) is to avoid it—to "pretend" to let go of the subtle soul and pass into the causal with a hidden soul fixation and addiction. This distorts the overall causal realm, its *Awareness-itself* (Brown's terminology), and what we can refer to as its Higher Self (using the following semantic definitions: the self of the gross is the ego; the self of the subtle is the soul; the self of the causal is the Higher Self; the self of the Witnessing state is the Real Self, or True Self; and the "self" of the Nondual is pure Suchness). I will return to this particular dysfunction (the distortion of the causal due to fixation to the subtle) when we discuss causal dysfunctions. Right now, I'll simply note, in regard to the subtle itself, that one of the dysfunctional ways that the subtle soul handles its "dark night" (where it must negotiate its own death) is by avoiding its death, or "pretending" to have undergone it, and trying to slip into the causal by directly identifying its soul with the Higher Self, which severely deforms the Higher Self and misnavigates the causal (and it often results in an abrupt cessation of any further development until adequately addressed). The difficulty here (again using Brown's terminology) is that the Higher Self operates by *Awareness-itself* (free of the soul or subtle personality), whereas the soul operates by *Awareness* (possessing soul or a subtle personality); fusing them drags *Awareness-itself* down into a denser, heavier, less expansive realm (mere *Awareness*) and deforms its actual contours and aims, which is to begin to be Aware of causal archetypes, thus making those subjects into objects, and readying the self to transcend them altogether in pure Emptiness, which, if development goes well, will happen in the next higher state-stage, the empty Witnessing realm.

This is an extremely important function—this overall Awareness-itself of archetypal material—and it is totally derailed when hijacked by the subtle soul, whose major wish is not to transcend all subtle and causal Form but to live forever in the realms of higher Form. The Higher Self is archetypal, formed of some of the most utterly subtle (that is, causal) Forms in existence, and, as noted, in turning its Awareness-itself on these causal Forms, or archetypes, it converts them into objects of Awareness-itself. "The subject of one stage becomes the object of the subject of the next," which is what the causal Higher Self is attempting to do—and this includes making the subtle soul, or *subtle subject* itself, into an *object* of Awareness-itself—thus dis-identifying and transcending the exclusive identity with the soul, and preparing for the major leap into Emptiness that is soon to occur, in the next state-stage. This momentous leap into Emptiness will be utterly derailed if the subtle soul, still hanging on to its subtle Forms and its very own life, refuses to allow those Forms—and itself—to become an object of Awareness-itself (and thus died to), and instead remains in (hidden) existence, attached to its subtle Forms, frightened deeply by its own dark night and its impending death. After all, what is being "let go of" and "died to" is an exclusive identity with the *everlastingness* of the soul, the *immortality* of the soul itself, in favor of the timeless Now of the causal Higher Self and Awareness-itself (which begins in the causal and finally culminates in the empty Witness), and until that jump is actually taken (and realized to be, in fact, a grand increase in consciousness, depth, openness, loving capacity, and spiritual embrace), it clearly appears as the loss of an *immortal* entity—what if it judges that wrongly? What is also being surrendered here, in the move from all subtle Forms to the near formlessness of the "dreamless" causal Higher Self, is virtually all of manifestation itself—what will be left for me? (Only a near infinitude of Grandeur and Glory.)[8]

The "dark night" aspect of the switch-points is generally of a double nature: it represents both the death of the self of the previous level—often experienced as a "dark night" or intensely felt fright of the life-lacking Abyss that the death of the present self-sense certainly appears to be—as well as another factor (which involves a regression back to the present stage after a leap forward to the higher stage, a regressive loss that is deeply depressing and "dark night" inducing;

we'll return to this shortly). Thus, there is a dark night of the senses—the death of the sensorimotor-reflecting gross ego as consciousness passes into the subtle realm, lets go of an exclusive identity with the physical body-mind, and opens into the luminous and visionary realm of the subtle; then a dark night of the soul—the death of the everlasting subtle personality (or soul) as consciousness releases an exclusive identity with the subtle realm and passes into the transpersonal causal and its "dreamless" Higher Self; then a dark night of the Self (which refers here to the causal and the Witnessing treated together, as they often are, as the formless causal/Witness, and with the causal Higher Self and the turiya True Self treated together as "the Self," namely, the ultimate and highest reach of a separate-self sense of *any* variety), which is the death, or release, of *any* experienced set-apart Self and its release into ultimate nondual Suchness as consciousness passes into Awakened Nonduality. In each of these cases, the dark night is synonymous with dis-identification, letting go of, dying to, releasing, transcending.

But there is also a second factor in these dark nights. It is often also the result of the person slipping back into its still present, soon-to-be-released self-sense ("slipping back" because it has not yet fully transcended this level) after having a preliminary experience of the next higher state—being bathed in its higher glories, wider expansiveness, luminous radiance, joy, and even bliss. Having once experienced a relative "heaven" and then having that heaven taken from him or her and being unceremoniously dumped back into the present squalid tenement housing (by comparison) often results in extreme pain, suffering, depression, or a feeling of hollowness (this is how, for example, St. John of the Cross generally uses "dark night").

The severity of any possible dark nights can often be best handled by a proper "Right View," which prepares the self for what is possible, even likely, in its higher growth, and lets it know that what appears to be a simple agonizing death is actually a death-and-rebirth, a death of its present self, yes, but a radiant resurrection on a higher level of a yet Freer and Fuller and more Liberated awareness—an advance forward in the process of Waking Up, not a retreat. But these dark nights, these death seizures, are one of the most common causes of developmental arrest in the growth process of Waking Up.

Another problematic approach of the subtle soul to the causal Higher Self is simply to denigrate and condemn a "Higher Self" in any form. Particularly in certain theistic traditions, for whom the soul is the highest self recognized, as well as for the zealous true believers of the anatta dogma, any "Higher Self" (especially, with the theistic traditions, one that is conceived as moving closer to a "Supreme Identity") is demonized and presented as a straightforward falsehood or, more sinisterly, as a demonic, evil, or heretical notion. We've seen that the soul spends a good deal of its time trying to extend its own life into a real everlastingness, hold on to its Awareness indefinitely, and deny the qualities of Awareness-itself (one of which is the death and transcendence of the subtle personality—the subtle subject or soul). The soul develops an "upwardly oriented" allergy to anything causal, including archetypes, original Forms of space-time, and occasionally the felt involutionary movement itself. This allergy to all things causal can, under certain circumstances, cause a rather problematic severing, or disruption, in the "downward causation" movement of involution per se, which shows up as actual disease processes in the physical and emotional realms, caused by the soul "choking off" subtler energies trying to "downwardly descend" from the causal realm. The many physical illnesses of a "spiritual" person are sometimes confused with the afflicted person being a "spiritual" person in the first place (as if it comes with the territory), whereas the real problem, in these cases, is often that these individuals are not being spiritual enough (they are not overly causal but lacking and avoiding the causal).

In the subtle state-stage itself, the soul can often dis-own, deny, dissociate, and project aspects of its own being and Awareness, and these can be either positive or negative qualities (recall that often the projection of positive qualities "flips" them into appearing as negative qualities, because the projection "flips" the direction of the quality as well, thus switching it from approaching others to others attacking oneself). To the soul that has projected its dis-owned aspects onto others, resulting in primarily negatively perceived qualities, the world appears full of such infected individuals, and the soul might take up various crusades to eradicate those qualities in the world (and sometimes, in extremis, to eradicate the infected individuals as well). This often happens when there is a previous dissociation of aspects of the lower realms (food, money, sex, power). The soul, having tasted some genuine transpersonal or spiritual or infinite qualities, misunderstands these lower aspects as barriers to further spiritual growth and hence tends to repress and project them (whereas the real barrier is these individuals' dysfunctional dis-owning of these qualities instead of healthily integrating them). So the soul takes up various anti-food, anti-money, anti-sex, anti-greed, or anti-power causes, zealously crusading against them (whereas the soul might do better to work for the *healthy* integration of these qualities into spiritual life). This is a fairly common problem with individuals who are sincerely spiritual (if "not religious") and are making excellent headway in their own state development of Waking Up—they get sidetracked with these dysfunctions and become zealously involved with all sorts of crusades, blowing them out of proportion, driven by this anti-money, anti-sex, anti-greed, anti-power, or any number of other rabidly pursued "anti-causes." They often achieve a fair amount of fame and name recognition for their "anti-crusade," because of the extraordinary energy and dedication they bring to the initiative (driven as it is by the inexhaustible energy of shadowboxing). This can be a particularly difficult issue to deal with, especially if they indeed become well known for promoting it; the shame of dropping it is terribly difficult to overcome.

The soul can dis-own, dissociate, and project either positive or negative soul qualities from *its own* state-stage (and not just a lower fixated stage), creating either a craving and hyperadmiration for (or hero-worshipping) those qualities in others when positive (Kosmic love, caring, compassion, greatness, humility, spiritual realization, equanimity, and peacefulness) or a loathing of those qualities in others when negative (Kosmic hatred, anger, alienation, jealousy, unethicality). This is a simple failure to integrate the qualities and traits of its own subtle level, and constitutes a miscarriage of development at that point. (A 3-2-1 or 3-2-1-0 process, or similar shadow work, is recommended; along with, as always, "Right View.")

The subtle is also the home, we have seen, of luminous forms that are easily interpreted as actual beings of light (or "alien" beings, angels, ascended teachers, and so forth), and if these forms (or beings) are projected, the individual will be in a stance of near-slavish worship of those onto whom the projection is made. One's entire life can be surrendered to such a hyperidealized person, usually with sad, sometimes dire, results, often of a cultic variety. Particularly if the individual has projected the sense of his or her own soul or Higher/True Self onto the other person, the results can be disastrous. The "Faust" legend is about an individual who sells his soul to the devil, and in effect, something similar happens here. The person onto whom the projection is made (often the spiritual teacher) now in effect "owns" the soul or Self of the individual; but this individual, instead of being paid (by the devil) for this extraordinary possession, is actually paying the devil for the privilege of surrendering his or her own soul/Self. Good teachers are used to this type of "Higher Self" transference and know how to interpret it so that the individual can recognize and awaken his or her own soul/Self as part of their ongoing spiritual practice. Some teachers, unfortunately, cultivate these types of transferences, encouraging their students to worship them exclusively as God, always with severe results.

The cure for these issues (and similarly related projections) resides, first, in finding a therapist or a group that has some understanding of these dynamics, or, at the least, practicing something like the 3-2-1 or 3-2-1-0 process adapted for higher states;[9] and, as always, embracing a more adequate, more inclusive, more comprehensive "Right View," such as, of course, the Integral.

The Need for a Soul Culture

If I might offer a short editorial at this point. Much of the criticism of Western culture rests entirely on critiques involving the gross, sensorimotor, waking state of manifestation. It's not that they're wrong. Some suggest that Western culture needs more feminine values, that its "patriarchal" orientation has committed it to much too aggressive, analytic, hierarchical, egocentric instead of ecocentric, relationship-focused instead of autonomy-focused, modes of being and awareness. There is some truth to this, as long as it is set in an Integral context. Western culture, for example, categorically does not need more feminine values per se. The first two stages of female moral development, recall, are (à la Carol Gilligan) the egocentric selfish and the ethnocentric care—and Western culture absolutely does not need more selfish and more prejudiced sexist/racist values. It's not enough to be female to contribute what Western society needs, because the very first two (and most common) stages of female values are exactly what the West needs less of, not more of. Those female values are actually damaging the West profoundly. What the West needs more of are the highest stages of female moral and value development—worldcentric universal care and integrated. But simply pushing female values is contributing to Western values decline. Others suggest that capitalism needs, if not to be jettisoned entirely, a drastically new face. John Mackey (cofounder of Whole Foods) and Raj Sisodia (coauthor of *Firms of Endearment*) take an explicitly Integral approach in *Conscious Capitalism*, using quadrants, levels, lines, and types to outline a much more compassionate and caring capitalism, ethical to its roots. There is much truth to those approaches, as well. And then there are the ever-present technophiles, waiting for the Singularity, at which point machines will take over not only providing the answers but also posing the questions facing Western culture, and provide such brilliant responses as to be beyond even human comprehension. There are at least some large grains of truth in this as well.

But I would like to add just one more point, at the least. We get few critiques focused on the West's *state* center of gravity. We get suggestions based on quadrants (Peter Senge's *Fifth Discipline*, which integrates the four quadrants); based on levels (Robert Kegan's and Lisa Laskow Lahey's *Immunity to Change*); based on lines (Alan Watkins's *Coherence* has ten lines that all his clients are expected to master—along with quadrants, levels, and types); and based on types (Helen Palmer's books on the nine Enneagram types). But virtually nothing on states. I agree with aspects of all of those critiques, and, of course, those of my Integral colleagues (such as Watkins and Mackey) who pull all of those together into genuinely Integral approaches (as my work attempts to do), but lacking in these mainstream suggestions are that any permanent transformations of the state center of gravity of the culture at large are needed.

This again slides into that iffy area of "this will work, but only if every man, woman, and child adopts my ideas," an area, I have indicated several times, of which I'm most wary. But it should at least be said that Western culture is long past the time that its predominantly ego-structured culture could and should become a *soul culture*. And by "soul," I don't mean in the sense of a fundamentalist mythic self-sense, locked into its ethnocentric, biased, in-group mentality, but in the sense of the actual subtle realm, which accepts interiors, is radiant with luminous creativity, and draws on the wisdom and virtue of, if not an actual string of past lives, then an extraordinary, unmatched learning process, or as a higher dimension of consciousness and culture beyond the ego's materialistic, exteriors-focused, self-centric, flatland orientation. The West has done everything that is necessary to make possible the emergence of this deeper, wider, higher dimension of reality. Particularly with the turn—and the jumpstart—that the process got in the sixties, the net result should have been that as individuals began to transform from around amber or orange to green (in structures), they would also have begun to "turn right" in states (referring to the layout of the Wilber-Combs Lattice), moving from being gross-ego oriented to subtle-soul oriented. Although the leading edge of culture in the Western world is today (on average) at orange/green altitude (in structures) with gross/egoic states (on average), it should be, at the least, at orange/green with a subtle-state center. We desperately need, in addition to any number of other important things, at the center, a *soul culture*. Now! (Don't you agree?)

There are two possible explanations of this. One is that, since Western culture has done everything required to be able to shift from gross to subtle—and yet it is not doing so—what is happening is that the subtle is, and has been for several decades (or longer), trying to emerge, but is actively being resisted, repressed, dis-owned (and thus shuttled into the repressed *emergent* unconscious, from which it would often be projected). If this were the case, we would expect to find an increase in hyperidealized individuals who the average citizenry virtually hero-worships, even in the face of a deconstructed gross-realm value system that makes idealization of anything virtually impossible, unless some sort of strong overriding factor is introduced (which is what this possibility suggests: what is being idealized is the greatness of a projected subtle-soul). We certainly see this in the millennials, who have made slobbering over the "famous"—and they are famous only for being famous—a character trait (why on earth does anybody even know who the Kardashians are?). What further makes this plausible is that most of the "famous," except for their fame, really have no special talent, skill, virtue, or shining characteristic that makes them any different from anybody else. They just happen to be famous, which polls of millennials show is ranked higher than having a good job, and this indicates that the soul's vertical *depth*, not any horizontal skill or talent, is what is driving this allure. Projecting their depth, they see it everywhere, and make following the famous a (almost literally) "religious" pursuit.

Another possibility is that the soul realm has actually already emerged in a fair number of people, but they have an enormous degree of ego addiction, so that the larger consciousness of the soul is being funneled (and narrowed downwardly) into merely gross egoic desires, wants, needs, and values. This becomes increasingly likely because, hundreds of years past the Enlightenment, as the ego continued its own growth and evolution, moving not only toward higher structures but higher states, the extraordinary growth in technology made the gross realm continue to yield up, in ever-increasing amounts, more and more material things that the ego craves—a highly technologized world is an ego's ultimate heaven. And thus, even as Eros pressure toward interior growth and evolution continued, the gross realm became more and more an obsessive dream of the egoic self, so that, as the profound allure of the deeper depth of the subtle-soul realm became more and more a reality, the capacity for addiction to the gross realm grew as well, sometimes even more rapidly. The only way to have your cake and eat it too was to transform to the subtle-soul realm, while remaining secretly addicted to the egoic-gross realm.

This certainly seems to hold true for the recent generation, which, research shows, value "money" and "fame" above all else (above job, relationships, self-realization)—quintessential egoic values, but invested with soul fervor and living through an extraordinarily developed technology and social media (the average millennial gets or sends eighty-eight messages a day). (The high rates of narcissism also point to an ego addiction.) But this phenomenon goes all the way back to the sixties and the Boomers, where so many leaders of the student rebellions couldn't wait to break into Wall Street, politics, or "business as usual," as if the awakening to interiors they had just so massively undergone was drained from them in a soul bleeding, leaving an ashen-white, bloodless, egoic face to rummage through the gross realm, trying to breathe life into a reality whose time had definitely come . . . and gone. So much of the hopes that the leading edge has today placed on technology—which is the single most exorbitant realm of substitute gratifications in today's world—are substitutes exactly for a conscious soul and Higher Self. They pound on the interior doors but are met by the gross-ego as it opens the entryway and points merely to the sensorimotor realm, hypertechnologized, for all things of value. And the majority duly follows this technologized egoic-gross Pied Piper—and with a subtle-soul "religious" fervor.

13

Dysfunctions of the Causal, Empty Witness, and Suchness States

Causal-State Dysfunctions

The causal also faces different dysfunctions depending upon which direction consciousness is facing when the disruption occurs: downward toward the subtle or upward toward Witnessing. I'll discuss them in that order.

We have already seen that one of the major subtle/causal disorders is when the subtle soul refuses to be relinquished and is carried, in disguised forms, into the causal, where it disrupts the form, function, and true goals and aims of the causal itself. Let's look at this problem from the view of the causal.

Subtle/Causal and Causal Dysfunctions

If all has gone well and proceeded in a functionally healthy fashion at the switch-point of the subtle to the causal state-stage, the subtle self (the subtle personality or soul) will have let go of itself, died to itself, and been reborn on the causal level of Awareness-itself, marked by one of the very subtlest (that is, causal) self-senses, that of the Higher Self and its capacity for Awareness-itself. The causal realm is the point at which the self and consciousness begin to develop an exhaustive awareness of all higher, or archetypal, forms in awareness—objectifying those potential subjects and thus preparing to transcend them altogether (in the next stage). This Awareness-itself begins to objectify the most subtle (that is, causal) forms in existence—namely, the archetypes—which include the very basic matrix of space-time itself. This activity is a type of "cleaning house," making into objects virtually all possible subjects, and thus clearing a space for Emptiness itself to arise (again, in the next state-stage).

If the casual Self retains any sort of hankering, grasping, or attachment to the positive delights of the previous subtle-soul realm, the first subphase of the subtle/causal switch-point (that of differentiation and dis-identification) will have been aborted to some degree, and the causal Higher Self will remain fixated on, addicted to, in disguised forms, the joys of the subtle soul (which, among numerous others, includes the feeling of projecting its inherently joyful self forward through space-time unendingly, or everlastingly, a true immortality addiction). If the Higher Self is attached (addicted) to that specific joy, as one example, then it will not be able to objectively witness, or become aware of, the archetypal space-time matrix itself (one of its primary missions), because it will be addicted to the everlasting joy of an everlasting space-time. It wants the security of time forever—literally, time stretching out before it in a never-ending duration—and not a moment without time. The causal Self will become addicted to space-time instead of witnessing and transcending it. Space-time will remain a hidden subject—a hidden lens through which consciousness *looks at* the world, and not a matrix at which consciousness looks, and thus objectifies (transcends). This causal fixation itself, if uncorrected, can even invade the next stage, the Empty Witnessing, and hence prevent true and genuine Emptiness from being realized. True eternity—which is not everlasting time but a moment free of time—will be confused with everlasting time (which is what the soul wants), and thus the genuine timeless Now and eternal Present will escape consciousness; the "timelessness" component of the Real will be conflated with an unlimited, everlasting series of temporal moments, thus never "ending." And this "never ending" will be taken as being truly free of death. It takes the "never-ending" nature of time as being in touch with the truly Undying—time never ends, hence death never occurs—whereas eternity actually is Undying because it never enters the stream of time to begin with, and hence, for that reason, it never experiences an ending. There is no ending because there's no beginning either, not because it goes on forever. Real timelessness, in short, is not continuing in time forever but being free of time altogether; it is the timeless Now and all-encompassing Present. As Wittgenstein said, "If we take eternity to mean not infinite temporal duration but timelessness, then eternal life belongs to those who live in the present."[1]

The causal Self's catastrophic confusion of eternity with everlastingness (via a space-time addiction) derails the recognition of Emptiness itself, or pure nirguna (unqualifiable) Spirit, because it is not actually free of time but is choking on time. It does not enter real Emptiness but an Emptiness contaminated and saturated with everlasting space-time, and—in a cascading, continuing series of catastrophes—this likewise prevents a genuine realization of Nonduality (the union of Emptiness and Form), since the "Emptiness" component is not truly Empty but is hiding everlasting time in the place of pure timelessness.

If, on the other hand, the causal Self goes too far, and instead of healthily dis-identifying with the soul, ends up dissociating and disowning the soul, a "soul allergy" will result, which will reverberate throughout the causal, effecting how the Higher Self per se experiences itself, since it has prematurely become wary of anything resembling a feeling of a self-sense or subjectivity (and a dissociation of subjectivity per se will lead directly to a rejection of Absolute Subjectivity, which we have seen is Zen master Shibayama's term for Buddha-mind—similar to Ramana's "I-I"). This can affect the functioning of Awareness-itself and prevent an even and equanimous witnessing of all causal objects, including all archetypes, because anything resembling a self-sense will be hyperavoided. This leaves "holes" in Awareness-itself—subjects that are not becoming objects because subjects are being avoided altogether, and thus remain as "hidden subjects" in Awareness-itself. If severe, the dissociated soul components can actually create a soul subpersonality, which will likely distort every single higher state-stage henceforth (because all forms of consciousness will be, to one degree or another, hijacked by the dissociated soul subpersonality, which injects its traits, drives, wants, and needs into consciousness at virtually every subsequent stage). This "soul allergy"—we have seen versions of this before—will also result in a loathing of anything perceived as a "soul"—in theology, in psychology, in spirituality, in oneself, in others. A new demon has arrived on the scene, and its name is "soul."[2]

On the causal level itself, any of its own qualities, traits, and characteristics (archetypes) can be dissociated, dis-owned, and projected. If positive qualities are projected, this generally results in an addiction to the person or phenomena onto which the positive quality has been displaced. These positive qualities, which are aspects of Awareness-itself and positive causal archetypes, include qualities such as Kosmic Love, Bliss, Being, Consciousness, Joy, Happiness, Open Energy, Flow, as well as any number of the causal forms traditionally interpreted as positive spiritual Beings, which we briefly summarized in chapter 5, such as Brahma, Vishnu, and Shiva. Notice that Spirit in 2nd person—for example, God the Father/Mother—is already *outside*, and external, in the 2nd-person perspective; what is projected "outside" here is one's *relationship* with Divine Being, which results in seeing so many others fruitfully and joyfully connected with the Divine, but not oneself. What needs to be re-owned here is not the Divinity but one's Higher Self's relationship with that Divinity. It is not the existence of God that is fundamentally and truly doubted; it is the possibility of one's actual *relationship* with God that is doubted in oneself, though admired in others.

Causal-to-Emptiness Dysfunctions

As for the problems with the causal in relationship to the next stage, the Empty Witness (turiya or "I-I"), one of the most significant difficulties again relates to the causal Higher Self letting go of itself, accepting its own death, and thus making room for the Real Self and empty Witnessing of the next state-stage. In other words, this is trouble with the causal/Witness's "dark night of the Self." If we treat the causal and the empty Witness as one realm (which is quite common), we can summarize this as one dark night process; if more accurately, we treat the causal and the empty Witness as the two realms that they technically are, this "dark night of the Self" has two major phases—the death of the Higher Self (here in the causal), and then the final death of the Real Self (the death of subjectivity in any form, including Absolute Subjectivity, as it gives way to pure nondual Suchness, the "headless" state we will return to in a moment), which occurs with the switching from the turiya Witness to turiyatita Suchness.[3] The death of the Higher Self involves accepting the death of items like the space-time matrix itself (and discovering the timeless Now—as a permanent transformation, or death to temporal alternatives, not just a quick "peak" experience). This occurs by strengthening the sense of being a pure Witness, an Observing Self, a true Seer under all conditions, a Mirror Mind that, anchored in the timeless Now, effortlessly and spontaneously witnesses all that arises, with as little Primordial Avoidance as possible. The Witness is an awareness of absolutely everything that is arising, moment to moment, whether pleasant or unpleasant, painful or pleasurable, sacred or profane, desired or despised; it witnesses the Total Painting of All That Is, without looking away, turning away, or moving away from a single thing.

If you are practicing that now, resting in the pure Observing Self or the true Witness, simply notice that there are very likely some items, however seemingly insignificant, that your awareness tends to avoid—some physical discomfort, some thought or idea, some impulse, some person, *something*—and you tend to "pull back" from that object, to flinch, to avoid. If you have pursued the Higher Self by practicing the Witnessing Self a fair amount, then those subtlest of avoidances will be closely involved with the contents of the Higher Self. The items that the deepest part of you is dedicated to avoiding actually comprise a part of the complex of the Higher Self, because the self structure is at bottom involved with the subject–object dichotomy, and that is built of things identified with the self, and not identified with the other. And "the other," at its very root, involves those items that are intentionally not identified with, or are intentionally avoided. These are especially important for you to give awareness to. Just let Awareness spread out across the Total Painting of All That Is, inwardly and outwardly, and let absolutely all of it (again, pleasant or unpleasant, desired or loathed, liked or disliked, wanted or hated, deeply painful or vaguely pleasant, near or far, within or without, happy or sad)—let all of them without exception arise equally and evenly in your conscious field, your mirror mind. This will make the Higher-Self subject into an object, thus transcending it, and thus shifting more of your fundamental identity to the Real Self or true Witness. I'll return to this point very shortly.

Really stepping into that "second self"—not the *observed* self, but the *Observing* Self—under all conditions, brings an extraordinary sense of peace, calm, imperturbability, the "peace that surpasseth under-standing," a sense of profound okayness with the world. As this capacity grows, fear diminishes greatly—there is nothing you can't Observe, and thus nothing you can't dis-identify with, and hence nothing you can't be free of. Of the Total Painting of All That Is, not one thing can-not be gazed upon equally, calmly, and spaciously, without looking away, turning away, moving away.

That first phase, or causal-to-Witness phase, of the dark night of the Self is a profound death in many ways, a complete dis-identification with all finite qualities, traits, tendencies, and characteristics of a self-sense. (The turiya Empty Witness is indeed "empty" of all contents, objects, and phenomena; it is qualified only by the beginning of the subject–object duality and the singular–plural duality—the 4 quad-rants—which, when seen as ornaments of Spirit or Suchness, are the radiant manifestations of ultimate Reality itself, but when not seen in conjunction with Spirit, are the last and highest obstacles to its real-ization.)

As the Real Self or true Witness begins witnessing the causal Self, converting it to an object of Boundless Changeless Awareness, the Real Self is experienced as the first "I" in the "I-I" experience—the Observ-ing "I" or Witnessing "I"—and the causal Higher Self, in the process of dying and being let go of, is the self-sense that is *being witnessed*, the second "I" in the "I-I" experience. That second "I," the causal Self-sense, can indeed become an object of Boundless Changeless Aware-ness, because it is not a, or the, Real Self, not the true Seer, the real Witness, and thus can be *seen as an object* whenever you take up the purely Observing Self or pure Witnessing stance and simply "feel your-self" at this state-stage. The self you feel is the causal Higher Self; the self doing the feeling is the Witness or Observing Self.

Whenever you practice Witnessing or resting in the Observing Self—and being aware of whatever self-sense is arising as an object of that awareness—the self-sense will tend to give way to higher and higher self-senses the more you stay with the practice. That is, because the various self-senses are connected to particular states—ego with gross, soul with subtle, Higher Self with causal, and then Real Self with the empty Witness itself—those self-senses are all available right now, be-cause their correlative states are all available right now. So when you first start practicing Observing-Self mindfulness, and doing it adequately, the first or Observing Self—the first "I" in the "I-I" experience of Observing or Witnessing—will be the true Witness, Absolute Subjectivity, the Real Self, and the second "I," the seen self, will start out as ego; if you persist, the seen ego will give way to the seen soul; continue to persist, and the seen soul will eventually give way to the seen Higher Self; and finally, you will be resting in the pure Witnessing Field, being aware of the Total Painting of all possible objects arising in your Witnessing Field, and the second self, having been moved from an "I" to an "it"—having been moved from part of the Seeing Self to a fully *seen* self—will become part of the entire object world or Total Painting. All that you will feel as a "subjective self" is the empty Opening or Clearing or Space in which all phenomena are arising moment to moment. That is the Real Seer, the True Self, the pure Witness, Absolute Subjectivity, an opening onto pure Emptiness itself.

In other words, as you begin practicing pure Witnessing, or "I-I" awareness, the first "I"—if you're doing it correctly—will indeed be the Real Self or the pure empty Witness or Absolute Subjectivity, and the second self or small "I" will be the self of your state center of gravity; to begin with, likely the ego, and the ego will be mistaken as the source of "I-ness" or real Subjectivity. As you Witness that ego, it will eventually—by being fully seen—be converted from a subject-self to an object-self; in other words, it will be converted from an "I" (and part of the "I-I") to a simple "it," and the "I-I" experience will become more and more an "I-it" experience. As that happens, it will create a vacuum, a space, into which the next-higher relative finite self-sense can emerge—namely, the soul. (The Real Self, or Witness, is still looking for a vehicle through which it can communicate, and this creates the "pull" that invites the next-higher finite self to emerge—via a shift in the state center of gravity—in this case from gross, and the ego, to subtle, and the soul.) If you then practice "I-I" awareness with the soul, the soul's own pretend subjectivity will be increasingly seen as a sham, an illusion, a pretend self—not a real self, not a real "I" but rather a seen self, an object self, a mere "it." Once again, the "I-I" experience shifts slowly but inexorably into an "I-it" experience, and the new "it-self" or "object-self"—in this case, the soul—switches over to the Total Painting side of the street, switches from being part of the Seeing Self to being part of the seen phenomena, to being part of the Total Painting of All That Is, and not something that is aware of the Total Painting (which it pretended to be its entire life). It is no longer—just as with the previous ego—part of that which looks at the Total Painting, but part of the Total Painting being looked at.

And again, if "I-I" awareness is continued, the "I-it" experience creates an opening, a clearing, in which the next-higher relative finite self can emerge, in this case, the Higher Self. As usual, the Higher Self emerges, in the "I-I" experience, as part of the Observing Complex or Seeing Self, and only slowly—as it is seen more and more as an object and thus stripped of its subjectivity—does it switch from being part of the "I" or Observing Self to being merely part of the overall "its" in the Total Painting.

We are, right now, discussing glitches in this particular switch-point. And this one is particularly important, because in all the previous "I-I" experiences (up to and including the causal Higher Self), the second "I" or small finite self has always ended up being a subject that could be made object, and doing so opened the door to the next higher state-stage and its new higher and wider self-sense (which starts out believing it is a true Subject). But when we get to the pure Witness or Observing Self or Real Self, it is always experienced—if experienced correctly—as a deep Subjectivity that can never itself become object. When we try to see the Real Self or pure Witness as an object, all that we will see (besides a lot of objects that aren't the pure Witness) is a vast Field of pure Freedom, a pure Emptiness free of any and all finite objects, an Opening or Clearing that is the utter Absence of all small objects (and small subjects). It is pure boundless changeless Awareness, and not any *contents* of Awareness. When we reach the pure Witness, or Absolute Subjectivity, in our attempts to make subject object, we realize, beyond a doubt, that we have run into a wall, into some sort of entirely different situation. We are an Observing Self, or pure Awareness, but now this Real Self can *never* be made an object. What is "entirely different" here is that we have finally made the jump from finite selves to an Infinite Self, from a relative self to an Ultimate Self, from a manifest/illusory/partial self to an Empty/Open/Infinite Self, free of all limitations, boundaries, qualities, characteristics, or confines. We are getting very, very close to our utterly most true and Real Condition (our own pure nondual Suchness, the next and final step after turiya/Witness). And the point, vis-à-vis dysfunctions here, is that it is a fixation to any finite subject (that is actually an object)—including the Higher Self—that prevents the clean emergence of this pure Empty Witnessing condition.

In other words, the true Witness, or pure Observing Self, cannot itself become an object of any sort. It can never be seen, because it is the true Seer; it is not a subject that can become object, because it is Absolute Subjectivity, the pure Subjective opening or clearing that can never be seen but is only the Seer itself; it can never be known but is the Knower itself; it can never be felt but is the Feeler itself. In itself, it is only an open empty Clearing (or Nothing or Absence), pure Emptiness as pure Consciousness without an object, which, as the Seer, can see all objects but cannot itself be seen—*Absolute* Subjectivity. Thus, as one rests in the pure Observing Self, or true Witness, and looks for that True Self, one won't see anything, but will instead feel a profound Freedom, a vast Openness, an infinite Spaciousness, a Clearing or Space, in which the entire manifest world is arising right now—all of it, moment to moment to moment. (And then, at the next higher—and last major—state-stage of unfolding, the entire Total Painting of what is being observed turns into that big blue pancake and falls on your head, uniting the Witness with all things Witnessed, and hence marking the disappearance, once and for all, of any form of the subject–object dichotomy. Daniel Brown calls the limiting factor in the Witnessing state "individuality"; that is, subjectivity in any form, including Absolute Subjectivity, because subjectivity, even in its ultimate form, is still dualistic, excluding within itself any objectivity—just what the Witness does when it objectively witnesses objects—exactly the duality overcome with Suchness.)

One of the primary goals of the Empty Witnessing state-stage, as I have noted, is to finish the exhaustive Witnessing of all the archetypes that was begun in the causal, so that these potential subjects finally become objects of the Real Self, or objects of Boundless Changeless Awareness. This includes all of the low- and high-causal phenomena that we previously discussed, including the space-time matrix (as well as any phenomenal objects remaining in the supracausal Witnessing stage itself). When all of causal space-time becomes an object of Boundless Changeless Awareness, time itself begins to move toward pure eternity (that is, *timelessness*, in which something that happened a million years ago is no further from the Now than a moment two minutes ago—there is *only* the timeless Present, which equally touches the past, present, and future); and space begins to move toward a pure infinity (that is, *spacelessness*; the space that particularly begins to disappear here is the space between subject and object, and that space finally disappears in pure nonduality as the world becomes a big blue pancake and falls on your head, totally "uniting" subject and object and getting rid of any space between them—there is then no space between you and the entire universe, all of which is arising within you, with no space between them).

"Be here now" is the cliché that fairly well describes this state of affairs. Since 100 percent of eternity, being itself timeless, is fully present at each and every moment of time, then all of eternity exists in *this* NOW moment. And since 100 percent of infinity, being itself spaceless, is fully present at each and every point of space, then all of infinity exists fully in *this* HERE, *wherever* that might be. The Empty Witness is a "be here now" Boundless Changeless Awareness, and for this to occur, all of the causal (except the two preexisting dualisms of subject–object and singular–plural) has to be objectified, witnessed, and made an object of Boundless Changeless Awareness, and thus let go, transcended, died to. (Of course, the Vantage Point caused by an exclusive identification with the causal is what will be permanently negated and transcended, while the causal realm itself will be retained, a partial subholon in the overall Self or Suchness of higher states and integrated with those higher states. State/realms remain; Vantage Points are replaced.) It is not the archetypes or space-time itself that is being dismantled, but consciousness's limited *identification* with those phenomena that is being disbanded. One can still be aware of space, time, and all the fundamental archetypes, but one no longer centrally identifies with them, or mistakes them for some sort of ultimate reality.

The successful negotiation of the first phase of the dark night of the Self—permanently dying to an *exclusive identity* with the Higher Self and most of the *exclusive* identities with any archetypes—can be particularly difficult because the Self that is dying here is the Self that possesses any content at all, and this is the first type of death that requires that degree of letting go. The Real Self, or Witness Self, is purely Empty (aside from its two defining dualisms of subject–object and singular–plural), and thus in many ways, this death to the causal is a death relating to any identity in the entire manifest, finite realm, and all of the causal Self's wants, desires, needs, wishes, traits, qualities, and characteristics (since all of those rest on the causal). This is a massive death! And it is made all the harder because Emptiness looks, from the outside, as if it were merely and only an infinite Absence, a Total Death, a horrifying Good-bye to any and all things ever cherished. It is not realized, therefore, that death to the causal Self and a leap into Emptiness is not a leap into a nastier Death but into an even greater Freedom and Liberation.

Not understanding this, the causal Higher Self can consequently develop an "Emptiness allergy" and will avoid any and all items that remind it of the Void, of the great Nothing, of the apparently ultimate Nonexistence. Meditation can start to be invaded by dread, fear, and trembling, by a "sickness unto death." Commonly, a feeling of interior "emptiness" can develop (often experienced as a profound hollowness and depression in the casual Self), and the causal Self, seeing a way out, will identify this interior emptiness with real Emptiness itself (it identifies a finite empty feeling with infinite Emptiness, which allows the finite at least to continue its existence). Worse, if there are any residues of lower fulcrum issues (particularly Fulcrum-2, the misnavigating of which can generate borderline disorders), these can be reactivated here, and the causal Self, already beginning to let go of many of its borders and boundaries, will slip into borderline-like fractured-boundary states. (Jack Engler found that many borderline individuals were attracted to the Buddhist notion of Emptiness, because it seemed to rationalize the hollowness that they constantly felt.) In the more extreme cases, the meltdown and loss of boundaries can reactivate subtle domains in a dysfunctional fashion, leading to near-psychotic hallucinations.

Further, the traditions generally maintain that it is in this causal realm that paranormal events are more likely to occur (since this is the realm where manifestation itself is coming into being, and therefore intentional control of this realm can, via the "downward causation" that comes with involution, paranormally influence lower domains). If one is undergoing causal meltdown problems, these paranormal capacities can be activated but with little, if any, conscious control or understanding, which can be totally unnerving and disturbing.

The teacher, faced with these problems, will usually and understandably (but regrettably) recommend "More meditation!" or "Back to the Zendo!," which unfortunately will usually intensify the meltdown (by intensifying boundary transcendence and hence fragility) and end up making matters worse. (Again, an Internet search for individuals or groups who specialize in "spiritual emergencies" is one of the few available sources of help.)

But if all goes well, intentionality and will and goal-driven activities in general will, at some point, simply and often suddenly "drop," and one will find oneself in a vast, pure, unmoving, unperturbed, unshakable, utterly even, equanimous, mirror-minded state, that of the pure Empty Witness, or Consciousness without an Object.

The Empty Witness Realm

The Witness, as with virtually all states and structures, finds itself faced with two fundamental navigation issues: dealing with that which has already emerged (generally, the previous stage, via Agape) and that which has not yet emerged, or is just now beginning to emerge (which generally involves the next higher stage, via Eros). I will discuss them in that order.

Causal-to-Emptiness Dysfunctions

We have already discussed many of the major dysfunctions that occur if the causal refuses to let go of its present Higher Self state-stage and Vantage Point in order to make room for the next higher realm and state-stage, that of the unqualifiable Real Self or Empty Witness, with its inherent, timeless Now, and Boundless Changeless Awareness. Let's look at these issues now *from the perspective of the Witness itself*:

A defining characteristic of the "Empty Witness" is, indeed, its "Emptiness"—or the fact that, with a few exceptions (particularly the two dualisms of subject–object and singular–plural), the Witness is radically free of any specific content or individual traits (except, again, for "individuality" itself). This is indeed like a mirror mind, which itself is free of all objects and merely reflects them in a nongrasping, nonrestricting fashion—just as the Observing Self (or Witness) is doing in you right now: there is some deep Awareness in you that spontaneously and without any effort at all hears the sounds arising around you, sees the phenomena arising in your visual field, notices the thoughts floating by in your mind, and is otherwise effort- lessly Aware of whatever is arising. You don't try and see your visual field; it is simply presented to you, spontaneously. The entire universe arises spontaneously in your Awareness, right now, right now, right now.

It is this pure equanimity and unflinchingly even reflective capacity that makes the Witness what it is—namely, the point at which infinite Consciousness as Such begins to enter the manifest realm and, in addi- tion to its inherently infinite dimensions, starts to take on specific finite forms. Emptiness, likewise, is the "space" where nothing starts to be- come something and is thus the Creative Matrix of the entire Kosmos. Resting as the pure Witness in oneself is to rest as pure infinite Spirit in oneself, the I AMness that "before Abraham was, I AM." Most forms of meditation, East and West, seek to establish a person in bare attention, pure choiceless Awareness, the pure Observing Self, or the infinite Witness per se, even if the meditation begins with gross objects themselves, and even if the aim of meditation is the higher nondual Suchness itself. The Witness is a crucial function and "in between point" in all of these.

Problems start when the Witness is not truly "Empty," but—in the dysfunction we are now discussing—remains embedded in, fixated on, attached to, or addicted to aspects of the previous causal realm. In the beginning phase of the dark night of the Self, the Higher Self has not fully died; Consciousness has not fully let go of its exclusive identity with the causal realm and its many near-infinite Joys (Radiance, Being, Bliss, Kosmic Love, Care, Creativity). Again, the problem is not, say, Creativity per se, but the Witness having an exclusive identity with Creativity and not with the rest of manifestation; that exclusive iden- tity and the Vantage Point created by the exclusiveness of that identity is what has to die. Just as with any basic structure, it is not the struc- ture itself but the exclusive identity with that structure and its View that has to be relinquished and died to. If, in the switch-point from causal to supracausal Witnessing, there is either a fixation (addiction) or a dissociation (allergy), then the Witness will not be able to function as a fully nonattached and clear mirror-mind Witness, but will either hanker after certain objects and events (addictive grasping) or avoid and deny them (allergic avoidance), both of which hamper and distort a bare and pure Witnessing of the world *just as it is*.

And seeing the world *just as it is* is the primary aim and goal of the Witnessing state-stage, which prepares Consciousness itself for its aware nondual union with ALL of manifestation (by identifying with *absolutely nothing* in particular, it becomes able to identify with *absolutely everything* equally). That is, Witnessing prepares Consciousness for its union of Emptiness and Form (or Godhead and manifestation)—or genuine Enlightenment by any other name. If the Witness remains attached to, or in avoidance of, any stretch of the manifest realm, or any part of the Total Painting of All That Is—which is therefore not Witnessed *just as it is*—then those stretches function as hidden subjects that refuse to become objects—subjects that might even form into sub-"I's" or (causal) subpersonalities, which encapsulate aspects of the *anandamayakosha* ("the sheath made of causal bliss") that the causal state supports. This bliss-driven grasping or avoiding is one of the major drives of the causal subpersonality and is often what makes it so hard to surrender in (or properly die to) the dark night of the Self.

The net effect of this dysfunction is that there are aspects of the manifest realm that the Witness cannot properly become aware of (subjects that won't become objects), and thus Boundless Changeless Awareness becomes distorted and disfigured. As a result, one of the Witness's own main goals becomes derailed—namely, beginning to witness individuality itself, thus turning that final subject into an object during the transition to the next and ultimate state of consciousness, nondual Suchness. The attached or avoided objects, now becoming some disfigured stretch of manifestation, generate in turn a disfigured stretch of witnessing Awareness, a (hidden) Higher Self parading as the True and Real Self, which, operating with Boundless Changeless Awareness, should be witnessing the entire manifest realm—the Total Painting of All That Is—with calm, clear, silent, even, equanimous, unwavering, unfaltering Consciousness as Such, but instead "wobbles" in the presence of the grasped or avoided phenomena, which deforms the very core of the Real Self and its Boundless Changeless Awareness. A causal subpersonality has embedded itself in the very center of Emptiness itself, malforming Emptiness and imbuing it with pseudo-Empty traits. This is a profoundly distorting, deforming, disfiguring occasion.

(And note that since it invades Emptiness, it also invades the union of Emptiness and Form—or Enlightenment itself. It is a deep scar on the face of Godhead, producing a tortured gnosis or broken jnana.)

Unfortunately, as with all such cases in states and structures, this is not something that Consciousness itself can easily become aware of, because you can't see what you can't see, and a subpersonality is a sub-subject, not an object, and thus won't enter the phenomenal field of Awareness (it's not an object!). It becomes a distorting part of that which is *looking at* the world, not something that itself can be *looked at*. This is particularly disastrous at this Empty Witnessing state-stage, where, as noted, one of the main goals is to begin to "objectivize" all remaining subjects (especially "individuality"), and thus prepare for the leap into trans-subject–object (nondual) Suchness. The very Clearing or Spaciousness or Emptiness road to the Ultimate itself is jammed, a fifty-car pileup that forces a disruptive detour on the Highway to Heaven.

In short, the problem with Higher Self fixations when it comes to the empty Witness is that the Higher Self refuses in all ways to become an object. It refuses to be *fully seen*, and thus remains embedded in the real Seer, a fixation in the Real Self or true Witness, which prevents the Witness from becoming a truly open Clearing or empty Space. If all goes the way it is meant to go, there is an awareness of "I-I," where—*as is always the case when correctly Witnessing the separate-self sense*—the first "I" is still experienced (as a pure Witnessing, pure Awareness, Absolute Subjectivity, or a pure, clear Open Spontaneous Spacious Awareness), but the second "I" has become an "it." It's no longer seen or felt as the source of Self-Awareness, but is something seen and felt as an *object* of Self-Awareness; it has been stripped of its official role as "my Self" or "my Real Subject," and has become instead "my Object," "my seen self, a mere finite convention," and thus "I-I" becomes directly felt as "I-it." When you rest as the Witness and the Higher Self is no longer "I" but "it," all forms of the observed or seen self have finally become "it," or the final subjects have been made into final objects. (In other words, the Higher Self is the highest of the centers of subjectivity that is really an object, an illusory self, a pretend self, a finite relative self—unlike the Real and True Self, which, as Absolute Subjectivity, is the ultimate-Truth Seer that can *never be made an object* but is only an Absence, a Clearing, an Emptiness, a Spaciousness, in which the entire manifest world is arising moment to moment.) When that Higher Self is fully seen, is fully objectified, then the second "I" in the "I-I" experience is totally evaporated as an active self-sense and is replaced, as object, by the Total Object of the whole Painting of All That Is. That Total Painting is now the object of the Observing Self, no longer the object of a small, relative, ultimately illusory self (including the Higher Self), which, as object, is now just an objective part of the Total Painting of All That Is and is seen as an "it" together with everything else seen. The Higher Self is no longer experienced as a real Self or an "I" that is part of the subjective complex of "I-I," which itself is now just an absolute "I" or Absolute Subjectivity, itself a mere Absence or Nothing-in-itself. The Higher Self has become simply one "it" among all the other "its" in the Total Painting, with the "I-I" having become an "I-it," with that "it" becoming one of all the overall "its" in the Total Painting of All That Is. The Higher Self is no longer looking at the Total Painting, but it is part of the Total Painting being looked at by the Real Self or Empty Witness.

In this condition, where the Real Self or true Witness has become nothing but an Absence or Opening or Clearing or Space in which the entire manifest world is arising moment to moment, then the Witness—in itself increasingly having become Nothing but this Opening—is ready to finally collapse into everything witnessed, as the big blue pancake falls on its head, and a simple nondual Suchness arises in its place.

Witness-to-Suchness Dysfunctions

As the Empty Witness faces the direction of nondual Suchness, it is faced with the last and major form of death that evolution has presented us with so far: the death of any form of felt individuality at all, and its replacement not by an exclusive identity with anything, Real Self or any kind of Self, but by a Supreme Identity with Spirit itself and all of Spirit's entire manifestation—one with the One and one with the Many and one with the All. This is not necessarily as initially appealing as it might sound.

Death is death, and it is an inability to "die before we die" that makes each fulcrum and switch-point a potential problem: each involves the death of the present self-sense and the rebirth of a yet-higher self, with a higher, wider, deeper identity, consciousness, creativity, care, and capacity for love, higher morals, and greater loving-kindness. But those higher characteristics are not generally experienced first— you have to get there first, which means death to the present address; and even if they were protoexperienced to some degree, the self still faces its own immanent death and transcendence, and that is never an easy task. For a fulcrum or switch-point to be properly navigated, there must be neither failed dis-identification and a resulting fixation (or addiction), nor overblown dis-identification (failed integration) and a dissociation resulting in avoidance (or allergy). The death of the separate self at whatever stage has to be fully, cleanly, clearly acquiesced to. Rare indeed is the individual who makes it through the entire spectrum of both states and structures without some sort of misnavigation or developmental miscarriage involving the avoidance of death. And it is death, not sex, that is the great and ultimate repression (resulting, as I suggested in *The Atman Project*, in various *immortality projects*, or pretend forms of death denial that allow the self to imagine its unending continuation forward in time however conceived at that stage).[4]

And here, at the culmination of the spectrum of major states of consciousness, the self—as True or Real Self—faces its final showdown: the death of the separate-self sense altogether, which is replaced by a nondual Suchness and Spirit that is not other to the entire world it sees.

The most common form of malfunction here is for the Witness to experience genuine fear as it faces its own death (fear, though greatly reduced in most higher states, is never fully absent as long as the subject–object dichotomy is present; as the Upanishads put it, "Wherever there is other, there is fear").[5] Eros collapses to Phobos, and the Witness develops a Suchness allergy in significant ways. It is not exactly "Suchness" that the Witness or Real Self fears directly, but any stretch of Awareness per se that feels as if the Witness is not present (and the Witness is not present wherever Suchness is). Awareness recoils in the face of a Witness-less infinity and thus deforms the overall developmental evolutionary process itself, right as it reaches into its own highest realms. Holding on to itself, it keeps out God.

I have previously pointed out that the Witness cannot imagine a future in which it does not exist, because even while imagining such a future, it is the Witness doing the imagining, and thus it can never get itself out of the picture (Descartes's point). But that is exactly what Suchness actually does—even though this cannot be imagined prior to it fully happening. But with Suchness, there is no longer the sense, in any direction, of a separate-self sense or "I"—or "I-I"—but rather, there is just the present moment, in whatever realm, gross, subtle, or causal, arising on its own, self-existing, self-aware, self-liberating, a "headless" condition taken into every dimension imaginable. This Suchness will still avail itself of the conventional finite self-sense of whatever realm it wishes to communicate with or through—the ego in the gross, the soul in the subtle, the Higher Self in the causal, the Real Self in the turiya realm—but these are no longer sources of a feeling of set-apartness, separate-selfness, or subjectivity; they are simply objective finite tools being used by the infinite to communicate and interact with the finite. As separate-self senses—and exclusive identifications—they have long ago been permanently negated, transcended, and let go of; as Gebser put it, the "self of one stage becomes the tool of the next," which is what these previous self-senses have become, tools of Suchness, tools of Spirit, for "touching" and "communicating" with any realm desired. The Total Painting of All That Is has likewise switched from the Total Display of All Objects of the Separate-Self and has become instead the Self-Aware Matrix of All Manifestation, which arises moment to moment just as it always has, but it is no longer the object of any subject—including Absolute Subjectivity—but rather is the nondual self-awareness of its own existing and self-liberating nature. And you are no longer a set-apart you looking at it; you *are* the totality of this Total Painting, as your own deepest and simplest Suchness. The Total Display is the final Form that becomes one with your Emptiness, your open Awareness, to disclose the ever-present Presence of turiyatita, or pure nondual Suchness, Thusness, Isness. All things are exactly as they are, just so.

For the Witness, objects or phenomena always appear "in front": they appear to be arising in front of the Witnessing Self (in all realms—gross, subtle, and causal, including, for example, the dream state), and the Self stands back as the Observer, or Looker—possessing a perfect equanimity, calm and unwavering, a radiant mirror-mind nature, imperturbable openness, and vast deep Awareness (if healthy). But in

Suchness, the Looker, the detached Observer, the standing-back Self, suddenly and completely drops out of existence altogether and becomes fully one with the Total Painting that it was just Witnessing so that a split-apart subject and object both disappear. They can still be observed, but are no longer split apart with one of them looking at the other; there is only the Present, timeless, nondual Now moment, or true Singularity, and all of its manifestations in any and all realms—nakedly self-seen, spontaneously self-existing, clear-light radiating, *non*dual to the core. "I see the world" switches to "I-see-the-world-sees-itself"; and there is no separate "I" or "world," just the seeing.

That seeing is what a Suchness allergy derails. And it is cured by the Witness finally looking deep into the Abyss, infinite Emptiness, vast Consciousness as Such, and letting go of that fundamental self-contraction known as the Looker or Observer, which is constructed by none other than the Primordial Avoidance, which splits the All into a world of relative, small, finite objects (and small finite subjects); namely, the "exterior" world of Matter, Prakriti, Mahamaya, Shakti, and a world of pure Empty Awareness, or Absolute infinite Subjectivity; namely, the "interior" world of Spirit, Purusha, Atman, turiya/Witness. But with Suchness, the radical Subject becomes not-two with all possible objects (all gross objects, all subtle objects, all causal objects) and thus both subject and object give way to the spontaneous flow of the Total World Process itself (turiyatita), radically seamless but not featureless, totally without borders but not without boundaries, radically free of separate individuals but not individual phenomena, all arising of-themselves-so, spontaneously and planned, unwilled and intentional, without time and temporal, without space and extended—that is, paradoxically uniting and synthesizing all possible opposites. The Witness, if it fears that leap to its own death, will often latch on to just one-half of any of those pairs, and thus rip nonduality in two, rather literally, and identify with half of the thus-disfigured Kosmos.

Allowing the Self (in any and all forms) to uncoil in the vast expanse of All Space is the fundamental cure to the Witness's unwillingness, or inability, to let go of itself, die to itself, and resurrect as the One-in-Allness of the Kosmos itself. When this death occurs, then right where it thought its head was, the entire universe itself is sitting, self-arising, self-shimmering, self-radiant, self-liberating. As it looks "out" at the world, the world "out there" is actually arising right on its shoulders, and its overall Awareness, which seemed to be on this side of its face, right behind and between its eyes, turns out to be the actual feel of the entire world itself, which is now arising exactly where its head used to be. The "subject" on this side of its face and the "object" on the other side are two sides of the same headless one-taste feeling. Exactly where the "behind-the-face" *feeling* once was is the *feeling* of the entire world itself, arising on its shoulders, inside and outside merging into one seamless whole, impossible to shake. Directly *feel* the Total Painting that seems to be on the "outside," and then directly *feel* the Looker that seems to be in here on the "inside," and they turn out to be exactly one and the same feeling. That is, *feel* the inside on "this side" of your face; now, still feeling the inside, *feel* the Total Painting on the outside—the *same* feeling! Move the outside feeling of the world to this side of your face; the entire world is arising *within you.* Then let your face go—there's only one feeling left, that of the entire world, with no separation between "you" and "it," just "it"; and you *are* that!

The individual self-contraction has vanished into the entire world arising moment to moment. You can *taste* the sky, in this one-taste state, swallow the Pacific Ocean in a single gulp. In place of the self-contraction is the Supreme Identity of Spirit itself, one with the inside and the outside, the simple Thusness, Suchness, or Isness of every single thing and event in this and every moment. The entire world is arising within you, and there's no "you" and no "world," just the arising. In all places, in all times, in any and every dimension imaginable, this is who and what you really are, timelessly and eternally and endlessly forever. And indeed, welcome home!

Suchness Dysfunctions

Suchness dysfunctions arise, as with all states, from one of two sources: problems with the state itself, or problems with the structures interpreting the state. (This is not the same as the two *directions* each problem involves—facing toward previously emerged phenomena or facing toward yet-to-emerge phenomena, Agape or Eros—but rather involves the *sources* of these problems, the present state itself or the structure interpreting it.) I have, in this chapter, been focusing on problems with the states themselves, as they deal with both a previous stage and an about-to-emerge higher stage. Here, let me say a few words about the second major source: problems with the structures doing the interpreting. (Once the general idea is grasped, which is fairly simple, interested readers can apply it to all other dysfunctions we have discussed.)

Dysfunctional Structures Interpreting States

These problems themselves are of two sorts: interpretation by a structure, even if healthy, that is inappropriately too low, and interpretation by a dysfunctional structure, no matter what its altitude.

The former is certainly one of the most common, although what one considers "too low" is a bit of a subjective judgment. I think most knowledgeable people would consider amber *ethnocentric* mythic to be too low for interpreting many things, certainly spiritually higher states (given the worldcentric universal rights of humankind introduced during the Enlightenment that are generally accepted everywhere today), although the ethnocentric mythic is regrettably the most common structure-stage that people are at worldwide, and it is certainly the most common altitude of most forms of spiritual intelligence itself. The mythic, traditional, fundamentalist level is one of the biggest problems facing the world today, and looking through its ethnocentrically prejudiced Views—or any other level less than at least worldcentric—is entirely inappropriate for an adequate interpretive structure for spirituality, certainly in today's world, where so many higher options are available.

Orange modern rational is at least the beginning of worldcentric, and thus on moral grounds alone would be the first structure open to being considered adequate. And that is probably the best way to view worldcentric orange: as the lowest acceptable altitude for spiritual intelligence and awareness in today's world.

More acceptable, because more developed—and yet, to many authorities, still not fully adequate—is green postmodern Pluralism. Green's advantages are its multicultural sensitivity, its openness to interiors, and its awareness of the dangers of marginalization and oppression (although its solutions are all variations on "accept my version of reality"). Its major disadvantage is that postmodern pluralism is still 1st-tier, and thus still convinced that its truth and values are the only truth and values worth embracing. A real problem with this level is that, when radical "unqualifiability," or "infinite Emptiness," is not understood adequately or is outright misunderstood, then stating ultimate Reality in words, no matter how metaphoric, often sounds much like the "egalitarian" nature of the postmodern Pluralistic stance, and thus Spirit or Ati or Godhead is taken as further proof of the ultimate truth of the pluralistic View. This is genuinely disastrous. Ultimate Truth itself is reduced to the pluralistic value set (namely, faux egalitarian, against all hierarchies, unaware of Two Truths, against all ranking judgments, rejects a genuine holarchy of consciousness, believes that "deconstruction" = Emptiness, is willing to see oppression in every difference noticed between any individuals or groups, and embraces Ground value but dismisses intrinsic value).[6] The majority of Buddhists and Buddhist teachers in the West are green postmodern pluralists, and thus Buddhism is largely interpreted in terms of the green altitude and the pluralistic value set, whereas the greatest Buddhist texts are all 2nd tier, teal (Holistic) or higher (for example, *Lankavatara Sutra*, *Kalachakra Tantra*, Longchenpa's *Kindly Bent to Ease Us*, Nagarjuna's Madhyamaka treatises, and so forth).

This makes teal (Holistic), or Integral 2nd tier in general, the lowest deeply adequate level with which to interpret Buddhism, ultimate Reality, and Suchness itself. Thus, interpreting Suchness in pluralistic terms (or lower) would have to be viewed ultimately as a dysfunction, certainly a case of arrested development, and one requiring urgent attention in any Fourth Turning.

These are some of the problems with interpreting states (in this case, Suchness states) with a too-low structure (in short, a severe misinterpretation and thus misunderstanding of the Ultimate). As for interpreting them with dysfunctional structures (of any altitude), the problem more or less speaks for itself. Whether the structure in itself is high enough or not, any malformation of the structure will be included in the interpretation of any state (or any other experience), and hence will deform the interpretation itself, usually in the same basic ways as the structure itself is deformed. Thus, for example, if there is a major Fulcrum-3 (red altitude) repression of various bodily states (sex, aggression, power, feelings), those repressions will be interpreted as *part of the higher state itself*, and so the state will thus be viewed as devoid of (whereas this is actually a repression of) any sex, aggression, power, feelings, or whatever it is that is dis-owned and pushed into the repressed submergent unconscious. If there is an orange altitude problem with self-esteem (Fulcrum-5), that problem will be magnified by the state experience, and the more intense the state experience, the greater the magnification. Too little self-esteem, and even profound spiritual experiences can be interpreted as "I'm not worthy, so this state—which seems to love me unconditionally—must be confused." If too much self-esteem, higher experiences are misinterpreted, not as a transcendence of the self, but as a reward for being the amazing self I am—"the wonder of being me."

To give another type of example, if there is a submerged green sub-personality existing in the turquoise stage, then any turquoise experience of a particular state will tend to be slanted into a nonhierarchical version of that state, even when that state is an experience of a greater love, greater value, greater consciousness, greater kindness, greater inclusiveness. The overtly "greater" experience (always the product of a growth holarchy) will be flattened and generally denied, by maintaining that all beings experience the same degree of these state phenomena—none are "greater" or "lesser." The Buddhist magazine *Tricycle* even carried an article (although it did not itself necessarily agree with it, but it is indicative of how widespread the green View is, including even Buddhism) declaring that *satori* itself was oppressive, since it assumed some people—those who had realized satori—were "better" than others, and thus satori or Enlightenment, the raison d'etre of Buddhism, was tossed into the garbage can. The greatest source of Freedom known to humans was declared a greatest source of oppression (say what?).

In short, since all states (and experiences in general) are interpreted by the present structure the person is at, any dysfunctions in those structures will be passed on to the interpretations that he or she makes of the world, including interpretations of states and higher states. A genuinely higher, causal, or nondual transpersonal state can thus, for example, be severely misinterpreted as being significantly malevolent, disturbed, evil, or otherwise construed or deciphered. As we will see in chapter 17, the signifier will end up bringing forth a less-than-accurate signified of the real referent, due to a disturbance in the signified's translation process, itself due to a fixation/dissociation (allergy/addiction) of the present structure that is doing the translating and interpreting. The higher state, put simply, will thus be interpreted or experienced in a less-than-adequate, distorted fashion, contaminated with shadow material. Since virtually everybody has some degree of repressed submergent unconscious (that is, some degree of shadow material), very few people escape this situation in some fashion. This is particularly sorrowful, since these higher states and structures are meant to contain more truth, more goodness, and more beauty than lesser stages, but are instead being misexperienced, misunderstood, and deformed due to shadow issues. This is, needless to say, another reason why shadow work (and Cleaning Up) is such an important part of any genuine growth and development, and certainly of any Integral Spirituality or Fourth Turning.

Suchness Dysfunctions Themselves

Let's now examine Suchness dysfunctions that are found in the state itself. We have already discussed a major one from the perspective of the Empty Witness—namely, the fixation of the Witness embedded in the state of Suchness itself, disfiguring Nonduality and tearing it in two, more or less literally. (That is, it converts Suchness into dualistic terms due to an inability to fully let go of, and die to, the Witness Self per se, which then invades Suchness and dualistically disfigures it; for example, seeing Suchness via the "individuality" of the Witness, or the embedded subject–object dichotomy, the root of all illusion.) Now let's look at that problem from the perspective of Suchness itself.

Suchness, or Thusness (*tathata*), is a profound reorganization of Consciousness as Such and of virtually all interpretations of the world. A radically Nondual world is radical indeed. Every single "opposite" is seen to be equally interwoven with its polar opposite—Emptiness and Form, infinite and finite, spiritual and material, enlightened and ignorant, awakened and asleep, timeless and temporal, subject and object, closed and open, one and many, inside and outside—and the undoing of such opposites undoes virtually every worldview. It doesn't mean that these opposites can't be distinguished or even acted on; it's that Consciousness itself neither inherently prefers one over the other nor exclusively identifies with one over the other (though it can still choose one over the other for any number of relative reasons). But the polar members of these pairs are seen to be mutually interdependent, mutually co-creating, and mutually reliant. It is as impossible to lead a life of all pleasure and no pain, or all happiness and no sorrow, or all enlightenment and no ignorance, as it is to live a life of all lefts and no rights, all ups and no downs, all insides and no outsides. And yet that is what consciousness and awareness and the self-sense attempt to do at every level other than Nondual Suchness—and the results are "suffering" by any other name and to whatever degree.

At the Witness level, the Witness itself inherently faces three major dualisms—subject versus object, singular versus plural (or individual versus collective), and absolute versus relative (among any number of others particular to the specific history of a given Witness). These are all ultimately overcome only in the Nondual Suchness realm. In the meantime, the Witness will generally select one of these paired opposites to identify with—usually the subject, individual, and absolute. Surrendering the exclusive identity with each of these is part of the death of the Real Self or observing Witness, and a failure to do so results in a fixation and addiction to the chosen half of the duality.

When that happens, that addiction to the chosen half of the duality is carried, usually in hidden and disguised forms, into the realm of Suchness itself—it is Suchness that comes to prefer the chosen half, and Suchness that becomes addicted to that dualistic opposite, which tears at the frame of its own Nonduality, rends the fabric of ultimate Reality, breaks the seamlessness of Thusness, and delivers up the Nondual in various subtly broken fragments and torn shards. Suchness itself, the realm of ultimate Awakened Awareness, delivers that Awareness in less than pristine forms, subtly infected with dualistic yearnings and a variously split and splintered Consciousness.

You can spot, for example, the dysfunctional reintroduction of the subject–object duality into a previously Nondual Awareness by—to use our "headless" example one more time—when the gap between the world and you as Looker suddenly reappears from the seamlessly interwoven nondual, or headless, "unity" Field of Awareness and the universe, which was seamlessly sitting right on top of your shoulders, effortlessly one with Awareness. Suddenly the world jumps out of the space that used to be your head and reappears as a separate realm, sitting, not right where your head used to be, but "out there" as an object of the Witness, which itself reappears "in" your head as a set-apart, distancing, "Observing" self-sense. The separation of the subject and object shows up as the reappearance of your head on "this side" of your face, with "the world" sitting "out there," on the other side, where previously they were one and the same feeling, with *everything* feeling as if it existed on this side of your face, so that "inside" and "outside" lost all meaning, and the entire world was arising *within* you. This reappearance of the subject–object split is the fixation/attachment/addiction of nondual Suchness to the "individuality" of the Witness, the self–other dichotomy inherent in the Witness.

Alternatively, Suchness can not only fail to differentiate adequately from some aspect of the previous Witnessing realm, it can go too far and not only differentiate and dis-identify but dissociate and dis-own some aspect of that realm, developing, of course, an avoidance and allergy to those aspects. This allergy basically has the same effect on the Nondual nature of Suchness as the previous addiction did (although, of course, from the opposite direction)—but the final result is similar: it tears Not-twoness into two, and pushes one member of a particular pair of polar opposites into the repressed submergent unconscious, even to the extent of creating a hidden subpersonality. When Suchness (prematurely) denies the Witness or "I-I" or Absolute Subjectivity, it cuts out the deepest dimension of Consciousness itself as it begins to manifest in, and as, the apparent world. Deepest Absolute Subjectivity is not let go of and gracefully released into nondual Suchness, but is split off, buried, and hidden, then covered with scar tissue. It's not now something that can be integrated into the overall Whole of Being and Becoming, but is something looking out at the world through its own dissociated and alienated corner of the Kosmos (where it has been sent and told to hide its face and look only at the walls in the corner it is facing, a punishment meted out by the subjugating force of dissociating repression, the result of one of the highest and final forms of Primordial Avoidance). Due to this Avoidance, one's full "I-I-ness" is not available in Awareness. Recall that in a healthy "I-I" experience, the true Witness, Real Self, or Absolute Subjectivity should be in the place of the first or Observing "I"—and being fully present as the open empty Subject of the field of Awareness (a pure "Absence" or empty "Clearing" or "Boundless Changeless" Space), it can be fully and straightforwardly transcended and let go of in Suchness. But as a result of Primordial Avoidance, that Absolute Subjectivity is pushed off the field, and in its place, in the first observing "I" spot (which should be "Empty" and "Open"), is the previous self, the causal Higher Self, which (with the True Self or Witness being off-line) is now the highest Self that is available anywhere to observe the Total Painting, or to try to; the point being that it will never do the full job that real Absolute Subjectivity would do were it available and not locked in the basement or sent to hide its head in the corner. (It cannot do the full job because the causal Higher Self is in part a Self of the very subtlest finite *Form*, whereas the Real Self is one of infinite Form-lessness, pure Emptiness or clear Openness. Since the Real Self is free of objects itself, it is ready to become "one" or "nondual" with ALL objects, giving way to the purely nondual, whereas the Higher Self is itself just *another object*, so it cannot become so empty of objects that it can be filled by ALL of them.) So there's a sclerotic fissure in Consciousness or Awareness itself, a fragmenting lesion that infests Being with a torn and ruptured witnessing function. The Suchness that rests on such a fractured base is not a full Suchness, because its Emptiness component is not fully Empty but has a hidden and distorted Absolute Subjectivity (distorted by a reactivated, reanimated, lesser-level Higher Self) jammed into its seamless seams. Instead of the graceful transcendence and inclusion of the Witness, the denial or dissociation of the Witness creates an Emptiness/Witness jammed with objects embedded in its own identity, and this Emptiness, now disfigured by objectification, can produce only an equally disfigured Enlightenment, since "the union of (now disfigured) Emptiness and Form"—the traditional definition of Enlightenment—becomes equally a "(now disfigured) Enlightenment."

The point is that, in normal and adequate state development, the pure Witness, or Absolute Subjectivity, is to be clearly located—through inquiry such as "Who am I?" "Who chants the name of the Buddha?" "What is my Original Face?" or "Allow Christ to fully fill Awareness," or simply the continued following of the practices of meditative unfoldment, which will eventually bring one to the Source of Awareness itself (that is, Absolute Subjectivity, by whatever name)—and having been directly located, the very *feeling of subjectivity* is given Awareness until any sense of a Feeler, Looker, or Observer is seen and felt to dissolve into everything that is being looked at. A *one taste* of all subjects and objects, *before* they arise, is recognized as the Tathagatagarbha (literally, "matrix of Thusness"). It is fully recognized and realized as the direct world of immediate Suchness or Thusness itself, the world *just as it is.* Suchness is not hacked into a part that sees the world and another torn and bloodied part as the world that is seen, but it arises only and always as The World, a seamless but not featureless, unified, nondual, open, clear, spontaneous Presence. As the Present in all directions, the Self-Aware Matrix of All Manifestation, self-arising, self-existing, self-aware, self-liberating, it is not fractured into any of the polarities, or dualities, that rip the fabric of the Total Interwoven Matrix into millions of shattered shards and shredded shavings.

This fracture can also arise due to an intense "anatta" belief that has been cutting off subjectivity from the beginning, a cutting and severing that culminates here with an absolute severing of Absolute Subjectivity, thus keeping the true nature of the self-contraction forever hidden from its awareness. When Zen describes satori as "the bottom of the bucket breaks," the "bottom" that "breaks" is the absolute, final, utter foundation of subjectivity altogether—or the very first floor of the separate-self sense—namely, a Primordial Avoidance, a self-contracting in the face of infinity, that shifts one's identity from the All to the skin-encapsulated ego. The "bottom" of the bucket (your separate ego) is the back of your head, because it is the area behind your eyes where you normally locate your separate self; and that "bottom" just falls out completely in boundless limitless Awareness when you totally lose your head and are instead one with the All— "the bottom of the bucket breaks." But if that subjectivity is simply denied all along (as with "anatta"), it leads not to actually locating the relatively real subjectivity, or the separate-self sense, but to a mushy sidestepping of the source of subjectivity by its simple denial. The result, especially in meditative states, is that one works toward a state, stretching from nirvana to nirodh, where true Nonduality is not understood or realized, but rather ends in a purely dualistic nirvana versus samsara, Emptiness *versus* Form, infinite formless versus finite form—and consciousness disappears into a formless, desireless, thoughtless, egoless, samsara-less, state of utter vacuity, a total nirvana utterly divorced from all samsara, or a pure cessation of all manifestation of any sort in a pure nirodh, which is the goal of Theravada Buddhism. All of this follows from the denial of the relative reality of atta, or atman (as in "anatta"; that is, "no atta" or "no self" whatsoever), which is part of a View that, with an equally tilted meditative-state development, drives toward a final meditative state that is not all-inclusive, not all-pervading, not all-embracing, and not all-liberating but is dualistic, partial, fragmented, siloed: nirvana (unmanifest) versus samsara (manifest), nirodh (total cessation) versus self-liberating (manifestation), "off the wheel (of reincarnating samsara)" versus "embracing the wheel (for the benefit of all)." This dualistic condition is where "anatta" in itself leads, and its final act of denying reality is to deny the very source of subjectivity itself—namely, Absolute Subjectivity, Purusha, Brahmanatman (as in the Vedanta), Mahatman (as in the *Nirvana Sutra*), Christ Consciousness, True Nature (as in Zen), pure I AMness. All of that is short-circuited as consciousness drives straight for the state of total cessation—not understanding manifestation and its mechanics but simply getting out of it. The bodhisattva vow is, in its purest form, a deep vow and promise *never* to do that—never to hide out in an unmanifest domain forever, afraid to show one's face in the real manifest world of Spirit's ornaments. It is a promise to gain Enlightenment as quickly as possible precisely so as to come back to the manifest realm of samsara, multiplicity, suffering, and sentient beings, beings in need of desperate help, and, indeed, to help them with the best skillful means one can muster for the benefit of all those beings, bar none. It's one of the easiest things in the world to simply turn one's back on all of suffering manifestation and its tortured sentient beings and hide away forever in a self-only (narcissistic) bliss realm—or even worse, a realm of total cessation, where absolutely nothing arises, there to spend the rest of everlasting time contemplating the wonder of oneself.

The fact that this can happen at this high realm shows that psycho-spiritual pathology most definitely can go all the way up and all the way down, and that shadow issues are never far from the development and evolution of Consciousness and Awareness, because development, or evolution, itself can miscarry at any of its major subphases. Wherever there is a further possible stage or step in evolution, there is a further possible pathology just waiting, ever eager, to happen.

Energy Malfunctions

I mentioned earlier that each disruption in Upper Left *consciousness* (states or structures) is accompanied by a correlative disruption in Upper Right *mass-energy* (or "bodies" in short, since each "body" contains matter, or mass, and energy—across a wide spectrum of gross to subtle to causal). Materialistic science reduces this rich multidimensional reality (of Left- and Right-handed events) to a flattened understanding that pictures any subjective (Left-hand, or emotional, mental, or spiritual) problem as actually being nothing but a problem with objective, Right-hand physical brain chemistry or neurophysiology, which can be treated, if at all, by treating nothing but the neurophysiology, usually with drugs/medication, but also surgery (for example, prefrontal lobotomy), electroconvulsive or "shock" treatment, or genetic treatments, which are increasingly available. But, in reality, any problem on any Upper Left level also involves some degree of gross, subtle, and possibly causal energy, or networks, in the Upper Right (with, in fact, some sort of correlation in all 4 quadrants—all dysfunctions are tetra-interwoven).

I'd like to focus on the two individual quadrants for a moment, Upper Left (consciousness or "mind") and Upper Right (mass-energy or "body").[7] Note that either quadrant can be the original source of the dysfunction and can transfer its malformations to the other quadrant through constant quadrant-to-quadrant tetra-interactions (since each quadrant is actually just a different perspective on the same phenomenon). So each of the major fulcrums of structure development (for example, those involving food, sex, power, love, self-esteem, self-actualization, or self-transcendence, to give one brief version of those 6-to-8 major levels) and each of the switch-points in the major states (gross, subtle, causal, witnessing, or nondual) will have a consciousness (mind) component (Upper Left) and a mass-energy (body) component (Upper Right). For example, on the mass-energy side, all Left-hand dysfunctions (in both structures and states) will have at least brain correlates (or some Right-hand physical exterior correlates). Those Left-hand dysfunctions (exactly the ones we have been investigating in structures and states over the past few chapters), as they show up in the Right-hand quadrants, will involve the actual physical or outward form that is their exterior (for example, a subjective rational thought in the Upper Left will correlatively light up the objective frontal cortex in the Upper Right), and—this is the point of this section—they will also have some sort of energetic component as well in the Right-hand or exterior quadrants, falling along that gross, subtle, causal, witnessing/nondual spectrum of energies—all of which, somewhat confusingly, are generally referred to as "subtle energy."[8] Thus, alongside the spectrum of consciousness in states and structures (in the Upper Left), there is a corresponding spectrum of energy of subtler and subtler dimensions (in the Upper Right). For example, a red altitude of consciousness in the Upper Left has a corresponding red altitude of material complexity (or mass-energy) in the Upper Right; a turquoise altitude of consciousness in the Upper Left has a corresponding altitude of material complexity (or mass-energy) in the Upper Right, and so on.

I have been focusing on the spectrum of consciousness and its dysfunctions (in the Upper Left), but now I want to say a few words here about the spectrum of energy (in the Upper Right) involved in dysfunctions. Since this can be rather dry and technical, I'll reserve most of it for a note, which the interested reader can pursue; and if not, no worries.[9] I'll just mention a few items in closing:

There is a common saying in the Energy Traditions, which reflects the ongoing nature of involution/evolution and the influence of the higher dimensions on the lower via "downward causation": "If you want to know what you were thinking yesterday, look at your body today; if you want to know what your body will look like tomorrow, look at your thinking today." That is, the higher realms, such as subtle soul and mind—and their thoughts—can have effects via downward involution all the way down to the gross physical body and its appearance, as well as its health and illness. What your body looks like today—as well as any illnesses it might have—are in part the result of what you were thinking yesterday; and what your body will be like tomorrow is in part the result of what you are thinking right now: the "downward causation" of involution . . .

In short, there is a spectrum of consciousness (including states, structures, and shadows) in the Upper Left quadrant, and each of those components has a correlate at the same altitude in the spectrum of mass-energy in the Upper Right quadrant. A dysfunction in either spectrum transmits to the other, and to one degree or another infects it as well. Thus, a problem at the green altitude in the Upper Left will also transmit to the green-altitude region of the mid-subtle mass-energy spectrum in the brain in the Upper Right, dysfunctionally infecting it. Via the process of downward causation of the moment-to-moment involutionary current, this energetic dysfunction can then transmit down the spectrum to any number of lower levels (thus, this subtle-soul illness can transmit/involve downward to generate a mental illness, which can transmit/involve downward to generate an emotional illness, which can end up transmitting all the way down to trigger a physical illness. In typically going all the way down and crashing at the lowest level, the gross material-physical dimension, it will likely manifest as actual physical illness—an illness that ultimately can be cured only by curing the origin point of the overall problem—in this case, the green altitude dysfunction and its mid-subtle-range energetic component).

We will return to this general notion in chapter 16.

Healthy and Unhealthy Drives

I have often pointed out that each state and structure faces in two directions vertically: looking "downward," it faces the previous stage (and all previous, lower, junior stages); looking "upward," it faces the next-to-emerge higher stage (and all higher, senior stages). The former is driven by Agape, or the loving embrace of the junior by the senior; the latter is driven by Eros, or the drive of the junior to reach even higher wholes and stages (a higher Love, as it were). The former (Agape) is a holon caringly embracing its own subholons; the latter (Eros), a holon looking to become a subholon in a yet-greater superholon.

Now, we have also seen, each of those drives can miscarry or malfunction. When Agape misfires, it doesn't just reach down and embrace its lower subholons, it fixates on or gets addicted to them (even *regressing* to them—a regression whose ultimate end point is all the way down to the lifeless, or "dead," material domain, a drive called "Thanatos" or "death drive," the pathological form of Agape). When Eros misfires, it doesn't just reach up for the higher, it does so because it denies, alienates, dis-owns, represses, or fears its present but soon-to-be "lower" holon, a drive called "Phobos," or fear, which creates an avoidance or allergy to that which it fears—the pathological form of Eros. Eros then doesn't "transcend and include," it "transcends and represses"—out of fear. Thus, generally speaking, all avoidances and allergies are "fear driven," and all fixations and addictions are ultimately "death driven."

Both of these are extremely common in spiritual pursuits, especially Eros as Phobos (although recently, with an extreme overemphasis on, and misunderstanding of, "Be here now," coupled with the need for narcissistic immediate gratification, regressive Agape as Thanatos is making a strong showing, as we'll see). Many individuals take up "spiritual transcendence" precisely as a way to avoid having to deal with various common problems and issues in ordinary life. Instead of working with these problems and integrating them, the temptation is to "spiritually bypass" them entirely and view their avoidance and denial as evidence of some superior spiritual attainment, whereas it is, or can be, alas, something much more mundane and shadow driven. It's common knowledge that in monasteries, for example, many individuals are there not only to find God but also to avoid conventional life and its problems—not only to "transcend and include" but also to "transcend and repress." Transcendence and repression become virtually indistinguishable. (Believers in, and advocates of, immanence and "embodiment" charge all transcendence with really being repression, oppression, and ultimately hate-driven, destruction-inducing denial. This can be true, but only in its pathological form.)

Because conflict was so widespread, Freud theorized that the ultimate cause of conflict had to be two instincts that were inherently at war with each other. At first he first proposed that these two were food and sex—where individual survival or food was clearly "contra" the collective survival of sex. His second pair of warring instincts were libido and aggression: pleasure-driven attraction is at war with the drives to hurt and destroy (a scheme that is still commonly used). His third formulation was the most controversial, and puzzling for many: Eros and Thanatos, or Life and Death.

I think that Freud's last formulation got this essentially vertical axis right, but he should have either described both drives in their pathological forms (Phobos and Thanatos) or described both drives in their healthy forms (Eros and Agape), instead of listing the healthy form of one and the unhealthy form of the other. But Freud was right that Thanatos is a real drive with real results, usually dysfunctional, in the human psyche.

Spiritually, "love of the lower" (for example, love of "lower" life forms, of "lower" feelings in one's own being, of "lower" sentient beings, of lower holons in any compound individual or superholon, of putatively "lower" or disadvantaged humans) can often start out as a genuine, loving, caring Agape. But if it's not balanced with an equal input from Eros, all of one's love ends up being aimed in the "junior" direction, and as that starts to feel slightly uncomfortable—because so unbalanced—one might simply intensify that form of love, not knowing any other course of action, and thus end up pushing into actually lower and lower states and realms of being and consciousness. If this downward spiral continues, the individual, in severe cases, can end up drinking a bit too much of the altar wine, or find dental trips for oxycodone more and more common, or one way or another, eventually end up with a full-blown addiction at the lowest levels—drug and substance abuse. (This is not an exaggerated claim, and seeing its truth depends upon getting the "feel" of full-blown Thanatos—a drive, or desire, to blot out one's painful sense of existence, an almost suicidal wish not to have to feel oneself confronting an uncaring world anymore, a need to "disappear" entirely in a totally numbed out, and in that sense "insentient," state—a state generally delivered by intoxication in its many forms; it's a short step from deeply wanting a love of the lower to actually finding it.)

Such intense addictions notoriously lead one down the nested hierarchy of motivations (and life in general): first surrendering 2nd-tier self-actualization (and a higher cause for spiritual pursuits), then surrendering orange self-esteem (many addicts can remember the exact point they spent the last ounce of their self-esteem to get drugs), then letting go of amber communal belonging (usually abandoning any genuine friends at all), then moving into merely egocentric and narcissistic levels, gripped by red power and finally infrared physiological drives alone, attempting merely to attain the desired state experience. This experience usually starts out even better than hoped for, not only blotting out the painful self's existence but also delivering a genuine taste and infusion of bliss-soaked subtle or causal or even nondual experience. This drive to experience self-transcendence in a positive, euphoric sense becomes a major, unacknowledged motivation for virtually all substance addictions. The individual takes a hit of crack, and for the first time in his or her life is ushered into a radically blissful state of experiential Wholeness—one hit of that, and he or she is hooked. Only when they hit bottom—the bottom of everything: relationships, love, work, sex, parenting, money, house—when there is nothing left to lose, does recovery begin. This is the grip of Thanatos— a desire to love malformed into a desire to die, and adopting means that are in effect slowly but surely suicidal.

But Agape turned Thanatos is not operative only in such extreme and severe cases; it is active and functioning in any regressive move downward from any level in the spectrum of development—a move, in whole or part, from violet to indigo, or teal to green, or orange to amber, or amber to red, and so on. Each regression is a death to a higher, more whole, more complex holon, and the embrace of its junior, less whole, less "alive" subholons. In evolution, as higher and higher holons are created that transcend and include their junior predecessors, and are built up in something like an archaeological layering of more and more complex strata, when regression occurs, it follows downward the same path that was created when moving upward, and does so strata by strata by strata, though now in the opposite direction.

Of course, in addition to the two vertical drives (Eros and Agape), there are the two "horizontal" drives—agency and communion—and they, too, can exist in healthy or unhealthy forms. Agency, in its healthy form, is functional autonomy—a healthy drive and function of wholeness, of being relatively whole (on whatever level); it is a "wholeness drive," and related to autonomy, there are the drives of justice, rights, independence, and freedom. But when agency becomes *dysfunctional*, it shows up, not just as working autonomy but as overblown autonomy—that is, as alienation, isolation, separation, repression, inability to commit and sometimes even an inability to communicate. (Both autonomy and alienated autonomy tend to be more masculine oriented, à la Carol Gilligan, hence the standard female complaint about the male: "He's afraid of commitment"; and the standard male complaint to the female: "I need more space.")

Communion, in its healthy form, is functional relationship—the drive to be a healthy part of a larger whole; it is a "relationship drive," a "partness drive," and with it, there is an emphasis on care, relational concerns, responsibility, and loving-kindness. But when communion becomes dysfunctional, it fosters not healthy relationships but morbidly fused relationships—the individual puts relationship entirely ahead of any individuality or self-autonomy; boundaries often melt down; there is not just a relationship but a fusion. (Both communion and meltdown communion tend to be more feminine oriented, also à la Carol Gilligan. Hence the standard male complaint about the female: "She's too needy; she defines herself by her relationships"; and the standard female complaint to the male: "You won't let me in.")

Any particular pathology or dysfunction—in states or structures—involves some mixture of these four drives in their healthy and unhealthy forms. Failure to differentiate and healthily dis-identify, for example, or failure to move to the next higher stage, is a failure of Eros—there's "not enough" Eros, leading to fixation and addiction. Failure to include, integrate, and embrace is a failure of Agape—there's "not enough" Agape, leading to avoidance and allergy. Dysfunctional agency and communion generate some of the problems we just outlined, from (with agency) alienation and narcissistic isolation, to (with communion) relationship meltdown and autonomy being swamped by relationships. I am not going to include an analysis of these in each of the dysfunctions that we are discussing, but interested readers can certainly make the necessary connections and spot the presence of these drives in each case. The functioning of these four drives in human beings illuminates how humans—as holons—share many characteristics possessed by all holons anywhere in the Kosmos, and these four drives are certainly some of those.

The Importance of Transference

A quick note about therapeutic interactions insofar as they pertain to dysfunctions on these levels (structures and states, with an emphasis on our present topic, state dysfunctions). Freud noted, early on, that his clients soon developed a "transference neurosis" with him, where their original neurosis (which brought them into therapy) was replaced by a neurosis that focused directly on the therapist. Instead of, for example, the client hating her father, she starts to hate the therapist; or, conversely, develops a "crush" on the therapist. For Freud, this was a positive occurrence, because whereas the direct causes of the original neurosis could not be directly seen or felt in the therapeutic situation (most having been set in motion years ago, long past the possibility of direct intervention), the transference neurosis was occurring right here, right now, in the therapist's office, plain enough for everybody to see. Further, the object of the transference—the therapist himself or herself—was there, present, able to work with this neurosis and inter-pret it with the client, and thus could aim to cure this present transfer-ence neurosis, returning the client to some sort of normality in his or her life. The therapist constantly draws attention to the transferred, or projected, material; explores with the client its real source and origins; and has the client particularly notice that the present reality does not, in fact, resemble the original situation at all—that the client is project-ing some past material onto the present reality, thus distorting the present unnecessarily. If the client sees this clearly enough, he or she stops transferring material from his or her own interior onto the real-ity of the therapist, thus "curing" the transference neurosis (and, to the extent that the transference neurosis was being driven by the orig-inal neurosis, this simultaneously puts a dent in that as well). Precisely because the original neurosis was replaced with the transference neu-rosis, and the transference neurosis could often be treated, there was a real chance that the client's original neurosis could be ameliorated.

Now, in virtually every higher transpersonal state (this occurs in structural realms, too, but here we are focusing on higher states, and once the general concept is grasped, it is easily applied to other areas), a similar process will almost always form between a spiritual student and his or her teacher—namely, the formation of a transference neuro-sis involving, in addition to any typical conventional shadow material, some transpersonal or spiritual material—a "spiritual transference neurosis."

The *original* or *root* spiritual "neurosis," if we can call it that, might be summarized this way: the students are caught in a case of mistaken identity, and identify some version of their infinite, Higher, Real, or True Self with their lower, finite, limited, and fragmented mental egoic self, which generates existential dukkha, or suffering, torment, terror, and tears. When these students come into contact with the teacher—and assuming that the teacher has, to some degree, awakened his or her own Higher or True Self (although this problem can happen, as can all projections, whether or not the "hooks" for the projection actually display the qualities about to be projected onto them; it's just that, if they do display the soon-to-be projected traits, the projection is all the more likely to occur with that particular person)—the students will transfer the intuition of their own Higher or Real Self onto the teacher, and thus see the teacher as possessing an abundance of Enlightened Awareness, Higher or Real Self, pure spiritual Emptiness, infinite Spirit itself (while the students, lacking the projected material, see themselves as possessing little, if any—as being totally unenlightened, ignorant, pathetic).

The goal of a good teacher is to spot this transference and "analyze" it by constantly reminding the students that they have an abundance of this Enlightened Awareness that they think only the teacher possesses; that the goal of the spiritual process is to Recognize their own Higher or Real Self (or Suchness) in themselves and not just see it in the teacher; that the goal of the teacher is, if anything, to help with this Recognition, to remind the students of their own inherent and ever-present infinite Spirit; that the aim of the practices that they do together is not to simply see the Real Self in the teacher, but to "join minds" with the teacher and thus realize that they both are displaying and perfectly manifesting the one and only Real Self and True Spirit in all the Kosmos ("Let this consciousness be in you which was in Christ Jesus, that we all may be one").

In short, the ordinary, typical, common spiritual neurosis—a case of mistaken identity with the mental ego instead of with the Higher or Real Self—is replaced by a "spiritual transference" to the teacher, who now possesses all Spirit and all True Self, whereas I, the student, completely lack such. The sophisticated teacher, who is used to working with such projections, will help the student to "analyze" this spiritual transference, pointing out that it is not true that the teacher, and only the teacher, possesses the Higher and Real Self, but rather the student completely, equally, and fully possesses and expresses this infinite Spirit, too. And, when that "analysis" is successful, the spiritual transference neurosis with the teacher, which replaced the original spiritual neurosis, is "cured," precisely because the spiritual transference neurosis is directly attacked, deconstructed, and undone, which also affects the original spiritual neurosis by returning the student to a direct realization of his or her own True Condition—namely, a Supreme Identity with the one and only infinite Spirit and True Self of the entire Kosmos.

There is a spectrum of selves or self-senses—from lowest to ultimate—each of which is marked by the possibility of various forms of dys-eases and dysfunctions, one of which is the projection of the intuition of the healthy self-sense of that level onto others, especially onto a teacher, therapist, master, coach, or spiritual guide. When this happens, it switches the typical neurosis of that particular level to a transference neurosis with the teacher at that level, which takes on specifically spiritual dimensions when higher states and structures are involved. The competent teacher knows how to spot these transference neuroses, and, in working with them, ameliorate or even "cure" them, returning the student to a healthy version of the self at that level, resulting ultimately, if the higher and highest levels are involved, in a complete, full, and profound Enlightenment, or Awakening, of the student to his or her own deepest, truest, highest, Ultimate Self or Suchness.

Spiritual transference neuroses are one of the most common—I would say, probably *the* most common—problem in spiritual communities (or in virtually any organization with an admired leader). Let me therefore gently suggest that students—and teachers—take a look at their own situations and see if they can sharpen their recognition and understanding of this occurrence, and thus help diminish this near-epidemic situation.

Concluding Remarks on the Shadow

All of the pathologies and dysfunctions just discussed can be treated to some degree with the 3-2-1 or 3-2-1-0 process, at least as a beginning program of shadow work, more extensive and sophisticated forms of which can certainly be sought if desired. Once individuals get a feel for this 3-2-1 process (or the 3-2-1-0 process), they often easily include it in any meditation practice they are using. Meditation, in general, often uses various forms of mindfulness practice—engaging the nonjudgmental or Witnessing mirror-mind with regard to the present stream of consciousness. If particularly attractive or repulsive images arise, running through a quick 3-2-1 exercise with them will often be enough to clear them, and you can actually feel the mind open and relax, decontracting in the face of what was alienated shadow material (but is now re-owned, integrated, and then let go of in a healthy, transcendental manner, opening the mind to a greater degree of relative freedom, spaciousness, and clarity). This fits nicely with mindfulness types of practice, since it helps reduce anger, fear, judgment, or reactivity to various mental images, increasing the equanimity and mindfulness possible. And having induced an increase in "relative relaxation" or relative openness or spaciousness (by returning the alienated and contracted material to its original state of undisturbed wholeness in the psyche), meditation can then help one move more easily into "ultimate relaxation" or radical Openness—the dissolution of the self-contraction or separate-self sense altogether—returning Awareness to its "thoughtless," "dreamless," "headless" state of unity consciousness, pure Nondual Suchness, and spontaneous Presence. This "double relaxation" can actually be directly felt in Awareness when one practices this type of "Integral" meditation.

But whatever shadow work that one adopts, take seriously the conclusion reached by so many teachers: meditation alone (or spiritual work in general) is not enough to fully handle shadow material. And having shadow material does not mean that you are not doing your spiritual practice correctly or that you are not being spiritual enough. (It is still much too common a presumption that if you have any emotional problems at all, it's because you're not being spiritual enough—you're not really putting your faith in Jesus, or you're not fully submitted to Allah, or you're not spending enough time with mindfulness practice, or not enough time in the Zendo, and so on—none of which is true; or, it may be true, but that's not the major cause of your emotional problems.) It simply means that you have some developmental fulcrum or switch-point problem, most likely created during development itself (including possibly your present meditative state-stage development), and it can usually be handled straightforwardly enough by some form of shadow work. Shadow work, then, should definitely be considered for inclusion in any Fourth Turning or Integral Spirituality.

Shadow work in general is a rehearsal of Enlightenment itself, a rehearsal of a direct realization of the Supreme Identity, where something that was felt to be other or outside or separate from me—which, in the case of the Supreme Identity, is Spirit itself and the entire manifest world appearing to arise and exist out there, separate and set apart from the little finite me in here—is recognized as one's true Nature. This Recognition heals that fragmented split and returns the Kosmos to its true condition, a seamless (not featureless) Whole reality hanging together in every direction. That which seemed utterly and absolutely alien to me is actually of one nature with me—the deepest me—and the entire universe is actually arising *within me*. And being free of that otherness, I am released likewise from fear, suffering, torment, terror (following the Upanishads, "Where there is other, there is fear"). I realize that I have, in the deepest source of my own being, broken a prior Wholeness into a subject in here and a world of objects out there, and then wrestling with that world of objects becomes my entire life— wanting them, fearing them, chasing them, avoiding them, all the while ignoring my prior, true, ultimately Whole and Real condition, the realization of which constitutes the Great Liberation.

Likewise, in a smaller degree, and almost as a type of rehearsal, with shadow work, I start with a sense of myself as a subject in here, which has become fraudulent and basically unreal because I have broken it into pieces in the deepest fashion, identified with some of the pieces and denied and projected the rest, converting the world out there into a world both even more dangerous and even more alluring than was previously the case, as my shadow falls over each and every one of the world's objects, casting a glimmering glow that is actually an illusion through and through. The illusion evaporates if, and only if, I re-identify with those pieces of myself that I have denied and tossed to the winds. Doing so is a miniature liberation, liberation from the small anxieties, petty depressions, and mediocre angst that were created with the original lie about myself, the lie that I contained none of those shadows but the world was full of them. The shadow, as the nexus of the finite lie, is returned to its proper home; a finite truth, freedom, unity, and wholeness results.

But even having done that, the greater lie, the larger projection, the bigger shade cast across the world is simply the entire world itself, which I have projected out of my own deepest and Truest Self. I have fundamentally lied about it, and then tossed it out to the rain and storms of a certain suffering, and now I am caught in the cross fire of a series of infinite lies about Spirit itself and my own deepest Being, and I am reduced to ducking and dodging, chasing and seducing, the fleeting, passing, finite, born and dying objects of that partial and broken world, instead of recognizing my own Original Face, Unborn and Undying, One and All, Whole and All-Embracing, Luminous and Clear. Upon taking back that entire world—the ultimate shadow of my ultimate Self—and recognizing my own Supreme Identity, then all tortured turmoil in the separate-self sense comes quietly to rest, as the separate-self sense itself simply evaporates and I am set free in an Ocean of infinity, a Sky of no scarcity, a Heart of All-Hallows, finished forever with the infinite lie about my own and truest Self, one with Spirit and one with All, here in the unending Light and Love of a true Infinity known as my Whole Being and Eternal Becoming; a larger Wholeness there exists nowhere in the known or unknown worlds, here and now, there and back, Only and All.

Part Four

Elements of an Integral Spirituality

14

Structures and States

An Integral Spirituality does not mean that all religions will be melted down into one, single, universal religion—any more than an "international style" of cuisine means that all food is melted down into Mexican. It does mean, however, that individuals at the Integral (and higher) stages of spiritual intelligence will demand Integral versions of their own faith. There are several somewhat different models of Integral— these stages of development, remember, aren't marked by their specific contents but by the degree of complexity of thinking and the degree of consciousness available at them (or the number of perspectives inherent at that level—Archaic through Magic-Mythic are 1st-person perspectives; Mythic adds a 2nd-person perspective; Rational adds 3rd-person; Pluralistic, 4th-person; Holistic and Integral, 5th- and 6th-person; Super-Integral, 7th-person and higher), and, within those degrees of complexity and consciousness, many different models are possible. But all of them, if truly Integral, will want to include the essentials of the others (to the extent that they are truly valid), and so these models tend to converge. That's what the Integral AQAL model attempts to do (and encourages others to do), and using that AQAL model as a metaframework, virtually any Integral Spirituality— whether Christian, Buddhist, Muslim, Hindu, Jewish, and so on—will therefore likely include certain elements, either as found in their own traditions or, if necessary, imported from other traditions and human disciplines, including the sciences. After having discussed many of these suggested elements somewhat randomly in previous chapters, in this part it's time to pull them all together and make specific recommendations.

This part consists of four chapters, chapters 14 to 17. Chapters 14 and 15 discuss what I think are the core issues that any Fourth Turning, or Integral Spirituality (or just Life itself) should include. Chapters 16 and 17 deal with "miscellaneous" items, which are not necessarily less important or less worthy of inclusion (many, in fact, are crucial), but if a prioritization were demanded, this is the general division I would suggest. Of course, almost everybody will have their own ideas and priorities, and all of them are welcome—truly, the more, the better—as this important dialogue is just now getting started, and the richer the voices, the better the outcome, undoubtedly. And so I trust that, in addition to reading about my suggestions and priorities, each of you will contemplate your own ideas and possibilities, and will bring them forward on any of the forums that will emerge to discuss this most significant of issues facing the modern and postmodern world, all around a common theme: "Just how inclusive do you *want* to be?"

Structures and Structure-Stages of Development

The acknowledgment of *structures and structure-stages of development*, or rungs and Views, is particularly crucial. Any Integral Spirituality would interpret its fundamental tenets in the language of each of the major developmental levels of Views. There would be a Magic teaching, a Magic-Mythic teaching, a Mythic-traditional teaching, a Rational-modern teaching, a Pluralistic-postmodern teaching, a holistic-Integral teaching, and a Super-Integral teaching (and possibly more, depending upon which sublevels are counted; but those seven are fundamental). This is needed because in virtually every culture on the planet, there are today a large number of individuals at each and every one of those stages, and they all see, hear, experience, and interpret a *different* version of whatever gospel, dogma, or dharma that they are presented with. These different interpretations are, quite literally, impossible to avoid or escape; each person engages in a different interpretation at each level of their overall development, no matter what it is. There-fore, spirituality can speak to that person either in the language of their own present level (which they will better understand) or in the language of a fixed level, usually a different level representing the of-ficial orthodox stance. (If indeed it is different from the level of the person receiving it, they will not fully or clearly understand it; in fact, it can be guaranteed that they will subtly but profoundly misunder-stand and distort various quite central issues.) Today, every spiritual system (bar none, except for today's pioneers, of course, who are deal-ing with some form of Integral model) teaches from basically one, pre-set, and predetermined level (usually Mythic, occasionally Rational, and sometimes, rarely, Pluralistic).

Instead of presenting their spiritual teaching from just one level-stage (an outmoded "one size fits all" view) and letting people at other level-stages make up their own versions (which they most definitely will; they have no choice but to interpret whatever they see through the lens of their present level), any conscientious spirituality would put its finest minds to work in creating the most understandable, appro-priate, and "correct" spiritual teaching for each and every structure and state available—the same basic gospel, dharma, or teaching but interpreted from at least seven different levels and five different states. Sound a little complicated? To some degree it is; but remember, *people are ALREADY making these different interpretations anyway right now!*—so we can either do this consciously and conscientiously, or haphazardly and blindly (and hence risk being blindsided by them). The choice is absolutely that simple.

The point is that, for any Integral faith in an ideal offering, one would start in early childhood with a Magical teaching, where a hero—a saint, sage, or adept—of the tradition is treated like any su-perman or superhero, much like the superheroes of any children's Sat-urday morning cartoon show today, most of which reflect the Magic View perfectly. The stories would be intentionally designed with that age and stage of development in mind: these cartoon superheroes can fly, walk on water, see through walls, bring dead beings back to life, cure illnesses, or any number of other magical events—all perfectly designed with the Magic Lens in mind. So we'd have Captain Chris-tian, Amazing Amir Man, Vanquishing Vedanta Venus, Super Mensch Kabbalah Guy, Krazy Power Kali Girl, Sri Mega Siddhi Siddhartha—

well, you get the point; *this is already how individuals at the Magic stage view their spiritual Adepts anyway* (and it is the only way they *can* view them!). They walk on water, heal the sick, raise the dead, turn water into wine, see flaming bushes, vanquish foes with the snap of a finger, cause rivers to be parted. This is how the Magic mind sees the world in general at this stage—including its spirituality! So why not appropriately address the mind as such—in those terms—at that stage? This is not to send the message that, in adulthood, this religion will make you a superman, only that the practice of religion brings many powerful benefits and will help you with many of Life's most difficult problems. There's a real magic secreted in spirituality—that's the lesson of this stage!

As the child grows into the elementary school years, Magic teaching gives way to Magic-Mythic, or "PowerGods," still reflecting the essentially egocentric nature of thinking, with the added drive and allure of newly emergent power drives. It will also shift the source of "miraculous" occasions from the self to powerful others, tentatively opening the dimension of Spirit as a Great Thou, and also teaching that there is good Help and Advice from knowledgeable Others—from adepts, teachers, saints, and sages from the tradition. Spirit in 2nd person comes hesitantly to the fore, and one's "imaginary friend"—quite common at this stage—can become oriented toward a True Friend and Creative Matrix of the Kosmos itself. Never again will the individual have to be alone in this often truly lonely world: listen carefully, and you will find the Great Thou of the Kosmos whispering in your ear, never leaving or abandoning you. That's a real superhero! God is not some gray-haired gentleman sitting on a throne high in the sky staring down at you but somebody, or some thing, that you can form an immediate, living, vital relationship with—starting right now! Reach out and touch anything—and there is Spirit, right here, right now. That's an important lesson of spirituality at this stage (even if God does tend to remain viewed as that gray-haired gentleman in the sky . . .). But the major lesson of religion at this "PowerGods" stage is that, throughout life, God can indeed be a profound and genuine source of power for you.

As the child enters middle-school years (ages seven to twelve), Magic-Mythic switches to pure Mythic, which, with its group-and-conformist orientation and the full emergence of 2nd person, fits the rule/role mind and peer pressure so characteristic of this period. This is also the first stage where a genuine interest in Truth can develop—given the concrete operational nature of cognition—and hence, in the Great Traditions, this is when the search for "absolute Truth" originates (Graves called this stage "absolutistic," and Spiral Dynamics calls it "TruthForce"), the "Truth that surpasseth understanding" and is redemptive or liberational. The Mythic-literal stage is where mythic truths are taken to be ultimately and absolutely true, and the notion of the "one true way" frequently emerges—and in an ethnocentric, "chosen peoples" form—the present "in" group. It is important at this stage to plant the seeds of *nonviolent ethnocentrism*. The mind is stuck with 2nd-person perspectives, and thus stuck with ethnocentrism, but the notion can be introduced that God speaks to all people as if they were the most special people in the whole world, because, to God, they are. So take the specialness of your faith as special indeed, because it is, but realize that God speaks to all peoples also, and they are special, too. In the meantime, use your specialness to enhance your attraction to, and love of, Spirit as it is conveying itself to you now, realizing that others, elsewhere, are doing the same—one big family speaking many different languages, all from the same Source. The "specialness" of one's particular group is an important nutrient at this stage of human development and shouldn't be simply denied. At this stage, let one's belly be filled with this specialness mana from Spirit, and thus prepare to become part of Spirit's truly one world, one family—one Source, many forms. One Spirit, many special families (especially yours!)—this is an important lesson at this stage of spiritual growth.

Midadolescence and early adulthood bring the crucial transformation from Mythic to Rational, perhaps the most important transformation prior to 2nd tier. Because of the shift from 2nd-person mythic and ethnocentric to 3rd-person rational and worldcentric, the teaching here emphasizes that, using reason and evidence, there is abundant support to believe in a universal spiritual dimension to the Kosmos, especially if one includes meditation and its direct, experiential, spiritual realizations (where one directly experiences Divine Presence, in a communion, union, or identity form—the closest thing to a direct, personal, experiential proof of Spirit's existence). The simple, outrageous improbability of an evolutionary unfolding to higher and higher and higher stages of unspeakable complexity continues to defy a mere "chance and natural selection" explanation. The astronomer Hugh

Ross calculated that "less than 1 chance in 10^{144} (trillion trillion trillion trillion trillion trillion trillion trillion trillion trillion trillion trillion) exists that even one such planet [a planet that supports life] would occur anywhere in the universe."[1] Einstein himself said that the universe evidences "an intelligence of such superiority that, compared with it, all the systematic thinking and acting of human beings is an utterly insignificant reflection."[2] Looking at all the evidence, Francis Crick, Nobel Prize–winning codiscoverer of the structure of DNA, concluded that "An honest man, armed with all the knowledge available to us now, could only state that in some sense, the origin of life appears at the moment to be almost a miracle, so many are the conditions which would have had to have been satisfied to get it going."[3] Miracle indeed.

Rational reasons to believe in this miraculous spiritual dimension to Reality include the following: (a) the "creative advance into novelty" that is demonstrated by evolution itself and is inexplicable by mere "chance mutation" (the evolution from strings to quarks to subatomic particles to atoms to small molecules to massively interconnected molecules to asexual cells and early organisms—just for starters—is an awful lot of evolution in a universe that is supposed to be "running down" but can easily be seen as yet more evidence of creative Eros or Spirit-in-action, "a self-organizing self-transcendent drive," as Erich Jantsch put it); (b) the evidence from numerous sciences on the interwoven, entangled, enacted, interconnected nature of all seemingly separate things and events (these are still 3rd-person deductions and should not replace 1st-person direct meditative evidence, but are further evidence of a self-organizing drive); (c) the presence of consciousness as an undeniable reality throughout the universe (the denial of which is a performative contradiction); and most significantly, (d) the experimental and injunctive proof of Spirit's existence by following paradigms, practices, and exemplars, from contemplation to highest yoga—this is not God taken on faith but based on direct personal experience, a "science of the interior," which, in every major culture the world over, has a practice leading to a "satori" or "Self-realization" that discloses a direct experience of Spirit itself, by whatever name.[4] A major aim of the Rational stage of spiritual intelligence is to demythologize the tradition, cleansing it of the magic and mythic elements that are characteristic of the infancy and childhood of humanity, a childhood experienced not only today but several thousand years ago when many of the major religions themselves were being laid down. Spirit has continued to evolve, and so should spirituality.

A major lesson of this stage is the very evolution or unfolding of spirituality itself from ethnocentric to worldcentric—so that Spirit is open to all peoples, not just to any one special family (since all families are most definitely special to God). So even though one's own faith may be "special," since to God they all are—what this means most centrally is that the only "chosen peoples" are ultimately *all* peoples everywhere—that regardless of race, color, sex, or creed, each sentient being is a being of Spirit, a direct and perfect manifestation—just as it is—of Spirit, and has Spirit as its own central core. Like waves in the ocean, or drops of rain from the sky, like rays from the sun, or bands in a rainbow—the metaphors are endless, the message the same: we are all outflowing manifestations of this infinite Spirit, with but one True Self looking out of the eyes of each and every sentient being alive, all the way down to atoms, with each evolutionary advance simply increasing the sensitivity of a being to the world around it—from atomic reactivity to cellular sensations, to neural nets and actual perception, to reptilian brain stems and active impulses, to early mammalian limbic systems and powerful emotions, to later mammalian cortexes and images and symbols, to the primate neocortex and early protoconcepts, to the human triune brain and its capacity for formal reason, to brain synchronization and "unity" states—in short, from subconscious to self-conscious to superconscious. In each we see a Spirit becoming more aware of itself, more conscious, more inclusive, more creative, more embracing, more loving and caring, more awakened, more capable of the Good and the True and the Beautiful—all the way to its own radical Self-Awakening and Self-Realization and Self-Remembering, which is the summum bonum, the ultimate Good, of a human being as well. The lesson here, at the Rational worldcentric stage, is that this Spirit "belongs" especially to no one chosen people but to all peoples, regardless of race, color, sex, or creed/religion. So choose your faith or spiritual practice, and find the one that is definitely "special" and the "best for you," but never think others cannot do the same with their faith and their spiritual practice. True, some spiritual practices are deeper, higher, wider, more effective, more

Whole than others—often seen even in different practices within the same tradition!—but no individuals, no people, are inherently better than another: all are God's children, loved equally by Him/Her, a Spirit available to anyone who, with loving heart and open mind surrenders his or her separate-self sense to the Divine One and All, the Goal and Ground and Condition of Everything That Is.

In short, in late adolescence and young adulthood, the Rational View appropriately expands spirituality from ethnocentric to worldcentric, from Spirit being available to a chosen "in-group" people to "all peoples," from "us" to "all of us"—"an us without a them." This is a massive leap in development, especially spiritual development, because it means giving up the belief that if I *don't* believe in this *particular* religion and this *particular* savior, then I am automatically bound for hell, no question about it. This demands the cognitive expansion from concrete operations to formal operations, the expansion of identity from 2nd-person ethnocentric to 3rd-person worldcentric, and the progression of morals from conventional/conformist to postconventional/universal. This does not mean, as noted, that everybody has to become a member of the same religion, but it does involve the recognition that, for example, if one is Christian, the words "from the Holy Spirit" in the statement "Whatsoever is true, by whomsoever it is said, is from the Holy Spirit" could be replaced by "from Brahman," "from Tao," "from Allah," "from Jehovah (Ayn Sof)," "from Godhead," or "from Dharmakaya" without altering its truth. This cognitive expansion also allows, say, a Christian, to make that crucial switch from thinking that Christianity, and it alone, is truly Divine, to seeing that whatever it is that makes Christianity divine ("the Holy Spirit") makes other spiritual systems divine as well, and that Spirit could not fail but speak to every human group and culture on the planet, but *in their own terms*, which, of course, will vary from culture to culture but leave none of them out. Certain ideas show up, in deep structure form, in all of them at particular stages of development and evolution—the same basic structures and major states are universally present, for example—but they will be expressed in unique and varying ways, which is just fine, which is just as it should be. The Rational View—which Graves called "multiplistic"—applies to spirituality as well: there are multiplistic forms of essentially similar Divine Truths (forms that vary according to the structure and state in which they originate, and their overall level of evolutionary development, which itself continues to unfold, becoming deeper and deeper, higher and higher, wider and wider, whether the religion accommodates to that fact or not).

The extreme green Pluralistic View that there is absolutely nothing at all in common between cultures (and thus no universal scientific, humanistic, or spiritual truths)—so that, for instance, it would be false to claim that different cultures have the same deep structures in both states and structures—not only makes no sense in its own right, it is a massive self-contradiction: It claims that all signifiers are contextually determined, that all referents are socially created, that all meaning is an interpretation, that no ranking system is anything but an oppressive prejudice, and that each culture has its own, incommensurable truths and values; in short, there are no universal truths, even in deep structures. Yet it also claims that those statements, its own statements, *are all universally true*. They are not merely interpretations but straightforward facts; its meaning system is not merely socially constructed by a particular society but is true for all societies in all eras; its ranking system, which is that its view is definitely better than others' views, isn't a ranking system but the unvarnished truth; its view is superior in a world where it also claims that nothing is supposed to be superior; and its truths, far from being culturally constructed meanings, are true for all people, in all cultures, at all places, in all times. Might as well write ten volumes claiming that writing doesn't exist.

Be that as it may, early adulthood is when, appropriately (and hopefully in a healthy fashion), the Rational View gives way to the Pluralistic View, as continuing life experiences show that there are often many more and different perspectives on an issue than monolithic rationality lets on—that "there are more things in heaven and earth than are dreamt of in your philosophy," as the Bard would have it. The healthy Pluralistic stage also acts to make sure the particular faith is trying to be inclusive, socially engaged, sustainable, nonoppressive, and environmentally sound. Pluralistic View spirituality is politically sensitive (usually liberal; or, increasingly, looking for a union of liberal and conservative), actively tolerant, and attempts to be inclusive (though it still dislikes other value systems—Mythic, Rational, Integral, and so on). It is interested in everything "conscious," from conscious capitalism to conscious parenting to conscious aging, and it is feminist, womanist, and more recently, masculinist, and relationship

502 | Elements of an Integral Spirituality

oriented ("The new Buddha will be the Sangha"). Again, it's important to remember that someone at the Pluralist View stage of spiritual intelligence may be totally atheist, theist, nontheist, or agnostic, as long as they reached their conclusions with a pluralistic mind and a 4th-person perspective.

The major problem with the Pluralistic stage is that it can (as can any stage) take extreme, or dysfunctional, forms, which I often call "the mean green meme" (MGM)—"mean" because that's just what it is. The Pluralistic stage includes such a sophisticated level of cognition (it is the highest altitude level in 1st tier, but that's the problem—it's still 1st-tier) that it is convinced, with this sophisticated cognitive capacity now backing it, that it is genuinely the one and only adequate truth and value system in existence, and that all others are not just wrong but generally detrimental and actively harmful to the world. (These value systems are usually maliciously conceived by the Pluralistic stage as some form of "ism"—racism, sexism, colonialism, imperialism, capitalism, speciesism, ageism, logocentrism—in fact, according to the Pluralistic View, no cultural beliefs prior to postmodernism existed apart from one or more of those "isms," and thus all of them house some degree or another of oppression.) It therefore feels justified in using almost any form of (nonphysical) attack to advance its own views. In most universities in the United States (as documented in the chilling book *The Shadow University*), all a student has to do is charge a teacher with racism, sexism, or almost any other "ism," and that teacher can (and usually will) simply be dismissed on the spot—without a trial, without being allowed to face his or her accusers or be allowed to present a defense or in any way allowed due process.⁵ It is the only place in the United States, *The Shadow University* points out, where due process of law has been systematically and widely suspended. As the authors of that book point out, in so many words, disagreeing with the green value system is now implicitly equated with being a terrorist—hence, as with actual suspected terrorists, due process can be indefinitely suspended. Recently, the president of Harvard made a small handful of perfectly reasonable hypotheses on the possible differences in brain biology between men and women, and the entire faculty darn near fainted and passed out. "I could not believe that in this day and age such thoughts were even being entertained," one female professor exclaimed, storming out of the room. Steven Pinker, almost alone, defended the president—given that lab research on hormones and neurophysiology had demonstrated the likely truth of his suggestions anyway. The Harvard president, of course, was fired. But that's the "mean green meme"—the MGM—in action. It is likely the result of the fact that green postmodernism is, as Terry Eagleton, a major leader in the field, put it, "About as dead as a philosophy can become." And it's only when a major worldview is threatened (and near extinction) that the Inquisition for that View comes out—as it did with the Spanish Inquisition during the Counter-Reformation and the amber View. You don't need the Inquisition when everybody believes the myths; you need it only when they start to doubt them.

That's what has happened to green—virtually everybody realizes that "postmodernism is dead," and the question, "What's next?" is on everybody's lips. What's next seems to be either some form of evolutionary philosophy—evolution has become so widely adopted—or some form of Critical Realism, with its hard-headed ontology; or occasionally, some form of Integral Theory and Practice, with something like its Integral Methodological Pluralism. However, as Max Planck, discoverer of "quantum" events, first pointed out a century ago, "A new scientific truth does not triumph by convincing its opponents and making them see the light, but rather because its opponents eventually die, and a new generation grows up that is familiar with it"[6]—in other words, "Old paradigms die when the believers in old paradigms die," which I have summarized as "The knowledge quest proceeds funeral by funeral." And so it is indeed likely that we will have to wait for this generation of Boomers to die in order for postmodernism to finally lose its "mean" grip. In the meantime, metaparadigms like Integral continue to grow (as does the percentage of people taking "that monumental leap of meaning" into 2nd tier).

It is possible to introduce simplified Integral models and maps as early as high school (and there is much to recommend doing so, and several places are actually doing this), but when development is left to its own devices, Integral stages tend to emerge in early midlife. The major reason is simply time. Robert Kegan, noted Harvard developmentalist, estimates that, on average, it takes about five years to move through any major level of development. Integral stages, which emerge roughly at the seventh major developmental level, would thus come in at thirty-five years old, generally. As more and more individuals move into Integral, we find more and more developing early or proto-Integral Views in late high school and early college. Be that as it may, the Integral View spiritual stance has the major characteristics I've briefly outlined in discussing the Integral stages in general. It might not want to literally include all other religions, but it wants its own religion to be all-inclusive, including the things I'm discussing now, starting with rungs and Views. Integral spirituality understands that individuals grow and develop through various stages, and this includes their View and understanding of spirituality. Spiritual teachings themselves should therefore be adapted and presented in the appropriate language and the appropriate level of difficulty for each individual stage—Magic to Mythic to Rational to Pluralistic to Integral to Super-Integral. Likewise, quadrants, lines (multiple intelligences), states and their Vantage Points, and various typologies all need to be included in a religion of tomorrow if it is to be inclusive and comprehensive enough to withstand the intense vibratory pressure of being catapulted into a future that is moving from conscious to superconscious, from Integral to Super-Integral, and from human to superhuman, and at an astonishing rate.

Stages in Buddhism Itself

We will return to the development of spiritual intelligence into the Super-Integral stages in a moment. But now, let's pause briefly and notice something that supplies profound supporting evidence for my basic thesis that structure-stages of spiritual intelligence (and thus of religions in general) exist, that stages of spirituality exist, and that, in today's world, every major religion *already exists* at every one of the basic structure-stages that we have discussed. (This is in addition to claiming that their contemplative branches all go through essentially the same major *state*-stages of development, a related thesis that I have already addressed and will also return to.) In other words, we don't have to work with the proposition "The human mind grows and develops through stages, including stages of spiritual intelligence, and thus the world's great religions ought to develop teachings that address each of these levels, thus forming a conveyor belt of spiritual transformation." Our proposition now is much simpler: "Every great world religion today *already* exists at each of the major stages of development (and spiritual intelligence), and thus all we need to do is recognize this fact. It's *already* happening."

And then, as an added bonus, we need to try and put the teachings of each religion at each structure-stage in some sort of developmental order, thus forming a conveyor belt.

Finally, there is the slightly tricky part: getting the religion's official authorities to acknowledge this fact and make it an intrinsic part of their overall gospel, dogma, doctrine, or dharma, and put all of the various level-stages and their interpretive Views under one roof, instead of having them, as they are now, falling all over the place with no central coordinating agency to arrange them in some sort of coherent order. (These Views already exist, so the choice isn't whether to provide these interpretations or not—it's done—but whether to consciously and explicitly recognize them and organize them, or let them remain chaotic, conflicting, random, and haphazard.)

In short, there are today examples of all of the world's great religious traditions functioning on virtually all of the levels and their Views that we have discussed, 1st to 2nd tier. But the fact that there are different-level Views is not itself understood (because structures and their Views, I have often pointed out, are not known or recognized by any tradition). In this regard I would like to mention the works of one of my very brightest students, Dustin DiPerna, who is also an original and creative theorist in his own right. In two volumes, *Streams of Wisdom: An Advanced Guide to Integral Spiritual Development* and *Evolution's Ally: Our World's Religious Traditions as Conveyor Belts of Transformation*, he sets out to supply more evidence to support some of the key tenets of Integral Spirituality, including that there are four major vectors of development (structures and structure-stages, or Views; states and state-stages, or Vantage Points).[7] He discusses stage/levels of Magic, Mythic, Rational, Pluralistic, and Integral Views; gross, subtle, causal, witnessing, and nondual state/realms (and their Vantage Points); and examples of all five stage/level Views in Christianity, Islam, Hinduism, and Buddhism.

Since we're looking at a possible Fourth Turning in Buddhism, I'll focus on his examples there, and add several of my own. In other words, we don't have to prove that there should be these level/stages in Buddhism—they *already* exist!

Buddhism began as a Rational system, one of the few of the world's Great Religions to do so. And remember how we are using "rational"—it doesn't mean dry, abstract, analytic, and alienated. It means capable of at least a 3rd-person worldcentric perspective; it can therefore introspect and reflect on its own awareness and experience, adopt a critical and self-critical stance, understand "what if" and "as if" worlds, and step back from the self and take a detached, nonattached view. The book title—*Buddhism: The Rational Religion*—says it all. There were few if any gods, goddesses, spirits, or mythological elements in original Buddhism—it was quite reasonable. And I think it is this rational nature (along with its core, of course, of Waking Up via state-stage development) that continues to make Buddhism so appealing to the modern West. As many have pointed out, Buddhism is closer to a psychology than a typical religion. Of course, most schools of Buddhism put a central emphasis on states, but when it comes to their interpretation, it is typically rational, objective, and evidence based.

Of course, not everybody is born at Rational. Actually, nobody is. All individuals start their development of basic rungs and Views at sensorimotor and Archaic, and move from there to Magic, then Magic-Mythic, then Mythic, then Rational, Pluralistic, and Integral (if they continue growing). And this means that individuals at all of those stages can be attracted to Buddhism, and over the centuries, actual schools of Buddhism have arisen that are based primarily at each of those Views, including Views lower than the original Buddhism.

Melford Spiro in his work *Buddhism and Society* divides Burmese Theravada Buddhism into three groups, and they are almost exactly Magic, Mythic, and Rational.[8] The first, which he calls "Apotropaic Buddhism," is primarily concerned with protection from evil spirits, using items such as magical charms and superstitious incantations. This is pure Magic. DiPerna adds the literal versions of some Pure Land schools, where it is believed that the single repetition of Buddha's name magically ensures rebirth in a Pure Land heaven. This is the equivalent of Christ's walking on water, or raising the dead, or turning water to wine, and so on; it is the earliest and "lowest" impulse of an interest in religion—namely, Magic, or the notion that some higher Power can interfere with history itself on my behalf, curing my ills, giving me boons, or otherwise miraculously altering my destiny (or, with core Magic, I myself can perform these feats!). Every child—early on, in its Magic-stage View—believes that this is possible (as I said, mummy could turn the yucky spinach into candy if she wanted), and humanity's earliest attitude to the Divine was the same.

Spiro's second group, "Kammatic Buddhism," is focused on generating merit for a future rebirth. This is a typically Mythic View with some magic elements. DiPerna points to the ethnocentric warfare of the Sinhalese Buddhists fighting in Sri Lanka as being primary examples. They possess all of Martin Marty and R. Scott Appleby's "family resemblances" of mythic-literal fundamentalists—a strong sense of religious identity (a "true believer"), strict social boundaries (us versus them), reliance on myth (absolutistic mythic-literal), and so on. (Marty and Appleby's influential work on the "family resemblances" between fundamentalisms wherever they appear around the world is yet further evidence of the ethnocentric Mythic-literal stage of development and its essentially similar deep structures across the globe. Virtually all of the fundamentalist approaches share these "family resemblances"; and using the notion of "family resemblances" is a fairly good way to characterize the deep structures of these universal or cross-cultural structure-stages, in this case, the Mythic-literal.) As for Sinhalese Buddhists in particular, they believe that they are the "owners and protectors of the Buddhist teachings"; Sri Lanka is the home of the true Dharma; they have control over the purity and right version of the Dharma; and they are "ethnic chauvinists" in constant warfare (holy war) with Tamil Hindus, the enemy of truth. Again, these are all typical characteristics of the deep features of the ethnocentric Mythic View.

Spiro's third group, "Nibbanic Buddhism," is interested in attaining Nirvana (Pali, *Nibbana*) through state realization as described by Theravada. This Rational Buddhism (also grounded in serious concern with state-stage development), as I noted, was probably the closest thing we have to Gautama Buddha's original teaching. The Rational nature of Early Buddhism also meant that it was not ethnocentric, as Mythic is, but worldcentric. Hence, Early Buddhism opened itself worldcentrically to the untouchables, usually excluded from the other religions of the time. This was a major factor in Buddhism's rapid spread throughout India. DiPerna adds D. T. Suzuki, the famous Japanese Zen author who probably did the most to introduce the West to Zen Buddhism, to those who expound Rational Buddhism. The historian Lynn Whyte said something to the effect that "the translation of

D. T. Suzuki's *Essays in Zen Buddhism* into English will rank with the translation of the Latin Bible into English." In over a dozen books, Suzuki patiently and rationally explained the nonrational core of Zen, and did so brilliantly. He fully acknowledged states, but did so from within a Rational interpretation.

The Pluralistic View is marked by deep social concern and powerful drives of social justice, is egalitarian and antihierarchical, is seriously concerned with environmental and ecological issues, argues for sustainability and renewable energy, downplays any sort of ranking, is antipatriarchal and antiwar, is profeminist, and is profoundly socially engaged. It is, in other words, the standard form of Buddhism in the Western world. DiPerna gives socially engaged Buddhism as a prime example of Buddhism at this green Pluralistic stage.

These Pluralistic values held by Western students, by the way, led to all manner of difficulties with the first wave of Eastern teachers in the 1960s and 1970s. Most Eastern teachers had come from Mythic cultures and ethnocentric backgrounds and were often very authoritarian, patriarchal, sexist, homophobic, and quite rigidly hierarchical. They were used to teachers being in positions of unquestioned authority, and they often acted that way. They were also unaccustomed to operating in the atmosphere of radical sexual openness, freedom, and ethical looseness of their students, who nonetheless expected a strict purity in the teacher (who often failed glaringly to meet those expectations—"when in Rome . . . well, have sex with a Roman," I suppose). These Mythic or occasionally Rational teachers met students who were largely Pluralistic, and a profound clash of Views resulted. This was extremely complicated by the fact that the teachers, although often lagging behind their students in structure development and View, were massively more developed than their students when it came to states and state-stages, many being at causal or nondual stages (with their students at gross or at most subtle). This caused profound confusion in the students, who couldn't tell if the advice from a teacher was coming from an outmoded and embarrassing Mythic View (patriarchal, sexist, homophobic, hierarchical, authoritarian) or a truly advanced state Vantage Point (on the ever-present nature of Spiritual Awareness, the timeless Now, the nature of pure Enlightenment, effective means for separate-self transcendence, the importance of Spirit in all areas of life). "How can he know so much about higher states yet be so homophobic? How can he be so awakened to equalizing Nonduality yet be so authoritarian and hierarchical? How can he be so liberated and yet take such advantage of his female students?"

And so the structure/state discrepancies went, causing enormous problems and heartaches on both sides. I know two fully transmitted American Zen masters (both, at one time, head of the largest Zen lineage outside of Japan itself) who faced a particularly difficult version of this, and who finally decided that the only way to get through their training was to "swallow the whole fish"—that is, to fully accept the outrageously coarse structural advice along with the truly advanced state advice (since they couldn't really tell which was which, and the spiritual tradition was certainly no help in this regard—and still isn't). All of that swallowing of the retarded structural advice left a very bad taste in their mouths, and they have both subsequently surrendered their mantles of orthodox authority, and barely even identify with their lineage. This is just sad.

And that points to exactly why an Integral Buddhism—a Fourth Turning of the Wheel—is so important for today's Buddhism. Understanding both the basic structure-rungs and their Views and the major state-realms and their Vantage Points would be an extraordinary revolution in our understanding of spirituality and its growth. States are interpreted by structures—and right there is a formula that unlocks a thousand mysteries. Incorporating that into Buddhism—or into any form of spirituality, for that matter—would be a monumental leap forward.

For now, the point is simply that there already exist entire schools of Buddhism at Magic, Mythic, Rational, and Pluralistic stages (and slowly, increasingly, at Integral stages, as I am attempting to demonstrate). So we don't need to prove that Buddhism can exist at these various stages—it already does, and has for centuries, in many cases. All that is required is to arrange them in their appropriate developmental sequence—the sequence of stages of spiritual intelligence that they display—and there are already some extremely helpful guidelines for how to do so, from James Fowler's absolutely pioneering work to my own Integral approach to Dustin DiPerna's creative application of both—to name just a prominent few. Plus other religious traditions are already applying an Integral Framework to convert their perspectives into Integral spiritual systems. (To mention just a few, I'd point to the superb work of, for example, Paul Smith, *Integral Christianity*[9] (there has been a recent explosion of books—a few dozen of them—by practicing ministers on a specifically Integral Christianity, all using the AQAL Framework in incredibly inspiring ways); or Marc Gafni on a "World Spirituality Based on Integral Principles," such as his *Radical Kabbalah*; or Amir Ahmad Nasr, *My Isl@m*.[10] All of the works in this area—there are many—have at their core the understanding of structures and structure-stages or Views (along with states and state-stages or Vantage Points), as well as lines and quadrants. (Jesus spoke in reference to ultimate Reality, which he called "Abba," which literally means "Daddy"—in 1st-, 2nd-, and 3rd-person terms: he spoke as God [1st person], he spoke *to* God [2nd person], and he spoke *about* God [3rd person]. All Christians are called to do exactly the same thing. Unity Church, something like the third or fourth largest "Protestant" congregation in the United States, has formally adopted the AQAL Integral Framework into its official teachings, and they are overseeing pragmatic explorations into how best to interweave an Integral Christianity into their congregations.)

Other things, in addition to the specific structures and Views that we have been focusing on, that Integral Spirituality should consider including are, of course, states of consciousness (and state-stages, or Vantage Points); the dual center of gravity of overall development (View and Vantage Point); quadrants (or the 1-2-3 of Spirit, discussed below); major typologies (such as Myers-Briggs or the Enneagram); shadow and shadow work; multiple intelligences (or developmental lines); technological breakthroughs in brain/mind connections and AI engaged in spirituality; polarity therapy; and a handful of other miscellaneous items. There are extensive arguments for each of these being an intrinsic aspect of any truly comprehensive or inclusive spirituality of tomorrow. An Integral Spirituality recognizes that human beings have several different but equally important dimensions to their makeup, such as their major perspective orientation (or quadrant, in Showing Up); their major level of development in general (or structure center of gravity, in Growing Up); their major state center of gravity (in Waking Up); various unconscious, or shadow, elements (in Cleaning Up); their predominant type of intelligence or line; their major personality type—and it also recognizes that *Spirit operates in and through all of these*. Failing to take any of those dimensions into ac-

count—at least in a simplified or introductory fashion—is to catastrophically ignore and deny that dimension of Spirit. It is to approach
the world spiritually blind in many of our eyes. It is to stumble numbed
and nearsighted into the universe, hobbled in some of the most important ways through which Spirit tries to reach us, touch us, speak to us,
speak through us, Awaken us, Awaken *as* us. An Integral Spirituality
demands that we fully approach matter, body, mind, soul, and Spirit in
self, culture, and nature—nothing less.

3rd-Tier Spiritual Intelligence

In these last sections, I want to occasionally give overview summaries
of topics that I have previously covered in some detail. I'm doing this
for several reasons, the simplest being that many people appreciate a
summary of material that might be new to them. But as you'll see as
we proceed, many of these summaries are of material that turns out to
be particularly important for any religion of tomorrow (or of today,
for that matter). These are areas and ideas that are almost entirely
neglected (or actively denied) by virtually all of today's spiritual systems (and by virtually all human disciplines as well). They deserve a
summary review.

I want to especially emphasize again that most of these ideas are the
result, not of a model of development, but of a metamodel of development. As I noted earlier, virtually every developmental model in existence starts with some general assumptions about development, and then
creates a basic metric, or test, and gives this test to hundreds, even thousands, of people. It then analyzes the test results and uses them to create a specific model of development in the line that is being investigated
(moral line, cognitive line, action-logics, self-concept, skill-functions,
and so forth). I take virtually every one of those models that have been
created and pull them all together into a meta-analysis that looks for
the basic patterns that they tend to display; I then put those patterns
together to arrive at a metamodel (using all the models to fill in the
gaps in any of them). So where the typical developmental model is a
model of people's awareness and actions, AQAL is a model of those
models (or a theory of theories—a metatheory; or a map of maps—a
metamap, and so on).

And the AQAL Integral Framework explicitly makes room for virtually each and every one of those models used individually as well.

Thus, an Integral Psychograph, besides presenting some of the common basic parameters found in most models (such as altitude, levels, lines, states, types, and so forth), will on different occasions include Piaget's stages, or Kurt Fischer's stages, or Jane Loevinger's stages, or Lawrence Kohlberg's stages, or Clare Graves's stages, or Terri O'Fallon's stages, since something specifically unique and useful can be found in every one of those models—each of them is presenting a unique perspective on the altitude and specifics of development in a particular line or group of lines—and this openness and inclusion is clearly something that none of those models, on their own, will do (Graves's model doesn't include Maslow's model; AQAL includes them both).

What we find in any model are several elements: there is, first and foremost, altitude itself, or the general tilt (or overall morphogenetic field) toward higher development (of greater complexity and more consciousness)—this is an overall directionality that cannot be reduced to any one line but is the common "driver" for all lines. There is then the line or lines that the model itself is covering (explicitly or implicitly); given the large number of lines, their permutations and combinations are near infinite. The researcher selects one or more of these lines, and then, watching as these lines move through the general field of increasing altitude, comes up with a model (a hypothesis) on what the specifics of these developmental shifts, or stages, are like. The intuition of altitude is given substance with the form of the proposed model. The researcher then devises various metrics or tests, and begins collecting data, which is then used to correct and tweak the proposed model. Given the number of variations and combinations among lines, and the number of metrics and models that can be created, no single model can hope to cover all the different lines, or all the ways that lines can be developmentally modeled.

This is why a metamodel is useful. By being a model of models, it looks at all of the different models and finds a framework that can accommodate most of the major elements of all of the various models (or the greatest number possible). As a model of these models, it thus captures what these models have in common, similar to the way that the models cover what a line or group of lines have in common. This is one of the things that makes the AQAL Metamodel so unique.

You will never, for example, find an explanation of Maslow's needs hierarchy that intrinsically includes the stages of Piaget, Kohlberg,

Loevinger, Kegan, S. Arieti, Commons, and so on—but that is exactly what you will find in the Integral Metamodel, with each of those models representing a different way to unpack the intuition of altitude in a different set of lines. So Integral Psychographs such as those given in figures 6.1 and 6.2 are common in Integral Metatheory, though you will see such psychographs nowhere else as a matter of course. This, again, is part of what makes the Integral Metamodel so unique.

Of course, this overall metamodel can then be used to apply to a specific line or group of lines. But notice, the metamodel then has to take on some of the specifics of the given line. So the orange altitude taken from the metamodel and applied to, say, the cognitive line, will use a different set of terms and structures than if it is applied to the aesthetic line. At this point, the metamodel is now acting like a model, and so it needs to apply directly to what the model covers (that is, the structure and function of a given line); it is not being applied primarily to other models in general. It is at this point that Integral Metatheory, if it is being applied to cognition (and related lines), might simply use the model of Kurt Fischer, or that of Piaget, or even Kegan. But this is the openness and comprehensiveness that a metamodel brings (it includes, but does not replace, other legitimate models).

Thus, the stages as presented by AQAL are not specifically found in any single model anywhere; rather they represent broad similarities that a majority of models generally have in common at given altitudes (using all the models to fill in the gaps in any). This gives the AQAL Metamodel, or Metatheory, a sturdiness not found in any single model. (And for detailed specifics, it will often refer to a specific model for those lines, always remembering that any single model is giving just one particular perspective out of dozens of different possible views.) Remember, at the very least, there are dozens of combinations of individual developmental lines—so there are not just different versions of the intuition of overall altitude itself, but different lines themselves moving through that altitude, and different models of development (knowingly or unknowingly) focus on one or a few of the overall lines and present increases in altitude as they appear in those lines. Other models will focus on other lines (using other intuitions of altitude)—this doesn't make one of them right and the other one wrong, it makes both of them right (if they are researched legitimately).

In the meta-analysis of the different structure-levels, I use aspects of virtually all the different lines—again, I am giving an overall orienting generalization and metamap of these altitude levels (levels that all of the lines share). So when I define "orange," for example, it will include aspects of such lines as cognitive, emotional, moral, aesthetic, interpersonal, and so forth, even though any actual specific model, not a metamodel, but a specific individual model, will NEVER include the elements from *all* of the lines, because each line has its own specific dynamics and specific structures—cognitive is different from emotional, and so on. Most of the lines have their own specific models, and thus no single developmental model does, or can, cover all lines directly, which is another reason to make room for all of them in a truly comprehensive Integral Metaframework and psychograph. The AQAL Metamodel includes generalizations across all of those lines, and thus one can speak of, for example, "orange cognition," "orange emotional intelligence," "orange morals," "orange aesthetics," and so forth, even though each of these has its own specific individual developmental pathways through those metalevels. But it's the metalevels we're interested in, because they are what all of the lines will have in common to some degree.

So as we go through each of the various elements in the AQAL Integral Framework—such as structures, states, lines, shadow material, and so on—remember that each of them is the result of a sophisticated metamodel and metatheory that has analyzed literally hundreds of different models and theories and then woven them into a coherent framework of orienting generalizations. No other model per se does this to this degree (with the explicit aim of *including* as many of them as possible; the aim of most theories is to exclude other theories; the aim of a good metatheory is to include all other legitimate theories). Each model is important, since it focuses on particular quadrants or levels or lines or states from a different perspective; but the AQAL Integral Metamodel takes all of them into account in a meta-analysis, which, again, is what makes AQAL Metatheory unique.

Finally, at the leading edge of evolution, we have three or four higher, at this point mostly potential, levels of development, including spiritual intelligence. Individually, I refer to their basic structure-rungs as para-mind (indigo altitude), meta-mind (violet), overmind (ultraviolet), and supermind (white or clear light); collectively, I refer to them as "3rd tier" or "Super-Integral." What all 3rd-tier structures have in common is some degree of direct transpersonal identity and experience, an emphasis on direct experience of some degree of Wholeness (becoming greater and greater at each higher level), and an "awareness of awareness." Further, each 3rd-tier structure of consciousness is integrated, in some fashion, with a particular state of consciousness (most often, but not necessarily, para-mind is integrated with the gross, meta-mind with the subtle, overmind with causal/Witnessing, and supermind with nondual). Previously, in 1st and 2nd tier, structures and states—although one *always* occurred with some version of the other—were relatively independent, although they could conjoin if state development were seriously undertaken (and then the state conjoined with whatever structure represented the individual's structure center of gravity at that time, which could itself grow and develop as state development increased). But one could have a state center of gravity at gross reflecting and yet evolve structurally all the way to turquoise Integral without fully objectifying the gross state (that is, without fully making it an object, without fully transcending it). But beginning with the 3rd-tier indigo para-mind, whenever you experience that structure itself, you also implicitly, or intuitively, understand or experience, at the minimum, the gross realm as objectified, which means that the objectified gross realm is intimately connected to the structure at this level. Objectifying the gross realm gives rise, or can give rise, to expanded states such as Nature mysticism (which can be experienced at earlier levels but not necessarily, and if it is, it will be interpreted according to the Views of those lower levels; but if it was not experienced before, then at this level it becomes an inherent reality and necessity).[11] Likewise, because of the conjunction with the objectified gross state, this level often carries variations of the realization that the physical world is not merely *physical* but is rather *psychophysical* in its true nature (more on that in a moment, along with the levels in 3rd tier). This can also evoke temporary higher-state presences, such as Witnessing states or even Nondual. And so on with the subtle state and meta-mind; causal/Witnessing and overmind; and nondual suchness and supermind.

The difference between Supermind and Big Mind (if we take Big Mind to mean nondual Suchness or turiyatita) is that Supermind is a structure but Big Mind is a state. Big Mind can thus be experienced or recognized at virtually any lower structure or level-rung, from Magic to Integral (as a peak-to-plateau experience). In fact, one can be at, say, the Pluralistic stage, and experience the entire sequence of state-stages (gross to subtle to causal to Witnessing to Nondual, resulting in a "*traditional* Enlightenment"), although, of course, the entire sequence, including nondual Suchness, will be interpreted in green Pluralistic terms (and thus is *not* an "*Integral* Enlightenment," which demands a structure at 2nd tier or higher; we'll explore this notion shortly). This lower-level interpretation is unfortunate in some ways—interpreting Dharma in less than 2nd-tier terms—and in this case, in merely Pluralistic terms (or it could be merely Mythic terms, or merely Rational terms, and so on). It is "unfortunate" since so much more is possible (I already established that the teal Holistic/Integral stage was the lowest fairly adequate level-rung for interpreting 3rd-tier structures and transpersonal states), but it happens all the time, given the relative independence of states and structures at 1st and 2nd tier, and the relatively few number of people who have actually moved into 2nd tier (around only 5 percent of today's population, although that percentage is fairly rapidly increasing daily).

Supermind, on the other hand, as a basic structure-rung (conjoined with nondual Suchness) can only be experienced once all the previous junior levels or structure-rungs have emerged and developed, and as in all development, stages cannot be skipped or bypassed. (Nor can they be peak experienced more than a stage or so higher than their present stage. If one is at moral-stage 2, for example, one cannot peak experience moral-stage 5; at most, one might peak experience moral-stage 3, if its construction has been completed and it is near ready for emergence.) Therefore, unlike Big Mind, Supermind can be experienced only after all 1st-, 2nd-, and 3rd-tier junior stages (all stages up to and including ultraviolet Overmind) have been passed through (all of which Supermind's own structure will transcend and include). While a Big Mind experience is available to virtually anybody (and will be interpreted according to the View of the person's current stage), Supermind is an extremely rare recognition (and is available only at white or clear light altitude, although it can begin to be peak experienced at the previous ultraviolet or Overmind stage). Supermind, as the highest structure-rung produced by evolution to date, has access (via "transcend and include") to all previous structures, all the way back to Archaic. (And the infrared Archaic itself, of course, has transcended and included, and now embraces, every major structure of evolution going all the way back to the Big Bang. As I have often noted, a human being literally enfolds and embraces all the major evolutionary unfoldings of the entire Kosmic history: a human being literally contains in its own makeup strings to quarks to subatomic particles to atoms to molecules to cells, and then all the way through the Tree of Life—from plant biochemistry to fish neural networks up to its latest evolutionary emergent, the triune brain, the most complex structure in the known natural world, which itself transcends and includes an amphibian/reptilian brain stem, a paleomammalian limbic system, and a primarily mammalian neocortex, as Paul Maclean has pointed out.) But all in all, this makes Supermind the single most "holistic" or "integral" structure in the known universe, transcending and including every major structure transformation since the Big Bang.

A Super-Integral Spirituality has many of the features of an Integral Spirituality, plus, among other things, an inherent conjunction of each higher stage with a given state; when the states themselves are higher, or transpersonal, this contributes to giving all 3rd-tier stages a transpersonal or spiritual flavor (in a continuum that runs from *communion* to *union* to *identity*). If one is at the identity end of the continuum, then the results are either gross nature mysticism, subtle deity mysticism, causal formless mysticism, or nondual Unity mysticism—any of which can be peak or plateau experienced at most earlier 1st- and 2nd-tier stages but can become structurally conjoined only at 3rd tier. These mystical states are, as just noted, available to virtually all the lower 1st- and 2nd-tier stages, although there are some significant differences in 3rd tier, given its inherent conjunction of structures and states. For example, one notable feature, verified by Terri O'Fallon's research, is that most 3rd-tier structures have a strong "awareness of awareness" component—consciousness is clearly becoming conscious of itself. The main reason for this, in my opinion, is that each 3rd-tier structure has "transcended and included" so many previous structures that the stacked "structure-upon-structure-upon-structure" nature sets up a major self-reflexive reverberating pattern by the time we reach 3rd tier, with the net result that an "awareness of awareness" becomes intrinsic in virtually all 3rd-tier levels.

The whole point of understanding the different forms that spirituality takes at each major View of development is that this enables us to create, in each tradition, a conveyor belt of spiritual teaching and practice—with different forms of teaching and practice at magic, magic-mythic, mythic, rational, pluralistic, holistic, and integral (and super-integral, which will become increasingly common in the future). This conveyor belt would pick up individuals in their early years, and transform with them—*and help them transform*—at each succeeding rung and View. As it is now, most major religions are stuck at some form of mythic View, while the other intelligences are free to move into rational, pluralistic, holistic, and even integral Views. This is a cultural catastrophe of the first magnitude. Spiritual intelligence is the only type of intelligence that evolved to interact with ultimate reality and ultimate truth and ultimate goodness itself—Spirit itself. All other intelligences interact only with relative truth; spiritual intelligence interacts with absolute truth. (As for those who make a big deal that there is no absolute truth, they generally believe *absolutely* that there is no absolute truth, thus showing us their version of absolute truth—absolute agnosticism. This is fine, as long as they acknowledge their own version of absoluteness).

But spiritual intelligence, because of its unique nature, ought to be leading the other intelligences by a stage or two, acting as a guiding beacon for all of them.[12] As it is, often stuck at Mythic, it usually lags a stage or two (or even more) behind most other intelligences, so that our growth and evolution is being hampered by our View of Spirit itself, an infinitely heavy lead albatross hanging around our developmental necks. Our View of God itself is slowing our evolution. Our View of the very source of evolution is hampering evolution! No wonder it's so easy for the "new atheists" to make so much fun of religion. In its typical Mythic-literal forms, for adults it's indeed laughable (although perfectly appropriate for a school-age child, as we have seen— but for a grown adult in today's world?).

It should be obvious by now that including vertical structures and Views is crucial, absolutely crucial, in any comprehensive spirituality. If states generally determine *what* it is that we can experience (gross objects, subtle objects, causal objects, and so forth), structures determine *how* we experience those objects—the very meaning, interpretation, experience, and value of those objects (at a magic level, a mythic level, a rational level, a pluralistic, an integral, a super-integral). Of the one hundred or so major developmental models and systems that I presented in *Integral Psychology*, about one-third of them dealt primarily with state-stages (with all of them showing a remarkable cross-cultural similarity, virtually all being variations on gross/waking, subtle/dreaming, causal/dreamless sleep, witnessing/mirror mind, and ultimate nondual/"unity") and about two-thirds of them dealt mostly with structure-stages, and, again, what is so remarkable is the essential similarity of almost all of these structure levels (with most being variations on the same basic 6-to-8 levels of development that I have been focusing on).

Again, let me briefly summarize these stages, because grasping their overall arc—in a single integrated sweep, as we will do now—really is crucial to understanding this whole topic of a spirituality that includes both structures and states in its inherent makeup. It's important to become at least generally familiar with the overall sweep of these major structure-stages—as a unified arc, from stage 1 to stage 8—so that they are easily recognized when any major points are made in reference to them.

And once more, let me just briefly note that these stages are the result, not of a model of development, but of a metamodel of development. This metamodel takes all of those hundred-plus models of developmental studies already mentioned in *Integral Psychology* and pulls them together into a meta-analysis that looks for the basic patterns that they tend to display; those patterns are then put together and integrated to arrive at a metamodel, using all the models to fill in the gaps in any of them. So where the typical developmental model is a model of people's awareness and actions, AQAL is a model of those models, a metamodel— or metatheory or metamap. These basic metalevels are what we are here summarizing, and the fact that they are the result of a meta-analysis of over one hundred different models gives them a great deal of credibility, and also gives them something that no single model possesses. Single models rely for their credibility on a specific type of metric, or test, that embodies a specific and given—and limited—perspective, and that model has legitimacy if the particular metric is correctly unfolded within that limited perspective. What gives a metamodel its credibility is the legitimacy it demonstrates in unfolding and pulling together all of these models based on all these different metrics.

So what we are largely (but not totally) focusing on in this section is a summary of the full spectrum of these metalevels (structures), particularly as they apply to spiritual intelligence (which is one line of a dozen or so multiple lines) and on their possible shadow elements as well (another dimension that is almost always neglected or denied in spirituality). Although I won't always explicitly address this issue, the implicit question as we run through these major levels of the line of spiritual intelligence is: what would spiritual intelligence look like from this particular altitude? We need to start to firmly realize that there is no single view of spirituality that is true for all people; at the very least, there are seven or eight quite different views! Which one is right?

Thus—and very briefly—all human beings start at a stage of fusion or symbiotic embeddedness, where the self is not yet differentiated from its surroundings (infrared, Archaic). This differentiation eventually occurs, and the self emerges as an egocentric, mostly impulsive, immediate gratification self-sense (at about eighteen months, often called "the psychological birth of the infant"; magenta, impulsive fantasy, Magic). This solidifies into an even more separate-self sense, with a keen desire for safety, self-protection, or power (red, Magic-Mythic, "PowerGods"). This egocentric series of selves eventually grows into an ethnocentric series of selves, as the self takes on the capacity of a 2nd-person perspective ("the *role* of other") and adopts conventional *rules*, producing a stage of sharp conformity (amber, the rule/role mind, Mythic-membership). Out of this conformist stage, with the arising of a 3rd-person universal perspective and, generally, the emergence of a rational capacity, the ethnocentric-identity-centered self gives way to a postconventional, postconformist, individuated, worldcentric self (autonomous, agentic, individualized, self-authoring, self-esteem desiring), capable of standing back both from itself and from its culture, to some degree, and reflecting on—and criticizing—both of them (orange, Rational, modern). This expands into a full-blown pluralistic, or even relativistic, self-sense (a 4th-person perspective, which reflects on 3rd-person worldcentric occasions), with multiple cultural sensitivities, a keen sense of marginalized, oppressed, and suppressed minorities, and a drive to correct those injustices (green, postmodern, Pluralistic). But lacking a truly global cognitive capacity, this pluralistic stage can at most criticize marginalizing but cannot conceive of integrative and unitive ways to overcome it (it deconstructs but cannot reconstruct). This occurs at the next major stage (usually noticed to be "a monumental leap of meaning"—because of its 5th-person perspective, which reflects on 4th-person fragmentations everywhere and hence introduces a unitive cognitive capacity, or vision-logic, that is capable of noticing universal common patterns and thus can provide unifying solutions to the marginalized fragments), a stage variously referred to as systemic, integrative, holistic, integral, autonomous, strategic, or similar such terms (teal, Holistic; and turquoise, Integral). It is this stage that the majority of structure-development models (in whatever multiple intelligence) list as the highest available level so far, although those models that continue further almost unanimously see any higher stages as being variations on "universal/mystical" or "self-transcending" or "transpersonal" stages (3rd-tier, super-integral).

I described each of the four postulated higher structure-stages in 3rd tier in chapter 7, and those interested can review those descriptions at this point if desired. Here is very brief summary of them in relation to spiritual intelligence:

The indigo para-mind (Fulcrum-9) is marked by a profound understanding that the world is not merely physical but *psychophysical* (which means, whether explicitly stated this way or not, that the individual understands that every occasion in existence, top to bottom, possesses 4 quadrants, or dimension-perspectives—that is, it possesses both objective or Right-hand exteriors, *and* subjective or Left-hand interiors, in a "body-mind" union, and these are co-creative or "tetra-enactive"). This level also includes a deep understanding of the *communion of all being*, the fundamental "we-ness" of every "I-ness" in existence, and the mutually interwoven nature of all sentient beings everywhere (in a holographic and holarchical fashion—"all in all, but some more 'all' than others" and not merely a holographic fashion—"all in all," which in itself doesn't include levels or waves and is deeply "flatland"). Identity itself includes a "gross body-mind dropped!" and a shift into at least a partially transpersonal sense of self (which marks all 3rd-tier levels), moving quite beyond the personal organism and into transcendental systems and mutual networks of being (a beginning Kosmocentric identity). Spirituality can, especially if conjoined with gross-realm reality, be open to forms of Nature mysticism or gross-unity mysticism. The individual feels directly one with—or at least deeply interwoven with—a gross-dimension, a Gaia-embedded multiplex, a sense of a flowing and fluid and interconnected self. Because it has objectified (transcended) most gross-oriented thinking, indigo has a clear understanding of the tenuous, hypothetical, even "arbitrary" nature of most of our theoretical models and pragmatic maps, and how what we "perceive" is deeply interwoven with what we "conceive"—so that all are to be held lightly. At the same time, a perceived or *seen Wholeness* dominates awareness, along with the beginning of an "awareness of awareness."

At violet meta-mind (Fulcrum-10), there is an increase in both "transcendence" and "inclusion," with "transcendence" particularly noticeable in the Visionary worldview available at this level, which involves a deep openness to realities beyond mere 1st or 2nd tier (the profound vastness and *extensiveness* of the "visionary" realm). And the increase in "inclusion" is seen in the emergence of a strong *feeling awareness*, tending to anchor consciousness in its embodied feeling modes (in addition to its "transbodily" Visionary modes). This feeling awareness discloses extensive tracks of *felt Wholeness*. This "transpersonal feeling" component is an important development given the increasing proportion of "heavenly" material compared to "earthly" material in 3rd tier—the "feeling" aspect anchors heavenly to earthly. Spirituality can tend toward something similar to forms of Deity mysticism (even if only a "union/identity with Light" or "Luminous Being"), more so if conjoined with the subtle state (home of Deity mysticism's deep features; also home of the state self-sense known as "soul," a subtle orientation that fits perfectly with the Visionary modes of this structure-stage and is easily incorporated/integrated with it).

With the ultraviolet Overmind (Fulcrum-11), a profound juncture point is reached, with Overmind lying, as it does, between the ultimate Supermind (and its conjoined Suchness), and all lower levels of earlier, junior-stage development—or simply put, it is a major juncture between heaven and earth altogether. As such, the spirituality of Overmind can wander in either of those directions, drifting toward an "other-worldly" heaven, in a decidedly transcendental direction—its strong inherent tendency—but it is never far from the sheer gravitas of all of the structure-stages that have previously emerged to date (a "this-worldly" earth). The Overmind is a crucial stage of involutionary/evolutionary interfacing and a key to balanced overall growth and development itself, learning, as it must, how to fully synchronize, in a state of coherence, all of heaven and all of earth, all of transcendence and all of inclusion, all of evolution and all of involution (a feeling that it is utterly beyond this world but also fully embraces it)—in order to stand ready for the shocking emergence of the radically superhuman Supermind. To reach Overmind is to stand at the crossroads of virtually every major possibility given to a collective humanity, possessing, as it does, the rung of every single, major, previous transformation involved in the evolution of humanity itself, and, indeed, the evolution of the universe itself, all the way back to the Big Bang, all laid out—figuratively or literally—to its inward eye, while also standing on its tiptoes and staring into tomorrow, into the world of a superhumanity that opens with the Supermind, lying before it as far as consciousness can see, a world of staggering possibilities and superhuman capacities and feats not seen by even the most gifted science-fiction visionaries. The Overmind, anchored in the all-temporal/timeless Now, faces these two worlds daily (the fullness of all of yesterday and the openness of all of tomorrow) and must seamlessly include both in the space of its "I-I" Heart.

Finally, at the white or clear light Supermind (Fulcrum-12), in conjunction with the nondual Suchness state, we have the highest structure of development yet produced by evolution, combined with the highest state produced as well. The Supermind is a fountain, flooding humanity with Divinity, leaning always to the unfolding of a genuine superhumanity in the making, the crossroads of a full Growing Up with a total Waking Up (to date), and the opening onto a future territory of unimaginable "Beyondness," a trans-transhumanism scarcely recognizable by any of today's standards or values. To feel the texture of Supermind—your own Source and Suchness—is to feel the interior of Godhead itself, is to see with Spirit's eyes, hear with Spirit's ears, touch with Spirit's skin. It is to breathe in the entire Kosmos and breathe it out as well, both bathed in the glorious grandeur of the ultimate All, a flight of the alone to the Alone—and in a mysterious ("unknowable"), spontaneous ("unplanned"), effervescent ("overflowing") fashion. To act as Supermind is to feel the Kosmos itself—all of it—acting through a vast clearing or opening that is your deepest Self and Suchness—all of the Kosmos stands up, all of the Kosmos walks across the room, all of the Kosmos sits at the table, all of the

Kosmos takes a bite of the sandwich. Looking at another person, all of the Kosmos is looking at itself; embracing another person, all of the Kosmos is holding itself; talking with another person, all of the Kosmos is talking with the Kosmos that is talking with itself. New forms are emerging in each moment, as the universe strains into the textures of tomorrow, and they are emerging through the very skin of your All-pervading, All-embracing, All-Kosmos Self and Suchness. You are not "looking at" anything; whenever something appears in Awareness, "you" are simply a "being Present with" that thing or event, and it is arising in that Total Painting Field that you are not observing but that is the texture of your very own Self and Suchness. It is arising *within You* (though "you" as a stand-apart Looker is not to be found anywhere; there is just "anywhere" arising moment to moment where "you" used to be, in the "headless" unity condition that is now your very Thusness). That Total Field Painting has long since turned into the big blue pancake and fallen on your head, and that big blue pancake contains every structure to have evolutionarily emerged since the origin of this universe, unfolding forms headed for exactly the Condition that you now are. As Supermind, when the Kosmos reaches out and touches the Kosmos, you feel a deep affinity, a solidarity, a union with all levels and dimensions of reality, top to bottom and everything in between. When you look at photos of deep space—some nebula or supernova or brilliant galaxy in full display—you are but feeling your own interiors; when you look down a microscope at the teeming thousands of cellular life forms, all wildly jerking in response to Life, you are but sensing your own cells, textures of your own Suchness; when a thunderstorm cracks on the horizon with lightning in the night, you are but seeing the insides of your brain, as neurons of your own Thusness light the way; when you see a map of Greenland, "take, eat, this is my body"; when you see the Pacific Ocean, "take, drink, this is my blood." Humanity is headed for a Superhumanity; this is the secret of Supermind.

And headed this way, Supermind is indeed.

On the Way to the Conveyor Belt

Returning now to the more typical stages of development in today's world, it is the overall similarity of virtually all the great developmental models (covering those first 6-to-8 major stages of evolutionary development) that makes such a striking impression and gives one near certainty that these developmental structures are real, important, and profound in their role in the human being and its experience of the world. The very Culture Wars themselves, as previously noted, are wars between three major structure-stages and their Views—the mythic traditional value structure, the modern rational value structure, and the postmodern pluralistic value structure. Another example of the role that structures play is that the stages of meditation are themselves interpreted in terms of the structures that are experiencing and moving through the meditative states (there is, for example, a magically interpreted subtle stage, a mythically interpreted subtle stage, a rationally interpreted subtle stage, a pluralistically interpreted subtle stage, an integrally interpreted subtle stage; and there is a magically interpreted causal stage, a mythically interpreted causal stage, a rationally interpreted causal stage, a pluralistically interpreted causal stage, an integrally interpreted causal stage; and so on, with each major state and its interpretation by a structure). This may sometimes sound a bit complex, but the point is that *this is already happening anyway!* We can be consciously aware of it, or we can keep our heads stuck in the sand—those really are our choices.

As we just saw, there are even entire schools of Buddhism (and every major religion) at each of the major structures of consciousness, each with their differing Views. To fail to realize this and take it into account is to fail miserably at inclusively grasping the dharma (or any other spiritual teaching—or any teaching at all) in its full range of possibilities, and this severely limits the appeal of that spirituality only to those who are *at the same stage-level as those who interpret it according to the orthodox View.*

We must pay keen attention to this inclusion of structures and their Views, especially given the generally conservative nature of most spiritual views. That is, most spiritual systems, realizing that they are dealing with some sort of ultimate truth, are understandably and correctly very slow to change their basic beliefs and practices, given the dire consequences of getting it wrong (whether they interpret it from a Mythic View, where "getting it wrong" means spending eternity in hell, or they interpret it from an Integral View, where "getting it wrong" means getting wrong the precise injunctions and interior practices most effective in producing nondual liberating states of Enlightenment and

Awakening). Spiritual systems are understandably slow to fiddle with the formula. And given that structures are not easily spotted, if at all, by introspection, meditation, or contemplation, then the only way they can be included is for spiritual teachers to study and understand the actual research being done by developmentalists on all the multiple intelligences and developmental lines, in all their developmental levels, that are already present in human beings, meditators being no exception. (Or spiritual teachers can simply begin with Integral Theory itself, which gives an adequate summary of all major levels and lines.)

An added benefit here is that research consistently shows that merely studying the stages of a developmental model increases the speed of development through those stages in the person doing the studying. Simply learning a developmental framework is "psychoactive" (as is, in fact, learning the AQAL Framework "psychoactive" across all of its major dimensions). But constant care and vigilance is mandatory to keep any spirituality authentically plugged into the levels, lines, and Views that all human beings are undergoing, so that all of those dimensions are open to Spiritual Awareness itself, with the overall human being—not to mention humanity itself, and, indeed, the Kosmos at large—enormously benefiting in the process.

Spirituality could then claim perhaps its most important and core function—not just to introduce the human being to Spirit itself, but to act as a conveyor belt for the developmental levels of increased Spiritual understanding and awareness—actually, the development of consciousness itself—all the way from the instinctual mind to the Supermind, and every level in between. This certainly includes spiritual intelligence itself, which, as the only multiple intelligence that deals with ultimate truth itself, could help humans plug into the process of GROWING UP spiritually, as their state practices can simultaneously help them WAKE UP to the increasing depths and heights of Spirit itself, with each of those state-stages being interpreted by the degree of structure-stage development and spiritual Growing Up that the person has accomplished to that point. The overall net effect is the highest, widest, deepest, most infinite state realization (Nondual) interpreted by the highest, widest, deepest, most inclusive structure realization (Supermind)—a dual center of gravity that is literally both fully in and fully out of this world.

States and State-Stages (or Vantage Points)

A Fourth Turning, or an Integral Spirituality, would also most definitely include states and state-stages (or Vantage Points). This is the very core of the process of Waking Up, which is the emancipatory core of the fundamental role of spirituality itself. Each stage of Waking Up involves, among other items, becoming more and more present to the Present, increasing one's Depth of Presence in any and all ways, until one attains a more or less permanent recognition of the Pure Presence of the Supreme Identity in a nondual "unity" consciousness—the Great Liberation, the Ground and Goal of all emancipatory spirituality.

Most schools of Buddhism already include state development (with some exceptions for Magic, Mythic, and Pluralistic Buddhism, as we saw earlier, with Magic focusing on superstitious rituals, Mythic focusing on ethnocentric mythic-literal narratives, and Pluralistic often denying all growth hierarchies, including those of state-stages). But, alas, most forms of Western religion today lack any recognition of direct peak experiences of transpersonal/spiritual states of consciousness, let alone include a full Waking Up via a contemplative system that spans the entire spectrum from gross to subtle to causal to emptiness to nondual states. This is odd, in many ways, because virtually all forms of Western (and Eastern) religions began as a series of mystical states and peak experiences had by the founder of the religion. The very first Christian gathering—the Pentecost—was marked by massive subtle-realm mysticism (flames encircling heads, later such things as doves descending, viewing Christ in a resurrected subtle light body), and for the first several hundred years, mystical experience defined Christian awareness ("Let this consciousness be in you that was in Christ Jesus, that we all may be one"). You sought out a Christian teacher if he or she were *sanctus*—sanctified, or awakened. But as the Church increased in power ("No one comes to salvation except by way of Mother Church"), Christianity increasingly switched from direct mystical experiences to mythic narratives, beliefs, and legalistic creeds (switched from spiritual Waking Up to early, lower levels of spiritual Growing Up). Mouthing the creeds replaced experiencing Spirit. By the time of the Counter-Reformation, virtually all of the contemplative branches of Christianity had been severely curtailed, and the Spanish Inquisition was fully in place to guard against any experiences of the Supreme Identity, or an identity of subtle soul and causal God in the nondual Godhead. Saints like Giordano Bruno were burned at the stake for stepping over the line, not to mention upward of perhaps three hundred thousand women burned at the stake for their experiential revels, charged with "witchcraft." Meister Eckhart, generally regarded as one of the greatest spiritual sages ever to live, East or West, was not himself excommunicated, but he did have his theses condemned (which means, as previously noted, that Eckhart is now in heaven, but his theses are burning in hell—which wouldn't give the poor man much to think about for all eternity, it seems).

The net result was that the Mythic structures of spiritual intelligence —which were perfectly adequate, as structures, for that prerational, pre–Western Enlightenment era, however pathologically they were occasionally expressed—were then permanently cemented into place as a dogma "for all time," and states of consciousness were in essence banned across the board, especially since states, unlike mythic creed-beliefs, could not be controlled by the Church. The double problem with this move was (a), Christianity lost all states (and thus, catastrophically, all access to Waking Up), and (b), the Mythic-literal View of spiritual intelligence was frozen into place and made everlasting dogma, never to be questioned henceforth, thus freezing spiritual intelligence in Growing Up at its childish Mythic stage. (In today's world, the previous pope, Pope Benedict XVI, announced, for example, that making a woman a minister would be equivalent to the sin of pederasty—which makes one wonder just which of those two things the Pope had experienced such that he could make that comparison. But this is typical of the ethnocentric mythic ethical codes that were in place two thousand years ago, and as the Mythic-literal was made dogma, became sealed into the Christian faith—entirely unnecessarily.)

During the Renaissance, as the other intelligences in the sciences, in medicine, in law, in art, in education and politics, began their moves into modern Rational, then postmodern Pluralistic, then unifying Integral, religion remained frozen at Mythic-literal—ethnocentric, racist, sexist, patriarchal, homophobic, authoritarian, absolutistic, dogmatic, unquestionable. The Western world, in effect, ceased its spiritual growth. Spiritual intelligence (that is, of *structures*), the way we spiritually GROW UP, was frozen at Mythic, or that of today's typical seven-year-old; and higher spiritual *states*, the way we WAKE UP, were banned in general. This is, in essence, the anemic state of Western spirituality today, a double catastrophe (low structures, no states). No wonder there has been such a rapidly declining Church membership in the postmodern world (on average, only 11 percent of northern Europeans are considered churched), as well as an avid interest in Integral Christianity and other forms of more comprehensive spirituality.

It should be emphasized that even in those spiritual schools that put states and Vantage Points front and center, historically none of them have included structure-rungs and Views, and thus they failed to see that each state and Vantage Point will be interpreted in important ways by the View of the structure-stage the person is at. Recall that a person can be at virtually any 1st- or 2nd-tier rung—Mythic or Rational or Pluralistic, for example—and, from that rung, meditatively develop through the entire sequence of state-stages; for example, from pluralistic gross to pluralistic subtle to pluralistic causal/witnessing to pluralistic nondual, or from rational gross to rational subtle to rational causal/witnessing to rational nondual. A person at, say, rational nondual, will indeed discover a pure union with their world, a union, or nonduality, of Emptiness and Form (in their nondual state), but that person's world of Form includes only all phenomena up to orange rational. The pluralistic world, the holistic world, the integral world, and the super-integral world are still "over their head" and not available in their awareness. The individual will NOT be one with those worlds because they are completely beyond the reach of their awareness. You can't be one with that which doesn't exist in any way for you. And so over the head of this individual—who is one with the entire physical world, one with the entire biological world, and one with the mental world from sensorimotor (infrared) to emotional-sexual (magenta) to conceptual (red) to concrete operational (amber) to formal operational (orange)—are the entire worlds of the pluralistic realm (green), the holistic realm (teal), the integral realm (turquoise), and the super-integral realm (indigo to white). If an object from any of those higher realms enters his or her awareness, they simply won't recognize it, or the object will appear puzzling and nonsensical, or in other ways it just won't register. So such a person, whether at mythic, rational, pluralistic, and so forth, is not one with the entire world, and their "unity consciousness," should they reach that state-stage, will not be a full "unity," either, because there are over their head entire structure-worlds of which they are completely unaware, even though otherwise they are in a genuine nondual state of the unity of Emptiness and Form—with the caveat, "one with all of the Form *that is actually in their world.*" For orange, that means *all* of the pre-orange Forms but *none* of the post-orange Forms (a fractured world indeed, and a similarly fractured Enlightenment).

Recall when we were experimenting with a "headless" state of unity consciousness. You might have noticed that being in that state did not carry any information about what structure-stage you were at. You could have been at amber Mythic, or orange Rational, or green Pluralistic, or turquoise Integral, and you still would have had that nondual, "headless," "unity" state experience. But if you were at, say, an amber Mythic stage, and you started talking with somebody at orange Rational, he or she might be saying things that made no sense to you, things that didn't enter your "oneness" state but just sort of passed through it, or over it, or outside it—but they certainly were not "in" it. It would be like talking to someone who is speaking a completely different foreign language—you might be "headlessly" one with the sounds, but you still have no idea what the sounds mean; you are definitely not one with the meaning, and so everything that person is saying to you is "over your head," is definitely *not* something that you are consciously one with. And that's the problem with states; they can't see structures, even though the states themselves are being interpreted by structures, by "hidden maps," by various types of grammar rules that simply cannot be seen by looking within and ordinarily never announce themselves to Awareness at all. This is why not one of the meditation systems worldwide has anything like the basic structure-rungs of Growing Up.

This is why it's so important for a truly comprehensive spirituality to include both structures and states. As one begins a state-development practice, such as meditation, one can also begin to learn about structure development, such as by reading Kegan and Lahey's work on languages and resistance to growth (see their *Immunity to Change*), or by engaging in the Integral Institute's metapractice, or some form of Zachary Stein's "operationalizing altitude," or the Human Program's integral workshops, or Integral Life's transformation programs.[13] This is important, because someone at, say, the Mythic View, who takes up

Buddhist meditation and eventually moves his or her state center of gravity all the way to nondual Suchness, will still interpret this state using mental tools that are limited to ethnocentric modes, with a correlative belief in a "chosen people" or a "chosen path"—the belief that their path alone can deliver a true Liberation (as we saw with the Sinhalese Buddhists of Sri Lanka). Even though they have taken the bodhisattva vow to liberate all beings, they can't help but have a hard time fully accepting a Muslim, or a Christian, even those with mystically nondual beliefs. The book *Zen at War* is full of purely ethnocentric beliefs from highly regarded Zen masters, which shows that this is not an isolated, negligible, or even rare problem but, in fact, happens all the time—and all of this is due primarily to the fact that structure development is not included with state development.

Jeffrey Martin's graduate thesis uses Hood's Mysticism Scale (which judges consistency and type of state experiences) and Susanne Cook-Greuter's Ego Development Scale (of structure-stage growth) and clearly demonstrates that structure-stages do not predict any sort of correlation with state development—they are indeed, as I have often pointed out, relatively independent. This is why including both state development and structure development—Vantage Points and Views (Waking Up and Growing Up)—is so crucial to any effective spirituality and would certainly be a central part of any Fourth Turning (or growth practice in general).

Most (but not all) schools of Buddhism have included states and state-stages (or Vantage Points), and often in exquisite detail. In fact, the Tibetan Buddhist schools of Buddhism are very likely the most comprehensive, inclusive, full-spectrum view of meditation and meditative stages in any of the world's paths of the Great Liberation. It is mostly other schools of spirituality, particularly the Western theological ones (as well as several schools of Buddhism, which, originating at Magic, Mythic, and Pluralistic levels, put little attention or awareness on states, as we have seen), that need to pay attention to the importance of states.

The process of WAKING UP is arguably what is most crucial in any spirituality—indeed, in life itself. The ultimate purpose of spirituality and spiritual practice is to discover one's fundamental Supreme Identity with Spirit, with the Ground of all Being, with the ultimate Reality of the Kosmos itself. It is odd, just odd, that anything exists at all. One of the most fundamental questions humans can ask themselves is, as Schelling's famous version has it: "Why is there something rather than nothing?" Why is this manifest universe arising at all? And, if I may borrow a phrase from Wittgenstein, while the answer to that question cannot be *said*, it can be *shown*—that is, it may be directly and immediately realized in the deepest reaches of one's own present Awareness. That which is Aware of this moment—that spacious, open, empty, deep, clear, unborn, and undying Presence that is reading this page and feeling this body and looking at this world—is itself none other than the Author, Creator, Source, and Suchness of the entire manifest universe; and you can know this Presence, this I AMness, this pure Self, this Big Mind, right here and right now with a simple act of recognizing it, just as you are right now.

It takes no effort to do this. Without trying at all, you are already aware of the sounds arising around you, you are already feeling the sensations arising in your body, you are already noticing the sights that arise moment to moment. All of them are spontaneously and effortlessly arising in the Spaciousness, the Presence, the Clearing and Opening, the deep I AMness of your very own Awareness, and have done so for as long as you can remember (which is to say, for as long as you were Aware, which, looking at it closely, is actually the everlasting timelessness of the pure Now moment—or eternity itself). This I AMness, this Presence, is your true and real Condition, present from since the Big Bang and before. (Can you *ever* specifically remember being without I AMness? Can you actually remember any moment at all that didn't have I AMness?) Simply recognizing That—which is *This*—is to Awaken to this ultimate Condition and radical Reality, and this is possible because this Reality, this Suchness, is utterly ever present, always already fully existing in the timeless Now moment itself. This ultimate Presence is not hard to reach but rather is impossible to avoid—it's just *this*, this *Presence*, nothing more. Simply notice what's aware of this page, and just that is it.

But having that ever-present Presence remain in Awareness can take a fair amount of practice (even though it's never *actually* not present). Like a muscle, the more you use it, the bigger and stronger it becomes, until its ever-present Reality is literally ever present. In that process of Waking Up, you will retrace the steps that this Reality took—that You took—as you threw yourself outward and pretended to be Other than

Who and What You really are, from pure Spirit to separate soul to individual mind to limited body to insentient and separated matter. In one large sneeze, you blew out the entire manifest universe as a hidden texture of your own True Self in a stunning Big Bang, and from there began the slow and sometimes tortuous growth back to your own Self-Realization, which occurs each and every time you recognize *This*, your own ever-present Presence and I AMness, just as you are doing now. This Presence doesn't require thought; it is aware of thoughts coming and going now. It doesn't require effort; it is effortlessly aware of effort and everything else arising right now. It doesn't require any specific action; it is spontaneously aware of all actions occurring moment to moment. And it takes no path to reach where you already are; this, your very own Awareness, just as it is right now, is IT. Too simple to believe; too close to achieve; too obvious to notice; to easy to be grasped; too present to be reached.

That process of Waking Up and its pragmatically useful (though ultimately unnecessary) accompanying state-stages are the core of any genuine spirituality, leading from the mistaken identity with a small, finite, born and dying, skin-encapsulated ego to an infinite, timeless, spaceless, unborn and undying True Self, and from there to an ultimate nondual "unity" consciousness or Suchness, which is one with Spirit per se, the Ground and Goal of the entire process. This is your birthright. This is your destiny. This is your daemon (inner genie or genius). This is your ultimate Being and Becoming, in a journey without goal and a path without destination and a means without effort, to a Home you have never left and a Welcoming that is already at hand.

15

Shadow Work, Quadrants, and Developmental Lines

Shadow Work

In these remaining sections, I will include some summaries of points that we have already covered in detail, particularly with those topics that are truly crucial to a religion of tomorrow, and ones that are almost always completely neglected (or actively denied) in most forms of today's spirituality. The neglect of these topics can be, and often is, just catastrophic. One such topic is the dynamically repressed unconscious, which I generally refer to as the "shadow." And the process of addressing the shadow I call "Cleaning Up." Cleaning Up has a negative and a positive aspect. The negative aspect involves taking something that is psychologically broken and fixing it—a process often called "shadow work." The positive aspect is often called "positive psychology" and refers to taking something that is working and making it work even better—with the result called "flourishing" or "thriveability." Both are important, and the Integral Metamodel includes both. Even so, with regard to spirituality, it is most often the negative aspect—the shadow and its trials—that cause the most resistance in orthodox religions, because the idea is that if you were really doing your spirituality correctly, you wouldn't need shadow work. If you were just praying harder, or meditating more often, or surrendering to the Divine more sincerely, you just wouldn't have any emotional problems. (This is why many people feel uncomfortable if they hear that their spiritual teacher is in therapy.)

But the point is that no amount of Growing Up practices and no amount of Waking Up practices will handle issues of Cleaning Up. Shadow work is simply a dimension of a human being that is almost entirely separate from any Growing Up or Waking Up—it has its own dynamic, its own patterns, and its own unique paths of healing the broken material. And what's worse, shadow material is extremely common—it's safe to say nobody fully escapes it—and it can infect and badly derail the processes of both Growing Up and Waking Up. Somebody involved in virtually any spiritual path will sooner or later hit issues that are shadow oriented, and if his or her tradition does not recognize this and make ample room for addressing it, that person's spiritual life is in for some very rough patches.

Although many models of shadow material believe that most shadow issues are generated at particular stages of Growing Up (for traditional Freudians, for example, all repression occurs by the end of the red stage and the beginning of amber), a metamodel of shadow material shows that shadow issues can occur at virtually any stage of both structure development (Growing Up) and state development (Waking Up). You can develop shadow issues not only at magenta and red, but at orange and green, at teal and turquoise, at indigo and violet (not to mention at subtle, causal, and witnessing states). So what I'd like to do here is give a brief summary of shadow genesis and shadow work spanning the full spectrum, and use this as a way to remind ourselves that shadow material is almost always, to some degree, generated by any major growth process—and thus to be aware of this, to be on the lookout for it, and to include some basic shadow therapeutic practices in any spiritual endeavor we engage in. If we fail to do so, we can almost be guaranteed that our spiritual path will run into numerous often insurmountable difficulties. (And notice as we review the full spectrum of shadow material, just how different the creation of shadow issues is from the dynamics of both Growing Up and Waking Up. Shadow material isn't created by the dynamics of Growing Up or Waking Up; it is created by *something going wrong* with the dynamics of Growing Up and Waking Up, and that has to be handled on its own, as a separate and different issue.)

Every transformation in every stage of evolution (or growth and development, in both structures and in states) occurs via a series of operations that have several subphases (dis-identification with the lower; identification with the higher; integration of both). In human consciousness development, for example, whether looking at a fulcrum of structure development or a switch-point of state development, there is a fundamental three-step process: the self (or consciousness) starts out identified with a particular stage (structure or state), and step 1 is to differentiate from, or *dis-identify with*, that stage (thus also letting go of the View/Vantage Point from that stage). The self then moves up to the next higher stage and *identifies* with it (step 2), thus generating a new self-identity and a new View/Vantage Point of the world. It then *integrates* (step 3) the previous structure-rung (or state-realm, not the View or Vantage Point, which has been let go of) with overall consciousness at the new stage (which itself has the new View/Vantage Point). The previous structure-rung or state-realm is included; the previous View or Vantage Point is let go of.

Something can go wrong at any of those subphases, and when it does, a specific type of dysfunction or pathology results. The point is simple: any step can break down. In particular, if the self fails to differentiate from, or adequately dis-identity with, the previous stage, then it will remain identified (or fused) with aspects of that stage, thus developing a fixation to them—and hence, will develop an *addiction to*—a grasping of, seeking for, desiring of—those aspects. If, on the other hand, the differentiation goes too far into dissociation, and the dis-identification swings into active dis-owning, then the self will develop an avoidance of various aspects of the previous stage, thus developing an *allergy* to them. Thus burdened with either addictions or allergies to elements of the previous structure or state, the self at its present stage will have its Awareness distorted and malformed, unable to relate simply and directly to those fixated or dissociated elements. It will thus not only be plagued by the various painful symptoms caused by those fixations or dissociations, but will also be unable to take up a stance of bare attention, mindfulness, or pure Witnessing in the face of those elements, either grasping after them or avoiding them.

It is the simple multiple-step process of the transformation dynamic itself—in all growth, development, and evolution—that makes malformations, miscarriages, and dysfunctions possible, indeed, to some degree likely. Evolution is not a featureless process with no curves, valleys, peaks, or basins, but a dynamic self-organizing and self-transcending process that can suffer breakdowns at virtually every one of its many moves and phases. Wherever there is a step in evolution, there is a potential dysfunction, a possible pathology, just waiting to happen.

If we focus again on humans, each time there is a misstep in a fulcrum or a switch-point, and various elements are either fixated or repressed—in other words, defended against—the actual nature and type of defense mechanism is determined largely by the tools available to the structure at that particular stage. If we look at human structural development, for example, problems at Fulcrum-1 (infrared chakra-rung 1, oral/anal, physiological needs) occur at a level of fairly weak cognitive capacity—after all, the boundary between self and other has not yet even been clearly drawn here, and thus the type of defense mechanism is one where material is pushed across a yet very porous and flimsy self-boundary as the easiest way to get rid of it. Thus prototypical projection or introjection—regurgitating material so it passes outside of the tenuous boundary or swallowing material so it moves inside it—are common defense mechanisms here (these mechanisms are so fundamental that they can be repeated at literally every subsequent stage, even if they become more and more complexified).

As we reach Fulcrum-2 (magenta chakra-rung 2, emotional-sexual drives, prana, fantasy cognition), the cognitive mind, though still weak, is strong enough to displace as well as deny items. Images and symbols have already formed, and thus they are aspects of the structure of the major defenses here: *displacement*, where, for example, anger at my dad (for being dangerous) is displaced onto anger at a friend for any perceived pushiness; and *denial*, where an uncomfortable or forbidden impulse or psychic content is simply denied existence (the word/symbol "No!" is already in place, ready to deny virtually anything). And the still relatively weak cognitive function cannot yet easily unify or integrate elements, leading to the defense mechanism of *splitting* (which is not so much a splitting of a prior unity but a failure to be able to bring together parts into a real unity).

At Fulcrum-3 (red chakra-rung 3, power drives, conceptual/intentional mind), concepts have begun to emerge, and the "language barrier" is in place, and thus the mind is strong enough to engage in classic, actual repression: the mind, threatened by bodily drives, feelings, impulses, desires, and so forth, actively pushes these threatening materials out of consciousness and into the repressed submergent unconscious —a classic mind-repressing-body situation (which produces traditional psychoneuroses such as anxiety, depression, obsession, and so forth).[1]

By Fulcrum-4 (amber chakra-rung 4, the rule/role mind, conformist mythic-membership), the self is no longer primarily threatened by the body; the role-self (connected with the rule/role mind), which has just emerged, is what is now threatened, and its role is threatened, not by the body, but by other roles (and by fitting in with other roles—peer pressure, for example). Likewise the rule-mind is worried about violating the rules, and thus it typically assumes a strongly conformist stance and will often simply lie about its violation of a particular role or its breaking of a particular rule (and if it does not lie to others, then it lies to itself). All of this is due to the newly emerging capacities of the rule/role mind and its specific defense mechanisms.

With Fulcrum-5 (beginning of chakra-5 or "self-expressive," orange rational, formal operational, worldcentric, "self-esteem"), the emergence of the 3rd-person rational structure allows for the development of a genuine depth perspective—in ideas as well as in actual perception. You'll likely recall the stick figures on the side of great ancient Egyptian buildings—humans depicted in only two dimensions, and thus lacking any real depth at all. But with the arrival of the Renaissance and then the Enlightenment, a 3rd-person perspective is added, and all of a sudden paintings jump out at you with their depth and perspective; the human face becomes a real face, with hills and valleys and creases and squints, and portraiture becomes popular. In the mind, "as if" and "what if" conditional worlds become possible to conceive (for example, "What if we outlawed slavery?" "What if we overthrew the monarchy and started a representative democracy instead?" "What if women were given universal rights?"). At the same time, any of the new phenomena in these new spaces could be dissociated, fragmented, repressed, dis-owned (producing new, more complex neuroses). The type of self that emerged with this new structure went beyond the previous conforming and conventional-rules-following self, to an independent, autonomous, and achievement-oriented self, driven in part by its own self-esteem drives—and as with all drives, any number of things could go wrong with this self-esteem, from not enough to way too much. Orange subpersonalities—dissociated and dis-owned because their particular orange tendencies were at fundamental odds with the goals, drives, and desires of the rest of the ego-self at this stage—retain their own ideas about merit, achievement, and accomplishment and continue to pursue those drives unconsciously, leaving the ego-self aware of only an inner turmoil, a rioting inner anxiety, or a hollowed-out depression. Ego alienation (an alienation or separation from the accurate self-image or authentic self-concept—not just a distorted self due to shadow dissociation, which can and does occur at virtually every stage, but a powerful, overall conscious sense of being alienated from one's authentic being and accurate self) becomes possible for the first time (as it does in adolescence today). Another common dysfunction is the repressed emergence of green pluralism—that is, as the green level begins to emerge, and because it diametrically disagrees with virtually all of orange, green can itself be repressed (in what I call the "repressed *emergent* unconscious"—which is the repression of something that has not yet emerged but is struggling to, unlike the "repressed *submergent* unconscious," which is the repression of something that has already emerged in awareness but been dis-owned; the former is the higher trying to come down, the latter is the lower trying to come up). All of these possible orange dysfunctions become particularly prominent with this new structure.

By the time of Fulcrum-6 (still chakra 5, since still "self-expressive," but otherwise pluralistic, multicultural, sensitive, aperspectival, green), not only has the self been introduced to the vast possibilities opened by numerous, multiple, new perspectives, but it is, in a sense, drowning in them. The central pathology (among many possible) at this level is *aperspectival madness*—being so aware of the multiple perspectives available with any situation that you can't decide which, if any, to believe, follow, or act on, and you become frozen in your tracks, like a deer caught in the headlights of the oncoming car (multiple perspectives) and blankly freezing in its tracks, wide eyed and fixedly staring. Pluralism maintains, largely correctly, that every perspective makes sense only in terms of its context, so that contexts always need to be taken into account. *Inadequate* pluralism (the most common type, alas) simply forgets that some contexts themselves are universal, and thus some truths are universal, too, and instead only fixates on the local context-bound nature of meaning, and thus maintains that there are no universal truths, no big pictures, no metanarratives at all—thus effectively paralyzing any real action it can take. This is why meetings run on green principles take forever and still don't reach any real conclusion. The meeting is considered a success if everybody has a chance to share their feelings; but no conclusion is reached because that would imply one view—as opposed to others—is true and correct, and that's just not possible, so, um, how do we feel? Why don't we just go around the room and everybody share their feelings? The 1960s had a saying: "Freedom is an endless process"; the "endless" was certainly right.

With aperspectival madness, where no values are allowed to be seriously embraced (since that would be to judge or rank other values as "not good enough"), the entire value structure tends to reduce to some of the lowest and basest values there are—with today's generation, for example, this is often fame and money, as we earlier noted. A *Newsweek* poll taken fifty years ago, in 1966, asked teenagers whom they most admired, and the results were John F. Kennedy, Abraham Lincoln, George Washington, Lyndon B. Johnson, and Helen Keller (in that order). A similar poll, taken today (2016), gave the following: Barack Obama, Taylor Swift, Beyoncé, and Selena Gomez tied with Abraham Lincoln (*Newsweek*, May 5, 2016).

In addition to aperspectival madness—which nowadays has become almost the de facto setting of green in general—there are numerous other dysfunctions at this stage. As with virtually all other levels, dis-owning (and then likely projecting) is possible with any of the newly emergent phenomena that come into existence at this level. More specifically, any component or aspect of a pluralistic thought or idea, a pluralistic feeling or emotion, or a pluralistic drive or need, can be either dissociated and dis-owned (and hence, likely projected)—producing an avoidance and hence an allergy to that element, in oneself or others—or fixated on and fused with—producing an attachment and hence an addiction. Precisely because of the multiple perspectives flooding awareness on almost any issue at this stage, and then driven by a simple need for coherence, a typical (but inadequate) solution is to push out of awareness many of the wildly multiple options so that only a single major one remains, thus reducing the confusion—but that actually simply represses the confusion, which then shows up as symptoms, symbolic (hidden) meanings, and all sorts of allergies of one flavor or another.

This is particularly true with feelings toward loved ones, those about whom we think we should have nothing but positive feelings, and yet negative perspectives also continually arise. Instead of incorporating all of them into a unity-in-diversity, we often simply deny the negative ones, pushing them into the repressed submergent unconscious, from whence they generate allergic neuroses of one variety or another (and they are often projected onto the loved one, who now seems to have these negative feelings toward us).

The shadow itself is most basically composed simply of the opposite tendencies that are presently held in awareness. The easiest way to contact your shadow feelings toward any object, person, or event is simply to assume the exact opposite of what you consciously think about it. If your conscious attitude is negative, your unconscious attitude is positive; if your conscious attitude is positive, your unconscious is negative (for example, if you consciously love your spouse, your unconscious loathes them—that's the whole, shocking point about the shadow). Keeping that opposite in mind—whatever it is—is the simplest way to prevent the creation of a repressed and dis-owned shadow concerning any issue or person (see "Polarity Therapy" in the next chapter).

In a sense, the pluralistic stage, with its multiple perspectives naturally arising in awareness as part of its inherent conscious structure possibilities, is a sign that consciousness is gaining in strength and is strong enough to include these multiple perspectives—positive and negative—in its own inherent awareness. This is something relatively new in development in general (although it tentatively begins to emerge with the orange "multiplistic" altitude), and is something that the self may—or may not—easily adopt. If not, it returns to its typical habit of repressing the opposing tendency, hanging on to the remaining conscious item with a special intensity, and thus creating a shadow element or even a subpersonality in the same move. It's at the next stage—the Integral—that multiple perspectives emerge *inherently* as aspects of a unifying wholeness, not just multiple perspectives, but coherent, integrally held multiple perspectives, or unities-in-diversities (although these, too, can be dissociated or fixated themselves, as we'll see).

A dysfunction that is very common in general at the intermediate stages (amber, orange, green, and integral 2ⁿᵈ tier) is to repress and alienate either *its previous stage or its immediately succeeding stage.* This is so common as to be accurately referred to as a "normal neurosis." Particularly aggravated by the Culture Wars (whose combatants are exactly those intermediate stages—traditional-religious amber, rational-modern orange, and multicultural-postmodern green, with integral occasionally thrown in), these specific stages, whose Views are already inherently contradictory, become, with the Culture Wars, exaggeratedly inflamed and disagreeable and mutually disgusting to each other.

The conflict here, as always, is between Views, not their underlying basic structures. For example, one view of the basic structure of the amber altitude (in the cognitive line) is called "concrete operational thinking" (or "conop"), which operates on the concrete world in a very direct manner. The cognitive structure at the next higher level, that of orange altitude, is "formal operational thinking" (or "formop"), which operates, not on the world but on thought itself (which then operates on the world). So conop and formop get along just fine—in fact, formop is directly operating on conop all the time (conop is called the "operand" of formop, or "that which is operated upon"). Basic structures or rungs are always compatible and thus are always included (in the "transcend and include"), and this is a good example of that.

But look at their respective Views—they couldn't be more contradictory or antagonistic. The amber View—and remember, "View" means, not the rung per se, but what happens when you are primarily identified with a particular rung and thus look at the world ONLY through its eyes—is one confined to conop, or the rule/role mind. Because of its concrete nature, it can take only a 2ⁿᵈ-person perspective, and is thus ethnocentric, sharply dividing people into "us" (the "chosen people") versus "them" ("infidels"); because it doesn't have a 3ʳᵈ-person capacity (for thought to operate on thought itself), it cannot stand "outside" of itself and criticize its own self or its culture, and thus it is locked into a strongly conformist, absolutistic View; and lacking 3ʳᵈ-person "objective" (or "scientific") methods, it has only the concrete mind to produce concrete Mythic-literal Views (the source of all fundamentalist religion).

Well, the View from formop disagrees with virtually all of that (even though its basic rung is fully inclusive of the previous basic rung as a subholon in its very own being). But as for what the world looks like when you look through the orange Rational structure, it's a different world indeed. First, the introduction of a 3rd-person "objective" capacity means that this stage can stand back, look at its own self and its own culture, and critically scrutinize them. It can propose "experiments" to discover truths and not rely on mere Mythic revelation to decide what's right (so it discovers that the world was not created in six days but has been slowly unfolding and evolving over 14 billion years). Chemistry replaces alchemy; astronomy replaces astrology; surgery replaces leeches. Science in general replaces Mythic-religion in general. In place of a *conformist* role self, there is an *autonomous individual* self. These two worldviews—these Views—could hardly be more different and contradictory; and, indeed, they form two of the intensely debating combatants in the Culture Wars.

The crucial point here is that one of the major reasons why basic rungs are included, or preserved, but basic Views are negated, transcended, or let go of in development and evolution is not only that a higher View is larger, higher, wider, with more consciousness and care and adequacy, but that the senior View and the junior View are, in almost every way, quite contradictory. You couldn't possibly believe both of them simultaneously (it is existentially impossible, for example, in the very same action, to be both an amber totally conformist self and an orange totally autonomous self—by definition, they're complete opposites).

This happens with Views up and down the entire spectrum of development—while the rungs of each stage are easily incorporated and included, the Views are wildly contradictory and couldn't be included even if desired (so they are successively negated and let go of, to make room for the next higher View). And, we were saying, it is particularly prominent with these intermediate levels (amber, orange, green, and integral), especially since their Views have become combatants in the Culture Wars, and hence are exaggeratedly even more contradictory in their stances.

Thus, amber represses and projects its own emerging "orange/objective/critical" capacities and thus sees the world itself as overwhelmingly "critical" of its mythic-religious Views (and if extreme, might even respond with various acts of terrorism—"The orange modern world makes no room for my religion, thus I have the right to blow it up"). Given the Erotic drive toward orange as the world's center of gravity, this dysfunction today is quite widespread with much of amber. Indeed, a quick review of the types of terrorism committed in the last several decades shows that fundamentalist religious drives are by far the most common ones.

Orange rational, for its part, can remain fixated to its own amber tendencies (addiction), or (more likely) repress and project its amber religious tendencies (allergy), thus seeing them "everywhere" and vehemently and even viciously reacting to the "dangerous, infantile, war-loving" fundamentalist religions choking the world. Avidly agreeing with the "new atheists," it sees mythic-religion as one of the most dangerous forces threatening the peace of the modern and postmodern world, and never tires of vehemently and scathingly attacking these forces wherever and whenever it can. It's not that what the new atheists are saying is totally wrong (indeed, many of their critiques, although severely limited in their view of just what constitutes spirituality, are quite accurate when it comes to fundamentalism); it's the hyperexaggerated emotionalism of their attacks that is the tip-off to their own shadow projection and hence shadow boxing.

Facing toward green, the next structure-stage to emerge, orange can, due to prior negative judgments about green postmodernism, repress and project any of its own green capacities as green attempts to emerge and descend into its awareness (hence, green allergy). The result is an orange modern View aggressively attacking anything flying under the banner of postmodern multiculturalism and the alarming "republic of feelings." Orange sees everything from the market to politics to education to social services as completely being ruined by a rampant green that will have nothing to do with real profit, actual accomplishment and merit, and a genuinely free market that is the greatest source of value creation ever invented by humans. Orange also believes that the educational system has been completely wrecked by replacing achievement with ersatz self-esteem practices that only increase narcissism, and sees an alarming drive to replace sharp analytic thinking with gooey self-centric feelings and "coming from the heart" in an "embodied fashion." Orange sees all of this with unadulterated horror—a tip-off that, in addition to whatever green qualities are actually out there, orange has added its own projected green qualities, which produces a world that appears to be totally (and "doubly") overrun by pathological green everywhere.

Green, for its part, when facing its junior elements—in this case, orange in particular—can remain stuck to, or fixated on, aspects of its own orange tendencies (addiction), or (much more likely) repress and project them (orange allergy). It then replays the orange antigreen anthem but in the opposite direction: green sees the world as absolutely overrun and overwhelmed with the totally destructive and disastrous systems of (orange) capitalism, business, profit in any form, crony financialism, ranking and "meritocracies" (instead of more equitable, totally "egalitarian" Views)—a culture that appears completely dominated by consumerism, greed, lust for money, wildly selfish and uncaring marginalization of anything appearing to be a "loser," and a system designed to serve the already wealthy "winners"—not to mention that orange in general is the single greatest contributor to, and cause of, everything from global warming to trafficking for profit. Absolutely everything to do with orange business, capitalism, profit, money, achievement, excellence, merit, accomplishment, intellect, and reason are reacted to with a tremendous animosity. The green self caught with such an orange subpersonality will often devote its life to various nonprofits meant to erase orange anything from the face of the planet. Since this is also and primarily an internal war, an interior battle, an inward split, the dissociated green self is open to a raft of unpleasant, sometimes disabling, dysfunctions, including an endemic unhappiness and depression, intense self-righteousness, and unacknowledged self-loathing. This nasty internal war between the green self and an orange subpersonality—a green View and an orange View—effectively reproduces one wing of the Culture Wars internally. (Of course, "painful neurotic symptoms" accompany *any* stage's allergies or addictions to either lower or higher stages in its own developmental unfolding.)

With this inner split or dissociation, a simple disagreement in values becomes intensified as an internal split and dis-owning—culture wars as a true interior civil war. As noted, this can happen whether the devaluing is aimed at the previous stage (aspects of which are split off and relegated to the repressed *submergent* unconscious), or oriented to the newly emerging stage (aspects of which are dissociated and relegated to the repressed *emergent* unconscious).

As for the latter dysfunction (repressing the emerging), if green is particularly attached to its View, and yet a certain amount of growth and development continues, the Integral levels will soon attempt to emerge, but because their View is so radically different from the green View in so many ways, the green self, even if on the verge of making that "monumental leap" to 2nd tier, will tend to contract in the face of the emerging 2nd-tier View, intensify its hold on green, and force any emerging Integral Views into the repressed emergent unconscious. This, if severe enough, can halt development almost entirely, resulting in a serious case of arrested development. Green will often, due to a type of pre/trans fallacy, confuse red premodern characteristics with green postmodern characteristics, and end up glorifying red tribal society, romantically giving red nothing but numerous positive and highly valued qualities (taken from green postmodern). As Don Beck put it, "Green never met a red it didn't love" (while it continues to loathe amber, orange, and 2nd tier altogether—as well as the *actual* characteristics of red). That is, green still despises several characteristics that in actual fact are characteristic of red, such as egocentric individuality, power, control, and domination. And these are the qualities that green misperceives whenever it looks at any Integral structure. Because the Integral altitude reintroduces hierarchies (in the form of growth hierarchies, or holarchies, not dominator or power hierarchies); because it reintroduces a type of individuality (but one conjoined with community); because it has the cognitive capacity to see beneficial universals, commendable Big Pictures, and effective metanarratives, whenever green looks at Integral, it sees red (the "nasty" aspects of red: it sees all of the unifying Integral qualities as actually being power driven, controlling, dominating). This drives green nearly insane with irritation, and it becomes as anti-Integral driven as the antigay zealots are antihomosexual (both of them, of course, shadowboxing their own internal impulses).

As I have noted, the possibility of this dually directed dis-owning (aimed at the previous stage or at the next-higher emerging stage) affects virtually all levels of development; and this happens because whereas the basic structures or rungs are included, enveloped, and embraced (the holon of each basic rung becomes a subholon in the next higher rung, and thus rungs are always compatible), the Views—precisely because they are generated by an *exclusive* identification with a basic rung, thus necessarily excluding the Views from any other rung—are therefore often incompatible, irreconcilable, discordant, and indeed contradictory. The cognitive *concepts* at the red altitude (part of its basic rung) are included in the cognitive rules of the amber altitude (part of its basic rung), but to *identify* with red concepts/intentionality gives a View of power, whereas to identify with the rules of amber concrete operational gives a View of strong conformity—and individual power does not mix well, or at all, with the unquestioning conformity required by membership in a group.

Thus, transcend and include, negate and preserve (the basic rungs are included and preserved, with no conflict at all; the Views are negated and transcended, since they conflict). The identity of the central, or proximate, self is moving onward, and you can't see the world from both the third rung of a ladder and the fourth rung of a ladder simultaneously, even though all the rungs themselves are present simultaneously. Likewise, as orange altitude emerges and the self begins to move toward identifying with that, the basic rungs are easily integrated (formal operational actually operates, we saw, on concrete operational), but the View from orange, which is highly individualistic, autonomous, self-authoring, self-criticizing, doesn't fit at all with the View from amber—conformist, other controlled, heteronomous, communal driven. And likewise with the basic rungs and Views of green pluralistic and orange rational (whose Views are, respectively, relativistic versus universal, communal versus individual, no metanarratives versus metanarratives, and so on); and of 2nd-tier Integral and green pluralistic (whose Views are, respectively, significant Big Pictures versus no big pictures at all; numerous metanarratives versus no metanarratives at all; universal contexts versus only local contexts, and so forth); and similarly with, as I said, virtually every developmental level (rungs are incorporated, Views are rejected). This is why it's so important to understand the difference between ladder/enduring rungs and temporary/transitional Views (something that most developmental models, such as Spiral Dynamics, don't do).

By the time we get to the Integral levels (teal Holistic and turquoise Integral), the fundamental conscious unit becomes a consciously recognized holon—a whole that is understood to be part of a larger whole. Wholeness becomes central at 2nd tier, and every Whole is always subsumed in a yet-greater Whole (even the Whole of this moment's universe becomes prehended, or included, in the next moment's Whole universe—the universe of this moment "transcends and includes" the universe of the previous moment). Of course, all previous levels are actually composed of holons (as is the Kosmos at large), but these start to become naturally conscious at 2nd tier (and in prominence at 3rd tier). The most common dysfunction here—at Integral levels—is denying, or being unaware of, either the wholeness aspect or the partness aspect of any occasion (any holon). The world is neither composed of wholes (as holism maintains) nor composed of parts (as atomism maintains); it is composed of whole/parts, of holons. Whole letters are parts of words; whole words are parts of sentences; whole sentences are parts of paragraphs; whole paragraphs are parts of whole treatises. None of those holons can be skipped or bypassed; none can be ignored.

The fact that the Integral levels are so, well, "integral," gives many people the impression that dysfunctions or pathologies simply don't occur here. But, I'm saying, that's simply not true. Although the phenomena of this stage tend to be whole/parts, or unities-in-diversities—in thoughts, ideas, feelings, emotions—various specific unities-in-diversities can themselves, in many instances, simply be alienated, repressed, dissociated. The shadow of the Integral levels is basically just a much more complex shadow (as are the subpersonalities), consisting occasionally of entire networks that become shadow.

With normal or healthy Integral, the multiple perspectives of an emotion tend to emerge simultaneously; but if that emotion is repressed, the multiple emotional perspectives can all be repressed, a networked shadow complex results. The same is true with ideas, thoughts, feelings, drives, needs, qualities, values. For example, if I am in love with a person, then at 2nd tier, I will experience that love as a richly contextualized feeling, interwoven not only with the loved individual but with humanity as a whole as the context. "I love this person as I love all humanity, even more so." That type of sentiment is typical at 2nd tier, either explicitly or implicitly—that whole/partness is simply how Integral inherently sees the world. And if that love relationship goes very badly, and I actively deny it by repressing all love for this person, I can simultaneously repress the love for all humanity, and suddenly my entire life seems devoid of love—it's simply gone, erased, out of awareness. A sweeping blackness descends on my life; interactions with people become labored; a certain joy has left my life, replaced with what seems an infinite hollowness. This is admittedly fairly severe; the point is, it's possible at these levels due to their very structure. Thus, at the Integral levels, holistic shadows—wholes that are broken parts of even larger wholes—are not uncommon. The same thing can happen with depression as learned helplessness; if I drop into a learned-helplessness state, and a particular future starts to look very gloomy, my vision-logic can extrapolate that extensively and see all sorts of futures not working and hence looking gloomy. My superholistic mind sees huge entire pictures all ruined, all gloomy, all depressing.

The central point here is that, at each level of development, *the elements that arise specifically at that level itself* are the elements that can become the shadow *at that level*. For orange, it's worldcentric emotions and traits; for green, it's multiplistic elements; for 2nd tier, it's whole/parts.

Also common at Integral, as previously noted, is a difficulty integrating green correctly. Most typically this is a green allergy. The Integral level had to engage in an enormously heroic battle to break through the sea of green surrounding it (and a green that despises Integral in almost every way, particularly its awareness of growth hierarchies, since green sees only dominator hierarchies and thinks that is what Integral is doing, which is enormously insulting to Integral, since in fact it is doing exactly the opposite and freeing awareness from domination drives). Most Integral individuals have had to courageously fight their way through a green swamp—and often, a mean green meme one at that—and crawl up and onto one of a few islands of slowly emerging Integral, there to finally find their new home. But the whole affair almost always leaves a very bad taste in the mouth, and if severe enough, the new Integral level will repress and dis-own any green View remaining in its system (before it can healthily transcend it). This sends green into the repressed submergent unconscious, from whence it is usually projected onto any person or event that even vaguely smells green, and leaves Integral with an active loathing, amounting even to a real hatred, of green anything (a hatred that is, of course, actually of aspects of its own interiors).

As we move into 3rd tier, new elements—particularly transpersonal ones, with an emphasis on an awareness of awareness and an experienced (not merely thought) Wholeness—begin to emerge, and dis-owned shadow material begins to focus on those. Again, the whole point about the shadow is that, at every level, numerous new, novel, and emergent phenomena come into existence, and as the self identifies with these new elements, it creates a new View of the world (by actually co-creating a new world); and virtually any elements of that View can be dissociated, dis-owned, alienated, or repressed, and the defense mechanisms that do this, at each particular level, are made of the very substances of the basic rungs of those levels. At the red concept/intentionality level, concepts themselves repress and dis-own feelings (and other elements); at the amber rule/role mind, dysfunctional rules act to alienate and distort various roles (giving ersatz "games people play," among other problems); at the orange rational level, rationality and rationalizations drive dissociation and dis-owning of worldcentric thoughts (and feelings and drives and other elements); at the green postmodern level, the mind pluralistically splits elements, dis-owning and distorting them; at the Integral levels, a malfunctioning vision-logic drives the repression of whole/parts (among other items). In each case, the root source of the dissociation and dis-owning is the general defense mechanism feature of the finite self-system, which functions ultimately to protect its own life and avoid an apparent death (see, for example, *The Atman Project* and *Up from Eden*).[2] The overall point is that the newly emergent elements of each new level of development bring new types of defense mechanisms, new forms of death-seizure, new phenomena to repress and dis-own, and new types of shadows and subpersonalities to be created. This occurs all the way up, all the way down.

All of this is still true at 3rd tier, but the picture becomes complexified because there are now also inherent transpersonal (or spiritual) elements involved, and thus, for example, whereas at the midlevel range of development, the *presence* of a belief in any infinity or spirit is often the sign of a dysfunction or inauthenticity (or Atman project), here at 3rd tier, the *lack* of awareness of infinity or spirit is often a dysfunction. Not only personal but transpersonal elements, and not only structures but states, are almost always involved in 3rd-tier dysfunctions to some degree.

The overriding focus of pathological orientation at 3rd tier—to speak of its levels generically for a moment—is the relation of heaven and earth, spiritual and conventional, infinite and finite, transpersonal and personal, eternity and time, otherworldly and this-worldly. All of these are now not only dimensions of a Kosmos out there but dimensions of one's own interior Being as well—now consciously available. What before was often an exterior conflict can, at these levels, become an interior civil war. Integration assumes as much, or more, importance as it has at any stage previously. And the unintegrated elements of those level's items become shadow elements here, often inhabiting subpersonalities that are starting to include transpersonal and genuinely spiritual components as well. It's not easy, bringing together heaven and earth. For the human being can, particularly at 3rd tier, deny or repress either one, as well as become attached or addicted to either one, and all four of those dysfunctions bring their own specific and often horrid suffering. I'll discuss them briefly one at a time.

To deny heaven (where "heaven" specifically means the higher, 3rd-tier structures and their conjoined states, a transpersonally or spiritually infused Wholeness) is to deny one's own higher nature, and not only one's higher-state condition (one's very soul and Self) but also the structures that otherwise should be uniting and joining these higher structures and Selves with their lower, conventional counterparts—the structures at 1st and 2nd tier that ideally become integrated into 3rd tier. The whole point of an evolutionary development taken to completion (complete at this time in history) is to let emerge each and every basic structure or major rung of consciousness, and simultaneously to strip it of any attachment or self-identification, so that all basic rungs and their motivations remain, but all separate-self senses and their Views are let go of and transcended. The only *motivations* left in a human being are those coming from the basic structures or rungs themselves, with *no motivations* left coming from any limited self-contractions or their partial Views. (Those have all been negated or transcended, structure-stage by structure-stage by structure-stage. Or, one could say, the only View left in existence is that of Supermind, just as the only Vantage Point left is that of nondual Suchness, but there is no self-contraction in any of those.)

Thus, at infrared, the capacity to eat and the need for food still arises, but there's no attachment to food (no addiction and no allergy); at magenta, the capacity for prana, general life energy and emotions, and the capacity for sex still arises, but there's no attachment to them (no addiction and no allergy); at red, the capacity for powerful intentionality still arises, but there's no attachment to it (no addiction and no allergy); at amber, the capacity for concrete thinking still arises, but there's no attachment to it (no addiction and no allergy); at orange, the capacity to think rationally still arises, but there's no attachment to it (no addiction and no allergy); at green, the capacity to view the world multiplistically still arises, but there's no attachment to it (no addiction and no allergy); at 2nd tier, the capacity for holistic and integral thinking still arises, but there's no attachment to it (no addiction and no allergy). Each of these basic structures is freed of grasping, clinging, attachment, addiction, pathological avoidance, allergy, a self-contracted identity with any of them, and a partial and limited View coming from any of them.

Instead, with each basic rung cleared of attachment, identification, and self-contracting distortions, each is left to perform its own natural, undefended, undistorted, unbroken functions and capacities, which aim particularly at connecting the human being with each and every corresponding level of development and complexity in the entire Kosmos—and giving the bodhisattva the tools and vehicles through which to touch, and ultimately serve and liberate, every sentient being in the universe, from quarks on up.

As I have often pointed out, but is worth repeating here in regard to this important point about vehicles through which ultimate Self and Suchness can express themselves: The human being is an exclamation mark to the entire story of evolution. Each human being contains, in his or her very makeup, every major holon that evolution has brought forth and that has emerged since the Big Bang itself—from quarks, to subatomic particles, to atoms, to molecules, to prokaryotic cells, to eukaryotic cells, to the fundamental biochemistry of plant life, to sensations of amphibian neural nets, to instinctual drives of food and sex of the reptilian brain stem, to paleomammalian emotions of the limbic system, to symbols of the cortex, to thoughts of the neocortex. In other words, every major level of the great Tree of Life has a corresponding level in the human compound individual, and human development consists of (1) the emergence of each and every one of those levels, followed closely, stage by stage, with (2) the identification of human consciousness or the self-sense with each and every one of those levels—incorporating and integrating its major messages and structures into the human being itself; and, soon thereafter (3) dis-identification of the human consciousness or self-sense from each and every one of those levels, while integrating their basic structures into overall consciousness itself, which frees each of those levels from human self-attachment, addiction, grasping, and distortion and yet leaves each of them fully present, as the vehicles and tools through which the Enlightened human being can reach out to, and touch, every sentient being at every level of existence in the entire Kosmos, liberating all sentient beings into the glorious condition of their own true nature. This is an overall Big Picture of Spirit-in-action in the very course of evolution itself.

To deny heaven is to deny the higher ends and reaches of that development and evolution. One may still connect with an ultimate Spirit via state-stage development (gross to subtle to causal to emptiness to nondual), but since, with the denial of the higher, that is now occurring only at lower levels, one's "unity consciousness" is actually limited in its Fullness by the fact that there are now structure-levels still "over one's head" that one has not identified with (namely—any of the 3rd-tier "heaven" levels being denied or repressed). Why would one deny heaven? In many cases, it is simple ignorance. Recall our oft-repeated point: states can be seen by introspection, structures can't.[3] Thus, one is often simply unaware of "heavenly structures" themselves, and thus doesn't know to look for them. Virtually every Path of the Great Liberation in all the world's wisdom traditions is aware of Big Mind (the state of Christ consciousness, Buddha-nature, Allah-being, Tao awakening, Brahmanatman, Ayn Sof, and so forth); none of them is aware of the Supermind (a structure like all other structures—undetected, unseen, undiscovered, and thus unknown to introspection). Recall also that maps of development are psychoactive: the simple awareness of the higher 3rd-tier "heaven" stages available in one's own growth and development activates and accelerates that growth. Simply learning something like the AQAL Framework is part of the cure for this ignorance and denial of heaven.

Another reason for the allergy to, or denial of, heaven is an addiction to earth. Here, a finite, sensory, exterior, temporal earth is identified with an infinite, transcending and including, eternal, ultimate Spirit. "Gaia" is taken to be ultimate reality, whereas it is actually just the Lower Right quadrant, starting with the emergence of prokaryotes, or early cells. (The planet Gaia only emerged several billion years after the Big Bang. If Gaia is ultimate reality, then where was Spirit all that time? James Lovelock's original Gaia hypothesis was an attempt to explain various factors influencing weather patterns over the planet. He suggested that a thin film of early living cells—prokaryotes, which stretch around the entire globe, and are also transcended and included in eukaryotes, or true cells, and thus exist inside your own body right now—forms a layer that acts as an interface between living and non-living realms, and thus, among other things, has an impact on the weather patterns displayed by the nonliving realm—an ingenious and almost certainly true suggestion. But from there "Gaia" somehow quickly came to mean the entire biosphere itself—deer and bunnies and crows and worms and fish and apes and forests—way beyond prokaryotes—and that came somehow to mean all of reality in a totalistic sense. Thus, Gaia = Spirit.) But when earth (or the overall gross realm) is taken to be the whole of Spirit, then we stop looking for the rest of Spirit, and arrested development can set in well before 3rd tier has a chance to emerge. In some cases, this confusion is due to actual fixations and attachments to earlier, sensorimotor-related realms (or at least gross-reflecting realms). In other cases, it is a simple matter, once again, of ignorance, of not recognizing the straightforward but profoundly important differences between finite and infinite, temporal and eternal (timeless), manifest and unmanifest—not recognizing that a samsara devoid of nirvana (that is, Gaia) should not be equated with Enlightenment.

Standing in opposition to earth addiction is earth allergy. This is a condition all too common and too easy to slip into in the meditative and contemplative traditions. "My Kingdom is not of this earth" is taken much too literally, and in some cases, earth itself is looked upon as the cause of illusion, sin, duality, nonenlightenment. In the First Turning of Buddhism, the earth is part of samsara, the world of Form that Awakening completely steps off of. I once heard a Theravada teacher respond to a question about ecological despolation with, "I don't care, I'm not coming back." He was getting off the round of birth and death altogether, never to return to this stinking place called earth again. No wonder Nagarjuna jumped all over that notion.

An addiction to heaven often has similar results, but for quite different reasons (it has similar results because it pushes out any regard for, or thought of, earth). But here, the transpersonal bliss, radiance, elation, luminosity, joy, and limitlessness of higher structures and states become an object of attachment; they are so overwhelmingly blissful that one never wants to return to ordinary reality in any way whatsoever. The exclusive love of heaven leaves little, if any, room for earth, and the results, again, are, in effect, an earth denial and allergy (even if there's not a definite earth repression in place, as there is with actual earth allergy). But this eventually acts to undermine considerably the blissful nature of the higher realms, because the earth remains a structural component of one's being in any event, and thus ignoring earth is ignoring a component of one's own makeup, an interior splitting that sooner or later is experienced as some degree of suffering, which certainly curtails the higher realm's happiness.

What is required to cure this particular dysfunction are often actual exercises, such as the following Taoist "microcosmic orbit": One breathes in the infinite spiritual Light (or heaven) at and beyond the crown through the crown of the head. One breathes that Light in and down through the front of the body, making sure that the mouth is closed and the tongue is on the roof of the mouth, and continues breathing it downward into the belly, the source of Life (or earth). Then one releases the energy on the out-breath up the spine and back through the crown, returning and releasing Life into infinite Light and Spirit above. This practice bodily brings heaven down and into earth, and releases earth back and up into heaven, completing their union and integration, or the "microcosmic orbit." (For more on this, see, for example, Mantak Chia's work.)

If "heaven" means not specifically the higher, 3rd-tier stages but simply any relatively higher yet-to-emerge stage (at whatever level), and "earth" means not specifically lower, 1st- and 2nd-tier stages but simply any lower and already emerged stage, then these four pathological orientations (addiction and allergy to heaven, addiction and allergy to earth) are possible, indeed common, at virtually every level of development (and we have been tracking many of them, particularly those involved in the Culture Wars). As we get into 3rd tier, these orientations start to take on the actual dimensions of the transpersonal and the personal, or a genuinely spiritual (transpersonal) heaven and a material (personal) earth, which are dimensions of one's own Being as well. (Earth is still a perfect manifestation of Spirit, just a junior dimension of such. Alternatively, seeing material earth as the Right-hand quadrants, earth becomes the exterior of each level of

Spirit. This is in keeping with our dual usage of "matter"—both the lowest level and the exterior of all levels.) Each 3rd-tier level will experience these personal and transpersonal dimensions slightly differently, depending on its actual form and structure. The specific defense mechanisms (denial of heaven and denial of earth) are built from the particular structures of each level, and once these distortions are created, they cause considerable problems, suffering, and—if severe—arrested development.

These problems are best dealt with by familiarizing oneself with the general characteristics of 1st-, 2nd-, and 3rd-tier structures and what can be expected at each, and then conscientiously helping to enact each structure-stage in its healthy and functional form. This should be accompanied by a deliberate and conscious state development (likewise one should familiarize oneself with the basic state-stages—gross to subtle to causal to emptiness to nondual—and what is to be expected at each state-stage, and then try to cooperatively and conscientiously enact each). In both cases (structures and states), being aware of the general types of shadow that can—and often will—be created through misdevelopment and its various defense mechanisms will help to head off many problems in advance, and allow one to spot actual problems, and address them, should they occur. "Right View"—specifically meaning "Right Integral View"—is, as always, foundational.

The problem with defense mechanisms—the basic reason that they don't work—is that they are a fundamental lie, an untruthfulness in the core of one's being, concerning exactly what exists in one's being itself. One has already identified with this material, which is generating a particular View at that stage, and precisely because one has already *identified* with it, then denying it (dissociating it, dis-owning it) is a blatant lie in the face of existence, a refusal of—a looking away from—an authentically present reality (however temporary it might be), which tears reality in two, right down the middle, and delivers up the broken shards as a false self-image and a hidden shadow, two aspects of a now-broken, previously unified authentic self (at whatever level, in structure or state). Because of that inherent falsehood, defense mechanisms are activities of the lie; they therefore—and this is the catch—they, the defense mechanisms, end up bringing about exactly what they were meant to ward off. Denying and dis-owning a quality, tendency, desire, or drive splits it off into a special realm of its own, where it is amplified, embellished, distorted, and hyped, which exaggerates its influence and reach and leaves a black hole in the conscious psyche and a white hole in the unconscious psyche, with the former sucking material out of awareness and the latter pumping it into unawareness, slowly draining consciousness off into a flooded basement, where it putrefies and stagnates. If I am trying to get anger out of my life, and hence I dissociate and deny it, I send it to the submergent unconscious, from whence it is likely to be projected onto any number of other individuals. I can, in fact, project it onto literally everybody I meet; and thus suddenly, instead of getting anger out of my life, I find it is absolutely everywhere in my life, surrounding me on all sides, and all of it is aimed directly at me (since that is its true source, to which it is attempting to return). Thus, defense mechanisms bring about exactly what they were meant to ward off.

In sum, although all of these dysfunctions can usefully be discussed in general terms such as fixation and addiction, or avoidance and allergy—and they are definitely true and accurate portrayals—the actual and specific forms that they take at each stage are determined by the actual and specific forms, or structures, that emerge with the rungs (or the states) at that particular stage. The very structure or pattern of a given stage contributes to a different type of defense mechanism, which is built out of that structure itself, at each stage—a defense mechanism built out of the fantasy mind, or the power mind, or the conceptual mind, or the rule/role mind, or the formal mind, or the pluralistic mind, or the vision-logic mind, or the para-mind, and so on; with states, the specific defense mechanism is built out of the structure that is experiencing the state. Just as there are nested hierarchies of structures and Views, and states and Vantage Points, so there are nested hierarchies of levels and types of defense mechanisms, specific dysfunctions, and symptoms, and specific treatment modalities for each level (and state) of consciousness and development. Integral Psychology and Psychiatry are interested in mapping out the full spectrum of all of these, from types of pathologies and defense mechanisms to the best (usually 4-quadrant) treatment modalities, and working not only with "what's broken" or "not working," but also with "what's right" and "how to make it even better" through flourishing.[4] "Cleaning

Up" includes both the more negative aspects of shadow work and symptom alleviation, as well as the more positive aspects of strength enhancement and ways to flourish.

In regard to all of these practices, I recommend keeping a journal. Here, you can keep track of dreams, various 3-2-1 and 3-2-1-0 exercises, each day's three-page "Daily Entry," practices of gratefulness and "Three Positive Things," forgiveness and "One Thing a Day" and "One Thing Each Yesterday," types of meditation practices and their unfolding experiences and insights, and general aspects from all the modules in an overall AQAL or Integral Life Practice. This journaling process can end up being one of the most powerful and effective growth and development tools you will ever use, powerfully helping subject to become object and thus accelerating the very process of development and evolution.

Lastly, in regard to "Cleaning Up," it is not necessary that an Integral Spirituality include an exhaustively in-depth approach to every single issue included in psychotherapy, in all its central theories and practices. A general awareness of the existence of various shadows (levels of subpersonalities correlated with levels of Views and Vantage Points) and an openness to be engaged in shadow work where necessary is generally plenty. A simple realization that the View, or Vantage Point, at any stage can exist in a healthy or unhealthy, functional or dysfunctional, fashion and that its unhealthy/dysfunctional version generates an addiction or an allergy revolving around that particular View—food, sex, power, love and belongingness, self-esteem and achievement, self-actualization and sensitivity, wholeness and integral drives, transpersonal and explicitly spiritual issues, and so forth—as well as shadow issues with each of the major states, as we discussed in chapters 12 and 13, is generally enough, when combined with simple exercises such as the 3-2-1 or 3-2-1-0 process. Individuals with significant or serious shadow issues can consult the appropriate specialist. It suffices generally to recognize the existence of shadow material and know how to spot it when and if it emerges—and to know simple practices for treating it, at least in an introductory fashion—and to begin establishing a network of the more integrally oriented professionals to work with individuals where necessary.

To put this all in perspective: Human beings didn't realize that they had evolved until around two hundred years ago. Likewise, they didn't learn that things could break down at every evolutionary step until shortly thereafter. Structures of consciousness weren't identified until around one hundred years ago. Yet most Great Traditions and systems of meditation are now at least a thousand years old—none of them had access to any of this information, and therefore lacked the opportunity to include these more recent discoveries in their approaches. Only with the discovery of evolution and the understanding that Spirit-in-action itself continues to unfold—producing new realities, new emergents, new truths, and new worlds entirely—does it become apparent that, not only a new Fourth Turning but ongoing future Turnings down the road are things that each and every spiritual system needs to recognize. Spirit-in-action *is* evolution, and neither one of them ever stops.

The 4 Quadrants

The quadrants are four perspectives and dimensions that all phenomena possess. You can look at any thing or event from both the interior and the exterior, and in both individual and collective forms. This gives us four major combinations (see figure 4.1 in chapter 4)—the interior of the individual; the exterior of the individual; the interior of the group or collective; and the exterior of the group or collective. These four dimensions/perspectives turn out to be incredibly important, because every phenomena in existence has these four orientations, and each of them gives unbelievably significant information. They each have very different but equally real truths, different validity claims, different types of phenomena or qualities or existent realities, and different approaches or methods for accessing them—and leaving out any one of them leaves a gaping hole in the universe.[5] Entire disciplines—medicine, spirituality, law, art, business, politics, organizational development, family systems, relationships, work, ecology—each have these 4 quadrants, without exception, and yet all four are rarely realized and included in any given approach, which automatically guarantees a partial, fragmented, broken, limited, patchy, splintered, disintegrated, prejudiced, and biased result—and these are everywhere!

To very briefly review, the 4 quadrants are (i) the *interior* of the *individual* (the "I" space, which is accessed by introspection and meditation, and contains thoughts, images, ideas, feelings, insights, emotions, satori, and the repressed submergent and emergent unconscious; this Upper Left quadrant includes structures and states of consciousness, as well as shadow material); (ii) the *exterior* of the *individual* (the "it" space, which is seen objectively by observation—a typical "scientific" view of the organism, which, in humans, contains atoms, molecules, cells, organ systems, lungs, kidneys, a triune brain with neurotransmitters, and so forth, plus the individual as seen from an "objective" or "exterior" view; for example, a fern, tree, frog, ape, and so forth, along with the individual's objective behavior, all in their singular, individual, objective forms); (iii) the *interior* of the *collective* (the "we" space, which contains shared values, ethics, worldviews, meanings, semantics, mutual resonance, and so forth); and (iv) the *exterior* of the *collective* (the "its" space—systems and collective structures, social institutions, family structures, organizations, environmental surroundings and ecological systems, techno-economic modes of production—foraging, farming, industrial, informational, and so on; the elements in the Lower Right quadrant are often referred to by sociologists as PESTLE—political, economic, social, technological, legal, environmental).

Integral Theory often reduces these four major dimension-perspectives to three, combining the two exterior realms into one major objective or 3rd-person realm of "it," with "you/we" being 2nd person and "I" being 1st person, giving us the "Big 3" of I, we, and it (or self, culture, and nature; or 1st-, 2nd-, and 3rd-person perspectives; or art, morals, and science; or Buddha, Sangha, and Dharma). Clearly, all three have been recognized for thousands of years; all three are equally and incredibly important; and rarely are all three included in any approach, sadly.

The quadrants are one of the most important and most often-used aspects of the AQAL Framework. One of the reasons is that virtually every discipline, as I was saying, has some school or subschool that focuses almost entirely on just one quadrant and builds all its theories around that one quadrant, dismissing or denying the others. I call this "quadrant absolutism," and it's an example of what can happen with any of the dimensions of AQAL. You can have "level absolutisms" (such as identifying all of spiritual intelligence with just the Mythic-literal level, and dismissing all others as unreal or unimportant); you can have "line absolutisms" (identifying just one line, or one multiple intelligence, as being the only real or important line, as education often does with cognitive intelligence); you can have "state absolutisms" (where only one state is given any reality, as scientific materialism does with the gross-physical state/realm); you can have any number of "type absolutisms" (where you knowingly latch on to just one typology and dismiss all others as insignificant).

But this is particularly prevalent with quadrants, and virtually every major human discipline has one or more subschools that absolutize just one or two quadrants, with the other quadrants being either denied entirely or, just as often, reduced to a minor subschool (which is usually dismissed or grudgingly acknowledged by the major and most influential school and its preferred quadrant). You can find examples of these subschools in virtually every major human discipline (at the very least, the discipline splits into two main subdivision contenders—the Left-hand quadrants, or the interior, interpretive "humanistic" approaches, versus the Right-hand quadrants, or the exterior, "scientific," positivistic approaches). In consciousness studies, for example, about half the schools of that discipline maintain that consciousness is nothing but a product of the material brain—the Upper Right quadrant alone is real; the other half maintain that you don't even know the material brain except as it is experienced in consciousness itself, that consciousness comes first—only the Upper Left quadrant is "really real." (Of course, some schools, particularly postmodernist ones, believe that consciousness itself is a cultural construction—only the Lower Left quadrant is real; and approaches from systems theory to extreme Marxism believe that consciousness is the product of a material-social system base—only the Lower Right quadrant is real.) And so it goes.

The important point is that all of those subschools have something very important to tell us! It is staggeringly unimaginable that only one quadrant would be latched on to and all the others totally denied or dismissed from existence just like that! What about all the evidence that one group has gathered showing that their quadrant is the only real and important quadrant, and what about all the evidence that others have collected showing that their favorite quadrant or quadrants alone are real—you can't just explain *all* of it away. But that is exactly what each camp does—it spends as much time trying to explain away the other camp's evidence as it does in presenting its own. Thus, the first move in making any discipline comprehensive, or integral, is to go through the discipline itself and find—in addition to the major school and its acknowledged-quadrant approach—all the small and often hidden schools that work with one or more of the other quadrants. Then take what each school has to say when working with its own quadrant, ignore what it says about other quadrants, and include them all in a 4-quadrant metatheory. (If some quadrants are completely left out, and no major or minor school deals with them, then import and incorporate approaches from outside the field—perhaps developmental psychology, cultural semiotics, or spiritual practices—into the final comprehensive product. Sometimes only the individual aspects of a particular quadrant need to be imported—as I am doing with structures, states, and shadows in the Upper Left of spirituality.) The goal is to include a full representation of all 4 quadrants. Integral Theory, of course, maintains that all 4 quadrants are equally real, and that they arise together, tetra-enact each other, and tetra-evolve together. The empirical fact is that there simply does not exist merely one of the quadrants without all the others—there's just no such thing.

A few extremely simple examples are given in figures 15.1 and 15.2. Figure 15.1 is a simple 4-quadrant version of a more truly inclusive or Integral Medicine. In the Upper Right quadrant, you can see standard, orthodox, objective, materialistic, "scientific" medicine—the way virtually all conventional medicine is practiced today, which focuses exclusively on gross-physical causes of illness and gross-physical treatments: physical causes such as bacteria, viruses, broken bones, plaque buildup in arteries, liver failure, various cancers, prostate hypertrophy, Alzheimer's, digestive ills, organ system failures (such as heart attacks), strokes, and so on; and concomitant gross-physical-only treatments such as surgery, antibiotics, radiation, drugs and medication, chemotherapy, behavioral modification, organ transplants, and so forth. The tip-off that this view alone is inadequate is that, of those complaints that bring patients into doctors' offices, less than 70 percent of them actually have real causes in the Upper Right. No wonder patient compliance with the cure that the doctor suggests is usually, and shockingly, less than 50 percent—many, in some cases most, of the treatments (particularly for that 70 percent) don't work, and patients know it. So do most doctors; a recent poll among oncologists—cancer specialists who often prescribe chemotherapy—showed that a slight

Figure 15.1. Integral Medicine.

majority of them would not take their own treatment if they got cancer. I asked one oncologist about this, and he said, "We have to offer them something, or they lose hope." Fine, but chemotherapy? A barbaric treatment with a cure rate of less than 5 percent (except for blood cancers), which is why doctors won't take their own treatment. So how about something equally ineffective but less brutal—say, leeches? The simple fact is that the other 70 percent of illnesses have causes in one of the *other* quadrants—such as a psychospiritual cause in the Upper Left (for example, being a type "A" personality, usually a red subpersonality), a cultural cause in the Lower Left (for example, minority disenfranchisement leading to endemic stress, and stress's role in illness is unquestioned), or a social system/institutional cause in the Lower Right (for example, environmental toxins, base and superstructure misfits, lack of affordability, asbestos in old walls, idiotic government regulations—a person with AIDS, testifying before Congress on the insanity of not allowing terminal patients to try whatever drug they thought might help, pleaded, "Please don't let my epitaph read 'He died of red tape'"—but that "red tape" will kill you just as surely as the virus will).

Various moves to "Integrative Medicine" (and considerably better,

"Integral Medicine") attempt to include factors—causes and treatments—from all 4 quadrants (and "Integral Medicine," from any factors in the AQAL Matrix). "Alternative care" treatments in the Upper Left include Energy Medicine, which has its actual source in the spectrum of subtle energies in the Upper Right, which I discuss in chapter 16, as well as imagery, visualization, Eastern medicine, yoga, meditation, psychotherapy, brain/mind machines (that harmonize Upper Left mind and Upper Right brain), chi machines (that also working with subtle energy), shadow work, spiritual development, and so on. Treatments in the Lower Left include support groups and group therapy. For example, research shows that women with breast cancer who attend group support sessions live an average of 100 percent longer! That is, they *double* their remaining expected life span. Orthodox doctors tend to overlook something like this because they can't control it, but if you've got a serious illness, the very first thing you can do to activate the Lower Left in your healing is join a support group for that illness. Another treatment in the Lower left is to work with the meaning of the illness and what your culture's *judgments* are about this illness. A culture's judgments convert an *illness* (a "scientific," objective entity) into a *sickness*. If you have this disease, you are not just ill, you are sick—and how and why you are sick is provided by background cultural frameworks and loaded meanings. Sadly, this sickness often contributes to the illness. Think about the judgments loaded on to getting HIV, when it first began spreading—you weren't just objectively ill, you had a moral sickness, and that sickness, as a pervasive, overpoweringly negative judgment, hung in the air with every diagnosis of HIV, so much so that, when HIV was first discovered, the average life span between the diagnosis of having HIV and death was six months. Intense negative cultural judgments ("sickness") can be internalized, which generates stress and eats away at one's health just as perniciously as a real cancer. We need to examine how these problems can be effectively handled. Treatments in the Lower Right include items such as cleaning up environmental toxins, city water systems, and housing environments, but also providing financial aid and social access to, and delivery of, the treatment. Many people are unable to drive or otherwise make it to the treatment center—and that's not a nice add-on; failure to have such access to medicine is exactly the same as having no medicine, and that will kill you just as quickly as a piano falling on your head. Again, orthodox doctors tend to overlook these issues, because "that's not part of the problem I'm responsible for"—which actually means "I'm not interested in that other 70 percent of the real causes of your illness, so lotsa luck, pal."

And, as mentioned, not just the quadrants but as many dimensions of the AQAL Framework as possible need to be taken into account, both as *cause* (in looking to pinpoint the causative factors for any illness, the cause of even physical illness can come from any and all elements in the overall AQAL Matrix) and *cure* (for example, if the cause comes from a particular element in the Matrix, its cure, or alleviation, might be found in a different location). The Left-hand quadrants or interiors are almost always considered outside the domain of orthodox medicine (and they certainly are outside of it the way it's presently practiced), but orthodox practitioners are bombarded and absolutely drenched with these domains at every point in their practice (yet they are almost always tossed—explicitly or implicitly—into that 70 percent "not my problem" bag). But, as a simple yet pertinent example, a person's structure center of gravity (mythic, rational, pluralistic, and so forth) will determine the meaning he or she gives not only to the illness but to the doctor's instructions, which will in many ways determine whether patient compliance reaches higher than that standard paltry 50 percent, or falls even lower. It depends entirely on how the doctor speaks about and frames the illness and the treatment. Somebody at Mythic will be motivated to take medicine for entirely different reasons than somebody at Pluralistic. A concrete Mythic conformist patient often simply wants to be told "what to do" with little further explanation (which can tend to confuse them and cause them to lose track of just what they are actually supposed to be doing), whereas a Pluralistic patient will more likely want to participate fully in his or her treatment and care as a "conscious partner" with the doctor (and, within forty-eight hours of the diagnosis, will have scoured the Internet and now know virtually as much, sometimes even more, than their doctor about their particular illness, and, by god, they intend to use it!). And if a doctor gives a Mythic patient a Pluralistic reason—or a Pluralistic patient is treated as Mythic—you can rest assured the patient will almost certainly not be sufficiently moved to follow the doctor's orders. That alarming 50 percent compliance rate is due much more to the doctor than the patient—and the causes of that problem lie in the Upper Left, not the Upper Right.

Integral Business is rapidly becoming more widespread as business-people themselves realize that everything from leadership to HR (human resource) functions to marketing depends on the psychograph (or the overall AQAL Kosmic Address) of the individuals engaged and targeted. Marketing an orange product in green terms will spell disaster, as will an amber product in orange terms. Figure 15.2 gives a very simplified 4-quadrant diagram of perhaps the four most common business and management theories now in existence and the quadrant from which they each typically originate. The venerable "Theory X" focuses on an "objective, scientific, behavioral" approach to individuals and their behavior, relying heavily on reinforcement ("carrot and stick") and objective "quality control" (in other words, pure Upper Right quadrant). "Theory Y," on the other hand, focuses on *interior* psychological factors and their needs and values, including things like emotional intelligence and Maslow's needs hierarchy (the Upper Left quadrant). For example, individuals at Maslow's "safety needs" (red altitude in the needs line) will work primarily for the salary, for the money; individuals at "self-actualization needs" (green/teal altitude) place *meaning* considerably above money, and want a meaningful workplace resonating with personal values and purposes more than any other feature. "Theory Y" focuses on all these interior factors in an individual, and has a phenomenal success rate in lowering absenteeism, the number of sick days, and health costs, and in increasing customer satisfaction and overall profit (one survey showed that, over the past fifteen years, the S&P Index went up 157 percent, whereas companies including Theory Y–type approaches went up a staggering 1,646 percent).[6] Theory Y approaches are clearly onto something important. "Cultural management" approaches, on the other hand, which deal predominantly with the Lower Left, became all the rage as postmodernism swept into prominence, stressing that an organization's culture (its shared values, goals, aims, and purposes) is the single most important thing that a manager should be managing, with all else stemming from how well that factor itself is handled. Peter Drucker, legendary leadership guru, reportedly said, "Culture eats strategy for breakfast"—in other words, it's more important than actual business plans for success!

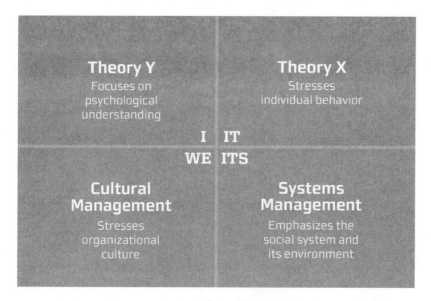

Figure 15.2. Integral Business.

It's estimated that up to 50 percent of a company's profit is dependent upon its culture—important indeed. And, for the last major management theory, "systems management" (which focuses on the Lower Right) is still one of the most widely used management philosophies now in existence, which treats the organization as a functionally unified system, the organizing of which is the single, largest, most influential element in the organization—fail at that, and the whole system collapses. But the systems approach, although it claims to be all-inclusive, actually includes few if any of the Left-hand quadrants—all of these are systematically ignored; the systems approach focuses almost exclusively on the Right-hand quadrants, highlighting the Lower Right of "functional fit." Open any book on systems theory, and you will find no discussion of morals, aesthetics, interior motivations and needs, intersubjective cultural factors, spirituality, shadow issues, art, music, and so forth—no 1st- or 2nd-person factors. However, in showing how all 3rd-person collective correlates (Lower Right) are indeed interwoven into vast systems of interrelated dynamic processes, systems theory shows, by implication, anyway, the interwoven, interconnected nature of all existence, while it actually works with those exterior, interobjective, collective, 3rd-person plural systems—which are an absolutely crucial component and "one-fourth" (the Lower Right) of the overall story.

Of course, Integral approaches to business—increasingly more widespread—simply asked the question "Aren't all of those factors present, and don't all of them therefore contribute to the success of a functioning organization?" The answer, of course, is a resounding "Yes," and as obvious as that is, it was only as individuals in authority in businesses began to make that "monumental leap of meaning" to 2nd tier that this "Yes" became functionally obvious—and seriously put into play. Integral Business and Leadership (and its correlates such as "Conscious Capitalism," although a fair amount of it is still green) is now one of the leading ventures at the most-advanced edge of business theory and practice.

In fact, well-known and highly respected developmentalist Robert Kegan, of Harvard University, refers to these leading-edge businesses as "DDOs"—"deliberately developmental organizations"—organizations that give interior development, in the individual and the group, the same priority as business development itself. He and his colleagues actually use the 4-quadrant Integral Framework to help businesses determine if they are being truly comprehensive and fully encompassing DDOs. Robert Kegan and Lisa Laskow Lahey write:

> Our colleague Ken Wilber has created a four-box model, which has been a valuable heuristic for a more comprehensive view of any complicated psychosocial phenomenon. . . .
> . . . The four-box heuristic invites people who are thinking about moving in the direction of a DDO to keep their eyes on all four boxes, what Wilber refers to as an "integral," or more adequately holistic, perspective.[7]

Later, they comment:

> The four-box model is another way of getting at the necessity to keep your eye on several realms at once as a setting—and its leadership—moves, however far it will, toward being a DDO. . . .
> A fledgling DDO must watch out for a tendency to hold on to only some, but not all, of these dimensions.[8]

Of course, an "Integral 4-quadrant approach" means including the major elements in each quadrant, too. A truly Integral Business, or

Integral Capitalism, takes into account the full range of elements in the overall AQAL Matrix. This includes, to point out an obvious one, encouraging Waking Up practices in the workplace, as incongruous as this might initially sound. But the simple practice of mindfulness, for example, can be brought into any activity in the business space and will not only sharpen and clarify the business practice itself, but also further the individual's spiritual path of Waking Up. This is indicative of a practice common to all forms of Integral Spirituality—namely, an active searching for ways that one's spiritual-awareness practice can be brought into virtually all areas of one's life—professional, personal, work, relationships, play—so one is, in effect, "a monk in the world." "Integral Awareness" is a mindfulness-like, mirror-mind alertness that is brought to bear on all areas of one's life, based on an AQAL composite map, in essence turning one's life into an unbroken series of flow states.

The 1-2-3 of Spirit

So what has all this "quadrant stuff" to do with spirituality, specifically? It's important because Spirit, too, can be viewed through these three or four major perspectives—and throughout history, it has been. The significant point is that all "Big 3" (or four) approaches to Spirit have different truths, different practices, different goals, and all three (or four) need to be included in any comprehensive spirituality. And all of these different perspectives are already in existence (although constantly at war with each other)! Recall that the 4 quadrants are four different dimension-perspectives of the same occasion, and that means that we have four different dimension/views—all equally real and important—of Spirit itself. But, like so many other disciplines, many spiritual systems get caught in "quadrant absolutism" and choose just one quadrant and then claim that Spirit in that quadrant alone is real, devastating other genuinely important dimensions of Spirit. Often this had dire consequences for individuals who stepped over that line.

Here's a quick example: In the Middle Ages, the Catholic Church allowed only conceptions of God in 2nd person—a great Thou; anybody who spoke of God in 1st person—as if they had experienced a Supreme Identity with God, so that their own 1st-person "I" (or "I-I") was one with Spirit—was straightforwardly accused of heresy (the *only* human who was allowed to have had a real experience of God in 1st person was Jesus of Nazareth). Thus, if they didn't repent—or often, even if they did—they were almost always drowned or burned at the stake. The Christian mystics—St. John of the Cross, St. Teresa, Meister Eckhart, the Victorine mystics—were always walking this terribly thin line, being careful not to express their own 1st-person experiences in anything but finely shaded 2nd-person terms. Eckhart stepped over the line; although he wasn't condemned, his theses were; Giordano Bruno, on the other hand, after a decade of torture at the hands of the Inquisition—remarkably, without recanting—was simply burned at the stake. A similar fate, in the Muslim world, met al-Hallaj for his "I am Truth!"

So, let me give some prominent examples of all three perspectives of Spirit (and, if you would, try to see the validity of each of them). Spirit in 3rd person is Spirit looked at objectively, as in the Great Web of Life, or Indra's Net (or something like "Gaia"). This is a very popular view in the modern and postmodern world (wherever spirituality is taken seriously and not confused with a merely Mythic-literal religion). It is behind everything from the Universe Story to Gaiacentric to "ecocentric" views. It is often combined with systems theory (which also tends to focus on collective exteriors, or the Lower Right). But it's a (partially) true perspective because it represents the objective dimensions of Spirit—objective dimensions that, however partial, do indeed exist and need to be included. Seeing Spirit as a Great Web of Life—with all beings, indeed all things, constituting inseparable strands in that remarkable Web—reminds us that Spirit is not just an interior realization or personal awareness but a concretely existing total manifest world that embraces each and every one of us, and, in fact, all sentient beings altogether, in a vast, mutually interdependent, mutually tetra-enacting, mutually evolving and dynamic network, a communion of all being in glorious grandeur and breathtaking wonder. Just look at it! A sense of exquisite Kosmic wonder is an appropriate response to this dimension of Spirit (perhaps start with the Grand Canyon or that stunning photo of the earth taken by the astronauts on the moon). The wonder of it!

Spirit in 2nd person is Spirit conceived as a Great Thou or Great Intelligence, the universe as a living, breathing, vital Reality, with which you can have a living relationship. This view can be seen in everything from many theistic traditions (whose "theism" can run the gamut from childish Mythic-literal views to actual, authentic subtle, or even causal, state realizations) to Guru Yoga, where the guru himself or herself—a present breathing "thou"—is seen as a living embodiment of Spirit in direct relationship with the student. It is also a reminder that ultimate Reality will always be, in some ways, a Great Mystery, a Great Other, a Great Openness. It is Spirit as disclosed in Martin Buber's beautiful notion of God as an I-Thou relationship, realized in gratitude and service. Metaphorically, Spirit is infinite Being and radiant Intelligence—and a Being with Intelligence is a Person, and in that metaphorical sense, Spirit in 2nd person is that dimension of Spirit that can be approached in a personal, living relationship, an I-Thou relationship. "Conversations with God" are possible whenever the Heart opens to the Voice of the Ultimate, consents to the Presence of the Divine, and listens in all humility and openness. Remembering Nagarjuna's lessons, these are ultimately just metaphors for Spirit—but then so is the Great Web of Life, Being-Consciousness-Bliss, Love, Total System, or any other quality or positive characterization that we can think of. Spirit in 1st person or the great "I" (or "I-I," which we will discuss next), Spirit in 2nd person (or Great Thou), and Spirit in 3rd person (or Great It) are all reminders that Spirit can be found as the Ground and Nature of *all dimensions* in the Kosmos—of all 4 quadrants. And to the extent that we visualize, imagine, or characterize Spirit, we need to include all available perspectives and dimensions, starting with the 4 quadrants or the Big 3—God as "I," God as "We (I-Thou)," and God as "It." God in 2nd person simply reminds us that Spirit can be found in every relationship that we humans have, and that every conversation we have is the sincerest form of worship—the "miracle of We."

Now imagine that Intelligence—which gave rise to the Big Bang, evolved into atoms and molecules and cells and living organisms, exploded throughout the heavens from supernovas to star dust, gave rise to Magic and Mythic and Rational and Pluralistic and Integral realms of culture, and pulses in each raindrop, shines in every moonbeam, cascades in every snowflake, and breathes as the Life of every sentient being—is now looking directly out of your eyes, touching this page with your fingers, listening with your ears, feeling with your senses, observing through your very Awareness. This is Spirit in 1st person,

Spirit as your one and only True Self, the same and only Spirit looking out of the eyes of each and every sentient being alive, the same True Self (there is only one in the entire Kosmos) beating in the Heart and riding the Breath of every being in existence. The very sense in you of I AMness is the same "Before Abraham was, I AM," the same I AMness prior even to the Big Bang, the same I AMness that never enters the stream of time and thus is found only in the timeless Now and hence is Unborn and Undying, Uncreate and Unmade, Unformed and Unlimited, the same I AMness that is the Self and Spirit of the entire Kosmos, even until the ends of the worlds. And may I introduce you? This is your Real Self.

We've seen some simple ways that you can find this Real Self very quickly: right now, simply be aware of what you feel is your self—your typical, ordinary, everyday self—simply be aware of it. But as you do so, notice that there are actually two selves involved. There is the self you are aware of—you're this tall, you weigh this much, you have this job, you're in this relationship, you're interested in these ideas, like these movies, and so on. But then there is the Self that is actually aware of all those objects—there is the Observing Self, the Witness, the Seer, the Looker. And the Seer cannot itself be seen, any more than a tongue can taste itself or an eye can see itself. If, in attempting to find the true Seer, you see anything, *that's just another object*; it's not a true subject, not a Real Self, not the true Seer. This Observing Self, or Real Seer, can never be seen as an object. As you look for the Real Seer, the true Witnessing Self, realizing that it's "neti, neti" ("not this, not that": "I see objects—mountains, trees, houses, cars—but I am not those objects; I have sensations, but I am not those sensations; I have feelings, but I am not those feelings; I have thoughts, but I am not those thoughts"), not any object that can be seen but *the Seer itself*—as you look for that, all you will experience is a sense of Freedom, of Release, of Openness, of Liberation—liberation from an identity with a bunch of small finite limited objects. This small objective self, which can be seen and felt, isn't even a real self, a real Subject, but is just a bunch of objects that you have mistakenly identified with. It is this case of *mistaken identity*—an identity with the skin-encapsulated ego, the separate-self sense, the self-contraction, instead of the open, infinite, free, liberated, empty Self-Awareness—that is the ultimate cause of all suffering, fear, angst, torment, turmoil, torture, terror. Patanjali (the codifier of yoga) defined ignorance (being unEnlightened) as "the identification of the Seer with the instruments of seeing." Or, quite simply, as Philosophia said to Boethius in his distress, "You have forgotten who you are."

And who you are is pure Spirit in 1st person: pure Consciousness without an object; the pure Subject, or Self, aware of small subjects and objects (what Zen master Shibayama calls "Absolute Subjectivity"—the pure empty Subject that can never be made an object); or as Madhyamaka-Yogachara has it, pure unqualifiable Awareness as pure radical Emptiness, or ultimate Freedom, Liberation, Release— open, transparent, naked, radiant, luminous, infinite, timeless, eternal, without boundary, separation, limitation, lack, want, desire, or fear. And where is this True Self? It's what's reading this page right now, hearing all these background noises, aware of this room, and looking out at this entire wondrous world, which is simply a texture of its own self-liberated nature. It's the same I AMness you can feel *right now*; the same I AMness you felt last week, and last month, and last year. In fact, it is the same I AMness of ten years ago, one hundred years ago, a million years ago, a billion years ago, prior even to the Big Bang. Existing only in the timeless Now, 100 percent of it is fully present at every point of time, beginninglessly, endlessly. It's the only experience you have that never ends or changes.

It takes no effort to realize this ever-present Awareness. Right now, without making any effort at all, you spontaneously hear sounds around you, naturally see the various sights arising, effortlessly feel the numerous feelings cascading through your body, spontaneously notice the many thoughts arising and racing across your mind. Your natural, effortless, spontaneous, ever-present Awareness, easily and with no exertion or force on your part, is readily aware of all of that. Your own sense of pure silent spacious Awareness behind all thoughts and feelings, your own ever-present I AMness, arises constantly and easily in the midst of manifestation and registers with no effort on your part at all. Simply sit back and let it all happen; let spontaneous Awareness arise *just as it is*. If the ego arises, let it arise, as a part of the texture of the total Painting of All That Is. If thoughts arise, let them arise, as part of the texture of the total Painting of All That Is. If feelings arise— positive or negative—let them arise, as a part of the texture of the total

Painting of All That Is. Thus, we noted, this ever-present Awareness is not hard to attain but impossible to avoid. This is the "always already" Enlightened mind that is your deepest Reality and truest Self and ultimate Spirit—fully present, right here, right now, always and everlastingly. The ultimate question is not how can I attain this enlightened mind, but am I ever actually without it? It is the you that you already *know* you are (right now!—you *already* know or feel yourself, right?)— and *that* is the *already* Enlightened mind. Right now, right here, in that fundamental Is-ness or Suchness that you feel—the simple feeling of Being—is the fully Awakened, timeless-Now Self, the 100 percent Enlightened mind. You have always known it (if not always admitted it). This is the awesome, enormous, and final secret of the Paths of the Great Liberation. As Ramana Maharshi put it:

> There is neither creation nor destruction,
> Neither destiny nor freewill,
> Neither path nor achievement;
> This is the final truth.

Spirit in 1st person, a Great "I" (or "I-I"), is as important as Spirit in 2nd person, a Great Thou, and Spirit in 3rd person, a Great It (such as the Great Web of Life). The ultimate infinite Spirit or Godhead manifests itself as an "I-I" (as well as countless "I's" in all sentient beings), and sees itself as "I-I" looking at itself in countless others as "You" (each of which has an "I-I") and also as a background "It," or objective dimension, arising in all directions. And your ultimate You (its Ground as infinite unlimited Spirit as Such) is the Thusness or ISness of all of them. Yet wars have been fought over which of these is the real Spirit; hundreds of thousands burned at the stake; millions killed in Crusades arguing its finer points. An Integral approach, of course, insists that all three or four of them are equally real, equally important, equally to be honored, awakened, realized, and included. The 1-2-3 of Spirit is also, from a slightly different angle, Buddha (the ultimate "I-I"), Sangha (the ultimate We), and Dharma (the ultimate It, or Thusness).

The 4 quadrants, or the 1-2-3 of Spirit, is a simple reminder of the many different forms these fundamental perspectives come in (secular to spiritual, profane to sacred) and a reminder to find room for all of them.

Developmental Lines (including Multiple Intelligences)

With regard to overall development, we have been discussing primarily general levels (structure-rungs) and states (with their realms). But a crucial point is that what is actually growing and moving through the various *levels* of development are the specific *lines* of development. The "levels" that we have been discussing are the generalized degrees of development—or "altitude"—of the various lines, what all of them have in common as a measure of the degree of growth and development that they have undergone. The notion that various developmental lines all proceed through the same basic developmental levels is a view fairly specific to Integral Metatheory, but a general scan of the various lines definitely suggests this. (Integral Metatheory is virtually the only developmental model, or metamodel, that is seriously interested in *all* of the various developmental models and how they all fit together, and it considers them more or less as they already are, without drastically altering any of them. Most models simply focus on their own line and don't pay much attention to how that line relates to all the others, whereas they are all formally included in a metatheory such as Integral's.) If you put all the various developmental models with their particular developmental lines (and their line's specific stages) next to each other and look at all of them together (as in figures 6.1 and 6.2), there is an unmistakable similarity across lines as their stages undergo increasing development. For example, the following all have an unmistakably similar "feel" to them—and, indeed, Integral Metatheory puts them all at amber altitude: various aspects of concrete operational cognition (Piaget), the conventional stages of moral development (Kohlberg), the conformist stages of ego development (Loevinger), the belongingness needs of motivational hierarchy (Maslow), the diplomat stage of action-inquiry (Torbert), the multiplicity stages of self-outlook (Perry), the sociocentric stage (Graves), the 3rd order of consciousness (Kegan), the representational system of skill theory (Fischer). "Altitude" is a concept that Integral Metatheory uses to represent the underlying "togetherness" of human being/awareness. It's like ten paths all going up the mountain, where each path has a very different view of the surrounding world (it's a "different line"), but for any position along one path, there is a position at the same altitude on each of the others. Positions on the path can all *share* the same degree of *altitude*—all can be said to be at 4,000 feet, or 6,000 feet, or 8,500 feet. The "levels of altitude"—each major one is assigned a different color—are represented by the vertical scale in, for example, figures 6.1 and 6.2.

The levels of altitude by themselves do not exist anywhere; what exists are specific developmental lines going through their own specific levels/stages, and those levels represent, in every case, a particular level of altitude (just as in the example, each of the particular stages in those specific lines can be referred to as at the "amber altitude" in their line). So we could use the technically specific name of the particular level in a given line (such as "concrete operational" for Piaget's cognition, or "conformist" for Loevinger's ego development, or "belongingness" for Maslow's needs/motivation hierarchy), but we could also simply say "amber cognition," "amber ego development," or "amber needs." This allows us to discuss development *in general* using stage/levels of altitude (as we have been doing), while realizing that the actual specifics will vary in precise detail from line to line.

And what of the various lines themselves—why are they even there? It appears that, in the course of evolution, as existence itself presented humans with many different, particular problems, humans evolved specific intelligences to deal with each of those major types of problems—a type of specialization that allowed humans to be much more successful in their living and problem solving than using a "one-size-fits-all" type of generalized intelligence. Life itself presented humans with a series of fundamental questions, and humans evolved specific intelligences to help answer each one. Table 2 lists some of the more common developmental lines (or "multiple intelligences") and the basic life questions that they have evolved to handle.

One of the important things to remember with regard to developmental lines is that the self-sense (using 1st-person terms) or the self-system (using 3rd-person terms) always has a dual center of gravity—every experience is experienced by a structure in a state (for example, speaking generally, amber/subtle, or turquoise/nondual, and so on). This is true, of course, of each developmental line or multiple intelligence.[9] Since levels do not exist apart from lines, the dual center of gravity, with reference to structures, refers to the *average level* of development of all lines; *or* it is sometimes used to refer specifically to the level of development of the self-line (which is the focal point of consciousness in an individual, and around which, generally, the other

Table 2. Lines (multiple intelligences) and life questions

Line	Life question	Typical researcher
Cognitive	What am I aware of?	Piaget, Kegan
Self	Who am I?	Loevinger
Values	What is significant to me?	Graves, Spiral Dynamics
Morals	What should I do?	Kohlberg, Gilligan
Interpersonal	How should we interact?	Selman, Perry
Spiritual	What is of ultimate concern?	Fowler, Wigglesworth
Needs	What do I need?	Maslow
Kinesthetic	How best to physically do this?	Gardner
Emotional	How do I feel about this?	Goleman
Aesthetic	What is attractive to me?	Housen
Linguistic	How best to word this?	Vygotsky

lines are arrayed). If we want to be specific, we can represent which line we are referring to as "cognitive amber/causal," or "emotional orange/subtle," or "aesthetic teal/nondual," and so on. Since individuals often use several lines simultaneously, they can all be listed; for example, cognitive orange, interpersonal amber, emotional red/subtle, which is just a detailed elaboration of the dual center of gravity (where the structure components of the dual center are presented in a "psychographic" fashion—that is, showing various lines at their specific levels). Notice that when we do so, all of the lines tend to be operating in the same state. The reason why is that states, generally (but not always), are exclusive—you can't be drunk and sober at the same time, or hypnogogic and wide awake simultaneously. Even if you lucid dream, you cannot be in a subtle dream sleep state *and* aware of the surrounding gross-physical world at the same time. So whatever major state the self-system is in, at any given time, will also tend to be the state that the lines that are active will likewise be in.

Individuals could be activating different multiple intelligences when they experience a particular altitude (for example, at a teal level, the individual could be activating cognitive intelligence, or emotional intelligence, or aesthetic intelligence, or moral intelligence, and so on). And likewise—and this becomes truly important in spiritual development—individuals could be emphasizing a particular multiple intelligence (or a combination of them) as they pass through the subtle state-stage, the causal state-stage, the witnessing state-stage, and so on. Since structures (or levels in particular lines) are responsible for *how experience is interpreted*, the structure/levels *as they actually appear in particular lines* will largely determine how those various states are experienced. Somebody experiencing the subtle state-stage using cognitive intelligence will have a significantly different experience than somebody who experiences the same subtle state-stage using aesthetic intelligence or moral intelligence.[10]

The traditions have a general notion of this important fact in that they usually distinguish several different types of paths, yanas, or yogas in general. In the Eastern traditions, for example, there is bhakti yoga (the yoga of devotional love, emphasizing emotional intelligence), jnana yoga (the yoga of the discriminating intellect, emphasizing cognitive intelligence), karma yoga (the yoga of physical action, emphasizing kinesthetic intelligence), Kundalini yoga (the yoga emphasizing subtle energy activation, emphasizing the spectrum of subtle energies in the Upper Right), hatha yoga (the yoga of physical body postures, emphasizing somatic intelligence), Raja yoga (the yoga of subtle energy combined with discriminating intellect, or prana and jnana, emphasizing cognitive intelligence and the subtle-energy spectrum).

Each of those paths still fully recognizes the general spectrum of state-stage development (from gross to subtle to causal to turiya to turiyatita), but the specific flavors of those stages, as well as specific insights and details, vary considerably from type of path to type of path (that is, from different line or multiple intelligence to different line). It behooves us to pay much more attention to the various ramifications of the fact that individuals are progressing through the general state-stages of meditative development, using primarily a particular multiple intelligence or a small number of them. Persons on these different paths experience the state-stages in noticeably different ways. Notice that individuals today are *already* facing this situation as they undergo meditative and contemplative development, since they are already approaching their specific path through one or more of a dozen or so multiple intelligences—this is already happening! A student who is fluent primarily in emotional intelligence and interpersonal intelligence will have a very hard time indeed with a school that emphasizes primarily cognitive intelligence.

Just as there is often a mismatch in levels between a student and a particular teacher or school, so there is likely to be a mismatch in lines (or different sets of multiple intelligences being primarily drawn on by each of them). This is something that any truly Integral, or Fourth-Turning, Spirituality would want to pay close attention to.

Just as each individual has a particular Kosmic Address—a specific combination of elements indicating where he or she is located in the overall AQAL Matrix, so each particular spiritual system *has its own generalized Kosmic Address*—its own mix of elements of the AQAL Matrix (for example, it generally relies on a particular quadrant; operates from, on average, a certain level of structure-altitude; draws on a particular set of lines or multiple intelligences; aims for a specific highest state-stage; and so on). The closer the student's address is to that of the school and path that he or she is following, the better the results, by far, that can be expected. The tendency till now has been to simply assume that any given spiritual path is right for anybody who wants to try it; but the more we look at all the various elements of a person's AQAL configuration—as well as the various elements in a particular spiritual path's AQAL configuration—the more we see the vast range of possibilities, and particularly the vast range of possible discrepancies and dissonances that can occur, and are already occurring, whether we know it or not, track it or not, want it or not, take it into account or not.

During the one to two thousand years from the founding of most spiritual systems up to today, there has been such a tremendous increase in information about the human system in general that it becomes negligent, in some cases almost criminally negligent, to keep overlooking and failing to include at least some of this information. One of the central aims of an Integral Spirituality and Fourth Turning would be, indeed, to begin redressing this unfortunate state of affairs.

Nothing less than our own *full* Awakening is at stake.

16

Miscellaneous Elements

I want to repeat that just because an element is characterized as "miscellaneous" doesn't mean it is less important or less worthy of consideration. Just the opposite, in some cases. In at least some instances, miscellaneous elements can be thought of as "very important, if core elements have already been addressed." However, with some exceptions, few of the following elements constitute, in themselves, fundamental areas of a Kosmic ontology (the way quadrants, levels, lines, and states do, for example). In some cases, these are simply additions or subdivisions within one of the five main AQAL elements (quadrants, levels, lines, states, and types). "Energy medicine" and "subtle energies," for example, are subdivisions within the Upper Right quadrant; "We practices" are exercises within the Lower Left quadrant; "accelerated development approaches" address state-stage development in the Upper Left quadrant; and so on.

So with that, let's get started.

Typologies

Typologies themselves are, in many ways, a core element in the AQAL recommendations for a Fourth Turning or Integral Spirituality ("types" are, after all, one of the five main elements in the "all quadrants, all levels, all lines, all states, all types" of AQAL). And while typologies in general are core, there are so many different typologies—hundreds, even thousands of them—that there isn't any single one or two or three that would necessarily always be included in any Integral Spirituality (or in any Integral approach in general). Rather, when addressing any particular area or topic, an individual can include one or more various typologies that are particularly appropriate for that area or topic. I've found that few typologies are ones that should without question be included in all Integral approaches to all topics (unlike, say, quadrants or levels). But that said, specific typologies offer incredibly important forms of information and data that can be profoundly significant in specific approaches, and so definitely need to be taken with utmost seriousness.

Briefly, *typologies*, from the simple, such as masculine/feminine, to the more complex, such as the Myers-Briggs or the Enneagram, are classification schemes that consist of characteristics that essentially remain the same throughout structure development and state development. If you are a five on the Enneagram, for example, you tend to remain a five at archaic, magic, mythic, rational, pluralistic, and integral. Typologies have become increasingly important the more we have seen how dramatically different the various types really are. For example, an Enneagram type 4 or type 7 really does see different worlds, have different characteristics, drives, needs, defenses, and fears. It becomes obvious that various spiritual systems, growth technologies, therapeutic techniques, and so on, essentially reflect the characteristics of the personality type of the founder or founders, and they work well for those who possess the same type but not as well for others, unless a specifically Integral approach is taken where the teaching is interpreted—differently and appropriately—according to how it appears for each type (not to mention how it appears at each level, to each line, and in each state), and that such a multiple-aware teaching is made available to all potential students.

Typologies can get complicated, and if you take into account the sheer number of them, attempting to include all of them is overwhelming, virtually impossible. The best one can do, for a particular area, is to select one or two typologies that are well suited, documented, and oft-used, having demonstrated their usefulness time and again. I have two I particularly favor in general—the simple masculine/feminine and the sophisticated Enneagram.

Various versions of the differences between masculine and feminine are as old as humanity itself. Many—most—of these are culturally molded and culture specific, although some very general features often show up cross-culturally (largely due to the biological universals found in the Upper Right quadrant), such as that men on average have a greater upper-body strength and women give birth and lactate. Simple as those different traits are, researchers such as feminist Janet Chafetz have demonstrated, using systems theory, that those two simple biological features alone are enough to be parlayed into significantly different sex roles in most cultures, with males tending toward the public/productive sphere and females the private/reproductive sphere, and these different roles are in many cases not due to any patriarchal oppression but to simple biology (according to Chafetz).

What became oppressive about those fixed roles—*equally oppressive* to men and women—was the tying of cultural roles to biological givens long past the time that biological factors were actually the primary constituents of cultural roles. For example, in agrarian societies—over 90 percent of which were "patriarchal"—women who practiced farming with a heavy animal-drawn plow had significantly higher rates of miscarriage; it was to their Darwinian advantage not to participate in that productive sphere; and such "muscular" tasks anyway fell generally to men, with their greater average upper-body strength. With industrialization, however, machines began doing the labor on nature that previously human bodies—usually male bodies—were forced to do. But men were not thereby released from their roles as production-sphere providers, breadwinners, "success objects," and such, and instead simply began, under the stress, to abandon existence (that is, die) a full decade sooner than women. Men alone were required to fight and die for their country; over 95 percent of work-related deaths were suffered by men; if somebody insulted a man's wife, he was expected to duel to the death for her honor—all this leading some scholars to refer to men in such cultures as "the disposable sex."

Meanwhile, most early liberal feminists, fearing that biology is destiny (which in some cases it had become—again, for men as much as for women), denied the importance, or even existence, of biological differences, believing, literally, that not all men but all humans were born equal. Legal, political, and educational equality is one thing, and a noble ideal; but overall functional equality doesn't make much sense, and flies in the face of most peoples' experience (for example, in most cultures, men, on average, are simply better at some things than women, such as tasks requiring physical body strength, and women, on average, are better at some things than men, such as acting with emotional sensitivity and communicating nonaggressively). Modern research into hormonal differences, as further examples, shows that testosterone, prevalent in men, is intimately connected with sex and aggression (testosterone's two main drives are "fuck it" or "kill it"), and oxytocin, prevalent in females, is a powerful "relationship drug," developed by evolution most likely to ensure a strong mother-infant bond, and giving women on average a much greater emotional sensitivity. I often joke that women recognize something like eighteen different degrees and types of emotion; men recognize two—forward and reverse.

But an Integral approach is not frightened by biological differences. They pertain to only one quadrant—the exterior-individual (the Upper Right or "it" quadrant), which can be modified, molded, or even reversed by the other quadrants—social systems, cultural worldviews, and psychospiritual orientations. But taking the biological quadrant into account, let's us at least acknowledge male and female evolutionary differences and their different needs, strengths, weaknesses, and preferences, as recognized by modern and postmodern researchers, starting most famously, perhaps, with Carol Gilligan. As we saw, Gilligan's work suggested that men tend to reason in terms of autonomy, rights, agency, justice, and ranking; and women in terms of relationship, care, responsibility, communion, and nonranking (with individual men and women capable of any of those across the whole spectrum). Gilligan also tracked what she referred to as the four major stages of female moral growth—going through *selfish* (egocentric), *care* (ethnocentric), *universal care* (worldcentric), and *integrated* (integral)—no surprise there!

This plays out in spirituality in many, many different ways. Men, for example, are comfortable sitting in a fixed posture, motionless, observing their interior experiences for hours in a detached, emotionless, unflinching fashion——the same motionless, emotionless, fixed stance that they have used all the way back to their time as hunters, waiting hours patiently for their prey to arrive. Women are often more comfortable with meditation in motion, moving and dancing, expressing their emotions as bhakti or loving relationship. Of course, both sexes can do either, it's just a matter of being aware of these native inclinations and taking them into account where appropriate. And, of course, these differences show up regularly in relationships, with men wrestling with their wandering sexual profligacy and women lamenting "the man's fear of commitment"—his drive mostly to agency, not so much communion; whereas women often tend to define themselves in terms of their relationships, and if taken too far, they "melt down" into fusion with their relationships, with little or no autonomy, agency, or self-power, totally defining themselves in the terms of the relationships that they have.

As a result of the Enlightenment and the Industrial Revolution, for the first time in history, the cultural gender roles in the Lower Left became decoupled from a necessary relationship with the biological givens in the Upper Right. Also, morally, in the Upper Left, individuals became open to a postconventional, worldcentric morality—a universal care—that unlike the previous ethnocentric and egocentric forms, treated all individuals fairly, regardless of race, color, sex, or creed. These developments combined to stimulate the various liberation movements of minorities, from slaves (the abolition of slavery) to women (the rise of feminism). White males, however, were not liberated from their traditional roles as "success objects," and hence continued dying a decade sooner than females. They were not decoupled from their Upper Right "greater upper-body strength" identities but instead were expected to apply that "greater strength" to all of their activities in whatever area, thus adopting a stance of aggressive, competitive, power over their fellows, which began infecting such things as the newly emergent capitalism with everything from cronyism to rampant greed.

By taking an Integral view of sex and gender, with at least its 4 major perspectives (quadrants) on any "biological givens," we can recognize that biological givens are only "one-fourth," so to speak, of the story. Although they should be fully taken into account, they should also be "transcended and included." We should recognize and account for them and then move beyond them and recognize attitudes and capacities of people that are not defined merely by their biological correlates. Nor should they be defined by previous eras' role identities, either, because they were almost always grounded in less-adequate stages of human development—archaic and magic and mythic—many elements of which can still be found in today's gender roles. Those earlier elements are still present to various degrees in today's cultures because everybody begins their development at square one and moves through each of those earlier stages, not all of which are navigated cleanly and without fixations, and thus they continue to influence how one sees one's present sex and gender. Taking all these factors into account is one of the central projects of the leading edge of Integral Sex and Gender Studies today.

Postmodern women *as well as* men need to continue working to free their presently available cultural roles from both their previous, especially mythic ethnocentric cultural roles, and their biological givens.[1] Both of these sources of role identities, however appropriate they might have been in earlier epochs, are completely out of date when it comes to the postmodern (and especially integral) world and men and women's place in it. We're on the verge of an entirely new world of relationships between men and women, based more on an Integral Tantra than on the mythic traditional View. One problem that continues to snarl feminists working on these more "partnership" cultures is what they feel is a need to find an earlier culture where these partnership relationships were widespread, so as to demonstrate that such relationships are possible. But these relationships are not something that existed yesterday in any widespread or sophisticated fashion; they are rather emergents, entirely new forms of relationship that come primarily from worldcentric and higher levels (just as Gilligan's "integrated" stage is a new and higher and completely emergent reality, not something being dug up from an earlier stage).

As for the Enneagram, it is a sophisticated typology consisting of nine basic types, numbered from 1 to 9, whose names describe them well: (1) the perfectionist, (2) the giver, (3) the performer, (4) the romantic, (5) the observer, (6) the questioner, (7) the epicure, (8) the protector, and (9) the mediator. You can see from the names how different each type is, and you can probably guess that they each have different healthy and unhealthy manifestations, different strengths and weaknesses, different functional and dysfunctional emotions and defenses, and different spiritual preferences and capacities, among others. Some spiritual practices work well with some types; in other cases, they are positively damaging. Helen Palmer does a particularly fine job working with the Enneagram (as does Russ Hudson), but there are many terrific books on the subject. Again, one doesn't have to be a profound master of the typology; just understand some of its basic features and realize their general significance. The importance of such typologies is that they remind us that a "one size fits all" approach to virtually anything—certainly spirituality—usually results in a grave limitation on, and even a distortion of, the teachings attempting to be conveyed. A truly comprehensive or integral approach is just a little more sophisticated than that.

Polarity Therapy

The original form of Polarity Therapy was introduced in the United States a half-century or so ago by Dr. Randolph Stone, and was heavily influenced by various Eastern healing traditions, such as Ayurveda (the ancient Hindu medicinal system) and subtle energy schools. Polarity Therapy maintains that the human organism has a fundamental subtle energy system that, through its various phases of attraction, repulsion, and neutrality, is responsible (via the "downward causation" of involution) for virtually all forms of physical illness. By adjusting the imbalances in this energy field, diseases could be fundamentally ameliorated or even cured.

From there, polarity therapy has recently expanded into a wide range of "therapeutic" approaches that essentially deal with the basic human proclivity to perceive the world in a series of opposites, dualities, or polarities—representing some of the basic dualities in the manifest, finite, relative world itself—and the general tendency to latch on to one-half of the duality, or polarity, and reject, deny, or otherwise downplay the other half. Now the way polarity therapy is generally practiced, these polarities do not include pairs of flat-out opposites—such as strong versus weak, health versus illness, confident versus insecure, kind versus mean, life versus death, and so on. Those are assumed to be essentially separate and nonintegrable. Rather polarity therapy addresses polarities and dualities of essentially positive but still opposite qualities such as ordered versus flexible, reflection versus action, stability versus change, knower versus learner, advocating versus inquiry, consistent versus adaptable, thinking versus doing, individual action versus collaboration, exploration versus security, and so on. The idea is that both halves of these polarities have positive and useful aspects, so instead of latching on to just one-half and denying or downplaying the other half, a both/and attitude and appropriate exercises for balancing these polarities can lead to a dramatic increase in overall capacity, skills, awareness, and inclusiveness.

Sophisticated versions of polarity therapy point out that each major level of consciousness and development tends to have a set of polarities that are particularly common at that stage. Thus, red is open to doing versus thinking, acting versus planning, selfish versus caring, and it tends to highly favor the first half of each of those polarities. Amber often has "us" versus "them," compliance versus assertion, fitting in versus standing out, stability versus change, with amber again strongly favoring the first term. Orange is open to planned versus spontaneous, linear versus chaotic, objective versus subjective, excellent versus average, achievement versus entitlement, with orange heavily preferring the first term. With green, there is a tendency to horizontal versus vertical, contextual versus standardized, pluralistic versus universal, interpretation versus given, with green, again, tending heavily to the first term. At 2nd tier, there is a widespread existence of whole versus part, system versus component, complex versus simple, comprehensive versus specific.

The general idea of polarity therapy is for the individual to carefully explore both the unacknowledged drawbacks, or weaknesses, of their favorite pole, and the unacknowledged advantages, or strengths, of the dismissed pole. (You can certainly pursue this type of exercise in your journal.) Instead of relying on given lists of complementary opposites and polarities from experts, spend some time thinking of a list for yourself. As you look at how you view the world, what do you consider your strengths, your positives, your cherished values, your deepest purpose? Write these out, and then think of what some of their opposite—but also valuable—poles might be. Write those down as well. And then practice exercising each pole—practice putting both into action, or if you don't practice putting them both in action, then imagine yourself doing so (really own *both* halves or both poles), and also practice finding the balance point between them. How can you begin to incorporate both halves of the polarity into your awareness and your behavior? Soften your attachment to your favorite pole, and increase your appreciation of your devalued pole. When this is done correctly, there is a feeling of "freeing" or "liberating" awareness from a previous limitation and contraction, and a new opening or expansiveness clearly comes into being. You have found a broader, deeper, wider space that has enlarged your skill set considerably and shown you a "bigger" you.

This "freeing" or "liberating" is even stronger with the next type of polarity therapy. If the first form of polarity therapy, which is the one that is almost exclusively used, might be called the "shallow version" (and that is not meant in a derogatory fashion—it's a very useful version!—but simply in a technically descriptive fashion), then the second version might be called "deep polarity therapy." Whereas Shallow Polarity deals with the relative finite realm and relative truth, Deep Polarity deals with ultimate realities and ultimate Truth. In effect, Deep Polarity deals with all opposites, even the ones not approached by Shallow Polarity—including exactly the apparently irreconcilable opposites such as life versus death, pleasure versus pain, transcendental versus immanent, infinite versus finite, eternal versus temporal, true versus false, reality versus appearance, one versus many, good versus evil, unmanifest versus manifest.

The balancing point of Shallow Polarity is some finite activity or quality that unites and synthesizes the two relative poles being considered, such as thinking versus doing is united in "types of activity"; stability versus change is united in "approaches to variation"; horizontal versus vertical is brought together in "general directions"; knower versus learner is united in "approaches to evidence"; consistent versus adaptable is brought together in "responses to challenges"; and so on. Uniting the relative poles explicitly or implicitly introduces you to a higher, broader, wider class of phenomena—an expansion of relative awareness and an increase in relative embrace (not to mention an actual expansion of one's skill set).

But the balancing point of Deep Polarity is Big Mind itself—either the pure Witnessing of the total Painting of All That Is, or the even deeper "headless" unity state with the entire Painting Itself. Both of those stances are free of every (or in the case of the Witness, virtually every) possible duality and polarity in existence. When you are aware of, and hold on to, a particular positive pole, such as life, or truth, or the good, you then bring up its opposite and hold it in mind as well, such as death, falsehood, and evil. Then you hold both these deeply positive and deeply negative poles in mind, side by side, and see both of them as equal and important aspects of the Total Painting of Manifestation. These opposites are the light and shade without which the Painting itself couldn't be seen at all ("life" would have no meaning if there wasn't also something called "death"; "truth" would have no meaning at all if "falsehood" didn't also exist; "health" makes no sense whatsoever without "illness"). The seemingly "bad" parts of all dualities (death, pain, illness, falsity, badness) are actually the dark shades and shadows without which the Painting of Life itself—and all its good "light" areas—would be utterly impossible. A Painting of all positives—all good, all light, all pleasure, all satisfaction, all lovable—would be no Painting at all, but something like the North Pole in the midst of a blanketing snowfall: a white background blur stretching featurelessly in all directions. The manifest universe is a universe of opposites, of dualities, of polarities; we can no more actually separate and isolate their poles than we can get all ups and no downs, all ins and no outs, all lefts and no rights gathered together in one spot. Can't be done. What can be done is to drop not just the negative pole, while chasing and desiring the positive, but both poles simultaneously, which opens us to the pure mirror mind of utter equanimity and all-inclusive, all-pervading, all-embracing nondual unity consciousness, a oneness with the Total Painting of everything that is arising in our Field of Awareness right now—*everything*.

The tendency of the self-contraction, of the separate-self sense, is to contract its awareness and subtly withdraw it from some content, no matter how seemingly insignificant, via a Primordial Avoidance—a turning away, a looking away, and hence a moving away from the Altogetherness of the All That Is, the Total Painting of Everything, right now, and right now, and right now. We shut our eyes to something that is arising, some feeling that doesn't seem right, some thought that doesn't feel good, some desire that seems unacceptable, some inclination that seems dangerous, some sensation that is simply uncomfortable. And in that first, single, simple contraction, lies the entire misery of humankind.

With that self-contracting motion, we think that the solution to our life's problems lies in gathering all the positive elements together, enhancing them, and cherishing them, while downplaying, denying, and dismissing any and all negatives. While that has some relevance in the realm of relative truth, we're now discussing ultimate Truth, where, as the Upanishads remind us, the aim is to be "free of the pairs"—that is, free of the pairs of opposites, *all* of them, positive and negative. If we approach the opposites separately and believe that—as a popular song used to put it, "You got to ac-cen-tu-ate the positive, e-lim-inate the negative"—this gives us exactly half of reality, half of the Total Painting of all manifestation, devastating the very nature of the manifest world itself. The problem with that "half approach" is that we think that it is going to give us radical, ultimate, absolute Truth, whereas it gives us only a broken, fragmented, decimated relative reality and world—a manifest toy completely broken right as we take it out of the box. Instead, we get "radical, ultimate, absolute Truth" by finding what is behind the opposites altogether, not just by grabbing the positives and ditching the negatives, but by dropping them both and finding a total Wholeness that goes staggeringly beyond what either half alone can offer.

And that Wholeness, a oneness with the Total Painting of All That Is, a oneness with the entire manifest universe, begins as we drop any conceptualization of Reality that is dualistic, that draws on half of a pair of opposites, any opposites, and relax attention into a radical oneness with everything arising moment to moment—*absolutely everything*—with no looking away, no turning away, no moving away. We simply allow every single thing and event in our Awareness to fully, completely, and spontaneously arise *just as it is*: inside and outside, pleasant and unpleasant, yours and theirs, us and them, me and thee, good and bad, likable and horrible, tensed and flowing—*everything*, just as it is. Allow it *all* to unfold, right now, with no looking away, turning away, or moving away.

This happens only when you recognize, simply but profoundly, that this is *already* happening. Look through your mind right now and try to spot that awareness that has been aware of whatever is arising as it arises. There is already a level of Awareness in you that is spontaneously and effortlessly aware of everything that is happening right now. Simply notice that there is already a background awareness, effortlessly present, of the objects arising in the world around you. (That's present now, yes?) You already feel the feelings in your body. (When you become aware of your feelings, you are actually becoming aware of an already present awareness of your feelings; that is, when you notice a feeling that you hadn't been paying attention to, notice that there previously was an ongoing awareness of that feeling; you simply weren't giving it any attention.) You already are aware of thoughts in your mind. (Simply notice that you are already noticing thoughts, even when you become absentminded. When a stretch of absentmindedness happens, there is no self-conscious awareness, definitely, but thoughts are self-aware as they continue to arise. Thoughts always know that they are present when they are, and you know this when you snap out of an absentminded state and yet still can remember some aspects of what you were thinking during your absentmindedness. How could that happen if there wasn't some sort of awareness the whole time? If there was no awareness, you'd simply have a total blackout—but you don't, because "unreflexive awareness" of thoughts continues, which is exactly why they can be remembered.) So as you introspect right now, simply and gently notice that, in your present awareness, objects in the world are already arising, spontaneously and effortlessly; feelings in your body are already arising, spontaneously and effortlessly; thoughts are already arising in your mind, spontaneously and effortlessly.

In other words, there is a present, ongoing, spontaneous *Awareness*, which is taking in everything around it, and then there is *attention*, which focuses and contracts awareness to specific, isolated things or events, and we tend to track that attention but forget the background ever-present Awareness. But that ever-present Awareness is the pure Witness in each of us, the true Seer, the Real Self, and it is never not present. And its object isn't a single thing or event or phenomenon, but the Total Painting of All That Is—that's what Awareness is aware of! So we can practice being "one with the Total Painting of Life" by simply noticing that this background Witnessing awareness is already evenly aware of all of the elements in this Total Painting. All you have to do, if you want to take it a step further, is allow that already present Looker to dissolve into everything it is Looking at, so that Subject and all objects, Awareness and all phenomena, Consciousness and all things, "you in here" and "all that out there" disappear into the ever-present "headless" Wholeness that is their Ground and Suchness (and the Total Painting turns into that big blue pancake and falls on your headless unity condition).

"The everyday mind, just that is the Tao," says Zen, and it means that literally. Your ever-present, already functioning, spontaneous mind is 100 percent of the Enlightened mind—right now! Not 95 percent of it, but 100 percent of it.

Practice this "everyday nonduality," this background all-encompassing Awareness, with any particular object or phenomenon arising in your Awareness. Take any big desire or wish that you have—a desire to love your mate, to get that promotion, to achieve a great accomplishment, to be fabulously rich, outrageously famous, inordinately adored—and then hold that desire along with its negative and destroying opposite. Alongside your love of your mate, entertain an equally strong hatred of your mate. Simply imagine the love; then imagine an equal hatred and simply hold that feeling; then place them right next to each other and hold them together—you'll find that the only way you can do that is to step back into Awareness, drop an identity with both of them, and simply Witness them as equal objects in your Awareness. You can let these "dual objects" arise either in a pure Witnessing, or Mirror Mind, equanimity—evenly Witnessing them, observing them both with Absolute Subjectivity or the Real Seer or true Witness—or you can hold these "dual objects" in your "headless" unity Field of All Space, where they will both arise as textures, as feelings, of your own Being/Awareness. Either way, you are identified with neither one of them alone (either you are equally dis-identified with both in the Witnessing state, or equally identified with both and the rest of the Total Painting in the "headless" unity state). Either is fine for this exercise, truly; practice whichever one comes more easily to you at this time.

Take another important item in your life, say, your desire to do well at your job, get the promotion, achieve widely recognized success. Then imagine actively not caring for the job or how you do at it, an utter indifference to your work; if pushed into it, an actual loathing. Feel one; then feel the other; then hold them both in your Awareness (either as Witness or as headless unity Field). Do this with at least a half-dozen major and important areas, values, goals, or desires in your life. (Enter these in your journal if you have one.) In each case, rest in the resultant equanimity of the Opening, or Clearing, "free of the pairs," and feel a nondual Spirit saturate your being. I AMness is "neti, neti"—not this opposite, not that opposite, but the ever-present, All-Pervading, All-Embracing, All-Encompassing Presence—with no looking away, turning away, or moving away. It is a profoundly relaxed, evenly hovering Awareness, which allows every single thing and event to arise just as it is, exactly as it is.

Notice the profound intimacy between both poles of these opposites, polarities, and dualities—they are literally mutually defining, mutually arising, mutually interdependent. The opposites lean on each other. The whole secret of the manifest realm of samsara—of illusion, suffering, sin, separation—lies in this hidden relation of all opposites to each other: when seen as separate and isolatable, with one-half capable of being pursued and the other half shunned, the manifest world is not seen as One and Whole; it is seen as Half and Partial. To say the same thing another way, it is not seen as a Total Painting manifestation of Spirit, with each and every phenomena, or brushstroke, being an ornament of Spirit, just as it is; rather, it is seen as existing entirely on its own, with no Ground and no Source and no Goal and no Suchness. Samsara seen apart from Spirit (apart from nirvana) degenerates into samsara as illusion, suffering, separation; whereas the very same samsara, seen as inseparable from Spirit (and nirvana)—Form inseparable from Emptiness—is samsara as the radiant, glorious expression of an Emptiness in a creatively exuberant and overflowing thrill.

So this ever-present, always aware, perfectly Witnessing (or even "headlessly" nondual) Awareness is the resolution point of Deep Polarity. It is the pure, infinite, ultimate Spirit, the Creatrix of All Reality, as it looks through your eyes and hears with your ears and touches with your hands, fully and completely present right now, Witnessing with its own Mirror Mind the entire Painting of the Manifest World that Spirit itself—your own deepest Condition—has created, *all of it*. By allowing "All of It" into your Awareness, you align your being with the Being of the Kosmos, in all directions and all at times, Unborn and Undying, Uncreate and Unmade, Fully Free and Fully Full, your own Original Face, "free of the pairs" because it embraces them all.

Subtle Energy Dimensions

Several schools of Buddhism have an explicit *subtle energy dimension*, particularly the tantric schools (such as Tibetan Buddhism). Others, such as Zen and Theravada, virtually never mention subtle energies at all. The great Zen Master Hakuin (who left behind eighty-three fully transmitted students, who together revitalized and reorganized Japanese Zen) tells of an event that he endured that was severely disturbing—namely, during meditation, he began to develop intense headaches, which eventually became so severe that they completely disrupted his meditation. His descriptions of these headaches make it almost certain that they were caused by a subtle-energy (kundalini) dysfunction generated, possibly, by the intensity of his meditation, which he performed without a proper knowledge of how to handle the subtle energy that it was releasing (since, in Zen, as noted, there is literally nothing about subtle energies—nothing about the chakras, their channels, meridians, or nadis, or exercises to deal with them, and so forth). So Hakuin set off on a journey to visit various mountain sages, looking for a cure. He finally found an old man who, versed in Taoist techniques, told Hakuin to coordinate his breath with an image of butter melting on the top of his head and running down the entire length of his body, taking all headache pain and suffering with it. Hakuin did so, and within weeks his headaches had vanished.

I have noted that states, being relatively independent—not only from structures but from other states—can be focused on relatively independently and to some degree can be cultivated independently. This is why Adi Da could categorize the world's meditative traditions into "The Path of Yogis," "The Path of Saints," and "The Path of Sages," depending on which state/realm they focused on—respectively, the gross, subtle, or causal/nondual. The Path of Yogis focuses on physical exercises and gross manipulations, or gross-reflecting states, working particularly with energy in the first six "gross-reflecting" chakras and then as it passes into more purely subtle realms, although sophisticated schools can continue beyond that. The Path of Saints often ignores the first six chakras *entirely* and starts with the seventh chakra and the four to seven subtle chakras at and beyond the crown—hence Saints are often pictured with haloes of light and luminosity surrounding their heads—the whole subtle luminous realm. Even more radical, the Path of Sages often skips all the gross and subtle realms and chakras and goes directly for the unmanifest or causal/nondual state, not even mentioning chakras or subtle energies, but aiming for the selfless Self condition directly. This is what Zen does with the witnessing/nondual state—"the Path of Sages"—it almost entirely avoids working with any subtle dimensions and subtle energies.[2] (Of course, these dimension/realms eventually become integrated in overall consciousness, since the integrating drive of consciousness itself will eventually and automatically reach down and embrace these lower state-realms, but if they are not engaged in a conscientious and deliberate fashion, this will often occur haphazardly and implicitly and often poorly.) This is primarily why, as I noted, there is in formal Zen teaching nothing explicitly said about the chakras, subtle energies, and meridians, or nadis, and no specific exercises or practices for evoking and developing these energies (a growth that therefore occurs "on its own," implicitly and often haphazardly). Nothing could speak more strongly for the relative independence of states than the existence of powerful meditative schools, like Zen, that leave out entire states and realms (such as subtle energy) and yet still develop powerful mystical state experiences that accurately reflect higher state-realms.[3]

The advice here, of course, is to include subtle energy awareness explicitly and directly in any spiritual system. It doesn't have to be exhaustive; but it does have to be enough to prevent someone like Hakuin, one of the three or four greatest Zen masters in history, from having to traipse through the mountains looking for some basic information that his own training should have routinely provided.

Nine Subtle Energy Systems

Donna Eden, in *Energy Medicine*, suggests that there are at least nine different subtle energy systems in the human body-mind.[4] This is one of the more inclusive systems that I've seen, although how they are integrated and fit with each other could be better detailed. In my opinion, there is an overall "altitude," or spectrum of degree of subtlety, that applies to all of these individual subtle energy systems. You can, and should, create an energy "psychograph" in the Upper Right quadrant, with the various subtle mass-energy "lines" in the Upper Right graphed against the developmental "levels" of energy altitude that use the *same* rainbow altitude of colors one finds running through all 4 quadrants. For each energy *at each altitude*, show the correlative structures and states of consciousness in the Upper Left as well as the correlatives in all the other quadrants as well, while also fully showing the rainbow levels of subtle energies in the Upper Right. The "rainbow altitude" of colors that I'm referring to here is the same rainbow that is shown in, for example, figures 6.1 and 6.2. It is also the same rainbow "tilt" of Eros found in *all* quadrants toward greater and greater consciousness and complexity, the "tilt" of the Kosmos itself that drives evolution to more and more Truth, Goodness, and Beauty in its overall unfoldings, which makes evolution indeed, as Jantsch defined it, "self-organization through self-transcendence," the ceaseless drive, à la Ilya Prigogine, of "order out of chaos," which marks that relentless drive of "creative advance into novelty"—all the ways that this universe is absolutely winding up, not simply winding down.[5] I'll provide a very brief summary of these different subtle energy systems or "lines" here:

1. *The meridians* are the body's subtle energy transportation system—a network of some fourteen pathways running throughout the body and connecting all organs and organic systems, as well as all the "acupuncture points" on the body's surface.

2. *The chakras* are major energy stations or centers, running up the body's spine from the root chakra at the base of the spine to the chakra at the crown of the head (and beyond). The chakras particularly organize Kundalini energy, or the subtle energy directly related to spirituality.

3. *The aura* is an energy shell surrounding the body, composed primarily of prana or bio-energy. Traditionally includes the etheric and astral bands of subtle energy.

4. *The electrics* is a basic energy grid connecting all subtle energy systems and consisting of what can be described as either the densest of the subtle energies or the subtlest of the physical energies. It's not a separate system itself—like the meridians or chakras—but the actual "electromagnetic" (or "densest") part of all the subtle energy systems.

5. *The Celtic Weave*, like the electrics, is not a system in itself but a part of all subtle energy systems, drawing them all together and allowing transfer of information between them.

6. *The basic grid* is the foundational grid supporting all of the other subtle energy systems, much like the steel frame on a skyscraper.

7. *The five rhythms*, more commonly known as the "five elements" (water, wood, fire, earth, and metal) but originally and perhaps most basically refer to (as the literal Chinese translation has it) "five walks"

or "five rhythms," represent five different fundamental patterns that subtle energies can take.

8. *The triple warmer* is a system of energies that aggressively organizes the body's energies to fight any invaders.

9. *The radiant circuits* is, in a sense, the opposite of the triple warmer; it organizes all the body's energies for positive health, well-being, and cooperation.

To understand the functioning of these subtle energy systems, recall the central function and activity of the involution/evolution (or Efflux/Reflux) movement: Spirit goes out of itself to produce causal awareness (Upper Left) and causal mass-energy (Upper Right), which go out of themselves to produce subtle awareness (Upper Left) and subtle mass-energy (Upper Right), which go out of themselves to produce gross/physical awareness (Upper Left) and gross/physical mass-energy (Upper Right). Dysfunctions on any higher level will, via the "downward causation" of involution/Efflux, be carried successively downward, producing the possibility, in turn, of dysfunctions in the soul, in the mind, in the bodily emotions, or—finally—in the physical body itself (and physical disease—cancer, heart disease, stroke, and so forth).

Subtle energies are, to speak of them in a narrower technical sense (that is, not all subtle energies generically from gross to nondual but those specifically lying *between* gross energies at the lower end and causal energies at the higher), those energies that are the exterior part of the specifically subtle domains themselves, those domains lying between the gross-physical and the causal. The subtle energies thus *support* emotions, mind, higher mind, and soul (as we saw with low, medium, and high subtle dimensions), and dysfunctions on any of those basic levels will be reflected in those subtle energies as a disturbance; and vice versa: specific subtle-energy disturbances can underlie and cause dysfunctions in any of those basic level-rungs (emotions, mind, higher mind, and soul), which in turn—via a further involutionary downward causation—can result in gross/physical dysfunctions and diseases. Subtle energies, in both the broad sense, as energies anywhere in the spectrum of energies running from gross to subtle to causal to nondual, or in the narrow technical sense of energies in just the subtle realm itself, can be used to both diagnose and help treat dysfunctions in any of the major states and structures, since all of them have a "mind" (consciousness, Upper Left) and a "body" (mass-energy, Upper Right) component.

To address specifically that broader meaning, "subtle energies" is often used to refer to *any* and *all* of the levels in any of the mass-energy systems in the human organism, from gross energy (strong and weak nuclear, electromagnetic, and gravitational forces) to subtle energy per se (in the subtle realms themselves) to causal energy (in the causal realms) to witnessing/nondual (in turiyatita). The same involutionary/evolutionary currents are at work in all of them, as I mentioned. Western medicine has been examining the correlation between gross energies (particularly electromagnetic) and various bodily dysfunctions, such as broken bones and their healing (which demonstrably involve electromagnetic fields). More recently, it has begun examining genuine subtle energies (such as in acupuncture, which has proven results that do not easily fit any orthodox medical models), and occasionally it is at least aware of causal energies (almost always associated with accompanying spiritual states). These correlations exist because any interior dimension on the "spectrum of consciousness" (Upper Left) has some sort of corresponding level in an exterior/objective dimension on the "spectrum of mass-energy" (Upper Right), a spectrum that itself (as with the interior, indeed all 4 quadrants) has a vertical holarchy (through the rainbow altitude spectrum) of lower to higher and yet higher levels of complexity (gross to subtle to causal to nondual). Every event in every quadrant has a correlative corresponding event in the Upper Right spectrum of mass-energy, and Integral Metatheory includes all of them without reducing any one to the others.

It is not necessary that any inclusive spiritual system be technically and fully aware of all of the details of all of these subtle energy systems (unless, of course, the particular school itself specializes in subtle energy practices). However, since most of these systems are very close to state phenomena, and since premodern cultures were, on balance, much more aware of state experiences and their anatomy than are the modern or postmodern worlds, some of the "true but partial" components that any Integral system would want to take from premodern cultures is their knowledge of states in general—including states of consciousness and their meditation state-stages (or Vantage Points), and subtle energy systems and their detailed anatomy and physiology, if you will. Exercising the subtle energy bodies is an intrinsic component of the body-mind-Spirit aspects of any Integral Life Practice (which, under the practice of "body," specifically includes practices of all major bodies—gross, subtle, and causal). The degree of detail that one should bring to subtle energy practice is similar to what I recommended for the shadow—namely, an exhaustively and totally inclusive practice of every known detail is not necessary (unless, again, the school itself specializes in subtle energy practice, as do some Tibetan schools, for example), but a general and at least introductory awareness of subtle energy is quite helpful and occasionally mandatory if actual disruptions develop. This introductory knowledge includes a simple recognition of the types of energy and shadows, their symptoms, and—importantly—where one can go for more detailed help should one need it. As is often the case with these types of topics, the Internet is as good a place as any to begin with.

Network Sciences

Up until recently, the most advanced developments in the systems sciences in the Upper Right and Lower Right quadrants have generally been in what is known as "the complexity sciences." Individuals such as Edgar Morin have pointed to the complexity sciences (including chaos and complexity theories) as being the most "leading edge" developments in these areas.[6] But, starting about ten years ago, even more sophisticated approaches to "systems" have been appearing under the name "network sciences." These have made many new and profound additions to our understanding of the interwoven (if still exterior) nature of phenomena. This, of course, is not to exclude chaos and complexity theories (for zone 8), or social autopoietic ("self-creating") systems and game theory (for zone 7)—any Integral Theory operates on a "transcend and include" basis, and so those theories would be included in any Integral understanding of the Right-hand quadrants. But network sciences take a fresh and profound look at the very nature of complex systems, nexus-agencies, and mass-energy-information interconnections. Network sciences are a centrally important component of any genuine Integral Metatheory.

In Integral Metatheory, the way complex systems and networks work is that, during tetra-evolution, various types of (for lack of a better name) "morphogenetic networks" tetra-evolve and are laid down as Kosmic habits or Kosmic grooves (if these can be said to be "stored" anywhere, it would be in the causal storehouse consciousness). "Interobjective" (collective exterior) networks particularly represent the Lower Right quadrant and exert their influence, as a Kosmic habit, via that quadrant in any holon.

During tetra-evolution, network patterns emerge, based on forces and pressures in all 4 quadrants, and are laid down as Kosmic habits, Kosmic grooves, or Kosmic memories. These Kosmic network morphogenetic patterns move, via downward causation during each moment-to-moment involutionary movement, from causal into subtle and then gross realms, and hence govern and shape the form, structure, and pattern of each and every manifest phenomenon. As Rupert Sheldrake has consistently (and very rationally) continued to point out, the one item that conventional science has been so very bad at explaining is the form, pattern, or structure of manifest things and events. A long protein molecule, for example, can fold into literally thousands of different forms, and yet, once it folds into one form, all subsequent protein molecules of that type everywhere in the world will fold into the identical form. Where on earth is that network pattern carried? For Integral Theory, it is a Kosmic habit (preserved in the storehouse), and it influences every subsequent protein by a downward involutionary causation each and every moment.

Several different theories, including the older chaos and complexity theories, can be used to help elucidate the concept of an evolutionary/involutionary Kosmic habit (or more generally, help to explain the nature and function of the Lower Right quadrant of "functional fit" in all holons). But we now have an added theory of great sophistication, known generally as the network sciences, which adds a corresponding sophistication to understanding the nature and structure, in particular, of the Right-hand components of these Kosmic habits themselves. This is of primary significance for Integral Theory itself; but, insofar as any Fourth Turning or Integral Spirituality is involved, precisely because it includes the 4 quadrants (as part of its integration of science and religion), new breakthroughs in any of those quadrants have at least a secondary impact on spirituality. The emergence of the network sciences is one such breakthrough.

Accelerated Developmental Approaches

As the state-developmental nature of spiritual experiences—including Enlightenment and Awakening experience—has become more obvious in the past decade or two, approaches to spiritual Awakening have started to emerge that take advantage of this new understanding, and techniques have been developed that at least appear to dramatically accelerate spiritual state development. Two in particular might be mentioned as examples.

One is the "Big Mind Process" developed by Genpo Dennis Merzel Roshi, a senior dharma successor of Maezumi Roshi. Based in part on the Stones' Voice Dialogue Technique, Big Mind engages the practitioner in a series of dialogue investigations of various types of self—from the controller to the seeker to the wounded child to the protector. The dialogue simply proceeds with things like, "Let me speak to the controller," the teacher requests. "Who are you?" "I'm the controller," the student responds, as the controlling self comes to the fore. "What is your goal? What do you do? How do you operate? What do you want?" and so on might be a few of the questions asked and responded to. Then next up might be, "Let me speak to the wounded child," and so on, as up to a dozen different selves are called forth and dialogued with. At the end of an hour or so of this, the teacher says, "Let me speak to Big Mind." And in something like over 95 percent of the cases, the individual will have a direct, immediate, authentic experience of ultimate Nondual Awareness, or Big Mind. I have participated in this process several times, and seen it done many more, and I am always stunned at how effective and profound the process really is, introducing individuals to a genuine experience of the Awakened Mind, in however an introductory fashion.

Of course, the process can work, at least theoretically, because ultimate Nondual Awareness is literally ever present. Many schools of Self-Liberation work with "pointing-out instructions" that point directly to such ever-present Awareness and help the individual immediately recognize it (I've been doing the same thing throughout this book by pointing out ever-present Witnessing and "headless" unity consciousness). But Genpo was the first to try using voice dialogue to simply call on Big Mind—and he noticed that, almost without exception, it simply and immediately appears. Of course, one of the keys to this process is the previous dialoguing with all the "relative selves"—all those small, object selves that are merely relative and finite, and that aren't even a Real Subject or Real Self because they can be seen as an object. By dialoguing with all of them, those "subjects" are made object, and thus cease to be directly identified with, making room for an experience of one's True Self or Big Mind. Big Mind is not seen as an object so much as experienced as a nondual Presence or Atmosphere. When asked questions like "Is there an inside or outside to Big Mind?" everybody answers, "No." "Is time present?" "Does Big Mind come or go?" "Do you see it out there?" are all answered, "No." By spending a good deal of time calling forth and talking to the small, relative, finite, object selves, consciousness itself more and more dis-identifies with them, seeing them as an object, and thus comes closer and closer to the pure Witness, or pure Observing Self, or Absolute Subjectivity per se, and thus is more and more open to falling into ever-present nondual Big Mind itself in a moment's notice.

Once Big Mind is called forth, Genpo walks individuals through a whole series of Zen koan-like questions, of increasing difficulty and subtlety, and the vast majority of individuals stay right with Big Mind and give "accurate" answers, even to koans that normally take years and years to solve. As a Zen student myself for fifteen years, I have been absolutely flabbergasted at the ease, quickness, and accuracy that most people solve koans that took me years to crack. But I love this process, certainly as a terrific and quick-acting introduction to Nondual Awareness and the Awakened Mind. See Genpo's book, *Big Mind/Big Heart* for more on this.

A similarly accelerated Awakening process can be found in Mondo Zen, developed by Jun Po Roshi, senior dharma successor to Eido Roshi. Jun Po reduced Rinzai Zen's 1,700 koans to 13 particularly essential ones, and—similarly to the Big Mind Process—goes straight to the heart of the koans by directly dialoguing with the student about them, giving the student not only the questions but also the answers, if necessary. He then discusses the answers via dialogue to further elicit and evoke the correct responses from pure, vast, deep, ever-present, Empty Awareness. ("Mondo," by the way, means "conversation" in Japanese.) Each successive Mondo koan points out a different aspect of this ever-present Awakened Mind, so that after a two- to three-hour session, even beginners have a profound introduction to this ultimate

Consciousness and true Suchness nature. See Keith Martin-Smith, *A Heart Blown Open*.[7]

What is amazing about both Big Mind Process and Mondo Zen is that they take seriously the idea that ultimate Nondual Awareness, or Awakened Mind, is 100 percent present in each and every moment of an individual's existence. There is literally no time at which the Awakened Mind is not always already fully present and fully obvious to you (and every other individual alive). "Too simple to believe" is a common Tibetan saying about this, and that's exactly right. Solving koans—or discovering God—is often so difficult not because the task itself is so hard but because it's so simple. It's so simple that it's incredibly easy to miss. As I hope some of the previous exercises that we've gone through in this book have pointed out, you are literally looking directly out of the fully Self-Liberated and 100 percent Awakened Mind right now, and all that is required is the simple recognition of this always already truth. It's the utter obviousness of it that makes it so difficult to see. You are staring *right at it* all the time, no exceptions, and so that ever-present experience tends to be one that sinks into the background and ceases to be noticed—but that certainly doesn't mean it isn't there; it means that you just have to look carefully and specifically for this, your Original Face. Both of these processes (Big Mind and Mondo Zen) take that truth at full face value, and simply proceed with that assumption, and in both cases, a genuine introductory glimmer of ultimate Nondual Awareness is virtually always the result.

These types of accelerated meditative processes will become more and more prevalent, particularly as it dawns on people that the last great Turning in almost any religion was well over a thousand years ago—we're well past the point where new approaches could have been introduced. Even the great, incredibly sophisticated nondual tantric schools (which, we've seen, some Buddhists already consider a Fourth Turning—opening the room for a Fifth) peaked in the eighth to the eleventh centuries CE, leaving some thousand years for new truths, new approaches, and new viewpoints to become possible. An Integral approach to Buddhism will certainly include many of these new developments. Both Genpo and Jun Po are very sympathetic to the AQAL Integral approach to spirituality as I'm outlining it, and several other Buddhist teachers, including Doshin (senior student of Jun Po), Diane Musho Hamilton (first graduate of Big Mind Process), and Patrick

Sweeney (Trungpa Rinpoche's direct-lineage successor), specifically use the AQAL Framework in their own teachings. Numerous other teachers, in other religions—including a good number in Christianity itself—are also using AQAL Integral approaches in their own variety of spiritual teaching. Of course, many other more inclusive approaches to spirituality are emerging, largely due, in part, to the direct impact that the emergence of Integral levels of consciousness are having on individuals' awareness everywhere. This is an incredibly hopeful and optimistic development.

The Technological Tie-In

There are at this time major revolutions occurring, or about to occur, in all 4 quadrants, something that has never happened in human history. I'll simply mention several of them, and then comment particularly on the computer intelligence (and Artificial Intelligence) revolution, especially as it relates to a religion of tomorrow.

We see profoundly accelerated changes occurring in the Lower Right quadrant, including what might be thought of as "negative revolutions," the foremost being climate change, which now seems to be accelerating faster than all previous predictions forecast. In order to avoid genuine disaster, it will require not only a rapid switch to non-fossil-fuel energy, but also the discovery of effective forms of carbon sequestration to remove existing carbon from the atmosphere. (I give us a fifty-fifty chance of avoiding serious catastrophe.) But the world is also on the brink, in the Lower Right, of profound discoveries relating to the actual structures of major global systems including economic systems (now acknowledged to intrinsically and steadily favor the wealthy); political systems (toward more truly equitable frameworks); financial systems (away from debt gambling to actual financial support); scientific systems (toward communal and communicative research protocols); legal systems (in ways not yet understood, of finding approaches that allow developmental depth to enter the system, instead of the flatland approach now dominant); and the complete remaking of virtually every major human institution and activity due to stunning technological advances headed this way. (Each of those Lower Right changes will have corresponding changes in the other quadrants, in addition to their own revolutions.)

In the Upper Right, stunning changes are particularly occurring in computer intelligence and Artificial Intelligence (AI), genomics (the study of the nature and behavior of DNA and nucleic codes), nanotechnology (the technology of the very small), robotics (the functioning of robots in virtually all areas of human activity), and cyborg-enhanced humans (individual organisms that are part human, part machine). Human history has always been an amalgam of human brain-powered creations (Left Hand consciousness and culture) and technological artifacts (Right Hand material and machine creations)—but never before has the technological started to run so far ahead of the human that many authorities maintain that within a few decades, machine intelligence and technology will so far surpass human intelligence and capacity that they will constitute, in effect, their own new species, very possibly exposing humans to extinction. (I also give this a fifty-fifty possibility.)

But there are indeed profound revolutions occurring in the Left Hand quadrants as well, and this book itself has been tracking several of them—stunning advances in our understanding of Growing Up, Waking Up, and Showing Up, understanding that has, in the last few decades, equaled or surpassed all that was understood of these areas in all of our prior history. The very emergence of 2nd-tier Integral levels, in both consciousness (Upper Left) and culture (Lower Left), constitutes something of a consciousness Singularity fully equal in profound implications to those of the proposed technological Singularity. Right now, humanity is in a desperate race between the 70 percent that remain at ethnocentric or lower levels, and the 30 percent or so at worldcentric and higher levels (with a special nod to the 5 percent now at Integral levels; watch for when that reaches the likely tipping point of 10 percent and the entire world's culture becomes background saturated with Integral values). As for that larger race (ethnocentric versus worldcentric), I also, seriously, give that a fifty-fifty chance of coming out in our favor. But to the extent that the ethnocentric levels win, we can look for significant increases in worldwide terrorism; foot-dragging on climate control; increased warfare between nations or subnations governed by fundamentalist factions; one or more nuclear incidents driven by ideological fanatics; continuing migration catastrophes as ethnocentric warlords keep up their battle cries; dramatically increased food shortages and famines as fundamentalist warfare detracts from effective agricultural activities; significant setbacks in women's rights world-wide; increased human trafficking; diminishment of human freedoms in general; increase in far-right political activity in the major developed countries; ideological zealots creating superviruses with likely one or more worldwide epidemics and millions dead; among literally dozens of other "us versus them" grimly dire actions and behaviors. In all of our disaster prediction scenarios, factors in the Right Hand quadrants are always focused on strongly, whereas these factors—stemming from the Left Hand quadrants—are almost completely ignored. We will likely come to regret this ignorance.

But my major point is that never, at any time in history, have there been this many fully revolutionary activities occurring in all quadrants all at once. It is a time the likes of which humanity has simply never, *ever*, seen. (And part of what makes them all so radically unique is the almost equal chance, which I keep putting at around fifty-fifty, that these revolutions could end up spelling either heaven or hell, depending on the quality of consciousness and culture that ends up controlling them, which is a factor almost never taken into account.)

As for machine intelligence and AI—and its connection with spirituality—this is an area where a potentially huge impact might be seen. It is already quite common, for example, to find brain-mind machines that, through various computer-generated means, help create specific brain-wave states (in the Upper Right) that then evoke correlative consciousness states (in the Upper Left). These brain waves are often set so that they match the major states of consciousness given by the meditation traditions, so that the evoked consciousness involves meditative and contemplative states. For example, the major states of waking (gross), dreaming (subtle), and deep dreamless sleep (causal) each have a signature brain-wave state (causal sleep: 0.1–4 Hertz; subtle dream: 4–8 Hertz; gross: 8–12 Hertz). By entraining brain-wave states at those frequencies, those meditative states of consciousness are correlatively evoked. These are very effective instruments for meditation, and research into them is continuing at a rapid pace.

The main drawback to all of this research (and AI in general) is that it is only investigating states, not also structures. Thus, individuals at egocentric and ethnocentric levels of structure in Growing Up can, in effect, plug into very high transpersonal states of Waking Up very quickly, which they will then interpret through their prejudiced ethnocentric viewpoints. This is not helping in that ethnocentric versus worldcentric race; it is hurting. What we desperately need are AI and machine intelligence researchers investigating the correlations in the Upper Right brain of the major Upper Left structures of consciousness (in other words, working not just with Waking Up but also with Growing Up). This type of feedback would be a profound breakthrough in developmental technologies that actually help get individuals into worldcentric and higher levels of consciousness—which would dramatically help in that specific consciousness race.

A major problem right now is that AI does not think the way that humans think (the same way that airplanes do not flap their wings when they fly). In fact, AI knows very little about how real human brains actually work; instead, it simply creates algorithms that give similar results to human thinking, and it uses those. But the reason— according to Integral Metatheory—that computer researchers do not understand human thinking is that they do not accurately understand its evolutionary constitution. That is, we have seen that, starting with the Big Bang, the Kosmos brought forth holon after holon, with each new and enduring holon "transcending and including" its predecessors. Further, each holon possessed at least some degree of "prehension" (or protoawareness). Thus, atomic protoawareness was taken up and included in molecular protoawareness; molecular protoawareness was taken up and included in cellular protoawareness; cellular protoawareness was taken up and included in organismic protoawareness. And from there, organismic protoawareness was taken up and included in increasingly complex and sophisticated structures with their own protoawareness and soon real awareness, all the way through the 6-to-8 major structures of human awareness, summating in the systemic teal or turquoise systems logic that the typical very smart machine intelligence and AI specialist uses as he or she investigates human thinking. But what they typically do is just skim off the top part of that 14-billion-year chain of hundreds of enfolded prehensions and only investigate the top layer of logical thinking, find algorithms that simulate that, and then try to get that to work, thinking it matches real human consciousness—and it does nothing of the sort, not even close. There are hundreds of layers of prehension, going all the way back to the Big Bang, that underlie every logical human thought in existence— and not one of those is included in the AI researchers' ideas about

608 | Elements of an Integral Spirituality

thinking. What is happening is that these researchers are creating a type of artificial thinking that is radically divorced from the rest of the Kosmos (whereas human thinking is in resonance with every level of existence produced by evolution from the very beginning, which is why human thought can indeed understand virtually any level of reality in existence—it is, in its own being, partially composed of those very levels, and their "minds" or prehensions all together summate in a human conscious thought, building on, and incorporating, all of them, and thus human thought is profoundly plugged into the Kosmos at all levels). AI, on the other hand, is an existential monster at this point; it has no resonance with the rest of existence at all; and this is a major reason that when this type of intelligence surpasses human intelligence, there is no reason that it would intrinsically feel any inherent sympathy with human thought and values, and thus would see no reason to keep humans around. This is why a great number of AI specialists increasingly believe that the creation of the first truly super-machine-intelligence will be the very last creation that the human species ever makes. (Yes, I give it fifty-fifty.)

But the general point for AI and spirituality is that if we focus on the creation of human-enhancing machine intelligence, instead of a simulated general artificial machine intelligence (capable of replacing humans), and then if we truly investigate the full range of human consciousness—including structures and not just states, as is now the case—then various forms of AI will very likely be viewed as indispensable and profoundly valuable adjuncts to human development, including human spiritual development. Verging on science fiction, we might even see things like the injection, into the human brain, of billions of nanotech transmitters plugged into the Cloud, in effect forming a new machine-intelligence-enhanced neocortex; and should the Cloud contain injunctions for accelerating the development of structures and states, we would see a true heaven on earth for virtually all human beings, since their brains would be plugged into a development-inducing system that results in a full Enlightenment for each. But in any event, entire branches of the religion of tomorrow would be devoted to machine intelligence and its spirituality-enhancing capacities for humans. Further, when it comes to the transhumanism belief—itself something of a default new religion in Silicon Valley—that humans will very soon be able to download their consciousness into machines and basically live forever, we will then have a much better answer than we do now to the question "Just which level of consciousness are you going to permanently download as your final and ultimate consciousness?" Today, the highest form of consciousness is generally taken by Silicon Valley to be some version of rationality; for the traditions, of course, that is actually some version of dukkha, suffering, sin, separation—do you really want to download that for all eternity? An everlasting, self-contracted, twisted form of inherent suffering? That's not a terrific heaven, if you think about it. Having a better map of consciousness would at least let us aim considerably higher, not a bad idea considering the stakes.

The Miracle of "We"

Another important technique, itself starting to get a fair amount of attention, is what is generally referred to as "We practices"—that is, serious group practices of group *as* groups, of groups taking up practices acting as a group, meant to evolve or transform or otherwise engage the entire group as a group entity. This is not just a group of individuals each doing an individual practice together, but a group practicing as a group itself. There is a common saying: "The next Buddha will be the Sangha (the group of Buddhist practitioners as a whole)." In some ways, this is nothing but the mouthing of a green platitude (inasmuch as, for some varieties of green, "individuality" itself is close to a sin, and only group, team, and collective activities are enthusiastically endorsed and actively engaged in). But in some cases, it is something much larger—it is the felt recognition that since there is already *an entirely new and higher type of "I" emerging at 2nd tier* (namely, inclusive, embracing, and Integral—and actively appreciating all previous stages of development, a historically unprecedented first, a genuine emergent novelty), then there will also be *an entirely new and higher type of "We" emerging as well*, made up of individuals at Integral and higher stages (simply because all phenomena have 4 quadrants, including an "I" and "We"—a higher "I" naturally goes with a higher "We"). What would this higher "We" be like? How can we engage it? What would it feel like? What practices specifically would help us contact this new and higher "We"?

One of the most astonishing, miraculous, stunning, and mysterious events in the entire Kosmos is that one being—let's say a human in this example—can actually reach a mutual understanding with another human being, that they can look each other in the eye and say, "I understand what you mean." The one and only Self of the Kosmos has illusorily "split" and "divided" itself into billions of individual selves, and two (or more) of those selves can, playing on the underlying unity between them, mutually resonate with and mutually understand each other. If you want to see evidence of Spirit, look no further than right here, in what I call "the miracle of the We." It's one thing for something to come from nothing; quite another for one of those somethings to look at another something and say, "I know what you mean." The ultimate One Mind showing up as two, and being able to establish that oneness through something like communication: what else is mutual understanding but a hidden reaffirmation of the singleness of Consciousness underlying the communication, a miracle if ever there was one, the miracle of We.

The "We" space is, of course, the Lower Left quadrant, the intersubjective domain, which I maintain goes all the way down, all the way up. What we find in human cultures is, in the Lower Left, a "layer cake" of holarchical dimensions of structure-Views in any situation where human beings congregate, work together, play together, or otherwise exist together. "Layer cake" (with reference to structures and Views, but it also applies to states and Vantage Points) means this: since every human is born at square 1 (the physiological rung and the Archaic View) and begins its growth and development from there, stage by stage by stage, each group or collective of humans consists of individuals at various stages of structure-View growth, who form a "layer cake" with various developmental strata (much like any geological formation, to switch metaphors, with the older layers at the bottom and the newer, higher levels at the top, and all sorts of developed levels in between, laid out in the chronological order in which they emerged). In most groups, there will therefore be a percentage of those at magenta Magic, a percentage at red Magic-Mythic, a percentage at amber Mythic, and then, depending on the group and its aims (and thus whom it attracts), possibly a percentage at orange Rational, a percentage at green Pluralistic, and a percentage at 2nd-tier Holistic/Integral.

In organizations, these layer cakes will often be predisposed and weighted to a particular stage (and thus possess a disproportionately thick layer at that level), depending on the job or the department or the area in which the individual works: so with on-the-floor or assembly line work, a greater percentage at amber Mythic (who excel at rote repetitive tasks); in middle management and sales, at orange Rational (who thrive on achievement, accomplishment, and success); in human resources and public relations, at green Pluralistic (whose "sensitive self" flourishes in helping and supporting customers); in upper management, at least a cognitive line at teal Holistic or turquoise Integral (or overall 2ⁿᵈ tier—the best of these often fit the descriptions of Jim Collins's "Fifth-Level Leaders" or Spiral Dynamics' "Spiral Wizards"). Elliott Jaques's work has documented the "layer cake" nature of most organizations, certainly when it comes to the level of cognitive development in people performing various jobs or tasks. His research indicates clearly that the greater the complexity of the task, the higher the level of cognitive development that one tends to find in individuals doing well (and thus succeeding) at that job. This is the "layer cake" in real action.

Often, the success of a company's culture depends upon (accidentally or intentionally) matching the individual who has a particular level of development with the job or office or task that especially draws on that specific level of development, so that the human skill set/aptitude and the complexity of the vertical job-task fit together nicely, matching *altitude* and *aptitude* (as in the preceding examples).

Many business consultants focus merely on "aptitude" and "skill" training to help business individuals become more successful—thus focusing only on the "horizontal" skill set of individuals and teaching them new behaviors or ways to refurbish their old skills to become more effective and more successful. But a newer class of business consultants also realize the profound importance not just of horizontal "aptitude" but also of vertical "altitude"—that is, the degree or level of consciousness possessed by the individual and thus the degree of complexity that individual can handle. And hence they focus, not just on teaching new skill sets (which focus on exterior behavior), but on practices that help individuals grow and evolve their altitude of consciousness (which focus on interiors: the level of their basic structures and Views). From Robert Kegan to Dave Logan to Dean Anderson to Stagen Associates to the Air Force Academy to—well, to many (rapidly increasing) numbers of others, who have taken due notice of the steadily increasing number of studies that show that the *degree or altitude of development* of a person is a crucial, and in many cases singularly indicative, determinant in the degree of his or her success in leadership.

There is also a small, but steadily increasing, number of consultants who realize the importance of states of consciousness in creative leadership. Otto Scharmer has developed a "U process" that actually draws on a very specific sequence of state capacities: it starts with the gross-realm problem, then moves to more creative subtle-realm ways of viewing it, then rests in causal formless creativity for a solution to arrive, then takes the initial form of the solution and fleshes it out by moving back into the subtle dimension, and then brings it into concrete life back in the gross-physical domain. When I pointed out that he was actually tapping into these states—the "U" in the "U Process" actually reflects that movement from gross to subtle to causal, which is the bottom of the "U," then back to subtle back to gross—and asked him if he agreed, he replied "100 percent." Increasing not only the degree of development in structures but also in states increases a person's capacity to handle more and more of Reality, thus increasing his or her capacities and talents in virtually any number of fields, which certainly includes leadership. As more and more people realize this, they will embed various practices to implement one or both of these growth sequences—in structures or states—in the organizational "layer cake" itself, ensuring both altitude and aptitude growth and development. (And we already saw the rapid growth of what Kegan calls "deliberately developmental organizations," which see business growth and employee growth as two aspects of a single ongoing process.)

The inclusion of the We-dimension as an inherent component of Reality in Integral Theory has meant that, virtually from the start, the We-dimension has been given special attention. One of the more recent movements in the worldwide Integral community has focused on the development of intensive practices and groups oriented especially toward common We-experiences and, to a certain degree, a common We-consciousness—although treading lightly is required here, since social holons do not possess an "I," or what Whitehead called a "dominant monad"; they possess instead a dominant mode of discourse or a dominant mode of resonance. When my dog gets up and moves across the room, 100 percent of its organs, cells, molecules, and atoms get right up and move with it; no group or society or organization has anywhere near that type of totalistic control, such that the governing mechanism of the group governs 100 percent of everything its members do. That's simply impossible. Rather, the governing "nexus"—or "nexus-agency"—of the group provides certain rules, values, guidelines, ethics, and semantics that influence, to one degree or another, its members. But there is no "super-I" that fully controls every member of the group. In other words, the relation of a member to a group is not the same as the relation of a cell to an organism, or a part to a machine—there is no "superorganism" or "Leviathan" to which all members are welded (and no social group, society, nation, and so forth, is a "big organism," because none of them have an "I" or dominant monad that is all-controlling). Rather, members are *partners* (not parts) in a network of intersubjective and interactive capacities, which governs some, not all, of the members' actions. We have to be careful here because there is a tendency to treat, for example, Gaia as a superorganism or super-I, whereas it is more like a song harmonizing its various members' notes, not a machine controlling all of its parts with perfect totalitarian control.

Thus, what we find in the real world—and in real groups, collectives, and "We's"—is a "layer cake" of different structures (and states) of development, with each layer containing a nexus-agency that exerts a significant influence on the members at that layer, and then a central cultural layer, or nexus-agency, which defines the group's overall characteristics and how the group officially defines itself (amber, orange, green, and so forth). This nexus-agency exerts a particularly strong influence on those members whose center of gravity is at the same basic level as the group's central level (and this set, or cluster, of individuals would, in most cases, be the cluster that we would expect to be the largest, since individuals are attracted to this particular group precisely because they share its particular value system and wish to participate in and advance it). Thus, to give an extremely simple example, take a fundamentalist church group. Given its likely Mythic-level View and characteristics, its "layer cake" will have a few individuals at Magic (who interpret the religion in Magic terms); a slightly higher percentage of individuals at Magic-Mythic (who interpret the religion in "PowerGods" terms); and the majority of individuals—probably close to 70 percent, 80 percent, even 90 percent—will have their structure center of gravity at Mythic-literal (the same as the group's central nexus), and thus that stratum of the "layer cake" will be particularly thick and influential; and finally, a smaller percentage at higher levels— a few at orange Rational, fewer still at green Pluralistic. Each of those layers will have (implicitly or explicitly) a nexus-agency that the members at that level tend to follow; and the social holon itself will have a central organizing level (in this case, Mythic-literal), which is the origin of a "dogma" nexus-agency, meant to govern all individuals who are members of that church's particular orthodox View of its religion. This "dogma" nexus-agency consists of the beliefs, values, ethics, worldviews, and semiotic meanings that are "kosher" for that church and are meant to be embraced by all those who identify themselves as members of that church (you are "in" the church when your religious thoughts are "internal" to the church's dogma nexus). The bulk of this "dogma" nexus-agency (in the Lower Left) will come from the deep structures of the Mythic-literal View; and of course will be strongly influenced by factors from the Upper Right (the actual behaviors that are allowed and that are banned or disallowed); the Lower Right (the actual physical forms and patterns of the church organization itself, including even things like the layout of the physical spaces used in worship); and the Upper Left (particularly the psychograph and character type of the "leader" of this particular congregation; and in general the "acceptable psychograph" that all members are expected to reflect). The particular features, or surface structures, of the dogmatic beliefs will include the church's actual version of the specific beliefs, stories, concepts, narratives, and notions of the particular religion itself at the Mythic-literal level of spiritual development, as interpreted through the idiosyncrasies (in all 4 quadrants) of this particular church and its leaders.

As individuals enter the topographical space in the AQAL Matrix that defines a particular religious service (for example, going to a Sunday church service), they will have their entire psychographic being-in-the-world temporarily merged, or conjoined, to one degree or another, with the church's sociograph (containing the ideal member's psychograph), and the nexus-agency of the resulting sociocultural holon will, for as long as the individual is in that topographical space, exert a strong (but not totalistic) governing influence on each individual's thoughts, feelings, ideas, awareness, and behavior.

What's interesting is that the members of this church, whose psychographs can shift significantly to fit with the overall dogmatic sociograph of the church itself while they are in its topographical space, will often find that a significantly different psychograph is activated when they are in different circumstances with different sociographs and different "layer cakes." Many scientists, for example, manage to segregate their religious and scientific views, and thus, while at their scientific job, will likely be in a social holon with a sociograph and "layer cake" that has the thickest layer of the cake at orange Rational (or higher), and thus they will, in that particular topographical space of the AQAL Matrix, resonate, not with their Mythic beliefs, but with their Rational scientific beliefs. The "layer cake" of the "We" at work is significantly different from the "layer cake" of the "We" when they are at church, and they manage to separate these different and contradictory beliefs, compartmentalizing their lives and handing each over to a different "layer cake," sociograph, and conjoined psychograph. Sometimes they will work at ways to "hold together" their differing beliefs—imagining, for instance, that when the Bible says that the Lord created the world in six days, a "day" for the Lord might be millions or billions of years, and thus their science and their religion can indeed fit together (other contradictions between the two are brought together in similar, not always convincing, ways).

The point is that all individuals exist in a wildly large number of different "We's," each with its own "fingerprint" or "layer cake" composed of different percentages of layers and Views at considerably different levels of development, and where the predominant defining nexus-agency of the social holon is at an altitude that a particular structure-level of the individual can resonate with in order that they can become a functioning member of that particular group or collective. If a specific group's dominant nexus-agency (or cultural center of gravity) is at, for example, orange, then that group will especially attract individuals at the orange level-stage of development.

In order to be a genuinely functioning member of a group, the individual must possess a structure-level and its View that is at least as developed as the central nexus-agency of that group. Thus, individuals whose structure center of gravity is red may be physically "in" a group whose nexus-agency is green, but those individuals' communications will not be "internal" to the group—or they will not be actual functioning members—because there are two or three levels of being and consciousness in the group that are "over their head" and whose communications will simply not make full sense to them. They'll never quite "get" what the group is about—its central values, aims, goals, or ethics. *Physically* they might be "in" the group, but *mentally* they are not, and thus they actually stand as outsiders to the group's main activities.

This is the problem, for example, with creating "teams" at work, when the only criteria for being a team member are exterior—a set of behavioral skills, physical proximity to the group, and so on—and do not take into account interior realities, such as the team member's actual center of gravity in vertical altitude. A team that is predominantly oriented around a green nexus-agency may have several team members working in the same physical area, but whose centers of gravity are red and amber, and those individuals will never be actual members of that team, no matter how closely together they are located. A member's "fitting" into a team is a matter of fitting into all 4 quadrants of the team's characteristics—including, of course, levels—and if that doesn't happen, the individual will never be a true member of the team, no matter how close in physical proximity the person is. This person will consistently fail to grasp the team's priorities and goals, and constantly be the source of the team continuing to perform poorly. This will confuse managers who don't take vertical dimensions into account, because this person's skill set might be exceptional.

A Higher "We"

One of the experiences of individuals practicing together, particularly when most of them are at 2nd tier or higher, is that of being in a "group mind" or something that *seems* like an individual organism. It's not actually that, as we have seen (it's physically impossible), but phenomenologically it feels almost as if it is; and the point is simply that, particularly with higher levels of development, the higher levels of consciousness involved can start to feel their intersubjective connections in a very strong, palpable way. Some groups have begun mapping the common stages that groups seem to go through, from things like preconventional to conventional to postconventional to integral and unified. What is happening, I believe, is that in these cases, higher and higher *state-realms* are being simultaneously experienced by the members, and as that heads toward the ultimate Nondual ("One Mind") condition, then that Unity condition is increasingly reflected through each and every individual, with a correlative feeling of each person being "part" of a "single" Consciousness (which is true in a certain sense, just not in a literal "single Leviathan" or "single organism" sense, because, even in these cases, there is no single "super-I" that controls all of the members' thoughts and actions).

The I-We-It dimensions of the AQAL Framework (the "Big 3" or the 4 quadrants) show up in Buddhism, we have noted, as Buddha-Sangha-Dharma, with Buddha being the ultimate "I-I" or consciousness domain, Sangha being the ultimate "We" or group/collective domain, and Dharma being the ultimate "It" or Thusness domain. The "We practices" outlined here are exploring the leading edge of the Sangha domain. This is an important, evolutionarily cutting-edge realm of recent research and practice, and any Fourth Turning might want especially to keep an eye on this Lower Left quadrant.

There are, at this time, several individuals who are actively exploring and experimenting with various "We practices." Perhaps one of the earliest (at least in today's age) and most influential was David Bohm, who maintained, in his book *On Dialogue*, that the world is in the dire state it is because of too much self-centered, fractured, fragmented thinking, and a new way of thinking, driven by dialogue, where we suspend assumptions and judgments, participate honestly and transparently, and stay connected, would open the door to more authentic, real, creative thinking capable of dealing with the world crisis.[8] Francisco Varela and Otto Scharmer (in work that Scharmer has particularly continued and deepened), recommended a group process based on (1) *suspension* of past associations and knowledge, (2) *redirection* of awareness to the timeless present source and away from the object, co-enacting a group field, and (3) *letting go* (and "*letting come*"), and away from "looking for." Scharmer expanded this into his U process, which, I noted, deals with the three major states of consciousness: getting a detailed overall awareness of the gross problem; shifting into subtle awareness and viewing the issue from that richer and fuller vantage point; then drawing on causal source, will, and creativity to allow new solutions; moving those back down into their subtle dimensions for fleshing out; and then finally materializing the solution in the gross realm (hence, gross to subtle to causal, back to subtle, back to gross). Andrew Cohen recommended a type of "intersubjective yoga" (Lower Left quadrant) where the individual lets go of self-identity and instead identifies with awareness itself (and "the ground of being") and especially identifies with the evolutionary impulse per se and its urgency, and then lets this evolutionary intelligence speak through every group member. When done correctly, this is often reported as feeling like a "group enlightenment."

Olen Gunnlaugson has done considerable work on "establishing second-person forms of contemplative education," examining intersubjectivity from numerous perspectives; and (with M. Moze) wrote an important article titled "Surrendering into Witnessing: A Foundational Practice for Building Collective Intelligence Capacity in Groups."[9] Stephan Martineau and Miriam Mason Martineau have done significant work on "We" practices involving transparent contact with each member, opening to forms of "ours" and not "mine." Thomas Hübl has done some profound work on, for example, taking gross shadow material and reading "behind" or "beneath" it into subtle and causal factors, and working with a field of a "We without a Them."

Decker Cunov and his colleagues at Boulder Integral Center have developed practices such as "circling," where members of the group are taught to focus on others and to openly, nakedly, honestly report all feelings and reactions moment to moment. This can lead to moments of extraordinary intimacy in the group as a whole. Dustin Di-Perna, mentioned earlier, has been working with "We practices" that seem to involve the "We" itself evolving through several levels ("conventional, personal, impersonal, interpersonal, transformational, awakened, evolutionary, and Kosmic." While I am in general and strong agreement with this work, it should at least be mentioned that this is a delicate and complicated issue, because the "We" itself does not possess a dominant monad but a dominant mode of resonance or discourse. As I explained earlier, when an individual holon, such as my dog, gets up and walks across the room, 100 percent of its cells, molecules, and atoms get right up and move across the room as well—because of its dominant monad (and governing agency). But no group or collective has anywhere near that sort of control over its members, who rather "resonate" with each other (in the "layer cake") depending upon their own Kosmic Address or psychograph. Thus, the levels that DiPerna discovered might very well be connected to a specific set of individuals with specific psychographs—all members were at green or teal or higher; all had access to higher states; all had done shadow work, and so on. It's not clear that a red group would—or even could—move through those same levels in that same order. But this is important exploratory research that I fully support.

Terry Patten (in addition to tracing the history of these exercises) has done a good deal of important theoretical research and living experimentation with "We practices," including many of those I just mentioned, and has come up with his own particular "We practice" that he calls "Integral Trans-Rhetorical Praxis," which focuses on "uplift" and "deepening" rather than "persuading" or even "teaching." His first step is to describe, in 3rd-person terms, the general Integral Theory involved; then he switches to a type of 1st-person confessional mode and talks about exactly how he is feeling in the moment as he tries to convey ideas that some people will find silly, threatening, unnecessary, and so on. This is an open, naked—and, as we noted, *confessional*—mode. This shifts the stage from abstract philosophical terms to deeply personal and intimate terms. He then addresses the group in a "ragged truth telling" and invites them to adopt a similar type of dialogue. If this actually connects—sometimes it does, sometimes it doesn't—the whole process leaps into a type of hyperspace of collective intelligence, where the "We" itself seems to be learning how to process and function in this new atmosphere. At this point, every perspective (1st, 2nd, and 3rd person), every type of discourse (framing, advocating, illustrating, inquiring), every mode of exploration (transrhetorical, transrational, transpersonal) can come into play, each under the aegis of this group intelligence. When it works, it generates—as do many of these practices—feelings of joy, inspiration, spiritual sacredness, creativity.

So much ragged excitement has been generated by these practices that Tom Murray wrote an understandable and helpful response, where he notes that much of the discussion in this area is diffuse, poorly defined, and nebulous.[10] These various practices can, he points out, actually be involved in (1) feelings, (2) shared meaning, (3) state experiences, (4) an emergent collective entity, or (5) collective action.

And, of course, he's right. And, in my opinion, that's not a problem, that's exactly as it should be.

The real problem confronting the "We practices" is simply the problem of evolution itself. Evolution has just barely poked its head into 2nd tier in individuals; of course, any number of individual "I's" at 2nd tier will of necessity generate a number of corresponding "We's" at the same altitude (teal or turquoise, in this case; occasionally higher). But, as a community, we don't yet know how to reliably transform individuals into 2nd tier. In fact, transformation is poorly understood in psychology on the whole. We just don't know exactly what factors consistently produce transformation, and which don't. Kegan correctly points out that developmental transformation involves "challenge and support"—but exactly what is challenged, and exactly what is supported? Psychoanalytic theories have always maintained that transformation involves "selective frustration"—but again, exactly what is frustrated (and what isn't)? Margaret Mahler, as I earlier noted, after watching infant and child development as closely as anybody in history, finally gave up trying to spot what helped produce highly developed individuals and concluded, "The lion's share of development rests with the infant." Parents who seemingly did everything wrong could still produce healthy and happy children; and parents who seemingly did everything right could produce mean-spirited little wretches. It was mostly up to the infant himself or herself—hence, "the lion's share of development rests with the infant." This is generally not what the average liberal parent or educator wants to hear, fervent believers that they are that they can actually do things that will help growth, learning, and transformation.

But, of course, this is no reason to stop trying to help growth or stop attempting to understand transformation more precisely (and there are important bits of data being added almost daily). People are almost always drawn to "integral" approaches because they first read an account of development and its higher Integral stages, and they got a profound "Aha!" experience—"This exactly describes me!" In most cases, that is not an arrogant overestimation but a profoundly relieving realization that they are not crazy, they are not insane, that their way of looking at the world—holistic, systemic, integrated, whole—is not off the wall, as almost everybody around them seems to think, but is in fact a genuine stage of human development that has more depth and more height and more width than any previous stage in history, and they have finally found something that makes sense of this to them.

But *exactly* how they came to be at an Integral stage, no psychologist really and fully understands. Everybody has some sort of theory—as I noted, for psychoanalysis, it's a consistently applied "selective frustration," giving the present level enough satisfaction to keep it healthy but not enough to keep it fixated or embedded; for Robert Kegan, it's the right combination of "challenge and support"—challenging the present level and supporting higher-level responses. But precisely how any of those actually applies to every action, nobody really fully understands.

At Integral Institute, we use a variety of practices collectively called "Integral Life Practice" (successor to an earlier version, still available, called "Integral Transformative Practice"). This operates under the principle of what might be called "dimensional cross-training." Studies show, for example, that if you take a group of meditators, and divide them into those doing just meditation, and those doing meditation combined with weight lifting (the overall number of practice hours being the same in each group), then, according to scoring by the meditation teachers themselves, those doing both meditation and weight lifting progressed more rapidly and to a greater extent *in meditation itself* than those doing just meditation alone. "Cross-training" seems to accelerate both dimensions. So we use the AQAL Framework and present practices in body (gross, subtle, and causal), mind, Spirit, and shadow—and in self ("I"), culture ("We"), and nature ("It"). See K. Wilber et al., *Integral Life Practice*, if you're interested.

When it comes to "We" practices, all that is certain is that with regard to the same "Aha!" experience that individuals had when they first discovered Integral, they absolutely know it must be possible to discover its correlate in the "We" dimension (every Upper Left quadrant has a correlate in the Lower Left quadrant, since all 4 quadrants tetra-enact). *This "higher I" that they have discovered must have a "higher We" as a correlate*, and they are hot on the trail of that. They also realize that the discovery and elaboration of this "Integral We" is something of a prerequisite for implementing Integral institutions in the Lower Right quadrant. People keep forgetting that Integral solutions to problems require individuals actually at Integral levels of development. This is not just learning a new theory or learning a new skill or implementing a new tool—it is an actual multidimensional *vertical stage in development* that must be lived, that must be actually grown and developed, and without that, all we have are Integral opinions, not Integral realities. Integral actions (in the Lower Right) require Integral individuals (in the Upper Left) and Integral "We's" (in the Lower Left) as actual developmental realities, not just theories. The urgency of finding Integral "We's" thus couldn't be greater given the general series of world crises we are now facing.

For the first time in history, virtually all of our truly serious and wicked problems are global in nature. Even fifty years ago, if a nation were facing serious problems, it could take actions itself to ameliorate them. Today, most serious problems are such that actions taken by any single nation are largely worthless—almost all nations have to participate: the problem is global, the solution must be global. The United States, for example, could completely cut its carbon emissions and that wouldn't affect global warming in any significant fashion at all. Virtually every nation—and every person—on the planet has to participate. The same is true of the world's financial crisis, environmental despoliation in general, starvation, the water crisis, global terrorism, overpopulation, species extinction, warfare, the planetary health crisis and runaway global viral infections, geopolitical conflicts, world governance. It is likely no accident that as humankind's problems, for the first time in history, have become global—requiring global solutions—humankind is also developing levels of consciousness that are, also for the first time in history, genuinely and deeply global, Kosmocentric, Integral. Global problems, global solutions, global consciousness—all of a piece. Integral is not just an armchair philosophy, but a clear-cut road to any inhabitable future at all.

But evolution moves as it does. Michael Murphy reminds us that evolution "meanders more than it progresses," and the same is true of the general Integral stages of evolution themselves—and in every quadrant (I, We, It, and Its).[11] Again, not much more than 5 percent of the population is today at Integral levels, and that population has not yet learned to self-identify as being at Integral (that is, most of the people at Integral stages don't know they are at those stages). So the fact that "We practices" can wander over all the areas pointed out by Tom Murray is not only understandable, it's desirable. We are learning how to address all of those areas—from feelings to shared meanings to state experiences to collective action—from Integral perspectives, and there are as yet no guide books here at all. All we can be assured of is that Eros will continue its unrelenting pressure to transform in all 4 quadrants, and human beings will respond to that drive, come what may. Evolution, like so many learning processes, operates through trial and error—and so, across the Integral board, we are seeing many trials, many errors, and a slow, inexorable growth to greater Truth, Goodness, and Beauty.

One last thing about "We's" in general and "We practices" in particular. The psychograph of *each individual* in a particular group will be a determining factor in the depth or height that the group itself can achieve. With 5 percent of the population at Integral, a group with only 5 percent of its members at Integral will never be able to form an Integral "We"—the mutual resonance (and governing nexus-agency) will be at considerably lower levels in the "layer cake." (Hence, "We practices" are mostly taken up by explicitly Integral organizations, where a good majority—over 50 percent—of individuals involved are likely at Integral levels or higher.) Integral is sometimes described as "an elitism"—and that's absolutely true, but it's an elitism to which all are invited. It is simply unavoidable that those individuals who find "Integral" ideas anywhere near attractive are largely those who are themselves at Integral levels of development in the first place, and at this time, that is relatively few (as I said, perhaps 5 percent). The same is true of "Integral We" practices, and these prerequisites simply must be acknowledged, delicate as the topic is. Although one of the points of an Integral approach to any problem is to language that issue in as large a number of levels as possible (Magic, Mythic, Rational, Pluralistic, Integral, and Super-Integral—as with the "conveyor belt" of spirituality), this doesn't mean to cavalierly overlook Integral itself.[12] It is a prerequisite that individuals must be at the Integral level for "Integral We" practices to be successful, although anybody can be invited to those practices; but realize that an "Integral" depth of the "We" will not be achieved in any group where the majority of those individuals are not themselves at Integral.

Terry Patten recognizes the importance of several prerequisites necessary to be "adequate" to the practice of "*Integral* We" practices. He gives several; they are:

Stage development in the self-related lines [must have developed] to "Exit Orange" [that is, on the verge of exiting Orange altitude for Green], "Exit Green," "Teal," or, for higher expressions of the praxis, "Turquoise" or "Indigo" levels; in state-stage growth, the relaxation of strict fixation of attention in the gross "waking state" levels of mind and emotion, and a basic inner Witnessing capacity; an ability to focus and direct attention and thus to stably rest it on others and the intersubjective field; some insight into shadow dynamics and ongoing sincere nondefensive inquiry into ongoing shadow dynamics; a basic capacity to endure discomfort and delay gratification; the integrity and courage necessary to transcend "looking good" in order to "make subject object" transparently; sufficient existential depth to be capable of remaining self-responsibly grounded while facing the world crisis and taking it seriously; and enough emotional intelligence, health, and compassion for self and others to be able to hold high levels of cognitive and emotional dissonance while remaining present with others in a fundamentally nonproblematic manner as a mostly friendly benevolent presence.[13]

All of those qualities—or certainly most of them—are required to establish perhaps the premier requirement of the group: the establishment of trust. This particularly demands that individuals be at 2nd-tier development, because those at 1st tier will not fundamentally respect anybody at any level other than their own, and thus a "rolled eyeball" group is what you get with mixed 1st-tier collectives. The capacity for "Witnessing" is also crucial, given that most "We" practices ask members to drop subject–object awareness and "surrender into Witnessing" or even Nondual states, and thus be able to remain focused and centered in the timeless Now and the presence of the freshness, aliveness, and novelty of the Present. With these types of prerequisites largely met, a fruitful "We" group exploration, experimentation, and learning process can occur.

What is especially important for an Integral Spirituality or Fourth Turning is the realization that, just as there is an entirely new and historically unprecedented "I" space emerging (with a radically new capacity for higher inclusiveness and caring—and a deeper Enlightenment process reflecting this higher "I"), so there is a new and higher "We" space, or Sangha, that is also emerging, and it, too, is historically unprecedented in many of its characteristics (including access to fundamental forms of intersubjective intelligence never before seen or experienced by humans). There's not only a new and higher "I" or Buddha (at higher structure-rungs of existence) and a new and higher "It" or Dharma (or Truth that includes not only that disclosed by states but also structures), there is also a new and higher "We" or Sangha (with a substantially more inclusive nature and vibrant group intelligence).

But what is central for an Integral Spirituality is not that it focus merely on the collective "We" but that it integrate all 4 quadrants in each and every moment: the "I," the "We," and the "It"—self, culture, and nature—are all brought together in the fresh aliveness and radiant Presence of the Present. The new Buddha is not going to be the Sangha, but the unification of the Buddha, Sangha, and Dharma in a single ongoing nondual Awareness and Awakening.

17

Integral Semiotics and a New God-Talk

Integral Semiotics

There is one item that ties together many of the topics that we have been discussing that goes by the name of "Integral Semiotics." I have pointed out on several occasions that the coming world—having gone from "God Everywhere" to "God Nowhere"—is now slowly entering "God Everywhere" again, but the "God" that is "everywhere" is a different God indeed, at opposite ends of the spectrum of development from the original "God," and possessing few, if any, similar characteristics. This demands an entirely new language of God talk; a completely new way to communicate about these ever-present, all-pervading realities; and totally different versions of signs and symbols representing these wildly new, astonishing, shocking realities. Our coming new world demands a new language altogether. And that means "semiotics"—and in particular, "Integral semiotics."

Semiotics is the study of signs and symbols, language, linguistic meaning-formation, and languages in general. And one of the first things you notice about virtually all schools of semiotics is that they are built around flatland ontologies. That is, take a simple example that I often use: the expressions "dog," "the square root of negative one," and "God." Now the only one of those items that is universally agreed to refer to things that exist is "dog," and that is because dogs exist in the physical, sensorimotor ("flatland") world. The other words are taken as iffy—maybe they refer to things that exist, maybe they don't; it depends on your philosophy and your religion, among other things. But "dogs"? Dogs are real because they exist in the one uncontestedly real worldspace—the physical sensorimotor.

The more one looks at this, the stranger it becomes. Ferdinand de Saussure, in his brilliantly pioneering *Course in General Linguistics*, pointed out that a sign actually has two components (three altogether): There is the original referent, the item that is being represented or evoked by the sign (such as the class of all dogs). Then there is the sign itself, and it has two aspects—a signifier and a signified. The *signifier* is the material (written or spoken) mark, or indicator, such as the words written on this page, or, if you're listening to me read this, the spoken words I'm using. And the *signified* is what comes to your mind when you read or hear a particular signifier. So if the signifier is "dog," the signified is whatever comes to your mind when you read or hear that word. Neither the signifier nor the signified, notice, is the same as the actual referent (in this case, the class of all actual dogs in the world). This is not dissimilar to Charles Peirce's division of a word into the sign (the signifier), the object (the referent), and the interpretant (the signified). Any sign *must* be interpreted before it will actually signify something; Peirce was insistent on this, and he agreed with Integral Theory that interpretants go all the way down, all the way up; which is the basis of his panpsychism.

Integral Theory adds a few other points, and then we get to the real punch line. The *signifier* is the Upper Right—the individual, exterior ("objective"), written or spoken material mark of the sign, word, or symbol. The *signified* is the Upper Left—what comes to mind when the sign or signifier is seen or heard (the individual, interior, "subjective" aspect). Now regularities governing the *sum total* of material signifiers is the system of *grammar* or *syntax* (the system or rules or patterns or nexus-agency that all signifiers follow in a given language— "the rules of grammar"—which specifies how the specific material marks, or signifiers, are used together as a system), which is the Lower Right. And the *sum total* of signifieds is *semantics* (the world of actual meanings, the collective "intersubjectivity" of the linguistic signs and their referents—the collective signifieds or total meaning space of all signifieds), which is the Lower Left. So the signifier is Upper Right, the signified is Upper Left, syntax or grammar is Lower Right, and semantics is Lower Left. None of those, note, is the actual referent, the actual subject or object or item being represented in the linguistic system.

So where, indeed, is the referent? Where is it "located"? Where can it be found? And right there is the punch line, the whole point that virtually all semiotic systems completely avoid or overlook. The assumption is generally that any real referent (as opposed to something imaginary, fantastical, or illusory) is located in the Right-hand sensorimotor world, the physical/material/gross world. And then around those existing *sensorimotor referents* (dogs, houses, guns, trees, stars, airplanes, apples, rivers, mountains, and so forth), a semiotic theory is built. If it has signifiers, they are all Right-hand sensorimotor items; syntax is all Right-hand sensorimotor (or physical systems of sensorimotor) information bits; semantics, for all real entities, all point to some Right-hand sensorimotor referent; and as for the signified, it is usually taken as some sort of mental picture or representation of the sensorimotor referent, even if a syntactical system is necessary to recognize it.

Now the only problem with that approach—and this does have meaning for an Integral Spirituality, among many other items, as we'll see—is that it completely privileges (and absolutizes) the physical sensorimotor worldspace. That is ultimately the only worldspace that is "really real." So, of course, all real referents exist in this physical sensorimotor worldspace. And that is *implicit* (if not plainly explicit) in virtually all semiotics.

Real problems start to arise as soon as we start asking about things like, say, the square root of negative one, or numbers in general. Most sciences would not, and do not, deny that numbers are real, in many cases as real as physical objects. For positivism, for example, the only real realities are physical things and numbers. And for positivism, the meaning of a proposition is the way, or ways, that we connect that proposition with a real physical object. If there is no way to do that— if the proposition or sentence cannot be verified by observation (that is, by sensorimotor observation)—then that proposition is not true. But it's not false, either—for positivism, it's *nonsensical*. (It's neither true nor false; it's completely without meaning—it would have to improve in order to be wrong.) It's just a meaningless string of words, and they sound like they have meaning only because words can be strung together to sound like almost anything—"Santa Claus stopped by last night"—but that doesn't mean it has a real meaning.

But the first thing you learn in developmental studies is that the physical sensorimotor worldspace is not the only real worldspace there is. In fact—and this is the dirty little secret of developmental studies, which explodes all traditional and typical ontologies (especially all forms of realism)—is that each major level of development *sees a different world*. We might say that it co-enacts a new, and in many ways different, world or worldspace—each with more complexity, more consciousness, more differentiation/integration; and these are not merely "different interpretations" of a single, pregiven, "real world" (the sensorimotor), but ontologically new worlds in many real ways. If each new level was instead simply a newer, more accurate interpretation of the single pregiven sensorimotor world,[1] then we would never actually or accurately know that or any world, because evolution is unending, and thus new and higher interpretations will always be emerging, with each making the previous level look "wrong." And this will happen forever—we never reach a higher level where evolution stops and promises never to introduce a new world, so that we can finally get an interpretation of the single pregiven world that would finally and actually be true. Thus, the idea that each new level is just a more accurate interpretation of the real sensorimotor world actually removes any chance of our knowing anything that is true about the sensorimotor world (or any other world)—all we ever know are partial and fragmented and "incorrect" (false) views of a reality that we can never know accurately, because evolution never ceases.

No, each level has a relative reality that, at that level, is as real as real can be (given all the circumstances and conditions of that level). As Hegel put it, "Each level is adequate; each higher level is more adequate." So, a sliding scale of truth ("Each level has truth; each higher level has more truth") is what evolutionary and developmental studies hand us. The correlative notion is that each level has a set of relatively real referents—real objects and phenomena that can be adequately enough represented by a particular signifier. If the individual has developed to the level where the specific referent exists, and has experienced that referent, then that individual will be able to have a fairly accurate *signified* emerge in his or her awareness when they see the *signifier*—in other words, they will be able to understand that signifier. If they have not developed to that level, then it's "all Greek to them," it's all "over their heads." They can't understand the *signifier* because they don't have a *developmental signified* that is up to the task.

So the sensorimotor worldspace is not the one, single, only real worldspace—it is simply one of numerous worldspaces (in structures and in states) that are also real, in some cases, more real (nondual ultimate Reality, for example). So all of a sudden, that sneaky "signified"—what comes to mind when you read or hear a word or sign—starts to slip into the picture in some very profound and irrevocable ways. Start by simply noticing the worldspaces that we have already briefly described in our tour of human development—in structures, we have the infrared (or sensorimotor) worldspace, the magenta worldspace, the red worldspace, the amber worldspace, the orange, the green, the teal, the turquoise, the indigo, the violet, the ultraviolet, and the white. In states we have the gross/physical (the sensorimotor), the subtle, the causal, the empty witness, and the ultimate nondual.

Each and every one of those worldspaces have phenomena in them that are seen, felt, and experienced as fully real when one is in that particular worldspace. The sum total of phenomena available (in all 4 quadrants) marks the total *worldspace* of that particular structure or state.[2] And now, the punch line. Where does a referent exist? *Every referent exists in a particular worldspace.* If a particular worldspace has a phenomenon that is a common experience or occurrence in a particular culture, then that culture will give that phenomenon (that referent) a word—a signifier. It is said that the Eskimos have twenty-eight words for snow—twenty-eight signifiers for the referent we refer to as "snow," which is a very common experience for Eskimos. If the typical Eskimo hears any one of those twenty-eight words (or signifiers), they will commonly understand more or less exactly what it means (a correct "signified" will arise in their mind); whereas if Americans hear almost any of those signifiers, they will have no idea (no signified) of what is meant ("It's just snow, you know, that white stuff?"). Contemplative traditions have numerous words (or signifiers) for various states of consciousness (for example, in Eastern traditions, we find *savikalpa samadhi, nirvikalpa samadhi, advaya samadhi, jnana samadhi, sahaja samadhi, nirodh,* and so forth), and the members of any meditation community quickly come to learn the appropriate signifiers of the state referents that they are seeking to contact.

Now let's go back to our three simple signifiers of "dog," "the square root of negative one," and "God." Take the last one—"God." "God" has numerous meanings, depending on the worldspace that is being referred to by the word. Thus, there is a mythic (or amber) worldspace God (and "God" is real in that particular worldspace—but only in that worldspace). In the Christian popular tradition, God is generally portrayed mythically as a highly anthropomorphic figure, often with the actual shape of a human being, usually a white-haired, gray-bearded, grandfatherly type individual, often pictured sitting on a royal throne in the sky surrounded by an entourage of the highly saved—various saints, martyrs, heroic proclaimers, prophets, sometimes angels who are flying around, and certainly His one and only Son. This view of "God" is unshakably and massively real for somebody at amber, and represents their intuition, as it presents itself at that structure-level, of a grand Spirit in 2nd person. This View, taken as almost self-evidently true at this level, is generally judged to be less real by higher structure-rungs. The amber *rung* itself—for example, concrete operational, the rule/role mind—is judged to be real, but less developed and less whole, by higher rungs, and it is, in fact, incorporated into the higher rung as a subpart of its being—the "include" part of "transcend and include." But the *View* from that rung, which is created by an exclusive identity with that rung, is judged to be inadequate for and from a higher rung, since it is a limiting of consciousness to that lower rung alone, giving a "smaller," "narrower," "less adequate" View than that from the higher rung—the "transcend" part of "transcend and include." Nonetheless, as I pointed out, the View from the amber rung is *true* as true can be for the individuals *at that rung*, but is judged less adequate by the Views of higher rungs and is thus rejected or "negated," while the rung itself is included.

But there is also the God that is, say, the formless Ground of all Being, and which exists—as a *real referent*—in the causal/emptiness domain; and it can be directly experienced as real by any who take up the meditative practices and injunctions to awaken the causal/emptiness worldspace in their own case. If that worldspace is *not* awakened and activated, the individual (assuming he or she has already rejected the mythic God) will firmly believe that all forms of God are dead, whereas what is really dead is their experiential access to the world-space in which that referent is most definitely quite real.

One of the most recent examples of this type of occurrence is given in the book *Proof of Heaven*, by the Harvard neurosurgeon Dr. Eben Alexander, who, in a coma with his frontal neocortex completely non-functional (as in zero—flatlined), nonetheless had what he described as the most profoundly real experience that he had ever had in his entire life. He said he couldn't find any description of it in any of the literature—that is, the scientific materialist literature he was used to reading—but he finally found a description of it by a mystic, which was something like "there is, some say, in God, a deep but dazzling darkness," which is actually quite a good description (signifier) of the formless causal domain (the real referent).[3] He had, in fact, had a direct experience of the causal God! He had experienced the real referent, and far from being a "mythic Santa Claus" type of experience, it was the "most real" experience that he had ever had. Because he had experienced the *real* referent, he therefore had a real signified that would adequately come to mind; what he lacked was a signifier—a symbol or string of symbols or words to describe the real referent, and this he finally found in a mystical text.

If his experience were a common experience in this culture, we would have something like twenty-eight words for it! As it is, we have virtually none; all we have are words that refer to the mythic world-space God, which is a real phenomenon for a seven-year-old, but not for rational or higher adults. (The real problem with the word "God" coming from that amber level is that the word is then used only in a way that can be generated by that level—that is, by the rule/role mind. Thus that amber God is unyieldingly and absolutistically pictured as giving very rigid and unvarying *rules* to be obeyed—such as the Ten Commandments, which have no contextuality at all. For example, there are some times when killing a human being is not only okay but recommended, such as in self-defense or family defense, in times of war, police actions, and so forth. This amber God is also pictured as defining a series of very rigid *roles* that one must take in regard to this absolute figure—mostly the roles of total submission and subservience—and of issuing a series of two-millennia-old ethical commands: a wife must submit to and totally obey her husband at all times; homosexuals are to be stoned; pork is taboo; Eve—and all women—are responsible for the Fall; the earth is the property of human beings, exploitable as desired; and on and on. Whenever this word "God" is used, all of that baggage comes with it in this culture.)

Thus semiotics—and this is really the point—has *a profound emancipatory element.* The higher structures and states that amount to our own liberation need to be named, need to be given signifiers, need to be acknowledged as just as real (sometimes more real, as Dr. Eben Alexander discovered) as any sensorimotor object, need to become part of a common Lower Left semantic worldspace. Of course the experience itself, like all experiences, will be beyond any words. All experiences, not just mystical experiences, are ineffable: you can't adequately describe a sunset, an orgasm, Bach's music, or vomiting by using words, any or all words; but words can be used to refer to them, and thus indicate their genuine reality. If a person has had the same experience, that is, has been exposed to the same referent—say, vomiting—then when you say, "I ate this huge sushi meal last night, and the whole thing just dumped out of my mouth and all over my date," the person will understand more or less exactly what you mean; they will have an adequate signified. If they have never experienced vomiting, they can only guess what it would be like. And if the referent is really uncommon—say, the same causal/formless/luminous experience that Dr. Eben Alexander had, or meditators might have—the person lacking any similar experience might, indeed, simply not believe it's really real—it's just some weird semihallucinated experience that you had. But that's just another good reason why we need to develop *a vocabulary for the experiences of higher structures and states.*

So, as we were saying, *we desperately need a new language* (not to mention the actual experiences represented by it). In that way only will people know that these higher referents exist, actually exist. "The Godhead," "the nondual One," "Buddha-nature," "Ayn Sof," "Dharmakaya," "Ayin," "the Supreme Identity," "the Tao," "Enlightenment," "Liberation," "infinite Freedom and Fullness," "radical Awareness," and "pure Consciousness" are all signifiers that have actual referents, and as you read them, if you have had any of those experiences, you will have a correct *signified* come to your mind, and you will know what I mean. Otherwise, it will be "all Greek" to you, meaningless words with no real referents and thus no signifieds and thus no reality for you. You will think that those referents don't exist; whereas what actually doesn't exist is your experiential access to the worldspace in which those referents are most definitely very real.

So "signifieds" aren't just "signifieds"—they are always "developmental signifieds." You have to develop to the worldspace in which the real referent exists in order to have a correct signified come to mind when you read or hear any of its signifiers. If a particular referent exists in the orange rational worldspace (as does the square root of negative one), you have to have developed to orange altitude in order to be able to see or feel that referent at all (through the study of orange mathematics, which you won't be able to understand at the lower amber, red, magenta, or infrared rungs). Otherwise, it will be "all Greek" to you; it will make no sense; it will be "over your head." If the referent exists in the indigo worldspace—such as the psychophysical nature of the real world (the co-creative, co-enactive nature of consciousness)—you have to have developed at least to indigo in order to be able to understand correctly what that means; otherwise, it's another referent "over your head." If a referent exists in the causal worldspace—such as the formless, timeless nature of ultimate Reality or Spirit—you have to either have a peak experience of that state (as Dr. Alexander did), or your state center of gravity has to have developed to that state-stage, usually because you have practiced some form of meditation or contemplation.

But typical semiotic theories overlook all of this entirely—overlook the fact that *referents always exist in particular worldspaces*, and you must have access to that worldspace in order to see and feel that referent and have a correct signified come to mind, and thus know for sure whether that referent really exists or not. (For example, the square root of negative one actually does exist in the orange worldspace, and you can discover this by studying orange mathematics. But not any ole phrase has truth—"the square root of integral calculus" is meaningless; it isn't true. In other words, each level has *real relative truth* and *real relative falsehood*, and that's what makes each worldspace a genuine *ontological reality* and not merely a reflection of a single, pregiven, sensorimotor worldspace. A theory that takes the most number of phenomena available at a given level into account and gives the best explanation of them is likely to be the most true theory at that level; ones that incorrectly represent or resonate with various phenomena are likely to be false at that level. Thus "true" and "false" have real meanings at each level, even though "truth" itself is a sliding scale, becoming "more" and "more" true with each increasing level.) Typical semiotics implicitly assumes that everybody is at the same basic stage of awareness—usually, a rational view that is confined to representing nothing but physical/sensorimotor objects and referents. ALL of the really interesting phenomena and items in human consciousness are thus totally dismissed, ignored, avoided, and overlooked, as flatland once again prevails.

And that's just what Integral Semiotics is all about. *Referents exist in worldspaces*—and there is a key that unlocks a thousand ontological puzzles and questions. Dogs exist in the infrared sensorimotor worldspace; the square root of negative one exists in the orange Rational worldspace; God as a formless Ground of all Being exists in the causal/empty worldspace, as a Nondual Ground exists in the turiyatita Suchness worldspace, and as a mythic-imaginal object exists in the Mythic-literal worldspace. With the exception of dogs, none of those very real entities exist in the infrared sensorimotor worldspace. They all exist in higher, wider, deeper, truer worldspaces, in structures and states (in all quadrants), whose phenomenological content is every bit as real as any other worldspace (and in some cases, as we keep seeing, even more real—meaning, containing more Being and Consciousness).

This, again, is why semiotics isn't just a dusty, academic, ivory tower relic. *Semiotics is a matter of emancipation.* It is driven, in its highest reaches, by an emancipatory interest. By naming and signifying the higher structures and states, it opens the doorway to our own growth and development into those states; it gives the mind permission to begin thinking in those directions; it reassures us that those realities are indeed really there. And to repeat, of course we don't want to confuse words or maps with the real territory—but we also don't want maps that leave out huge sections of the real territory, so that we don't even suspect they exist. Get a complete map first—and then let it go for your direct experience of that territory!

This is why what is really required is what I have called a "gigaglossary": a list, a dictionary, an encyclopedia of the various phenomena that we have good evidence exist in each worldspace—each structure and View, and each state and Vantage Point (and each quadrant, each line, and so forth). If Eben Alexander, our Harvard neurosurgeon, had

had such a giga-glossary available to him, he would not have had to spend hours wondering if he had gone temporarily insane or had, in fact, seen heaven—the real heaven, the real Ground of Being, as disclosed from the higher structures and states that have evolved to date, and not a remnant of the mythic childhood of men and women. He could have simply looked it up in the giga-glossary and found not only a matching description of his state experience but a whole history of those branches of human discipline (particularly the contemplative sciences, East and West) that have, over the centuries and often millennia, developed not only fairly complete phenomenologies of these worldspaces but injunctions (paradigms, exemplars, practices) for actually and directly contacting these spaces and seeing for oneself if the referents there are real. It would be a comprehensive Wikipedia of the real world, in all of its quadrants, levels, lines, states, and types—not a resource that provides implicit, strong, unspoken support for the flatland reality of a scientific materialism and a belief in nothing but the single pregiven reality of the sensorimotor world. (The "big data" movement is an attempt to put all the known "facts" on computer systems. This is a fine idea in many ways but deeply flawed in at least one essential component—the only realms considered real and worthy of inclusion are the standard positivistic realms: physical objects and mathematical numbers and systems. All other equally real worldspaces are ignored—magenta, red, amber, green, teal, turquoise, indigo, violet, ultraviolet, and white. If "big data" were to include the giga-glossary, this would be a truly revolutionary movement, instead of the essentially reactionary movement it now is.)

This whole topic—semiotics in general—is, as I said, a matter of emancipation. *Integral semiotics is emancipatory!* And in some cases, it references the very deepest and highest emancipation that men and women have yet realized, a condition where humans discover Spirit, as Spirit discovers itself—in all its quadrants, and in its highest structure-levels, and in all its lines, and in its highest states, a truly Full or Integral emancipation! Men and women have wondered, puzzled, and agonized for ages over these deepest questions, starting with "What is ultimate Reality" and "Who am I, most deeply?"—and humans the world over have come up with essentially similar practices and road maps of the worldspaces that disclose answers to those questions (via state-stage developments into deeper and deeper Presence, recently complemented by understandings from higher and highest structures, in all lines, with all quadrants).

Name it!—is the key to all realities. If we don't adequately name it (the signifier), then for all intents and purposes, it (the real referent) doesn't exist, or won't commonly exist. We will go to the grave with that song still in our hearts. Of course, to say it one last time, nobody wants to confuse the map (signifier) with the territory (referent); at the same time, we don't want to have maps that leave out some of the most important territories of our lives so that we have no way to indicate that these important territories are even there! Most people in this culture are completely unaware of the fundamental structure-stages, the "hidden maps," that govern so much of their lives; they are unaware of the progress through state-stages that they can engage and that can result in the shocking resurrection of their own Truest and Deepest Selves, a Supreme Identity with the Divine itself, in all its radiant, infinite, timeless and eternal, glorious, sumptuous, superabundant grandeur. They are the victims, not of confusing a map with the territory, but of having no map whatsoever to alert them to these stunning territories. Lacking an Integral Semiotics, they are cut off from an emancipated future. This is the core sadness at the very heart of our human culture.

Languages of the Divine

Integral Semiotics is about recognizing that every thing or event (every referent) has a Kosmic Address—it exists in some particular world-space somewhere in the AQAL Matrix—and that if you want to be able to see that real thing or event (the real referent), you have to put yourself in the same vicinity as the Kosmic Address of the event you want to see or experience; your Kosmic Address must generally align with the Kosmic Address of the thing you want to experience, or it won't happen. Thus, if you want to know if "God as the formless Ground of all Being" really exists, you have to orient yourself in the Upper Left quadrant, take up a practice that moves your state center of gravity from gross to subtle to causal, and then, using a 1st-person perspective in that causal state in the Upper Left quadrant, *look*. And if you are like 95 percent of people who have done so, you will experience this vast, clear, infinite, formless, empty, "dark" (because it transcends the world) but radically "luminous" (because it is infused by radiant Spirit) ultimate Reality—and you will know for yourself as to the reality of this groundless Ground of Being. You put your Kosmic Address into the same general vicinity as the Kosmic Address of the referent of that signifier ("formless Ground of Being"), and so you could directly experience that referent, with a "knowledge by acquaintance" flooding your being. Or possibly you could be thrown into the vicinity of that worldspace, or that Kosmic Address, by a near-death experience, or perchance a drug experience, or a walk in nature, or making love, or listening to Bach, and so on. The point is that all actual referents—including dogs, the square root of negative one, and formless God—exist in particular worldspaces; they have specific Kosmic Addresses. They aren't lying around in a flatland pregiven world waiting to be perceived by all and sundry, but the particular worldspaces have to be contacted (the particular Kosmic Addresses have to be looked up and followed), in order for you to be put in close enough vicinity to the referent to be able to directly experience it. (Not even a dog is open to being perceived by all beings—a single cell, for example, can't see the dog because it can't get anywhere near its Kosmic Address, so the dog doesn't exist for it.)

Now, let me briefly return to one important point. As I noted, it is often said that mystical experience is "ineffable," beyond all words and symbols. And in some cases, particularly with radically ultimate Truth, there is a certain sense to that. (Ultimate Truth, being metaphorically "nondual," cannot easily be put into concepts, since virtually all concepts have meaning only in terms of their opposites—infinite versus finite, ultimate versus relative, good versus evil, pleasure versus pain, and so on—and Reality has no opposite, being, again metaphorically, "all-inclusive"; and even that term is dualistic, excluding as it does "all-exclusive." This is why Nagarjuna, who establishes that the Ultimate itself cannot be said to exist, or not exist, or both, or neither, would have to say something like, "It can be called neither Void, nor not Void, nor both, nor neither, but in order to point it out, we call it the 'Void.'") But there is another, more common reason that it is often said that mystical experience is ineffable, and it's not because there is something especially different about mystical experience itself. All experiences, I noted, are in fact, and strictly speaking, ineffable—watching the sun set, riding a bike, eating oatmeal, going swimming—none can be satisfactorily described in words, such that a person who had never had the experience would know what you meant. But if enough people have had an experience of one of these, then we attach "names" or "signifiers" to those experiences, those referents. When you hear the signifier or have the referent described, you will know exactly what that means. Again, it's like the twenty-eight names for snow. Zen masters have twenty-eight words for variations on Emptiness (tathata, shunyata, dharmakaya, alaya-jnana, chittamatrata, tathagatagarbha, svabhavikakaya, advaya, prajnaparamita, ri, satori, jnana, prajna, and so on, each with a slightly different connotation)—the point being, Zen masters talk about "ineffable" Emptiness all the time!

Throughout the ages, mystics have come up with around four different types of language that can be used to speak about the unspeakable (each of which I also indicate with a particular symbol). There is positive, assertoric, or kataphatic language—saying *what Spirit is*—for example, "Spirit is infinite (+)." There is negative, apophatic, *via negative* language—saying *what Spirit is not*—for example, "Spirit is neti, neti; not this, not that—it is not infinite, not loving, not inclusive, not any concepts (–)." There is metaphoric language—saying *what Spirit is like*—for example, "Spirit is more luminous than the light of a thousand suns blazing off the top of a snow-capped mountain (*)." And, most importantly, and ultimately the only technically "correct" type of language, is injunctive, which provides the instructions and directions for the practices, paradigms, and actions required to put consciousness in the same vicinity as the Kosmic Address of the specific dimension of Spirit being sought, there to experience the referent directly for oneself. Such injunctive language might take this form: "Sit in a comfortable position, cross your legs, put your hands in your lap, lower your eyes, and count your breath from one to ten, then repeat; do this twenty to thirty minutes twice a day to begin with (!)." The symbol (!) is meant to emphasize that these are all actions, real activities that elicit and enact real worldspaces with real phenomena possessing real Kosmic Addresses. The positive sign (+) indicates that the statement is attempting to say what Spirit is; the negative sign (–), that the statement is attempting to say what Spirit is not; and the metaphoric star sign (*), that the statement is attempting to say what it is like.

A Kosmic Address, as I have noted, is the sum total of the AQAL dimensions of any given phenomenon. We live in a universe that is, formally, without a given center—it is a universe where any thing or event can be taken as the center of the universe, and everything else related to its location. But "its location" cannot itself be given in a single and fixed fashion, since it is not located in relation to any fixed center; it itself can be located only in relation to the sum total of all other phenomena in the universe. Therefore, its "address"—its "Kosmic Address"—can be indicated only by giving a list of its relative relations to other known phenomena. The AQAL Matrix does exactly this. Thus, a simple Kosmic Address of a given emotional state might be that it exists in quadrant 1 (Upper Left), in the emotional intelligence line, at an amber altitude, in a gross state, with an Enneagram type five, and defiling emotion type 4. In the known universe, that is enough information to identify the general "location" of that particular emotional state—along with its major qualities and characteristics. Or, for a jet fighter as a social product or artifact, it exists in quadrant 4 (Lower Right), in the military-defense line, at a teal altitude, in a gross state, of a fighter F-16 type, of an United States type. God as Loving Ground (Great Thou) is quadrant 2 (Lower Left), ultraviolet altitude, bhakti line, low-causal state, Spirit-in-2nd-person type, saguna type. And so on. All three of those referents are real; they exist in particular, real worldspaces; and the location, or Kosmic Address, of each can be indicated in relation to the sum total of other real referents in the Kosmos, which the AQAL Matrix dimensions do. Any number of identifying "locating" elements can be given; the five AQAL elements are a simple minimum. Further, the knower, or experiencer, of any of those referents also has its own particular Kosmic Address, and that, too, needs to be stated for a full picture. (Somebody at the amber altitude structure-level who is attempting to understand an indigo-level phenomenon will not do a very adequate job, and might mistranslate it badly; this needs to be taken into account with any knowing process, and the "location" of any referent will include both the referent's and the knower's Kosmic Address.)

The central point is that the sensorimotor worldspace, which is generally taken as the only real worldspace in existence, is but one of dozens of real worldspaces, each with a plethora of real phenomena or *real referents*. And each of those real referents can be given a *signifier*, and if you have actually experienced that referent, you will have a generally correct *signified* arise in your mind as you hear or read the signifier (and you will know, for yourself, whether that referent is real or not). As higher and higher worldspaces emerge and evolve, the components of the lower, junior worldspaces are seen as less inclusive but not totally unreal; they are real in those worldspaces, and, further, their enduring components are likely some of the actual components of the holons or phenomena in the higher worldspaces (for example, atoms, molecules, cells, and organisms become fundamental components of their successors). The Views from the lower worldspaces are seen as less real, but again, not totally unreal. They are perfectly real as the actual View from those worldspaces themselves (a View adopted by every single sentient being, or individual holon, who has that worldspace as a center of gravity), even if those junior Views are negated or transcended by higher Views (as we saw Hegel put it, "Each level is adequate; each higher level is more adequate").

But there are always—literally *always*—some number of sentient beings (individual holons) at every level of worldspace (with its particular View) that has ever emerged since the Big Bang. In Upper Right terms, for example, there is still an atomic View of the world (the panpsychic prehension that an atom has of its worldspace), a molecular View of the world, a cellular View of the world, an organismic View of the world, and so on. Each lower View is less inclusive, less conscious, has less Being, and is, in that sense, less real compared to any higher View—but again, not totally unreal, certainly not to the sentient holons still inhabiting that worldspace! Except for those sentient beings whose species has gone extinct, there is *no worldspace that has emerged and evolved since the Big Bang that is not still in existence to some degree somewhere*, and this means that it is populated by panpsychically aware sentient holons with that given View. This includes interiors as well as exteriors, and it is the interior worldspaces that, in particular, tend to be completely overlooked, ignored, or flat-out denied reality by sensorimotor materialists (including those who embrace both scientism and scientific materialism).

The main problem with spirituality in today's world is a semiotic problem; most modern and postmodern cultures simply do not have a vocabulary for any 3rd-tier structure-Views of Spirit or any higher-state experiences of Spirit. Spirit—as an actual referent—is confined almost solely to the Magic and Mythic Views of reality. Again, although they are not unreal occasions for the individuals at those levels, they are less real compared to higher, rational and transrational, personal and transpersonal, structures and states. And the transrational realms are explicitly NOT prerational; they transcend and include rationality, but these realms are as far above rationality as the tooth fairy is beneath it. Yet we treat virtually all Spiritual concerns as if they were, indeed, not much more than tooth fairies of one sort or another. God is an adult's great imaginary friend in the sky. This is pathetic, truly.

This is why semiotics is a matter of emancipatory interest. Semiotics is the doorway to Freedom, Liberation, Release, Fullness, Abundance, Overflowingness, Outrageous Love and Joy and Bliss and Beauty and Being, Unborn and Undying, Unmade and Uncreate, Infinite and All-Pervading, Eternal and All-Inclusive. Those are just words. But they are part of the twenty-eight words for Spirit, and the richness of our vocabulary points to the richness of our very Being. Of course, it's worth repeating, we do not want to confuse words with reality, map with territory, sign with referent, theory with fact. At the same time, while not wanting to confuse map and territory, we don't want to have a totally screwed-up map either (or no map at all!). And a map of Spirituality that stops at Mythic-literal and deliberately excludes all higher structures and states is about as screwed-up a map of ultimate Reality as the modern and postmodern world could possibly produce.

So we try instead to achieve eternity, not by experiencing the timelessness of this Now moment, but by looking to download our consciousness into silicon chips and megacomputers, shedding our bodies of carbon and adopting ones of silicon instead, thus living everlastingly (which is actually the opposite of real eternity; "everlasting" is a stream of all time, endlessly and forever; while real "eternity" is a moment without time, totally present in the timeless Now—and from there, fully present at all points of time, though not requiring them). So we download ourselves into a computer frame—just, you know, make sure nobody drops your particular computer, for as it shatters into a thousand pieces, your immortality goes with it. I am entirely in favor of exploring a transhuman dimension of technology—or any dimension of technology for that matter—but not if we do so by continuing to forget the real Ground of Being and attempting to build our immortality projects as mere substitute gratifications for a real timeless Eternity and a genuine spaceless Infinity. (Not to mention the problem that most of the "consciousness" that is going to be downloaded into computer frames is just orange Rational awareness. What of the higher levels? Are we going to be eternally denied them?) What's the point in substituting a short and pain-ridden, torture-dominated life for a very long pain-ridden and torture-dominated life? Do we think it's a good thing to live a long and miserable life, the longer the better?

Perhaps not. Perhaps we should start instead with a real gigaglossary, a genuine taking stock of the sum total of real and actual phenomena that humans have available to them at all structures and in all states. So much of what we are looking for already exists! At this point, it is simply a matter of naming it, of locating it, of finding its Kosmic Address and following the injunctions and directions for finding that Kosmic Address ourselves and directly experiencing it, and all that that brings with it. It is nothing less than our own Emancipation that we are talking about.

The Real Impact of Interior Thinking

Thoughts are real things. It's common to hear in Integral circles that although Integral is causing a big intellectual splash, Integral approaches aren't making much of an impact on the "real" world. First, I disagree strongly. The gains that Integral approaches have made, even in the last five years, are rather startling: for an entire year, the *Architectural Review* published an article each month on an AQAL Integral reformulation of architecture itself (called "The Big Rethink"); a front-page review of the Wachowski's film *Cloud Atlas* in the *New York Review of Books* (November 2, 2012) used the AQAL Framework to explain the review; the government of the United Kingdom released its official report on the British capacity to respond to climate change, a several-hundred-page review using an AQAL Integral Framework as its basis; the Unity Church officially adopted the AQAL Integral Framework to create its main teaching of an Integral

Christianity; Ubiquity University, a worldwide university founded across the board on Integral principles, was created; there has been a strong impact by Integral approaches on the creation of an Integral Spirituality in many of the Great Traditions, from Integral Kabbalah to a widely discussed conference on a possible "Fourth Turning" in Buddhism to a surprisingly strong interest—and over a dozen books— on an Integral Christianity (not to mention the Unity Church); numerous business and leadership consulting firms are using an Integral Framework to organize their work (including such well-known approaches as Dave Logan's, Dean Anderson's, and Alan Watkins's, all supportive of an Integral view); leaders in the Ukraine asked for assistance to "rebuild the Ukraine from the ground up based on Integral principles, a project we see taking at least ten years"; there are several publishing imprints devoted to Integral books (from Integral Publishers to the SUNY Integral series); and there have been numerous worldwide mainstream articles and essays and existing practices on Integral Medicine, Integral Nursing, Integral Economics, Integral Psychology, Integral Spirituality, Integral Politics, Integral Education, Integral Art, Integral Criminology; and an astonishing sixty or so disciplines have been completely reformulated using AQAL Integral approaches in the *Journal of Integral Theory and Practice*. And these are only a small sampling of the advances that relate to just my own work, not to mention hundreds of other scholars worldwide.

But these examples miss the point rather entirely. The saying that we "are playing a game of miles and yet are seeing progress in only inches and feet" completely misses what real progress actually means. All of these "lack of progress" complaints equate the real world with the mere sensorimotor world and overlook the existence and fundamental reality of all of the interior worldspaces—from infrared to magenta to red to amber to orange to green to teal to turquoise to indigo to violet to ultraviolet to white—and the very real phenomena that can be found in each and every one of those very real worldspaces (worldspaces every bit as real as the sensorimotor worldspace). Then when progress isn't made in the sensorimotor world, all of the other progress being made in the other worldspaces is completely overlooked, and the whine of "no progress at all" rises up, deafeningly.

Real progress in the real world starts, in virtually all cases, by first, the creation, in a particular interior worldspace (amber, or orange, or green, and so forth) of a growing set of real objects or real phenomena having to do with whatever it is that is under consideration (often a particular problem requiring a solution, a particular invention that is needed, a particular approach to an issue, or some red-hot conflict area, and so on). These objects that are created in the particular world-space are, as I said, utterly real and ontologically there. Where are they stored? Well, take morphogenetic fields in general. As I noted earlier, when a new protein is first synthesized, it could fold in literally thousands of different ways. But once it folds in a particular way, and once that way is repeated, then every single instance of that protein type, anywhere in the world, will henceforth fold in exactly the same way. Where is that "form" stored? How do the proteins know the correct form, since it's given *nowhere* in the protein itself? Well, we might say it is stored in the storehouse consciousness of the casual realm, as per the *Lankavatara Sutra* (or perhaps in what some Eastern traditions call "the Akashic record"). But wherever it is stored, it is clearly stored somewhere in the real Kosmos, and it clearly has a *real causative impact* on the sensorimotor world—in this case, the folding of every protein of that particular type all over the world.

The same thing happened when—say, the red structure first emerged. At first, its deep structures could have gone in any number of different ways. All that was required was that they "transcend and include" their predecessors. But having done that, they could have developed in any number of quite different ways. But once they began forming in one way, red structures around the world began forming in an identical fashion. That was some perhaps fifty thousand years ago; and now, today, wherever you find red around the world (and in its cognitive forms, it has been investigated in over forty diverse populations, from Amazon rain forest tribes, to Australian Aborigines, to Russian workers, to Mexican nationals), and in every case, it has exactly the same deep structures. Where is that form being stored? Well, probably in the same place that the protein's morphogenetic field is being stored (and we might as well say it's the causal-realm storehouse, but it is somewhere very real in the very real Kosmos).

Those red structures began as some red thoughts—some real red interior phenomena—in the Upper Left quadrant (the interior "I" space) of a handful of individuals, and through their Upper Right quadrant behavior, they communicated them to other individuals who might understand, and as those numbers grew, red "We" structures in the Lower Left quadrant (the intersubjective field) began to form— real red "We" objects or things or phenomena began to form in the Lower Left quadrant. As those continued to take hold, then around the world, as the red structure was starting to emerge in other places, its structure tended to be the same as had grown in this original group (thus, Magic cultures that emerged halfway around the world at that time emerged with the same basic deep structures, as Jean Gebser made so clear). These interior objects were real forms having a real causative impact on other beings around the world. As these interior red objects continued to build, and individuals continued to think in red terms, those objects eventually spilled out of individuals' interiors and began to create material, sensorimotor, social institutions in the Lower Right. Empires began to form, and each in turn, particularly as it gave way to amber, conquered most of the known world in its time.

All of this came from interior thoughts as utterly real objects, or ontologically real phenomena, stored in their primary forms some- where in the real Kosmos, reaching down and having an absolutely real causative impact on the sensorimotor world (just as the form of the folding protein reaches down and creates the form of every single one of those proteins wherever it occurs). And so creativity goes. When representative democracy first began in the modern West, it was just a thought in the minds of a few Renaissance thinkers—the notion of "individual freedom" was novel indeed, at least in that era, with amber mythic-membership conformity and monarchical rule the gen- eral order of the day. But a handful of individuals began creating inter- nal orange objects—worldcentric objects, rational objects, transmythic objects. Did they run out and create a democratic revolution on the spot? Of course not. The internal objects weren't nearly clear enough yet in all their forms. In fact, it would take a few hundred years of continuing to build these orange interior objects—real phenomena in the real orange worldspace—that had the names of "individual free- dom," "democratic representation," "nonmonarchical government," and so on.

Those interior thought objects continued to grow, up to the time of the Paris salons and "café society," where these orange objects began to inhabit a larger and larger number of orange "We" spaces, and became real objects, real phenomena, in the orange "We" worldspace. And finally, after several hundred years of interior object building, these objects spilled out into the sensorimotor world with the American and the French revolutions, creating institutions in the Right-hand quadrants that were materializations of the orange interior objects of the Left-hand quadrants, which had been building and building for hundreds of years—and had been stored in the real Kosmos—eventually to have absolutely real and stunning effects.

Individuals clamoring for "Integral progress" are like those who, during the Renaissance, as orange "individual freedom" objects began to first form, would run out in the streets and try to start a democratic revolution right there on the spot, simply because a few of them thought that that was a grand idea. The problem was that the idea hadn't yet had the time, or the number of individuals, to continue to build and build internal objects representing individual freedom and representative government. It would take hundreds of years for those ideas, those internal objects, to become fleshed out enough, and elaborate enough, and complex enough to be able to create forms that, wherever they were stored in the Kosmos, would one day be able to reach right down and hammer the sensorimotor world into submission.

And so it is with Integral. Every time you think an Integral thought, every time you read or write an Integral sentence, every time an Integral feeling runs through your body, every single time, you are building internal Integral objects that literally are being stored in the real Kosmos; and one day they will have such force that they, too, will reach down from their storage area and pound the sensorimotor world into submission. And that will be directly *because* of those thoughts that *you* had, those ideas that ran across *your* mind, those feelings that made *your* heart beat a little faster. Progress? Progress!!! You are engaged in one of the most monumentally progressive movements that has ever been seen in history. The very activity in your consciousness is building internal objects and ontologically real phenomena of an Integral nature that literally are being stored in the real Kosmos and that will one day reach down and bring men and women to their knees with joy and gratitude and grace and awe, will rewrite history as we know it, and will shape the world with a greater Truth and Goodness and Beauty than has ever been conceived or seen or known.

YOU, my friend—by every Integral thought that you have, conceive, read, write, share, hear, pass on, dream, or envision, by the very fact of your interiorly entertaining that Integral object of awareness—YOU are driving a progress that will one day bring the world to a shuddering surrender of gratitude and grace and all-caring embrace.

Nobody knows how many interior Integral objects are required in the "I" and the "We" before they begin to spill out into the sensorimotor world and hammer it into a new form, the likes of which have never been seen. But consider the sheer magnitude of that transformation in literally all walks of life—and you think that we aren't *progressing* enough??? Have you *any* idea of what is happening here? Have you the slightest notion of the far-reaching transformations that your own internal Integral thoughts are in process of building? Run out and start a revolution now? Are you insane? Have you really thought through the massive changes in government, education, medicine, politics, law, business, technology, energy, food, transportation, law enforcement, the justice system—to name a pitiful few—that will be required for this Integral revolution?

And yet . . . it is a certainty. We know this because every developmental model we have has, beyond the pluralistic/relativistic stage of development, a holistic/integral stage of development—and those models are usually based on various forms of actual research in the real world. This revolution is now built into the very fabric of human growth, development, and evolution. Its deep features, at least in its early (teal) forms, have been laid down (enough to show up on test after test after test). You have already thought enough interior Integral thoughts to build enough Integral objects to reach down from their Kosmic storage bin and causatively influence developmental schemes and tests and research. This is a level that is already laid down in the Kosmos as a stage headed our way. It's in the mail; its delivery is on its way; it can't be halted. It is a tsunami that is, today, still thousands of miles offshore—but it's headed in this direction, and nothing can stop it. That's the thing about stages of human development—real stages are cut into the Kosmos, they cannot be skipped, bypassed, or altered by social conditioning. Their deep structures are Kosmic grooves—actual ontological grooves cut into the universe by *repeated human actions*—and they are as real, and unalterable, as Jupiter's orbit, an electron's structure, or the mechanism of DNA action.

Which human actions? Why, yours, of course. Integral thinking is, on any sort of even modestly wide scale, not much older than fifteen or twenty years—just about as long as many of you have been interested in it. In other words, your thoughts, ideas, visions, and works have been building these Integral deep structures, to the point that their basic (teal) forms are being set as Kosmic grooves—and therefore they are coming our way, like it or not, want it or not. Ever since you had your first Integral encounter, you have been building the interior objects that have coalesced into a set of deep structures now stored as Kosmic grooves and cut into the universe irrevocably, ready to descend on the sensorimotor world with a thunderous crescendo that will shake people to their deepest core and will affect every known area of human activity (just as have, for example, amber and orange and green before it). Look at the world around you, and behold the landscape, behold the site, where the revolution is about to occur, and shudder with the realization of what you have already accomplished in this little amount of time. The Integral changes that have already occurred have happened with lightning speed, in evolutionary terms. Expect this to speed up on some occasions, slow down on others—as evolution continues to meander more than progress. But don't overlook the stunning progress that has already occurred, and is continuing to occur, as individuals—and "We's"—continue to grow interior Integral objects that are set to refashion the world at large.

And what can you do to help bring this historical revolution? Right now, this moment? Every time you think an Integral thought; every time you conceive an Integral idea; every time your pulse quickens with the thought of a more beautiful, more truthful, more ethical world tomorrow; every time you read and study, or create and write, Integral notions; every time you even ask, "What can I do to bring this about, to speed this up?"; every time you dream the dream of a more inclusive tomorrow, the dream of a more harmonious future, the dream of a more balanced and cherished earth, the dream of a Spirituality that touches the God in each and every being alive, and gives that God an embodied home in your own being; every time you reach out for a future that is even just a little more Whole than the one today; every time you imagine any human activity—from education to parenting to medicine to government to law—redrawn in a more inclusive and Integral fashion; every time you look into the eyes of a young child, perhaps even your own, and wish for them a future of greater love and compassion, care and concern, and see them smile in the radiant halo of that embracing tomorrow; every time you think a moment a little more Whole than the previous one, or see partialities brought together in the patterns that connect, or reach out to a future where all God's children are judged in Kosmic terms, not parochial or prejudiced ones; every time you make a choice that is in favor of the betterment of humankind and all living beings in their entirety; every time you see broken pieces and fractured shards and torn and tortured human beings brought together in a more unified, inclusive, and caring embrace; and every time you yearn for a tomorrow even slightly more unified and inclusive and embracing than today—every time, every single time, you do anything like any of those, you are yourself directly, immediately, and irrevocably building interior Integral objects that are instantly being stored in the real Kosmos, adding a few inches to the size of that tsunami racing in our direction now. Welcome to your place in history. It is richly deserved.

• • • • •

In this and the previous three chapters, I have presented some of the central elements of any Integral Spirituality, and this would include any Fourth Turning of the Wheel of Dharma. In the coming years, virtually all the world's Great Religions will be faced with a choice of whether to continue their thousand-year-old dogmas, or move into a future that transcends and includes their essential ideas, while embracing the new truth and new goodness and new beauty that Spirit's continuing evolution is itself increasingly bringing to the fore.

The advantages of this move are legion. I'll mention only a very few, just as a rough summary. In including all 4 quadrants, the war between science and spirituality is ended. The Right-hand quadrants, whose validity claims include truth and functional fit, cover all the major sciences, physics to biology to chemistry to ecology to geology to sociology, and the Left-hand quadrants, whose validity claims include truthfulness and justness, cover all major aspects of spirituality, from structures to states. The Right-hand quadrants include a spectrum of mass-energy (gross energy to subtle energy to causal energy to nondual) arrayed in a spectrum of complexity, and the Left-hand quadrants include a spectrum of consciousness and culture (including Views, Vantage Points, morality, typologies, shadow elements, interior therapies, and so on). A spectrum of development, in all quadrants, allows every major discipline to be coordinated with human growth and evolution. A view that includes all quadrants, all levels, all lines, all states, and all types makes room for virtually everything in the Kosmos and generously includes them. Ultimate Enlightenment, and the ways we WAKE UP; relative levels and lines, and the ways we GROW UP; shadow therapies and flourishing, and the ways we CLEAN UP; and the ultimate nondual Unique Self and Suchness in all 4 quadrants, and the ways that we SHOW UP—there is a warm outreach to, and glad inclusion of, them all.

Such would be true of a Fourth Turning in Buddhism as well. Buddhism, which throughout its history has shown strong interests in evolutionary, integrated, and systemic ways of thinking, along with an interest in a panoply of profound practices for state Awakening, is ready for yet another profound unfolding, which would retain all the essentials of its previous turnings and add the new elements that have unfolded as Spirit-in-action has continued its unrelenting evolution.

And, last but certainly not least, the practice of a Fourth Turning Buddhism, or, for that matter, of any genuinely Integral Spirituality, or Integral Practice, in any field or area, would allow an individual to participate in the creation of interior Integral objects, now being formed and stored in the Kosmos, and due to reach right down and hammer the sensorimotor world into a more compassionate, inclusive, and Enlightened realm. It would allow an individual—it would allow you—to participate in perhaps the greatest single transformation in all of humanity's history. This is not just a *stage* transformation, as in the transformation from archaic foraging to magic horticultural to mythic traditional agrarian to rational modern industrial to pluralistic postmodern informational, but also a major *tier* transformation: from a 1st tier of stages built by deficiency needs, scarcity motivations, absolutistic thinking, noninclusive and exclusionary practices, and hence human conflict and suffering to a 2nd tier of stages built by inclusiveness, embrace, abundance motivation, being values and caring kindness in its actions, tender mercies in its thoughts, exquisite patterns that connect in its ideas, and wholes upon wholes upon wholes in its awareness. By including Growing Up, Waking Up, Cleaning Up, and Showing Up, humanity would be able to imagine a future unbearably close to the Fullness of Being and the Freedom of Emptiness: where all sentient beings are treated with dignity, care, concern, and loving-kindness; where people find the Divine in their own Deepest Self and see Spirit unfolding in every detail of the world around them; where human hearts all sing harmoniously in a radiant realm the vibrant songs of dignity, care, and brilliant luminosity; where human-computer linkages serve not the everlastingness of the separate ego but only the harmonious resonance of the deepest unity of all humanity itself, indeed, all sentient life in toto; where "transhumanism" means not the end of flesh but its radiant transmutation into supermind forms of gorgeous beauty etched into the Kosmos; where "suffering" is a word that has lost all meaning; where torment, torture, tears, and terror are things of a world long past; where a radiant Great Perfection is the Ground and Goal of every sentient being in every realm in every world, a smile of loving-kindness etched on the heart of each and every one. All of the above—*all* of it—is the birthright of every being in every domain in the radiant Kosmos itself. In each and every realm arising in this wondrous universe, there is this, *just this*, in each and every moment, nothing more. *This* you have known from before you were born; *this* will self-liberate you into your own radiant Condition; *this* is your everlasting welcome home—just *this*, nothing more.

And *this*—just *this*—this you always already know, don't you?

Conclusion
The Evolution of Nonduality

Emptiness is universally maintained, by the Paths of the Great Liberation, to be not-two with the world of Form. The ultimate Nondual
estate (Godhead, Advaya, Ayn Sof, Brahman/rupa, ultimate One) in
its pure Emptiness (Shunyata, Ayin, nirguna Brahman, infinite Abyss,
Primordial Nature of God) transcends and includes the entire world of
Form (Rupakaya, saguna Brahman, manifest universe, Consequent
Nature of God). And whereas Emptiness is a matter of states and Freedom, Form is a matter of structures and Fullness. (As the title of one
book wonderfully words it, *Divine Emptiness and Historical Fullness.*)
And while Emptiness has not changed since the Big Bang (or before),
Form and Fullness have definitely changed, as the universe continued
to evolve into more and more complex Forms, hence becoming Fuller
and Fuller. As I noted earlier, we can see the universe get Fuller and
Fuller (for example, in the Upper Right) as it evolves from subatomic
particles to atoms to molecules to cells to organisms, and from there
to photosynthetic organisms, to organisms with neural nets, to ones
with reptilian brain stems, to limbic systems, to the triune brain, whose
neural synapses outnumber all the stars in the universe. The interiors
of these holons (that is, in the Upper Left) have been evolving into
more and more complex, Fuller and Fuller forms, as well, from prehension, to protoplasmic irritability, to sensation, perception, impulse,

image, emotion, to—with humans—concepts, schemas, rules, formal metarules, vision-logic, para-mind, meta-mind, and higher (pushing into overmind and supermind).

These basic interior holons support various worldviews, as we have seen, starting at sensorimotor and instinctive Archaic, and moving to image and symbol Magic, conceptual Magic-Mythic, rule/role Mythic, formal Rational, postformal Pluralistic, vision-logic Integral, and 3rd-tier Super-Integral.

But this leads to an inescapable conclusion: when compared to the Enlightened sages of, say, three thousand years ago, whose dual center of gravity was generally (Mythic, Nondual)—giving them the benefit of the doubt about being Nondual instead of the more common causal at that time—a fully Enlightened sage of today is not more Free (Emptiness is still the same Emptiness, and hence the same Freedom), but today's sage is definitely Fuller (since there have evolved, from the time when Mythic was the highest structure, at least three new and higher structures—Rational, Pluralistic, and Integral—which today's fully evolved sage would include). Genuine Enlightenment, in other words, is being one with *both* the highest state and the highest structure to have emerged and evolved at a given time in history. Assuming both sages achieved the Nondual state, and the earlier sage achieved at best the Mythic structure (while the modern sage achieves Integral structure), then for that Mythic/Enlightened sage, there are "over his or her head," so to speak, at least three higher very real structures of the Kosmos (Rational, Pluralistic, and Integral), which the earlier sages were *not* one with, because those ontological levels hadn't yet even emerged in any significant fashion. Today's sage, on the other hand, realizing the same nondual Emptiness, is no Freer than the early sage but is certainly Fuller, having included in his or her Supreme Identity, at least three higher ontologically real levels of the Kosmos. The Emptiness of both confers the same Freedom, but the greater and more complex Form of the latter gives the modern sage a significantly greater Fullness, or more Being (although not more Emptiness). The earlier sages were fully Enlightened *for their time*; but would not be fully Enlightened for today, which the later sages are. (I like this definition of Enlightenment—being one with all states and structures at any given time—since it gives both sages their due, while also recognizing the undeniable gains of evolutionary unfolding.) This is something a

Fourth Turning of the Wheel would want to take advantage of. Emptiness and Form are still nondual or not-two, but the world of Form has evolved—and is still evolving—following that inexorable "creative advance into novelty" via a process of "transcend and include," and therefore the very identity of our modern sage is Fuller. He or she actually contains in his or her being up to three or so greater levels of reality, and a correspondingly greater, Fuller degree of Being. Of course, our modern sage might only be at Magic structurally, and hence would actually have less Fullness than our ancient Mythic sage. But by defining "full (or Integral) Enlightenment" as *being one with all states and all structures that have emerged and evolved at a given point in history*, the evolved sage of today would be no Freer, but significantly Fuller, than yesterday's sage—and yet both would be considered Enlightened for his or her time, since both are one with the highest structure and highest state to have evolved at that time in history. (As I said, I really like this orientation, because it allows both modern and ancient sages to be "equally accomplished," although one of them is "more evolved.")

And that is perhaps the final thing that we would want to include in any Buddhism undergoing a Fourth Turning. Evolution carries on. Spirit-in-action carries on. The unfolding of higher and higher, more complex, and more conscious structures of reality carries on. And since Enlightenment involves a oneness with the entire universe, Enlightenment itself becomes richer and richer. What Whitehead called "the Consequent Nature of God" is quite similar to our Total Painting of All That Is, or the Totality of All Evolving Form (as opposed to the "Primordial Nature of God," or our pure Emptiness, which doesn't evolve, or enter the stream of time, at all). The Total-Painting God becomes Fuller and Fuller (as the Total Painting evolutionarily adds more and more levels of Being), and hence a oneness or union (or not-twoness) of Primordial-Emptiness God with that Total-Painting God also become richer and richer. Or one can think of it as the total union of Emptiness/Freedom and Form/Fullness. The Emptiness/Freedom of the Primordial Nature of God itself remains unchanging, or timeless (the Emptiness of a billion years ago is not different than the Emptiness of today—Empty is Empty),[1] but the Form/Fullness nature of the Consequent Nature of God becomes evolutionarily Fuller and Fuller— and hence their union, their not-twoness, likewise becomes Fuller and

Fuller. By including structure-rungs and their Views in a Fourth Turning, the Fullness of Buddha-nature (the Consequent Nature of God, the increasingly evolving Fullness of the Total Painting) becomes able to be tracked, thus increasing the Depth of our Enlightenment and the Degree of our Awakening (as Fullness becomes greater and greater), which is one of the primary goals of Buddhism from its very inception.

In short, since Enlightenment is the union of Emptiness and Form, although Emptiness (and its Freedom) doesn't evolve, Form (and its Fullness) most certainly does, and thus the *union* of Emptiness and Form likewise must evolve in some ways—Enlightenment itself becomes richer and richer, Fuller and Fuller, one with a universe that itself is becoming bigger and bigger, larger and larger, wider and wider. This is not easily seen if you track only states leading to Emptiness and its emancipatory Freedom (because you track only the Emptiness of Form, not its increasing Fullness), but if you add structures and their path to increasing Fullness, you can begin following this increase in the depth, the richness, the Fullness of Enlightenment itself—real Enlightenment as the sum total of Waking Up *and* Growing Up.

A Fourth Turning of Buddhism is consistent with Buddhism's history and its own self-understanding and has much to recommend it (as does an integral orientation for every spirituality looking to become more inclusive). I join those students and teachers who argue that now, indeed, the time is ripe for such a Turning. The world is at a place in its overall evolution where, in the grand unfolding arc from subconscious to self-conscious to superconscious, or from prerational to rational to transrational, or from submental to mental to supramental, or from 1st tier to 2nd tier to 3rd tier, we are now on the verge of the unfolding of superconscious, transrational, supramental, 3rd-tier stages. We are standing on the edge of an Integral, then Super-Integral, revolutionary transformation. And what is conspicuously lacking is a conventional, cultural, common knowledge and understanding of the general stages of development in general, and the stages of spiritual development in particular. We are bereft of a true and comprehensive God; if ever there was a time that a real God or Goddess or Spirit was required, that time is now. We are moving into a period where "God is Everywhere," and yet we have no idea whatsoever about what or where or how this God could even be. We are walking totally blindfolded into the future, and yet we are chatting and smiling and talking frivolously about how fine things are: "You know, we have this amazing Singularity coming our way!" and "We're getting close to being able to go transhuman!" and "All we have to do is take care of this little pesky climate problem—which technology surely will—but otherwise, Wow!"

We are, in the meantime, stuck with a Spirit that is, in most circles, and at best, Magic or Mythic, which are Views that are categorically rejected by virtually everyone who is at Rational or higher. Our entire vocabulary, our semiotics, is woven around a Mythic-literal (or magical) View of ultimate Reality, a View laughably rejected by the majority of educated and more developed individuals—precisely those individuals who most ought to be including a developed Spiritual Intelligence (as well as state experience) into their own worldviews and decision-making processes. We need an entirely new language, a new vocabulary, an Integral Semiotics to replace the old, most definitely worn-out, millennia-treaded words and symbols that were generated in the childhood of humanity and are fully rejected by its adult stages (which unfortunately also reject all of spirituality with it—the level/line fallacy). We are truly lost in the wilderness with no compass that points to true North as ultimate Reality; it merely spins its needle in the face, not of Infinity, but an infinite number of finite, relative, conventional truths, the half of the Two Truths doctrine that means the less. We are a humanity without a Ground, a race of mammals that has only itself—and thus is in the process of ruining the planet for everything else, a race that is truly dedicated to the surface and superficial and stupid and stupefied, stumbling numbed and narcoticized into a tomorrow of outrageously hazardous dimensions. And we cannot find a Ground that we can trust because the only words and images that we have involve utterly unbelievable "tooth fairy" narratives and childish "miracles"—of water turned into wine, supermen raising the dead and walking on water, an Old Man in the Sky raining down everything from locusts to vengeance with a malice unmatched. How could any thinking person believe any of that???

Well, they don't have to. Almost from the beginning of all that "religion," there have been rare communities that were devoted to "spirituality"—not to fairy tales, but to psychotechnologies of consciousness transformation. These communities had contemplative sciences, which, like all good sciences, rested on injunctions or paradigms (actual social practices or experiments), which resulted in direct data accumulation (direct experiences of real phenomena elicited by following the injunctions—namely, in this case, direct spiritual experiences, satori, gnosis, or kensho), which were themselves checked (validated or refuted) by a community of the adequate (those who had completed the first two strands, following injunctions and collecting data). The findings of these contemplative sciences are, as we have repeatedly seen, essentially similar around the world in their overall conclusions and their maps of consciousness and reality, running from gross to subtle to causal to witnessing to nondual realms—however differently they were actually worded and however differently subdivided. Variations on these states can be found in St. Teresa's seven interior mansions; Zen's ten Ox-Herding pictures; Plotinus's levels of mind; the Victorine mystics' "eye of flesh, eye of mind, eye of spirit"; Kashmir Shaivism's ten emanation levels; Kabbalah's ten levels of Sefirot; Yogachara Buddhism's nine rungs of consciousness; Mahamudra's six state-stages of practice; to name just a very few. Arthur Lovejoy pointed out that this view is "held by the greater number of the subtler speculative minds" East and West in all founding cultures,[2] and it is still open to public verification by any who wish to take up the direct experiment in consciousness and find out for themselves. To repeat that beautiful quote from Machen's fictional character Hampole:

> Some have declared that it lies within our choice to gaze continually upon a world of equal or even greater wonder and beauty. It is said by these that the experiments of the alchemists of the Dark Ages . . . are, in fact, related, not to the transmutation of metals, but to the transmutation of the entire Universe. This method, or art, or science, or whatever we choose to call it (supposing it to exist, or to have ever existed), is simply concerned . . . to enable men [and women], if they will, to inhabit a world of joy and splendour. It is perhaps possible that there is such an experiment, and that there are some who have made it.[3]

Some have, indeed. At the same time, evolution itself has been pushing forward with its relentless "creative advance into novelty," producing epoch after epoch after epoch, each being more complex, more conscious, more caring, more inclusive and embracing, less violent, and moving closer and closer to transpersonal, spiritual, transrational stages of *structure* development itself (not only states). Every major model of human structure development runs (at a minimum) from an initial symbiotic fusion to an impulsive to a protective to a conformist to a rational to a pluralistic to a systemic structure-stage of development. And many developmentalists, looking at the obvious directionality of that sequence (more inclusive, more conscious, more caring and embracing, less violent and aggressive, and overall more Whole), have postulated the existence of even higher stages beyond those, and when they do so, those higher stages are almost always maintained to be deeply transpersonal, mystical, transcendental, or spiritual in some higher sense (from Abraham Maslow to Lawrence Kohlberg to Jenny Wade to Susanne Cook-Greuter to Terri O'Fallon). And these are all developmentalists who have seen the earlier Magic and Mythic stages and know that this *new spirituality* looks *nothing* like those prerational Magic and Mythic forms at all, and yet these new forms exist, waiting there on the horizon for us, waiting for us to reach out and embrace them, download them, bring them in and down, embody them, and embrace the entire world with them. Spiritual awareness, previously available only if someone took up a state-stage practice and developed into higher states, will become part of the basic rungs of existence itself, and hence inevitable, natural, and normal. Spiritual awareness will become part of the universal *structure-stages* of growth, occurring as one's structure development continues, and thus it will be patently present and given in *all* human beings with continued development (and not just in those who voluntarily take up meditation, but to ALL who simply continue normal growth and development—hence, "God everywhere").

In both structures and states, an entirely new type of evolutionary Spirit is seen to be emerging—a Spirit that, as it discloses itself, has clearly been here from the beginning (and before), but in a more nascent, un-self-reflexive fashion. But it is now, through the vehicle of awakened humans, awakening to itself as well (a Spirit that sleeps in nature, awakens in humans, and fully realizes itself in Spirit—with humans having access to all three of those domains as dimensions of their own structural Being or compound individuality). It is a new dawn, it is a new world, it is a new man, it is a new woman, it is a new horizon altogether.

We need a new language. We need a new vocabulary. We need an Integral Semiotics. The very structure-stages of growth are headed toward a new individual Emancipation, a new and deeper Freedom and Fullness, infinite Emptiness and finite Form, a Great Liberation more gloriously dazzling, sumptuously inclusive, and luxuriously comprehensive than has ever before been seen on this earth. All indications, all evidence, and all data are that this will be an absolutely staggering transformation in almost every way conceivable—in medicine, politics, art, education, therapy, religion, economics, business, leadership, relationships, parenting, and play—among others. A Fourth Turning in Buddhism (or a similarly Integral Spirituality in any major Great Tradition) would help to ensure that Spiritual Self-Realization is part of humanity's higher and further *inevitable structure-stage* development (that is, not just a voluntary *state*-stage development that you can take up or not as you choose, but a universally given *structure*-stage of growth that exists in all humans). Individuals would pass through these structure-stages without exception, if they continue to grow, beginning at turquoise and indigo, just as individuals today pass, without exception, through magenta, red, amber, and up to turquoise integral. These structure-stages would supply not only higher states of consciousness but also higher structures of consciousness. This would very likely be the single greatest revolutionary transformation that humanity has experienced to date—and by a staggering margin—not only moving (and GROWING UP) into a truly Integral 2nd tier (and beginning 3rd tier) for the first time in its history, but also including a state WAKING UP to its own deepest nature and real condition for the first time in the modern and postmodern eras. Taken together (both higher structures *and* higher states, not just higher states), this development would be so radically new and (r)evolutionary as to defy comparison with any other period in our entire history. Add to this transformation the technological singularities, including robotics, nanotechnology, and genomic revolutions in the Right-hand quadrants, which are all headed our way with undeniable certainty and speed (including renewable energy discoveries, new Gaia-cleansing capacities, and the extension of the average life span into hundreds of years) and humanity will indeed begin to think, in all sincerity, about something resembling a real heaven on earth, a true intervention of Spirit in history—a union of this-worldly and otherworldly, samsara and nirvana, Emptiness and Form, heaven and earth—as a normal, natural, universal stage or stages of human development in general. The implications truly and deeply defy imagination in virtually every way. We will look back on this (and all previous) ages as being the Darker-than-Dark Ages, which was followed by the dawn of a new Light, a new world, a new man, a new woman, a new horizon altogether —as Spirit continues its unstoppable, undeniable, irrevocable evolution, dragging us with it.

Thus, a new Freedom in Waking Up; a new Fullness in Growing Up; a new Flourishing in Cleaning Up; and a new Fully Functioning in Showing Up—this is the astonishing face of a new Spirit headed in our direction with unstoppable fury. For this, indeed, we need a new language, a new vocabulary, a new inclusive view for the new man and new woman—in many ways, the superman and superwoman—powered by a supermind whose brain is directly plugged into the total technological infrastructure of the entire planet (not to mention Spirit itself!), uniting the Right-hand technological realities with the Left-hand consciousness and culture realities, resurrecting a Being that is Becoming while riding the very edge of a ray of light traveling at the limit of velocity itself, racing to a rendezvous with a tomorrow the likes of which has never even been imagined anywhere on this earth.

We need a new critical theory, a new Holistic/Integral Critical Theory (or, more accurately, metatheory), which criticizes existing cultures, not only when they fail to produce communication undistorted by domination or economic exchanges not dominated by force and prejudice, but also when they fail to open human development to genuine Wholeness—to postpluralistic, post-postmodern stages of development, at least 2nd-tier Integral and hopefully 3rd-tier Transpersonal levels in each and every line (individual and collective). Culture needs to resume its primary function as a pacer of transformation, with the bar set beyond hyperindividuality to transindividuality (Integral and Super-Integral Awareness), and religious systems recalibrated as conveyor belts, picking people up at prepersonal levels, helping them move into personal levels, and then delivering and releasing them into transpersonal and superconscious levels altogether—a wholeness upon wholeness upon wholeness, everlastingly.

And you already know this Wholeness, don't you? You already immediately recognize the ever-present I AMness in you right now, do you not? You, the very *feeling of you*, right here, right now, just as it is; engaging that feeling-awareness fully is the experiment that Machen's character Hampole spoke of, the one that transmutes the entire Universe and delivers men and women to a world of even greater joy, beauty, and splendor. There is indeed a new dawn, a new world, a new man, a new woman, a new horizon altogether—and it exists nowhere but in the texture of this very *you*, unfolding timelessly, eternally.

Take your seat as ever-present I AMness (opening onto Suchness), this present utterly obvious feeling of *being you*, and ride it into the future, bringing your own specific, unique, one-of-a-kind gifts and talents with you, therein to work on transmuting this earth into a radiant heaven of outrageous love and foolishly offered-everywhere kindness. Rest in both the timeless Being of your ever-present Self and the raging urgency of evolution's unfolding Eros as it races through the world of Becoming, recognizing that your Being and Becoming, your Emptiness and Form, your Eternal Thusness and your temporal Eros, is Spirit's own way of continuing to realize more and more of its own true Self and real Condition in and through the only vehicle it could ever use to do so: *You.*

• • • • •

And so now, go out and remake the world. And start to do so by *rethinking* the world, using a better, more comprehensive, more ultimately accurate map of this extraordinary territory you call your life. The AQAL Matrix has likely made you aware of areas and dimensions of yourself that you didn't fully realize were there, and indicated ways that these are simply more avenues and perspectives through which Spirit itself can inhabit and fulfill your own being. The Total Painting of All That Is just got bigger for you—wider, deeper, higher, with all of it evenly being observed by your own true Witness, your own "I-I," even now. And that empty Witness can spill out of itself and into a "headless" union with the Total Painting itself, as the *entire universe* is seen truly to be arising *within you*. The remaking and rethinking of the world is a remaking and rethinking of your very own Self and its own deeper Suchness, even now again, which is why you can undertake this extraordinary task in the first place.

It is possible to remake this world because you—the very *deepest you*—are its one and only Author, its sole Creator. But it—you—are not alone, because the deepest Self of this deepest you is looking out through the eyes of every sentient being alive, including all 9 billion humans on the planet. You can remake the world because you possess 18 billion hands, more than enough to reshape and refigure all that needs to be done. Feel the unimaginable creative power of this one and only I AMness, and know that anything is possible. Grab the very best map you can possibly find, and strike out in the direction of this radically new territory, knowing that the entire Creative Force of the whole Kosmos is your constant companion. Grab your Self, find the World, reawaken and remake both. This is now your own deepest moral imperative—by whatever lights you can find, shine on the World, radiate the World, illuminate the World, enlighten the World. If you can't do it, it can't be done—so please hurry and engage in this. We're all anxiously awaiting, and deeply depending on *you* for our own salvation . . .

Notes

Introduction

1. Arthur Machen, *Delphi Collected Works of Arthur Machen (Illustrated)* (Hastings, UK: Delphi Classics, 2013).
2. Adam Bucko and Rory McEntee, *The New Monasticism: An Interspiritual Manifesto for Contemplative Living* (Maryknoll, NY: Orbis Books, 2015), 22.
3. Ken Wilber, *Integral Spirituality: A Startling New Role for Religion in the Modern and Postmodern World* (Boston: Integral Books, 2007).
4. Alfred North Whitehead, *Process and Reality: An Essay in Cosmology*, ed. David Ray Griffin and Donald W. Sherburne (New York: Free Press, 1978), 28.
5. Machen, *Delphi Collected Works of Arthur Machen*.

Chapter 1:
What Is a Fourth Turning?

1. T. R. V. Murti, *The Central Philosophy of Buddhism: A Study of the Madhyamika System* (New York: Routledge, 1955).
2. Whitehead, *Process and Reality*.
3. Sung Bae Park, *Buddhist Faith and Sudden Enlightenment* (Albany: State University of New York Press, 1983), 127.

4. The five M's originated in the Hindu tantric tradition where they are called the *Panchamakara*: *madya* (wine), *mamsa* (meat), *matsya* (fish), *mudra* (farina, cereal grain), and *maithuna* (sexual intercourse).

5. *Brihadaranyaka Upanishad* 1.4.2.

Chapter 2:
What Does a Fourth Turning Involve?

1. "Kosmos" is a Greek word meaning the entire world—the physical, the emotional, the mental, and the spiritual. It has sadly been reduced to "cosmos," which the modern world still claims to be "the whole world," but it only includes the physical realm—materialistic reductionism, in other words. In Integral Theory, *Kosmocentric* (Kosmos centered) refers to a general stage-realm of development, following *egocentric* (me centered), *ethnocentric* (us centered), and *worldcentric* (all-of-us centered—all human beings). Kosmocentric (all-world centered) includes not just all humans but all sentient beings, all of reality itself. Every important developmental line and multiple intelligence develops through variations on at least these four major level-stages (which, in various models, including my own more detailed version, are subdivided into anywhere from six to fourteen major level-structures. I will be outlining these specific level-stages as we continue).

2. Clare W. Graves, "Human Nature Prepares for a Momentous Leap," *The Futurist* April (1974): 72–87.

3. These "worldview" transformations—the archaic transition from apes to humans, to magic tribal, mythic traditional, rational modern, pluralistic postmodern, and so forth—that occur in what we will see are the interiors of the collective, what we will call the Lower Left quadrant (or the "we" space), are each correlated with transformations in all the other quadrants at the same time ("quadrants" are the major irreducible dimensions of manifestation, as we'll see in detail soon). Thus, for example, in what we call the Lower Right quadrant (or the collective group looked at from the outside or the exterior in an objective stance), those collective interior worldviews (archaic, magic, mythic, rational, pluralistic) are correlated with, or occur alongside of, transformations

in the techno-economic base, such as foraging (magic) to horti-cultural (magic-mythic) to agrarian (mythic) to industrial (ratio-nal) to informational (pluralistic).

4. Paulos Mar Gregorios, *A Light Too Bright: The Enlightenment Today: An Assessment of the Values of the European Enlighten-ment and a Search for New Foundations* (Albany: State Univer-sity of New York Press, 1992).

5. This is part of the notorious claim by the Boomers that of all gen-erations, they alone had finally gotten the right answers—the widely noticed, and criticized "Culture of Narcissism" of the Baby Boomers. Christopher Lasch, *The Culture of Narcissism: American Life in an Age of Diminishing Expectations* (New York: W. W. Norton, 1979). This "Boomer greatness" was often indicated in books that had "conscious" in the title, such as "Con-scious Business," "Conscious Parenting," "Conscious Aging," "Conscious Relationships," "Conscious Working," "Conscious Marketing," "Conscious Medicine," all with the clear implica-tion that all the previous attempts in those areas were "uncon-scious"—that is, wrong, goofed up, half-awake, incorrect. I'm speaking myself as a Boomer, of course; I'm actually very fond of this crazy generation, but a concerned critic as well, evidenced in my presentations such as *Boomeritis*. Ken Wilber, *Boomeritis: A Novel That Will Set You Free* (Boston: Shambhala Publications, 2002).

6. These models can be found in any of the major works by these theorists. See, for example, Jean Gebser, *The Ever-Present Origin*, trans. Noel Barstad and Algis Mickunas (Athens: Ohio University Press, 1986); Graves, "Human Nature Prepares for a Momentous Leap"; Abraham H. Maslow, *The Farther Reaches of Human Nature* (New York: Penguin, 1993); Jean Piaget and Bärbel Inhel-der, *The Psychology of the Child* (New York: Basic Books, 1969); Jane Loevinger and Ruth Wessler, *Measuring Ego Development* (San Francisco: Jossey-Bass, 1970); Lawrence Kohlberg, *Essays on Moral Development*, 2 vols. (San Francisco: Harper and Row, 1981–84); Will Durant and Ariel Durant, *Rousseau and Revolu-tion*, vol. 10 of *The Story of Civilization* (New York: Simon and Schuster, 1967); James W. Fowler, *Stages of Faith: The Psychology*

of Human Development (New York: HarperCollins, 1995); Melvin E. Miller and Susanne R. Cook-Greuter, *Transcendence and Mature Thought in Adulthood: The Further Reaches of Adult Development* (Lanham, MD: Rowman and Littlefield, 1994); Jenny Wade, *Changes of Mind: A Holonomic Theory of the Evolution of Consciousness* (Albany: State University of New York Press, 1996).

7. Ken Wilber, *Integral Psychology* (Boston: Shambhala Publications, 2000).

8. Dale Ahlquist, *The Complete Thinker: The Marvelous Mind of G. K. Chesterton* (San Francisco: Ignatius Press, 2012), 110.

9. Wilber, *Integral Spirituality*.

10. "Experience" is not the best word for these types of spiritual realizations. "Experience" implies a subject experiencing an object, with a beginning in time and an ending in time, and many of the higher spiritual states have neither of those. It's more accurate to say, "This *moksha* (Freedom) realization is neither an idea nor an experience but a direct and presently immediate recognition of a space or clearing in which both ideas and experiences arise, itself beyond both feelings and thoughts, though including them if they do arise." But unless the author has the luxury of the room to explain all this, "experience" at least gets across the "not-merely-a-concept" nature of this awareness. And as for the "unity" in quotes, it is to emphasize that ultimate Truth is not directly and literally a "unity" state—"unity" itself being a dualistic notion, making sense only compared to its opposite, "multiplicity." This is why Zen says "not two, not one," to emphasize the Emptiness of the Ultimate. But "unity" is a commonly used term and gives a metaphoric hint as to its real nature, and so I use it, but almost always in quotes.

11. I use the phrase "multiple intelligence" to refer to a class or group of types of intelligences. You can thus refer to one member of this group as "a" multiple intelligence, just as you can refer to a member of the group of dogs as "a dog." A multiple intelligence is a type of intelligence; it does not imply that the intelligence is itself multiple.

12. Paul Smith, *Integral Christianity: The Spirit's Call to Evolve* (St. Paul, MN: Paragon House, 2011).

13. See his work in Ken Wilber, Jack Engler, and Daniel P. Brown,

Transformations of Consciousness: Conventional and Contemplative Perspectives on Development (Boston: New Science Library, 1986). The book also contains a chapter by Harvard theologian John Chirban, comparing the state-stages of a half-dozen Desert Fathers and finding a basic similarity in their stages (which are similar to the Eastern stages found by Brown). As we'll see, these are also similar to the stages first clearly outlined by Evelyn Underhill in her classic *Mysticism*. My thesis is that these state-stages of meditation are similar worldwide because they reflect the biologically given similarities of things like the waking, dream, and dreamless sleep state. When these are experienced *consciously* (instead of unconsciously as is typically and normally the case), they become stages in the meditative path—and hence their similarity worldwide. We will be exploring this notion in detail in subsequent sections.

14. Fowler, *Stages of Faith*.
15. Evelyn Underhill, *Mysticism: A Study in the Nature and Development of Man's Spiritual Consciousness* (Charlottesville, VA: Noonday Press, 1955).
16. Howard Gardner, *Multiple Intelligences: New Horizons in Theory and Practice* (New York: Basic Books, 2006).
17. An understanding and experience of states of consciousness does indeed go back at least fifty thousand years to some of the earliest shamans and medicine folk. Arguments can be made, however, that the depth of these states continued to grow and evolve. As structures were evolving from Magic to Magic-Mythic to Mythic to Rational to early Pluralistic and proto-Integral, states were moving from gross conscious states and types of nature mysticism, to subtle states of consciousness and types of deity mysticism, to causal/witnessing states of consciousness and types of formless mysticism, to nondual states of consciousness and types of "unity" mysticism. These advancements generally coincided with growth in structures of consciousness, with gross mysticism occurring up to magic-mythic (shamans and yogis), subtle mysticism occurring with mythic (saints), causal formless mysticism occurring with rational (sages), and nondual mysticism occurring with early pluralism and proto-integral (siddhas).
18. Brian Daizen Victoria, *Zen at War* (New York: Weatherhill, 1997).

19. Ken Wilber, ed., *Quantum Questions: Mystical Writings of the World's Great Physicists* (Boston: Shambhala Publications, 2001).
20. Ibid., 3.

Chapter 3:
The Fundamental States of Consciousness

1. An entheogen is a substance that, when ingested by a human, tends to lead to various altered and peak state experiences, many of a decidedly spiritual or divine flavor ("theo" = "god"; "en" = "within"; "gen" = "generated"). Even some of the earliest religious texts often refer to substances such as "soma," which induce God visions; entheogens used today include mescal cactus, mushroom psilocybin, ayahuasca, and LSD-25.

2. One has to be extremely careful in noting exactly how many states/realms the particular tradition is allowing in order to understand the three highest of the five states. All the traditions include some versions of the two lowest states (gross/physical and subtle). And then, if they allow all five states, the definitions of each are as I have given them, which are the "narrow," "technically correct" definitions. But sometimes the tradition will (for simplicity's sake, or sometimes because it is unaware of alternatives) acknowledge only four states, and if so, almost always *the causal is combined with turiya*, the Empty Witness, and the resultant state is given the characteristics just of turiya; it's the open, empty, clear, pure Witnessing Awareness, itself free of all form, all objects, all thoughts ("imageless," "formless," and "dreamless"), and is a pure Emptiness that is also pure ultimate Consciousness as Such. Again, these are qualities usually assigned to just turiya or Mahatman, but here combined with the causal dreamless sleep state—probably because the "dreamless" state itself is very close to an imageless, thought-free, pure and empty awareness, and when displaying those "dreamless" aspects, it is for all practical purposes the state of formless Emptiness, and thus the two states are easily confused and combined—or sometimes done so intentionally just to simplify things.

  On the other hand—and this is fairly common, so watch out for it—if only three states are recognized, then the characteristics of the two highest states (turiya and turiyatita, or Emptiness/Witness and Nondual Suchness) are all "smooshed" into the causal or Dharmakaya, and that Dharmakaya becomes the ultimate realm, awakening to which is awakening to the nondual Enlightened state (and thus it comes to represent everything from the true Witness to pure nondual Suchness, even though technically "Suchness" is beyond the Witness). Even more confusing, some systems (such as Buddhism) will often do all three of these things: sometimes talking as if there are only three states (and three bodies, which is called the "Trikaya" doctrine, the "Three Body" doctrine), whereas at other times four states (and four bodies) are given, and in yet still others, five states (and five bodies). You simply have to watch carefully the context and make your determination from there. There is, after all, in technical detail, a staggering number of differences between these three highest states, and their realizations in consciousness are the difference between being ignorant (if you only know three of the five states), having a dualistic realization (the fourth state of an Emptiness divorced from Form, a nirvana split from samsara), or having a fuller Enlightenment (the 5th state of pure nondual or "unity" consciousness). So it's important to keep any eye on just how many states are being acknowledged (and, for any truly inclusive or comprehensive system, to include all five, even if sometimes simplifying to a fewer number just for convenience).

3. The *waking mind* or state of consciousness (the radio content, sound, or actual thought) is being carried or supported by the gross realm or the *gross body* (the gross mass-energy component; in Buddhism, the Nirmanakaya). Thus the gross mind has a gross body (although the terms "gross," "subtle," "causal," and so forth, *technically* refer only to the body or mass-energy realm; but since there are only so many terms to go around, they are often also used for the corresponding mind—hence, the gross mind is supported by the gross body). The *dream mind* or state of consciousness is being carried or supported by the *subtle body* (the subtle mass-energy component; in Buddhism, the Sambhogakaya). Subtle mind, subtle body. The *deep-sleep mind* is being carried or supported by the *causal body* (causal mass-energy component; in Buddhism, the Dharmakaya). The *Witnessing/Nondual mind* (to combine those two, as is often done) is being carried or supported

by the *integrative body* (nondual mass-energy component; in Buddhism, the Svabhavikakaya). The realms, or bodies, are "concrete" mass-energy dimensions (and they are named after the type of "body," which is the literal meaning of the word "kaya," as in "Sambhoga*kaya*" or "Dharma*kaya*," because they actually exist in the concrete world, although they get, of course, subtler and subtler). Therefore you can actually point to them, you can "put your finger" on them (you can point to your physical body and actually touch it; with subtler awareness, you could actually see or "touch" your subtle body with its auras, chakras, acupuncture meridians, and so on). The "minds" or "states" (or "sheaths") are the nonmaterial awareness components, which don't exist in the concrete world. Where, for example, is "mutual understanding," "love," "care," "insight," or "satori"? You can't put your finger on them, like you can a body. And yet do we really doubt their existence?

4. *Brihadaranyaka Upanishad* 1.4.2.

5. I usually put "unity" in quotation marks when referring to "unity" consciousness because the ultimate state is conceived, by virtually all the Great Paths of Liberation, as being purely nondual—the "not-twoness" of infinite and finite, spirit and flesh, ultimate and relative, subject and object, nirvana and samsara, Emptiness and Form—but that doesn't mean a direct and simple identity, or unity, either. What the dualistic terms (infinite and finite, ultimate and relative, and so forth) refer to cannot be separated or divorced from each other, but neither can they be directly and simply identified with each other either. There is a "unity-in-diversity," if you will—or what Zen calls "not-two, not-one." So that "not-one" part is why I usually put "unity" in quotes (and if I don't, it's implied).

6. Wilber, Engler, and Brown, *Transformations of Consciousness*.

7. Traditionally, the chakras are referred to primarily as "subtle energy centers," and that is how they are generally presented and worked with. These energy centers are part of the anatomy of the subtle body and its subtle energies—with the first chakra, at the base of the spine, starting in the gross realm of food and matter and typically the highest chakra, the seventh chakra at and beyond the crown of the head, moves from subtle into causal/ultimate re-

ality. As energy centers, they are primarily "bodies," or mass-energy swirls, each becoming subtler and subtler. These chakras are primarily discovered through meditative introspection, and they are not traditionally known as what we are calling "structures" (at most, they are what the traditions often call "sheaths," which have an implicit correlation with structures, although that correlation is not presented or directly spelled out by any of the traditions, since, again, structures cannot be seen by mere introspection). But since all phenomena have all 4 quadrants (as I'll explain later) and the chakras are technically part of the "spectrum of energies" in the Upper Right quadrant, they definitely have correlates in the Upper Left quadrant—including states and structures—and thus the structure correlates of the chakras (were the traditions to postulate them) can be fairly easily deduced from the characteristics that are generally ascribed to each chakra as an energy swirl. It is this implicit correlation of the Upper Left with the Upper Right that I am referring to when I refer to the "structure" component of each chakra—and, as we would expect, the structure correlation is quite accurate in general (that is, the way the energy swirls in the Upper Right are defined by the traditions is very compatible with the way the structures in the Upper Left are defined by modern developmental psychology, since the 4-quadrant correlations are so generally similar in virtually all cases). Finally, since, according to Integral Theory, every phenomenon in one quadrant has correlates in all 4 quadrants, the mass-energy swirls, or chakras, in the Upper Right can be taken as direct examples of the correlates in the Upper Right of the structures in the Upper Left as they are being presented.

8. Georg W. F. Hegel, *Phenomenology of Mind*, trans. J. B. Baillie (Mineola, NY: Dover Publications, 2003), 64.

9. Robert Kegan, *The Evolving Self* (Cambridge, MA: Harvard University Press, 1982).

10. Can't we just use chakras for integral mindfulness and be aware of them? Not exactly. As I have often noted, basic structures can't be seen by simply introspecting; the aspects of the chakras that you can actually see by looking within are essentially just their energy signatures, or subtle energy swirls, and the qualities and traits associated with them. The subtle energy swirls are the

Upper Right mass-energy, or "body," correlates of the Upper Left, or "mind," structures; but the actual characteristics of these structures, such as their magical thinking, or their mythic thinking, or their rational thinking, and so on, are found in none of the texts on chakras and cannot be seen by looking within at the chakras. You can't tell if you are at moral-stage 1 or moral-stage 2 or moral-stage 3 by looking within—you'll never see a thought that says, "I'm at moral-stage 3." You can feel a charka energy that says, "I love the entire world!" But each basic structure's characteristics are ones that I am taking from modern research, from Western models of growth and development, and I am combining these "mental" characteristics with the "body" energies of the chakras. As for the subjects that need to be made objects, here, in the Upper Left, or consciousness dimension itself, these "hidden maps" or "hidden structures" are being revealed by Western models that have been incorporated into an overall Integral Framework. Concentrating on the chakra energies would not, in and of itself, be making subjects of awareness into objects of awareness. Working directly on the chakras is part of working with energy states—it is more part of Waking Up than Growing Up, and follows its own path of growth and development, which I will focus on next. No, the "hidden maps" and "hidden structures" are things that modern developmental psychology has discovered, and it is these otherwise hidden and unknown structures and maps that we need to make conscious. These are the hidden subjects that need to be made objects, in order for Growing Up to be accelerated and increased.

11. Geshe Kelsang Gyatso, *Mahamudra Tantra: The Supreme Heart Jewel Nectar* (Glen Spey, NY: Tharpa Publications, 2005), 99. Geshe Gyatso uses the standard three-state/body classification: Nirmanakaya, Sambhogakaya, and Dharmakaya—or gross, subtle, and very subtle (the Tibetan term for "causal" is "very subtle," so instead of "gross," "subtle," "causal," it's "gross," "subtle," "very subtle"; I used "causal" in keeping with my general terminology). This three-state classification, as it usually does, implicitly collapses the 4th-state empty witnessing mind and the 5th-state nondual mind, both of which are fully recognized by the Tibetans. But they often include them in the Dharmakaya or the very subtle (or

"causal"), which I have therefore summarized as "causal/non-dual." This is simple semantics (as I indicated when I first described the Dharmakaya state in defining the five states). The point is that "gross," "subtle," "causal" is well recognized by this tradition. Further, each of these "three worlds" (and actually, all five worlds) are said to consist of a realm, or *dhatu* ("ontology"); the body experiencing it, or the "kaya," as in the "Trikaya" or "Three Body" classification Geshe Gyatso uses (gross Nirmanakaya or Form, subtle Sambhogakaya or Transformation, and very subtle Dharmakaya or Emptiness/Truth); the state of consciousness supported by it (waking, dreaming, dreamless; or "epistemology"); and the level of consciousness knowing it, as in the eight or nine levels of Yogachara (also "epistemology"). Integral Theory includes all four of these dimensions (realm, body, state, and level).

12. Dustin DiPerna, *Streams of Wisdom: An Advanced Guide to Integral Spiritual Development* (Tucson, AZ: Integral Publishing House, 2014).

13. Ruchira Avatar Adi Da Samraj, *Real God Is the Indivisible Oneness of Unbroken Light* (Loch Lomond, CA: Dawn Horse Press, 1999), 18–19.

14. The stages of meditation, in other words, like virtually everything else, are a 4-quadrant affair. I mentioned the quadrants earlier, as helping to situate science and spirituality. I will soon be returning to them and will explain them more fully, where we will see that the 4 quadrants are four major perspectives, or dimensions, inherent in any situation, and all four need to be included for a full or comprehensive view of any topic. These quadrants include areas such as biological, psychological, cultural, economic, technological, environmental, and social factors—all of which play a role in how the surface features of these meditative stages appear and are experienced. As I've said, it's fairly well recognized that cultural and social factors play an important role in how human experience is actually experienced. This is true for transpersonal universal features as well—they are interpreted by structures in all 4 quadrants. Thus, for example, it is common to find in Western mystical literature innumerable references to beings of light, often with two wings—in other words, angels. (Whether they are viewed as actually distinct ontological beings, or something more

like radiant luminous forms found in the subtle state, depends in large measure on the structure-stage doing the experiencing.) But in either case, there is not a single mention in the Western mystical texts of a being of light with ten thousand arms; and yet that is an incredibly common image in Tibet, representing the bodhisattva of compassion, Avalokiteshvara, of whom, for instance, the Dalai Lama is said to be an incarnation. The point is not that these figures are *merely* cultural constructions—rather, the brain state and the subtle-consciousness state from which both images originate are very real, and are found universally—and with universally similar deep features; but they are interpreted by factors that include cultural and social molding factors, which result in different surface features and actual experiences, hence the "two-armed" and "ten-thousand-armed" *interpretations* of subtle-state *realities*.

15. This view strikes a balance between naive realism and subjective idealism. We start with the developmental component—and if you do include a developmental component (which critical realism acknowledges is one of its significant lacks), the first thing that you face is the fact that every structure-stage of development *sees a different world* (a magic world, a mythic world, a rational world, a pluralistic world, an integral world, and so forth). Now, there are three basic ways that that discovery can be viewed: (1) there is only one, real, pregiven world or ontology, and each level is giving a different interpretation of that world (realism); (2) the structure of the knowing subject is itself creating the phenomenon that is seen, thus each level sees something different (idealism); and (3) a middle way between the two—integral pluralistic enaction—which sees epistemology and ontology as being two correlative aspects of the same Whole reality. In this view, the knowing subject, through its own inherent epistemology (or its chosen form of methodology—see below) co-enacts or co-creates the known object—with subject and object co-enacting, co-influencing each other. In each moment-to-moment prehensive unification, as the new subject prehends the previous subject, incorporating it into its own being, its own being is obviously altered to some degree by that prehensive incorporation (the object influences the subject). But likewise, as the subject prehends the object, and incorporates

it in its own being, the being of the object is influenced by the structure of the knowing subject doing the incorporating. Thus, different levels of consciousness perceive co-enactedly different worlds.

The epistemic fallacy assumes that the knowing subject has no impact or influence on the ontology of the known object; thus, there is only one, single, pregiven world that each level of development interprets differently. But if you describe that "one, single, pregiven" world to me, I will show you that you are actually describing an orange world, or a green world, or a teal world, or a turquoise world, and so on. You are implying, whether you know it or not, that each level of development co-creates a different object world (although you are unaware of the "hidden map" or rules of grammar of the level doing the co-enacting). If there is only one, single, true, pregiven world, and yet each higher level of development sees more and more of that world and thus interprets it more and more accurately, then no single level would itself ever have truth, because evolution never reaches a specific level and says, "That's it, I've had enough; no more evolution; what we see here is final truth." No, there are always higher levels of evolution coming, and thus if there is only one real and true world and one real ontology, this present level's view—and every level's view—of reality will always be wrong, will always be less than the highest level would see, because there is NEVER a highest level. And since there is no one highest level, nobody ever sees anything true at all, *ever*. Everything you see now is wrong, and will be proven so by future evolution (think of how the world will look five thousand years from now). Think of how the Magic View saw the world, and how little of that is accepted by today's higher levels (it had no atoms, no molecules, no cells, no evolution, and so forth); or how the Mythic View saw it. For the Magic View, atoms did not "ex-ist." By "ex-ist," I mean that the phenomenon in question—in this case, atoms—existed nowhere in the awareness of Magic tribal consciousness. Atoms, in fact, did not ex-ist until orange Rational and modern science. But were atoms totally nonexistent in the Magic world? No, atoms *subsisted* in reality; they just didn't ex-ist in awareness. If that's so— and it is—then this view avoids the epistemic fallacy in any form.

So, then, what is the nature, or the "truth," of atoms themselves? What is their ontological status? That will be determined by which level of development answers the question, and again, here we say either that there is only one true, pregiven nature of atoms, or that the nature of atoms is co-enacted by the level of consciousness answering the question. That seems like it would reintroduce the epistemic fallacy, but consider: When atoms were first conceived by orange, atoms were pictured as being literally little planetary systems, with a sun/nucleus and planets/electrons. With pluralistic/multiplistic green, this gave way to a rambling quark theory and the view that subatomic particles were actually probability waves consisting of various types of multiple quarks. With teal and 2nd tier, these quarks were brought together in a unified fashion (the so-called Eightfold Way, recently given a boost by the discovery of the Higgs boson). But this theory still couldn't unite all four physical forces (strong and weak nuclear, electromagnetic, and gravitational), only three of them (it left out gravity). With turquoise, this gave way to string theory or M theory—the belief that subatomic particles are actually particular manifestations of ten-dimensional "strings" from this particular multiple universe—a view, although wildly abstract, that nonetheless managed to unite all four forces, although everybody agreed it was so abstract that no possible empirical proof would ever be possible.

Which of these views of atoms is true? If we want to "save" ontology and anchor science in ontology by making ontology the one real unchanging world of which science makes increasingly accurate maps and models, and thus say that there is only one, single, pregiven true nature, or ontology, of atoms, then we will have to say that, frankly, we can't say what the true ontology of atoms is now, because the next level of development will continue to see atoms differently, and presumably more accurately. Thus, only the ultimate and absolutely final level of development or evolution will actually have the real truth; all lesser levels—including our own present view—will NOT have any truth at all, just partial, limited, distorted illusions of the real atom. The ontology-privileging realist approaches, which want to save ontology by making it the one real unchanging domain, and ground epistemology in ontology, end up absolutely destroying any chance of ever getting at that one true ontological domain, because evolution is unending, thus we will never get an accurate view of that ontological reality. OR, we can abandon the ontic fallacy of "one true world" and say, as Hegel said, "Each stage is adequate, each higher stage is more adequate," so that "each stage is true (for the 4-quadrant conditions and overall phenomena given at that stage), and each higher stage is 'more true' (for the new conditions and new emergent phenomena given at its stage)." This is what developmental studies reveal with unmistakable clarity in any event—each new level of consciousness has (and co-enacts) a different world.

To be more precise, at each given level, or worldspace, the epistemology (the knower), the methodology (the "how" of knowing), and the ontology (the "what" that is known) are all mutually interwoven, co-creative, and integrally enactive. All three of them tetra-interact to produce or disclose the final phenomenon that comes to ex-ist instead of merely subsist. And by convention (whether consciously realized or not), what "subsists" is virtually always taken to be what "ex-ists" at the highest major level generally doing the knowing. Today, what subsists in the world is basically what ex-ists at the turquoise worldspace, since that is the "most true" or "most evolved" View of all the levels that have developed so far. Since nobody will ever know the ultimate level of evolution, because there are no indications that evolution will ever reach an end point, the only meaning of "truth" becomes "most true"—the View seen from the worldspace of the highest level that is doing the seeing. In today's world, "the most, most, most true" View would be that of Supermind, but since so few people are anywhere near that level, and fewer still of them are investigating atoms, the highest expectable level/View of an atom is, as noted, that of turquoise. The tetra-enacted ontology of the turquoise worldspace thus becomes the reality that is implicitly said to be the "one true" subsisting reality at all previous times and places—including the "real world" of the magic tribal societies, the "real world" of the mythic traditional societies, the "real world" of the rational modern societies, and the "real world" of the pluralistic postmodern societies (whereas it is, of course, simply what *ex-ists* in the tetra-enacted turquoise worldspace, which is then conventionally and implicitly assumed to be the single *subsisting* reality of this and all other worlds, and the reality taken to be the one and only "really real" or ontologically true reality by realism). But as soon as you describe what you maintain "subsists" according to today's most advanced theories, you will only be describing what ex-ists in the turquoise worldspace, unavoidably.

This approach thus steers between the one, single, pregiven true view of realism and its single ontology, and the subjective idealist view that all objects are created by the knowing subject. No, there is a reality that subsists apart from any knowing or method of knowing it (the one exception being if the object of knowing is itself some aspect of the human knowing system/process, which obviously does not exist or subsist independently), and for any aspect of that subsisting reality to ex-ist in any human's awareness, that subsisting object has to be known by a subject or group of subjects (at a particular developmental level of consciousness) using a particular method of knowing (the senses, a microscope, a cloud chamber, a telescope, and so forth). A pluralistic subject using a pluralistic methodology will co-create, or integrally enact, a pluralistic object. If any one of multiple factors is missing, the phenomenon fails to ex-ist in any awareness at all. And again, as for what it is, exactly, that *subsists*—what is actually ontologically there—that is taken to be whatever the View is, of the highest level doing the viewing (since that will be the "most true" version of subsistence available). This might sound like the Integral view introduces a *ding an sich*—an unknowable "thing in itself"—that different levels enact differently, but not so. Rather, the realist view that there is a single ontology that grounds epistemology or knowing actually turns out to be the one that is implicitly postulating a *ding an sich*, since the real object, as evolutionary developmentalism shows, will only appear at the ultimately highest level ever to evolve, which is something that will never be known, *ever*—and right there is the unknowable thing in itself that realism implicitly postulates. Whereas, defining "true" as "true for a given level or worldspace" allows the human being to actually know something true—the phenomena that ex-ist at its level are true phenomena (at that level, and if studied adequately by the methodologies at that level). To qualify truth by saying "at that level" doesn't deny or reduce "truth," it simply situates it; having done so, truth is as true as true can be— at that level. The Integral view also assumes that "each stage is true, each higher stage is more true"—that subsistence will be seen more and more clearly and enacted more and more adequately as development unfolds, making ex-istence more and more adequate as well. It also claims that the "most true" version of subsistence is the ex-isting View of the highest level of evolution to date that is doing the looking, so that "most true as true can be" is "the highest level's truth" for that issue. The highest level's ex-istence is *true* subsistence for that point in history/evolution—"truth" has no *real* or actually workable meaning other than that. Unlike realist and idealist versions, this approach allows truth to be genuinely grounded in a mutually interwoven process of epistemology, methodology, and ontology, with none of them reduced to an unknowable, single, pregiven ontology or abstracted into an ultimate radical subjective epistemology, neither of which adequately account for evolutionary/developmental issues at all.

Some view like this is what is necessitated as soon as we look at developmental studies and take them seriously. Because the first thing you learn from developmental research is that every level sees a different world—every level *has* a different world. This smashes all realist ontologies to pieces and demands a sliding scale of real truth as developmentally true, which itself calls for an integral, pluralist, enactive paradigm, which, in my opinion, alone can respond adequately to these issues.

I have since added the fact that if we look at the quadrants from the viewpoints of "zones"—namely, a holon in each quadrant can be looked at from "without," or "from the outside," in an objective/universal/rational stance, or looked at from "within," or "from the inside," in a subjective/cognitive/local/enacted stance— this gives us 8 zones, 4 within and 4 without. I give evidence (in volume 2 of the Kosmos Trilogy, "Sex, Karma, Creativity," unpublished ms.) that disciplines in each quadrant break down into these two major approaches. This turns out to pinpoint which approaches emphasize a realistic (objectivist) component to being and knowing, and those that emphasize an idealist (cognitive/en-active) approach, and each of these 8 zones have very well-known approaches indeed. It is by bringing an Integral ("all-zone") approach to this issue that a balanced, comprehensive, truly holistic viewpoint can be derived, as just presented. (And it also suggests something that is an Integral truism, namely, that each of these approaches are "true but partial"—if you take up the particular perspective that generates a zone, then the world will actually look to you to be fundamentally realist or fundamentally idealist, depending upon the zone from which you are observing that world. Integral, as usual, draws together the "true but partial" truths—realist AND idealist—into a larger "true but partial" view—Integral—which represents the "most true" and "most large" view at this point in evolution.) See chap. 11, n. 1, for further elaboration.

Chapter 4:
The Gross and Subtle States of Consciousness

1. Bubba Free John (Adi Da), *The Paradox of Instruction: An Introduction to the Esoteric Spiritual Teaching of Bubba Free John* (San Francisco: Dawn Horse Press, 1977).

2. One of the ongoing topics of discussion in any Integral Psychology/Spirituality is when various states can be objectified (made conscious) in relation to overall structure development—both the earliest or lowest point this can happen, and the highest point at which it must happen for development to continue at all. Thus, as for the "earliest," if you recognize the five major natural states of consciousness, you also recognize that all except for the lowest—the gross waking state—are "unconscious" in the earliest stages of development (that is, infancy). What happens in overall state development leading to Enlightenment (or a full course of Waking Up) is that Wakefulness, or Consciousness as Such, or pure Awareness, moves from being identified with, and stuck in, the gross waking state, to being conscious in, or aware of, the subtle dream state (either with "lucid dreaming," or certain states of meditation such as Brown's "Awareness," or possibly both, thus turning the unconscious subtle subject-self, or "soul," into an object of awareness, thus transcending and including it in Con-

sciousness). Then Wakefulness, or Consciousness, moves into the causal or very subtle state (either remaining tacitly aware during deep dreamless sleep, or experiencing certain states in meditation development such as Brown's "Awareness-itself," thus turning the hidden, unconscious, causal subject into an object of awareness, hence transcending and including it). From there Wakefulness moves into pure Emptiness, formless insight/awareness, pure Witnessing mirror-mind awareness, or True Self consciousness, thus starting to transcend and include that ultimate source of dualism and moving toward the "final" stage, the pure Awakened nondual Suchness.

The question as to "earliest" is: what is the earliest structure-stage at which any of this, as well as all of this, can occur? Clearly, it takes a fairly strong and developed self-sense to be able to move through those difficult and demanding state-stages, and the self at its very earliest levels would almost certainly not be strong enough to do so. So what are the correlations here? My educated guesses are (I'll explain the colors in chapter 6; no need to remember them now): The self needs to be at magenta Magic/impulsive to be able to even begin its journey into subtle-state awareness, and more commonly it will be at the red Magic-Mythic. It must be at the amber Mythic to begin journeying into causal, and even more commonly, at the orange Rational. It needs green Pluralistic, and more likely teal Holistic, to reach truly nondual state-stages. Part of the data used to generate these suggestions is taken from the historical record and the correlation between the average mode, or structure center of gravity, of a particular era and the highest state realizations that also emerged and were present in those eras. Thus, Magic foraging saw the rise of low-to-medium subtle-state shamanism; amber Mythic saw the rise of high subtle-state mysticism and "one manifest spirit" priestly religion; early incursions into orange Rational saw the rise of truly causal, or formless-state, mysticism, such as nirvana divorced from samsara, One divorced from Many; and the early glimpses of Pluralism, and especially 2nd tier, saw the rise of Tantra and the pure nondual schools.

As for the "other end" (that is, what is the highest/latest structure-stage in which a particular state has to be objectified, or made conscious, in order for development to continue?), I have simply, for the time being (as research continues to come in), followed, among other sources (including my own experience), Aurobindo regarding the four higher (and highest) structures in 3rd tier or Super-Integral. I assigned each structure a state that must be made conscious *at the latest* by that structure in order for development to continue at all: thus, Aurobindo's "illumined mind" (my indigo para-mind) finally objectifies gross and gross-reflecting; his "intuitive mind" (my violet meta-mind) finally objectifies subtle; his "overmind" (my ultraviolet overmind) finally objectifies causal/witnessing; and his "supermind" (my white or clear light supermind) finally objectifies nondual. In many, probably most, cases, this happens earlier (anywhere after the minimum-requirement structures just given have been reached).

These are "theoretical framing limits" to the Wilber-Combs Lattice—both the earliest and the latest that a particular structure can experience a particular state. But within those wide limit points, it is still generally true that almost any state can be experienced by almost any *structure*; Waking Up and Growing Up are indeed two very different axes of development, both of which need equal tending.

3. Whitehead's view of moment-to-moment reality is fleshed out, by Integral Theory, to cover all 4 quadrants, and evolution is a product of all 4 of those quadrants. For Whitehead, each moment (or "drop of experience" at any level) comes to be as a new subject of experience, and in doing so, it "feels," or prehends, the previous moment's subject, thus making it object. This constitutes the "causal" component of the past on the present—obviously if the present moment is enfolding, embracing, and prehending the previous moment, that previous moment will have an impact on the present one. This is the "include" part of the "transcend and include" that, for Integral Theory, marks each moment's unfolding. But if that were all that happens, this would be a strictly causal, deterministic universe, with the past fully causing the present. But, says Whitehead, the new present moment, after prehending the previous one, then adds its own degree of novelty, newness, or creative addition, and that, Integral Theory adds, constitutes the "transcend" part of the "transcend and include." In holons that have little novelty or creativity—especially insentient holons, like

atoms—the very low degree of novelty makes a sequence of unfolding that involves atoms look very deterministic; but, Whitehead maintains (correctly, I believe) that "low novelty" is not the same as "no novelty," and so the universe, at all levels, is NOT a deterministic machine but a creative, vital unfolding, with consciousness (prehension), or interior dimensions (Left-hand), and a material or exterior form (Right-hand), with inherent creativity in every moment. After all, atoms managed to bring forth molecules, an enormously creative act. So the very modest amount of novelty (that is, Eros) given to atoms nonetheless accumulated over millions of years to leap forward as emergent molecules.

For Integral Theory, this moment-to-moment unfolding is occurring, not just in a single subject–object stream, but in all 4 quadrants. Each quadrant has to mesh with its predecessor; there is thus a selection pressure placed by each quadrant on the ongoing existence of a particular holon, a pressure based on the validity claim of that quadrant (truth in Upper Right, truthfulness in Upper Left, justness in Lower Left, and functional fit in Lower Right). "Natural selection" is simply a subset of functional fit in the Lower Right. This inherent process of quadrant-to-quadrant meshing (with a creative/transcending subject prehending a previous subject and making it object, in all 4 quadrants—"transcending and including") was operative since the very beginning of the Big Bang, and thus evolution (Eros-in-action, Spirit-in-action) was operative from the start; it didn't require the emergence of sexual organs, spontaneous mutations, and then natural selection, because none of those were present when quarks evolved into atoms, and then atoms evolved into molecules, which evolved into cells. That's an awful lot of evolution occurring before anything even vaguely Darwinian had emerged. Thus, evolution really is an omnipresent "self-organization through self-transcendence" drive present throughout the Kosmos from the very beginning, and all the ingredients necessary to run this "transcend and include" process are fully given in the Neo-Whiteheadian account of moment-to-moment unfolding (as hooked to an AQAL Framework): causality, creativity, and directionality (toward greater and greater "transcend and include," which means greater and greater differentiation/integration, or wholeness, and greater Truth, Beauty, and Goodness—the selection pressures from the 4 quadrants), and not only the general characteristics that were present from the start but also the incalculable number that emerged as a result of evolutionary unfolding.

4. The dual meanings of "physical" or "material"—the lowest level *and* the exterior of all levels—often lead somebody who accepts only the material realm in the lowest sense as real; that is, only the lower or lowest sensorimotor realm as real, to end up accepting the exteriors of *interior realities* that themselves are quite beyond the sensorimotor, and realities that the person will never accept *on their own* as being real (but will accept as part of the package of matter in the larger definition as the *exterior* of those realms). Thus, in figure 4.1, if we look at the Right-hand quadrants, moving from eukaryotic cells to the complex neocortex and its "structure-functions" (SF1, SF2, SF3), materialists will accept all of those *exteriors* (for example, the triune brain) as real, but will not accept their corresponding interiors as real—interiors such as emotions and concepts and formal-operational or rationality. They accept their exteriors as real because the exteriors are all made of the "same" material form as the lowest sensorimotor level is, and thus these people are being faithful materialists. This is funny.

And, by the way, in Integral Theory, when we say that the lowest level is physical, we still mean only the exterior of the lowest level. The interior of the lowest level is the first form of awareness or consciousness—called there "prehension" (as shown in figure 4.1). So for Integral Theory, "matter" or "physical" itself means just the exterior forms of all phenomena, their Right-hand components; their Left-hand, or interior, components all are prehension or its evolutionary elaborations.

5. A "holon" is a whole that is also a part of a larger whole—as whole atoms are parts of whole molecules, whole molecules are parts of whole cells, whole cells are parts of whole organisms, and so on. The universe is composed fundamentally of holons, or whole/parts, in all realms. Each holon has proto-consciousness, perspective, or what Whitehead called "prehension," which means "feeling-touch"; and each has four major drives, two "horizontal drives" operating on any given level: (1) agency (the

drive to be an individual whole; an autonomy drive, a wholeness drive) and (2) communion (the drive to be part of a larger whole; a relationship drive, a partness drive) and two "vertical drives" operating between levels: (3) Eros (the drive to higher wholes) and (4) Agape (the drive to embrace lower subwholes, such as its own components).

6. Unlike the elements in the low and middle subtle, whose characteristics, by themselves, tend toward a prepersonal and personal experience, respectively. For example, there is little in the mid-subtle energy range that would itself pull the egoic-mental levels higher or above themselves; thus when they are experienced by transpersonal structures, they have a tendency to pull them *down*, although the likely outcome will still depend profoundly on the contribution of the structure itself. Likewise with low subtle, its energies (etheric and astral) tend to support prepersonal, prerational structures (for example, vital life, emotional-sexual), although again, the likely outcome depends significantly on the structure experiencing it—a transpersonal structure will tend to find the transpersonal aspects of those lower dimensions in any event and experience them as such (or certainly experience them from a transpersonal perspective). Although low, middle, and high subtle have tendencies that, on their own, gravitate toward prepersonal, personal, and transpersonal experiences, respectively, in the final outcome of the always conjoined structure/state experience, the general type of what that is experienced is contributed by the state, but the *how*—the interpretation and thus much of the actual experience tone itself—is contributed by the structure.

This is important since the traditions, unaware of the structures of Growing Up, tend to define the state merely by its contents, overlooking the determining influence of the structure-level on the state-experience. This shows up most dramatically in how, for example, the radiantly luminous forms of the subtle (one of the subtle's most widespread general characteristics) are ultimately interpreted by the experiencers of those radiant forms. A prepersonal structure tends to merge or fuse with them and consequently assigns them purely human, anthropomorphic qualities. An early personal structure, such as Mythic-literal (and this is extremely common, as I have been noting), will tend to interpret these radiant forms as literal, ontologically real and separate beings (asuras, devas, angels, and so forth), and gives them largely anthropo-familar features (or perhaps a mixture of various features, such as in a unicorn, a centaur, a fairy, a supernatural angelic being). A 3rd-tier structure will tend to interpret them, not as anthropomorphic 2nd-person beings (although there are 2nd-person 3rd-tier forms of Spirit—that is, the Lower Left quadrant in the 3rd tier), but as archetypal, evolutionary, collective 3rd-person forms, patterns, or morphic fields (akashic record, vasanas of the collective storehouse consciousness, and so forth). Again, the same state is seen differently according to the structure doing the seeing, in the always complex structure/state conjoint that is experience.

7. This is why Fulcrum-2 (the Magic impulsive stage) is the cornerstone of the narcissistic and personality disorders (this is, of course, in addition to contributions always made by the other three quadrants, particularly genetics and brain chemistry in the Upper Right, family values and cultural aspects in the Lower Left, and social systems—from environmental to political to economic in the Lower Right). As James Masterson and others have pointed out, if traumatic fixation occurs prior to the rapprochement subphase, when the self is still narcissistically one with the surrounding others, it remains narcissistically structured, seeing the whole world as an extension of its glorious self. If the problem occurs during the rapprochement subphase, the result contributes to the borderline disorders; the self, having problems with creating a firm and clear boundary between self and other (if the rapprochement subphase is correctly navigated, it results in the creation of a strong and clear self-boundary), lives its life as if it is one constant rapprochement crisis, with no strong self to handle it. The self splits into fragmented part-selves and, outwardly, part-objects (for example, the all-good mother and the all-bad, devouring mother). These are all problems that can occur when development in the self-line is misnavigated through the basic developmental levels, in this case level 2 (Fulcrum-2, "fulcrum" is the name of any one of the major developmental levels as they appear in the self-line).

Chapter 5:
The Causal, Empty Witness, and
Nondual States of Consciousness

1. Besides, since the only way the "contents" of these higher realms, such as the high subtle and the causal, were known by the ancients was by introspection, as we have seen, then their list or survey of the contents of these higher realms would have been much more accurate and inclusive than they in fact are if all forms had been truly created first by involution and were thus open to discovery by meditative introspection (since they would have already fully existed in the higher unconscious, awaiting emergence, and thus would have been open to discovery by meditative introspection). If everything that has emerged in evolution were already potentially present—put there by involution—and ready to unfold in evolution, then the traditions would have had a very complete, very accurate view of everything that has indeed emerged in human history (since it would have all been there, available to profound introspection). But every major traditional metaphysical and meditative text will give lists and lists of beings such as I outlined that are to be found in the high-subtle realm (devas, asuras, hungry ghosts, titans, gods and goddesses, and so forth, not to mention that their description of the entities found in the gross and gross-reflecting realm contains abundant lists of items found only in their own cultures), yet there is no mention in any of their lists of items created by involution of anything that was later discovered in the modern and postmodern eras. Although proponents of the view that everything is first created in involution would claim that these artifacts are all produced during involution, nonetheless there is no mention at all—in any of the mystical texts—of telephones, cell phones, iPods, computers, airplanes, internal combustion engines, steam mills, baseball, ocean liners, skyscrapers, elevators, automobiles, football, gas chambers, land mines, hand grenades, guns, satellites, rockets, jets, and so on. If all of these had been produced by involution and were sitting there, in the storehouse unconscious, waiting to emerge at the appropriate time in evolution (waiting, as Huston Smith put it in *Forgotten Truth*, "to fall out of the sky"), then

why was not a single one of these items introspected or intuited and then mentioned by a single ancient Adept? The reasonable answer, of course, is that they had not, in fact, been produced during involution (even though the Big Bang had already occurred—and therefore ALL of involution had already occurred—and we were collectively about halfway back to our horizonless Omega Point of resurrected Spirit). There's no mention of these modern or postmodern items anywhere—because, it now seems, they were not in fact created during involution but during evolution, and evolution itself had not, during premodern times, yet produced modern and postmodern inventions. They weren't listed because they didn't yet exist and had not yet emerged.

2. Erwin Schrödinger, *What Is Life?: With Mind and Matter and Autobiographical Sketches* (Cambridge: Cambridge University Press, 2012), 89.

3. Ludwig Wittgenstein, *Tractatus Logico-Philosophicus*, trans. David Francis Pears and Brian McGuinness (New York: Routledge, 2001), 6.4311.

4. Douglas E. Harding, *On Having No Head: Zen and the Rediscovery of the Obvious* (Carlsbad, CA: InnerDirections Publishing, 2002).

5. Chögyam Trungpa, *Journey without Goal: The Tantric Wisdom of the Buddha* (Boston: Shambhala Publications, 1981), 136.

Chapter 6:
The Hidden Structures of Consciousness

1. A "structure of consciousness" is a probability wave of finding a particular event—thought, emotion, or behavior—in a particular region of the AQAL Matrix specified by that structure. Thus, if we say that a person has a cognitive center of gravity at orange rational, that means that if we look in the Upper Left quadrant of the AQAL Matrix, the probability that a person's next thought, when faced with a specific challenge, will be of the pattern of a formal operational (formop) thought is around 50 percent (there is also a probability of 25 percent or so that it will be of the level higher than formop, and a probability of around 25 percent that it will be of the level lower than formop). Thus, "structures" are

not rigid rungs in a ladder or concrete steps in a staircase (as our metaphors unfortunately suggest), but are free-floating "probability waves" in any region (quadrant, level, line, state, type) of the AQAL Matrix. When 4-quadrant "causes" come together simultaneously to trigger a particular quadrant, level, line, state, or type, the probability wave governing that particular region is activated, and the probability that the resultant holon will "materialize" (emerge out of the pure Empty Ground of ongoing Being and Becoming via the storehouse or Ground unconscious) gives the likelihood of actually finding the emerging holon in that particular space (the particular quadrant, particular level, particular line, particular state, or particular type—or any combination). Moreover, all of these probability waves are governed by something like a Heisenberg uncertainty principle: the more the time-related characteristics of the holon can be determined (goal, aims, drives, needs, tendencies), the less the space-related components can be (relationships, communions, agencies, forms), and vice versa. This occurs because the "measurement" of the holon involves the consciousness of the measurer invading the consciousness (prehension) of the measured emerging holon, and consciousness interfering with consciousness changes the nature of the emerging holon itself to some degree, ensuring that all of its components can never be totally determined, because measuring the holon will always involve smashing into it one way or another, thus affecting and altering it. This is simply part of the "tetra-enaction" of the overall AQAL Matrix and all of its phenomena.

2. The actual order of the colors of the developmental spectrum turn out to be important, for reasons given by the traditions themselves—each chakra, for example, has a color, and these colors occur, from lowest to highest, in the same order as in a natural rainbow, because the actual energies of the chakras are said to be manifestations of the same Kosmic energies producing rainbows—reflecting the "unified" nature of the Kosmos itself. So there is a reason that the chakras run from "infrared" (or more accurately, "crimson") and "red" at the low end, which are low frequencies of raw, "violent" color associated with anger, hatred,

and so forth, to green smooth colors in the middle, representing more advanced/evolved levels, or bands, of both colors and consciousness, to blue and indigo at the highest end, with their smooth, soothing, peaceful tones. As more and more research is done into "energy medicine" and "subtle energies," machines evoking various levels will be based, in some cases, on directly eliciting a particular level of consciousness by resonating with a particular color; it's therefore very important that these colors are in the correct order if we are to elicit the levels we actually want. Spiral Dynamics also uses colors for its 6-to-8 basic levels in the values line, but its color assignments are totally off according to the tantric traditions. Violet or purple, for example, is assigned by Spiral Dynamics to one of the very lowest levels (Magic), whereas for the traditions it is one of the very highest levels, in some cases, *the* highest level of all. Likewise, blue is put right in the middle by Spiral Dynamics, whereas according to the traditions it is one of the highest of all levels. Spiral Dynamics has yellow as one of its two highest levels, whereas the traditions put it toward the lower end of the spectrum, in the red/orange range. When I first started using Spiral Dynamics as an easy introduction to the levels in one particular line (the values line), the comment I got most often was "Yeah, but they got the colors wrong," and I'd always say, "Yes, but that can be easily addressed." Turned out to be not so easy to address, so I had to make explicit a color spectrum that is more accurate, according to the traditions (a color spectrum that was implicit in my work going back all the way to my first book, because I would always draw parallels with the chakra yoga system—and implicitly, its colors). With *Integral Spirituality, The Integral Vision*, the eBook *The Fourth Turning*, and so on, I explicitly introduced a more adequate spectrum of colors that match a real rainbow—and thus, according to Tantra, more accurately match the actual energies at these various levels of development. I regret not addressing this colors problem from the moment I started using Spiral Dynamics as an example of my work on levels and lines—it has contributed to an inadequate scheme becoming fairly widely dispersed; but, I suppose, better late than never to correct it. I'll be using the more adequate color scheme in this presentation.

Chapter 7:
The Structure-Stages of Development

1. Fowler, *Stages of Faith*.
2. Carol Gilligan, *In a Different Voice: Psychological Theory and Women's Development* (Cambridge, MA: Harvard University Press, 1982).
3. A "stage" is an ontologically, genuinely existing level or structure of consciousness and complexity, a real structure in the Kosmos. A "tier" is a conventional grouping of structures, which doesn't exist in and of itself as a separate thing but is simply a conventional grouping made by researchers to indicate and emphasize a major and profound shift in the nature of the structures themselves at each tier. Thus, for example and from one perspective (taken by Kohlberg, for example), 1st tier itself already has three tiers: morality, for example, has egocentric or preconventional tier, ethnocentric or conventional tier, and worldcentric or postconventional tier structures. All of these are different enough to warrant being grouped as tiers (with what I am now calling "2nd tier" becoming "4th tier," and so on). The basic tier division I am presently using, with the first six major structure-rungs (archaic to pluralistic) being 1st tier, the next two or three rungs (from holistic to integral) being 2nd tier, and the final three or four rungs (para-mind to Supermind) being 3rd tier, is based on the fundamental nature of truth and self-identity at each rung: 1st-tier structures self-centrically believe that their truth and values are the only real truth and values in existence (and thus are separate, fragmenting, and partial); 2nd-tier structures are holistic and systemic and thus inclusive, embracing, and relatively comprehensive—these 2nd-tier structures are the first structures that think all structures have some importance (whereas 1st-tier structures think that only they are important); and 3rd-tier structures are marked by deep Wholes and "awareness of awareness," as the self moves from personal to transpersonal in its makeup, inherently united with states to incorporate states themselves into ongoing structural evolution. I am using this particular version of tiers (though I don't deny the validity of other ones such as Kohlberg's) because it powerfully indicates the nature of a person's

identity and view of truth—fragmented and partial, personally holistic and inclusive, or transpersonally holistic and superconscious. As Graves used to point out, 2nd tier is the true beginning of a real and genuine humanity. I add that 3rd tier (not recognized by Graves) marks a superhumanity and that 1st tier remains (for Graves and others) deficiency-needs based, partial, broken, and fragmented—the sole state of humankind until, basically, today's emergence of 2nd tier, which is why today's evolutionary unfoldings into Integral levels are so utterly unprecedented, profound, and far-reaching: The emergence of 2nd tier today is the first major tier change (as just outlined) and significant transformation of human identity anywhere in humankind's entire history, the likes of which have never been seen before, anywhere—"a chasm of meaning, a monumental leap in meaning." It is this monumental leap that I want to make available so it can be incorporated by the richness of Buddhism (as well as, hopefully, by all major religions, if they are to shake off their infantile, childish, and adolescent notions and enter the full adulthood of human possibilities).

4. Kegan, *The Evolving Self.*
5. The same goes for the concept of "bioequality," the notion popular with green, but hanging on in some dysfunctional forms all the way to indigo, and prevalent as well in inadequately interpreted states of nature mysticism—namely, the notion that we should regard all species in a radically egalitarian way, so that each species is a purely equivalent strand in the Great Web of Life, including humans, and thus each species gets the same "one vote" in any actions we should take toward the biosphere or Gaia. On this view, how we respond to the AIDS epidemic is a hugely moral decision. After all, the average AIDS patient produces 1 billion HIV viruses a day, and so if we decide to treat a person's AIDS, it would be one vote against AIDS and 1 billion votes in favor of it. Clearly, AIDS is one of the most moral events ever to occur in history, for which we should be enormously thankful—at least according to bioequality. Likewise, using bioequality, one virus particle has the same moral worth as one Siberian tiger—at which point the silliness of the concept just becomes obvious. Each higher-emergence holon, since it transcends and includes its predecessor (the result of each subject becoming object of each new

subject), has all of the being of its predecessor plus adds some new and novel aspects or being, and thus it has more being, more reality, in its own makeup, and thus is more valuable in terms of its intrinsic or wholeness value. Hence it has more significance, since it signifies or includes more reality in its own being. But the lower or junior holon is a necessary component of many more higher holons (atoms are needed to make molecules, cells, organisms, and so forth, but organisms are not needed to make atoms or molecules or cells). Thus atoms have more *fundamentalness*, or "part," value ("extrinsic value"), and organisms have more *significance*, or "wholeness," value ("intrinsic value"). In general, the more junior a holon is, the more *fundamental* it is (the more other holons depend on it for their very makeup), whereas the more senior a holon is, the less fundamental but the more *significant* it is (it includes more holons in its very makeup, thus including and signifying more reality; but there are fewer holons that include it, so it is less fundamental). I refer to fundamentalness as extrinsic, or "part," value and significance as intrinsic, or "wholeness," value. And, finally, all holons also have "Ground value," which is the purely equal value that all of them have as being perfect manifestations of the Great Perfection, or pure Spirit, just as they are. In a growth holarchy, the lower levels are more fundamental, the higher levels are more significant, and all have equal Ground value. The Kosmos is not just holographic (all have only equal value) or merely holarchical (all have different value); the Kosmos is rather holographic/holarchic.

Further, you can tell when you have a real holarchy (a real growth hierarchy) and that the order of your holarchy is real (and not merely a product of biased ranking or judging but an actually existing, ontologically real hierarchy) by using this criterion: in a real hierarchy, whenever you destroy a particular type of holon, all of the lower (less significant but more fundamental) holons are NOT destroyed, but all of the truly higher (more significant but less fundamental) holons ARE destroyed. Thus, in the real hierarchy of atoms to molecules to cells to organisms, if you destroy all molecules, none of the truly lower holons will be destroyed (in this case, none of the atoms), but all of the higher holons will be (in this case, cells and organisms). That is obviously true, because this is a real hierarchy. This "thought experiment" will show, in every case, the ontological existence of the particular ranking scheme in a real hierarchy: in a real hierarchy, destroy a particular level, and all the higher, more significant levels are also destroyed, but none of the lower, more fundamental ones are.

6. Thus, even if the universe started with a perfect hologram in its first nanosecond, the next moment's universe—the next moment's overall newly arising subject that prehends the previous moment's subject, now as object—that second moment's universe is already a holarchical event; it transcends and includes the previous moment (à la the Neo-Whiteheadian 4-quadrant view). And the next moment's subject would transcend and include this present moment's subject, making it object, and enfolding it into its own larger, deeper, wider existence. And so vertical levels of *depth* (holarchies) are built into the Kosmos by its very structure (as outlined in the 20 tenets and simplified in the "transcend and include," "subject becomes object" overview). Each holographic world becomes a junior level in a more senior level's holographic world, so that holographs are related holarchically—not as equivalent points, but as nested hierarchies or holarchies. This is the utterly core structure of the Kosmos's evolutionary unfolding—transcending and including, transcending and including—and not the popular, flatland, holographic universe.

7. Frances E. Vaughan, *Awakening Intuition* (New York: Doubleday, 1979).

8. We have seen that many traditions combine the causal and turiya into one "empty pure Self" awareness, and I am doing that here. We can certainly divide this structure-rung into two—one conjoined with causal, the higher conjoined with turiya; or do the same thing and simply refer to the "low" and "high" Overmind. But I am treating them as one major structure-rung, in part to retain resonance with Aurobindo, but also because probably the most common presentation is of 4 states and not 5—thus, gross, subtle, causal/turiya, and nondual. But this is a simple convenience, nothing more.

9. The involution/evolution (or Efflux/Reflux) sequence originally and in some ways primarily refers to the unfolding and enfolding

of the major states. That is, the nondual microgenetically, or moment to moment, gives rise to the primary dualism of subject versus object, and thus pure Witnessing awareness (on the "subject" side), then passes out (amnesia or "forgetting" of the higher) and gives rise to a reduced version of itself called the causal—or the first actually manifest world—which itself then passes out and awakens as a reduced version called the subtle, which finally passes out and gives rise to the densest level, the gross; and then, moment to moment, returns via that sequence to pure nondual awareness, with the person's *state* center of gravity *determining how much of those stages, in either direction, will be conscious.* Somebody with a subtle state center of gravity will be aware of gross and subtle levels, in both involution and evolution, but unaware of causal, witnessing, and nondual; somebody permanently at witnessing will be aware of gross, subtle, causal, and witnessing, in both directions, but unaware of nondual, and so on.

This sequence is also intimately involved with the growth and unfolding of structures, although in a somewhat secondary or derivative fashion. All individuals, at any given time in history, are born possessing the potential Forms of all the levels of consciousness that have emerged and evolved up to that particular point in evolution, enfolded as unconscious potential in their Ground unconscious (or the collective storehouse unconscious). Today, individuals are born possessing all the potential Forms of all structure/levels all the way up to turquoise, with faint possibilities of 3rd tier, which are yet to be fully formed and thus are not available in their final Form in the storehouse or Ground unconscious. As the already present and stored structure/levels emerge into consciousness (following the order of the fixed deep structures already stored in the Form storehouse—that is, in sequence, stage by stage, from infrared to turquoise), those structures slot into the involution/evolution sequence that is already occurring in states. Depending on individuals' *structure center of gravity*, they will be conscious of all the rungs up to their structure center of gravity. If they are, for example, consciously at orange, then in both involution and evolution of structures, they will be aware of infrared, red, amber, and orange rungs (but only orange Views, the others having been negated, transcended, and let go of); but as involution/evolution continues to microgenetically move through the remaining levels made available by evolution, they will remain unaware of them—in this case, unaware of green, teal, and turquoise, even though they are present in their Ground unconscious and are microgenetically active, not to mention some traces of 3rd tier, which hasn't fully formed yet. The involution/evolution sequence is thus consciously occurring in them, on the evolution side, from infrared to orange—or mid-mind—and then continuing unconsciously to turquoise in structures, where it trails off. (The only structure, at that point in evolution, that is present beyond turquoise is an Erotic impulse to go beyond turquoise, but there are no actual Forms or structures adequately ready to receive that movement—individuals who evolve beyond turquoise will have to do so on their own in a pioneering fashion, with some traces as general guiding forms.) If the individual's state center of gravity is subtle, then he or she will pick up the realms of reality from gross to subtle, while the involution/evolution sequence continues unconsciously through causal, witnessing, and nondual—in both directions. Overall then, in moment-to-moment microgeny, the involutionary sequence starts out at nondual in states and at turquoise in structures, and in this person, will become conscious at an orange structure and a subtle state. In both directions, structures/states higher than orange/ subtle will be unconscious, but starting at orange and subtle, the structures and states in consciousness up to them will unfold or enfold together in both involution and evolution.

As structure evolution moves into Overmind, causal/Witnessing states consciously enter the picture as well (if they haven't previously), so that structures all the way to ultraviolet Overmind and states from gross to witnessing are now all correlatively involved in the evolution/involution sequence. Since Witnessing, or Emptiness, is "right next" to ultimate Nondual, the Overmind starts to get preliminarily involved with that, as well, which is why the Overmind forms such a crucial link in overall evolution/ involution and the relation of Supermind to all lower levels.

10. The original involutionary sequence is not of structures but of

states (moving from nondual to Witness to causal to subtle to gross; see previous note). Thus the first introduction of dualisms is the turiya/Witness's introduction of the subject–object duality (Brown's "individuality") and the singular–plural dualism—or the 4 quadrants, when manifesting a world, which is part of Spirit's creative play when seen as such, but part of illusory maya when seen apart from Spirit. Supermind is the product of evolutionary "transcend and include" and not a product of creative involution—involution produces the necessary ingredients for evolution to return to a Spiritual awakening that happens to include ALL of Spirit's stages (its structure-rungs) of its own evolutionary reawakening to its own Self-Being or Suchness—that is, Supermind. The structures of consciousness are the levels of being and awareness that were created by Spirit in its own evolutionary unfolding, whereas the states are the product of Spirit's own involutionary infolding. Supermind is thus the product, not known beforehand by Spirit, of the structure-levels of Spirit's return to itself via evolution, which is a return made possible, and necessary, by its own involutionary "getting lost" in its own lowest levels—namely, matter. Then, using the involutionary givens for this universe (such as the 20 tenets, including "Eros" and "transcend and include"), Spirit created the evolutionary sequence of unfolding through higher and higher, more and more whole, more and more conscious levels or structures of unfolding to Spirit's own Self-Realization and Self-Liberation—a process that, at this point in evolution, has produced, as the highest summation of these structures to date, the Supermind. Thus, the Overmind is not a "movement away" from Supermind as part of the involutionary sequence; it is produced by evolution as the highest stage just prior to Supermind, increasingly overcoming all previous dualisms created by the unfolding of Spirit from its own lowest levels of manifestation (that is, starting with matter). Thus, the Overmind does not introduce the subject–object dichotomy but is the structure that is the closest to finally overcoming it, a process fully completed with the next step to Supermind.

11. William Blake, *The Marriage of Heaven and Hell* (London: Camden Hotten, 1868), 14.

Chapter 8:
Shadow Work

1. Although with one important difference: Jung's archetypes are some of the earliest forms of *evolution*; the Great Traditions' archetypes are the earliest forms in *involution*. It's a big difference. For Jung, archetypes are "forms devoid of content," but when you asked him, "What kind of form?" he almost always answered "mythic forms, particularly as seen in the world's great mythologies and religions"—by which he meant everything from Zeus, Oedipus, Venus, and Mars, to Ishwara, Brahma, Kali, the Great Mother, uroboros, the warrior, the wise old man or woman, the king or queen, the trickster, and so forth. Jung's idea was that, as human beings began their evolution, certain early and fundamental forms and images and symbols were repeated enough that they became central to the human psyche, and were inherited by all humans in the collective unconscious. Thus, if you look at a book like Jean Shinoda Bolen's *Goddesses in Everywoman*, for example, you will find almost a dozen feminine "archetypes" like Venus or Aphrodite. But all that those mythic "archetypes" really represent are early fundamental *roles* that the rule/role mind, or mythic mind, first took in human development for women. They have nothing to do with the fundamental forms, or patterns, upon which *all of manifestation* is based—the first forms in involution (the "real" archetypes, according to the traditions). They are rather some of the first forms in human evolution—the King, the Queen, the Warrior, Death, and various central psychological functions/forms as well, including the ego, the shadow, the anima and animus, the Self. The Great Traditions' involutionary archetypes instead refer to the first forms in involution, or the first forms in the creation of this manifest universe—the forms that are needed in order to create a universe in the first place, and the forms upon which all other forms are based and depend: space, time, geometric form, color, and so on (this sometimes includes the sum total of all human thoughts and actions, or even all sentient beings' thoughts and actions, collected and retained in a "storehouse" unconscious). Thus, the traditions' involutionary archetypes and Jung's evolutionary archetypes come from oppo-

site ends of the spectrum of consciousness and definitely should not be confused. (Jung's archetypes might more accurately be called "prototypes.")

2. Kegan, *The Evolving Self*.

3. Technically, it's not enough to say that "the subject of one stage becomes the object of the subject of the next stage," because that "object" could itself be alienated, dis-owned, and projected, so that one could be fully aware of that object but imagines that it belongs to others, to someone else—that is, it's a projected object of the present subject, which fits the definition but is not an example of development! This is actually the definition of a pathology, not a healthy development—that subject has indeed become object but in a perfectly dysfunctional fashion. So this really won't work as a definition. Rather, and more accurately, development occurs when "the subject in the 1st-person subjective stream ('I') becomes an object in the 1st-person objective stream ('me') and eventually in the 1st-person possessive stream ('mine')—and an objective/possessive object ('me' or 'mine') of the next stage's subject in the 1st-person subjective stream ('I')." The pathological version occurs when "the subject in the 1st-person subjective stream ('I') of one stage becomes the object in a 2nd- or 3rd-person objective stream ('you,' 'him,' 'her,' 'it') of the next stage's subject in the 1st-person subjective stream ('I')"—in other words, it becomes dissociated and projected. That possibility still fits with the broader definition "the subject of one stage becomes the object of the next," but that's clearly not an adequate definition of development. For simplicity's case, I sometimes still use that wording. and, indeed, in *The Atman Project* (1980), I formulated it as "the subject of one stage becomes object of the next," two years before Kegan suggested it in his *The Evolving Self* (1982)—not that he borrowed it (the general concept itself is implicit in Baldwin and Piaget, among others), but simply that I'm very familiar with this notion, and thus what can be inadequate with it, too.

4. See Ken Wilber et al., *Integral Life Practice: A 21st-Century Blueprint for Physical Health, Emotional Balance, Mental Clarity, and Spiritual Awakening* (Boston: Integral Books, 2008).

5. Martin E. P. Seligman, *Flourish: A Visionary New Understanding of Happiness and Well-Being* (New York: Free Press, 2011).

702 | Notes to Chapter 9

6. Ibid.

7. Helen Schucman, *A Course in Miracles: Combined Volume* (Glen Elen, CA: Foundation for Inner Peace, 1992).

8. Wilber et al., *Integral Life Practice*.

Chapter 9:
Dysfunctions of the 1st-Tier Structure-Views

1. I am largely tracking specific defense mechanism lines, as well as problems in lines such as the psychosexual or pranic or affective/ emotional line (that is, specific fulcrums), but when the self-line is involved with archaic pathologies—whether created in the Upper Left quadrant or, just as likely, in conjunction with factors in the other quadrants, including family dynamics in the Lower Left, social factors in the Lower Right, and especially genetics and brain physiology in the Upper Right—the results, in Fulcrum-1, are usually the various psychoses, where the self boundary fails to form adequately and the self is open to flooding by states, particularly the subtle in actual hallucinations. Likewise, at the next fulcrum, Fulcrum-2, if the standard pranic or affective line is disturbed, the problems are usually emotional disturbances in general (splitting) or, a bit higher, psychosexual (allergies or addictions), but if the self-line is involved, we have the narcissistic-borderline disorders (if the problem occurs before the rapprochement subphase, where the self–other boundary solidifies, the self remains stuck in its narcissistic self-only orbit; if the problem occurs at the rapprochement subphase, the results are the borderline conditions, where the self lives its life as one continuing rapprochement crisis, with weak self and weak self-boundaries poorly adapted, where the defense mechanism of splitting—the incapacity to integrate self and other at a higher level—is common). At Fulcrum-3, typical pranic or affective line pathologies involve allergies or addictions to power, and traditional repressions of any bodily feelings by the newly emerged conceptual mind (classic repression and its psychoneuroses); if the self-line is involved, the pathologies tend to be similar, and revolve around traditional repression of bodily states by the conceptual mind, as these various lines start to come loosely together in the "self-related lines" in general. In the first three fulcrums, dysfunctions with dis-owned or denied feelings

result in standard psychopathologies—fixations/addictions to food, sex, or power (or other bodily feelings). But if the self-line itself is directly involved—given that these first three fulcrums are where the self is itself forming—we have, respectively, the generation of psychoses, narcissistic/borderline disorders, or psychoneuroses. Once a relatively strong self is formed—at red Fulcrum-3—then dysfunctions tend to be the classical repression found in typical psychoneuroses (and then the amber rule/role mind and its script dysfunctions, having to do with problems related to the social rules or social roles; then orange self-esteem and its dysfunctions, then green self-actualization and its problems, and so forth).

2. Recall that, for Freud, sex is a basic overall life-pleasure energy; the infant starts out "polymorphously perverse," which means it can get pleasure from all surfaces and activities of its body. As it develops, it restricts this general sexual energy-pleasure to just certain areas of the body. At the oral stage, the infant gets pleasure from the oral cavity, putting things in its mouth, sucking, and so forth. At the anal stage, it gets pleasure from controlling the body and especially its defecation. At the phallic (genital) stage, it localizes pleasure to the genital region, which is where it will stay localized for its adult life (unless there has been fixation/repression at one of these earlier stages). The second basic structure-stage is often called "emotional-sexual" with this general idea in mind, that the infant and child are developing precursors to adult sexuality in their own emotional and pleasure development. Of course, the adult form of sexuality doesn't come online, generally, until adolescence; but its precursors in psychosexual development go all the way back to these developments in early childhood.

3. At this point, let me note that as we talk about a specific pathology at a particular *level*—so far, in food, sex, power, or love, to put them almost unforgivably generically—most of these are also developmental *lines* that themselves *continue to unfold* at even higher levels and sometimes begin at even earlier developmental levels (as does, to give but one example, love) and then continue their development into higher levels. For example, love begins in its egocentric forms at the earliest levels of Archaic and infrared; it expands to some degree at the next level, Fulcrum-2 or magenta

Magic View, as the self expands, but is still egocentric; it expands again at Fulcrum-3, Magic-Mythic, still retaining its egocentric, 1st-person perspective View; finally, at Fulcrum-4, the heart chakra, amber Mythic View, which adds a 2nd-person perspective, love can begin to take on its defining characteristic as love of an other, not just oneself, so that love expands from *egocentric* to *ethnocentric* forms, a major expansion; love expands yet again at fulcrums-5 and 6, or orange Rational and green Pluralistic—both self-expressive, worldcentric chakra 5—as love expands from *ethnocentric* to *worldcentric* (or love of all humans, regardless of sex, color, race, or creed), a profound expansion; and it then leaps mightily at fulcrums-7 and 8, or Holistic and Integral (chakra 6), in its truly integral and inclusive forms; and leaps mightily once again as it enters the higher and highest levels of 3rd tier and Super-Integral (chakra 7), as love takes on universal/Kosmic and eventually infinite dimensions. The point is that the same expansion is happening with sex, power, and the other structures/ chakras. In each case, the particular quality defining that chakra usually has lower- and higher-level expressions, or lower and higher developmental levels to what are in fact these particular developmental lines. Pathologies can occur at any of these lower or higher levels, even when the main chakra at an earlier or higher level is primarily defined by another quality or trait or developmental line (as, for example, the second chakra is with psychosexual and the third chakra is with power). So the "integral psychographic" nature of these lines and qualities should be kept in mind.

We commonly see a failure to take this into account in many models, such as Spiral Dynamics and consultants who are using it. It's common to hear people say, for example, of an organization just getting started, that "It needs more blue vMEME (amber altitude "values" meme) *order or structure*" (which first emerges at amber altitude or blue values) or "That person needs more blue order." But blue/amber (mythic-membership) order is marked by ethnocentric, extremely absolutistic, very conformist, very rigid thinking (such as found in groups like the Nazis or in fundamentalist religions)—exactly what these organizations and individuals do NOT need. It's like saying, "What we need here are more

Nazis!" This happens because Spiral Dynamics confuses an "intelligence" (like order) with stages of development, failing to see that the intelligence that emerges at a particular stage—like blue/amber order—can itself continue its unfolding line by developing to higher levels/stages. There is blue order, for sure, but there is also orange order, green order, teal order, and so on, and the organization or person who needs more order needs more of some of those higher levels of order, not primitive, lower, blue/amber order (Nazis!). Virtually nobody needs to be more prejudiced, ethnocentric, biased, absolutistic, racist, sexist, rigidly hierarchical, incapable of taking 3rd-person perspectives and thus incapable of thinking scientifically—*all* those ethnocentric qualities that blue "order" (and its vMEME) has an abundance of. An organization that actually incorporated more of that "blue order" would collapse tomorrow. This problem results primarily from the very common failure, found also in Spiral Dynamics, to differentiate basic structures and their Views, and thus those who fail to make this distinction get confused as to what is "negated" and what is "preserved" in higher development. Spiral Dynamics maintains that, for example, the "purple" Magic View that a three-year-old develops can be directly contacted by any adult thrown into similar Life Conditions. It is indeed possible to recontact that lower *structure-rung* or chakra at any time in subsequent development, since they are on the "include" side of the street and remain in existence; but their *Views* do not. This is the distinction that Spiral Dynamics and so many other theories fail to make. For an adult to directly recontact and experience the Magic View (instead of the images/symbols of the basic structure-rung that originally supported that View when the self exclusively identified with that structure-rung and created that View) would mean that an adult at—say, orange, would instantly lose all access to reason, all access to concrete operational capacities, all access to concepts and any intentionality at all, and, most alarming, would lose all access to language of any sort and would simply blubber in a fantasized magical world. This never, but never, happens (unless, as I noted, there is severe brain damage, highly advanced Alzheimer's, and so on). This is just a poorly thought-through theory when it comes to the basics of ladder, climber, and View, confusing basic structures and their generated Views and treating them as if they were both the same in all ways.

4. Roger Walsh, "A Big Picture View of Human Nature and Wisdom," unpublished ms.

5. In these examples, the Lower Right dysfunctional factors can damage and even cripple not only the health of the physical body at the same level (with nutritional diseases and physical illnesses) but also, via emergent development and "transcend and include," *higher emergent levels as well*, including emotional, psychological, and spiritual, due to the "include" part of the "transcend and include"—so that higher levels almost always include some degree of lower-level dysfunction and malformation.

6. Seligman, *Flourish*, 47.

7. Seligman, *Flourish*.

8. To correct the Lower Right institutionalization of comfort food (meaning, mostly junk food), a central place to start is with the schools. The federal government, under sway of special interests of the junk-food industry, aligns school food programs with a nutritional diet that is almost universally condemned as not only inadequate but actually harmful. Sugary drinks, highly processed "white" foods (white flour, white rice, white sugar), along with candy-dispensing machines, are staples, with little or no servings of fresh fruits or vegetables. Organizations like Whole Foods, whose founder, John Mackey, is a strong proponent of Integral approaches to business—and, of course, food—are starting school food programs, with the aim of changing this dismal state of affairs. The national government could—and yes, should—get behind these efforts and offer their own. It's not exactly hard to find a consensus on what's good and what's bad nutrition. And likewise, national education efforts—aimed at families and kids themselves—can help provide some of these generally accepted guidelines for good eating (along with guidelines for exercise and other practices that promote physical health). Breakfast in the United States is still frightfully poor in nutrition value—starting with the cereals that push the "refined white" foods excessively. Mothers and fathers, not knowing any better, serve what advertisements suggest they serve, not what good nutrition suggests.

As for the Lower Left quadrant, that central mechanism of cultural maintenance, *shame*, should be slowly reintroduced with nationwide, federally assisted if necessary, educational systems teaching the simple facts—almost totally not known or understood at large—about what constitutes the difference between healthy shame (also known as a functioning *conscience*) and unhealthy shame (a neurotic, overcritical driver). The national tendency is to take *any self-critical voice* whatsoever and decommission it, toss it, get rid of it; instead, if that inner voice is pointing *away* from overly self-centered, self-promoting, self-glorifying tendencies, and away from tendencies that hurt, degrade, humiliate, or repress and dominate others, then *listen to that voice*—it is not only how to treat others admirably, it is how you yourself can grow and evolve to even higher levels of consciousness. It is the doorway to your own Self-liberation, not its denial. Parents, in particular, need to know this difference, and apply it diligently and consistently to the raising of their children. A decent, beginning conscience should be in place before the child starts typical education (and, in many cases, it will have to be reinforced because of the "nonshaming" attitude most schools will take, with their "I am special" green-stage-derived campaigns). Shame is a layer existing between the first three levels of development (food, sex, power) and all higher levels (love, self-esteem, self-actualization, self-transcendence), and acts as a buffer keeping one down, and the other up. Listen to it!

As for Upper Right genetics, in many cases, gene expression is governed by many factors outside of the gene itself, including the organism's behavior. For those who have likely inherited a gene or genes for the factors leading to overeating or being overweight (which often does not involve overeating, but simple metabolic rates), it's important not to prime the pump in childhood by overeating, or eating highly refined white foods that cause insulin-release flooding (which in turn causes insulin-receptor insensitivity, leading to adult-onset diabetes, which we are seeing in more and more children, something never before seen in history; this is a first, alas). But until actual genetic manipulation becomes possible (not that far off!), not priming the genetic pump is definitely recommended.

708 | Notes to Chapter 9

As for the Upper Left quadrant, I will indeed be bold enough to suggest that individuals take an Integral view to the problem, thus helping them see the real 4-quadrant (or overall AQAL Matrix) forces driving their problem, and thus at least making those hidden subjects theoretical objects, lessening to that degree their influence or control over them. Both structure and state development is recommended, increasing in each case the reach and influence of the "I" space and diminishing the power of the "it" drive (the food addiction).

9. "Neti, neti" is Sanskrit for "not this, not that"—meaning that Spirit is ultimately beyond all forms, ideas, categories, qualities, or characteristics that can be applied to it. This is maintained, not just because of various theoretical arguments (although these are abundant—from Kant to Nagarjuna) but because the direct realization and awakening of Spirit itself shows all concepts and notions to be totally inadequate by comparison. When St. Thomas Aquinas had his realization later in his life, he said everything he had written before that was worth "straw." As Spirit manifests itself in and as the world, in involution, and then begins its Refluxing evolutionary unfolding, it identifies with a particular item, then breaks that exclusive identification to make room for an ever-larger identity that includes the previous item but adds new ones—thus negating and transcending, but including and preserving, all phenomena, until, in any particular case, it has, by transcending and including the entire universe, come to its own shocking Self-Realization, beyond All, yet one with All. This is the best we can metaphorically get at Spirit-in-action as Eros, driving every stream and river and ocean of outrageous evolution, always pushing higher and higher, itself becoming more complex and more complex, more unified and more unified, more whole and more whole, more conscious and more conscious, until the entire World Process is transcended and included in its own Goal, Ground, and Creatrix. The various streams of psycho-development are likewise streams of "transcend and include," and pathology is a disorder in this magnificent overall display of Spirit's own evolution—or, if you wish, simply the universe's own drive to "self-transcendence through self-organization" (Jantsch). This "transcend and include" is the basic form of evolution in all domains.

10. Nora Ephron, *Heartburn* (New York: Knopf, 1983), 13.

11. The esoteric or hidden teachings were involved with paths of Waking Up; whereas the larger, exoteric, outward, and public teachings were involved with Growing Up in spiritual intelligence, usually from Magic up to Mythic. The esoteric cores included Kabbalah and some forms of Hasidim in Judaism, Gnostic and contemplative traditions in Christianity, Sufism in Islam, Vedanta in Hinduism, and contemplative Taoism in Taoism. Buddhism was, from the start, primarily a path of Waking Up, as interpreted from the orange level; later schools showed more Growing Up (with some significant texts pushing into 2nd tier), and a large number of sects also developed at lower levels of spiritual intelligence (Magic and Mythic), as we'll see. The esoteric schools were almost always fewer in number, were held to be "secret" and worthy only of special students, and were much more demanding (one of the reasons that fewer individuals were drawn to them).

12. Especially when you basically have Darwin on your side against the Neo-Darwinians. David Loye as done a series of superb books that show—with extensive and direct quotes from Darwin himself—that the Darwin of the "selfish gene" and "survival of the fittest" is about as far from the real Darwin as you can get. For starters, Darwin did not believe that "survival of the fittest" was the sole or even the primary driver of evolution. In *The Descent of Man*, Darwin's final and definitive statement of evolution as it worked in humans, he specifically mentions "survival of the fittest" exactly two times—once to apologize for ever using the term! Instead, he mentions "love" ninety-five times and "moral sensitivity" ninety-two times. He makes it clear that this a hierarchy of evolutionary drives, with survival of the fittest on the very bottom; then sexual selection, where the female selects the mate she will have sex with (Darwin doesn't call it the "mating season," he calls it the "season of love"—for all animals, not just humans). Here, female choice selection is actually what determines what will be passed on by evolution, so this powerful force is governed entirely by females. Then there is a type of parental selection and social selection. And then directly to the two highest forces of selection and evolution—love and moral sensitivity. Selection of the fittest is

710 | Notes to Chapter 9

a pure Upper Right and Lower Right force, that of "functional fit." The introduction of female selection introduces the Upper Left desires and choices; the introduction of love introduces the Lower Left and the I-thou love relationship. And Darwin leaves no doubt that he thinks this is real love, even in lower animals such as birds. And then finally, the introduction of moral sensitivity points not just to the Lower Left quadrant but to *higher levels* of development in that quadrant—this is moral sensitivity at its best, not its worst. Loye is now working on a book called *Integral Darwin*, which shows, as I just briefly outlined, that Darwin was applying an Integral framework to make sure he had a comprehensive sense of evolution in all 4 quadrants. "Tetra-evolution" (4-quadrant evolution) is simply how *this moment* must unfold in order to make room for the *next moment*—namely, the subject of this moment becomes the object of the subject of the next, a process that must "fit" in all 4 quadrants in order to be "selected" and passed on by evolution. But this is also a theory of evolution that does not depend primarily on random mutations of genetic material and selection only by "functional fit" in the Lower Right but can explain evolution being in operation from the moment of the Big Bang forward, and continuing to operate in all 4 quadrants (society, culture, individual anatomy, psychology, spirituality, and so forth) with or without genetic mutations. We hear so often today that "evolution touches everything, nothing is outside its reach." I agree, and simply point out the AQAL Integral approach is the only approach that explains how that is possible—all the rest of them assume the Neo-Darwinian explanation lying in the background somewhere, which is not capable, even in Darwin's actual version, of explaining the vast majority of changes and improvements that we see in the world. Darwin's theory of evolution is a minor subset of this overall AQAL process, and is not, especially in today's world, even capable of coming close to explaining the vast number of evolutionary changes that we see in the world—in culture, technology, business, medicine, and education and in individuals, societies, and planetary processes. None of these can be explained by mere genetic mutations. The assumption is that Darwinian evolution perfectly covers all of biology (it absolutely does not), and then, accordingly, it actually covers all of the universe in all its dimensions (not even close!). Evolution does cover the entire universe but only in something like its "AQAL-driven" version, beyond mere genetics and natural selection, and anchored in the very structure of the dynamics of moment-to-moment unfolding existence, of Being and the actual form of its Becoming.

13. As part of the basic structure of orange, "rational" refers to various types of 3rd-person, reflective, abstract, multiple-perspective-taking cognitions, such as formal operational thinking ("formop"). As an enduring basic structure, formop remains in existence and is operated on (is an "operand" of) by vision-logic and is always available to focus in on this level of existence (the beginning "abstract" realm, using "abstract" in the very best possible sense). Even if one is at, say, meta-mind, this level of existence—and those existing at this level—can be selectively approached by activating and focusing on formop, on orange cognition. The fifth chakra, whether one identifies with it or not, always remains in existence after it is activated. When "Rational" is used as a transitional View, it means the worldview that results when one looks at the world exclusively with formop (or some similar orange cognitive tool). Both exclusive preformal and postformal modes are denied, and the Rational mind sees a world run on rationality and only rationality (along with its many associated qualities and capacities, from self-esteem to achievement to excellence to merit to progress). That View is negated and transcended with the emergence of the next higher stage (that is, green). The same is true of "the pluralistic mind" and the Pluralistic View—the former is an enduring basic cognitive structure, which remains in existence after its emergence, and the latter is a transitional View that is negated and transcended with the next higher stage, teal 2nd tier. In both cases, the former (enduring structures) are the "include" part of "transcend and include," and the latter (transitional Views from *only* that structure) are the "transcend" part of "transcend and include." In most cases, I try and find different names for the enduring basic structures and the transitional Views—with orange, "reason" and "rationality" are good choices, and with green, "pluralistic" and "relativistic"—but these end up narrowing options too drastically, and I end up reverting to using similar names; but clearly, as I have spent much time stressing, the one is

preserved or included, and the other negated or transcended, in overall ongoing development and evolution.

14. As I discussed in chapter 7, there are two very different types of hierarchies—dominator hierarchies and actualization, or growth, hierarchies—and this Pluralistic stage thoroughly confuses them. Pretty much all the bad things that are said about dominator hierarchies are true—they are oppressive, marginalizing, politically corrupt, and socially repressive. The higher you go in a dominator hierarchy, the more oppressive and domineering you are. Growth, or actualization, hierarchies are virtually the opposite in every way. Each level "transcends and includes" its predecessor, so it becomes more and more inclusive, more unified, more whole—and psychologically, tests show—people in them become more loving, more caring, more embracing, and less domineering, less oppressive, less controlling, the higher up they go in them. Most hierarchies in nature are growth hierarchies, with each stage as one ascends in the hierarchy—from egg to chicken, from acorn to oak, from infrared to supermind—being more and more inclusive and whole. In the typical growth hierarchy in nature—from quarks to atoms to molecules to cells to organisms, for example—each level transcends and includes its predecessor (all of an atom is in a molecule; all of a molecule is in a cell; all of a cell is in an organism, and so on). Cells don't oppress molecules or hate molecules—they include them, they embrace them, if anything, they love them. Arthur Koestler, noticing this, said growth hierarchies should be called *holarchies*, since each level is more and more holistic, and is composed of *holons* (another term he coined, also adopted by Integral Theory, which means a whole that is a part of a larger whole, as in the sequence quarks to atoms to molecules, and so on—each of those is a holon, and the sequence is a holarchy). Carol Gilligan's hierarchy (her term) for female moral growth is a growth hierarchy, a holarchy, as are the eight or so major level-stages of human growth I am outlining. Postmodern pluralism confuses these two types of hierarchies, and thus treats all hierarchies as if they were dominator hierarchies, a genuine catastrophe, since in throwing out all growth holarchies, it threw out all means of growth and development. Pluralism itself is at least the sixth major stage in a growth hierar-

chy or holarchy, and in cutting out all hierarchies, it cut out all paths to its own existence.

Chapter 10:
Dysfunctions of the 2nd-Tier Structure-Views

1. Victoria, *Zen at War*.

2. *Defense mechanisms in general*. This particular type of "Wholeness association" is one of the definitions of biased or prejudiced thinking—treating one thing as if it were the same as all similar things (which means, treating Wholes with similar parts as being the same)—and defense mechanisms in general tend to do exactly that (it's just that, at Integral levels, the "size" of the Wholes are substantially larger). But we saw this going all the way back to the earliest type of cognition, the so-called primary process, which confuses all wholes that have similar parts—for example, if one Asian person is bad luck, all Asian people are bad luck (all people with the partness "Asian-ness" are equated). This type of biased confusion is still operative in some of the defense mechanisms of 2nd tier; it's often part of the general nature of shadow repression—the shadow, recall, is "the locus of the lie." It's how we lie to ourselves about ourselves, and prejudiced and biased thinking is one of the elements that many defense mechanisms have in common, because they are fundamentally a distortion, a lie. Add to the fact that this 2nd-tier level is itself composed primarily of Wholes, and you have the pretty obvious result that dysfunctions at this level are Wholeness dysfunctions.

We see this whole/partness confusion (that is, a deformed holon) in defense mechanisms such as displacement, where if, for example, a young child is repeatedly traumatized by a red-haired nurse, the child might displace this fear onto all red-headed people. Whole individuals with their many differences, or different "parts," who simply happen to share the single "partness," or the quality, of being red-headed are equated and treated identically—again, the essence of biased, or prejudiced, thinking is treating the member of a general class as if that person has all the characteristics of that class, without getting to know that person individually. Thus, it is an empirical fact that white people score an average of five points lower on IQ tests than Asians. Thinking that is not prejudice, it's a simple empirical fact. But thinking that the white person you just met will score five points lower on an IQ test than an Asian is prejudiced thinking—you have "pre-judged" the individual person by applying general characteristics of a class to that individual person without actually checking it out. This type of prejudiced, or biased, thinking—equating wholes with similar parts (for example, white people as wholes with the "part-ness" of "scoring five points lower than Asians," or, more negatively, "being five points stupider than Asians")—goes all the way back, we saw, to the primary process, and the primitiveness of this type of thinking often shows up repeatedly in defense mechanisms even at quite high levels, as with some of the Integral levels, as we just saw (the major difference being, as I noted, that the "size" of the dissociated Wholes at Integral levels is considerably "larger"). Another common example is denial, where often a characteristic of one item that is being denied is spread to any item with that characteristic and then that thing, too, is denied, and again wholes with similar parts are confused.

Much of this has to do with the primitive nature of defense mechanisms themselves, on no matter what level. None of them work without difficulties and unintended side effects—the worst of which is that defense mechanisms in general bring about that which they were meant to ward off. Of course, if we knew that, we'd never use them, but the whole point is that their operation is unconscious, outside of our awareness in general. Defending against fear increases fear—it's a fear of fear. Defending against anxiety increases anxiety—it's displaying an anxiety about anxiety. Defending against depression increases depression—it's being depressed about being depressed. Lying about the existence of some interior material doesn't get rid of it but simply highlights it, so it gets more attention than if it hadn't been highlighted. Defense mechanisms are inherently danger-driven emergency measures, and quick, seat-of-the-pants measures are rarely as effective or efficient as well-thought-out, carefully planned ones. Defense mechanisms are just intrinsically primitive and half-baked lies, at whatever level.

3. Integral Metatheory, as might be expected, tends to look for the "true but partial" aspects of all of these. When we do so, as is

often discovered, the overall number of approaches tends to shake down to four to eight major classes of theories, which happen to match the 4 quadrants (and 8 zones). The 4 quadrants, as the basic dimension-perspectives of reality itself, are naturally the dimensions that anchor most specific approaches in most areas—including psycho-theories. In terms of the quadrants, there are approaches that focus on the Upper Left. Original psychoanalysis is an archetypal example; it sees the symptoms and symbols as the product of factors occurring in the individual psyche or "I" space, in particular, Eros and Thanatos (which are essentially the two vertical drives in all holons—ascending Eros and descending Agape—but with Agape interpreted in its pathological form, which is the drive not just to reach down and embrace all junior holons with love and care, but to regress to lower and ultimately the lowest of all holons, insentient matter, or death). Positive Psychology has recently had a large impact on these Upper Left schools by stressing an emphasis on what is going right and not just focusing on what is going wrong.

There are approaches that focus on the Lower Left, and, as I briefly mentioned, they tend to see all symptoms and symbols as really being a disturbed and oppressive culture speaking through an individual who is basically a scapegoat for the society's ills that it refuses to face consciously. Every major "transformation" advocate is based largely in this quadrant and assumes that culture at large is now operating from an old, outdated, destructive, and harmful set of assumptions, and that a "new paradigm" will replace that "old paradigm" and usher in a worldwide global transformation in consciousness and culture. Noting that humans have already gone through some major transformations—from hunting to farming, from farming to industrialization, from industrialization to information—they announce that humanity is now undergoing a profound new transformation, which, if worldwide culture everywhere were simply to start following their recommendations, would be earthshaking. (There is considerable disagreement as to what it is that every man, woman, and child needs to believe in order for this to happen—in large measure, I have suggested, because most of these theorists are coming from green Pluralistic stages, which excel at deconstructing present realities but are less helpful when it comes to constructive and truly Integral possibilities.)

Other major approaches, particularly in the past few decades, see all symptoms and symbols as due to factors in the Upper Right quadrant, the organic body and its brain, neurotransmitters, and brain functions. Treatments involve not interior insight or understanding, as do virtually all the Left-hand quadrant approaches, but physical interventions in the brain itself, the most common being medications, but they have included electric shock and brain surgery. The "symbols" that are being released by the gaping hole in the psyche do not have any deep interior meaning but are simply signs that the brain is broken, and all that is required is to address that broken brain. For this, medication is most often recommended, and Big Pharma is spending a fortune pushing these drugs and the major, scientific materialist paradigm behind this approach.

Wishing for more wholeness, but still within the exterior, sensorimotor, "scientific" purview, many significant approaches view the problem through a Lower Right quadrant lens, with approaches ranging from family systems therapy to eco-psychology. The idea is that reality is actually a series of dynamic, mutually interdependent, interwoven processes at all levels, and although this approach conspicuously leaves out all interior, Left-hand realities, it often uses a variety of systems theories to approach these dynamic unities. The general idea is that individuals suffering symptoms and sending up symbols have severed themselves from these mutually interwoven holistic systems—starting with the family system and stretching all the way to the entire biosphere (or Gaia)—and that ecocentric (or other systemic) approaches instead of egocentric approaches are the only real cure, because only they get at the actual and real causes.

And, indeed, all of these approaches are "true but partial." They each have an important piece of the overall puzzle, and their insights need to be carefully "transcended and included" in a more comprehensive, inclusive approach. Most of them make relatively accurate assessments and appraisals when working within their own quadrant but start to make horrific errors when, using an approach appropriate for one quadrant, they start applying it to all of them. "Truthfulness" (in the Upper Left) is confused with "truth" (in the Upper Right); or "functional fit" (in the Lower Right) is confused with "cultural meaning" (in the Lower Left); and thus, with quadrant absolutisms firmly in hand, these approaches end up wreaking havoc, not on their one-quarter of the picture, but on the other three-quarters.

Chapter 11:
Dysfunctions of the 3rd-Tier Structure-Views

1. What we "see out there" is a product, not just of a given ontology of the item seen, but of the methodology and epistemology we bring to see it (see chap. 3, n. 15). Again, this is not saying that the characteristics of the known object are fully created by the knowing subject (this is NOT subjective idealism); simply that the characteristics of the object that are disclosed depend in part upon the means of disclosure. If we have an iron rod, and we start heating that rod, there is no way to know that the rod is becoming hot by simply looking at it. Vision does not disclose the hotness. Touching, however, does—touch it (change your methodology), and you will see that the "hotness" is disclosed. Even more, if we look at the rod through an infrared-detecting device, we will see the rod lit up and radiating in all directions—those radiating fields cannot be detected by any human visual sense; but change the methodology (in this case, with an infrared-detecting device), and those fields are disclosed. To say that there is "just a single rod in existence" is to privilege one or more detecting methodologies (or types of epistemologies). We could say that "the single" rod is what is disclosed by the sum total of detecting devices used on it, and that would be fine as long as we include human epistemology in the equation of detecting devices, and then realize that the epistemological subject itself grows through upward of a dozen different real levels, and each of those levels will see something different about the rod and its surroundings: we have a magenta rod (an elemental spirit), a red rod (tool of a PowerGod), an amber rod (creation of an almighty Creator), an orange rod (made of atoms and crystals), a green rod (made of multiple quarks), a turquoise rod (made of eleven-dimensional strings), and so on, indefinitely. Every rod that we know is the product of the ontology of the rod

(endlessly expanding), the methodology used to detect it, and the epistemology used to know it—all three are inseparable aspects of the single Wholeness of whatever the rod actually is. There is no such thing as "*the* rod." The closest thing to it would be the rod "at the end of time," when all known methodologies would have been discovered and used, and the highest level of evolution would have been reached for epistemology; the sum total of all these would be "the" rod. However, if we say that, then, of course, we never have anything resembling any sort of truth, ever, because until "ultimate truth" is reached at the end of time, everything we know is shot through with some sort of falsehood. Far from anchoring our ontology—as virtually all realist schools attempt to do in this fashion, by postulating "the rod"—we have actually destroyed ontology, destroyed any hope of ever having any truth at all. Rather, each Whole rod (a phenomenon that is a product of a particular epistemology X a particular methodology X the ontology thus disclosed) is a *true* version of the rod *at that particular level* if all the given phenomena at that level are fully taken into account and then the best possible view of the rod is determined given the actual realities of that particular AQAL address. Less than that, and we have a false view of the rod (and ontology and epistemology). More than that is not possible. Similar (but not identical) to the way Hegel put it, "Every level is adequate, every higher level is more adequate," we have "Every level is true, every higher level is more true." Thus, truth is on a sliding evolutionary scale, with each level capable of truth, and each higher level capable of a wider truth. Any other option—from realist to idealist to materialist to positivist—unconvincingly privileges one component of this overall process.

Another way to look at all of this is that the above is an integral overview of the results of taking all of the methodologies generated in all 8 zones and including all their central features, in order to arrive at the "most correct" view of epistemology and ontology possible (or the view "most likely" true at this stage of history/evolution). "Zones" or "hori-zones" are where holons in each of the 4 quadrants are looked at from within ("subjectively") and from without ("objectively")—giving 8 zones altogether. These are "ontologically" real realities, the products of perspectives of perspectives. Thus each zone has different types of real phenomena and is accessed by different types of real methodologies (the sum total of which is referred to as *Integral Methodological Pluralism*). Just as the view from any quadrant is called a "quadrivium" (and their total, "quadrivia"), so the view from any zone is referred to as an "octavium"—to completely butcher the Latin involved—and their total, "octavia." Thus, the 8 zones can be thought of as "8" quadrants—and they are all very, very important.

The central idea is that each zone generates—and is accessed by—a *different family of methodologies*. Zone #1 (the subjective view of the interior of an individual) is accessed by interior phenomenology (phenomenology has applications in several zones, but it is one of the few that also accesses zone #1, and thus is listed as exemplary here), meditation, contemplation, and introspection. Zone #2 (the outside/objective view of the interior of an individual) is accessed by developmental structuralism and evidence-based maps and models of the interior of an individual's psyche. Zone #3 (the inside/subjective view of the interior of the collective) is accessed by hermeneutics, interpretive sociology, Heideggerian Dasein-analysis, Wilhelm Dilthey's *geist* sciences, Max Weber's *verstehen* aspects of sociology, and so forth. Zone #4 (the outside/objective view of the interior of the collective) is accessed by cultural semiotics, cultural studies, ethnomethodology, Foucault's genealogy, and so forth. Zone #5 (the inside/subjective view of the exterior of the individual) is accessed by cognitive behaviorism, cognitive science, Humberto Maturana and Varela's enactive/autopoietic biological paradigm, and so forth. Zone #6 (the outside/objective view of the exterior of the individual) is accessed by empiricism, behaviorism, positivism, empirical natural sciences (chemistry, biology, physics), and so on. Zone #7 (the inside/subjective view of the exterior of the collective) is accessed by game theory, Niklas Luhmann's social autopoiesis, social values theory, enactive systems theories, and so forth. And zone #8 is accessed by general system theory, complexity theory, chaos theory, network sciences, and so on. The point with all of them is that they are perspectives of perspectives of perspectives, where each perspective—being subjective or objective—creates, enacts, and brings forth a different dimension of reality. An integral pluralistic multiple methodology goes hand in hand with an integral pluralistic epistemology and integral pluralistic ontology, all three of which also vary from altitude to altitude to altitude. This gives an indication of the complexity and richness of Integral approaches to everything from epistemology to ontologies to research agendas.

In particular, note that each zone is especially delimited by being an "inside" or an "outside" view of a prior perspective already chosen as especially real—that is, the inside or outside view of a holon "in" the Upper Right (that is, zones #5 and #6); or the inside or outside of the Lower Right (that is, zones #7 and #8); or the inside and outside of the Upper Left (that is, zones #1 and #2); or the inside and outside of the Lower Left (that is, zones #3 and #4). These zones appear in quadrants where, in most cases, it has already been decided which one is the "ultimate reality," and once one has decided on what quadrant is "really real" (for example, material objects are what is "really real"—the Upper Right; or social systems—the Lower Right; or inner empiricism/constructivism—the Upper Left; or cultural constructivism—the Lower Left, and so forth), after one has made that fundamental selection, then one will generally further select the zone, the inside view or the outside view, of that "really real quadrant." One doesn't necessarily even have to choose a quadrant; but one will still very likely—and almost all existing epistemologies do—select either an *inside view* (subjective, enactive, phenomenological, autopoietic, cognitive [meaning the view "from within" as the organism's own cognition sees it, compared to a "rational" scientific view "from without" as the scientists themselves see it]), or select that *outside view* (objective, "totalistic" or some form of 3rd-person "holism," "rational" [meaning, as the scientists themselves see the overall reality]). These two basic views—inside/subjective and outside/objective—are also behind the major "competing" epistemologies in history, such as materialism/realism versus idealism (outside/objective versus inside/subjective); body versus mind (outside/objective versus inside/subjective); matter versus spirit (outside/objective versus inside/subjective); and so on.

The point is that, since the perspective "inside/outside" is universally available (all the way up, all the way down—it's what creates the "zones" in each quadrant), it fits into the typical human inclination to choose one side of a duality and proclaim it to be real, while denying reality to its opposite, and then basing its entire methodology on the "really real" zone (inside or outside) in whatever quadrant (or quadrants) that has already been chosen as the ultimately "really real" reality there is.

Some examples will show the importance (and reality) of this distinction between the "inside view" and the "outside view." Two of the most important theorists in postmodern theory are Martin Heidegger and Michel Foucault, and while both of them acknowledged the reality of the intersubjective (Lower Left) view, they did so from exactly an inside versus an outside view. Hubert Dreyfus and Paul Rabinow do an excellent job of summarizing Foucault's approach and differentiating it from Heidegger's:

> Foucault's devotion to the description of concrete structures understood as conditions of existence bears a striking similarity to what Heidegger, in *Being and Time*, calls an existential analytic. But there is an important difference here too. For although both Heidegger and Foucault attempt to disengage and relate the "factical" principles which structure the space governing the emergence of objects and subjects [that is, enact a world], Heidegger's method is hermeneutic or *internal*, whereas Foucault's is archaeological or *external*. (emphases mine; *Michel Foucault: Beyond Structuralism and Hermeneutics*, 2nd ed. [Chicago: University of Chicago Press, 1983], 57n)

And they also comment that "Foucault is explicitly rejecting both Husserlian phenomenology and Heideggerian hermeneutics when he opposes to the exegetical account the *exteriority* of the archaeological attitude" (emphases mine; ibid., 57). It could hardly be put plainer. Heidegger is focusing on zone #3 (the inside or "internal" of the collective interior); Foucault, on zone #4 (the outside or "external" of the collective interior).

We can see precisely the same thing in today's battles between the different schools of systems theory. Virtually all of them make the prior judgment that the "ultimately really real" reality is the Lower Right quadrant (the sum total, Whole, or collective of all objective interwoven dynamic "its"), but then they split, almost down the middle, as to which view within the Lower Right is the truly ultimately real perspective—the inside (cognitive, enactive, autopoietic, relative) versus the outside (objective, rational, universal, realist).

Those who choose the *inside view* will put a great deal of emphasis—sometimes, a total emphasis—on the creative power of the interior, cognitive, subjective, enactive capacity of the organism to create or co-create its own reality/environment. Thus, well-respected systems evolutionary researcher Derek Bickerton maintains that what any organism "sees"—including humans—depends upon its evolutionary history, and thus all knowing is "species-specific" (that is, subjective/inside); there simply is no "objectively single and real" view of a reality that is "out there." As he puts it, "It is meaningless to talk about a 'true view of the world.' To attain such a view, a minimum prerequisite would be for the viewer not to belong to any particular species" (quoted in Kenneth Bausch, *The Emerging Consensus in Social Systems Theory* [New York: Springer Science and Business Media, 2001], 52) and "It is absurd to speak about a 'true view of the world' because it is not true for any creature that what it perceives is the world itself. What constitutes any creature's view is essentially a system of categories" (ibid., 54). (In other words, it is an enacted/co-created/inside view.) As Kenneth Bausch summarizes this view,

> Our representations have no reality independent of our minds and languages. They do not re-present an existing reality that is present to us. In the course of evolution and ontogeny, we have fabricated these representations, imposed them on our experience, justified them, and come to rely upon them. With all these representations, however, and all our refinements of self-observation, self-description, reflection, and theories of reflection, we never achieve a privileged access to knowledge. We remain bound to self-observation. (ibid., 374)

In short, there is (*from this perspective*—zone #7) no single, pregiven, true "outside view" because there is no single pregiven "outside"; there are only the ways that the organism co-creates its "outside" reality/environment according to its own systems of autopoietic cognitions. This perspective is the way reality *actually looks* to somebody emphasizing a collective "inside view" (that is, somebody viewing reality via zone #7) and—especially given the impact of autopoiesis theory—it is a very common view in modern systems theories and evolutionary theories. This means that individuals who emphasize one or more of zones #1, #3, #5, or #7 will have a great affinity with each other; all of them maintaining, in their own ways, that the structure of the knowing subject is fundamental in creating/enacting the ontology of the given object, and, indeed, that there is no "pregiven single reality" that is simply "out there" awaiting perception by all and sundry. What we call "reality" is primarily co-enacted by the perceiving organism (and its culture), and otherwise has no substantial, characterizable existence. Recall that generally a theorist will have previously selected one quadrant as being the "really real" quadrant, and so only one zone—either the inside zone or the outside zone of that quadrant—will generally be postulated as being the "really real" zone; so it's not required that all of the "inside" zones are included in any single theory. Usually the theorist will select just one zone, which is a zone in the preselected "really real" quadrant, and then will argue that the opposite zone in that quadrant—if the inside view is selected, then the outside view, and vice versa—is unreal or mistaken or just plain wrong (not to mention the similar view from all the other already rejected quadrants). If two quadrants are felt to be "really real," then both inside—or both outside—views will be the "really real" ones, and so on. Critics of this "inside view" typically charge it with "the epistemic fallacy," the putative fallacy being to claim that the structure of the subject has a substantial hand in the formation of the ontology of any object it knows. The view that charges and criticizes this "epistemic fallacy" is generally held by all those who adopt the opposite stance—that is, the outside, rational, realist, objective view. For Integral Metatheory, both are "true but partial," depending primarily on the perspective/view that one takes. So we do acknowledge a "real ontology"—*but this is the way reality looks only from the outside views*—the inside views instead tend to see autopoietic, co-enactive, co-creative realities. BOTH of these are real, and Integral Metatheory refuses to choose just one and reject the others. Doing that is just a perspective absolutism. And that can be seen as false: all you have to do is adopt the perspective—the particular quadrant and zone—and look at reality the way the proponents of that view are looking at it, and you will see just what they are seeing. Your claim that they are "wrong" comes, not from the perspective itself, but from your preselection of just one of them as the only true one—the "wrongness" is in your narrow and limited viewpoint, not in the viewpoint itself, which is perfectly "true but partial."

And, indeed, as Bausch himself points out clearly, almost exactly half of the other systems theorists (that is, those who don't hold the inside, co-creative, enactive, autopoietic views) do indeed adopt the given "objective reality" view, giving us the two major views on the nature of systems themselves: inside/enactive and outside/realist (we just saw these two views, inside and outside, in the Lower Left with Heidegger and Foucault; now we see them in the Lower Right with the two main schools of overall systems theory). As Bausch, in his full summary of systems thinking, points out: there are today "two grand unifying theories of present-day systems thinking: complexity/bifurcation/components systems and autopoiesis" (ibid., 15)—which he also points out are exactly the outside/realist/objective reality view and the inside/enactive/co-creative autopoietic view.

Bausch summarizes these two major approaches as follows:

> These two strands of thinking advance systems theory beyond the bounds of mechanical (closed) models and organic (open) models and move it into the arena of emergent models. Component-systems thinking, which is propounded by Csanyi, Kampis, and (to some extent) Goertzel, is an outgrowth of Bertalanffy's General Systems Theory (GST). GST "enabled one to interrelate the theory of the organism, thermodynamics, and evolutionary theory" (Luhmann). Component-system theory loosely includes the bifurcation thinking of Prigogine, the molecular biology of Eigen, the complexity thinking of Kauffman and Gell-Mann, the physics of infor-

mation theory, and the sociology of cognitive maps. It describes the processes that generate increasing unity and complexity in specific details that are alleged to have universal application [external, objective, realist, universal; ontology favoring].

Autopoiesis in its biological form, proposed by Maturana and Varela, considers organisms as systems that are closed in their internal organization, but open on the level of their structural composition and metabolism. Autopoiesis in its sociological form, proposed by Luhmann, focuses on the difference between system and environment and identifies autopoietic systems with the unity of contradiction that derives from their being simultaneously autonomous from their environment and totally dependent upon it. In our thinking about autopoietic and component-systems, we discover vistas of new and possibly fruitful explanations of physical, organic, social, and cultural processes. It turns out that these ideas [component-systems and autopoiesis—the outside view and the inside view of the Lower Right quadrant] comprise the bulk of the ideas that are considered and evaluated in this research. (emphasis mine; ibid., 16)

The first approach is the more standard *dynamic systems theory*, which (for this simple classification) includes a wide variety of approaches such as general systems theory, cybernetics, dissipative structures, component systems, chaos theories, complexity theories, and so on. As we will see, dynamic systems theory is often actually called the "*outside*" (or *rational*) view, because it attempts to give the overall view seen from the outside: "detached, objective, systemic, reconstructive, universal."

The second major approach attempts to give an account, not of the system seen from without by a detached (scientific) observer, but the inner choices made by an individual organism as it actively participates with (and enacts) its environment—this is the *autopoietic* perspective, also specifically called the "*inside*" (or *cognitive*) view.

By the way, all of those terms—*autopoietic, cognitive, inside; systems, rational, outside*—are used *by the theorists themselves*—including "inside" and "outside"—as ample quotes will show. At this point, I am not giving my own interpretation of these schools, simply reporting how they see themselves. I will eventually maintain, of course, that they are actually focusing on different zones —the inside versus the outside zones, respectively—or, for systems (Lower Right quadrant), zone #7 and zone #8, respectively, *with both being true when addressing their own zone.*

So we have a systems/rational/objective/outside view, and an autopoietic/enactive, cognitive/inside view. And virtually all of present-day systems theory is divided almost equally between these two major views. Some people are confused by the use of "rational" and "cognitive" in this scheme, because often these two words mean the same thing, so why in this case are they diametrically opposed to each other? As employed by the theorists themselves, "cognitive" is used not to specifically mean "rational" or "intellectual," but in its wider and more inclusive meaning, which is any organism's attempt to register its environment (for example, an amoeba reacts to light, so it has a rudimentary cognition of light, but it does not, of course, have a "rational" view of light). In this sense, if I take a "cognitive" view of biology (à la Varela and Humberto Maturana), then I will try to explain, *from the inside view of the organism,* the types of reactions, behaviors, and cognitions that the organism itself makes as it encounters, enacts, and brings forth its world. This is also sometimes called *biological phenomenology* (a phrase Maturana and Varela themselves use), because it attempts to describe the phenomenal world of the organism itself. This is what the autopoietic approaches, pioneered by Maturana and Varela, attempt to do (and Maturana and Varela actually call their approach "biological phenomenology" and "the view from within," and they explicitly exclude any form of standard dynamic systems theory from their view, since no biological organism actually has that view, except the human scientific organism). Thus, we have the autopoietic, cognitive, enactive, co-creative, inside view.

This inside view accuses the outside/objective/realist schools of committing the "ontic fallacy," the putative fallacy of believing that the entire structure of the knowing process is created by (or dependent upon) the object as it is reflected on or known by the knowing subject—that the object is "really real," pregiven, single, intransitive, and universal. The object may be interpreted in different ways, but it is, underneath all that, one and the same object, and the aim of all true knowledge is to accurately reflect, or represent, this pregiven ontology, and that is exactly what is denied by virtually every inside-view approach. The inside/auto-poietic view also charges this realist/objectivist view with believing in "the myth of the given"—the myth that there is, in fact, only a single pregiven world, just waiting to be known by one and all (that pregiven world might be confused, misinterpreted, covered up, or denied, but it is still the same, single, pregiven world or ontology). The realist schools claim to be plugged into this ontology.

"Rational" is merely one type (or level) of cognition; as used by these theorists, it means the rational activity of the scientists themselves as they attempt to explain phenomena in terms of, say, complex dynamic systems of mutual interaction. In this general systems approach—the "rational/outside" approach—the attempt is not made to "get inside" the organism, but to stand back and try to see the whole picture, the total system, or web of relationships, as they mutually interact with and influence each other. This "rational" view is not saying that the Web of Life is merely a rational entity, but simply that scientists attempt rationally to study that Web. This "rational," 3rd-person view is taken only by the scientists themselves; only a scientist sees a "big picture systems view"—it is definitely not the cognition of, say, a frog (and thus it is a view that is "outside" of the frog's view). Thus, we have the systems, rational, universal, objective, realist, outside view.

This is the outside view that charges the inside/subjective/auto-poietic view with the "epistemic fallacy"—the putative fallacy of believing that substantial aspects of the known object are imposed/enacted/co-created by the structure of the knowing subject (instead of there being one, fundamentally real ontology, which, no matter how many different ways it might be interpreted, is basically the same single, invariant, universal, intransitive reality).

So we see there are these two basic, historically dominant, fundamental views of epistemology and ontology, and the Integral claim is that they are both right to the extent that they are adequately describing whichever of the zones they have focused on (the inside/autopoietic/subjective views focus on such zones as #5 and #7, and the realist/objective/outside views focus on such zones as #6 and #8). Each view is *right* or *correct* when it is focusing on its particular views or zones (assuming it is doing it correctly, of course), and if so, then it has a "true but partial" reality (and this needs to be included in an overall Integral approach). And possible views are *false* or *incorrect* when they violate the exclusion principle and criticize other views for what they are supposedly "doing wrong." In other words, the Integral View rejects both the epistemic and the ontic fallacies in principle (unless, of course, they are actually being committed, which means, for Integral Metatheory, that either specific characteristics of the subject are being imported onto [or ascribed to] the correlated object in ways that are truly wrong and largely fabricated [epistemic fallacy] or specific characteristics of the object are being imported onto [or ascribed to] the correlated subject in ways that are truly wrong and largely fabricated [ontic fallacy]). Integral Metatheory rejects both the view that it is always a mistake to claim that the subject never enacts/co-creates objects and the view that it is always a mistake to claim objects never impact/ co-create the structure of knowing itself. For Integral Metatheory, the epistemic fallacy applies to any overapplication of the inside view, which occurs when the substantive (subsisting) aspects of the outside/objective reality are denied entirely (or made to totally depend upon human knowing). In other words, the epistemic fallacy is the false idea that there is *only* the inside/ subjective/enactive world (and all objects are nothing but enacted), which is simply not true (every quadrant, after all, has an inside AND an outside—how much clearer could that be?). And the ontic fallacy, for Integral Metatheory, applies to any overapplication of the outside view, when the significant additions/creations/enactions of the structure of the knowing subject are totally denied and their enactive impacts glibly charged with being an "epistemic fallacy." The theorists who charge others with committing these fallacies can assume that they are always correct and that those who commit these fallacies are always mistaken For example, some critical realists charge Integral Metatheory with always committing the epistemic fallacy, simply because it maintains that all 4 quadrants are tetra-enacted, which means that all four of them have a contributing reality, and not just one, as the epistemic fallacy stunningly maintains. That "epistemic view" of all of Integral simply involves broken, partial, fragmented aspects of the real and Whole world, which has both *subsistence* ("objectively real ontological realities") and "ex-istence" ("subjectively real and enacted phenomenal realities")—*both equally real.*

These two stances (subsistence and ex-istence) are integrated via the notion that the best understanding of any reality's subsistence ("real ontological being," which is indeed *real*, and apart from any particular human knowing, unless the object in question is part of a particular human's knowing itself, and then of course it's involved) is best given by the highest level of consciousness development at any given time in history/evolution (for example, the "actual nature" or "subsistence" of an atom is best given, not by magenta or red or amber or orange, but by turquoise, the highest expectable level of development in today's world—that is our closest chance of getting at the *real* subsistence of an atom today). Hence, the *outside/objective view* is fully included.

At the same time, the highest view today (generally, that of turquoise) is itself involved in the enaction or co-creation of whatever it is that it happens to know—a structure can know only what will actually impact or influence that structure, and thus all knowing is, in part, an interpretation (one of the partial truths we take from postmodernism, itself representing the subjective/constructive/enactive zone, the other side of the street, which we are integrating). That is, any item that appears in consciousness is something that "ex-ists" or stands out in consciousness, and does so with the imprints of that structure of consciousness. Thus, for example, although atoms had a subsistence during tribal times, no atom ex-isted in the mind of any tribal individual, and thus, for all intent and purposes, the atom did not ex-ist for tribal people. This is the autopoietic/inside view—although we acknowledge that, nonetheless, during tribal times, atoms did indeed subsist (they subsisted in reality, they just did not "ex-ist" in human reality; this is the outside/realist view, fully included). And, as soon as we are asked to describe exactly what these atoms were that *subsisted* in tribal times, we will actually use whatever views of the atom that *ex-ist* in the finest turquoise minds today. Thus, subsistence and ex-istence are always linked (and outsides and insides are always correlative/united). Thus, for us today, what we believe is the *subsistence* of an atom (that is, its "real existence" both today and all the way back to tribal times and before) is actually the *ex-istence* of the atom as it appears to turquoise (in today's accepted science). Each higher level of development will get us closer to the "truth," but this is a sliding scale. Again, as Hegel said, "Each level is adequate; each higher level is more adequate," and this is the same for truth: "Each level has truth; each higher level has more truth (or, 'even more accurate truth')."

This does not undercut ontology, it actually saves it. Suppose there is indeed only "one pregiven intransitive reality." Now couple this with the fact of ongoing evolution, each stage of which sees reality "more clearly" or "with more truth" (the way each higher level of consciousness has seen atoms more accurately and more clearly over time, from orange little "planetary systems" to green quarks to teal unified quark theory to turquoise strings—the "most real" truth of atoms today is given by the highest structure to evolution today, that is, turquoise strings). But that being the case, if there is only one, single, pregiven reality that is seen more and more clearly with every higher developmental stage, *and* evolution never ends, then we would never know any meaningfully real truth at all. We would have to wait until the very end of evolution in order to see "final truth." In the meantime, we will only know partial falsehoods for all time (because evolution never ends, and thus we will never have "ultimately real truth"). However, by recognizing that this Integral unity of inside/subjective and outside/objective views gives us a sliding scale of truth ("Each level is true, each higher level is more true"), then each level is allowed to know a *real* truth—*as true as true can be* (as best as truth can, at this time, with this level's given tools and techniques, be adequately known). That is "truth" as far as it can have any actual or real meaning at all. And all of these truths can be expected to grow and evolve and thus make "more truth" at each higher level, which does not deny truth as it presents itself at any lower level, but simply situates it within a total Wholeness of reality in which epistemology and ontology (inside and outside) are two aspects of the same underlying, unfolding Wholeness. In this way—and this way only—can we escape the one-sided approaches of those who charge others with committing epistemic and ontic fallacies. And in this way only can those two archetypal enemies—idealism versus realism, spiritualism versus materialism, subjective versus objective, empirical versus rational, epistemic versus ontic—both be fully acknowledged and fully integrated.

This view comes from a sustained look at developmental studies—which critical realism does not take into account, and which they now acknowledge to be one of their significant weaknesses. The first thing that you learn in developmental studies is that every level has a different world. And there are basically only two ways you can handle that fact. You can say that there is one, given, intransitive, "realist" ontology and that each higher level of development sees that ontology more and more clearly. That definitely puts ontology front and center and allows Karl Popper, for example, to explain how science can put a person on the moon by appealing to science's access to the one real ontology. This is the outside/rational/realist/objective ontology that guides all "outside" views. The only problem with this is that you haven't saved ontology, you've deleted it, destroyed it. By acknowledging that every higher level of development and consciousness and cognition sees that pregiven ontology more clearly—and sees that what was taken for truth at the previous stage is actually seen as false, or very limited, from a higher stage/view—you realize that you will NEVER see this full ontology in a complete and adequate way. Because only the highest level of evolution will ever see that full ontology, and evolution never ends, knowledge of ontology is NEVER, but NEVER, really known. All we know are various falsehoods and illusions, and humanity is removed from ever being able to know any genuine reality. Ontology is not saved; it is utterly destroyed. Anchoring truth in just outside/objective/ontological/realist/universal/intransitive views does exactly that.

If, on the other hand, we adopt a developmental, "sliding," "evolutionary" view of truth, then every level has a degree of truth judged by the reality and the phenomena of that level. If all phenomena are brought together carefully and adequately and worked together into a hypothesis that accounts for all known facts and truths *at that level*, then that is as close to truth as "truth" can possibly mean at that point in evolution. But this also means that we stop claiming that there is only one, single, given truth, which is known by disciplines such as science (because even if there were a single truth, those truths that are known keep changing with every new developmental level—and we will still NEVER get an adequate truth). As for "every level is adequate, but every higher level is more adequate" and likewise "every level is true, every higher level is more true," we already know that that is true for consciousness, ethics, love, awareness, cognition, morals, aesthetics, and on and on (that is, "Each level has consciousness, each higher level has more consciousness"; "Each level has ethics, each higher level has greater ethics"; "Each level has love, each higher level has more love"—we have research on all that almost ad infinitum). But this means that each level is helping to enact and co-create the phenomena at its level (all 4 quadrants tetra-arise). Both epistemology and ontology play together in a mutually unified and unifying Wholeness in this endeavor. Charging proponents of epistemology with the "epistemic" fallacy or proponents of ontology with the "ontic" fallacy is pure idiocy, if you'll excuse my French.

In my own presentations—and largely just for space considerations—I will often argue for the reality of either the inside view or the outside view, without always taking time to argue for their unity (which is simply assumed, anyway, to be a fairly obvious assumption of Integral Metatheory). When I emphasize the inside view, I usually focus on the realities of enaction (usually identified as "tetra-enaction" to emphasize the important role of all 4 quadrants and all inner zones), as well as the fact that phenomena are co-created by the subject (epistemology) and the paradigm/exemplar/injunction (methodology), which together bring forth a real and different world at each level of development/evolution (thus, overall, there are multiple epistemologies, multiple methodologies, and multiple ontologies, integrated in AQAL)—and THAT is the overall view of Integral Metatheory. I'll often focus especially on the importance of perspectives in the whole epistemic/ontic process: the fact that the meaning of a statement is the injunction (perspectival action) of its enaction. "The world is built of sentient beings with perspectives" is a typical shorthand of the view as Integral summarizes it.

On the other hand, when I focus on the outside ("ontological") view, I focus on the actually existing elements of the AQAL Framework (quadrants, levels, line, states, types, and so forth), the 20 tenets (such as that "reality is composed of holons"; when emphasizing the unity of inside and outside, I'll often say "reality is composed of holons with perspectives") and will not mention that, for example, AQAL is a summary view of reality as explained via vision-logic at the turquoise or indigo level/perspective, is grounded in a nondual state, and is in part an interpretation co-created by those structures/states of consciousness.

As I generally present them, the inside view emphasizes the centrality of epistemology and methodology (Who and How), and the outside view focuses on ontology (the What). The When and Where are likewise inherent in the AQAL Framework, inasmuch as one cannot fully give all the elements of the AQAL Framework without indicating the temporal When (with the overall evolutionary/developmental component being a part of that temporal dimension) and the Where (with dimensions such as the entire Lower Right quadrant being dependent upon the systematic physical/material location of the overall occasion with a particular Kosmic Address). What I will never do is suggest that any of those five elements (Who, What, When, Where, How) can exist without the others; "Integral" means exactly what the word says.

And finally, briefly, these two major views, the inside/enactive/autopoietic/co-creative and the outside/rational/universal/realist, are present, as I mentioned, in all 4 quadrants, although I focused on examples from the Lower Left and Lower Right. But the Upper Right is where Varela and Maturana first made their breakthrough discoveries on autopoiesis and the enaction paradigm (working primarily from the inside of the Upper Right—or "biological phenomenology" or the "view from within"). This was primarily a pure zone #5. They contrasted this, in their writings, with approaches such as positivism, realism, materialism, empiricism, and rationalism, which are the outside views of the Upper Right (namely, zone #6); as well as with systems theory in general, which is the outside view of the Lower Right; a biological organism does NOT see the world as a Web of Life as general system theory does, and thus that is one of the first things they rejected in their "biological phenomenology." Niklas Luhmann picked up this enactive paradigm and applied it to social systems in the Lower Right (as I extensively noted). So the inside/outside dialectic "battle" we have been tracing is at work in the Upper Right as well.

And likewise in the Upper Left. The inside/enactive view (the view from zone #1) is often characterized as "prehension," and this means that in each holon, the subjective/cognitive/co-creative dimension is highlighted; its own given awareness (or protoawareness) brings forth a world of distinctions that are its primary reality. This means that there is also an emphasis on the "constructivist" capacity of each sentient holon (or level of consciousness). When this constructivist capacity is viewed from without or from the outside view (zone #2), what it sees are the resultant structures that have been enacted/co-created, but because it is looking at these "constructed structures" through a perspective that sees universal/objective/realist realities, these constructed structures are given a very real ontology and are not viewed as "merely subjective" or "just fantasy," but rather are as real as any objectively real entity; this is, in fact, the core of authentic structuralism. At the same time, because structuralism follows the developmental/evolutionary unfolding of these constructed structures over time, it sees that each new level of constructed structures (each new level of consciousness) sees a different world, or actually *has* a different world because it creates a (partially) different world at each new constructed level. This is a move in the direction of uniting inside/creative/enactive and outside/realist/universal; but generally speaking, most structuralism treats these structures, once having been created, as being largely given structures with little if any variation from individual to individual, reflecting the zone-#2 perspective of objective universal realities that is its main focus. It is Integral Metatheory that explicitly pulls together the inside/enactive/interpretative/creative zone #1 with the outside/ontological/realist/universal zone #2 (as it does with the inside and outside zones in all quadrants).

Of course, other forms of methodologies are possible in these major zones in the Upper Left, but all of them follow these basic characteristics derived from the dimension/perspective/holonic reality of each. Thus, other zone-#1 methodologies include pure awareness, phenomenology, meditation, contemplation, naked introspection (and other 1st-person of 1st-person of 1st-person views), and other zone-#2 methodologies include any major theoretical map or model of the interior of the individual being, from psychoanalysis to Jungian psychology to Five Factor theory to aspects of spiritual psychologies (and other 1st-person of 3rd-person of 1st-person views, including the common but somewhat awkward application of systems theory to the individual psyche—awkward, because systems theories, both inside and outside versions, deal with social holons without a dominant monad or "I," which is a primary datum in the Upper Left; still, it has a moderate usefulness in helping track the networked capacities of the interwoven subholons of the human psyche).

Integral Metatheory combines the inside and outside views from all 4 quadrants (which also gives us levels, lines, states, and types)—and we have seen that each of the quadrants has an inside and outside view (and not only that, but that the inside and outside views are often the predominant views available at that quadrant). This is the general meaning of "Integral" itself. (See also chap. 3, n. 15.)

2. See, for example, John Dupuy, *Integral Recovery: A Revolutionary Approach to Alcoholism and Addiction* (Albany: State University of New York Press, 2013), and Guy du Plessis, *An Integral Guide to Recovery: Twelve Steps and Beyond* (Tucson, AZ: Integral Publishers, 2015).

3. John M. Broughton, "The Development of Natural Epistemology in Adolescence and Early Adulthood" (PhD diss., Harvard University, 1975).

4. Blake, *The Marriage of Heaven and Hell*, 14.

5. Henry David Thoreau, *Walden* (Las Vegas: Empire Publishing, 2013), 4.

6. *Tractatus Logico-Philosophicus*, 6.4311. So that is the relation of

736 | Notes to Chapter 11

the ultimate Reality (incorrectly itself referred to as the "Whole") and all the "parts"—each part is not a part of infinity, each part IS the infinite; each finite point contains 100 percent of the infinite (since the infinite is itself without any dimensions, *all* of it can fit into any dimension—and does so). And then there is the relation of the parts themselves to the other parts, and in that *relative* and *finite* dimension (which pantheism mistakes for the infinite), each part is indeed part of the Totality of parts. Moreover, this is not a flatland situation, where each part has exactly the same amount of "Wholeness" as every other part; rather, the parts are parts in a *holarchy*—all parts transcend and include others, so each part has more and more Wholeness than other parts. These parts thus stretch in a vast holarchy of the Total Whole, with each higher level of parts in the holarchy containing more and more parts, more and more Wholeness—each holon in the higher level has more holons than those of the lower levels. Each level is manifest Spirit; each higher level is "more manifest Spirit" (while all of them "contain" 100 percent of infinite Spirit). Thus, there is the infinite, unmanifest, unqualifiable Spirit ("nirguna" Brahman —100 percent present at every finite point); and then, in the realm of manifestation, there is the finite sum Total-of-all-Things Spirit, the highest rung in the ladder of manifestation, with each level of manifestation stretching in a spectrum from the lowest and least Whole to the highest and most Whole ("saguna" Brahman). Infinite Spirit is the wood or Condition of the entire ladder, and "woodness" (the infinite) is fully present at each and every finite rung, no matter how finitely Full or Shallow. Rungs can be higher or lower, more or less Whole, but no rung has more "woodness" than any other rung—all are equally "woody." The "most Spirit" a climber can have is to be *standing on the highest rung* AND to be fully aware of the *woodness of all*. This "woodness" realization can be had on any rung—since any and all are equally wood—but that realization will be united with the amount of finite Wholeness on the particular rung itself; the "highest rung" awareness can be had only at and from the highest-level rung, where the "fullest totality" of all manifest Spirit can alone be realized, along with the 100 percent of infinity realization available at any rung.

7. This might be called a type of "multidimensional Suchness," a practice that adds developmental depth to present Awareness or mindfulness. To get a simple sense of this, do the following: as vividly as possible, imagine, right above your head, an incredibly brilliant, radiant Light, stretching in all directions, all the way to infinity. Don't *think* about that Light, just look at it, observe it (if you can shift into actually identifying with that Light, go right ahead). Now, shift down and into your mind/brain, and indeed start thinking—about the Light, or about the world around you, or about work, friends, films, anything—just mentally *think*. Then shift down again, and pay attention to the *feelings* in your body; just notice any feelings that are arising—warmth, a subtle joy, a tension, a desire, a sexual feeling, anything like that—whatever your body is feeling. Then shift down again, into the densest, "deadest" level, that of insentient matter, starting in your own body with bones and skeleton—feel their heaviness, their density—and then the deadness of the dirt under your feet or of the floor beneath you and the entire physical realm.

   That is a very simple reverse run through matter, body, mind, and spirit; and an Awareness that includes depth will include an Awareness of each of those dimensions (in more specific and detailed fashion than these simple examples). But that gives you an idea of the "multidimensionality" that comes when you add developmental depth to present-level Awareness. Most people end up spending much of their time on just one of these levels or dimensions, mistaking it for the whole of their being. Avoiding such restriction is what taking into account developmental depth does.

   As regards developmental depth, notice its inherent conjunction with time. Whenever you think of a yesterday, that yesterday has, in almost all cases, less depth than today. The universe, moment to moment, continues to "transcend and include" in its ceaseless "creative advance into novelty," and thus every moment, adding something extra to the previous universe, produces a universe that is just that much Fuller. And the farther back you go, the less Full—the more shallow—is the world that you are thinking about. But that also means that, as you think of past worlds, you are including worlds that possess lower dimensions

than your present world; so "historical thinking," or "evolutionary thinking," is a way to, realized or not, add developmental
depth to your awareness. The key is, while remaining in the timeless Now, to allow a developmental past to arise in your awareness, with all of its lower dimensions (however you conceive
them) arising as well. As another overly simple example, if you
are starting at a soul level, then your past will include all earlier
and lesser soul levels, and from there down into mind, starting at
its highest levels, and then moving down into its middle and finally its lowest mental levels, and from there into the vital body,
its higher levels of feelings and awareness and down to its own,
earlier, lower levels, and from there into the insentient, "dead,"
densest levels of matter, through its lower and lower levels all the
way to the Big Bang. Bringing these types of "vertical awareness"
capacities into your own Awareness, in countless different and
more sophisticated ways than in these examples, is a crucial
component of Integral and higher levels of consciousness, and
actually adds a depth dimension—and a *depth feeling* and *depth
perception*—that becomes more and more obvious.

8. *Brihadaranyaka Upanishad* 1.4.2.
9. The Integral approach is, so far, the only approach anywhere,
East or West, that includes and unites Waking Up and states, and
Growing Up and structures. However, a small handful of Western
psychological models have attempted to integrate Eastern models
of a Higher or True Self (or "no self") into Western models of
psychotherapy. There aren't more than a dozen or so serious attempts to do so, and I support the aims of all of them, although
of course I have my own ideas about the details of how that
should be done (a central core being the inclusion of both Waking
Up and Growing Up, which not one of those approaches does).

Chapter 12:
Dysfunctions of the Gross and Subtle States

1. Notice that I have said that, most fundamentally, there are no
intrinsically prepersonal, personal, or transpersonal states—those
adjectives are usually supplied by the structure doing the experiencing. But this does not prevent there being a general "spectrum"
of increasingly transpersonal dimensions, moving from gross to

subtle to causal modes; and thus the higher one moves on this spectrum, the more transpersonal the experience is likely to be, looking at just that factor. But in order to have an actual transpersonal state experience, the ego, or personal self, has to have itself emerged and been formed, in order for it to be transcended at all into any sort of "transpersonal" state—Engler's "you have to be somebody before you can be nobody." But once the personal egoic self is in place, then higher states themselves—particularly high subtle, causal, and nondual—can hit the egoic self and tend to temporarily dissolve its boundaries, and when that happens, the self is at least temporarily opened to experiencing those higher states in a transpersonal fashion. If it is at teal, turquoise, or higher, it will almost certainly experience them as transpersonal, since its own structure is lying right on the border of such transpersonal structures anyway, and thus to experience "something bigger" (in a peak state experience) is often interpreted as a "transpersonal" bigger, and the self will often respond by eventually reacting with its own tentative, higher, initial transpersonal structures, such as indigo. This at least tentative transpersonal structure thus receives the state peak experience as a transpersonal state, and the peak experience proceeds with few glitches or long-term problems. Indeed, one of the problems with inflation at lower structures is that a higher, subtle or causal, state hits the personal egoic self, and that self cannot meet the influx with a higher transpersonal-structure response but instead simply absorbs the higher state into its own personal being, thus inflating that being enormously. In the example we're talking about in the main text, the egoic self doesn't transcend to a transpersonal oneness with all of Nature, but simply crams all of Nature into its own egoic being, blowing its ego up nearly to the size of Nature itself—not ego lost in Nature but Nature crammed into ego—resulting in pure inflation.

Generally, if the impact of the influx of a higher state into a particular structure results in an experience that involves the next-higher, soon-to-emerge structure, at least to some degree, the pressure for inflation is siphoned off; if not, then it tends to expand and inflate the present structure as it attempts to adapt to the sudden increase in consciousness and energy. Thus, even at a prepersonal structure-stage, where the ego is already in fusion with the entire physical world, the higher-state peak experience might help the prepersonal self experience a higher personal structure, which it can do because the higher structure has more depth, and the "more depth" is a perfect way to translate the "greater consciousness" that is being pumped into the system. The personal realm—where the self is identified now with only the individual organism, but as including the mental and emotional aspects of the organism and not just its physical components—has more being and more significance than a oneness with the entire physical realm, because it has more depth ("span," remember, is "the number of holons on a given level"; "depth" is "the number of levels in a given holon"). Thus, when the self shifts from physical fusion with all of the physical world to an identity only with the individual psycho-emotive-physical organism, there is indeed less span, but also much greater depth, and thus it is a fine way to translate higher-state influxes into a structure reception consonant with the influxing higher energies. Thus, a state peak experience (high subtle, causal, or nondual) might drive a personal structure to a temporary transpersonal experience, or the identical state peak experience (high subtle, causal, or nondual) might help a prepersonal structure open to a personal structure. The latter is not the way peak experiences are usually thought of (which always is as "transpersonal"), but given the actual structures of development, it is a possible and actually common experience.

You can also think of this "personal structure peak experience" in terms of a dis-identification that peak experiences often involve—namely, a peak experience, involving "higher" and "wider" experiences and energies than the typical self-structure is used to, often causes a temporary dis-identification with the present self-structure and an opening to higher structures ready to emerge. When this happens with a prepersonal structure, the next-higher structures ready to emerge are all personal structures—so again, the result of the peak experience can be a personal experience. Finally, since there is, in the prepersonal realms, no strong and independent, personal egoic self that has yet formed, it is not possible for this system to have a transpersonal experience of any sort anyway; the system will either absorb the peak experience into itself, resulting in an inflation of an already highly narcissistic self, or will be opened to the experience of a soon-to-emerge personal structure, which does indeed happen relatively often, especially given the "dis-identification" drive inherent in higher peak experiences. Of course, that "dis-identification" drive can also contribute to a resultant pathology, if a weak and struggling-to-be-formed self is deconstructed and dis-identified with due to a peak experience, exactly when dynamics in the opposite direction are needed. This is one of the most common forms of "inflation" at these lower levels, where "inflation" means that the prior fusion state of adualism and oceanic immersion has been inflated—in the worst case scenarios, this contributes to psychotic risk factors, as the self–other boundary is exposed to forces that destroy it.

2. Rhonda Byrne, *The Secret* (New York: Atria Books, 2006). Transcendental Meditation has a specific meditative program called "the siddhis program," where it is claimed that traditional siddhis (for example, walking through walls, omniscience, levitating and flying) are taught. Nonetheless, after enormous scientific investigation and tracking, no genuine siddhis have been believably reported. The one emphasized the most by the movement, that of "bumping," which is a fairly impressive bouncing through the air, coming off the ground in the lotus position, itself a near impossible feat, has nonetheless not been able to demonstrate anything other than ballistic motion—that is, all of the power of the bumping is put into the body at take-off by bodily muscles themselves, and no "psychic power" alters the course of flight at all after that. Many of these siddhis are simply the imaginative product of a mind in meditation—reaching infinite stretches of expansion and feelings of power—that are understandably taken too literally. This is not to say that all paranormal phenomena themselves are unreal, however. Roger Walsh (private communication) has studied meta-analyses of experiments on various paranormal events (ESP, remote viewing, precognition) at numerous prestigious institutions (for example, Duke University) and reports a near 100

percent certainty that several of these do exist. This is what I mean when I speak of any of these paranormal phenomena as being "real."

3. Michael Murphy, *The Future of the Body: Explorations into the Further Evolution of Human Nature* (Los Angeles: J. P. Tarcher, 1992).

4. By saying that the subtle realm, unlike the gross, is a product of development, this simply means that the gross realm does not it-self emerge after some other realm—rather, it is where everybody starts, and thus there are no developmental dysfunctions at the "beginning" point of the gross, unless one counts prior rebirth states. (Some models, such as Stanislav Grof's, include the pre-birth state and the neonatal and perinatal state, tracking the birth trauma in all its stages; I call this Fulcrum-0, and it is the move-ment from a predifferentiated state where gross, subtle, and causal states are all interfused, moving into a birthed condition where the primary goal is the adaptation of the organism—struc-tures and states—to the gross sensorimotor realm. In some ways this can be thought of as a "beginning to the gross realm.") But in general, "not having an obvious developmental beginning to the gross" doesn't mean that the gross is outside of development en-tirely, since it can indeed developmentally give way to the subtle, and thus get caught in developmental snarls at that point. And, of course, the self-sense (the ego at this point) is exclusively identi-fied with this state—namely, the gross-reflecting state—thus cre-ating this state's Vantage Point, which is to say, being identified with the physical gross realm and seeing and thinking the world from that viewpoint (that is, Vantage Point). As I noted, this state is, by default, the starting state-stage in any further state-stage development. So, by default, the gross is stage 1 in any meditation model of state-stages, and it has a gross-realm Vantage Point, which involves an identity with the gross physical body and gross-reflecting thoughts. As the self's state center of gravity switches to subtle (at the subtle state-stage of development), the gross Vantage Point is dropped and replaced by a subtle Vantage Point that includes an identity with the subtle personality (or soul); the gross realm remains, and the individual can still see the physical sensorimotor world. As usual, structures and states re-

main; Views and Vantage Points are let go of and replaced. Thus the gross state can suffer developmental snarls, but only in regard to higher emergent levels, not to lower levels, since there are no lower levels in gross states (except if "neonatal" is taken as such).

5. Margaret S. Mahler, Fred Pine, Anni Bergman, *The Psychological Birth of the Human Infant: Symbiosis and Individuation* (New York: Basic Books, 2000), 63n4.

6. Western Buddhism is often caught in considerable misunderstandings of the anatta or "no-self" doctrine prevalent in original or Theravada Buddhism, which maintains that the ultimate reality of nirvana is directly a no-self state; the dharmas, or moment-to-moment existing realities, are taken to be real, but any conventional self, or subject, viewing or experiencing them is unreal, and attachment to that illusory self is the major cause of all dukkha, or suffering. Nagarjuna, the basic founder of Mahayana Buddhism, challenges this notion in a fundamental way. The relative self, he maintains, is as real as the momentary dharmas—it makes no sense to have a stream of objects and no subjects. So Theravada is wrong when it comes to that relative truth, he maintains. And as for ultimate reality (or Shunyata), it most definitely is neither (1) self nor (2) no-self nor (3) both nor (4) neither. Identifying ultimate Emptiness with a no-self condition is itself a fundamentally dualistic notion, and thus is itself part of the very causes of suffering. Thus Theravada is wrong when it comes to that ultimate Truth as well, Nagarjuna claims. Hence, overall, the anatta doctrine is wrong when it comes to relative truth and wrong when it comes to ultimate truth.

Francisco Varela got into a friendly "argument" with the Dalai Lama. Varela kept saying that "Buddhism doesn't believe in a self," and the Dalai Lama kept saying, "Um, well, yes it does." And Francisco would come back, "No, you don't understand, Buddhism maintains . . ." and then he would "explain" Buddhism to the Dalai Lama! Finally the translator stepped in, and informed Francisco to the effect that "Buddhism believes in the relative reality of a subjective self but believes ultimate reality can be defined as neither self nor no-self." I don't think Varela ever got it.

Indeed, only a fairly small number of Western Buddhists seem to have understood this. For some reason, the anatta, or no-self, notion has become almost dogmatic to many, perhaps most, forms of Western Buddhism. The anatta notion directly identifies ultimate Emptiness with a specific set of qualities, which is a pure and immediate violation of the fundamental doctrine (Shunyata) of all the higher schools of Buddhism. This seems to be part of that confusion between the relative self and the Real Self that is so common, where the Real Self, in this case, is interpreted as "no self" and then all relative selves in all domains are claimed to be illusory, leaving no room for the importance of an accurate, authentic, finite self as the vehicle of pure Emptiness (an Emptiness called *mahatman* or "Great Self" by the *Nirvana Sutra*, one's "True Nature" by Zen, and the "nature of the mind" by Dzogchen). This has made it particularly hard to integrate Buddhism with Western schools of psychology and psychotherapy, since there is no movement going from false self to authentic self that is recognized by these "Buddhist" Westerners (there is only no-self in all domains, a notion that itself smashes the Two Truths doctrine of relative truth and ultimate truth), and thus precious little common ground with any form of Western psychology/therapy. This is not useful.

7. The emergent unconscious consists of two basic phenomena: (1) those things placed there (in the emergent unconscious) during involution, and awaiting the appropriate point of evolutionary emergence (the so-called involutionary givens), and (2) things that have been creatively formed by evolutionary Eros, tetra-evolving in all 4 quadrants (and all other involved dimensions of the AQAL Matrix), inherited at birth by subsequent generations, and awaiting emergence at particular points in development (for example, all humans inherit the deep structures of the basic rungs all the way, at this point in evolution, to the Forms of 2nd tier, and fainter traces of Forms up to Supermind; although not all of those will emerge in any given individual, all individuals inherit those potentials—that is, not all involutionary and all inherited givens will emerge, even though the potential is present). The emergent unconscious is related to a larger phenomenon called the "Ground unconscious." The emergent unconscious contains items that, as the name implies, are due to emerge sometime during the individual's lifetime, whether they do or not; the "Ground" unconscious contains the emergent unconscious plus a series of collectively in-

herited items that may or may not actually emerge in the consciousness of a given individual. Thus, the Ground unconscious includes items such as the storehouse consciousness and phenomena such as Kosmic habits (and also includes all aspects of subsistence that don't ex-ist)—all of them are things that are collectively related to individuals or groups but whose existence is generally not apparent in any obvious ways (until and unless they "emerge" and "ex-ist" in awareness). This is related to what we have called the "Neo-Whiteheadian" view of evolution, where the past AQAL configuration is tetra-prehended (or prehended in all 4 quadrants in a quadrant-to-quadrant fashion), which is the "include" part of "transcend and include," and then any new, novel, and creative components are added to the configuration by the newly emerging and evolving moment, a process of novel "emergence," or the "transcend" part of "transcend and include"; and aspects of the Ground unconscious can be included in this "emergent" part of the process. "Natural selection" becomes merely one of numerous selection processes, each of which operates according to the validity claims specific to each quadrant (with natural selection being merely a subset of the selection pressures in the Lower Right quadrant—whose main validity claim is "functional fit," of which natural selection is obviously an example). If there is a "mutual resonance" of the previous AQAL holon with the new, emergent, and creative AQAL holon—and this mutual resonance must occur in all 4 quadrants (all AQAL elements, actually)—then that new and novel holon becomes part of the ongoing evolutionary movement. It becomes a Kosmic habit or Kosmic groove and is incorporated into the AQAL Matrix as a new and enduring holon, individual or social, to be passed on to its successor, which undergoes the same general process all over again, moment to moment to moment.

8. By the way, when the self dis-identifies with the subtle soul and switches its identity to the causal Higher Self, that doesn't mean reincarnation stops. (And again, this assumes that one believes in reincarnation itself. An alternative explanation as to why individuals believe in reincarnation is that when one experiences some of the higher and highest states and structures, those dimensions are definitely experienced as being quite "beyond" the present state of

the self, and this "beyondness" can be experienced as being beyond this present life and stretching to other lives, when it is actually just stretching to other, higher dimensions, not actual lifetimes. Either interpretation is acceptable to Integral Metatheory. We'll simply assume the reincarnation interpretation for the present point.) Rather, reincarnation still continues through the vehicle that is the subtle realm, but that is now the vehicle OF the Higher Self, which reincarnates with and through the subtle dimension; it's just that the set point of the state development sequence has now notched up from subtle to causal, and the individual will be reborn with a strong disposition to develop in that new lifetime all the way to the causal in state development. The same happens if and when the turiya Witness is realized—the set point notches up to that. Only with nondual Suchness does the forced nature of reincarnation come to an end and leaves reincarnation a choice that the Enlightened mind makes or not. If it has taken the Bodhisattva vow, it has promised to come back, to reincarnate, endlessly to help others gain their realization.

9. See Wilber et al., *Integral Life Practice.*

Chapter 13:
Dysfunctions of the Causal, Empty Witness, and Suchness States

1. *Tractatus Logico-Philosophicus,* 6.4311.

2. Let me remind Buddhists of Nagarjuna's actual thoughts on the "self" itself. Most Buddhists retain a Theravada notion of anatta or "no self." Nagarjuna did not. He pointed out that, in fact, the anatta doctrine is wrong on both the relative and absolute planes. On the relative plane, a conventional self, or subject, is just as real as the conventional object or "dharma." (In the Theravada tradition, the moment-to-moment flashes of experience, called "dharmas," are held to be ultimately real; but the self perceiving them is held to be an illusion, much like, in the dark, spinning a flashlight in a circle gives the illusion of a real circle existing.) Nagarjuna maintained that that was an incoherent doctrine and that the conventional subject/self and object/dharmas each have a *relative reality.* Thus, the anatta doctrine is incorrect on the relative plane. As for the absolute plane, the ultimate Emptiness is *neither* (1)

self (atman) *nor* (2) no-self (anatman or anatta) *nor* (3) both *nor* (4) neither. Thus, the anatta doctrine is incorrect on the absolute plane as well. Hence, being wrong on both relative and absolute planes, the anatta doctrine is altogether incorrect.

This anatta doctrine has been consistently misunderstood and misconstrued by Western Buddhists. It's fine to characterize Emptiness as being without self; you just cannot claim that what *is* real *is* selflessness—that the Ultimate is selfless or is anatta—that is just another opposite that is also denied ultimate reality (nor can you deny both of them, according to Nagarjuna; that would be just more dualistic concepts). Westerners keep forgetting the second part (that you cannot *identify* the Ultimate with selflessness). In some cases, this is the direct result of a "soul allergy."

3. The subject–object duality is the first duality, arising originally in the supracausal turiya Witnessing state and manifesting in the causal. To the subject–object duality required for the creation of a universe, Integral Theory adds the "singular–plural" duality—for a total of 4 quadrants—pointing out that it makes no sense for a single subject and single object to exist, since the boundary between them would run everlastingly in both directions; it must itself have a boundary, and this is the "individual-collective" boundary. The Witness embodies this "individuality" as well, which agrees with Brown's identification of "individuality" as the main obstacle in the Witnessing stage of *Boundless Limitless Awareness*.

4. Ken Wilber, *The Atman Project: A Transpersonal View of Human Development* (Wheaton, IL: Quest Books, 1996).

5. *Brihadaranyaka Upanishad* 1.4.2.

6. All holons have at least three different types of value: Ground value, intrinsic value, and extrinsic value. "Ground value" is the same for all holons, and comes from the fact that all holons are equal manifestations of the Divine itself—they are, in fact, the Divine itself in essence. "Intrinsic value" is the value a holon has by virtue of being a "whole" (or the "wholeness" aspect of the whole/part nature of every holon). The more holons are included in the wholeness of a given holon, the more intrinsic value that holon has. Thus, in the actualization holarchy atoms to molecules to cells to organisms, organisms contain all of the previous ho-

lons in their own makeup, and thus they have "more being," more "wholeness value," or more "intrinsic value" in their own makeup than any of the previous, junior holons. On the other hand, atoms—which contain none of the higher holons—are nonetheless themselves parts, subholons, or components of all the higher holons, and thus atoms have more "partness value," or "extrinsic value," than any of the other holons (since more other holons depend upon them). Organisms, although they have much intrinsic value, have much less extrinsic value since they are "parts" of very few higher holons. Atoms have enormous extrinsic value, being components, or parts, of virtually all higher holons and yet little intrinsic value, since they include only a few other holons in their makeup (quarks, subatomic particles). The typical pluralist, denying holarchies in general, denies levels of intrinsic and extrinsic values, and sees everything as egalitarianly possessing the same Ground value—which is only part of the truth of various types of value.

7. Referring to the Upper Left quadrant as "mind" in general and the Upper Right quadrant as "body" in general is just that, a generalization. Remember that the "lowest" level itself—the gross, physical, or material level—has two very distinct meanings: it is the very lowest level of reality or manifestation (represented by, say, subatomic particles such as quarks or atoms themselves), and it is the exterior, or outer dimension (the Right-hand dimension) of every higher level (except formlessness or literal emptiness). But the physical—as the lowest level—still has correlates in all 4 quadrants. Thus, in the individual or Upper quadrants, if we take a quark as it appears in the Upper Right, namely, the outward form of that physical quark—the actual look and form of the quark itself, its material (or mass-energy) qualities and aspects—then correlative with that, in the Upper Left quadrant, is the correspondingly low level of its interior levels, namely, prehension. Further, those prehensions are intersubjectively woven together in the Lower Left quadrant (or cultural "we," which quark prehensions most definitely have), just as the material outward forms of the quarks themselves in the Upper Right (including their mass-energy aspects) are interobjectively interwoven together in the Lower Right quadrant (as various "systems" or "social holons," marked by their own specific mass-energy finger-

prints). Thus, the physical level—as the very lowest level in reality, in the "great chain of being," has correlates in all 4 quadrants, including a proto-consciousness (or "prehension" or proto-"I") in the Upper Left, an intersubjective mutual resonance (or proto-"we") in the Lower Left, a specific outer mass-energy form (or "it") in the individual exterior or Upper Right, and an interobjective functional fit system or social holon (or "its") in the Lower Right. In this overall generalization of "mind" and "body," the lowest or physical level, in its Left-hand or interior quadrants (of "I"-consciousness and "we"-culture), is a subjective "mind," and in its Right-hand or exterior quadrants (individual object form, or "it," and collective objective system-form, or "its") is an objective "body." Thus, even here at the lowest levels, every mind has a body, every interior has a correlative exterior, in all 4 quadrants.

8. Also somewhat confusing is that the names of the states of consciousness, such as "subtle" consciousness, "causal" consciousness, and so forth, technically refer only to the bodies, or energies, of these occasions—only to their Right-hand aspects, not their Left-hand aspects, which are *technically* called "dream" state, not "subtle," "deep dreamless sleep," not "causal," and so on. But because so many of the states, like "dreaming" and "deep dreamless," can and often do occur during nonsleeping or waking states, the names given to their Upper Right energetic or bodily components—that is, "subtle," "causal"—are often also used for their Upper Left state names as well, since they don't imply sleep.

This is not a problem as long as we remember the actual differences between Left-hand and Right-hand entities. All Right-hand entities, such as mass-energy, whether gross, subtle, or causal, have some sort of actual location in the concrete, space-time universe. It might be a subtle or a causal location, not a gross physical one, but it has "coordinates" or is a real field with real dimensions, no matter how subtle they might be. There is some world where you can "put your finger on them." But no Left-hand entities have a simple location, and you can't "put your finger on them." Where does "mutual understanding" exist? Where do "desire," "pride," "love," "purpose," "happiness," or "depression" exist? The Left-hand quadrants ("I" and "we") have no simple location, but both the Right-hand quadrants ("it" and "its") have some sort of location in some existing world or another. The reason why the "mind-body" problem has been so difficult is that it involves getting things that have no location hooked up with things that do have location—"the ghost in the machine"—but for Integral Metatheory, they are two different perspectives on the same underlying Wholeness. The two different perspectives prevent this from being a mere identity thesis, which ends up equating them, and the "of an underlying Wholeness" prevents it from being merely another dualism.

9. Of paramount importance here is the concept of involution/evolution (Efflux/Reflux), because it is a fundamental tenet of most of the Great Traditions that many, indeed most, of the pathologies on a given level have their source in pathologies originating in higher levels, which, via the "downward causation" of involution/Efflux, transmit their dys-eases downward, level by level, until a particular level ends up being the primary manifestation point of the illness. A sickness of the soul, for example, can translate downward into a mental illness; a mental illness can translate downward into an emotional illness; an emotional illness can translate downward into the final manifestation as an actual physical illness—cancer, heart disease, arthritis, and so on.

Since structures that have not manifest yet generally have no explicit influence *but states do* (since all major states are generally ever present—meaning, for example, that even if a person has not reached the causal state-stage in state development, the causal is still present and is experienced in one of its forms each night in deep dreamless sleep), it is particularly the state dysfunctions that become involved in the energy component of all dysfunctions. That is, if a person is at, say, a red structure center of gravity (which would correlate with, as just one example, moral-stage 2), then he or she can't have problems with moral-stage 5, since that higher structure doesn't exist as anything but a potential form in the emergent unconscious. But that same person, who also might have only a gross-state center of gravity, will nonetheless still wake, dream, and sleep, and even though the person is not directly conscious of them, they are manifest, in existence, and thus can have actual effects and causes—including illnesses that infect all other quadrants and all lower dimensions with their own dysfunctional energy (via "downward causation" and "tetra-interaction").

Thus, even if these states have not become fully available to consciousness (in state-stage training and development), because they are present and functioning, any malformations in any of the states can become an energetic dysfunction that not only affects the state at which the malformation occurs, but also, via downward causation of involution/Efflux, transmits the effects of that malformation downward to all lower states (and structures). Energetic malformations in the causal-state Higher Self can transmit downward to the subtle-state soul (and likewise to a corresponding basic structure, anything from the meta-mind or violet altitude to the power-mind or red, among others). As another example, energetic malformations of the subtle soul can transmit downward to the mental ego (or to a corresponding gross, or gross-reflecting, basic structure, perhaps the rational mind or orange altitude).

Likewise, as higher, especially 3rd-tier, basic structures come online, then any deformation in their fulcrum can result not only in a consciousness dysfunction (in the Upper Left) but also in a corresponding subtle energetic dysfunction (in the Upper Right), and that can, via downward causation of involution as it appears in the structure-stream, be transmitted to any lower or previous structure-rung. This is actually fairly common in meditation and higher developmental practices.

For the traditions, these illnesses are best dealt with by attacking them at their place of origin, particularly if those are in higher states (higher structures being poorly understood by the traditions). Causal archetypal distortions can transmit downward to subtle-realm distortions, which can transmit downward to various gross-reflecting distortions (mental or emotional), which finally can transmit downward to direct physical gross distortions of physical illness. Psychiatrists are used to dealing with mental or emotional problems showing up in psychosomatic physical disorders, affecting virtually any and all organs and organ systems in the body. They can chase one shadow illness down medically in one area, only to have it show up, in another form, as another physical illness. That can go on almost indefinitely, until and unless the original mental or emotional shadow problem is itself directly dealt with, which usually puts an end to the psychosomatic chicken chase.

But the typical psychiatrist is unaware of the higher transmental state (and structure) problems that themselves might be causing the mental or emotional problems in the first place (higher subtle, causal, turiya, or nondual states). These can be appropriately dealt with only using more sophisticated, complete, and inclusive maps of the mind, body, and consciousness itself, maps that include the higher territories of transpersonal states and structures, as well as the spectrum of subtle energies that are now already operating in every human alive. The traditions are unanimous that these higher dimensions aren't merely somebody's theories that you can take or leave as you wish, but direct, real, actual, living realities already present in the body-mind of every individual now breathing. Any inclusive or comprehensive shadow work should most definitely take these higher dimensions into account, in both their Effluxing and Refluxing movements, and hence, any truly Inclusive Spirituality, wishing to cover the shadow-work side of the street, would want to keep this in mind, too.

Higher states of consciousness (including transpersonal, spiritual states) can be evoked directly by eliciting the Upper Left state itself (via spiritual, often meditative, exercises), or by eliciting the corresponding Upper Right energy state (via techniques such as Tantra, which addresses subtle energy, starting with its emotional-sexual form, and elicits that as a way to bring forth the correlative consciousness state). Thus, a particular "bodymind" union level, or state, can be reached via a "mind/consciousness" approach or via a "body/energy" approach (both are possible). We see some innovative "body/energy" approaches in such newer technologies as binaural beat technology (which involves stereo earphones that play a different-rate beat in each ear, which the brain handles by synchronizing itself to their difference), which brings forth various brain-wave energetic vibration states in the Upper Right, which then very quickly bring forth the correlative consciousness state in the Upper Left. For example, to use a standard correlation map that every major binaural beat company the world over uses:

a brain-wave pattern of 7 Hertz (7 cycles/second) usually corresponds with a theta brain state in the Upper Right, which is often experienced in dream states, and hence subtle states in general, which indeed persons will begin experiencing in their Upper Left consciousness when you apply 7 Hertz patterns to their Upper Right brain; 3 Hertz usually corresponds with the delta brain state in the Upper Right, or deep dreamless sleep (the causal state), which persons will likewise begin experiencing in their Upper Left consciousness when you apply 3 Hertz patterns to their Upper Right brain; and so on. These are all phenomena easily understood via the AQAL Framework and the correlation between the spectrum of consciousness in the Upper Left and the spectrum of mass-energy in the Upper Right.

See chapter 16 for a fuller outline of subtle energies, their many different forms, and their overall importance.

Chapter 14:
Structures and States

1. Hugh Ross, *The Creator and the Cosmos: How the Greatest Scientific Discoveries of the Century Reveal God* (Colorado Springs, CO: NavPress, 2001), 198.

2. Albert Einstein, *Ideas and Opinions*, ed. Carl Seelig (New York: Three Rivers Press, 1995), 40.

3. Francis Crick, *Life Itself: Its Origin and Nature* (New York: Simon and Schuster, 1981), 88.

4. There is no rational proof or disproof for Spirit itself, for the same reason that there is no identifiable beginning to Spirit—to point to a beginning in time is to make Spirit itself strictly temporal, which it is not. A rational proof, which operates with various finite variables according to finite laws of logic and deduction would have to apply qualities and characteristics that do not, in themselves, apply to unqualifiable Spirit; a purported proof of Spirit might be proof of something, but it wouldn't be a proof of Spirit but a disfigurement of Spirit. Disfigurements are fairly easy to prove; they just have nothing to do with Spirit per se. No rational argument for Spirit's existence has been offered that compelled consent by all who heard it. And several philosophers—from Kant to Nagar-

juna—have given strong reasons for the conclusion that proofs of Spirit involve contradictions that defeat the whole purpose.

On the other hand, there is a type of proof of Spirit, but it involves activating modes of knowing other than rational ones, and thus they are always suspect by rationality. The aforementioned Nagarjuna, essentially the founder of Mahayana Buddhism, believed that the awakening of prajna, or nondual awareness, directly reveals the ultimate reality of spiritual nature just as it is, and anybody who wants to take up the interior experiment of meditation (the exemplar or paradigm) would have a series of direct experiences (satori), or direct data, that included spiritual suchness. Moreover, this spiritual reality could be checked—confirmed or refuted—by a community of the adequate (those who had completed the first two strands, namely, following the exemplar and gathering data). This is as close to a scientific experiment and proof of spirit that has ever been offered anywhere in history, and seems perfectly acceptable to me. But it's not a rational proof; it's an injunctive proof—"If you want to know this, do this . . . ," as all scientific proofs are. This is an injunctive proof of Spirit, not a rational proof.

5. Alan Charles Kors and Harvey A. Silverglate, *The Shadow University: The Betrayal of Liberty on America's Campuses* (New York: Free Press, 1998).

6. Max Planck, *Scientific Autobiography and Other Papers* (New York: Philosophical Library, 1968), 33–34.

7. DiPerna, *Streams of Wisdom* and *Evolution's Ally: Our World's Religious Traditions as Conveyor Belts of Transformation* (Tucson, AZ: Integral Publishing House, 2015).

8. Melford E. Spiro, *Buddhism and Society: A Great Tradition and Its Burmese Vicissitudes*, 2nd, expanded ed. (Berkeley: University of California Press, 1982).

9. Smith, *Integral Christianity*.

10. Marc Gafni, *Radical Kabbalah* (Tucson, AZ: Integral Publishers, 2012); Amir Ahmad Nasr, *My Isl@m: How Fundamentalism Stole My Mind—and Doubt Freed My Soul* (New York: St. Martin's Press, 2013).

11. What happens if an individual has, at a previous level(s), already

moved his or her state center of gravity from, say, gross to subtle to causal, and then, as structure development continues, moves into indigo 3rd tier (which is prepared to force gross objectification only)? These states, when first realized or objectified, were being interpreted from the structure center of gravity that the individual possessed at the time. For example, while at Pluralistic, for example, those states were interpreted in pluralistic terms and qualities; at turquoise, they were interpreted in turquoise terms and qualities. When that self-complex then moves into indigo, those states will, again, start to be interpreted in indigo terms. Since indigo vision (its cognitive component) evolved to master an objectified (transcended) gross realm, the indigo level will begin to directly draw out of the state-realized complex of gross/subtle/causal states (already objectified to some degree when they were first realized) all of the gross elements, as it focuses on them in terms of its direct psychophysical vision understanding. It will directly integrate its structure components with the only state components it fully and completely recognizes—namely, the objectified gross and gross-reflecting state material. The other states will not be directly and structurally integrated into indigo structure (only loosely integrated or brought into the overall self-complex), since indigo does not possess the cognitive capacity to directly do so. Higher 3rd-tier levels do, and if those higher levels are reached, their cognitive capacities will begin integrating the state components that they are capable of handling—violet metamind, the subtle; ultraviolet overmind, the causal/witnessing; and white supermind, the nondual. In the meantime, the indigo structure/gross state conjoined/integrated complex will begin to interpret the remaining objectified (but only loosely incorporated) states that are in its own being (in this example, subtle and causal) according to the terms and values and qualities of the integrated indigo/gross complex self-sense.

12. It is generally acknowledged, by most developmentalists, that cognitive intelligence is "necessary but not sufficient" for other intelligences (but not for all other lines, especially in other quadrants—the development of the physiological line of the brain in the Upper Right, for example, occurs largely unconsciously, and

thus does not rest on cognitive intelligence; in fact, it is necessary but not sufficient for the development of cognitive intelligence itself). The reason that cognitive intelligence is necessary but not sufficient for most conscious multiple intelligences is that if, for example, I am going to respond using moral intelligence, I have to be aware of my moral inclinations in the first place, and that means a cognitive awareness/intelligence is needed. Therefore, in most psychographs, cognitive intelligence is the highest level of any multiple intelligence, with the other intelligences falling anywhere from immediately behind it, to several levels behind it. When I say spiritual intelligence ought to be leading the other intelligences, I mean that the cognitive/spiritual complex should be on the leading edge, setting the other intelligences in a context that includes ultimate concern, so that an individual's fundamental priorities are not forgotten.

13. See, for example, the website of Integral Life, www.IntegralLife.com.

Chapter 15:
Shadow Work, Quadrants, and Developmental Lines

1. A brief reminder that any dysfunction in any quadrant—including the Upper Left quadrant that we are tracking now—has correlative, contributing dysfunctions in all other quadrants. Whether family dynamics from the Lower Left or brain chemistry malfunction in the Upper Right or problems with social institutions in the Lower Right, all quadrants "tetra-interact" to form a problem, or dysfunction, in any of them. Here I am simply focusing on the factors in the Upper Left, but contributing factors in all quadrants (indeed, in all dimensions of the AQAL Matrix) should at least be kept in mind.

2. Wilber, *The Atman Project*; Ken Wilber, *Up from Eden: A Transpersonal View of Human Evolution* (Wheaton, IL: Quest Books, 1996).

3. How does this fit with the tenet that, during structure-stage evolution (as well as state-stage), "The subject of one stage becomes the object of the subject of the next"? Doesn't that imply that structures can be seen, since they become objects of the new sub-

ject? Yes and no. What is seen as objects are the surface structures of the previous stage, but not the characteristic deep structure or defining pattern. Thus, for example, as one moves from amber rule/role (with its conformist drives) to orange rationality (with its autonomous drives), one can indeed now see conformist tendencies as objects, and feel the tendency to blindly follow the rules. But one doesn't see—and can't see—the actual structure of the amber stage, its rule/role nature, its actual grammar or syntax, the specific form and detailed characteristics of the stage itself. That can only be determined by specific experimental research, usually of a developmental nature—often through question-and-answer investigation of a large number of people over long periods of time, and then deducing the pattern or structure of the mind that would itself produce the discovered data. None of this is open to simple introspection or mindfulness, and thus none of that "becomes object" of the new subject—unless the new subject actually learns a developmental map and knows specifically what to look for.

4. See R. Elliott Ingersoll and Andre Marquis, *Understanding Psychopathology: An Integral Exploration* (London: Pearson, 2015).

5. If a phenomenon (all the way up, all the way down) is an individual holon or compound individual, then it actually *possesses*—as dimensions of its very makeup—all 4 quadrants or perspectives: it has an "I" or proto-"I" world (its own prehension); a "we" world or worlds (mutual resonance with other "I's" of its world); an "it" world (its own existence seen and felt as an objective gathering of subholons); and an "its" world or worlds (the systems of which it is a member and upon which it depends for its existence). It possesses all these dimensions in its own being and it looks at and approaches the Kosmos through any of those perspectives. If it is a social holon, or an artifact, then it doesn't possess all 4 quadrants (a social holon doesn't possess an "I" quadrant, for example), but it can be *looked at* through all 4 quadrants or perspectives (I call this overall "looking at" a "quadrivia," the former, a "quadrant"). The point is that all phenomena can be looked at either from (quadrant) or through (quadrivia) these dimension-perspectives. Thus, a deer has 4 quadrants—its own

"I" space, its "we" space, its "it" space, and its "its" space; a painting of a deer doesn't have consciousness or awareness in itself, but it can be looked at through any of these four perspectives: I can look at it and form my own subjective opinion of it; you and I (we) can look at it and discuss it and form a consensus opinion about it; it can be looked at as composed of objective atoms and molecules, or analyzed according to its formal patterns and techniques of painting (an objective "it" perspective); and it can be looked at as part of any number of systems, including its owner's economic system, the market system that sold it, the legal system governing its use, and so on ("its" systems and social structures, including eco-social systems). All of these dimension-perspectives give very real, very important information; and virtually all human disciplines have at least one branch that focuses almost exclusively on just one of these quadrants, maintaining that the others are completely unreal, or at best, quite secondary. Integral Metatheory, of course, claims all are equally important and should be equally included.

6. John Mackey and Rajendra Sisodia, *Conscious Capitalism: Liberating the Heroic Spirit of Business* (Boston: Harvard Business Review Press, 2014), 278.

7. Robert Kegan and Lisa Laskow Lahey, *An Everyone Culture: Becoming a Deliberately Developmental Organization* (Boston: Harvard Business Review Press, 2016), 242.

8. Ibid., 273–74.

9. Multiple intelligences are a subset of developmental lines; they particularly refer to lines that, as the name implies, are involved with a conscious activity of intelligence or brightness. There are lines, especially in other quadrants, that are not involved directly with consciousness or intelligence in any aware fashion. In the Lower Right, for example, biologists recognize "grades" and "clades"—a "grade" is a level of development in reference to species, a "clade" is a line of development in reference to species. In the Upper Right, a "degree of complexity" refers to levels of development in the physical entity, whereas something like "organ systems" refers to specific developmental lines in that entity, such as the muscular system, nervous system, endocrine system, digestive system, and so

on, each of which develops through levels, or degrees, of complexity. None of these are multiple intelligences.

10. This raises the intriguing question whether particular lines or multiple intelligences can become Enlightened, with other lines not having those experiences. Is that even possible? What seems to be the case is that when consciousness, in any line or multiple intelligence, manages to move the self-line through all of the major state-stages (making each of those subjects object) all the way to standard traditional Enlightenment, then all of the lines or intelligences are simultaneously exposed to the objectified version of the states—if the person achieved Enlightenment primarily in the cognitive line, even the aesthetic line would have access to, say, the causal realm as a conscious object, simply because that is now how that state/realm exists in that individual. But the aesthetic line would not be specifically "line-Enlightened," that is, it would not have put its own processes through the discipline of a subject becoming object in each of the various states, and so, although having generic access to the awakened states, would not have access to how to fully function in each of those states—as cognitive intelligence would, since it was trained to do so as the self passed through each of them. This suggests that there is a "generic line Enlightenment" that all lines or multiple intelligences are opened to if any line succeeds in passing through the major states, and a "specific line Enlightenment" that the individual's lines that were used as they developed through the various state-stages possess by virtue of having been specifically trained in the processes marking the illumination of each state-stage—these are now part of the line's own specific knowledge repertoire, something that the lines that did not participate in this could claim.

We can see this is in the various ways that Enlightened individuals act and respond after their Enlightenment. Some, for example, are quite eloquent, even poetical, upon their Enlightenment; others not at all, sometimes almost incoherent or indecipherable. The former almost certainly included linguistic intelligence in their "package" of lines that were trained for Enlightenment and specifically moved through each state-stage (a "specific line Enlightenment"), whereas the latter almost certainly did not, and so their linguistic intelligence only benefits from a "generic line Enlightenment"—that line recognizes higher illuminated states and has access to them, but is not trained in moving through them or expressing them in detail or with any fluency. The same with emotional intelligence, interpersonal intelligence, moral intelligence, and so on—some Enlightened individuals are very strong in some of those, others quite weak.

Chapter 16:
Miscellaneous Elements

1. Gender scholars distinguish between biological factors, which in men and women are referred to as "sex" and listed as male and female, and sociocultural factors, which are referred to as "gender" and listed as masculine and feminine. In other words, male and female sex is the Upper Right; masculine and feminine gender is the Lower Left. Both, of course, are important to take into account. As usual, most scholars prefer one quadrant and downplay or totally deny the other—evolutionary psychology tending to see nothing but biological male and female sexual elements, and feminists seeing nothing but culturally induced masculine and feminine gender elements.

2. I have further divided Da's scheme by differentiating between causal/Witnessing, which remains the "Path of Sages," and the pure nondual, which I call the "Path of Siddhas," a "siddha" being a tantric practitioner. A typical Path of Siddhas is Nyingma Tibetan Buddhism, whose "nine yanas" include gross-reflecting, subtle, causal/witnessing, and nondual states in a superbly comprehensive system of states and state-stages (although again, no structures or structure-stages).

3. Different state/realms, such as gross, subtle, and causal, are not, in themselves, related as "transcend and include" (which otherwise marks *all* forms of evolution and development). What unites these state/realms in a "transcend and include" fashion is the self-system (or consciousness per se) *as and when it develops through these state/realms*. As the self-sense evolves from gross to subtle, it negates or transcends its exclusive identity with the gross realm, identifies primarily with the subtle, and then includes

or integrates the gross realm itself in its overall being, but not its exclusive identity with, or Vantage Point of, the gross realm, which is negated and let go of. Thus, the gross itself is "transcended and included" not by the subtle, but by the self-system at the subtle. Hence, all of the state/realms are unified by the self-system's development through them, with development, as always, involving "transcend and include."

When a particular state/realm—due to its relative independence and separation from other realms—is exclusively approached with a conscious discipline, as any one of the Paths of Yogis, Saints, or Sages does, it is retroactively integrated by the integrating function of the self-system (consciousness), since normal development through all the realms has been avoided. This means that any potential subjects still residing in a particular state/realm are permeated by awareness, explicitly or implicitly, and thus become object, and hence capable of being included (as in "transcend and include") in the overall self-system. If this occurs retroactively and automatically and implicitly—without an explicit conscious practice—it is often a haphazard, somewhat rocky, occasionally poorly effected process. Further, what generally ends up missing in these cases is the development of any specific skills or aptitudes with regard to the particular state/realm—as Hakuin, whose Path of Sages had exposed him to an implicit retroactive inclusion of gross and subtle realms, still knew nothing of specific practices or exercises for handling his Kundalini issues. This is one of the many reasons that the more complete the nature of a particular meditative or contemplative path—moving from, and explicitly covering, gross, subtle, causal and witnessing, and nondual state-stages—the more adequate and fully accomplished is that path.

Finally, precisely because of the relative independence of the state/realms, any overall meditative path can be very selective and only sporadically focused on various elements from different realms. A Tibetan practitioner, for example, might begin with shamatha/vipassana training (gross-reflecting), then move to inner heat (subtle realm *tummo*), then—in this particularly designed path—move straight to causal/nondual *trekchod*. The subtle realm is very meagerly represented in this path by inner heat—most of the chakras are bypassed, and *tögal* (high-subtle practice) is not included, so the subtle is definitely shortchanged here. But precisely because the states are relatively independent, this type of thing happens all the time. One of the aims of a truly Integral Spirituality is to help determine exactly which elements from the various state/realms would be considered basically mandatory in a complete Waking Up development, and which are auxiliary or elective. The point is that we now have an Integral Framework that can hold all of these features and thus help guide us through this important process.

4. Donna Eden and David Feinstein, *Energy Medicine* (New York: J. P. Tarcher, 1998).

5. This spectrum of subtle energies (using "subtle energy" in the broad sense to refer to the spectrum of energies running from gross physical to subtle to causal to nondual) will, of course, span the entire spectrum in the Upper Right (where it is "located") with full correlations in the Upper Left and all other quadrants. In order to represent this, holonic fields should be shown surrounding each holon in the Upper Right, that is, surrounding atoms, molecules, prokaryotes, eukaryotes, neuronal organisms, neural cord, and so forth. So atoms would show fields of the strong and weak nuclear forces, and electromagnetic and gravitational fields. In addition to these, and "surrounding" them, in prokaryotes would be the first specifically subtle energy, the etheric; then, with the emergence of the limbic system, the organism would be shown with its physical energy fields, then its etheric field, and then emerging, and holonically surrounding that, would be the astral subtle energy field. Then as the simple neocortex (or just cortex) emerges, all of those energies would be present, plus an emerging degree of subtle Thought energy holonically surrounding all of them. Then when the "dreamless, formless" state and Overmind emerges, causal energy holonically emerges and surrounds all the previous energy fields, all the way to Supermind and nondual holonic energy.

The point is that the "spectrum of subtle energy" is not a separate spectrum apart from the existing holons already in manifestation but a more accurate depiction of the full terrain of all of these holons—each is intrinsically surrounded by a subtle energy field, each of which "transcends and includes" its predecessors, and is an inherent part of the exterior, Right-hand structure of each and every holon in existence. The gradient of increasing consciousness, increasing complexity (and increasing of the Good, True, and Beautiful) is inherently tied to a spectrum of increasing subtlety of subtle energy, which is an inherent aspect of the nature of each and every holon in existence, which all possess 4 quadrants, two of which, the exterior quadrants (Upper Right and Lower Right), contain subtle energy fields within fields. These are not present in the interiors—the interiors do not have simple location, as do all exteriors—but they have correlates in each interior quadrant, for example, Upper Right "etheric/prokaryotic" correlates with Upper Left "irritability," and Upper Right "prana/limbic" correlates with Upper Left "emotional-sexuality," and so on.

6. Edgar Morin has created a "holistic" philosophy that includes, for example, the Good, the True, and the Beautiful, but only as looked at through a "scientific" (or ultimately, an implicitly objectivistic) lens. In other words, even if Morin grants that there are higher interior realities, he describes them only in 3rd-person terms, thus giving only knowledge by description. Where are the discussions of the actual injunctions and paradigms needed to directly contact these higher realities (such as the developmental stages themselves)? These are given scant, if any, attention by Morin, who thus leaves out knowledge by acquaintance. There is an important distinction between authentic inclusion of interiors and mere subtle reductionism, that is, acknowledging interiors only as seen in exterior terms, which is no interior at all, but the colonization of the interiors by scientific materialism. (Morin essentially takes a zone-5 and zone-7 approach to zone-1 and zone-3 realities.) His approach is, in most cases, exemplary of subtle reductionism. This is essentially the problem that results when a scientifically embedded theorist attempts an integral overview; the net result is both a distortion of the interiors, which are deformed and disfigured by being shoved through a 3rd-person lens, and the distortion of the Lower Right, which has to "cram"

all the other quadrants into it, which is like trying to put ten pounds of mud into a five-pound sack.

Again, I have written the least about the Right-hand quadrants, simply because they are the quadrants acknowledged and accepted by official Western knowledge systems and modes of research. *Everybody* is working on these quadrants! There is much less novel and creative work to be done in those domains; and it doesn't take much effort or genius to take all the established facts of the Right-hand quadrants and include them in an AQAL Framework. Of course that needs to be done, and I've always assumed individuals with such an interest would gladly take up the task, and many have started doing so. The Left-hand quadrants, however, are largely orphans; even Upper Left psychologies—zone-2 maps and models—are more zone-5 cognitive behavioral constructions than real zone-2 revelations. And when it comes to both structures of consciousness and states of consciousness, the amount of work done on that has been precisely zero—even though it is arguably the single most important topic for all of humankind (the integration of Waking Up with Growing Up). So I have always concentrated and focused my attention on areas that, in my opinion, need the most work. To express a bit of a personal peeve here, what is slightly irritating is when critics claim that I simply have nothing to say about these Right-hand quadrants. What about the 20 tenets for all individual holons, or theories of tetra-evolution, or the difference between dominator and actualization hierarchies, or self-organization through self-transcendence in these domains? But for heaven's sakes, I got my graduate degrees in biochemistry and biophysics, and I have volumes of things to say about these quadrants—but none of that is nearly as pressing as the discoveries that attention to the Left-hand quadrants will reward one with. We have an entire civilization working full speed on the Right-hand quadrants, and a minuscule number *authentically* working on the Left-hand. Of course, I address the Right-hand quadrants often and sometimes in much detail, particularly as they are related to the tetra-arising of all quadrants and their co-enaction. But my primary focus remains where attention itself is most needed today—the Left-hand interiors. The Right-hand quadrants are doing fine—there are new discoveries almost daily, headed toward a technological Singularity; genome secrets are being cracked faster than you can say "deoxyribonucleic acid"; computer science is producing a computer that could win the game of "Jeopardy!"—a much harder task than Big Blue beating Kasparov in chess; nanotechnology is pushing forward at lightning speed; and on and on and on. And ALL of these are meant to be included in the Right-hand quadrants of the AQAL Framework (they certainly are in my version, anyway). How could they not be? But what all of that science is not supposed to do is interpret in its objectivistic, 3rd-person, exterior terms the Left-hand factors of the Good and the Beautiful, art, morals, and literature, spirituality, hermeneutics, and cultural studies, and 1st-person consciousness itself (as opposed to its 3rd-person correlates). This would be a subtle reductionism that destroys both sides of the reduction (the reducer and the reducee). This is just more of the fundamental Enlightenment paradigm, the "myth of the given," which, however useful three hundred years ago, gets us nowhere today as we try to move toward a genuine Integral Age.

7. Keith Martin-Smith, *A Heart Blown Open: The Life and Practice of Zen Master Jun Po Denis Kelly Roshi* (Studio City, CA: Divine Arts, 2011).

8. David Bohm's contributions to physics need to be taken with a bit more skepticism. He worked in the quantum mechanics field, where the "measurement problem" was already causing a puzzle. The idea was that, according to the Schrödinger wave equation, the location of the particle being tracked couldn't be said to exist until it was actually measured, whereupon the wave equation collapsed to give a particular result. And the Heisenberg Uncertainty principle indicated that you couldn't tell the values of two variables of the particle—such as position and momentum—with complete certainty; the more you knew of one, the less you knew of the other. In any event, strict causality was therefore ruled out. So if not causality, what was behind the collapse of the wave equation? Bohm postulated "hidden variables"—supersmall variables—that themselves caused the collapse, so causality was

saved; a somewhat obvious move that Einstein himself called "the cheap way out." Bohm went on to suggest that physics illustrates that there are two realities: the first he called "the implicate order," which was the sum total of all things interwoven and entangled as one before they emerged and separated, and the second he called the "explicate order," which was the world of separate things and events that conventional reality recognizes. The collapse of the wave equation is the moving of the particle from the implicate to the explicate order. The problem is that some people (including Bohm on occasion) connected "pure spirit" with the implicate order and the "material realm" with the explicate order. Laypeople everywhere certainly took his theory this way, and started talking about physics "proving" the "spiritual implicate order" underlying all our ordinary, separate, isolated things and events (of the "explicate order"). The problem with that view is that it violates nonduality in its very first step; it postulates two, separate, different realms—one dualistic realm is spirit, and one dualistic realm is matter, and that dualism is inherent in the universe, something that no mystic anywhere would agree with. As Bohm became aware of this, he actually added a "super-implicate realm," which was the underlying reality of both the implicate and explicate realms, although now, of course, there wasn't even poorly interpreted evidence from physics to support that view (thus killing the whole excitement about these "physics proves mysticism" notions—the hardest of sciences is proving mysticism!—but there was nothing anywhere that even vaguely supported a "super-implicate order"). The simplest study of Nagarjuna would show that the "super-implicate order" was, in any event, still dualistic, as it made sense only in contrast to a reality that excluded both the implicate and explicate orders (it was falling prey to the problem with all dualistic approaches, which use concepts to rope the ultimate, when concepts make sense only in terms of their opposites, and are thus intrinsically dualistic). I even had a conversation with Bohm where he added yet a fourth realm to try and overcome the problems—still failing to get the actual problem to begin with, and simply becoming a very sloppy metaphysician. But you still hear that "modern physics shows a totally unified world." Well, actual modern physics—

string and M theories—postulate a world of literally hundreds of different universes, with little if anything in common among them, the farthest thing from a "unified world" you could imagine. This is what happens when you confuse 3rd-person approaches with 1st-person approaches, knowledge by description with knowledge by acquaintance.

9. *Journal of Integral Theory and Practice* 7, no. 3 (2012): 105–15.

10. "Meta-Sangha, Infra-Sangha: Or, Who Is This 'We,' Kimo Sabe?" *Beams and Struts*, http://www.beamsandstruts.com/essays/item/ 1181-meta-sangha-infra-sangha-or-who-is-this-we-kimo-sabe.

11. Murphy, *The Future of the Body*, 61.

12. Technically, the word "integral" applies to the highest, most complex, most unified and integrated level in existence—at this time, white, or clear light, Supermind. But the term is also used in a relative, sliding sense: a molecule is more integral than an atom, a cell is more integral than a molecule, an organism is more integral than a cell, and so on. Thus, when developmentalists began studying the various available stages of development—where the highest stages with any sort of significantly noticeable population were 2nd-tier stages—many of them (for example, Gebser and Loevinger) called 2nd tier by terms such as "integral," "integral-aperspectival," or "integrated," since those were the most integral of any stages they found. Of course, had 3rd tier been in existence to the degree that 2nd tier is now, then 3rd tier would have been labeled "integral." "Integral Theory" applies to all levels known to exist (1st to 2nd to 3rd tier); but it also keeps the historical term "integral" for 2nd tier in general and turquoise in particular and uses "super-integral," among others, for 3rd tier. The relative nature of the term should be kept in mind.

13. "Enacting an Integral Revolution" (lecture, Integral Theory Conference, 2013).

Chapter 17:
Integral Semiotics and a New God-Talk

1. For example, the magenta structure, which marks the completion of the emergence of sensorimotor intelligence, can see the "single, pregiven" sensorimotor world for the first time, since it understands "object constancy"—hide an object under a pillow, and

magenta will believe it still exists when hidden from sight. But it can't understand conservation of volume or mass (pour water from a short fat glass into a tall thin glass, and it will think that the tall glass has more water). The concrete operational (amber) structure introduces that understanding, and so amber sees infrared sensorimotor more accurately than magenta does. Likewise, the formal operational structure (orange), by introducing an understanding of abstract prioritization of physical qualities, sees the infrared world even more accurately—and so on. It's not that those lower levels are wrong, but they inherently overlook (and effectively deny) the real realities of each of those higher levels *in themselves*; they overlook and deny the emergent, real realities that these higher levels bring into existence. The higher levels not only reflect or interpret the sensorimotor world in increasingly better fashions ("each higher stage is more adequate"), they are indeed themselves higher stages, higher worldspaces, *higher worlds*—just as real as (in some ways more real than) the infrared sensorimotor world. And those higher worldspaces not only see the sensorimotor in more and more adequate ways, they also have their own phenomena, objects, events, and processes that are without doubt just as phenomenologically real as the phenomenological sensorimotor worldspace—and therefore can be the real referents of real signifiers. If an individual has developed to the particular higher level where the referent exists, that individual will be able to have a correct signified emerge in his or her awareness when he or she sees the particular signifier; and if not, that signifier's real meaning—the real referent and the correct signified—will remain "over his or her head," being "all Greek to him or her." And since the typical realist ontologist thinks that the sensorimotor world is the one, true, real world, then just which sensorimotor world does this ontologist believe in? The magenta sensorimotor? The amber sensorimotor? The orange sensorimotor? The violet sensorimotor? Which is it? Each higher level sees a more adequate sensorimotor world, so we'd have to say that the highest level of all is the sensorimotor realm that the ontologist believes in—but there is no highest level, as evolution is endless. So this ontologist, far from saving ontology, has demolished it—we will never know the true sensorimotor realm.

That's what we get from the myth of the given. Way to go, guy! See also chap. 3, n. 15; and chap. 11, n. 1.

2. More technically, a "worldspace," which I often identify simply with its altitude (for example, red worldspace, amber worldspace, orange worldspace, 3rd-tier worldspace, and so forth), is actually defined by the *complete* Kosmic Address of a phenomenon at that altitude, and a "Kosmic Address" is the actual quadrant, level, line, state, and type of the particular phenomenon at that address. In our multivalent universe, there is no "center" of the total universe (we're not even sure we're aware of all of the universe—its farther reaches and deeper dimensions have still to be fully investigated). In other words, there is no "foundation location" which can be used to define "where" to find a particular phenomenon, so the location of any known phenomenon can be defined only in relation to the sum total of all other known phenomena—that is, its location as specified in the AQAL Matrix. That specific AQAL Matrix location (its quadrant, level, line, state, and type) is the phenomenon's *Kosmic Address*. (Abbreviated versions of a phenomenon's Kosmic Address can be given, such as noting just its quadrant and its level, or its level and its state, or its quadrant, line, and type, and so on. But the full Kosmic Address, which effectively "locates" a phenomenon in relation to the known Kosmos, consists of all the AQAL Matrix features.) Thus, an overall "red worldspace" identifies all the elements existing at the red altitude in all of the AQAL Matrix—it is the sum total of the phenomena at the red altitude in all quadrants, in all lines at that level, all states experienced at that level, and any types at that level. The "Upper Right quadrant worldspace" is all of the elements of the AQAL Matrix existing as the Upper Right quadrant—all of the altitudes in that quadrant (all rainbow levels of all altitudes, which are fully present in this and every quadrant), all lines in this quadrant, all states that are experienced from this quadrant's perspective, and all types that can apply to phenomena in this quadrant. Every real phenomenon, or referent, has a Kosmic Address—that is, it exists in a particular worldspace and *is real in that worldspace*. Signifiers indicate these referents that are each located in a specific worldspace, and if you want to be able to see or experience that referent yourself, you must take

steps *to put yourself in that same worldspace*, or you will never be able to see the referent and will likely think it doesn't exist. For example, a "causal formless God" can be directly experienced if a person gets into a consciously experienced causal state (usually, via meditation, such as nirvikalpa samadhi); otherwise, it is "over their head" and remains "all Greek" to them, and they will erroneously claim that all forms of God are dead, whereas what is really dead is their experiential access to the worldspace in which that referent is most definitely quite real. *Referents exist in worldspaces* (that is, have Kosmic Addresses)—this is the super secret of Integral Semiotics, and indicates its profound emancipatory power and emancipatory interest.

3. Eben Alexander, *Proof of Heaven: A Neurosurgeon's Journey into the Afterlife* (New York: Simon and Schuster, 2012), 48.

Conclusion

1. Emptiness per se is not a separate realm lying around somewhere different from other realms, such as the manifest realm of Form. Emptiness, rather, is simply the Emptiness of whatever realm it is present with—it is the Emptiness of God, the Emptiness of self or Self, the Emptiness of Form, the Emptiness of the entire universe at any given time in evolution, and so on. It is not different from any of them, it is the Emptiness of any of them. The reason that "Emptiness doesn't change" is not because it is ensconced in a separate realm set aside from time but because the pure Emptiness present, say, a billion years ago—Emptiness as (or "qua") Emptiness—is the pure Shunyata of the entire manifest universe, whatever its Form was a billion years ago. Likewise, the Emptiness of today's entire manifest universe is the pure Shunyata of all of today's universe, whatever its Form. The Emptiness of both universes is the same, identical Emptiness; it's not a realm apart from the universe but the "transparency" or "openness" (or, more precisely, the "shunyata-ness") of each and every thing in the universe. Like the wetness of the ocean, it is not something set apart from the ocean or existing in its own separate realm, but is the nature of the ocean and each and every one of its waves—they are all equally "wet," equally "suchness" (tathata) or "emptiness" (shunyata). The Emptiness as Emptiness of the universe a billion

years ago isn't something different from the Emptiness as Emptiness of today's universe. Emptiness didn't change its nature, Emptiness didn't evolve or mutate over those billion years—it is the same "transparency" or "openness" ("shunyata-ness") that it has always been. That's what I mean by saying that Emptiness (and its Freedom) hasn't changed over time, or doesn't enter the stream of time. Not a set-apart realm, but the same quality or understanding of any thing, event, or process that is seen to be "Empty" in its true nature—this is unchanging, unevolving.

There are at least two common uses of "Emptiness," both of which are recognized by Integral Metatheory. The first is a bit more literal, and is close to the meaning of "formlessness" or "unmanifest" (as in "formless Spirit," "unmanifest Spirit," or "unqualifiable Spirit"—nirguna Brahman—where, in the word "nirguna," "guna" means qualities or characteristics, and "nir" means "without"). This is Emptiness in its narrower sense. It is from this infinite formless Spirit that the entire manifest realm arises, and the very first quadrants to arise are still very close to this utterly divine Emptiness. The Upper Left quadrant is the spiritual Self, "I-I," Purusha, Christ consciousness, Brahman-Atman, Mahatman—or Spirit in 1st person, the divine "I." The Lower Left quadrant is personal God, Ishvara, the Great Thou—Spirit in 2nd person, or the divine "Thou/We." The Right Hand quadrants are the entire material Form (or mass-energy) of the total universe, Mahamaya, Shakti, Prakriti, Kundalini—Spirit in 3rd person, or the divine "It." In the standard AQAL diagram, Emptiness, meaning "formless, unqualifiable, unmanifest," is the paper on which the 4 quadrants are drawn, and the 4 quadrants, in their first manifestation, are as I have just indicated. Each of these dimensions can actually be experienced virtually on its own (and there are different meditative states that actually focus on each one of them); they can also be experienced in various combinations. It is common to see different religious schools select one of these dimensions and make it the "most real," with the others being assigned lesser realities.

Other options (based on various of those dimensions) include pantheism, which equates Spirit with the sum total of the manifest universe (and doesn't understand or include the infinite, formless, unmanifest, spaceless domain that is fully present at each point of manifest space). Pantheism does include that dimension, but often does not understand that this overall reality cannot be grasped by normal, conventional modes of thought or consciousness, but requires a transformation in consciousness to realize this reality directly. Various modes of theism equate Spirit with the Great Thou, or Spirit in 2nd person, and tend to ignore other perspectives on Spirit (and often the formless unmanifest empty Ground). Monism selects one dimension in the manifest domain (usually one quadrant) and equates that with Spirit or ultimate Reality.

Then there is Emptiness in the broadest sense, which is not formless versus the world of form, but the Transparency (or Emptiness) of both united. This total nondual Emptiness is the "ultimate of ultimates," the unmanifest paper plus the entire manifest 4-quadrant universe. One of several "experiences" of this ultimate Ultimate is to experience Spirit in 1st or 2nd or 3rd person (I, Thou/We, or It), but "from" the vast open infinite/finite total Emptiness. Its most common "unqualifiable quality" is Unsurpassed Inclusiveness that transcends and includes the sum total of all dimensions through all perspectives in all domains, an "experience" that is one of a simple, direct, immediate Suchness, Thusness, or Itness—this moment, as it is, just as it is, in any and all of its infinite possibilities.

2. Arthur O. Lovejoy, *The Great Chain of Being: A Study of the History of an Idea* (New Brunswick, NJ: Transaction Publishers, 2009), 26.

3. Machen, *Delphi Collected Works of Arthur Machen*.

Bibliography

Adi Da Samraj, Ruchira Avatar. *Real God Is the Indivisible Oneness of Unbroken Light*. Loch Lomond, CA: Dawn Horse Press, 1999. *See also* Bubba Free John.

Ahlquist, Dale. *The Complete Thinker: The Marvelous Mind of G. K. Chesterton*. San Francisco: Ignatius Press, 2012.

Alexander, Eben. *Proof of Heaven: A Neurosurgeon's Journey into the Afterlife*. New York: Simon and Schuster, 2012.

Bausch, Kenneth C. *The Emerging Consensus in Social Systems Theory*. New York: Springer Science and Business Media, 2001.

Blake, William. *The Marriage of Heaven and Hell*. London: Camden Hotten, 1868.

Broughton, John M. "The Development of Natural Epistemology in Adolescence and Early Adulthood." PhD diss., Harvard University, 1975.

Bubba Free John. *The Paradox of Instruction: An Introduction to the Esoteric Spiritual Teaching of Bubba Free John*. San Francisco: Dawn Horse Press, 1977. *See also* Adi Da Samraj, Ruchira Avatar.

Bucko, Adam, and Rory McEntee. *The New Monasticism: An Interspiritual Manifesto for Contemplative Living*. Maryknoll, NY: Orbis Books, 2015.

Byrne, Rhonda. *The Secret*. New York: Atria Books, 2006.

Crick, Francis. *Life Itself: Its Origin and Nature*. New York: Simon and Schuster, 1981.

DiPerna, Dustin. *Evolution's Ally: Our World's Religious Traditions as Conveyor Belts of Transformation*. Tucson, AZ: Integral Publishing House, 2015.

———. *Streams of Wisdom: An Advanced Guide to Integral Spiritual Development*. Tucson, AZ: Integral Publishing House, 2014.

Dreyfus, Hubert, and Paul Rabinow. *Michel Foucault: Beyond Structuralism and Hermeneutics*. 2nd ed. Chicago: University of Chicago Press, 1983.

Durant, Will, and Ariel Durant. *Rousseau and Revolution*. Vol. 10 of *The Story of Civilization*. New York: Simon and Schuster, 1967.

Eden, Donna, and David Feinstein. *Energy Medicine*. New York: J. P. Tarcher, 1998.

Einstein, Albert. *Ideas and Opinions*. Edited by Carl Seelig. New York: Three Rivers Press, 1995.

Ephron, Nora. *Heartburn*. New York: Knopf, 1983.

Fowler, James W. *Stages of Faith: The Psychology of Human Development*. New York: HarperCollins, 1995.

Gafni, Marc. *Radical Kabbalah*. Tucson, AZ: Integral Publishers, 2012.

Gardner, Howard. *Multiple Intelligences: New Horizons in Theory and Practice*. New York: Basic Books, 2006.

Gebser, Jean. *The Ever-Present Origin*. Translated by Noel Barstad and Algis Mickunas. Athens: Ohio University Press, 1986.

Gilligan, Carol. *In a Different Voice: Psychological Theory and Women's Development*. Cambridge, MA: Harvard University Press, 1982.

Graves, Clare W. "Human Nature Prepares for a Momentous Leap." *The Futurist* April (1974): 72–87.

Gregorios, Paulos Mar. *A Light Too Bright: The Enlightenment Today: An Assessment of the Values of the European Enlightenment and a Search for New Foundations*. Albany: State University of New York Press, 1992.

Gunnlaugson, Olen, and Mary Beth G. Moze. "Surrendering into Witnessing: A Foundational Practice for Building Collective Intelligence Capacity in Groups." *Journal of Integral Theory and Practice* 7, no. 3 (2012): 105–15.

Gyatso, Geshe Kelsang. *Mahamudra Tantra: The Supreme Heart Jewel Nectar*. Glen Spey, NY: Tharpa Publications, 2005.

Harding, Douglas E. *On Having No Head: Zen and the Rediscovery of the Obvious*. Carlsbad, CA: InnerDirections Publishing, 2002.

Hegel, Georg W. F. *Phenomenology of Mind*. Translated by J. B. Baillie. Mineola, NY: Dover Publications, 2003.

Kegan, Robert. *The Evolving Self*. Cambridge, MA: Harvard University Press, 1982.

Kegan, Robert, and Lisa Laskow Lahey. *An Everyone Culture: Becoming a Deliberately Developmental Organization*. Boston: Harvard Business Review Press, 2016.

Kohlberg, Lawrence. *Essays on Moral Development*. 2 vols. San Francisco: Harper and Row, 1981–84.

Kors, Alan Charles, and Harvey A. Silverglate. *The Shadow University: The Betrayal of Liberty on America's Campuses*. New York: Free Press, 1998.

Lasch, Christopher. *The Culture of Narcissism: American Life in an Age of Diminishing Expectations*. New York: W. W. Norton, 1979.

Loevinger, Jane, and Ruth Wessler. *Measuring Ego Development*. San Francisco: Jossey-Bass, 1970.

Lovejoy, Arthur O. *The Great Chain of Being: A Study of the History of an Idea*. New Brunswick, NJ: Transaction Publishers, 2009.

Machen, Arthur. *Delphi Collected Works of Arthur Machen (Illustrated)*. Hastings, UK: Delphi Classics, 2013.

Mackey, John, and Rajendra Sisodia. *Conscious Capitalism: Liberating the Heroic Spirit of Business*. Boston: Harvard Business Review Press, 2014.

Mahler, Margaret S., Fred Pine, and Anni Bergman. *The Psychological Birth of the Human Infant: Symbiosis and Individuation*. New York: Basic Books, 2000.

Martin-Smith, Keith. *A Heart Blown Open: The Life and Practice of Zen Master Jun Po Denis Kelly Roshi*. Studio City, CA: Divine Arts, 2011.

Maslow, Abraham H. *The Farther Reaches of Human Nature*. New York: Penguin, 1993.

Miller, Melvin E., and Susanne R. Cook-Greuter. *Transcendence and Mature Thought in Adulthood: The Further Reaches of Adult Development.* Lanham, MD: Rowman and Littlefield, 1994.

Murphy, Michael. *The Future of the Body: Explorations into the Further Evolution of Human Nature.* Los Angeles: J. P. Tarcher, 1992.

Murti, T. R. V. *The Central Philosophy of Buddhism: A Study of the Madhyamika System.* New York: Routledge, 1955.

Nasr, Amir Ahmad. *My Isl@m: How Fundamentalism Stole My Mind—and Doubt Freed My Soul.* New York: St. Martin's Press, 2013.

Park, Sung Bae. *Buddhist Faith and Sudden Enlightenment.* Albany: State University of New York Press, 1983.

Piaget, Jean, and Bärbel Inhelder. *The Psychology of the Child.* New York: Basic Books, 1969.

Planck, Max. *Scientific Autobiography and Other Papers.* New York: Philosophical Library, 1968.

Ross, Hugh. *The Creator and the Cosmos: How the Greatest Scientific Discoveries of the Century Reveal God.* Colorado Springs, CO: NavPress, 2001.

Schrödinger, Erwin. *What Is Life?: With Mind and Matter and Autobiographical Sketches.* Cambridge: Cambridge University Press, 2012.

Schucman, Helen. *A Course in Miracles: Combined Volume.* Glen Elen, CA: Foundation for Inner Peace, 1992.

Seligman, Martin E. P. *Flourish: A Visionary New Understanding of Happiness and Well-Being.* New York: Free Press, 2011.

Smith, Paul. *Integral Christianity: The Spirit's Call to Evolve.* St. Paul, MN: Paragon House, 2011.

Spiro, Melford E. *Buddhism and Society: A Great Tradition and Its Burmese Vicissitudes.* 2nd, expanded ed. Berkeley: University of California Press, 1982.

Thoreau, Henry David. *Walden.* Las Vegas: Empire Publishing, 2013.

Trungpa, Chögyam. *Journey without Goal: The Tantric Wisdom of the Buddha.* Boston: Shambhala Publications, 1981.

Underhill, Evelyn. *Mysticism: A Study in the Nature and Development of Man's Spiritual Consciousness.* Charlottesville, VA: Noonday Press, 1955.

Vaughan, Frances. *Awakening Intuition*. New York: Doubleday, 1979.

Victoria, Brian Daizen. *Zen at War*. New York: Weatherhill, 1997.

Wade, Jenny. *Changes of Mind: A Holonomic Theory of the Evolution of Consciousness*. Albany: State University of New York Press, 1996.

Walsh, Roger. "A Big Picture View of Human Nature and Wisdom." Unpublished manuscript.

Whitehead, Alfred North. *Process and Reality: An Essay in Cosmology*. Edited by David Ray Griffin and Donald W. Sherburne. New York: Free Press, 1978.

Wilber, Ken. *The Atman Project: A Transpersonal View of Human Development*. Wheaton, IL: Quest Books, 1996.

———. *Boomeritis: A Novel That Will Set You Free*. Boston: Shambhala Publications, 2002.

———. *Integral Psychology*. Boston: Shambhala Publications, 2000.

———. *Integral Spirituality: A Startling New Role for Religion in the Modern and Postmodern World*. Boston: Integral Books, 2007.

———, ed. *Quantum Questions: Mystical Writings of the World's Great Physicists*. Boston: Shambhala Publications, 2001.

———. *Up from Eden: A Transpersonal View of Human Evolution*. Wheaton, IL: Quest Books, 1996.

Wilber, Ken, Jack Engler, and Daniel P. Brown. *Transformations of Consciousness: Conventional and Contemplative Perspectives on Development*. Boston: New Science Library, 1986.

Wilber, Ken, Terry Patten, Adam Leonard, and Marco Morelli. *Integral Life Practice: A 21st-Century Blueprint for Physical Health, Emotional Balance, Mental Clarity, and Spiritual Awakening*. Boston: Integral Books, 2008.

Wittgenstein, Ludwig. *Tractatus Logico-Philosophicus*. Translated by David Francis Pears and Brian McGuinness. New York: Routledge, 2001.

Index